Malleus Maleficarum

The classic study of witchcraft

HEINRICH KRAMER AND JAMES SPRENGER

Translated with an introduction, bibliography and notes by
MONTAGUE SUMMERS

BRACKEN BOOKS
LONDON

Malleus Maleficarum

First published in 1928 by John Rodker

This edition published in 1996 by Bracken Books, an
imprint of Random House UK Ltd, Random House,
20 Vauxhall Bridge Road, London SW1V 2SA

ISBN 1 85170 539 2

Printed and bound in Guernsey by The Guernsey Press Co. Ltd

CONTENTS

THE FIRST PART

TREATING OF THE THREE NECESSARY CONCOMITANTS OF WITCHCRAFT
WHICH ARE THE DEVIL, A WITCH, AND THE
PERMISSION OF ALMIGHTY GOD

PART ONE

CONTENTS

THE SECOND PART

TREATING OF THE METHODS BY WHICH THE WORKS OF WITCHCRAFT ARE
WROUGHT AND DIRECTED, AND HOW THEY MAY BE
SUCCESSFULLY ANNULLED AND DISSOLVED

Resolved in but two Questions, yet these are divided into many Chapters.

THE THIRD PART

RELATING TO THE JUDICIAL PROCEEDINGS IN BOTH THE ECCLESIASTICAL AND CIVIL COURTS AGAINST WITCHES AND INDEED ALL HERETICS

Containing XXXV Questions in which are most Clearly set out the Formal Rules for Initiating a Process of Justice, how it should be Conducted, and the Method of Pronouncing Sentence.

INTRODUCTION

IT has been observed that "it is quite impossible to appreciate and understand the true and inner lives of men and women in Elizabethan and Stuart England, in the France of Louis XIII and during the long reign of his son and successor, in Italy of the Renaissance and the Catholic Reaction —to name but three European countries and a few definite periods—unless we have some realization of the part that Witchcraft played in those ages amid the affairs of these Kingdoms. All classes were affected and concerned from Pope to peasant, from Queen to cottage girl."

Witchcraft was inextricably mixed with politics. Matthew Paris tells us how in 1232 the Chief Justice Hubert de Burgh, Earl of Kent, (Shakespeare's "gentle Hubert" in *King John*), was, amongst other crimes, openly accused by Peter de Roches, Bishop of Winchester, of having won the favour of Henry III through "charms and incantations". In 1324 there was a terrific scandal at Coventry when it was discovered that a number of the richest and most influential burghers of the town had long been consulting with Master John, a professional necromancer, and paying him large sums to bring about by his arts the death of Edward II and several nobles of the court. Alice Perrers, the mistress of Edward III, was not only reputed to have infatuated the old King by occult spells, but her physician (believed to be a mighty sorcerer) was arrested on a charge of confecting love philtres and talismans. Henry V, in the autumn of 1419, prosecuted his stepmother, Joan of Navarre, for attempting to kill him by witchcraft, "in the most horrible manner that one could devise." The conqueror of Agincourt was exceedingly worried about the whole wretched business, as also was the Archbishop of Canterbury, who ordered public prayers

for the King's safety. In the reign of his son, Henry VI, in 1441, one of the highest and noblest ladies in the realm, Eleanor Cobham, Duchess of Gloucester, was arraigned for conspiring with "a clerk", Roger Bolingbroke, "a most notorious evoker of demons", and "the most famous scholar in the whole world in astrology in magic", to procure the death of the young monarch by sorcery, so that the Duke of Gloucester, Henry's uncle and guardian, might succeed to the crown. In this plot were further involved Canon Thomas Southwell, and a "relapsed witch", that is to say, one who had previously (eleven years before) been incarcerated upon grave suspicion of black magic, Margery Jourdemayne. Bolingbroke, whose confession implicated the Duchess, was hanged; Canon Southwell died in prison; the witch in Smithfield was "burn'd to Ashes", since her offence was high treason. The Duchess was sentenced to a most degrading public penance, and imprisoned for life in Peel Castle, Isle of Man. Richard III, upon seizing the throne in 1483, declared that the marriage of his brother, Edward IV, with the Lady Elizabeth Grey, had been brought about by "sorcery and witchcraft", and further that "Edward's wife, that monstrous witch," has plotted with Jane Shore to waste and wither his body. Poor Jane Shore did most exemplary penance, walking the flinty streets of London barefoot in her kirtle. In the same year when Richard wanted to get rid of the Duke of Buckingham, his former ally, one of the chief accusations he launched was that the Duke consulted with a Cambridge "necromancer" to compass and devise his death.

One of the most serious and frightening events in the life of James VII of Scotland (afterwards James I of England) was the great conspiracy of 1590, organized by the Earl of Bothwell.

James with good reason feared and hated Bothwell, who, events amply proved, was Grand Master of a company of more than one hundred witches, all adepts in poisoning, and all eager to do away with the King. In other words, Francis Stewart, Earl of Bothwell, was the centre and head of a vast political plot. A widespread popular panic was the result of the discovery of this murderous conspiracy.

In France as early as 583, when the infant son and heir of King Chilperic, died of dysentery, as the doctors diagnosed it, it came to light that Mummolus, one of the leading officials of the court, had been secretly administering to the child medicines, which he obtained from "certain witches of Paris". These potions were pronounced by the physicians to be strong poisons. In 1308, Guichard, Bishop of Troyes, was accused of having slain by sorcery the Queen of Philip IV of France (1285–1314), Jeanne of Navarre, who died three years before. The trial dragged on from 1308 to 1313, and many witnesses attested on oath that the prelate had continually visited certain notorious witches, who supplied him philtres and draughts. In 1315, during the brief reign (1314–1316) of Louis X, the eldest son of Philip IV, was hanged Enguerrand de Marigny, chamberlain, privy councillor, and chief favourite of Philip, whom, it was alleged, he had bewitched to gain the royal favour. The fact, however, which sealed his doom was his consultation with one Jacobus de Lor, a warlock, who was to furnish a nostrum warranted to put a very short term to the life of King Louis. Jacobus strangled himself in prison.

In 1317 Hugues Géraud, Bishop of Cahors, was executed by Pope John XXII, who reigned 1316–1334, residing at Avignon. Langlois says that the Bishop had attempted the Pontiff's life by poison procured from witches.

Perhaps the most resounding of all scandals of this kind in France was the La Voison case, 1679–1682, when it was discovered that Madame de Montespan had for years been trafficking with a gang of poisoners and sorcerers, who plotted the death of the Queen and the Dauphin, so that Louis XIV might be free to wed Athénais de Montespan, whose children should inherit the throne. The Duchesse de Fontanges, a beautiful young country girl, who had for a while attracted the wayward fancy of Louis, they poisoned out of hand. Money was poured out like water, and it has been said that "the entire floodtide of poison, witchcraft and diabolism was unloosed" to attain the ends of that "marvellous beauty" (so Mme. de Sévigné calls her), the haughty and reckless Marquise de Montespan. In her thwarted fury she well nigh resolved to sacrifice Louis himself to her overweening ambition and her boundless pride. The highest names in France— the Princesse de Tingry, the Duchesse de Vitry, the Duchesse de Lusignan, the Duchesse de Bouillon, the Comtesse de Soissons, the Duc de Luxembourg, the Marquis de Cessac—scores of the oldest aristocracy, were involved, whilst literally hundreds of venal apothecaries, druggists, pseudo-alchemists, astrologers, quacks, warlocks, magicians, charlatans, who revolved round the ominous and terrible figure of Catherine La Voisin, professional seeress, fortune-teller, herbalist, beauty-specialist, were caught in the meshes of the law. No less than eleven volumes of François Ravaisson's huge work, *Archives de la Bastille,* are occupied with this evil crew and their doings, their sorceries and their poisonings.

During the reign of Urban VIII, Maffeo Barberini, 1623–1644, there was a resounding scandal at Rome when it was discovered that "after many invocations of demons" Giacinto Contini, nephew of the Cardinal d'Ascoli, had been plotting with various accomplices to put an end to the Pope's life, and thus make way for the succession of his uncle to the Chair of Peter. Tommaso Orsolini of Recanate, moreover, after consulting with certain scryers and planetarians, readers of the stars, was endeavouring to bribe the apothecary Carcurasio of Naples to furnish him with a quick poison, which might be mingled with the tonics and electuaries prescribed for the ailing Pontiff, (Ranke, *History of the Popes,* ed. 1901, Vol. III, pp. 375–6).

To sum up, as is well observed by Professor Kittredge, who more than once emphasized "I have no belief in the black art or in the interference of demons in the daily life of mortals", it makes no difference whether any of the charges were true or whether the whole affairs were hideous political chicanery. "Anyhow, it reveals the beliefs and the practices of the age."

Throughout the centuries witchcraft was universally held to be a dark and horrible reality; it was an ever-present, fearfully ominous menace, a thing most active, most perilous, most powerful and true. Some may consider these mysteries and cantrips and invocations, these sabbats and rendezvous, to have been merest mummery and pantomime, but there is no question that the psychological effect was incalculable, and harmful in the highest degree. It was, to use a modern phrase, "a war of nerves". Jean Bodin, the famous juris-consult (1530–90) whom Montaigne acclaims to be the highest literary genius of his time, and who, as a leading member of the Parlement de Paris, presided over important trials, gives it as his opinion that there existed, not only in France, a complete organization of witches, immensely wealthy, of almost infinite potentialities, most cleverly captained, with centres and cells in every district, utilizing an espionage in every land, with high-placed adherents at court, with humble servitors in the cottage. This organization, witchcraft, maintained a relentless and ruthless war against the prevailing order and settled state. No design was too treacherous, no betrayal was too cowardly, no blackmail too base and foul. The Masters lured their subjects with magnificent promises, they lured and deluded and victimized. Not the least dreaded and dreadful weapon in their armament was the ancient and secret knowledge of poisons (*veneficia*), of herbs healing and hurtful, a tradition and a lore which had been handed down from remotest antiquity.

Little wonder, then, that later social historians, such as Charles Mackay and Lecky, both absolutely impartial and unprejudiced writers, sceptical even, devote many pages, the result of long and laborious research, to witchcraft. They did not believe in witchcraft as in any sense supernatural, although perhaps abnormal. But the centuries of which they were writing believed intensely in it, and it was their business as scholars to examine and explain the reasons for such belief. It was by no means all mediæval credulity and ignorance and superstition. Mackay and Lecky fully recognized this, as indeed they were in all honesty bound to do. They met with facts, hard facts, which could neither have been accidents nor motiveless, and these facts must be accounted for and elucidated. The profoundest thinkers, the acutest and most liberal minds of their day, such men as Cardan; Trithemius; the encyclopædic Delrio; Bishop Binsfeld; the learned physician, Caspar Peucer; Jean Bodin; Sir Edward Coke, "father of the English law"; Francis Bacon; Malebranche; Bayle; Glanvil; Sir Thomas Browne; Cotton Mather; all these, and scores besides, were convinced of the dark reality of witchcraft, of the witch organization. Such a consensus of opinion throughout the years cannot be lightly dismissed.

The literature of the subject, discussing it in every detail, from every point of view, from every angle, is enormous. For example, such a Bibliography as that of Yve-Plessis, 1900, which deals only with leading French cases and purports to be no more than a supplement to the Bibliographies of Græsse, the Catalogues of the Abbé Sépher, Ouvaroff, the comte d'Ourches, the forty-six volumes of Dr. Hoefer, Schieble, Stanislas de Guaita, and many more, lists nearly 2,000 items, and in a note we are warned that the work is very far from complete. The *Manuel Bibliographique*, 3 vols., 1912, of Albert L. Caillet, gives 11,648 items. Caillet has many omissions, some being treatises of the first importance. The library of witchcraft may without exaggeration be said to be incalculable.

It is hardly disputed that in the whole vast literature of witchcraft, the most prominent, the most important, the most authoritative volume is the *Malleus Maleficarum* (*The Witch Hammer*) of Heinrich Kramer (Henricus Institoris) and James Sprenger. The date of the first edition of the *Malleus* cannot be fixed with absolute certainty, but the likeliest year is 1486. There were, at any rate, fourteen editions between 1487 and 1520, and at least sixteen editions between 1574 and 1669. These were issued from the leading German, French and Italian presses. The latest reprint of the original text of the *Malleus* is to be found in the noble four volume collection of Treatises on Witchcraft, "sumptibus Claudii Bourgeat", 4to., Lyons, 1669. There is a modern German translation by J. W. R. Schmidt, *Der Hexenhammer*, 3 vols., Berlin, 1906; second edition, 1922–3. There is also an English translation with Introduction, Bibliography, and Notes by Montague Summers, published John Rodker, 1928.

The *Malleus* acquired especial weight and dignity from the famous Bull of Pope Innocent VIII, *Summis desiderantes affectibus* of 9 December, 1484, in which the Pontiff, lamenting the power and prevalence of the witch organization, delegates Heinrich Kramer and James Sprenger as inquisitors of these pravities throughout Northern Germany, particularly in the provinces and dioceses of Mainz, Cologne, Tréves, Salzburg, and Bremen, granting both and either of them an exceptional authorization, and by Letters Apostolic requiring the Bishop of Strasburg, Albrecht von Bayern (1478–1506), not only to take all steps to publish and proclaim the Bull, but further to afford Kramer and Sprenger every assistance, even calling in, if necessary, the help of the secular arm.

This Bull, which was printed as the Preface to the *Malleus*, was thus, comments Dr. H. C. Lea, "spread broadcast over Europe". In fact, "it fastened on European jurisprudence for nearly three centuries the duty of combating" the Society of Witches. The *Malleus* lay on the bench of every judge, on the desk of every magistrate. It was the ultimate, irrefutable, unarguable authority. It was implicitly accepted not only by Catholic but by Protestant legislature. In fine, it is not too much to say that the *Malleus Maleficarum* is among the most important, wisest, and weightiest books of the world.

It has been asked whether Kramer or Sprenger was principally responsible for the *Malleus*, but in the case of so close a collaboration any such inquiry seems singularly superfluous and nugatory. With regard to instances of joint authorship, unless there be some definite declaration on the part of one of the authors as to his particular share in a work, or unless there be some unusual and special circumstances bearing on the point, such perquisitions and analyses almost inevitably resolve themselves into a cloud of guess-work and bootless hazardry and vague perhaps. It becomes a game of literary blind-man's-buff.

Heinrich Kramer was born at Schlettstadt, a town of Lower Alsace, situated some twenty-six miles southwest of Strasburg. At an early age he entered the Order of S. Dominic, and so remarkable was his genius that whilst still a young man he was appointed to the position of Prior of the Dominican House at his native town, Schlettstadt. He was a Preacher-General and a Master of Sacred Theology, P.G. and S.T.M., two high distinctions in the Dominican Order. At some date before 1474 he was appointed an Inquisitor for the Tyrol, Salzburg, Bohemia, and Moravia. His eloquence in the pulpit and tireless activity received due recognition at Rome, and for many years he was Spiritual Director of the great Dominican church at Salzburg, and the right-hand of the Archbishop of Salzburg, a munificent prelate who praises him highly in a letter which is still extant. In the late autumn or winter of 1485 Kramer had already drawn up a learned instruction or treatise on the subject of witchcraft. This circulated in manuscript, and is (almost in its entirety) incorporated in the *Malleus*. By the Bull of Innocent VIII in December, 1484, he had already been associated with James Sprenger to make inquisition for and try witches and sorcerers. In 1495, the Master General of the Order, Fr. Joaquin de Torres, O.P., summoned Kramer to Venice in order that he might give public lectures, disputations which attracted crowded audiences, and which were honoured by the presence and patronage of the Patriarch of Venice. He also strenuously defended the Papal supremacy, confuting the *De Monarchia* of the Paduan jurisconsult, Antonio degli Roselli. At Venice he resided at the priory of Santi Giovanni e Paolo (S. Zanipolo). During the summer of 1497, he had returned to Germany, and was living at the convent of Rohr, near Regensburg. On 31 January, 1500, Alexander VI appointed him as Nuncio and Inquisitor of Bohemia and Moravia, in which provinces he was deputed and empowered to proceed against the Waldenses and Picards, as well as against the adherents of the witch-society. He wrote and preached with great fervour until the end. He died in Bohemia in 1505.

His chief works, in addition to the *Malleus*, are: *Several Discourses and Various Sermons upon the Most Holy Sacrament of the Eucharist*; Nuremberg, 1496; *A Tract Confuting the Errors of Master Antonio degli Roselli*; Venice, 1499; and *The Shield of Defence of the Holy Roman Church Against the Picards and Waldenses*; an incunabulum, without date, but almost certainly 1499-1500. Many learned authors quote and refer to these treatises in terms of highest praise.

James Sprenger was born in Basel, 1436-8. He was admitted a novice in the Dominican house of this town in 1452. His extraordinary genius attracted immediate attention, and his rise to a responsible position was very rapid. According to Pierre Hélyot, the Franciscan (1680-1716), *Histoire des Ordres Religieux*, III (1715), ch. XXVI, in 1389 Conrad of Prussia abolished certain relaxations and abuses which had crept into the Teutonic Province of the Order of S. Dominic, and restored the Primitive and Strict Obedience. He was closely followed by Sprenger, whose zealous reform was so warmly approved that in 1468 the General Chapter ordered him to lecture on the Sentences of Peter Lombard at the University of Cologne, to which he was thus officially attached. A few years later he proceeded Master of Theology, and was elected Prior and Regent of Studies of the Cologne Convent, one of the most famous and frequented Houses of the Order. On 30 June, 1480, he was elected Dean of the Faculty of Theology at the University. His lecture-room was thronged, and in the following year, at the Chapter held in Rome, the Master General of the Order, Fra Salvo Cassetta, appointed him Inquisitor Extraordinary for the Provinces of Mainz, Trèves, and Cologne. His activities were enormous, and demanded constant journeyings through the very extensive district to which he had been assigned. In 1488 he was elected Provincial of the whole German Province, an office of the first importance. It is said that his piety and his learning impressed all who came in contact with him. In 1495 he was residing at Cologne, and here he received a letter from Alexander VI praising his enthusiasm and his energy. He died rather suddenly, in the odour of sanctity—some chronicles call him "Beatus"—on 6 December, 1495, at Strasburg, where he is buried.

Among Sprenger's other writings, excepting the *Malleus*, are *The Paradoxes of John of Westphalia Refuted*, Mainz, 1479, a closely argued treatise; and *The Institution and Approbation of the Confraternity of the Most Holy Rosary, which was first erected at Cologne on 8 September in the year 1475*, Cologne, 1475. Sprenger may well be called the "Apostle of the Rosary". None more fervent than he in spreading this Dominican elevation. His zeal enrolled thousands, including the Emperor Frederick III, in the Confraternity of the Most Holy Rosary, which was enriched with many indulgences by a Bull of Sixtus IV. It has been observed that the writings of Father James Sprenger on the Rosary are well approved by many learned men, Pontiffs, Saints and Theologians alike. There can be no doubt that Sprenger was a mystic of the highest order, a man of most saintly life.

The Dominican chroniclers, such as Quétif and Echard, number Kramer and Sprenger among the glories and heroes of their Order.

Certain it is that the *Malleus Maleficarum* is the most solid, the most important work in the whole vast library of witchcraft. One turns to it again and again with edification and interest. From the point of psychology, from the point of jurisprudence, from the point of history, it is supreme. It is hardly too much to say that later writers, great as they are, have done little more than draw from the seemingly inexhaustible wells of wisdom which the two Dominicans, Heinrich Kramer and James Sprenger, have given us in the *Malleus Maleficarum*.

What is most surprising is the modernity of the book. There is hardly a problem, a complex, a difficulty, which they have not foreseen, and discussed, and resolved.

Here are cases which occur in the law-courts to-day, set out with the greatest clarity, argued with unflinching logic, and judged with scrupulous impartiality.

It is a work which must irresistibly capture the attention of all men who think, all who see, or are endeavouring to see, the ultimate reality beyond the accidents of matter, time and space.

The *Malleus Maleficarum* is one of the world's few books written *sub specie aeternitatis*.

MONTAGUE SUMMERS.

7 October, 1946.
In Festo SS. Rosarii.

NOTA.— *To Dr. H. J. Norman I wish to express my grateful thanks for his kindness in having read through the proofs of the* Malleus Maleficarum. *Those who realize the labour and sacrifice of time such a task demands will best appreciate the value of such generous assistance.*

M. S.

THE BIBLIOGRAPHY OF THE MALLEUS MALEFICARUM IS EXTREMELY INTRICATE AND difficult, as many of the earlier editions both folio and quarto are without place or date. Thus the British Museum possesses a copy (Press-Mark I B, 1606), folio, which in the catalogue stands as "1485?", but this can hardly be correct. The British Museum has five editions of the fifteenth century: 4to, 1490? (IA 8634); folio, 1490 (IB 8615); 4to, 1494 (IA 7468); folio, 1494 (IB 5064); 4to, 1496 (IA 7503).*

Graesse, *Bibliotheca Magica*, Leipzig, 1843, gives the editions of the fifteenth century as Nuremberg, both 4to and folio, 1494 and 1496. He also mentions an early folio and an early 4to without date or place. He further records a 4to published at Cologne in 1489, and a folio published at Cologne, 1494.

Malleus Maleficarum, 8vo, Paris, an edition to which the British Museum catalogue assigns the date "1510?".

Malleus Maleficarum, 8vo, "Colonie. Per me Henricū de Nussia," 1511.

Malleus Maleficarum, 8vo, *Coloniae*, J. Gymnicus, 1520. (Copies of these two Cologne editions are in the British Museum.)

Malleus Maleficarum . . . per F. Raffaelem Maffeum Venetum et D. Jacobi a Judeca instituti Seruorum summo studio illustratus et a multis erroribus vindicatus . . . Venetiis Ad Candentis Salamandrae insigne. MD. LXXVI, 8vo. (This is a disappointing reprint, and it is difficult to see in what consisted the editorial care of the Servite Raffaelo Maffei, who may or may not have been some relation of the famous humanist of the same name (d. 25 January, 1522), and who was of the monastery of San Giacomo della Guidecca. He might have produced a critical edition of the greatest value, but as it is there are no glosses, there is no excursus, and the text is poor. For example, in a very difficult passage, *Principalis Quaestio II, Pars II*, where the earliest texts read "die dominico sotularia iuuenum fungia . . . perungunt," Venice, 1576, has "die dominica solutaria iuuenum fungia . . . perungunt.")

Malleus Maleficarum, Impressum Francofurti ad Moenum apud Nicolaum Bassaeum . . . 8vo, 1580.

Malleus Maleficarum, . . . Francofurti . . . apud Nicolaum Bassaeum . . . 8vo, 1582.

Malleus Maleficarum, . . . Francofurti . . . apud Nicolaum Bassaeum, 2 vols., 8vo, 1588. This edition also contains in Vol. I extracts from Nider's *Formicarius*. Vol. II, which is dedicated to John Mündzenberg, Prior of the Carmelite House at Frankfort, contains the following nine Tractates:

Bernard Basin, *De artibus magicis*. (1482.)
Ulrich Molitor, *De lamiis*. (1489.)
Girolamo Menghi, O.S.F.C., *Flagellum Daemonum*. (1578.)
John Gerson, *De probatione Spirituum*. (*circa* 1404.)
Thomas Murner, O.M., *De Pythonico contractu*. (1499.)
Felix Hemmerlin, *De exorcismis*. (*circa* 1445.)
Eiusdem, *De credulitate Daemonibus adhibenda*. (1454.)
Bartolomeo Spina, O.P., *De strigibus*. (1523.)
Eiusdem, *Apologiae III aduersus Ioann. Franc. Ponzinibium*. (1525.)

The title-page announces that these works are "Omnes de integro nunc demum in ordinem congestos, notis & explicationibus illustratos, atque ab innumeris quibus ad nauseam usque scatebant mendis in usum communem uindicatos." It is true that the earlier editions did swarm with errors, and some of

---

* *Jules Baissac, "Les grands Jours de la Sorcellerie," 1890, p. 19, says—I do not know on what authority—"La 1re édition du 'Malleus Maleficarum' est de 1489, in —4, Cologne, cinq ans après la publication de la Bulle Summis desiderantes."*

these blemishes have been duly corrected, but there still remains much to be done in the way of emendation. It is to be wished that even the little care given to Vol. II had been bestowed on the text of the *Malleus Maleficarum* in Vol. I, for this is very poor and faulty.

Malleus Maleficarum, Lyons, 8vo, 1595. (Graesse.)

Malleus Maleficarum, Friburg, 1598.

Malleus Maleficarum, Lyons, 8vo, 1600.

Malleus Maleficarum, Lyons, "multo auctior," 8vo, 1620.

Malleus Maleficarum, Friburg, 8vo, 1660.

Malleus Maleficarum, 4to, Lyons, 1666. (Graesse.)

Malleus Maleficarum, 4 vols., "sumptibus Claudii Bourgeat," 4to, Lyons, 1669. This would appear to be the latest edition of the *Malleus Maleficarum*, and the text has here and there received some revision. For example, in the passage to which reference has already been made, *Principalis Quaestio II, Pars II*, where the former reading was "sotularia iuuenum fungia . . . perungunt," we have the correct "axungia"* instead of "fungia." I have given in the Introduction a list of the collections contained in these four noble volumes.

Quétif-Echard, *Scriptores Ordinis Praedicatorum*, 2 vols., Paris, 1719, Vol. I, p. 881, mention a French translation of the *Malleus Maleficarum*, *Le Maillet des Sorcières*, as having been published, quarto, at Lyons by Stephanus Gueynard. No date, however, is given, and as this book cannot be traced, it seems highly probable that one of the many Lyons reprints of the *Malleus Maleficarum* was mistakenly supposed to be a French rendering of the original. In answer to my inquiries M. le Directeur of the Bibliothèque Nationale has kindly informed me: "L'ouvrage de Sprenger, *Le Maillet des Sorcières*, édition de Lyon, ne se trouve point à la Bibliothèque Nationale. Mais, de plus, je me suis reporté à l'excellente *bibliographie lyonnaise* de Baudrier, XIᵉ série, 1914, et là non plus, l'édition de Stephanus Gueynard ne se trouve point." *Le Maillet des Sorcières*, 4to, Lyons, by Stephanus Gueynard, does not occur in the valuable *Essai d'une Bibliographie Française méthodique et raisonnée de la Sorcellerie* of R. Yve-Plessis, Paris, 1900.

There is a modern German translation of the *Malleus Maleficarum* by J. W. R. Schmidt, *Der Hexenhammer*, 3 vols., Berlin, 1906; second edition, 1922-3.

In 1912 Oswald Weigel, the famous "Antiquariat & Auktions-Institut" of Leipzig, sold an exceptionally fine, if not—should it be once permissible to use a much over-worked word—a unique collection of books dealing with witchcraft. This Library contained no fewer than twenty-nine exemplars of the *Malleus Maleficarum*, of which the dates were catalogued as follows: (1) Argentorati (Strasburg), J. Prüss, *ca.* 1487. (2) Spirae, Peter Drach, *ca.* 1487. (3) Spirae, Peter Drach, *ca.* 1490; or Basle, J. von Amorbach, *ca.* 1490?. (4) No place nor date. With inscription "Codex moāsterij scti Martini prope Treuirim." (5) Köln, J. Koelhoff, 1494. (6) Nürnberg, Anton Koberger, 1494. (7) Nürnberg, Anton Koberger, 1496. (8) [Paris], Jehan Petit, *ca.* 1497. (9) Cöln, Henricus de Nussia, 1511. (10) [Paris, Jehan Petit, no date.] (11) Lyon, J. Marion, 1519. (12) Nürnberg, Frederick Peypus, 1519. (13) Köln, J. Gymnicus, 1520. (14) Venetiis, Io. Antonius Bertanus, 1574. (15) Venetiis, *ibid.*, 1576. (16) Francofurti, apud Nicolaum Bassaeum, 1580. (17) Francofurti, *ibid.*, 1582. (18) Lugduni, apud Ioannam Iacobi Iuntae, 2 tomi, 1584. In this edition the title is misprinted *Malleus Maleficorum*. (19) Francofurti, Sumptibus Nicolai Bassaei, 1588. (20) Duplicate of 19. (21) Lugduni, Petri Landry, 2 tomi, 1595. (22) Francofurti, Sumptibus Nicolai Bassaei, 2 tomi, 1600. (23) Lugduni, Sumptibus Petri Landry, 3 tomi, 1604. (24) Lugduni, *ibid.*, 1614. (25) Lugduni, *ibid.*, 1615. (26) Lugduni, Sumptibus Clavdii Landry, 3 tomi, 1620. (27) Lugduni, 3 tomi, 1620-21. (28) Lugduni, 4 tomi, 1669. (29) The modern German translation of the *Malleus Maleficarum* by J. W. R. Schmidt, *Der Hexenhammer*, 3 vols., Berlin, 1906.

---

* *Axis-ungo. See Palladius, I, xvii, 3. Also Vegetius, "De Arte Ueterinaria," IV, x, 3; also IV, xii, 3.*

THE BULL OF INNOCENT VIII

Innocent, Bishop, Servant of the servants of God, for an eternal remembrance.

DESIRING with the most heartfelt anxiety, even as Our Apostleship requires, that the Catholic Faith should especially in this Our day increase and flourish everywhere, and that all heretical depravity should be driven far from the frontiers and bournes of the Faithful, We very gladly proclaim and even restate those particular means and methods whereby Our pious desire may obtain its wished effect, since when all errors are uprooted by Our diligent avocation as by the hoe of a provident husbandman, a zeal for, and the regular observance of, Our holy Faith will be all the more strongly impressed upon the hearts of the faithful.

It has indeed lately come to Our ears, not without afflicting Us with bitter sorrow, that in some parts of Northern Germany, as well as in the provinces, townships, territories, districts, and dioceses of Mainz, Cologne, Trèves, Salzburg, and Bremen, many persons of both sexes, unmindful of their own salvation and straying from the Catholic Faith, have abandoned themselves to devils, incubi and succubi, and by their incantations, spells, conjurations, and other accursed charms and crafts, enormities and horrid offences, have slain infants yet in the mother's womb, as also the offspring of cattle, have blasted the produce of the earth, the grapes of the vine, the fruits of trees, nay, men and women, beasts of burthen, herd-beasts, as well as animals of other kinds, vineyards, orchards, meadows, pastureland, corn, wheat, and all other cereals; these wretches furthermore afflict and torment men and women, beasts of burthen, herd-beasts, as well as animals of other kinds, with terrible and piteous pains and sore diseases, both internal and external; they hinder men from performing the sexual act and women from conceiving, whence husbands cannot know their wives nor wives receive their husbands; over and above this, they blasphemously renounce that Faith which is theirs by the Sacrament of Baptism, and at the instigation of the Enemy of Mankind they do not shrink from committing and perpetrating the foulest abominations and filthiest excesses to the deadly peril of their own souls, whereby they outrage the Divine Majesty and are a cause of scandal and danger to very many. And although Our dear sons Henry Kramer and James Sprenger, Professors of Theology, of the Order of Friars Preachers, have been by Letters Apostolic delegated as Inquisitors of these heretical pravities, and still are Inquisitors, the first in the aforesaid parts of Northern Germany, wherein are included those aforesaid townships, districts, dioceses, and other specified localities, and the second in certain territories which lie along the borders of the Rhine, nevertheless not a few clerics and lay folk of those countries, seeking too curiously to know more than concerns them, since in the aforesaid delegatory letters there is no express and specific mention by name of these provinces, townships, dioceses, and districts, and further since the two delegates themselves and the abominations they are to encounter are not designated in detailed and particular fashion, these persons are not ashamed to contend with the most unblushing effrontery that these enormities are not practised in those provinces, and consequently the aforesaid Inquisitors have no legal right to exercise their powers of inquisition in the provinces, townships, dioceses, districts, and territories, which have been rehearsed, and that the Inquisitors may not proceed to punish, imprison, and penalize criminals convicted of the heinous offences and many wickednesses which have been set forth. Accordingly in the aforesaid provinces, townships, dioceses, and districts, the abominations and enormities in question remain unpunished not without open danger to the souls of many and peril of eternal damnation.

Wherefore We, as is Our duty, being wholly desirous of removing all hindrances and obstacles by which the good work of the Inquisitors may be let and tarded, as also of applying potent remedies to prevent the disease of heresy and other turpitudes diffusing their poison to the destruction of many innocent souls, since Our zeal for the Faith especially incites us, lest that the provinces, townships, dioceses, districts, and territories of Germany, which We have specified, be deprived of the benefits of the Holy Office thereto assigned, by the tenor of these presents in virtue of Our Apostolic authority We decree and enjoin that the aforesaid Inquisitors be empowered to proceed to the just correction, imprisonment, and punishment of any persons, without let or hindrance, in every way as if the provinces, townships, dioceses, districts, territories, yea, even the persons and their crimes in this kind were named and particularly designated in Our letters. Moreover, for greater surety We extend these letters deputing this authority to cover all the aforesaid provinces, townships, dioceses, districts, and territories, persons, and crimes newly rehearsed, and We grant permission to the aforesaid Inquisitors, to one separately or to both, as also to Our dear son John Gremper, priest of the diocese of Constance, Master of Arts, their notary, or to any other public notary, who shall be by them, or by one of them, temporarily delegated to those provinces, townships, dioceses, districts, and aforesaid territories, to proceed, according to the regulations of the Inquisition, against any persons of whatsoever rank and high estate, correcting, mulcting, imprisoning, punishing, as their crimes merit, those whom they have found guilty, the penalty being adapted to the offence. Moreover, they shall enjoy a full and perfect faculty of expounding and preaching the word of God to the faithful, so often as opportunity may offer and it may seem good to them, in each and every parish church of the said provinces, and they shall freely and lawfully perform any rites or execute any business which may appear advisable in the aforesaid cases. By Our supreme authority We grant them anew full and complete faculties.

At the same time by Letters Apostolic We require Our venerable Brother, the Bishop of Strasburg,* that he himself shall announce, or by some other or others cause to be announced, the burthen of Our Bull, which he shall solemnly publish when and so often as he deems it necessary, or when he shall be requested so to do by the Inquisitors or by one of them. Nor shall he suffer them in disobedience to the tenor of these presents to be molested or hindered by any authority whatsoever, but he shall threaten all who endeavour to hinder or harass the Inquisitors, all who oppose them, all rebels, of whatsoever rank, estate, position, pre-

---

* *Albrecht von Bayern, 1478–1506.*

eminence, dignity, or any condition they may be, or whatsoever privilege of exemption they may claim, with excommunication, suspension, interdict, and yet more terrible penalties, censures, and punishment, as may seem good to him, and that without any right of appeal, and if he will he may by Our authority aggravate and renew these penalties as often as he list, calling in, if so please him, the help of the secular arm.

Non obstantibus . . . Let no man therefore . . . But if any dare to do so, which God forbid, let him know that upon him will fall the wrath of Almighty God, and of the Blessed Apostles Peter and Paul.

Given at Rome, at S. Peter's, on the 9 December of the Year of the Incarnation of Our Lord one thousand four hundred and eighty-four, in the first Year of Our Pontificate.

The translation of this Bull is reprinted by permission from " The Geography of Witchcraft," by Montague Summers, pp. 533-6 (Kegan Paul).

MALLEUS MALEFIC ARUM

THE FIRST PART TREATING OF THE THREE NECESSARY CONCOMITANTS OF WITCHCRAFT, WHICH ARE THE DEVIL, A WITCH, AND THE PERMISSION OF ALMIGHTY GOD

✧

PART I

QUESTION I

Here beginneth auspiciously the first part of this work. Question the First.

WHETHER the belief that there are such beings as witches is so essential a part of the Catholic faith that obstinately to maintain the opposite opinion manifestly savours of heresy. And it is argued that a firm belief in witches is not a Catholic doctrine: see chapter 26, question 5, of the work of Episcopus. Whoever believes that any creature can be changed for the better or the worse, or transformed into another kind or likeness, except by the Creator of all things, is worse than a pagan and a heretic. And so when they report such things are done by witches it is not Catholic, but plainly heretical, to maintain this opinion.

Moreover, no operation of witchcraft has a permanent effect among us. And this is the proof thereof: For if it were so, it would be effected by the operation of demons. But to maintain that the devil has power to change human bodies or to do them permanent harm does not seem in accordance with the teaching of the Church. For in this way they could destroy the whole world, and bring it to utter confusion.

Moreover, every alteration that takes place in a human body—for example, a state of health or a state of sickness—can be brought down to a question of natural causes, as Aristotle has shown in his 7th book of *Physics*. And the greatest of these is the influence of the stars. But the devils cannot interfere with the movement of the stars. This is the opinion of Dionysius in his epistle to S. Polycarp. For this alone God can do. Therefore it is evident the demons cannot actually effect any permanent transformation in human bodies; that is to say, no real metamorphosis. And so we must refer the appearance of any such change to some dark and occult cause.

And the power of God is stronger than the power of the devil, so divine works are more true than demoniac operations. Whence inasmuch as evil is powerful in the world, then it must be the work of the devil always conflicting with the work of God. Therefore as it is unlawful to hold that the devil's evil craft can apparently exceed the work of God, so it is unlawful to believe that the noblest works of creation, that is to say, man and beast, can be harmed and spoiled by the power of the devil.

Moreover, that which is under the influence of a material object cannot have power over corporeal objects. But devils are subservient to certain influences of the stars, because magicians observe the course of certain stars in order to evoke the devils. Therefore they have not the power of effecting any change in a corporeal object, and it follows that witches have even less power than the demons possess.

For devils have no power at all save by a certain subtle art. But an art cannot permanently produce a true form. (And a certain author says: Writers on Alchemy know that there is no hope of any real transmutation.) Therefore the devils for their part, making use of the utmost of their craft, cannot bring about any permanent cure—or permanent disease. But if these states exist it is in truth owing to some other cause, which may be unknown, and has nothing to do with the operations of either devils or witches.

But according to the Decretals (33) the contrary is the case. "If by witchcraft or any magic art permitted by the secret but most just will of God, and aided by the power of the devil, etc. . . ." The reference here is to any act of witchcraft which may hinder the end of marriage, and for this impediment to take effect three things can concur, that is to say, witchcraft, the devil, and the permission of God. Moreover, the stronger can influence that which is less strong. But the power of the devil is stronger than any human power (*Job* xl). There is no power upon earth which can be compared to him, who was created so that he fears none.

Answer. Here are three heretical errors which must be met, and when they have been disproved the truth will be plain. For certain writers, pretending to base their opinion upon the words of S. Thomas (iv, 24) when he treats of impediments brought about by magic charms, have tried to maintain that there is not such a thing as magic, that it only exists in the imagination of those men who ascribe natural effects, the causes whereof are not known, to witchcraft and spells. There are others who acknowledge indeed that witches exist, but they declare that the influence of magic and the effects of charms are purely imaginary and phantasmical. A third class of writers maintain that the effects said to be wrought by magic spells are altogether illusory and fanciful, although it may be that the devil does really lend his aid to some witch.

The errors held by each one of these persons may thus be set forth and thus confuted. For in the very first place they are shown to be plainly heretical by many orthodox writers, and especially by S. Thomas, who lays down that such an opinion is altogether contrary to the authority of the saints and is founded upon absolute infidelity. Because the authority of the Holy Scriptures says that devils have power over the bodies and over the minds of men, when God allows them to exercise this power, as is plain from very many passages in the Holy Scriptures. Therefore those err who say that there is no such thing as witchcraft, but that it is purely imaginary, even although they do not believe that devils exist except in the imagination of the ignorant and vulgar, and the natural accidents which happen to a man he wrongly attributes to some supposed devil. For the imagination of some men is so vivid that they think they see actual figures and appearances which are but the reflection of their thoughts, and then these are believed to be the apparitions of evil spirits or even the spectres of witches. But this is contrary to the true faith, which teaches us that certain angels fell from heaven and are now devils, and we are bound to acknowledge that by their very nature they can do many wonderful things which we cannot do. And those who try to induce others to perform such evil wonders are called witches. And because infidelity in a person who has been baptized is technically called heresy, therefore such persons are plainly heretics.

As regards those who hold the other two errors, those, that is to say, who do not deny that there are demons and that demons possess a natural power, but who differ among themselves concerning the possible effects of magic and the possible operations of witches: the one school holding that a witch can truly bring about certain effects, yet these effects are not real but phantastical, the other school allowing that some real harm does befall the person or persons injured, but that when a witch imagines this damage is the effect of her arts she is grossly deceived. This error seems to be based upon two passages from the Canons where certain women are condemned who falsely imagine that during the night they ride abroad with Diana or Herodias.* This may be read in the Canon. Yet because such things often happen by illusion

and merely in the imagination, those who suppose that all the effects of witchcraft are mere illusion and imagination are very greatly deceived. Secondly, with regard to a man who believes or maintains that a creature can be made, or changed for better or for worse, or transformed into some other kind or likeness by anyone save by God, the Creator of all things, alone, is an infidel and worse than a heathen. Wherefore on account of these words " changed for the worse " they say that such an effect if wrought by witchcraft cannot be real but must be purely phantastical.

But inasmuch as these errors savour of heresy and contradict the obvious meaning of the Canon, we will first prove our points by the divine law, as also by ecclesiastical and civil law, and first in general.

To commence, the expressions of the Canon must be treated of in detail (although the sense of the Canon will be even more clearly elucidated in the following question). For the divine law in many places commands that witches are not only to be avoided, but also they are to be put to death, and it would not impose the extreme penalty of this kind if witches did not really and truly make a compact with devils in order to bring about real and true hurts and harms. For the penalty of death is not inflicted except for some grave and notorious crime, but it is otherwise with death of the soul, which can be brought about by the power of a phantastical illusion or even by the stress of temptation. This is the opinion of S. Thomas when he discusses whether it be evil to make use of the help of devils (ii. 7). For in the 18th chapter of Deuteronomy it is commanded that all wizards and charmers are to be destroyed. Also the 19th chapter of Leviticus says : The soul which goeth to wizards and soothsayers to commit fornication with them, I will set my face against that soul, and destroy it out of the midst of my people. And again, 20: A man, or woman, in whom there is a pythonical or divining spirit dying, let them die: they shall stone them. Those persons are said to be pythons in whom the devil works extraordinary things.

Moreover, this must be borne in mind, that on account of this sin Ochozias fell sick and died, IV. Kings i. Also Saul, i Paralipomenon, 10. We have,

---

* "Diana or Herodias." This decree, which was often attributed to a General Council of Ancyra, but which is now held to be of a later date, was in any case authoritative, since it passed into the "De ecclesiasticis disciplinis" ascribed to Regino of Prum (906), and thence to the canonists S. Ivo of Chartres and Johannes Gratian. Section 364 of the Benedictine Abbot's work relates that "certain abandoned women turning aside to follow Satan, being seduced by the illusions and phantasms of demons, believe and openly profess that in the dead of night they ride upon certain beasts with the pagan goddess Diana and a countless horde of women, and that in these silent hours they fly over vast tracks of country and obey her as their mistress, while on other nights they are sullen to pay her homage." John of Salisbury, who died in 1180, in his "Policraticus," I, xvii, speaks of the popular belief in a witch-queen named Herodias, who called together the sorcerers to meeting at night. In a MS., "De Sortilegis," the following passage occurs: "We next inquire concerning certain wicked crones who believe and profess that in the night-time they ride abroad with Diana, the heathen goddess, or else with Herodias, and an innumerable host of women, upon certain beasts, and that in a silent covey at the dead of night they pass over immense distances, obeying her commands as their mistress, and that they are summoned by her on appointed nights, and they declare that they have the power to change human beings for better or for worse, ay, even to turn them into some other semblance or shape. Concerning such women I answer according to the decrees of the Council of Alexandria, that the minds of the faithful are disordered by such fantasies owing to the inspiration of no good spirit but of the devil."

moreover, the weighty opinions of the Fathers who have written upon the scriptures and who have treated at length of the power of demons and of magic arts. The writings of many doctors upon Book 2 of the *Sentences* may be consulted, and it will be found that they all agree, that there · are wizards and sorcerers who by the power of the devil can produce real and extraordinary effects, and these effects are not imaginary, and God permits this to be. I will not mention those very many other places where S. Thomas in great detail discusses operations of this kind. As, for example, in his *Summa contra Gentiles*, Book 3, c. 1 and 2, in part one, question 114, argument 4. And in the *Second of the Second*, questions 92 and 94. We may further consult the Commentators and the Exegetes who have written upon the wise men and the magicians of Pharao, *Exodus* vii. We may also consult what S. Augustine says in *The City of God*,* Book 18, c. 17. See further his second book *On Christian Doctrine*.† Very many other doctors advance the same opinion, and it would be the height of folly for any man to contradict all these, and he could not be held to be clear of the guilt of heresy. For any man who gravely errs in an exposition of Holy Scripture is rightly considered to be a heretic. And whosoever thinks otherwise concerning these matters which touch the faith that the Holy Roman Church holds is a heretic. There is the Faith.

That to deny the existence of witches is contrary to the obvious sense of the Canon is shown by ecclesiastical law. For we have the opinions of the commentators on the Canon which commences: If anyone by magic arts or witchcraft . . . And again, there are those writers who speak of men impotent and bewitched, and therefore by this impediment brought about by witchcraft they are unable to copulate, and so the contract of marriage is rendered void and matrimony in their cases has become impossible. For they say, and S. Thomas agrees with them,

that if witchcraft takes effect in the event of a marriage before there has been carnal copulation, then if it is lasting it annuls and destroys the contract of marriage, and it is quite plain that such a condition cannot in any way be said to be illusory and the effect of imagination.

Upon this point see what Blessed Henry of Segusio ‡ has so fully written in his *Summa*: also Godfrey of Fontaines § and S. Raymond of Peñafort,‖ who have discussed this question in detail very clearly, not asking whether such a physical condition could be thought imaginary and unreal, but taking it to be an actual and proven fact, and then they lay down whether it

‡ "*Blessed Henry.*" *Blessed Henry of Segusio, usually called Hostiensis, the famous Italian canonist of the thirteenth century, was born at Susa, and died at Lyons, 25 October, 1271. After a most distinguished career, on 4 December, 1261, he became Cardinal-Bishop of Ostia and Velletri, whence his name Hostiensis. His "Summa super titulis Decretalium" (Strasburg, 1512; Cologne, 1612; Venice, 1605), which was also known as "Summa aurea," or "Summa archiepiscopi," since it was written whilst he was Archbishop of Embrun, won for its author the title "Monarcha iuris, lumen lucidissimum Decretorum." One portion of this work, the "Summa, siue Tractatus de poenitentia et remissionibus," was very popular, and is continually referred to as of high authority. The book was written between 1250 and 1261.*

§ "*Godfrey.*" *Godfrey of Fontaines, Doctor Uenerandus, scholastic philosopher and theologian, was born near Liège within the first half of the thirteenth century; he became a canon of his native diocese, and also of Paris and Cologne. In 1300 he was elected to the See of Tournai, which he declined. During the last quarter of the century he taught theology with great distinction at the University of Paris. His vast work, "XIV Quodlibeta," which in manuscript was extensively studied in the mediaeval schools, has recently been published for the first time with an ample commentary.*

‖ "*S. Raymond.*" *One of the most distinguished names of the Dominican Order. Born in 1175, he professed Canon law at Barcelona and Bologna. At the request of his superiors he published his "Summa Casuum," of which several editions appeared in the sixteenth and seventeenth centuries. His reputation as a jurist was so great that in 1230 he was called to Rome by Gregory IX, who directed him to rearrange and codify the ecclesiastical canons. Having completed the work, he refused all honours, and returned to Spain. He died at Barcelona, 6 January, 1275. His feast is celebrated on 23 January.*

* "*The City of God.*" *S. Augustine's great work "De Ciuitate Dei" was written 413–26.*

† "*On Christian Doctrine.*" *The "De Doctrina Christiana" was originally written in 397, but S. Augustine revised his work with addition in 427, leaving a monument of hermeneutics.*

is to be treated as a lasting or temporary infirmity if it continued for more than the space of three years, and they do not doubt that it may be brought about by the power of witchcraft, although it is true that this condition may be intermittent. But what is a fact beyond dispute is that such impotency can be brought about through the power of the devil by means of a contract made with him, or even by the devil himself without the assistance of any witch, although this most rarely happens in the Church, since marriage is a most excellent sacrament. But amongst Pagans this actually does happen, and this is because evil spirits act as if they had a certain legitimate dominion over them, as Peter of Palude* in his fourth book relates, when he tells of the young man who had pledged himself in wedlock to a certain idol, and who nevertheless contracted marriage with a young maiden, but he was unable to have any connexion with her because the devil always intervened, actually appearing in bodily form. But nevertheless in the Church the devil prefers to operate through the medium of witches and to bring about such effects for his own gain, that is to say, for the loss of souls. And in what manner he is able to do this, and by what means, will be discussed a little later, where we shall treat of the seven ways of doing harm to men by similar operations. And of the other questions which Theologians and Canonists have raised with reference to these points, one is very important, since they discuss how such impotence can be cured and whether it is permissible to cure it by some counter-charm, and what is to be done if the witch who cast the spell is dead, a circumstance of which Godfrey of Fontaines treats in his *Summa*. And these questions will be amply elucidated in the Third Part of this work.

This then is the reason why the Canonists have so carefully drawn up a table of the various differing penalties, making a distinction between the private and open practice of witchcraft, or rather of divination, since this foul superstition has various species and degrees, so that anyone who is notoriously given to it must be refused Communion. If it be secretly practised the culprit must do penance for forty days. And if he be a cleric he is to be suspended and confined in a monastery. If he be a layman he shall be excommunicated, wherefore all such infamous persons must be punished, together with all those who resort to them, and no excuse at all is to be allowed.

The same penalty too is prescribed by the civil law. For Azo,† in his *Summa* upon Book 9 of the Codex, the rubric concerning sorcerers, 2 after the *lex Cornelia*,‡ concerning assassins and murderers, lays down: Let it be known that all those who are commonly called sorcerers, and those too who are skilled in the art of divination, incur the penalty of death. The same penalty is enforced yet again. For this is the exact sentence of these laws: It is unlawful for any man to practise divination; and if he does so his reward shall be death by the sword of the executioner. There are others too who by their magic charms endeavour to take the lives of innocent people, who turn the passions of women to lusts of every kind, and these criminals are to be thrown to the wild beasts. And the laws allow that any witness whatsoever is to be admitted as evidence against them. This the Canon treating of the defence of the Faith

---

† "*Azo*." *Early in the thirteenth century Portius Azo stood at the head of the Bolognese school of law which was accomplishing the resuscitation of the classical Roman law. He was the pupil of the celebrated Johannes Bassianus, and his fame so eclipsed all his contemporaries that in 1205 Thomas of Marlborough, afterwards Abbot of Evesham, spent six months at Bologna hearing his lectures every day. Azo was saluted as "Master of all the Masters of the laws," and the highest praise that could be given another canonist was to declare him to be "second only to Azo." Savigrey says that Azo was alive as late as 1230. His chief work is a "Summa" of the first nine books of the Code, to which he added a "Summa" of the Institutes. No less than thirty-one editions appeared between 1482 and 1610; of which five are earlier than 1500. Throughout the Middle Ages these treatises were in highest repute.*

‡ "*Lex Cornelia.*" *De Sicariis et Ueneficis. Passed circa 81 B.C. This law dealt with incendiarism as well as open assassination and poisoning, and laid down penalties for accessories to the fact.*

---

* "*Peter of Palude.*" *Peter of Palude, who died 1342, of the Order of S. Dominic, was one of the most distinguished Thomistic theologians during the first half of the fourteenth century.*

explicitly enjoins. And the same procedure is allowable in a charge of heresy. When such an accusation is brought, any witness may come forward to give evidence, just as he may in a case of lese-majesty. For witchcraft is high treason against God's Majesty. And so they are to be put to the torture in order to make them confess. Any person, whatever his rank or position, upon such an accusation may be put to the torture, and he who is found guilty, even if he confesses his crime, let him be racked, let him suffer all other tortures prescribed by law in order that he may be punished in proportion to his offences.

Note: In days of old such criminals suffered a double penalty and were often thrown to wild beasts to be devoured by them. Nowadays they are burnt at the stake, and probably this is because the majority of them are women.

The civil law also forbids any conniving at or joining in such practices, for it did not allow a diviner even to enter another person's house; and often it ordered that all their possessions should be burnt, nor was anyone allowed to patronize or to consult them; very often they were deported to some distant and deserted island and all their goods sold by public auction. Moreover, those who consulted or resorted to witches were punished with exile and the confiscation of all their property. These penalties were set in operation by the common consent of all nations and rulers, and they have greatly conduced to the suppression of the practice of such forbidden arts.

It should be observed that the laws highly commend those who seek to nullify the charms of witches. And those who take great pains that the work of man shall not be harmed by the force of tempests or by hailstorms are worthy of a great reward rather than of any punishment. How such damage may lawfully be prevented will be discussed in full below. Accordingly, how can it be that the denial or frivolous contradiction of any of these propositions can be free from the mark of some notable heresy? Let every man judge for himself unless indeed his ignorance excuse him. But what sort of ignorance may excuse him we shall very shortly proceed to explain. From what has been already said we draw the following conclusion: It is a most certain and

most Catholic opinion that there are sorcerers and witches who by the help of the devil, on account of a compact which they have entered into with him, are able, since God allows this, to produce real and actual evils and harm, which does not render it unlikely that they can also bring about visionary and phantastical illusions by some extraordinary and peculiar means. The scope of the present inquiry, however, is witchcraft, and this very widely differs from these other arts, and therefore a consideration of them would be nothing to the purpose, since those who practise them may with greater accuracy be termed fortune-tellers and soothsayers rather than sorcerers.

It must particularly be noticed that these two last errors are founded upon a complete misunderstanding of the words of the Canon (I will not speak of the first error, which stands obviously self-condemned, since it is clean contrary to the teaching of Holy Scripture). And so let us proceed to a right understanding of the Canon. And first we will speak against the first error, which says that the mean is mere illusion although the two extremes are realities.

Here it must be noticed that there are fourteen distinct species which come under the genus superstition, but these for the sake of brevity it is hardly necessary to detail, since they have been most clearly set out by S. Isidore* in his *Etymologiae*, Book 8, and by S. Thomas in his *Second of the Second*, question 92. Moreover, there will be explicit mention of these rather lower when we discuss the gravity of this heresy, and this will be in the last question of our First Part.

The category in which women of this sort are to be ranked is called the category of Pythons, persons in or by whom the devil either speaks or per-

---

* "*St. Isidore.*" The "*Etymologiae*," or "*Origines*" as it is sometimes called, must be regarded as the most important and best known of the works of S. Isidore of Seville, born circa 560; died 4 April, 636. It has been described as "a vast storehouse in which is gathered, systematized, and condensed, all the learning possessed by that time." Throughout the greater part of the Middle Ages it was the text-book most in use in educational institutions. Arevalo, who is regarded as the most authoritative editor of S. Isidore (7 vols., Rome, 1797–1803), tells us that it was printed no less than ten times between 1470 and 1529.

forms some astonishing operation, and this is often the first category in order. But the category under which sorcerers come is called the category of Sorcerers.

And inasmuch as these persons differ greatly one from another, it would not be correct that they should not be comprised in that species under which so many others are confined : Wherefore, since the Canon makes explicit mention of certain women, but does not in so many words speak of witches ; therefore they are entirely wrong who understand the Canon only to speak of imaginary voyages and goings to and fro in the body and who wish to reduce every kind of superstition to this illusion : for as those women are transported in their imagination, so are witches actually and bodily transported. And he who wishes to argue from this Canon that the effects of witchcraft, the infliction of disease or any sickness, are purely imaginary, utterly mistakes the tenor of the Canon, and errs most grossly.

Further, it is to be observed that those who, whilst they allow the two extremes, that is to say, some operation of the devil and the effect, a sensible disease, to be actual and real, at the same time deny that any instrument is the means thereof; that is to say, they deny that any witch could have participated in such a cause and effect, these, I say, err most gravely: for, in philosophy, the mean must always partake of the nature of the two extremes.

Moreover, it is useless to argue that any result of witchcraft may be a phantasy and unreal, because such a phantasy cannot be procured without resort to the power of the devil, and it is necessary that there should be made a contract with the devil, by which contract the witch truly and actually binds herself to be the servant of the devil and devotes herself to the devil, and this is not done in any dream or under any illusion, but she herself bodily and truly co-operates with, and conjoins herself to, the devil. For this indeed is the end of all witchcraft; whether it be the casting of spells by a look or by a formula of words or by some other charm, it is all of the devil, as will be made clear in the following question.

In truth, if anyone cares to read the words of the Canon, there are four points which must particularly strike him. And the first point is this: It is absolutely incumbent upon all creatures and Priests, and upon all who have the cure of souls, to teach their flocks that there is one, only, true God, and that to none other in Heaven or earth may worship be given. The second point is this, that although these women imagine they are riding (as they think and say) with Diana or with Herodias, in truth they are riding with the devil, who calls himself by some such heathen name and throws a glamour before their eyes. And the third point is this, that the act of riding abroad may be merely illusory, since the devil has extraordinary power over the minds of those who have given themselves up to him, so that what they do in pure imagination, they believe they have actually and really done in the body. And the fourth point is this: Witches have made a compact to obey the devil in all things, wherefore that the words of the Canon should be extended to include and comprise every act of witchcraft is absurd, since witches do much more than these women, and witches actually are of a very different kind.

Whether witches by their magic arts are actually and bodily transported from place to place, or whether this merely happens in imagination, as is the case with regard to those women who are called Pythons, will be dealt with later in this work, and we shall also discuss how they are conveyed. So now we have explained two errors at least, and we have arrived at a clear understanding of the sense of the Canon.

Moreover, a third error, which mistaking the words of the Canon says that all magic arts are illusions, may be corrected from the very words of the Canon itself. For inasmuch as it says that he who believes any creature can be made or transformed for the better or the worse, or metamorphosed into some other species or likeness, save it be by the Creator of all things Himself, etc. . . . he is worse than an infidel. These three propositions, if they are thus understood as they might appear on the bare face of them, are clean contrary to the sense of Holy Scripture and the commentaries of the doctors of the Church. For the following Canon clearly says that creatures can be made by witches, although they necessarily must be very imperfect creatures, and probably in some way deformed. And it is plain that the sense of the Canon agrees with what S. Augustine tells us concerning the magicians at the court of Pharao, who turned their rods into serpents, as the holy doctor writes upon the 7th chapter of *Exodus*, ver. 11, —and Pharao called the wise men and the magicians. . . . We may also refer to the commentaries of Strabo, who says that devils hurry up and down over the whole earth, when by their incantations witches are employing them at various operations, and these devils are able to collect various germs or seeds, and from these germs or seeds they are able to cause various species to grow. We may also refer to Blessed Albertus Magnus,* *De animalibus*. And also S. Thomas, Part 1, question 114, article 4. For the sake of conciseness we will not quote them at length here, but this remains proven, that it is possible for certain creatures to be created in this way.

With reference to the second point, that a creature may be changed for better or for worse, it is always to be understood that this can only be done by the permission and indeed by the power of God, and that this is only done in order to correct or to punish, but that God very often allows devils to act as His ministers and His servants, but throughout all it is God alone who can afflict and it is He alone who can heal, for " I kill and I make alive" (*Deuteronomy* xxxii, 39). And so evil angels may and do perform the will of God. To this also S. Augustine bears witness when he says: There are in truth magic spells and evil charms, which not only often afflict men with diseases but even kill them outright. We must also endeavour clearly to understand what actually happens when nowadays by the power of the devil wizards and witches are changed into wolves and other savage beasts. The Canon, however, speaks of some bodily and lasting change, and does not discuss those extraordinary things which may be done by glamour of which S. Augustine speaks in the 18th book and the 17th chapter of *Of the City of God*, when he reports many strange tales of that famous witch Circe, and of the companions of Diomedes and of the father of Praestantius. This will be discussed in detail in the Second Part.

Whether it be a Heresy to Maintain that Witches Exist.

The second part of our inquiry is this, whether obstinately to maintain that witches exist is heretical. The question arises whether people who hold that witches do not exist are to be regarded as notorious heretics, or whether they are to be regarded as gravely suspect of holding heretical opinions. *It seems* that the first opinion is the correct one. For this is undoubtedly in accordance with the opinion of the learned Bernard. And yet those persons who openly and obstinately persevere in heresy must be proved to be heretics by unshaken evidence, and such demonstration is generally one of three kinds; either a man has openly preached and proclaimed heretical doctrines; or he is proved to be a heretic by the evidence of trustworthy witnesses; or he is proved to be a heretic by his own free confession. And yet there are some who rashly opposing themselves to all authority publicly proclaim that witches do not exist, or at any rate that they can in no way afflict and hurt mankind. Wherefore, strictly speaking those who are convicted of such evil doctrine may according to the commentary of Bernard be excommunicated, since they are openly and un-

---

* *"Blessed Albertus."* Albert the Great, the Dominican doctor, scientist, philosopher, and theologian. Born circa 1206; died at Cologne, 15 November, 1280. He is called "the Great" and "Doctor Uniuersalis" on account of his extraordinary genius and encyclopaedic knowledge, for he surpassed all his contemporaries in every branch of learning cultivated in his day. He is certainly one of the glories of the Order of Preachers. Ulrich Endelbert speaks of him as: "Uir in omni scientia adeo diuinus, ut nostri temporis stupor et miraculum congrue uocari possit" ("De summo bono," III, iv). Perhaps at the present day his extraordinary genius is not sufficiently recognized, for he was certainly one of the most learned men of all time. The latest edition of his complete works, Paris (Louis Vives), 1890–99, in thirty-eight quarto volumes, was published under the direction of the Abbé Auguste Borgnet, of the diocese of Reims. "De animalibus" will be found in Vols. XI–XII. The feast of Albertus Magnus is celebrated on 15 November. He was beatified by Gregory XV in 1622, so in this translation I call him "Blessed" by anticipation.

mistakably to be convicted of false doctrine. The reader may consult the works of Bernard, where he will find that this sentence is just, right, and true. Yet perhaps this may seem to be altogether too severe a judgement mainly because of the penalties which follow upon excommunication: for the Canon prescribes that a cleric is to be degraded and that a layman is to be handed over to the power of the secular courts, who are admonished to punish him as his offence deserves. Moreover, we must take into consideration the very great numbers of persons who, owing to their ignorance, will surely be found guilty of this error. And since the error is very common the rigor of strict justice may be tempered with mercy. And it is indeed our intention to try to make excuses for those who are guilty of this heresy rather than to accuse them of being infected with the malice of heresy. It is preferable then that if a man should be even gravely suspected of holding this false opinion he should not be immediately condemned for the grave crime of heresy. (See the gloss of Bernard* upon the word *Condemned.*) One may in truth proceed against such a man as against a person who is gravely suspect, but he is not to be condemned in his absence and without a hearing. And yet the suspicion may be very grave, and we cannot refrain from suspecting these people, for their frivolous assertions do certainly seem to affect the purity of the faith. For there are three kinds of suspicion—a light suspicion, a serious suspicion, and a grave suspicion. These are treated of in the chapter on Accusations and in the chapter on Contumacy, Book 6, *On Heretics.* And these things come under the cognizance of the archidiaconal court. Reference may also be made to the commentaries of

Giovanni d'Andrea,† and in particular to his glosses upon the phrases *Accused; Gravely suspect;* and his note upon a presumption of heresy. It is certain too that some who lay down the law on this subject do not realize that they are holding false doctrines and errors, for there are many who have no knowledge of the Canon law, and there are some who, owing to the fact that they are badly informed and insufficiently read, waver in their opinions and cannot make up their minds, and since an idea merely kept to oneself is not heresy unless it be afterwards put forward, obstinately and openly maintained, it should certainly be said that persons such as we have just mentioned are not to be openly condemned for the crime of heresy. But let no man think he may escape by pleading ignorance. For those who have gone astray through ignorance of this kind may be found to have sinned very gravely. For although there are many degrees of ignorance, nevertheless those who have the cure of souls cannot plead invincible ignorance, nor that particular ignorance, as the philosophers call it, which by the writers on Canon law and by the Theologians is called Ignorance of the Fact. But what is to be blamed in these persons is Universal ignorance, that is to say, an ignorance of the divine law, which, as Pope Nicholas‡ has laid down, they must and should know. For he says: The dispensation of these divine teachings is entrusted to our charge: and woe be unto us if we do not sow the good seed, woe be unto us if we do not teach our flocks. And so those who have the charge of souls are bound to have a sound knowledge of the Sacred Scrip-

* *"Bernard."* Junior, or Modernus, a canonist who lived in the middle of the thirteenth century, called *"Compostellanus"* from the fact that he possessed an ecclesiastical benefice in Compostella. He was also known as Brignadius from his birthplace in Galicia, Spain. Bernard was chaplain to Innocent IV, who reigned 1243–54, and was himself a noted canonist. Bernard's Commentaries on Canon law are very copious and very celebrated. He is termed Modernus to distinguish him from Bernard Antiquus, a canonist of the early thirteenth century, a native of Compostella, who became Professor of Canon law in the University of Bologna.

† *"Giovanni d'Andrea."* This distinguished canonist was born at Mugello, near Florence, about 1275; died 1348. He was educated at the University of Bologna, where he afterwards became Professor of Canon law. He had previously taught at Padua and Pisa, and his career as a lecturer extended for nearly half a century. His works are *"Glossarium in VI decretalium librum,"* Venice and Lyons, 1472; *"Glossarium in Clementinas"; "Nouella, siue Commentarius in decretales epistolas Gregorii IX,"* Venice, 1581; *"Mercuriales, siue commentarius in regulas sexti"; "Liber de laudibus S. Hieronymi"; "Additamenta ad speculum Durand"* (1347).

‡ *"Pope Nicholas."* Nicholas V, 1397–1455, the great patron of learning.

tures. It is true that according to Raymond of Sabunde* and S. Thomas, those who have the cure of souls are certainly not bound to be men of any extraordinary learning, but they certainly should have a competent knowledge, that is to say, knowledge sufficient to carry out the duties of their state.

And yet, and this may be some small consolation to them, the theoretical severity of the law is often balanced by the actual practice, and they may know that this ignorance of the Canon law, although sometimes it may be culpable and worthy of blame, is considered from two points of view. For sometimes persons do not know, they do not wish to know, and they have no intention of knowing. For such persons there is no excuse, but they are altogether to be condemned. And of these the Psalmist speaks: He would not understand in order that he might do good. But secondly, there are those who are ignorant, yet not from any desire not to know. And this diminishes the gravity of the sin, because there is no actual consent of the will. And such a case is this, when anyone ought to know something, but cannot realize that he ought to know it, as S. Paul says in his 1st Epistle to Timothy (i, 13): But I obtained the mercy of God, because I did it ignorantly in unbelief. And this is technically said to be an ignorance, which indirectly at least is the fault of the person, insomuch as on account of many other occupations he neglects to inform himself of matters which he ought to know, and he does not use any endeavour to make himself acquainted with them, and this ignorance does not entirely excuse him, but it excuses him to a certain degree. So S. Ambrose,† writing upon that passage

in the *Romans* (ii, 4): Knowest thou not, that the benignity of God leadeth thee to penance? says, If thou dost not know through thine own fault then thy sin is very great and grievous. More especially then in these days, when souls are beset with so many dangers, we must take measures to dispel all ignorance, and we must always have before our eyes that severe judgement which will be passed upon us if we do not use, everyone according to his proper ability, the one talent which has been given. In this way our ignorance will be neither thick nor stupid, for metaphorically we speak of men as thick and stupid who do not see what lies directly in their very way.

And in the *Flores regularum moralium* the Roman Chancellor commenting upon the second rule says: A culpable ignorance of the Divine law does not of necessity affect the ignorant person. The reason is this: the Holy Spirit is able directly to instruct a man in all that knowledge essential to salvation, if these things are too difficult for him to grasp unaided by his own natural intellect.

The answer to the first objection then is a clear and correct understanding of the Canon. To the second objection Peter of Tarentaise (Blessed Innocent V‡) replies: No doubt the devil, owing to his malice which he harbours against the human race, would destroy mankind if he were allowed by God to do so. The fact that God allows him sometimes to do harm and that sometimes God hinders and prevents him, manifestly brings the devil into more open contempt and loathing, since in all

---

* "*Raymond of Sabunde.*" *Born at Barcelona, Spain, towards the end of the fourteenth century; died 1432. From 1430 to his death he taught theology, philosophy, and medicine at the University of Toulouse. Of his many works only one remains, "Theologia Naturalis." It was first written in Spanish, and translated into Latin at various times: Deventer, 1487; Strasburg, 1496; Paris, 1509; Venice, 1581, etc. Montaigne, who translated the book into French, Paris, 1569, bears witness to the extraordinary popularity it enjoyed in his own day.*

† "*S. Ambrose.*" "*On désigne depuis le XVIᵉ siècle sous le nom d'Ambrosiaster (= pseudo-Ambroise) l'auteur anonyme d'un commentaire sur les Epîtres de saint Paul (à l'ex-*

clusion de l'Epître aux Hébreux), qui au moyenâge, peut-être même dès l'époque de Cassiodore, fut imputé inexactement à saint Ambroise. Cette paraphrase est tout à fait remarquable; c'est l'une des plus intéressantes que l'antiquité chrétienne nous ait léguées." Labriolle, "*Histoire de la Littérature Latine Chrétienne,*' c. III.

‡ "*Innocent V.*" *Petrus a Tarentasia, born in Tarentaise, towards 1225, elected at Arezzo, 21 January, 1276; died at Rome, 22 June, 1276. At the age of sixteen he joined the Dominican Order, and he won great distinction as a Professor at the University of Paris, whence he is known as Doctor Famosissimus. He is the author of several works dealing with philosophy, theology, and Canon law, some of which are still unpublished. The principal of these is the "Commentary on the Sentences of Peter Lombard." I have used the edition, Toulouse 1652.*

It seemed they made a habit of showing where concessions were allowed & then going to extremes to invalidate, Ex: heretical level of knowledge.

things, to the manifestation of His glory, God is using the devil, unwilling though he be, as a servant and slave. With regard to the third objection, that the infliction of sickness or some other harm is always the result of human effort, whereby the witch submits her will to evil, and so actually as any other evil-doer, by the volition of her will can afflict some person or bring about some damage or perform some villainous act. If it be asked whether the movement of material objects from place to place by the devil may be paralleled by the movement of the spheres, the answer is No. Because material objects are not thus moved by any natural inherent power of their own, but they are only moved by a certain obedience to the power of the devil, who by the virtue of his own nature has a certain dominion over bodies and material things; he has this certain power, I affirm, yet he is not able to add to created material objects any form or shape, be it substantial or accidental, without some admixture of or compounding with another created natural object. But since, by the will of God, he is able actually to move material objects from place to place, then by the conjunction of various objects he can produce disease or some circumstance such as he will. Wherefore the spells and effects of witchcraft are not governed by the movement of the spheres, nor is the devil himself thus governed, inasmuch as he may often make use of these conditions to do him service.

The answer to the fourth objection. The work of God can be destroyed by the work of the devil in accordance with what we are now saying with reference to the power and effects of witchcraft. But since this can only be by the permission of God, it does not at all follow that the devil is stronger than God. Again, he cannot use so much violence as he wishes to harm the works of God, because if he were unrestricted he would utterly destroy all the works of God.

The answer to the fifth objection may be clearly stated thus: The planets and stars have no power to coerce and compel devils to perform any actions against their will, although seemingly demons are readier to appear when summoned by magicians under the influence of certain stars. It appears that they do this for two reasons. First, Because they know that the power of that planet will aid the effect which the magicians desire. Secondly, They do this in order to deceive men, thus making them suppose that the stars have some divine power or actual divinity, and we know that in days of old this veneration of the stars led to the vilest idolatry.

With reference to the last objection, which is founded upon the argument that gold is made by alchemists, we may put forward the opinion of S. Thomas when he discusses the power of the devil and how he works: Although certain forms having a substance may be brought about by art and the power of a natural agent, as, for example, the form of fire is brought about by art employed on wood: nevertheless, this cannot be done universally, because art cannot always either find or yet mix together the proper agents in the proper proportions, and yet it can produce something similar. And thus alchemists make something similar to gold, that is to say, in so far as the external accidents are concerned, but nevertheless they do not make true gold, because the substance of gold is not formed by the heat of fire which alchemists employ, but by the heat of the sun, acting and reacting upon a certain spot where mineral power is concentrated and amassed, and therefore such gold is of the same likeness as, but is not of the same species as, natural gold. And the same argument applies to all their other operations.

This then is our proposition: devils by their art do bring about evil effects through witchcraft, yet it is true that without the assistance of some agent they cannot make any form, either substantial or accidental, and we do not maintain that they can inflict damage without the assistance of some agent, but with such an agent diseases, and any other human passions or ailments, can be brought about, and these are real and true. How these agents or how the employment of such means can be rendered effective in co-operation with devils will be made clear in the following chapters.

It seemed they stretched the "if God allows" a lot, It seemed to me some of their own arguments in the beginning on why not to believe in witchcraft were just as valid.

QUESTION II

IF it be in accordance with the Catholic Faith to maintain that in order to bring about some effect of magic, the devil must intimately co-operate with the witch, or whether one without the other, that is to say, the devil without the witch, or conversely, could produce such an effect.

And the first argument is this: That the devil can bring about an effect of magic without the co-operation of any witch. So S. Augustine holds. All things which visibly happen so that they can be seen, may (it is believed) be the work of the inferior powers of the air. But bodily ills and ailments are certainly not invisible, nay rather, they are evident to the senses, therefore they can be brought about by devils. Moreover, we learn from the Holy Scriptures of the disasters which fell upon Job, how fire fell from heaven and striking the sheep and the servants consumed them, and how a violent wind threw down the four corners of a house so that it fell upon his children and slew them all. The devil by himself without the co-operation of any witches, but merely by God's permission alone, was able to bring about all these disasters. Therefore he can certainly do many things which are often ascribed to the work of witches.

And this is obvious from the account of the seven husbands of the maiden Sara, whom a devil killed. Moreover, whatever a superior power is able to do, it is able to do without reference to a power superior to it, and a superior power can all the more work without reference to an inferior power. But an inferior power can cause hailstorms and bring about diseases without the help of a power greater than itself. For Blessed Albertus Magnus in his work *De passionibus aeris* * says that rotten sage, if used as he explains, and thrown into running water, will arouse most fearful tempests and storms.

Moreover, it may be said that the devil makes use of a witch, not because he has need of any such agent, but because he is seeking the perdition of the witch. We may refer to what Aristotle says in the 3rd book of his *Ethics*. Evil is a voluntary act which is proved

by the fact that nobody performs an unjust action merely for the sake of doing an unjust action, and a man who commits a rape does this for the sake of pleasure, not merely doing evil for evil's sake. Yet the law punishes those who have done evil as if they had acted merely for the sake of doing evil. Therefore if the devil works by means of a witch he is merely employing an instrument; and since an instrument depends upon the will of the person who employs it and does not act of its own free will, therefore the guilt of the action ought not to be laid to the charge of the witch, and in consequence she should not be punished.

But an opposite opinion holds that the devil cannot so easily and readily do harm by himself to mankind, as he can harm them through the instrumentality of witches, although they are his servants. In the first place we may consider the act of generation. But for every act which has an effect upon another some kind of contact must be established, and because the devil, who is a spirit, can have no such actual contact with a human body, since there is nothing common of this kind between them, therefore he uses some human instruments, and upon these he bestows the power of hurting by bodily touch. And many hold this to be proven by the text, and the gloss upon the text, in the 3rd chapter of S. Paul's Epistle to the *Galatians:*† O senseless Galatians, who hath bewitched you that you should not obey the truth? And the gloss upon this passage refers to those who have singularly fiery and baleful eyes, who by a mere look can harm others, especially young children. And Avicenna†

---

* "*De passionibus.*" *This treatise on physical science may be found in Vol. IX. of Abbé Borgnet's edition of the "Opera omnia."*

† "*Galatians.*" iii, i. *The original Greek is* Ὦ ἀνόητοι Γαλάται, τίς ὑμᾶς ἐβάσκανεν τῇ ἀληθείᾳ μὴ πείθεσθαι; *Curtius doubts the etymological connexion between* βασκαίνω *and Latin* "*fascino*" *as from a root* ΦΑΣ. *In classical times the charm was dissolved by spitting thrice. Cf. Theocritus, VI, 39:* ὡς μὴ βασκανθῶ δέ, τρὶς εἰς ἐμὸν ἔπτυσα κόλπον.

‡ "*Avicenna.*" *Abn Ali Al Hosian Ibn Addallah Ibn Sina, Arabian physician and philosopher, born at Kharmaithen, in the province of Bokhara, 980; died at Hamadan, in Northern Persia, 1037. It should be noted that the Schoolmen were aware of the pantheistic tendencies of Avicenna's philosophical works, and accordingly were reluctant to trust to his exposition of Aristotle.*

also bears this out, *Naturalium*, Book 3, c. the last, when he says: "Very often the soul may have as much influence upon the body of another to the same extent as it has upon its own body, for such is the influence of the eyes of anyone who by his glance attracts and fascinates another." And the same opinion is maintained by Al-Gazali* in the 5th book and 10th c. of his *Physics*. Avicenna also suggests, although he does not put this opinion forward as irrefutable, that the power of the imagination can actually change or seem to change extraneous bodies, in cases where the power of the imagination is too unrestrained; and hence we gather that the power of the imagination is not to be considered as distinct from a man's other sensible powers, since it is common to them all, but to some extent it includes all those other powers. And this is true, because such a power of the imagination can change adjacent bodies, as, for example, when a man is able to walk along some narrow beam which is stretched down the middle of a street. But yet if this beam were suspended over deep water he would not dare to walk along it, because his imagination would most strongly impress upon his mind the idea of falling, and therefore his body and the power of his limbs would obey his imagination, and they would not obey the contrary thereto, that is to say, walking directly and without hesitation. This change may be compared to the influence exercised by the eyes of a person who has such influence, and so a mental change is brought about although there is not any actual and bodily change.

Moreover, if it be argued that such a change is caused by a living body owing to the influence of the mind upon some other living body, this answer may be given. In the presence of a murderer blood flows from the wounds in the corpse of the person he has slain. Therefore without any mental powers bodies can produce wonderful effects, and so a living man if he pass by near the corpse of a murdered man, although he may not be aware of the dead body, is often seized with fear.

Again, there are some things in nature which have certain hidden powers, the reason for which man does not know; such, for example, is the lodestone, which attracts steel and many other such things, which S. Augustine mentions in the 20th book *Of the City of God*.

And so women in order to bring about changes in the bodies of others sometimes make use of certain things, which exceed our knowledge, but this is without any aid from the devil. And because these remedies are mysterious we must not therefore ascribe them to the power of the devil as we should ascribe evil spells wrought by witches.

Moreover, witches use certain images and other strange periapts, which they are wont to place under the lintels of the doors of houses, or in those meadows where flocks are herding, or even where men congregate, and thus they cast spells over their victims, who have ofttimes been known to die. But because such extraordinary effects can proceed from these images it would appear that the influence of these images is in proportion to the influence of the stars over human bodies, for as natural bodies are influenced by heavenly bodies, so may artificial bodies likewise be thus influenced. But natural bodies may find the benefit of certain secret but good influences. Therefore artificial bodies may receive such influence. Hence it is plain that those who perform works of healing may well perform them by means of such good influences, and this has no connexion at all with any evil power.

Moreover, it would seem that most extraordinary and miraculous events come to pass by the working of the powers of nature. For wonderful and terrible and amazing things happen owing to natural forces. And this S. Gregory points out in his *Second Dialogue*.† The Saints perform miracles,

---

* "*Al-Gazali.*" *Abu Hamid Mohammed Ibn Mohammed, the celebrated Arabian philosopher, born at Tous in Khorasan in 1038; died at Nissapour in 1111. He passed through complete scepticism to the mysticism of the Sufis. It is often said that Blessed Albertus Magnus wrote thus: "Non approbo dictum Auicennae et Algazel de fascinatione, quia credo quod non nocet fascinatio, nec nocere potest ars magica, nec facit aliquid ex his quae timentur de talibus." But this passage is more than suspicious.*

† "*Second Dialogue.*" *The "Dialogorum Libri IV" is one of the most famous of S. Gregory's works, and very many separate editions have appeared.*

sometimes by a prayer, sometimes by their power alone. There are examples of each: S. Peter by praying raised to life Tabitha, who was dead.* By rebuking Ananias and Sapphira, who were telling a lie, he slew them without any prayer. Therefore a man by his mental influence can change a material body into another, or he can change such a body from health to sickness and conversely.

Moreover, the human body is nobler than any other body, but because of the passions of the mind the human body changes and becomes hot or cold, as is the case with angry men or men who are afraid: and so an even greater change takes place with regard to the effects of sickness and death, which by their power can greatly change a material body.

But certain objections must be allowed. The influence of the mind cannot make an impression upon any form except by the intervention of some agent, as we have said above. And these are the words of S. Augustine in the book which we have already quoted: It is incredible that the angels who fell from Heaven should be obedient to any material things, for they obey God only. And much less can a man of his natural power bring about extraordinary and evil effects. The answer must be made, there are even to-day many who err greatly on this point, making excuses for witches and laying the whole blame upon the craft of the devil, or ascribing the changes that they work to some natural alteration. These errors may be easily made clear. First, by the description of witches which S. Isidore gives in his *Etymologiae*, c. 9: Witches are so called on account of the blackness of their guilt, that is to say, their deeds are more evil than those of any other malefactors. He continues: They stir up and confound the elements by the aid of the devil, and arouse terrible hailstorms and tempests. Moreover, he says they distract the minds of men, driving them to madness, insane hatred, and inordinate lusts. Again, he continues, by the terrible influence of their spells alone, as it were by a draught of poison, they can destroy life.

And the words of S. Augustine in his book on *The City of God* are very much to the point, for he tells us who magicians and witches really are. Magicians, who are commonly called witches, are thus termed on account of the magnitude of their evil deeds. These are they who by the permission of God disturb the elements, who drive to distraction the minds of men, such as have lost their trust in God, and by the terrible power of their evil spells, without any actual draught or poison, kill human beings. As Lucan says: A mind which has not been corrupted by any noxious drink perishes forspoken by some evil charm. For having summoned devils to their aid they actually dare to heap harms upon mankind, and even to destroy their enemies by their evil spells. And it is certain that in operations of this kind the witch works in close conjunction with the devil. Secondly, punishments are of four kinds: beneficial, hurtful, wrought by witchcraft, and natural. Beneficial punishments are meted out by the ministry of good Angels, just as hurtful punishments proceed from evil spirits. Moses smote Egypt with ten plagues by the ministry of good Angels, and the magicians were only able to perform three of these miracles by the aid of the devil. And the pestilence which fell upon the people for three days because of the sin of David who numbered the people, and the 72,000 men who were slain in one night in the army of Sennacherib, were miracles wrought by the Angels of God, that is, by good Angels who feared God and knew that they were carrying out His commands.

Destructive harm, however, is wrought by the medium of bad angels, at whose hands the children of Israel in the desert were often afflicted. And those harms which are simply evil and nothing more are brought about by the devil, who works through the medium of sorcerers and witches. There are also natural harms which in some manner depend upon the conjunction of heavenly bodies, such as dearth, drought, tempests, and similar effects of nature.

It is obvious that there is a vast difference between all these causes, circumstances, and happenings. For Job was afflicted by the devil with a harmful disease, but this is nothing to the purpose. And if anybody who is too clever

---

* "S. Peter." "Acts of the Apostles," ix, 36–42; and v, 1–11.

and over-curious asks how it was that Job was afflicted with this disease by the devil without the aid of some sorcerer or witch, let him know that he is merely beating the air and not informing himself as to the real truth. For in the time of Job there were no sorcerers and witches, and such abominations were not yet practised. But the providence of God wished that by the example of Job the power of the devil even over good men might be manifested, so that we might learn to be on our guard against Satan, and, moreover, by the example of this holy patriarch the glory of God shines abroad, since nothing happens save what is permitted by God.

With regard to the time at which this evil superstition, witchcraft, appeared, we must first distinguish the worshippers of the devil from those who were merely idolaters. And Vincent of Beauvais* in his *Speculum historiale*, quoting many learned authorities, says that he who first practised the arts of magic and of astrology was Zoroaster,† who is said to have been Cham‡ the son of Noe.

And according to S. Augustine in his book *Of the City of God*, Cham laughed aloud when he was born, and thus showed that he was a servant of the devil; and he, although he was a great and mighty king, was conquered by Ninus the son of Belus, who built Ninive, whose reign was the beginning of the kingdom of Assyria in the time of Abraham.

This Ninus, owing to his insane love for his father, when his father was dead, ordered a statue of his father to be made, and whatever criminal took refuge there was free from any punishment which he might have incurred. From this time men began to worship images as though they were gods; but this was after the earliest years of history, for in the very first ages there was no idolatry, since in the earliest times men still preserved some remembrance of the creation of the world, as S. Thomas says, Book 2, question 95, article 4. Or it may have originated

---

* "*Vincent.*" *Little is known of the personal history of this celebrated encyclopaedist. The years of his birth and death are uncertain, but the dates most frequently assigned are 1190 and 1264 respectively. It is thought that he joined the Dominicans in Paris shortly after 1218, and that he passed practically his whole life in his monastery at Beauvais, where he occupied himself incessantly upon his enormous work, the general title of which is "Speculum Maius," containing 80 books, divided into 9885 chapters. The third part, "Speculum Historiale," in 31 books and 3793 chapters, brings the History of the World down to A.D. 1250.*

† "*Zoroaster.*" *Pliny, "Historia Naturalis," XXX, ii, says of magic: "Sine dubio illic orta in Perside a Zoroastre, ut inter auctores conuenit. Sed unus hic fuerit, an postea et alius, non satis constat." Apuleius, "De Magia," XXVI, mentions Zoroaster and Oromazus as the inventors of sorcery: "Audistisne magiam . . . artem esse dis immortalibus acceptam . . . a Zoroastro et Oromazo auctoribus suis nobilem, caelitum antistitam?"*

‡ "*Cham.*" "*A.V.*" *Ham. Lenglet du Fresnoy in his "History of the Hermetic Philosophy" repeats an old tradition: "Most alchemists pretended that Cham, or Chem, the son of Noe, was an adept in the art, and thought it highly probable that the words 'Chemistry' and 'Alchemy' are both derived from his name." Lactantius, "De Origine Erroris," II, says of the descendants of Cham: "Omnium primi qui Aegyptum occu-*

pauerunt; caelestia suspicere, atque adorare coeperunt."
"Réalité de la Magie et des Apparitions," Paris, 1819 (pp. xii–xiii), has: "Le monde, purgé par le déluge, fut repeuplé par les trois fils de Noé. Sem et Japhet imitèrent la vertu de leur père, et furent justes comme lui. Cham, au contraire, donna entrée au démon dans son coeur, remit au jour l'art exécrable de la magie, en composa les règles, et en instruisit son fils Misraim.

"Cent trente ans après le déluge, Sem habitait la Perse. Ses enfans pratiquaient la religion naturelle, que Dieu mit dans le coeur du premier homme; et leurs vieillards se nommaient mages, qui veut dire "sages" en notre langue. Dans la suite, les descendans de Cham se partagèrent, et quelques-uns passèrent en Perse; Cham, qui vivait encore, était à leur tête. Il opéra tant de prodiges par ses charmes et ses enchantements, que les Bactriens lui donnèrent le nom de Zoroastre, c'est-à-dire, 'astre vivant'; et transportèrent à ceux de sa secte le nom honorable de "mages," que les adorateurs du vrai Dieu abandonnèrent, dès qu'ils le virent ainsi profané: et c'est de là que nous est venu le nom de 'magie,' pour signifier le culte du démon.

"Cham, ou Zoroastre, fut encore l'inventeur de l'astrologie judiciaire; il regarda les astres comme autant de divinités, et persuada aux hommes que tout leur destin dépendait de leurs bonnes ou mauvaises influences. Ainsi l'on commença à leur rendre un culte religieux, qui fut l'origine de l'idolâtrie. La Chaldée fut le premier théâtre de ces égaremens; et alors, 'Chaldéen, astrologue et magicien' étaient trois mots synonymes."

with Nembroth,* who compelled men to worship fire; and thus in the second age of the world there began Idolatry, which is the first of all superstitions, as Divination is the second, and the Observing of Times and Seasons the third.

The practices of witches are included in the second kind of superstition, which is to say Divination, since they expressly invoke the devil. And there are three kinds of this superstition:—Necromancy, Astrology, or rather Astromancy, the superstitious observation of the stars, and Oneiromancy.

I have explained all this at length that the reader may understand that these evil arts did not suddenly burst upon the world, but rather were developed in the process of time, and therefore it was not impertinent to point out that there were no witches in the days of Job. For as the years went by, as S. Gregory says in his *Moralia*, the knowledge of the Saints grew: and therefore the evil craft of the devil likewise increased. The prophet Isaias says: The earth is filled with the knowledge of the Lord (xi, 6). And so in this twilight and evening of the world, when sin is flourishing on every side and in every place, when charity is growing cold, the evil of witches and their iniquities superabound.

And since Zoroaster was wholly given up to the magic arts, it was the devil alone who inspired him to study and observe the stars. Very early did sorcerers and witches make compacts with the devil and connive with him to bring harm upon human beings. This is proved in the seventh chapter of Exodus, where the magicians of Pharao by the power of the devil wrought extraordinary wonders, imitating those plagues which Moses had brought upon Egypt by the power of good angels.

Hence follows the Catholic teaching, that in order to bring about evil a witch can and does co-operate with the

devil. And any objections to this may briefly be answered thus.

1. In the first place, nobody denies that certain harms and damages which actually and visibly afflict men, animals, the fruits of the earth, and which often come about by the influence of the stars, may yet often be brought about by demons, when God permits them so to act. For as S. Augustine says in the 4th book *Of the City of God:* Demons may make use of both fire and air if God allow them so to do. And a commentator remarks: God punishes by the power of evil angels.

2. From this obviously follows the answer to any objection concerning Job, and to any objections which may be raised to our account of the beginnings of magic in the world.

3. With regard to the fact that rotten sage which is thrown into running water is said to produce some evil effect without the help of the devil, although it may not be wholly disconnected with the influence of certain stars, we would point out that we do not intend to discuss the good or evil influence of the stars, but only witchcraft, and therefore this is beside the point.

4. With regard to the fourth argument, it is certainly true that the devil only employs witches to bring about their bale and destruction. But when it is deduced that they are not to be punished, because they only act as instruments which are moved not by their own volition but at the will and pleasure of the principal and agent, there is a ready answer: For they are human instruments and free agents, and although they have made a compact and a contract with the devil, nevertheless they do enjoy absolute liberty: for, as has been learnt from their own revelations—and I speak of women who have been convicted and burned at the stake and who were compelled to wreak vengeance and evil and damage if they wished to escape punishments and blows inflicted by the devil—yet these women do co-operate with the devil although they are bound to him by that profession by which at first they freely and willingly gave themselves over into his power.

With regard to these other arguments, in which it is proved that certain old women have an occult knowledge which

---

* "*Nembroth.*" S. Augustine, "*De Ciuitate Dei,*" XVI, 3, quotes: "*Chus autem genuit Nebroth; hic coepit esse gigans super terram. Hic erat gigans uenator contra Dominum Deum.*" Nebroth is the English Nimrod, who was considered a past master of magic, and even by later ages a demon. So we have: "*Nembroth. Un des esprits que les magiciens consultent. Le mardi lui est consacré, et on l'évoque ce jour-là: il faut, pour le renvoyer, lui jeter une pierre; ce qui est facile.*" Collin de Plancy ("*Dictionnaire Infernal,*" sixième édition, 1863).

enables them to bring about extraordinary and indeed evil effects without the aid of the devil. It must be understood that from one particular to conclude a universal argument is contrary to all sound reason. And when, as it seems, throughout the whole of the Scriptures no such instance can be found, save where it speaks of the charms and spells old women practise, therefore we must not hence conclude that this is always the case. Moreover, the authorities on these passages leave the matter open to question, that is to say, whether such charms have any efficacy without the co-operation of the devil. These charms or fascinations seem capable of division into three kinds. First, the senses are deluded, and this may truly be done by magic, that is to say, by the power of the devil, if God permit it. And the senses may be enlightened by the power of good angels. Secondly, fascination may bring about a certain glamour and a leading astray, as when the apostle says: Who hath bewitched you? *Galatians* iii, 1. In the third place, there may be a certain fascination cast by the eyes* over another person, and this may be harmful and bad.

And it is of this fascination that Avicenna and Al-Gazali have spoken; S. Thomas too thus mentions this fascination, Part 1, question 117. For he says the mind of a man may be changed by the influence of another mind. And that influence which is exerted over another often proceeds from the eyes, for in the eyes a certain subtle influence may be concentrated. For the eyes direct their glance upon a certain object without taking notice of other things, and although the vision be perfectly clear, yet at the sight of some impurity, such as, for example, a woman during her monthly periods, the eyes will as it were contract a certain impurity. This is what Aristotle says in his work *On Sleep and Waking*,† and thus if anybody's spirit is inflamed with malice or rage, as is often the case with old women, then their disturbed spirit

looks through their eyes, for their countenances are most evil and harmful, and often terrify young children of tender years, who are extremely impressionable. And it may be that this is often natural, permitted by God; on the other hand, it may be that these evil looks are often inspired by the malice of the devil, with whom old witches have made some secret contract.

The next question arises with regard to the influence of the heavenly bodies, and here we find three very common errors, but these will be answered as we proceed to explain other matters.

With regard to operations of witchcraft, we find that some of these may be due to mental influence over others, and in some cases such mental influence might be a good one, but it is the motive which makes it evil.

And there are four principal arguments which are to be objected against those who deny that there are witches, or magical operations, which may be performed at the conjunction of certain planets and stars, and that by the malice of human beings harm may be wrought through fashioning images, through the use of spells, and by the writing of mysterious characters. All theologians and philosophers agree that the heavenly bodies are guided and directed by certain spiritual mediums. But those spirits are superior to our minds and souls, just as the heavenly bodies are superior to other bodies, and therefore they can influence both the mind and body of a man, so that he is persuaded and directed to perform some human act. But in order yet more fully to attempt a solution of these matters, we may consider certain difficulties from a discussion of which we shall yet more clearly arrive at the truth. First, spiritual substances cannot change bodies to some other natural form unless it be through the mediumship of some agent. Therefore, however strong a mental influence may be, it cannot effect any change in a man's mind or disposition. Moreover, several universities, especially that of Paris, have condemned the following article:—That an enchanter is able to cast a camel into a deep ditch merely by directing his gaze upon it. And so this article is condemned, that a corporeal body should obey some spiritual substance if this be understood simply, that is to say, if the obedience

---

* *"Cast by the eyes."* In Ireland it was supposed that certain witches could cast a spell at a glance, and they were commonly called "eyebiting witches."

† *"On Sleep."* This is one of the smaller treatises connected with Aristotle's great work *"On the Soul,"* περὶ ψυχῆς.

entails some actual change or transformation. For in regard to this it is
God alone Who is absolutely obeyed.
Bearing these points in mind we may
soon see how that fascination, or influence of the eyes of which we have
spoken, is possible, and in what respects
it is not possible. For it is not possible
that a man through the natural powers
of his mind should direct such power
from his eyes that, without the agency
of his own body or of some other
medium, he should be able to do harm
to the body of another man. Nor is it
possible that a man through the natural
powers of his mind should at his will
bring about some change, and by
directing this power through the
mediumship of his eyes entirely transform the body of a man, upon whom
he fixes his gaze, just as his will and
pleasure may be.

And therefore in neither of these ways
can one man influence and fascinate
another, for no man by the natural
powers of his mind alone possesses such
an extraordinary influence. Therefore,
to wish to prove that evil effects can be
produced by some natural power is to
say that this natural power is the power
of the devil, which is very far indeed
from the truth.

Nevertheless, we may more clearly
set forth how it is possible for a careful
gaze to do harm. It may so happen that
if a man or a woman gaze steadfastly at
some child, the child, owing to its power
of sight and power of imagination, may
receive some very sensible and direct
impression. And an impression of this
kind is often accompanied by a bodily
change, and since the eyes are one of
the tenderest organs of the body, therefore they are very liable to such impressions. Therefore it may well happen that the eyes receive some bad
impression and change for the worse,
since very often the thoughts of the
mind or the motions of the body are
particularly impressed upon and shown
by the eyes. And so it may happen that
some angry and evil gaze, if it has been
steadfastly fixed and directed upon a
child, may so impress itself upon that
child's memory and imagination that it
may reflect itself in the gaze of the
child, and actual results will follow, as,
for example, he may lose his appetite
and be unable to take food, he may
sicken and fall ill. And sometimes we
see that the sight of a man who is

suffering from his eyes may cause the
eyes of those who gaze upon him to
dazzle and feel weak, although to a
large extent this is nothing else but the
effect of pure imagination. Several
other examples of the same sort might
be discussed here, but for the sake of
conciseness we will not discuss them in
any further detail.

All this is borne out by the commentators upon the Psalm, Qui timent te
uidebunt me.* There is a great power
in the eyes, and this appears even in
natural things. For if a wolf see a man
first, the man is struck dumb. Moreover, if a basilisk see a man first its look
is fatal; but if he see it first he may be
able to kill it; and the reason why the
basilisk is able to kill a man by its gaze
is because when it sees him, owing to
its anger a certain terrible poison is set
in motion throughout its body, and this
it can dart from its eyes, thus infecting
the atmosphere with deadly venom.
And thus the man breathes in the air
which it has infected and is stupefied
and dies. But when the beast is first
seen by the man, in a case when the
man wishes to kill the basilisk, he furnishes himself with mirrors, and the
beast seeing itself in the mirrors darts
out poison towards its reflection, but
the poison recoils and the animal dies.
It does not seem plain, however, why
the man who thus kills the basilisk
should not die too, and we can only
conclude that this is on account of some
reason not clearly understood.

So far we have set down our opinions
absolutely without prejudice and refraining from any hasty or rash judgement, not deviating from the teachings
and writings of the Saints. We conclude, therefore, that the Catholic truth
is this, that to bring about these evils
which form the subject of discussion,
witches and the devil always work
together, and that in so far as these
matters are concerned one can do
nothing without the aid and assistance
of the other.

We have already treated of this fascination. And now with reference to the
second point, namely, that blood will
flow from a corpse in the presence of a
murderer. According to the *Speculum
naturale* of Vincent of Beauvais, c. 13, the

---

* "*Qui timent.*" Psalm li, 8: *Uidebunt
iusti et timebunt.*

wound is, as it were, influenced by the mind of the murderer, and that wound receives a certain atmosphere which has been impressed by and is permeated with his violence and hatred, and when the murderer draws near, the blood wells up and gushes forth from the corpse. For it would seem that this atmosphere, which was caused and as it were entered the wound owing to the murderer, at his presence is disturbed and greatly moved, and it is owing to this movement that the blood streams out of the dead body. There are some who declare that it is due to some other causes, and they say that this gushing forth of the blood is the voice of the blood crying from the earth against the murderer who is present, and that this is on account of the curse pronounced against the first murderer Cain. And with regard to that horror which a person feels when he is passing near the corpse of a man who has been murdered, although he may not be in any way cognizant of the vicinity of a dead body, this horror is psychic, it infects the atmosphere and conveys a thrill of fear to the mind. But all these explanations, be it noted, do not in any way affect the truth of the evil wrought by witches, since they are all perfectly natural and arise from natural causes.

In the third place, as we have already said above, the operations and rites of witches are placed in that second category of superstition which is called Divination; and of this divination there are three kinds, but the argument does not hold good with reference to the third kind, which belongs to a different species, for witchcraft is not merely any divination, but it is that divination, the operations of which are performed by express and explicit invocations of the devil; and this may be done in very many ways, as by Necromancy, Geomancy, Hydromancy, etc.

Wherefore this divination, which is used when they are working their spells, must be judged to be the height of criminal wickedness, although some have attempted to regard it from another point of view. And they argue thus, that as we do not know the hidden powers of nature, it may be that the witches are merely employing or seeking to employ these hidden powers: assuredly if they are employing the natural powers of natural things to bring about a natural effect, this must be perfectly

lawful, as indeed is obvious enough. Or even let us conceive that if they superstitiously employ natural things, as, for example, by writing down certain characters or unknown names of some kind, and that then they use these runes for restoring a person to health, or for inducing friendship, or with some useful end, and not at all for doing any damage or harm, in such cases, it may be granted, I say, that there is no express invocation of demons; nevertheless it cannot be that these spells are employed without a tacit invocation, wherefore all such charms must be judged to be wholly unlawful.

And because these and many other charms like to them may be placed in the third category of superstition, that is to say, idle and vain observing of times and seasons, this is by no means a relevant argument as to the heresy of witches. But of this category, the observing of times and seasons, there are four distinct species: A man may use such observations to acquire certain knowledge: or he may in this way seek to inform himself concerning lucky or unlucky days and things: or he may use sacred words and prayers as a charm with no reference to their meaning: or he may intend and desire to bring about some beneficial change in some body. All this S. Thomas has amply treated in that question where he asks, Whether such observing be lawful, especially if it be to bring about a beneficial change in a body, that is to say, the restoration of persons to health. But when witches observe times and seasons, their practices must be held to belong to the second kind of superstition, and therefore, in so far as they are concerned, questions concerning this third class are wholly impertinent.

We now proceed to a fourth proposition, inasmuch as from observations of the kind we have discussed certain charts and images are wont to be made, but these are of two separate sorts, which differ entirely one from the other; and these are Astronomical and Necromantic. Now in Necromancy there is always an express and particular invocation of demons, for this craft implies that there has been an express compact and contract with them. Let us therefore only consider Astrology. In Astrology there is no compact, and therefore there is no invocation, unless by chance there be some kind of tacit invocation, since the figures of demons and their names sometimes appear in Astrological charts. And again, Necromantic signs are written under the influence of certain stars in order to counteract the influence and oppositions of other heavenly bodies, and these are inscribed, for signs and characters of this kind are often engraved upon rings, gems, or some other precious metal, but magic signs are engraved without any reference to the influence of the stars, and often upon any substance, nay, even upon vile and sordid substances, which when buried in certain places bring about damage and harm and disease. But we are discussing charts which are made with reference to the stars. And these Necromantic charts and images have no reference to any heavenly body. Therefore a consideration of them does not enter into the present discussion.

Moreover, many of these images which have been made with superstitious rites have no efficacy at all, that is to say, in so far as the fashioning of them is concerned, although it may be that the material of which they are made does possess a certain power, although this is not due to the fact that they were made under the influence of certain stars. Yet many hold that it is in any case unlawful to make use even of images like these. But the images made by witches have no natural power at all, nor has the material of which they are formed any power; but they fashion such images by command of the devil, that by so doing they may, as it were, mock the work of the Creator, and that they may provoke Him to anger so that in punishment of their misdeeds He may suffer plagues to fall upon the earth. And in order to increase their guilt they delight especially to fashion many such images at the more solemn seasons of the year.

With regard to the fifth point, S. Gregory is there speaking of the power of grace and not of the power of nature. And since, as S. Jóhn says, we are born of God, what wonder then that the sons of God enjoy extraordinary powers.

With regard to the last point we will say this, that a mere likeness is irrelevant, because the influence of one's own mind on one's own body is different from its influence upon another body. For since the mind is united to the body as though the body were the material form of the mind, and the emotions are an act of the body, but separate, therefore the emotion can be changed by the influence of the mind whensoever there is some bodily change, heat or cold, or any alteration, even to death itself. But to change the actual body, no act of the mind is sufficient by itself, unless there can be some physical result which alters the body. Whence witches, by the exercise of no natural power, but only by the help of the devil, are able to bring about harmful effects. And the devils themselves can only do this by the use of material objects as their instruments, such as bones, hair, wood, iron, and all sorts of objects of this kind, concerning which operation we shall treat more fully a little later.

Now with regard to the tenor of the Bull of our Most Holy Father the Pope, we will discuss the origin of witches, and how it is that of recent years their works have so multiplied among us. And it must be borne in mind that for this to take place, three things concur, the devil, the witch, and the permission of God who suffers such things to be. For S. Augustine says, that the abomination of witchcraft arose from this foul connexion of mankind with the devil. Therefore it is plain that the origin and the increase of this heresy arises from this foul connexion, a fact which many authors approve.

We must especially observe that this heresy, witchcraft, not only differs from all other heresy in this, that not merely by a tacit compact, but by a compact which is exactly defined and expressed it blasphemes the Creator and endeavours to the utmost to profane Him and to harm His creatures, for all other simple heresies have made no open compact with the devil, no compact, that is, either tacit or exactly expressed, although their errors and misbelief are directly to be attributed to the Father of errors and lies. Moreover, witchcraft differs from all other harmful and mysterious arts in this point, that of all superstition it is essentially the vilest, the most evil and the worst, wherefore it derives its name from doing evil, and from blaspheming the true faith. (*Maleficae dictae a Maleficiendo, seu a male de fide sentiendo.*)

Let us especially note too that in the practice of this abominable evil, four points in particular are required. First, most profanely to renounce the Catholic Faith, or at any rate to deny certain dogmas of the faith; secondly, to devote themselves body and soul to all evil; thirdly, to offer up unbaptized children to Satan; fourthly, to indulge in every kind of carnal lust with Incubi and Succubi and all manner of filthy delights.

Would to God that we might suppose all this to be untrue and merely imaginary, if only our Holy Mother the Church were free from the leprosy of such abomination. Alas, the judgement of the Apostolic See, who is alone the Mistress and the Teacher of all truth, that judgement, I say, which has been expressed in the Bull of our Holy Father the Pope, assures us and makes us aware that these crimes and evils flourish amongst us, and we dare not refrain from inquiring into them lest we imperil our own salvation. And therefore we must discuss at length the origin and the increase of these abominations; it has been a work of much labour indeed, but we trust that every detail will most exactly and most carefully be weighed by those who read this book, for herein will be found nothing contrary to sound reason, nothing which differs from the words of Scripture and the tradition of the Fathers.

Now there are two circumstances which are certainly very common at the present day, that is to say, the connexion of witches with familiars, Incubi and Succubi, and the horrible sacrifices of small children. Therefore we shall particularly deal with these matters, so that in the first place we shall discuss these demons themselves, secondly, the witches and their works, and thirdly, we will inquire wherefore such things are suffered to be. Now these demons work owing to their influence upon man's mind and upon his free will, and they choose to copulate under the influence of certain stars rather than under the influence of others, for it would seem that at certain times their semen can more easily generate and beget children. Accordingly, we must inquire why the demons should act at the conjunction of certain stars, and what times these are.

There are three chief points to discuss. First, whether these abominable heresies can be multiplied throughout the world by those who give themselves to Incubi and Succubi. Secondly, whether their actions have not a certain extraordinary power when performed under the influence of certain stars. Thirdly, whether this abominable heresy is not widely spread by those who profanely sacrifice children to Satan. Moreover, when we have discussed the second point, before we proceed to the third, we must consider the influence of the stars, and what power they have in acts of witchcraft.

With regard to the first question there are three difficulties which need elucidation.

The first is a general consideration of these demons, which are called Incubi.

The second question is more particular, for we must inquire, How can these Incubi perform the human act of copulation?

The third question is also a special one, How do witches bind themselves to and copulate with these devils?

☆

QUESTION III

Whether children can be generated by Incubi and Succubi.

AT first it may truly seem that it is not in accordance with the Catholic Faith to maintain that children can be begotten by devils, that is to say, by Incubi* and Succubi: for God Himself, before sin came into the world, instituted human procreation, since He created woman from the rib of man to be a helpmeet unto man: And to them He said: Increase and multiply, *Genesis* i, 28. And again Adam being inspired by God said: They shall be two in one flesh, *Genesis* ii, 24. Likewise after sin had come into the world, it was said to Noe: Increase, and multiply, *Genesis* ix, 1. In the time of the new law also, Christ confirmed this union: Have ye not read, that he who made man from the beginning, *Made them male and female?* S. *Matthew* xix, 4. Therefore men cannot be begotten in any other way than this.

But it may be argued that devils take their part in this generation not as the essential cause, but as a secondary and artificial cause, since they busy them-

* *"Incubi." For a very full discussion of the whole subject see Sinistrari's "Demoniality" with my Commentary and glosses, Fortune Press, 1927.*

selves by interfering with the process of normal copulation and conception, by obtaining human semen, and themselves transferring it.

Objection. The devil can perform this act in every state of life, that is to say, in the matrimonial state, or not in the matrimonial state. Or he can perform it in one only state. Now he cannot perform it in the first state, because then the act of the devil would be more powerful than the act of God, Who instituted and confirmed this holy estate, since it is a state of continence and wedlock. Nor can he effect this in any other estate: since we never read in Scripture that children can be begotten in one state and not in another.

Moreover, to beget a child is the act of a living body, but devils cannot bestow life upon the bodies which they assume; because life formally only proceeds from the soul, and the act of generation is the act of the physical organs which have bodily life. Therefore bodies which are assumed in this way cannot either beget or bear.

Yet it may be said that these devils assume a body not in order that they may bestow life upon it, but that they may by the means of this body preserve human semen, and pass the semen on to another body.

Objection. As in the action of angels, whether they be good or bad, there is nothing superfluous and useless, nor is there anything superfluous and useless in nature. But the devil by his natural power, which is far greater than any human bodily power, can perform any spiritual action, and perform it again and again although man may not be able to discern it. Therefore he is able to perform this action, although man may not be able to discern when the devil is concerned therewith. For all bodily and material things are on a lower scale than pure and spiritual intelligences. But the angels, whether they be good or whether they be evil, are pure and spiritual intelligences. Therefore they can control what is below them. Therefore the devil can collect and make use as he will of human semen which belongs to the body.

However, to collect human semen from one person and to transfer it to another implies certain local actions. But devils cannot locally move bodies from place to place. And this is the argument they put forward. The soul is purely a spiritual essence, so is the devil: but the soul cannot move a body from place to place except it be that body in which it lives and to which it gives life: whence if any member of the body perishes it becomes dead and immovable. Therefore devils cannot move a body from place to place, except it be a body to which they give life. It has been shown, however, and is acknowledged that devils do not bestow life on anybody, therefore they cannot move human semen locally, that is, from place to place, from body to body.

Moreover, every action is performed by contact, and especially the act of generation. But it does not seem possible that there can be any contact between the demon and human bodies, since he has no actual point of contact with them. Therefore he cannot inject semen into a human body, and therefore since this needs a certain bodily action, it would seem that the devil cannot accomplish it.

Besides, devils have no power to move those bodies which in a natural order are more closely related to them, for example the heavenly bodies, therefore they have no power to move those bodies which are more distant and distinct from them. The major is proved, since the power that moves and the movement are one and the same thing according to Aristotle in his *Physics*. It follows, therefore, that devils who move heavenly bodies must be in heaven, which is wholly untrue, both in our opinion and in the opinion of the Platonists.

Moreover, S. Augustine, *On the Trinity*, III, says that devils do indeed collect human semen, by means of which they are able to produce bodily effects: but this cannot be done without some local movement, therefore demons can transfer the semen which they have collected and inject it into the bodies of others. But, as Walafrid Strabo says in his commentary upon *Exodus* vii, 11: And Pharao called the wise men and the magicians: Devils go about the earth collecting every sort of seed, and can by working upon them broadcast various species. See also the gloss on those words (Pharao called). And again in *Genesis* vi the gloss makes two comments on the words: And the sons of God saw the daughters of men. First, that by the sons of God are meant the sons of Seth, and by the daughters of men, the daughters of Cain. Second, that Giants were created not by some incredible act of men, but by certain devils, which are shameless towards women. For the Bible says, Giants were upon the earth. Moreover, even after the Flood the bodies not only of men, but also of women, were pre-eminently and incredibly beautiful.

Answer. For the sake of brevity much concerning the power of the devil and his works in the matter of the effects of witchcraft is left out; for the pious reader either accepts it as proved, or he may, if he wish to inquire, find every point clearly elucidated in the second *Book of Sentences*, 5. For he will see that the devils perform all their works consciously and voluntarily; for the nature that was given them has not been changed. See Dionysius* in his fourth chapter on this subject; their nature remained intact and very splendid, although they cannot use it for any good purpose.

And as to their intelligence, he will find that they excel in three points of understanding, that is, in the subtlety of their nature, in their age-long experience, and in the revelation of the higher spirits. He will find also how, through the influence of the stars, they learn the dominating characteristics of men, and so discover that some are more disposed to work witchcraft than others, and that they molest these chiefly for the purpose of such works.

---

* *"Dionysius."* A series of famous writings was attributed to S. Dionysius the Areopagite ("Acts" xvii, 34), who was also popularly identified with the Martyr of Gaul, the first Bishop of Paris. The writings themselves form a collection of four treatises and ten letters. These will all be found in Migne, "Patres Graeci," III. The treatises are generally referred to under their Latin names, "De Diuinis nominibus"; "Caelestis hierarchia"; "Ecclesiastica hierarchia"; "Theologia mystica." The main source from which the Middle Ages obtained a knowledge of Dionysius and his doctrine was undoubtedly the Latin translation by Scotus Eriugena, made about 858. There are ample commentaries by many writers such as Hugh of Saint-Victor, Blessed Albertus Magnus, S. Thomas, and Denys the Carthusian. The works of Dionysius the Areopagite and the identification of this writer with S. Denys were accepted by Saints and Schoolmen, and perhaps we should do well to follow them without curious questions and impertinent discussion.

And as to their will, the reader will find that it cleaves unchangeably to evil, and that they continuously sin in pride, envy, and gross covetousness; and that God, for his own glory, permits them to work against His will. He will also understand how with these two qualities of intellect and will devils do marvels, so that there is no power in earth which can be compared to them: *Job* xli. There is no power on the earth which can be compared with him, who was created that he should fear no one. But here the gloss says, Although he fears no one he is yet subject to the merits of the Saints.

He will find also how the devil knows the thoughts of our hearts; how he can substantially and disastrously metamorphose bodies with the help of an agent; how he can move bodies locally, and alter the outward and inner feelings to every conceivable extent; and how he can change the intellect and will of a man, however indirectly.

For although all this is pertinent to our present inquiry, we wish only to draw some conclusion therefrom as to the nature of devils, and so proceed to the discussion of our question.

Now the Theologians have ascribed to them certain qualities, as that they are unclean spirits, yet not by very nature unclean. For according to Dionysius there is in them a natural madness, a rabid concupiscence, a wanton fancy, as is seen from their spiritual sins of pride, envy, and wrath. For this reason they are the enemies of the human race: rational in mind, but reasoning without words; subtle in wickedness, eager to do hurt; ever fertile in fresh deceptions, they change the perceptions and befoul the emotions of men, they confound the watchful, and in dreams disturb the sleeping; they bring diseases, stir up tempests, disguise themselves as angels of light, bear Hell always about them; from witches they usurp to themselves the worship of God, and by this means magic spells are made; they seek to get a mastery over the good, and molest them to the most of their power; to the elect they are given as a temptation, and always they lie in wait for the destruction of men.

And although they have a thousand ways of doing harm, and have tried ever since their downfall to bring about schisms in the Church, to disable charity, to infect with the gall of envy the sweetness of the acts of the Saints, and in every way to subvert and perturb the human race; yet their power remains confined to the privy parts and the navel. See *Job* xli. For through the wantonness of the flesh they have much power over men; and in men the source of wantonness lies in the privy parts, since it is from them that the semen falls, just as in women it falls from the navel.

These things, then, being granted for a proper understanding of the question of Incubi and Succubi, it must be said that it is just as Catholic a view to hold that men may at times be begotten by means of Incubi and Succubi, as it is contrary to the words of the Saints and even to the tradition of Holy Scripture to maintain the opposite opinion. And this is proved as follows. S. Augustine in one place raises this question, not indeed as regards witches, but with reference to the very works of devils, and to the fables of the poets, and leaves the matter in some doubt; though later on he is definite in the matter of Holy Scripture. For in his *De Ciuitate Dei*, Book 3, chapter 2, he says: We leave open the question whether it was possible for Venus to give birth to Aeneas through coition with Anchises. For a similar question arises in the Scriptures, where it is asked whether evil angels lay with the daughters of men, and thereby the earth was then filled with giants, that is to say, preternaturally big and strong men. But he settles the question in Book 5, chapter 23, in these words: It is a very general belief, the truth of which is vouched for by many from their own experience, or at least from hearsay as having been experienced by men of undoubted trustworthiness, that Satyrs and Fauns (which are commonly called Incubi) have appeared to wanton women and have sought and obtained coition with them. And that certain devils (which the Gauls call Dusii) assiduously attempt and achieve this filthiness is vouched for by so many credible witnesses that it would seem impudent to deny it.

Later in the same book he settles the second contention, namely, that the passage in Genesis about the sons of God (that is Seth) and the daughters of men (that is Cain) does not speak only of Incubi, since the existence of such is not credible. In this connexion there is the gloss which we have touched upon before. He says that it is not outside belief that the Giants of whom the Scripture speaks were begotten not by men, but by Angels or certain devils who lust after women. To the same effect is the gloss on *Esaias* xiii,* where the prophet foretells the desolation of Babylon, and the monsters that should inhabit it. He says: Owls shall dwell there, and Satyrs shall dance there. By Satyrs here devils are meant; as the gloss says, Satyrs are wild shaggy creatures of the woods, which are a certain kind of devils called Incubi. And again in *Esaias* xxxiv, where he prophesies the desolation of the land of the Idumeans because they persecuted the Jews, he says: And it shall be an habitation of dragons, and a court for owls. The wild beasts also of the desert shall meet . . . The interlinear gloss interprets this as monsters and devils. And in the same place Blessed Gregory explains these to be woodland gods under another name, not those which the Greeks called Pans, and the Latins Incubi.

Similarly Blessed Isidore, in the last chapter of his 8th book, says: Satyrs are they who are called Pans in Greek and Incubi in Latin. And they are called Incubi from their practice of overlaying,† that is debauching. For they often lust lecherously after women, and copulate with them; and the Gauls name them Dusii,‡ because they are diligent in this beastliness. But the devil which the common people call an Incubus, the Romans called a fig Faun;§

---

* "*Esaias.*" *See my gloss upon this passage,* "*Demoniality,*" *Introduction, xxvi–xxviii.*

† "*Overlaying.*" *Nider,* "*Formicarius,*" *ix, writes:* "*Incubi dicuntur ab incumbendo, hoc est struprando.*"

‡ "*Dusii.*" "*De Ciuitate Dei,*" *XV, 23, where S. Augustine has:* "*Et quosdam daemones, quos Dusios Galli nuncupant, adsidue hanc immunditiam et tentare et efficere, plures talesque adseuerant, ut hoc negare impudentiae uideatur.*"

§ "*A Fig Faun.*" "*Jeremias*" *l, 39, the desolation of Babylon, has: Propterea habitabunt dracones cum faunis ficariis: et habitabunt in ea struthiones: et non inhabitabitur ultra usque in sempiternum, nec exstruetur usque ad generationem, et generationem. Which Douay translates:* "*Therefore shall dragons dwell there with the fig fauns: and ostriches shall dwell therein, and it shall be no more inherited for ever, neither shall it be built up from generation to generation.*" *The English gloss says:* "'*Fig fauns.*' *Monsters* to which Horace said, "O Faunus, lover of fleeing nymphs, go gently over my lands and smiling fields."

As to that of S. Paul in I. *Corinthians* xi, A woman ought to have a covering on her head, because of the angels, many Catholics believe that "because of the angels" refers to Incubi. Of the same opinion is the Venerable Bede in his *History of the English*;* also William of Paris† in his book *De Uniuerso*, the

of the desert, or demons in monstrous shapes: *such as the ancients called 'fauns' and 'satyrs': and as they imagined them to live upon wild figs, they called them 'fauni ficarii' or 'fig fauns.'"* Mirabeau, "Erotika Biblion" (pseudo-Rome), 1783, under "Béhémah" writes: "Les satyres, les faunes, les égypans, toutes ces fables en sont une tradition très remarquable. Satan en arabe signifie bouc; et le bouc expiatoire ne fut ordonné par Moyse que pour détourner les Israélites du goût qu'ils avoient pour cet animal lascif. (Maimonide dans le More Nevochin, p. 111, c. xlvi, s'étend sur les cultes des boucs.) Comme il est dit dans l'Exode qu'on ne pouvoit voir la face des dieux, les Israélites étoient persuadés que les démons si faisoient voir sous cette forme. . . . On a ensuite confondu les incubes et les succubes avec les véritables produits. Jérémie parle de faunes suffoquans. (Jérém., l, 39. Faunis sicariis et non pas ficariis. Car des faunes qui avoient des figues ne voudroit n'en dire. Cependant Saci la traduit ainsi; car les Jansénistes affectent la plus grande pureté des moeurs, mais Berruyer soutient le 'Sicarii' et rend ses faunes très actifs.) Héraclite a décrit des satyres qui vivoient dans les bois, et jouissoient en commun des femmes dont ils s'emparoient."* But the Vulgate has *"Fauni ficarii," which settles the point. That the reading was very disputed is clear from Nider, "Formicarius," who has: "Quem autem uulgo Incubonem uocant, hunc Romani uicarium dicunt. Ad quem Horatius dicit: Faune Nympharum fugientium amator meos per fines et aprica rura lenis incedas. Insuper illud Apostoli I Cor. xi. Mulier debet uelamen habere super caput suum propter Angelos: Multi Catholici exponunt quod sequitur, propter angelos, id est Incubos."* The quotation from Horace is "Carminum," III, 18.

* "Bede." Born 672 or 673, died 735. This great work, "Historia Ecclesiastica Gentis Anglorum," giving an account of Christianity in England from the beginning until his own day, has been recognized as a masterpiece by the scholars of all ages and countries. An authoritative edition was published by Plummer, two vols., Oxford, 1896.

† "William of Paris." William of Auvergne, the celebrated philosopher and theologian, was born at Aurillac in Auvergne towards the end of the twelfth century, and died at Paris, of which city he had in 1228 been consecrated Bishop, in 1249. Although not a "Summa theologica," his "de Universo" is a practical endeavour to found

last part of the 6th treatise. Moreover, S. Thomas speaks of this (I. 25 and II. 8, and elsewhere; also on *Esaias* xii and xiv). Therefore he says that it is rash to deny such things. For that which appears true to many cannot be altogether false, according to Aristotle (at the end of the *De somno et uigilia*, and in the 2nd *Ethics*). I say nothing of the many authentic histories, both Catholic and heathen, which openly affirm the existence of Incubi.

But the reason that devils turn themselves into Incubi or Succubi is not for the cause of pleasure, since a spirit has not flesh and blood; but chiefly it is with this intention, that through the vice of luxury they may work a twofold harm against men, that is, in body and in soul, that so men may be more given to all vices. And there is no doubt that they know under which stars the semen is most vigorous, and that men so conceived will be always perverted by witchcraft.

When Almighty God had enumerated many vices of luxury rife among the unbelievers and heretics, from which He wished His people to be clean, He says in *Leviticus* xviii: Defile not ye yourselves in any of these things: for in all these the nations are defiled which I cast out before you: and the land is defiled: therefore I do visit the iniquity thereof upon it. The gloss explains the word "nations" as meaning devils who, on account of their multitude, are called the nations of the world, and rejoice in all sin, especially in fornication and idolatry, because by these are defiled the body and the soul, and the whole man, which is called "the land." For every sin that a man commits is outside his body, but the man who commits fornication sins in his body. If anyone wishes to study further the histories concerning Incubi and Succubi, let him read (as has been said) Bede in his *History of the English*, and William, and finally Thomas of Brabant in his book *About Bees*.

To return to the matter in hand.

a science of reality on principles opposed to those of the Arabian commentators upon and perverters of Aristotle. His theological works are particularly interesting as devoting much attention to a refutation of the Manichees, whose heresies had been recently revived. There is a good study by Valois, "Guillaume d'Auvergne," Paris, 1880.

And first for the natural act of propagation instituted by God, that is, between male and female; that as though by the permission of God the Sacrament of Matrimony can be made void by the work of the devil through witchcraft, as has been shown above. And the same is much more strongly true of any other venereal act between man and woman.

But if it is asked why the devil is allowed to cast spells upon the venereal act, rather than upon any other human act, it is answered that many reasons are assigned by the Doctors, which will be discussed later in the part concerning the divine permission. For the present the reason that has been mentioned before must suffice, namely, that the power of the devil lies in the privy parts of men. For of all struggles those are the hardest where the fight is continuous and victory rare. And it is unsound to argue that in that case the work of the devil is stronger than the work of God, since the matrimonial act instituted by God can be made void: for the devil does not make it void by violence, since he has no power at all in the matter except as he is permitted by God. Therefore it would be better to argue from this that he is powerless.

Secondly, it is true that to procreate a man is the act of a living body. But when it is said that devils cannot give life, because that flows formally from the soul, it is true; but materially life springs from the semen, and an Incubus devil can, with God's permission, accomplish this by coition. And the semen does not so much spring from him, as it is another man's semen received by him for this purpose (see S. Thomas, I. 51, art. 3). For the devil is Succubus to a man, and becomes Incubus to a woman. In just the same way they absorb the seeds of other things for the generating of various things, as S. Augustine says, *de Trinitate* 3.

Now it may be asked, of whom is a child so born the son? It is clear that he is not the son of the devil, but of the man whose semen was received. But when it is urged that, just as in the works of Nature, so there is no superfluity in the works of angels, that is granted; but when it is inferred that the devil can receive and inject semen invisibly, this also is true; but he prefers to perform this visibly as a Succubus and an Incubus, that by such filthiness

he may infect body and soul of all humanity, that is, of both woman and man, there being, as it were, actual bodily contact.

Moreover, devils can do invisibly more things which they are not permitted to do visibly, even if they so wished; but they are allowed to do them invisibly, either as a trial for the good, or as a punishment for the wicked. Finally, it may happen that another devil may take the place of the Succubus, receive the semen from him, and become an Incubus in the place of the other devil; and this for a threefold reason. Perhaps because one devil, allotted to a woman, should receive semen from another devil, allotted to a man, that in this way each of them should be commissioned by the prince of devils to work some witchcraft; since to each one is allotted his own angel, even from among the evil ones; or because of the filthiness of the deed, which one devil would abhor to commit. For in many inquiries it is clearly shown that certain devils, out of some nobility in their natures, would shrink from a filthy action. Or it may be in order that the Incubus may, instead of a man's semen, by interposing himself on to a woman, invisibly inject his own semen, that is, that which he has invisibly received. And it is not foreign to his nature or power to effect such an interposition; since even in bodily form he can interpose himself invisibly and without physical contact, as was shown in the case of the young man who was betrothed to an idol.

Thirdly, it is said that the power of an angel belongs in an infinite degree to the higher things; that is to say, that his power cannot be comprehended by the lower orders, but is always superior to them, so that it is not limited to one effect only. For the highest powers have most unbounded influence over creation. But because he is said to be infinitely superior, that is not to say that he is indifferently powerful for any work that is propounded for him; for then he might just as well be said to be infinitely inferior, as superior.

But there must be some proportion between the agent and the patient, and there can be no proportion between a purely spiritual substance and a corporeal one. Therefore not even the devils have any power to cause an effect, except through some other active medium. And this is why they use the seeds of things to produce their effects; see S. Augustine, *de Trinitate*, 3. Wherefore this argument goes back to the preceding one, and is not strengthened by it, unless anyone wishes for S. Augustine's explanation why the Intelligences are said to have infinite powers of the higher and not of the lower degree, given to them in the order of things corporeal and of the celestial bodies, which can influence many and infinite effects. But this is not because of the weakness of the inferior powers. And the conclusion is that devils, even without assuming bodies, can work transmutations in semen; although this is no argument against the present proposition, concerning Incubi and Succubi, whose actions they cannot perform except by assuming bodily shape, as has been considered above.

For the fourth argument, that devils cannot move bodies or semen locally, which is substantiated by the analogy of the soul. It must be said that it is one thing to speak of the spiritual substance of the actual angel or devil, and another thing to speak of the actual soul. For the reason why the soul cannot locally move a body unless it has given life to it, or else by contact of a living body with one that is not living, is this: that the soul occupies by far the lowest grade in the order of spiritual beings, and therefore it follows that there must be some proportionate relation between it and the body which it is able to move by contact. But it is not so with devils, whose power altogether exceeds corporeal power.

And fifthly, it must be said that the contact of a devil with a body, either in the way of semen or in any other way, is not a corporeal but a virtual contact, and takes place in accordance with the suitable proportion of both the mover and the moved; provided that the body which is moved does not exceed the proportion of the devil's power. And such bodies are the celestial bodies, and even the whole earth or the elements of the world, the power of which we may call superior on the authority of S. Thomas in his questions concerning Sin (quest. 10, *de Daemonibus*). For this is either because of the essence of nature, or because of condemnation for sin. For there is a due order in things, in accordance both with their very nature and with their motion. And just as the higher heavenly bodies are moved by the higher spiritual substances, as are the good Angels, so are the lower bodies moved by the lower spiritual substances, as are the devils. And if this limitation of the devils' power is due to the essence of nature, it is held by some that the devils are not of the order of those higher angels, but are part of this terrestrial order created by God; and this was the opinion of the Philosophers. And if it is due to condemnation for sin, as is held by the Theologians, then they were thrust from the regions of heaven into this lower atmosphere for a punishment, and therefore are not able to move either it or the earth.

This has been said on account of two easily dispelled arguments:—One, regarding the heavenly bodies, that the devils could also move these, if they were able to move bodies locally, since the stars are nearer to them in nature, as also the last argument alleges. The answer is that this is not valid; for if the former opinion holds good, those bodies exceed the proportion of the devils' power: and if the second is true, then again they cannot move them, because of their punishment for sin.

Also there is the argument that objects that the motion of the whole and of the part is the same thing, just as Aristotle in his 4th *Physics* instances the case of the whole earth and a clod of soil; and that therefore if the devils could move a part of the earth, they could also move the whole earth. But this is not valid, as is clear to anyone who examines the distinction. But to collect the semen of things and apply it to certain effects does not exceed their natural power, with the permission of God, as is self-evident.

In conclusion, in spite of the contention of some that devils in bodily shape can in no way generate children, and that by the "sons of God" is meant the sons of Seth and not Incubi devils, just as by the "daughters of men" is meant the descendants of Cain; nevertheless the contrary is clearly affirmed by many. And that which seems true to many cannot be altogether false, according to Aristotle in his 6th *Ethics* and at the end of the *de Somno et Uigilia*. And now also in modern times we have the well-attested deeds and words of witches who truly and actually perform such things.

Therefore we make three propositions. First, that the foulest venereal acts are performed by such devils, not for the sake of delectation, but for the pollution of the souls and bodies of those to whom they act as Succubi or Incubi. Second, that through such action complete conception and generation by women can take place, inasmuch as they can deposit human semen in the suitable place of a woman's womb where there is already a corresponding substance. In the same way they can also collect the seeds of other things for the working of other effects. Third, that in the begetting of such children only the local motion is to be attributed to devils, and not the actual begetting, which arises not from the power of the devil or of the body which he assumes, but from the virtue of him whose semen it was; wherefore the child is the son not of the devil, but of some man.

And here there is a clear answer to those who would contend that there are two reasons why devils cannot generate children:—First, that generation is effected by the formative virtue which exists in semen released from a living body; and that because the body assumed by devils is not of such a sort, therefore, etc. The answer is clear, that the devil deposits naturally formative semen in its proper place, etc. Secondly, it may be argued that semen has no power of generation except as long as the heat of life is retained in it, and that this must be lost when it is carried great distances. The answer is that devils are able to store the semen safely, so that its vital heat is not lost; or even that it cannot evaporate so easily on account of the great speed at which they move by reason of the superiority of the mover over the thing moved.

☆

QUESTION IV

By which Devils are the Operations of Incubus and Succubus Practised?

IS it Catholic to affirm that the functions of Incubi and Succubi belong indifferently and equally to all unclean spirits? *And it seems* that it is so; for to affirm the opposite would be to maintain that there is some good order among them. It is argued that just as in the computation of the Good there are degrees and orders (see S. Augustine in

his book on the nature of the Good), so also the computation of the Evil is based upon confusion. But as among the good Angels nothing can be without order, so among the bad all is disorder, and therefore they all indifferently follow these practices. See *Job* x.: A land of darkness, as darkness itself; and of the shadow of death, without any order, and where the light is as darkness.

Again, if they do not all indifferently follow these practices, this quality in them comes either from their nature, or from sin, or from punishment. But it does not come from their nature, since they are all without distinction given to sin, as was set out in the preceding question. For they are by nature impure spirits, yet not so unclean as to pejorate their good parts; subtle in wickedness, eager to do harm, swollen with pride, etc. Therefore these practices in them are due either to sin or to punishment. Then again, where the sin is greater, there is the punishment greater; and the higher angels sinned more greatly, therefore for their punishment they have the more to follow these filthy practices. If this is not so, another reason will be given why they do not indifferently practise these things.

And again, it is argued that where there is no discipline or obedience, there all work without distinction; and it is submitted that there is no discipline or obedience among devils, and no agreement. *Proverbs* xiii.: Among the proud there is always contention.

Again, just as because of sin they will all equally be cast into Hell after the Day of Judgement, so before that time they are detained in the lower mists on account of the duties assigned to them. We do not read that there is equality on account of emancipation, therefore neither is there equality in the matter of duty and temptation.

But against this there is the first gloss on I *Corinthians* xv: As long as the world endures Angels are set over Angels, men over men, and devils over devils. Also in *Job* xl it speaks of the scales of Leviathan, which signify the members of the devil, how one cleaves to another. Therefore there is among them diversity both of order and of action.

Another question arises, whether or not the devils can be restrained by the good Angels from pursuing these foul practices. It must be said that the

Angels to whose command the adverse Influences are subject are called Powers, as S. Gregory says, and S. Augustine (*de Trinitate*, 3). A rebellious and sinful spirit of life is subject to an obedient, pious and just spirit of life. And those Creatures which are more perfect and nearer to God have authority over the others: for the whole order of preference is originally and in the first place in God, and is shared by His creatures according as they approach more nearly to Him. Therefore the good Angels, who are nearest to God on account of their fruition in Him, which the devils lack, have preference over the devils, and rule over them.

And when it is urged that devils work much harm without any medium, or that they are not hindered because they are not subject to good Angels who might prevent them; or that if they are so subject, then the evil that is done by the subject is due to negligence on the part of the master, and there seems to be some negligence among the good Angels: the answer is that the Angels are ministers of the Divine wisdom. It follows then that, as the Divine wisdom permits certain evil to be done by bad Angels or men, for the sake of the good that He draws therefrom, so also the good Angels do not altogether prevent wicked men or devils from doing evil.

Answer. It is Catholic to maintain that there is a certain order of interior and exterior actions, and a degree of preference among devils. Whence it follows that certain abominations are committed by the lowest orders, from which the higher orders are precluded on account of the nobility of their natures. And this is generally said to arise from a threefold congruity, in that such things harmonize with their nature, with the Divine wisdom, and with their own wickedness.

But more particularly as touching their nature. It is agreed that from the beginning of Creation some were always by nature superior, since they differ among themselves as to form; and no two Angels are alike in form. This follows the more general opinion, which also agrees with the words of the Philosophers. Dionysius also lays it down in his tenth chapter *On the Celestial Hierarchy* that in the same order there are three separate degrees; and

we must agree with this, since they are both immaterial and incorporeal. See also S. Thomas (ii. 2). For sin does not take away their nature, and the devils after the Fall did not lose their natural gifts, as has been said before; and the operations of things follow their natural conditions. Therefore both in nature and in operation they are various and multiple.

This harmonizes also with the Divine wisdom; for that which is ordained is ordained by God (*Romans* xiii). And since devils were deputed by God for the temptation of men and the punishment of the damned, therefore they work upon men from without by many and various means.

It harmonizes also with their own wickedness. For since they are at war with the human race, they fight in an orderly manner; for so they think to do greater harm to men, and so they do. Whence it follows that they do not share in an equal manner in their most unspeakable abominations.

And this is more specifically proved as follows. For since, as has been said, the operation follows the nature of the thing, it follows also that those whose natures are subordinate must in turn be subordinate to themselves in operation, just as is the case in corporeal matters. For since the lower bodies are by natural ordination below the celestial bodies, and their actions and motions are subject to the actions and motions of the celestial bodies; and since the devils, as has been said, differ among themselves in natural order; therefore they also differ among themselves in their natural actions, both extrinsic and intrinsic, and especially in the performance of the abominations in question.

From which it is concluded that since the practice of these abominations is for the most part foreign to the nobility of the angelic nature, so also in human actions the foulest and beastliest acts are to be considered by themselves, and not in relation to the duty of human nature and procreation.

Finally, since some are believed to have fallen from every order, it is not unsuitable to maintain that those devils who fell from the lowest choir, and even in that held the lowest rank, are deputed to and perform these and other abominations.

Also it must be carefully noted that, though the Scripture speaks of Incubi and Succubi lusting after women, yet nowhere do we read that Incubi and Succubi fell into vices against nature. We do not speak only of sodomy, but of any other sin whereby the act is wrongfully performed outside the rightful channel. And the very great enormity of such as sin in this way is shown by the fact that all devils equally, of whatsoever order, abominate and think shame to commit such actions. And it seems that the gloss on *Ezekiel* xix means this, where it says: I will give thee into the hands of the dwellers in Palestine, that is devils, who shall blush at your iniquities, meaning vices against nature. And the student will see what should be authoritatively understood concerning devils. For no sin has God so often punished by the shameful death of multitudes.

Indeed many say, and it is truly believed, that no one can unimperilled persevere in the practice of such vices beyond the period of the mortal life of Christ, which lasted for thirty-three years, unless he should be saved by some special grace of the Redeemer. And this is proved by the fact that there have often been ensnared by this vice octogenarians and centenarians, who had up to that time ruled their lives according to the discipline of Christ; and, having once forsaken Him, they have found the very greatest difficulty in obtaining deliverance, and in abandoning themselves to such vices.

Moreover, the names of the devils indicate what order there is among them, and what office is assigned to each. For though one and the same name, that of devil, is generally used in Scripture because of their various qualities, yet the Scriptures teach that One is set over these filthy actions, just as certain vices are subject to Another. For it is the practice of Scripture and of speech to name every unclean spirit Diabolus, from Dia, that is Two, and Bolus, that is Morsel; for he kills two things, the body and the soul. And this is in accordance with etymology, although in Greek *Diabolus* means shut in Prison, which also is apt, since he is not permitted to do as much harm as he wishes. Or Diabolus may mean Downflowing, since he flowed down, that is, fell down, both specifically and locally. He is also named Demon, that is, Cunning over Blood, since he thirsts for and procures

sin with a threefold knowledge, being powerful in the subtlety of his nature, in his age-long experience, and in the revelation of the good spirits. He is called also Belial, which means Without Yoke or Master; for he can fight against him to whom he should be subject. He is called also Beelzebub, which means Lord of Flies, that is, of the souls of sinners who have left the true faith of Christ. Also Satan, that is, the Adversary; see 1 *S. Peter* ii: For your adversary the devil goeth about, etc. Also Behemoth, that is, Beast, because he makes men bestial.

But the very devil of Fornication, and the chief of that abomination, is called Asmodeus, which means the Creature of Judgement: for because of this kind of sin a terrible judgement was executed upon Sodom and the four other cities. Similarly the devil of Pride is called Leviathan, which means Their Addition; because when Lucifer tempted our first parents he promised them, out of his pride, the addition of Divinity. Concerning him the Lord said through Esaias: I shall visit it upon Leviathan, that old and tortuous serpent. And the devil of Avarice and Riches is called Mammon, whom also Christ mentions in the Gospel (*S. Matthew* vi): Ye cannot serve God, etc.

To the arguments. *First*, that good can be found without evil, but evil cannot be found without good; for it is poured upon a creature that is good in itself. And therefore the devils, in so far as they have a good nature, were ordained in the course of nature; and for their actions see *Job* x.

Secondly, it can be said that the devils deputed to work are not in Hell, but in the lower mists. And they have here an order among themselves, which they will not have in Hell. From which it may be said that all order ceased among them, as touching the attainment of blessedness, at that time when they fell irrecoverably from such rank. And it may be said that even in Hell there will be among them a gradation of power, and of the affliction of punishments, inasmuch as some, and not others, will be deputed to torment the souls. But this gradation will come rather from God than from themselves, as will also their torments.

Thirdly, when it is said that the higher devils, because they sinned the more, are the more punished, and must therefore be the more bound to the commission of these filthy acts, it is answered that sin bears relation to punishment, and not to the act or operation of nature; and therefore it is by reason of their nobility of nature that these are not given to such filthiness, and it has nothing to do with their sin or punishment. And though they are all impure spirits, and eager to do harm, yet one is more so than another, in proportion as their natures are the further thrust into darkness.

Fourthly, it is said that there is agreement among devils, but of wickedness rather than friendship, in that they hate mankind, and strive their utmost against justice. For such agreement is found among the wicked, that they band themselves together, and depute those whose talents seem suitable to the pursuit of particular iniquities.

Fifthly, although imprisonment is equally decreed for all, now in the lower atmosphere and afterwards in Hell, yet not therefore are equal penalties and duties equally ordained for them: for the nobler they are in nature and the more potent in office, the heavier is the torment to which they are subjected. See *Wisdom* vi: "The powerful shall powerfully suffer torments."

☆

QUESTION V

What is the Source of the Increase of Works of Witchcraft? Whence comes it that the Practice of Witchcraft hath so notably increased?

IS it in any way a Catholic opinion to hold that the origin and growth of works of witchcraft proceed from the influence of the celestial bodies; or from the abundant wickedness of men, and not from the abominations of Incubi and Succubi? And it seems that it springs from man's own wickedness. For S. Augustine says, in Book LXXXIII, that the cause of a man's depravity lies in his own will, whether he sins at his own or at another's suggestion. But a witch is depraved through sin, therefore the cause of it is not the devil but human will. In the same place he speaks of free-will, that everyone is the cause of his own wickedness. And he reasons thus: that the sin of man proceeds from free-will, but the devil can-

not destroy free-will, for this would militate against liberty: therefore the devil cannot be the cause of that or any other sin. Again, in the book of Ecclesiastic Dogma it is said: Not all our evil thoughts are stirred up by the devil, but sometimes they arise from the operation of our own judgement.

But it is submitted that the true source of witchcraft is the influence of the celestial bodies, and not devils. Just as every multitude is reduced to unity, so all that is multiform is reduced to some uniform beginning. But the acts of men, both in vice and in virtue, are various and multiform, therefore it seems that they may be reduced to some beginnings uniformly moved and moving. But such can only be assigned to the motions of the stars; therefore those bodies are the causes of such actions.

Again, if the stars were not the cause of human actions both good and bad, Astrologers would not so frequently foretell the truth about the result of wars and other human acts: therefore they are in some way a cause.

Again, the stars can influence the devils themselves in the causing of certain spells; and therefore they can all the more influence men. Three proofs are adduced for this assumption. For certain men who are called Lunatics are molested by devils more at one time than at another; and the devils would not so behave, but would rather molest them at all times, unless they themselves were deeply affected by certain phases of the Moon. It is proved again from the fact that Necromancers observe certain constellations for the invoking of devils, which they would not do unless they knew that those devils were subject to the stars.

And this also is adduced as a proof; that according to S. Augustine (*de Ciuitate Dei*, 10), the devils employ certain lower bodies, such as herbs, stones, animals, and certain sounds and voices, and figures. But since the heavenly bodies are of more potency than the lower bodies, therefore the stars are a far greater influence than these things. And witches are the more in subjection in that their deeds proceed from the influence of those bodies, and not from the help of evil spirits. And the argument is supported from 1 *Kings* xvi, where Saul was vexed by a devil, but was calmed when David struck his harp before him, and the evil spirit departed.

But against this. It is impossible to produce an effect without its cause; and the deeds of witches are such that they cannot be done without the help of devils, as is shown by the description of witches in S. Isidore, *Ethics* VIII. Witches are so called from the enormity of their magic spells; for they disturb the elements and confound the minds of men, and without any venomous draught, but merely by virtue of incantations, destroy souls, etc. But this sort of effects cannot be caused by the influence of the stars through the agency of a man.

Besides, Aristotle says in his *Ethics* that it is difficult to know what is the beginning of the operation of thought, and shows that it must be something extrinsic. For everything that begins from the beginning has some cause. Now a man begins to do that which he wills; and he begins to will because of some pre-suggestion; and if this is some precedent suggestion, it must either proceed from the infinite, or there is some extrinsic beginning which first brings a suggestion to a man. Unless indeed it be argued that this is a matter of chance, from which it would follow that all human actions are fortuitous, which is absurd. Therefore the beginning of good in the good is said to be God, Who is not the cause of sin. But for the wicked, when a man begins to be influenced towards and wills to commit sin, there must also be some extrinsic cause of this. And this can be no other than the devil; especially in the case of witches, as is shown above, for the stars cannot influence such acts. Therefore the truth is plain.

Moreover, that which has power over the motive has also power over the result which is caused by the motive. Now the motive of the will is something perceived through the senses or the intellect, both of which are subject to the power of the devil. For S. Augustine says in Book 83: This evil, which is of the devil, creeps in by all the sensual approaches; he places himself in figures, he adapts himself to colours, he attaches himself to sounds, he lurks in angry and wrongful conversation, he abides in smells, he impregnates with flavours and fills with certain exhalations all the channels of the understanding. Therefore it is seen that it is in the devil's power to influence the will, which is directly the cause of sin.

Besides, everything which has a choice of two ways needs some determining factor before it proceeds to action. And the free-will of man has the choice between good and ill; therefore when he embarks upon sin, it needs that he is determined by something towards ill. And this seems chiefly to be done by the devil, especially in the actions of witches, whose will is made up for evil. Therefore it seems that the evil will of the devil is the cause of evil will in man, especially in witches. And the argument may be substantiated thus; that just as a good Angel cleaves to good, so does a bad Angel to evil; but the former leads a man into goodness, therefore the latter leads him into evil. For it is, says Dionysius, the unalterable and fixed law of divinity, that the lowest has its cause in the highest.

Answer. Such as contend that witchcraft has its origin in the influence of the stars stand convicted of three errors. In the first place, it is not possible that it originated from astromancers and casters of horoscopes and fortune-tellers. For if it is asked whether the vice of witchcraft in men is caused by the influence of the stars, then, in consideration of the variety of men's characters, and for the upholding of the true faith, a distinction must be maintained; namely, that there are two ways in which it can be understood that men's characters can be caused by the stars. Either completely and of necessity, or by disposition and contingency. And as for the first, it is not only false, but so heretical and contrary to the Christian religion, that the true faith cannot be maintained in such an error. For this reason, he who argues that everything of necessity proceeds from the stars takes away all merit and, in consequence, all blame: also he takes away Grace, and therefore Glory. For uprightness of character suffers prejudice by this error, since the blame of the sinner redounds upon the stars, licence to sin without culpability is conceded, and man is committed to the worship and adoration of the stars.

But as for the contention that men's characters are conditionally varied by the disposition of the stars, it is so far true that is it not contrary to reason or faith. For it is obvious that the disposition of a body variously causes many variations in the humours and character of the soul; for generally the soul imitates the complexions of the body, as it is said in the Six Principles. Wherefore the choleric are wrathful, the sanguine are kindly, the melancholy are envious, and the phlegmatic are slothful. But this is not absolute; for the soul is master of its body, especially when it is helped by Grace. And we see many choleric who are gentle, and melancholy who are kindly. Therefore when the virtue of the stars influences the formation and quality of a man's humours, it is agreed that they have some influence over the character, but very distantly: for the virtue of the lower nature has more effect on the quality of the humours than has the virtue of the stars.

Wherefore S. Augustine (*de Ciuitate Dei,* V), where he resolves a certain question of two brothers who fell ill and were cured simultaneously, approves the reasoning of Hippocrates rather than that of an Astronomer. For Hippocrates answered that it was owing to the similarity of their humours; and the Astronomer answered that it was owing to the identity of their horoscopes. For the Physician's answer was better, since he adduced the more powerful and immediate cause. Thus, therefore, it must be said that the influence of the stars is to some degree conducive to the wickedness of witches, if it be granted that there is any such influence over their bodies that predisposes them to this manner of abomination rather than to any other sort of works either vicious or virtuous: but this disposition must not be said to be necessary, immediate, and sufficient, but remote and contingent.

Neither is that objection valid which is based on the book of the Philosophers on the properties of the elements, where it says that kingdoms are emptied and lands depopulated at the conjunction of Jupiter and Saturn; and it is argued from this that such things are to be understood as being outside the free-will of men, and that therefore the influence of the stars has power over free-will. For it is answered that in this saying the Philosopher does not mean to imply that men cannot resist the influence of that constellation towards dissensions, but that they will not. For

Ptolemy in *Almagest** says: A wise man will be the master of the stars.† For although, since Saturn has a melan-

---

* "*Almagest.*" Claudius Ptolemaus was a celebrated mathematician, astronomer, and geographer. Of the details of his life nothing appears to be known beyond the facts that he was certainly at Alexandria in A.D. 139, and since he survived Antoninus Pius he was alive later than March, 161. His "Geography," Γεωγραφικι υφήγησις, is very famous, but perhaps even more celebrated was the Μεγάλη σύνταξις τῆς ἀστρονομίας, usually known by its Arabic name of Almagest. Since the "Tetrabiblus," the work on astrology, was also entitled σύνταξις, the Arabs, to distinguish the two, called the greater work μεγάλη, and afterwards μεγίστη; the title "Almagest" is a compound of this last adjective and the Arabic article. The work is divided into thirteen books, of which VII and VIII are the most interesting to the modern astronomer, as they give a catalogue of the stars. The best edition of the "Almagest" is considered to be that by Halma, Paris, 1813–16, two vols., 4to.

† "*Sapiens homo dominabitur astris.*" This famous tag is continually quoted. Cf. Tomkis' "*Albumazar*" (acted at Cambridge, March, 1615), I, 7, where Albumazar says:

> Indeed th' Ægyptian Ptolemy, the wise,
> Pronounc'd it as an oracle of truth,
> Sapiens dominabitur astris.

In Book III, Epigram 186, of John Owen's first published volume, we get:

> "*Fata regunt reges; sapiens dominabitur astris.*"

Sir Sampson Legend in Congreve's "Love for Love," produced at Lincoln's Inn Fields, 30 April, 1695, II, 1, bantering old Foresight, who loudly acclaims the influence of the stars, throws at him: "I tell you I am wise; and sapiens dominabitur astris; there's Latin for you to prove it." According to W. Aldis Wright's note on Bacon's "Advancement of Learning," II, xxiii, 12: "Mr. Ellis says this sentence is ascribed to Ptolemy by Cognatus." The reference is to Cognati's collection of Adages, which together with the "Adagia" of Erasmus and other famous repertories of saws and proverbs may be found in the volume "Adagia" compiled by Joynaeus. Joannes Nevizanus, "Sylva Nuptialis," II, 96, notes: "Dicit tamen Bal. in c.j. at lite pand. quod sapiens dominabitur astris." Bal. is Baldus, Baldo degli Ubaldi (b. 1327), the most famous canonist of his day and Professor utriusque iuris at the Universities of Padua, Perugia, and Piacenza, who wrote ample glosses on the "Corpus Iuris Ciuilis." Burton, "Anatomy of Melancholy," quotes "sapiens," etc., and A. R. Shilleto in his notes says that it is also cited by Jeremy Taylor, and that C. G. Eden, his best editor, could not trace the origin of the phrase.

choly and bad influence and Jupiter a very good influence, the conjunction of Jupiter and Saturn can dispose men to quarrels and discords; yet, through free-will, men can resist that inclination, and very easily with the help of God's grace.

And again it is no valid objection to quote S. John Damascene* where he says (Book II, chap. vi) that comets are often the sign of the death of kings. For it will be answered that even if we follow the opinion of S. John Damascene, which was, as is evident in the book referred to, contrary to the opinion of the Philosophic Way, yet this is no proof of the inevitability of human actions. For S. John considers that a comet is not a natural creation, nor is it one of the stars set in the firmament; wherefore neither its signification nor influence is natural. For he says that comets are not of the stars which were created in the beginning, but that they are made for a particular occasion, and then dissolved, by Divine command. This then is the opinion of S. John Damascene. But GOD by such a sign foretells the death of kings rather than of other men, both because a king is a public person, and because from this may arise the confusion of a kingdom. And the Angels are more careful to watch over kings for the general good; and kings are born and die under the ministry of the Angels.

And there is no difficulty in the opinion of the Philosophers, who say that a comet is a hot and dry con-glomeration, generated in the higher part of space near the fire, and that a conjoined globe of that hot and dry vapour assumes the likeness of a star. But unincorporated parts of that vapour stretch in long extremities joined to that globe, and are a sort of adjunct to it. And according to this view, not of itself but by accident, it predicts death which proceeds from hot and dry infirmities. And since for the most part the rich are fed on things of a hot and dry nature, therefore at such times many of the rich die; among which the death of kings and princes is the most notable. And this view is not far from the view of S. John Damascene, when carefully considered, except as regards the operation and co-operation of the Angels, which not even the philosophers can ignore. For indeed when the vapours in their dryness and heat have nothing to do with the generation of a comet, even then, for reasons already set out, a comet may be formed by the operation of an Angel.

In this way the star which portended the death of the learned S. Thomas was not one of the stars set in the firma-ment, but was formed by an Angel from some convenient material, and, having performed its office, was again dissolved.

From this we see that, whichever of those opinions we follow, the stars have no inherent influence over the free will, or, consequently, over the malice and character of men.

It is to be noted also that Astronomers often foretell the truth, and that their judgements are for the most part effective on one province or one nation. And the reason is that they take their judgements from the stars, which, according to the more probable view, have a greater, though not an inevitable, influence over the actions of mankind in general, that is, over one nation or province, than over one individual person; and this because the greater part of one nation more closely obeys the natural disposition of the body than does one single man. But this is men-tioned incidentally.

And the second of the three ways by which we vindicate the Catholic stand-point is by refuting the errors of those who cast Horoscopes and Mathe-maticians† who worship the goddess of

---

* "S. John." S. John Damascene, Doctor of the Church, was born at Damascus about 676, and died some time between 754 and 787. The quotation is from Ἔκδοσις ἀκριβὴς τῆς ὀρθοδόξου πίστεως, which is the third part of the most important of all his works, Πηγὴ γνώσεως, Fountain of Wisdom. This third part, "The Orthodox Faith," to which reference is made here, must be considered the most notable of all the writings of S. John Damascene, and it is in this treatise that he discloses so compre-hensive a knowledge of the astronomy of his day. It may be pointed out that Sprenger regards the authority of S. John far too lightly, for the Doctor's words carry great weight. The only complete edition of the works of S. John Damas-cene is that by Michael Lequien, O.P., published at Paris, 1717, and Venice, 1748. Migne has reprinted this, "Patres Græci," XCIV–XCVI, with the addition of certain works by some attributed to the same author.

† "Mathematicians." Although in Cicero and in Seneca "mathematicus" means a mathema-tician, in later Latin it always signifies an

fortune. Of these S. Isidore (*Ethics*, VIII. 9) says that those who cast Horoscopes are so called from their examination of the stars at nativity, and are commonly called Mathematicians; and in the same Book, chapter 2, he says that Fortune has her name from fortuitousness, and is a sort of goddess who mocks human affairs in a haphazard and fortuitous manner. Wherefore she is called blind, since she runs here and there with no consideration for desert, and comes indifferently to good and bad. So much for Isidore. But to believe that there is such a goddess, or that the harm done to bodies and creatures which is ascribed to witchcraft does not actually proceed from witchcraft, but from that same goddess of Fortune, is sheer idolatry: and also to assert that witches themselves were born for that very purpose that they might perform such deeds in the world is similarly alien to the Faith, and indeed to the general teaching of the Philosophers. Anyone who pleases may refer to S. Thomas in the 3rd book of his *Summa* of the Faith against the Gentiles, question 87, etc., and he will find much to this effect.

Nevertheless one point must not be omitted, for the sake of those who per-haps have no great quantity of books. It is there noted that three things are to be considered in man, which are directed by three celestial causes, namely, the act of the will, the act of the intellect, and the act of the body. The first of these is governed directly and solely by God, the second by an Angel, and the third by a celestial body. For choice and will are directly governed by God for good works, as the Scripture says in *Proverbs* xxi: The heart of the king is in the hand of the Lord; he turneth it whithersoever he will. And it says "the heart of the king" to signify that, as the great cannot oppose His will, so are others even less able to do so. Also S. Paul says: God who causeth us to wish and to perform that which is good.

The human understanding is governed by God through the mediation of an Angel. And those bodily actions, either exterior or interior, which are natural to man, are regulated by God through the mediation of the Angels and the celestial bodies. For Blessed Dionysius (*de Diuin. nom.*, IV) says that the celestial bodies are the causes of that which happens in this world; though he makes no implication of fatality.

And since man is governed as to his body by the celestial bodies, as to his intellect by the Angels, and as to his will by God, it may happen that if he rejects God's inspiration towards goodness, and the guidance of his good Angel, he may be led by his bodily affections to those things toward which the influence of the stars inclines him, that so his will and understanding become entangled in malice and error.

However, it is not possible for anyone to be influenced by the stars to enter upon that sort of error in which the witches are ensnared, such as bloodshed, theft or robbery, or even the perpetration of the worst incontinences; and this is true of other natural phenomena.

Also, as William of Paris says in his *De Uniuerso*, it is proved by experience that if a harlot tries to plant an olive it does not become fruitful, whereas if it is planted by a chaste woman it is fruitful. And a doctor in healing, a farmer in planting, or a soldier in fighting can do more with the help of the influence of the stars than another who possesses the same skill can do.

Our third way is taken from the

---

astrologer, a diviner, a wizard. The "Mathematici" were condemned by the Roman law as exponents of black magic. Their art is indeed forbidden in severest terms by Diocletian (A.D. 284-305): "Artem geometriae discere atque exercere publice interest, ars autem mathematica damnabilis interdicta est omnino." The word "mathematician" was used in English sometimes to denote an astrologer, a fortune-teller. So in Shirley's comedy "The Sisters," III, licensed April, 1642, when the bandits disguised as diviners visit the castle, Giovanni enters crying out: "Master Steward, yonder are the rarest fellows! In such fantastical habits too; they call themselves mathematicians." "What do they come for?" the steward asks. "To offer their service to my Lady, and tell fortunes," is the reply. When Antonio sees them he grumbles:

Her house is open for these mountebanks,
Cheaters, and tumblers, that can foist and flatter
My lady Gewgaw. . .
What are you, sir?
    Strozzo. One of the mathematicians, noble signior.
    Antonio. Mathematicians! mongrel,
How durst thou take that learned name upon thee?
You are one of those knaves that stroll the country,
And live by picking worms out of fools' fingers.

refutation of the belief in Fate. And here it is to be noted that a belief in Fate is in one way quite Catholic, but in another way entirely heretical. For Fate may be understood after the manner of certain Gentiles and Mathematicians, who thought that the different characters of men were inevitably caused by the force of the position of the stars, so that a wizard was predestined to be such, even if he were of a good character, because the disposition of the stars under which he was conceived or born caused him to be such as he was. And that force they called by the name of Fate.

But that opinion is not only false, but heretical and altogether detestable on account of the deprivation which it must entail, as was shown above in the refutation of the first error. For by it would be removed all reason for merit or blame, for grace and glory, and God would be made the author of our evil, and more such incongruities. Therefore such conception of Fate must be altogether rejected, since there is no such thing. And touching this belief S. Gregory says in his Homily on the Epiphany: Far be it from the hearts of the faithful to say that there is any Fate.

And although, on account of the same incongruity which is detected in both, this opinion may seem to be the same as that concerning the Astrologers, they are yet different inasmuch as they disagree concerning the force of the stars and the influx of the seven Planets.

But Fate may be considered to be a sort of second disposition, or an ordination of second causes for the production of foreseen Divine effects. And in this way Fate is truly something. For the providence of God accomplishes His effects through mediating causes, in such matters as are subject to second causes; though this is not so in the case of some other matters, such as the creation of souls, glorification, and the acquisition of grace.

Also the Angels may co-operate in the infusion of Grace by enlightening and guiding the understanding and the capability of the will, and so a certain arrangement of results may be said to be one and the same as Providence or even Fate. For it is considered in this way; that there is in God a quality which may be called Providence, or it may be said that He has ordained intermediary causes for the realization of some of His purposes; and to this extent Fate is a rational fact. And in this way Boethius speaks of Fate (*de Consolatione* IV): Fate is an inherent disposition in things mobile, by which Providence binds things to that which It has ordained.

Nevertheless the learned Saints refused to use this name, on account of those who twisted its meaning to the force of the position of the stars. Wherefore S. Augustine (*de Ciuitate Dei*, V) says: If anyone attributed human affairs to Fate, meaning by Fate the Will and Power of God, let him keep his opinion but amend his tongue.

It is clear, then, that what has been said provides a sufficient answer to the question whether all things, including works of witchcraft, are subject to Fate. For if Fate is said to be the ordainment of second causes of foreseen Divine results, that is, when God wills to effect His purposes through second causes; to that extent they are subject to Fate, that is, to second causes so ordained by God; and the influence of the stars is one of these second causes. But those things which come directly from God, such as the Creation of things, the Glorification of things substantial and spiritual, and other things of this sort, are not subject to such Fate. And Boethius, in the book we have quoted, supports this view when he says that those things which are near to the primal Deity are beyond the influence of the decrees of Fate. Therefore the works of witches, being outside the common course and order of nature, are not subject to these second causes. That is to say, that as regards their origin they are not subject willy-nilly to Fate, but to other causes.

Witchcraft is not caused by the Powers that Move the Stars.

It follows that, just as witchcraft cannot be caused in the manner that has been suggested, so also it is not caused by the separate Essences which are the Powers that move the stars; although this was believed to be the case by Avicenna and his school, for the following reasons. For they argued that those are separate Essences of a higher power than our souls; and the soul itself can sometimes, by the force of imagination, or merely through fear, effect a change in its own body, and even sometimes in another body. For example, a man walking on a plank placed at a great height easily falls, but in his fear he imagines that he will fall; but if the plank were placed on the ground he would not fall, for he would have no reason to fear falling. So by the mere apprehension of the soul the body grows hot in the case of the concupiscent and wrathful, and cold in the case of the fearful. It can also, by strongly imagining and fearing such things, be affected with illnesses, such as fever and leprosy. And as with its own body, so it can influence another body either for health or sickness; and to this is ascribed the cause of bewitchment, of which we have spoken above.

And since according to that view the deeds of witches have to be attributed to the Powers that move the stars, if not precisely to the stars themselves; therefore we must add to what we have already said on this subject, that this also is impossible. For the Powers that move the stars are good and intelligent Essences, not only by nature but also by will, as appears from their working for the good of the whole universe. But that creature by whose aid witchcraft is done, although it may be good by nature, cannot be good by will. Therefore it is impossible to hold the same judgement of both these Essences.

And that such an Essence cannot be good in respect of will is proved as follows. For it is no part of a well-disposed intelligence to extend patronage to those who act against virtue; and of such sort are the actions of witches. For it will be shown in the Second Part that they commit murders, fornications, and sacrifices of children and animals, and for their evil deeds are called witches. Therefore the Intelligence by whose aid such witchcraft is performed cannot be well-disposed towards virtue; although it may be good in its original nature, since all things are so, as is evident to anyone who thinks about it. Also it is no part of a good Intelligence to be the familiar spirit of criminals, and to extend patronage to them and not to the virtuous. For they are criminals who use witchcraft, and they are known by their works.

Now the natural function of the Essences that move the stars is to influence any creature for good, although it often happens that it becomes corrupted by some accident. Therefore those Essences cannot be the original cause of witches.

Besides, it is the part of a good spirit to lead men to that which is good in human nature, and of good repute; therefore to entice men away from such, and to betray them into evil things, belongs to an evilly-disposed spirit. And by the wiles of such a spirit men make no headway in those things which are worthy, such as the sciences and virtues, but rather in that which is evil, such as the knowledge of theft and a thousand other crimes; therefore the origin is not in these separate Essences, but in some Power evilly disposed toward virtue.

Besides, that cannot be understood to be a well-disposed spirit which is invoked as a helper in the commission of crimes. But this is what happens in the deeds of witches; for, as will be shown by their performances, they abjure the Faith, and slay innocent children. For the separate Essences which move the stars do not, on account of their goodness, provide help in these works of witchcraft.

In conclusion, then; this kind of works can no more arise from the Movers of the stars than from the stars themselves. And since they must originate from some Power allied to some creature, and that Power cannot be good in its will, although it may be naturally good, and that the devils themselves answer to this description, it follows that it is by their power that such things are done.

Unless, indeed, anyone should bring forward the trifling objection that witchcraft originates in human malice, and that it is effected by curses, and the placings of images in a certain place, the stars being favourable. For example, a certain witch placed her image and said to a woman, "I will make you blind and lame"; and it happened so. But it happened because the woman from her nativity was destined by the stars for such an affliction; and if such words and practices had been used against anyone else, they would not have been effective. And to this I shall answer in detail; first, that such witchcrafts cannot be caused by human malice; secondly, that they cannot be caused by magic words or images, whatever stars may be in concurrence.

Witchcraft does not operate from Human Malice alone.

And first to prove that witches' works cannot arise from human malice, however great. For a man's malice may be either habitual, inasmuch as by frequent practice he acquires a habit that inclines him to commit sin, not from ignorance but from weakness; in which case he is held to sin from wickedness. Or it may be actual malice, by which is meant the deliberate choice of evil, which is called the sin against the Holy Ghost. But in neither case can he, without the help of some higher Power, work such spells as the mutation of the elements, or the harming of the bodies both of men and beasts. And this is proved first as to the cause, and secondly as to the effect of witchcraft.

For a man cannot effect such works without malice, that is, a weakening of his nature, and still less when his nature has already been weakened; as is clear, since his active virtue is already diminished. But man, through all sorts of sin and wickedness, becomes weakened in his natural goodness. Both reason and authority prove this. For Dionysius (*de Diuin. Nom.* IV) says: Sin is the effect of natural habit; and he speaks of the sin of guilt. Wherefore no one who is conscious of sin commits it, unless he does so out of deliberate revolt.

I answer thus. The sin of guilt stands in the same relation to the good of nature as does the good of grace to the sin of nature. But by grace is diminished natural sin, which is as a tinder prone to guilt; therefore much more is natural good diminished by guilt. And it is not valid to put forward the objection that a bewitchment is sometimes caused by an old woman evilly looking at a child, by which the child is changed and bewitched. For, as has already been shown, this can only happen to children because of their tender complexion. But here we speak of the bodies of all sorts of men and beasts, and even the elements and hailstorms. If anyone wishes to inquire further, he may refer to S. Thomas in his questions concerning Evil: Whether sin can corrupt the whole natural good, etc.

And now as regards the effects of witchcraft. From the effects we arrive at a knowledge of the cause. Now these effects, as they concern us, are outside the order of created nature as known to us, and are done through the power of some creature unknown to us, although they are not miracles, which are things done outside the order of the whole of created nature. As for miracles, they are wrought by His power Who is above the whole order of the entire natural creation, Which is the Blessed God; as it is said: Thou art He Who alone workest great marvels. So also the works of witches are said to be miraculous only inasmuch as they are done by some cause unknown to us, and outside the order of created nature as known to us. From which it follows that the corporeal virtue of a man cannot extend itself to the causation of such works; for it has always this quality, that the cause with the natural effect is, in the case of man, recognized naturally and without wonder.

And that the works of witches can in some way be called miraculous, in so far as they exceed human knowledge, is clear from their very nature; for they are not done naturally. It is shown also by all the Doctors, especially S. Augustine in Book LXXXIII, where he says that by magic arts many miracles are wrought similar to those miracles which are done by the servants of God. And again in the same book he says that Magicians do miracles by private contract, good Christians by public justice, and bad Christians by the signs of public justice. And all this is explained as follows. For there is a Divine justice in the whole universe, just as there is a public law in the State. But the virtue of any creature has to do with the universe, as that of the private individual has to do with the State. Therefore inasmuch as good Christians work miracles by Divine justice, they are said to work them by public justice. But the Magician, since he works through a pact entered into with the devil, is said to work by private contract; for he works by means of the devil, who by his natural power can do things outside the order of created nature as known to us, through the virtue of a creature unknown to us; and it will be for us a miracle, although not actually so, since he cannot work outside the order of the whole of created nature, and through all the virtues of creatures unknown to us. For in this way only God is said to work miracles. As it is said: Thou art God Who alone workest great marvels. But bad Christians work through the signs of public justice, as by invoking the Name of Christ, or by exhibiting certain sacraments. If anyone pleases, he can refer to S. Thomas in the first part of the questions, III, art. 4. He can also study the conclusions in the Second Part of this work, Chapter VI.

That Witchcraft is not exercised and wrought by Voices and Words under a favouring Influence of the Stars.

Neither does witchcraft proceed from words uttered over images by men under favourable constellations. For the intellect of a man is of such a nature that its knowledge springs from things, and phantasms must be rationally examined. It is not in his nature, simply by thought or by the intrinsic operation of his intellect, to cause things to happen just by expressing them in words. For if there were men who had such power, they would not be of the same nature as we, and could only equivocally be called men.

But it is said that they effect these things by words when the stars of the nativity are favourable; from which it would follow that they would be able to act by the power of words only under certain conditions, and that they would be powerless without the help of the stars of their victim's nativity. But this is clearly false from what has been said before concerning Astromancers, casters of Horoscopes and Fortune-tellers.

Besides, words express the conception of the mind; and the stars cannot influence the understanding, neither can the Powers that move them, unless they wish on their own account, and apart from the motion of the stars, to enlighten the understanding; and this would only happen in regard to good works, for not enlightenment but darkness is given to the understanding for the performance of evil works; and such is the function not of good, but of evil spirits. Therefore it is clear that if their words are in any way effective, it is not by virtue of any star, but by virtue of some Intelligence, which may be naturally good, but

cannot be good in respect of will, since it always works for evil; and such is the devil, as has been shown above.

And they cannot effect such things by images influenced, as it were, by the stars. For such images, marked with whatever characters and figures, are the result of a man working by art. But the stars cause natural effects; a term which cannot be applied to the effects caused by evil witches, to the harm of creatures, proceeding apart from the accustomed order of nature. Wherefore this argument is not relevant.

Again, it has been shown above that there are two kinds of images. Those of the Astrologers and Mages are ordained not for corruption, but for the obtaining of some private good. But the images of witches are quite different, since always they are secretly placed somewhere by the command of the devil for the hurt of a creature; and they who walk or sleep over them are harmed, as the witches themselves confess. Wherefore whatever they effect is done by means of devils, and is not due to the influence of the stars.

To the arguments. For the first, we must understand the words of S. Augustine, that the cause of man's depravity lies in man's will, meaning the cause which produces the effect; which is properly said to be the cause. It is not so, however, with the cause which permits the effect, or arranges or advises or suggests it, in which sense the devil is said to be the cause of sin and depravity; God only permitting it that good may come of evil. As S. Augustine says: The devil provides the inner suggestion, and persuades both inwardly and outwardly by more active stimulation. But he instructs those who are entirely in his power, as are witches, whom there is no need to tempt from within, but only from without, etc.

And through this we come to the second argument, that everyone is, by direct understanding, the cause of his own wickedness. And concerning this it is to be said that, though it would be contrary to the doctrine of free-will to believe that a man may be influenced by direct command, it is not so to say that he is influenced by suggestion.

Thirdly, impulses to good or evil can be caused to be suggested by the influence of the stars, and the impulse is received as a natural inclination to human virtue or vice. But the works of witches are outside the common order of nature, and therefore they cannot be subject to those influences.

The fourth argument is equally clear. For though the stars are a cause of human acts, witchcraft is not properly a human act.

For the fifth argument, that the Powers that move the stars can influence souls. If that is understood directly, they do so influence them by enlightening them towards goodness, but not to witchcraft, as has been shown above. But if it is understood mediately, then through the medium of the stars they exert an indirect and suggestive influence.

Sixthly, there are two reasons why devils molest men at certain phases of the Moon. First, that they may bring disrepute on a creature of God, namely, the Moon, as S. Jerome and S. John Chrysostom say. Secondly, because they cannot, as has been said above, operate except through the medium of the natural powers. Therefore they study the aptitudes of bodies for receiving an impression; and because, as Aristotle says, the brain is the most humid of all the parts of the body, therefore it chiefly is subject to the operation of the Moon, which itself has power to incite humours. Moreover, the animal forces are perfected in the brain, and therefore the devils disturb a man's fancy according to certain phases of the Moon, when the brain is ripe for such influences.

And there are two reasons why the devils are present as counsellors in certain constellations. First, that they may lead men into the error of thinking that there is some divinity in the stars. Secondly, because they think that under the influence of some constellations corporeal matter is more apt for the deeds that they counsel.

And as to what S. Augustine says in *de Ciuitate Dei*, XXXVI: Devils are attracted by various kinds of stones, herbs, trees, animals, songs, and instruments of music, not as animals are attracted by food, but as spirits by signs, as if these things were exhibited to them as a sign of Divine honour, for which they are themselves eager.

But it is often objected that devils can be hindered by herbs and music from molesting men; as it is alleged in the argument from Saul and the music of the harp. And hence an attempt is made to argue that some men can work witchcraft through certain herbs and occult causes, without the help of devils, but only of the influence of the stars, which have more direct power over matters corporeal for corporeal effects than over the devils for effects of witchcraft.

Now, though this must be answered more widely, it is to be noted that herbs and music cannot by their own natural virtue entirely shut out the molestation which the devil can inflict upon men, with the permission of God and the good Angels. Yet they can mitigate that molestation; and this can even be of so slight a nature that they can entirely remove it. But they would do this, not by acting against the devil himself, since he is a separate spirit against whom nothing corporeal can naturally act, but by acting against the actual molestation of the devil. For every cause that has limited power can produce a more intense effect on a suitable than upon an unsuitable material. See Aristotle *De Anima*. They who act do so upon a predisposed patient. Now the devil is an agent of limited power; therefore he can inflict a fiercer affliction on a man disposed to that affliction or to that which the devil means to inflict, than upon a man of a contrary disposition. For example, the devil can induce a fiercer passion of melancholy in a man disposed to that humour than in a man of the contrary disposition.

Moreover, it is certain that herbs and music can change the disposition of the body, and consequently of the emotions. This is evident in the case of herbs, since some incline a man to joy, some to sadness, and so with others. It is evident also in the case of music, as Aristotle shows (*Politics*, VIII), where he says that different harmonies can produce different passions in man. Boethius also mentions this in his *Music*, and the author of the *Birth of Knowledge*, where he speaks of the usefulness of music, and says that it is of value in the cure or alleviation of various infirmities. And thus, other things being equal, it may help to weaken the affliction.

But I do not see how herbs or music can cause a man to be of such a disposition that he can in no way be molested by the devil. Even if such a thing were permissible, the devil, moving only in local vapour of the spirit, can grievously afflict men supernaturally. But herbs and harmonies cannot of their own natural virtue cause in man a disposition by which the devil is prevented from creating the aforesaid commotion. Nevertheless it sometimes happens that the devil is permitted to inflict only so small a vexation on a man that, through some strong contrary disposition, it may be totally removed; and then some herbs or harmonies can so dispose a man's body to the contrary that the vexation is totally removed. For example, the devil may at times vex a man with the affliction of sadness; but so weakly that herbs or harmonies which are capable of causing a swelling and uplifting of the spirits, which are contrary emotions to sadness, can totally remove that sadness.

Moreover, S. Augustine, in his Second Book *On the Christian Doctrine*, condemns amulets and certain other things of which he there writes much, attributing their virtue to magic art, since they can have no natural virtue of their own. And this is clear from what he says. To this sort belong all amulets and charms which are condemned by the School of Physicians, which condemns very clearly their use, in that they have no efficacy of their own natural virtue.

And as for that concerning 1 *Kings* xvi: that Saul, who was vexed by a devil, was alleviated when David played his harp before him, and that the devil departed, etc. It must be known that it is quite true that by the playing of the harp, and the natural virtue of that harmony, the affliction of Saul was to some extent relieved, inasmuch as that music did somewhat calm his senses through hearing; through which calming he was made less prone to that vexation. But the reason why the evil spirit departed when David played the harp was because of the might of the Cross, which is clearly enough shown by the gloss, where it says: David was learned in music, skilful in the different notes and harmonic modulations. He shows the essential unity by playing each day in various modes. David repressed the evil spirit by the harp, not because there was so much virtue in the harp, but it was made in the sign of a cross, being a cross of wood with the strings stretched across. And even at that time the devils fled from this.

☆

QUESTION VI

Concerning Witches who copulate with Devils.

Why it is that Women are chiefly addicted to Evil Superstitions.

THERE is also, concerning witches who copulate with devils, much difficulty in considering the methods by which such abominations are consummated. On the part of the devil: first, of what element the body is made that he assumes; secondly, whether the act is always accompanied by the injection of semen received from another; thirdly, as to time and place, whether he commits this act more frequently at one time than at another; fourthly, whether the act is invisible to any who may be standing by. And on the part of the women, it has to be inquired whether only they who were themselves conceived in this filthy manner are often visited by devils; or secondly, whether it is those who were offered to devils by midwives at the time of their birth; and thirdly, whether the actual venereal delectation of such is of a weaker sort. But we cannot here reply to all these questions, both because we are only engaged in a general study, and because in the second part of this work they are all singly explained by their operations, as will appear in the fourth chapter, where mention is made of each separate method. Therefore let us now chiefly consider women; and first, why this kind of perfidy is found more in so fragile a sex than in men. And our inquiry will first be general, as to the general conditions of women; secondly, particular, as to which sort of women are found to be given to superstition and witchcraft; and thirdly, specifically with regard to midwives, who surpass all others in wickedness.

Why Superstition is chiefly found in Women.

As for the first question, why a greater number of witches is found in the fragile feminine sex than among men; it is indeed a fact that it were idle to contradict, since it is accredited by actual experience, apart from the verbal testimony of credible witnesses. And without in any way detracting from a sex in which God has always taken great glory that His might should be spread abroad, let us say that various men have assigned various reasons for this fact, which nevertheless agree in principle. Wherefore it is good, for the admonition of women, to speak of this matter; and it has often been proved by experience that they are eager to hear of it, so long as it is set forth with discretion.

For some learned men propound this reason; that there are three things in nature, the Tongue, an Ecclesiastic, and a Woman, which know no moderation in goodness or vice; and when they exceed the bounds of their condition they reach the greatest heights and the lowest depths of goodness and vice. When they are governed by a good spirit, they are most excellent in virtue; but when they are governed by an evil spirit, they indulge the worst possible vices.

This is clear in the case of the tongue, since by its ministry most of the kingdoms have been brought into the faith of Christ; and the Holy Ghost appeared over the Apostles of Christ in tongues of fire. Other learned preachers also have had as it were the tongues of dogs, licking the wounds and sores of the dying Lazarus. As it is said: With the tongues of dogs ye save your souls from the enemy.

For this reason S. Dominic,* the leader and father of the Order of Preachers, is represented in the figure of a barking dog with a lighted torch in his mouth, that even to this day he may by his barking keep off the heretic wolves from the flock of Christ's sheep.

It is also a matter of common experience that the tongue of one prudent man can subdue the wrangling of a multitude; wherefore not unjustly Solomon sings much in their praise, in *Proverbs* x.: In the lips of him that hath understanding wisdom is found. And

again, The tongue of the just is as choice silver: the heart of the wicked is little worth. And again, The lips of the righteous feed many; but fools die for want of wisdom. For this cause he adds in chapter xvi, The preparations of the heart belong to man; but the answer of the tongue is from the Lord.

But concerning an evil tongue you will find in *Ecclesiasticus* xxviii: A backbiting tongue hath disquieted many, and driven them from nation to nation: strong cities hath it pulled down, and overthrown the houses of great men. And by a backbiting tongue it means a third party who rashly or spitefully interferes between two contending parties.

Secondly, concerning Ecclesiastics, that is to say, clerics and religious of either sex, S. John Chrysostom† speaks on the text, He cast out them that bought and sold from the temple. From the priesthood arises everything good, and everything evil. S. Jerome in his epistle to Nepotian says: Avoid as you would the plague a trading priest, who has risen from poverty to riches, from a low to a high estate. And Blessed Bernard in his 23rd Homily *On the Psalms* says of clerics: If one should arise as an open heretic, let him be cast out and put to silence; if he is a violent enemy, let all good men flee from him. But how are we to know which ones to cast out or to flee from? For they are confusedly friendly and hostile, peaceable and quarrelsome, neighbourly and utterly selfish.

And in another place: Our bishops are become spearmen, and our pastors shearers. And by bishops here is meant those proud Abbots who impose heavy labours on their inferiors, which they would not themselves touch with their little finger. And S. Gregory says concerning pastors: No one does more harm in the Church than he who, having the name or order of sanctity, lives in sin; for no one dares to accuse him of sin, and therefore the sin is widely spread, since the sinner is

---

* "*S. Dominic.*" *Before the birth of S. Dominic, his mother, Blessed Joanna d'Aza, dreamed that she had brought forth a black-and-white dog carrying in his mouth a lighted torch. The dog with the torch is accordingly the pictorial attribute of the Saint. Nor must the play upon the name of his sons be forgotten—Dominicani, Domini canes, Hounds of the Lord.*

† "*S. John Chrysostom.*" *Born at Antioch 347; died at Comana in Pontus, 14 September, 407. His fifty-nine homilies "On the Psalms" (iv–xii, xli, xliii–xlix, cviii–cxvii, cxix–cl) are very famous. For a full study of these see Baur's "Der ursprüngliche Umfang des Kommentars des hl. Joh. Chrysostomus zu den Psalmen" in* Χρυσοστομιχά, *fasc. I, Rome, 1908.*

honoured for the sanctity of his order. Blessed Augustine also speaks of monks to Vincent the Donatist: I freely confess to your charity before the Lord our God, which is the witness of my soul from the time I began to serve God, what great difficulty I have experienced in the fact that it is impossible to find either worse or better men than those who grace or disgrace the monasteries.

Now the wickedness of women is spoken of in *Ecclesiasticus* xxv: There is no head above the head of a serpent: and there is no wrath above the wrath of a woman. I had rather dwell with a lion and a dragon than to keep house with a wicked woman. And among much which in that place precedes and follows about a wicked woman, he concludes: All wickedness is but little to the wickedness of a woman. Wherefore S. John Chrysostom says on the text, It is not good to marry (*S. Matthew* xix):* What else is woman but a foe to friendship, an unescapable punishment, a necessary evil, a natural temptation, a desirable calamity, a domestic danger, a delectable detriment, an evil of nature, painted with fair colours! Therefore if it be a sin to divorce her when she ought to be kept, it is indeed a necessary torture; for either we commit adultery by divorcing her, or we must endure daily strife. Cicero in his second book of *The Rhetorics* says: The many lusts of men lead them into one sin, but the one lust of women leads them into all sins; for the root of all woman's vices is avarice. And Seneca says in his *Tragedies*: A woman either loves or hates; there is no third grade. And the tears of a woman are a deception, for they may spring from true grief, or they may be a snare. When a woman thinks alone, she thinks evil.

But for good women there is so much praise, that we read that they have brought beatitude to men, and have saved nations, lands, and cities; as is clear in the case of Judith, Debbora, and Esther. See also 1 *Corinthians* vii: If a woman hath a husband that believeth not, and he be pleased to dwell with her, let her not leave him. For the unbelieving husband is sanctified by the believing wife. And *Ecclesiasticus* xxvi: Blessed is the man who has a

virtuous wife, for the number of his days shall be doubled. And throughout that chapter much high praise is spoken of the excellence of good women; as also in the last chapter of *Proverbs* concerning a virtuous woman.

And all this is made clear also in the New Testament concerning women and virgins and other holy women who have by faith led nations and kingdoms away from the worship of idols to the Christian religion. Anyone who looks at Vincent of Beauvais (*in Spe. Histor.*, XXVI. 9) will find marvellous things of the conversion of Hungary by the most Christian Gilia,† and of the Franks by Clotilda,‡ the wife of Clovis. Wherefore in many vituperations that we read against women, the word woman is used to mean the lust of the flesh. As it is said: I have found a woman more bitter than death, and a good woman subject to carnal lust.

Others again have propounded other reasons why there are more superstitious women found than men. And the first is, that they are more credulous; and since the chief aim of the devil is to corrupt faith, therefore he rather attacks them. See *Ecclesiasticus* xix: He that is quick to believe is light-minded, and shall be diminished.

---

† *"Gilia." Rather Gisela, the devout sister of Duke Henry of Bavaria (the future Emperor S. Henry II); in 995 married S. Stephen of Hungary, who succeeded to the throne in 997. She was untiring in her efforts to spread the Faith throughout the kingdom. The coronation mantle of Hungary, a purple damask cope, embroidered in silk and gold by Queen Gisela, dated 1031, is preserved at Budapest.*

‡ *"Clotilda." Born probably at Lyons about 474; died at Tours, 3 June, 545. The feast of S. Clotilda is celebrated 3 June. From the sixth century onwards, the marriage of Clovis I, King of the Salic Franks, and Clotilda, which took place in 492 or 493, was made the theme of epic narratives and many legends. Clotilda soon acquired a great ascendancy over her husband, and she availed herself of this influence to win him to the Catholic Faith. For a time her efforts seemed unavailing, but Clovis, who in a great battle against the Alemanni saw his men on the point of defeat, invoked the God of his wife, promising to become a Christian if only victory should be granted to the Franks. The tide instantly turned, and, true to his word, he was baptized at Reims by S. Remigius at Christmas, 496. His sister and three thousand of his noblest warriors at the same time embraced the Faith. Thus S. Clotilda was the instrument in the conversion of a mighty people.*

---

* *"S. Matthew." The ninety Homilies on S. Matthew were written about the year 390.*

The second reason is, that women are naturally more impressionable, and more ready to receive the influence of a disembodied spirit; and that when they use this quality well they are very good, but when they use it ill they are very evil.

The third reason is that they have slippery tongues, and are unable to conceal from their fellow-women those things which by evil arts they know; and, since they are weak, they find an easy and secret manner of vindicating themselves by witchcraft. See *Ecclesiasticus* as quoted above: I had rather dwell with a lion and a dragon than to keep house with a wicked woman. All wickedness is but little to the wickedness of a woman. And to this may be added that, as they are very impressionable, they act accordingly.

There are also others who bring forward yet other reasons, of which preachers should be very careful how they make use. For it is true that in the Old Testament the Scriptures have much that is evil to say about women, and this because of the first temptress, Eve, and her imitators; yet afterwards in the New Testament we find a change of name, as from Eva to Ave (as S. Jerome says), and the whole sin of Eve taken away by the benediction of Mary. Therefore preachers should always say as much praise of them as possible.

But because in these times this perfidy is more often found in women than in men, as we learn by actual experience, if anyone is curious as to the reason, we may add to what has already been said the following: that since they are feebler both in mind and body, it is not surprising that they should come more under the spell of witchcraft.

For as regards intellect, or the understanding of spiritual things, they seem to be of a different nature from men; a fact which is vouched for by the logic of the authorities, backed by various examples from the Scriptures. Terence* says: Women are intellectually like children. And Lactantius (*Institu-*

tiones, III): No woman understood philosophy except Temeste.† And *Proverbs* xi, as it were describing a woman, says: As a jewel of gold in a swine's snout, so is a fair woman which is without discretion.

But the natural reason is that she is more carnal than a man, as is clear from her many carnal abominations. And it should be noted that there was a defect in the formation of the first woman, since she was formed from a bent rib, that is, a rib of the breast, which is bent as it were in a contrary direction to a man. And since through this defect she is an imperfect animal, she always deceives. For Cato says: When a woman weeps she weaves snares. And again: When a woman weeps, she labours to deceive a man. And this is shown by Samson's wife, who coaxed him to tell her the riddle he had propounded to the Philistines, and told them the answer, and so deceived him. And it is clear in the case of the first woman that she had little faith; for when the serpent asked why they did not eat of every tree in Paradise, she answered: Of every tree, etc. —lest perchance we die. Thereby she showed that she doubted, and had little faith in the word of God. And all this is indicated by the etymology of the word; for *Femina* comes from *Fe* and *Minus*, since she is ever weaker to hold and preserve the faith. And this as regards faith is of her very nature; although both by grace and nature faith never failed in the Blessed Virgin, even at the time of Christ's Passion, when it failed in all men.

Therefore a wicked woman is by her nature quicker to waver in her faith, and consequently quicker to abjure the faith, which is the root of witchcraft.

And as to her other mental quality, that is, her natural will; when she hates someone whom she formerly loved, then she seethes with anger and impatience in her whole soul, just as the tides of the sea are always heaving and boiling. Many authorities allude to this

---

* "Terence." "Hecyra," III, i, 30–32:
Pueri inter sese quam pro leuibus noxiis iras gerunt!
Qua propter? quia enim, qui eos gubernat animus, infirmum gerunt.
Itidem illæ mulieres sunt ferme, ut pueri, leui sententia.

† "Temeste." "Denique nullas unquam mulieres philosophari docuerunt praeter unam ex omni memoria Themisten." III, xxv. But on this Xistus Betulaeus (ed. 1556) glosses: "Putat fortasse Leontii coniugem, ad quam Epicurus scripsisse legitur. Quid dicemus de Thermistoclea, Pythagorae sorore? quid de aliis pluribus quarum bene longum catalogum Textor recenset?"

cause. *Ecclesiasticus* xxv : There is no wrath above the wrath of a woman. And Seneca (*Tragedies*, VIII) : No might of the flames or of the swollen winds, no deadly weapon, is so much to be feared as the lust and hatred of a woman who has been divorced from the marriage bed.*

This is shown too in the woman who falsely accused Joseph, and caused him to be imprisoned because he would not consent to the crime of adultery with her (*Genesis* xxx). And truly the most powerful cause which contributes to the increase of witches is the woeful rivalry between married folk and unmarried women and men. This is so even among holy women, so what must it be among the others? For you see in *Genesis* xxi. how impatient and envious Sarah was of Hagar when she conceived: how jealous Rachel was of Leah because she had no children (*Genesis* xxx): and Hannah, who was barren, of the fruitful Peninnah (I. *Kings* i) : and how Miriam (*Numbers* xii) murmured and spoke ill of Moses, and was therefore stricken with leprosy: and how Martha was jealous of Mary Magdalen, because she was busy and Mary was sitting down (*S. Luke* x). To this point is *Ecclesiasticus* xxxvii : Neither consult with a woman touching her of whom she is jealous. Meaning that it is useless to consult with her, since there is always jealousy, that is, envy, in a wicked woman. And if women behave thus to each other, how much more will they do so to men.

Valerius Maximus tells how, when Phoroneus, the king of the Greeks, was dying, he said to his brother Leontius that there would have been nothing lacking to him of complete happiness if a wife had always been lacking to him. And when Leontius asked how a wife could stand in the way of happiness, he answered that all married men well knew. And when the philosopher Socrates was asked if one should marry a wife, he answered: If you do not, you are lonely, your family dies out, and a stranger inherits; if you do, you suffer perpetual anxiety, querulous complaints, reproaches concerning the marriage portion, the heavy displeasure of your relations, the garrulousness of a mother-in-law, cuckoldom, and no certain arrival of an heir. This he said as

one who knew. For S. Jerome in his *Contra Iouinianum*† says : This Socrates had two wives, whom he endured with much patience, but could not be rid of their contumelies and clamorous vituperations. So one day when they were complaining against him, he went out of the house to escape their plaguing, and sat down before the house; and the women then threw filthy water over him. But the philosopher was not disturbed by this, saying, "I knew that the rain would come after the thunder."

There is also a story of a man whose wife was drowned in a river, who, when he was searching for the body to take it out of the water, walked up the stream. And when he was asked why, since heavy bodies do not rise but fall, he was searching against the current of the river, he answered : "When that woman was alive she always, both in word and deed, went contrary to my commands; therefore I am searching in the contrary direction in case even now she is dead she may preserve her contrary disposition."

And indeed, just as through the first defect in their intelligence they are more prone to abjure the faith; so through their second defect of inordinate affections and passions they search for, brood over, and inflict various vengeances, either by witchcraft, or by some other means. Wherefore it is no wonder that so great a number of witches exist in this sex.

Women also have weak memories; and it is a natural vice in them not to be disciplined, but to follow their own impulses without any sense of what is due; this is her whole study, and all that she keeps in her memory. So Theophrastus says : If you hand over the whole management of the house to her, but reserve some minute detail to your own judgement, she will think that you are displaying a great want of faith in her, and will stir up strife; and unless you quickly take counsel, she will prepare poison for you, and consult seers and soothsayers; and will become a witch.

But as to domination by women, hear what Cicero says in the *Paradoxes*. Can he be called a free man whose wife governs him, imposes laws on him, orders him, and forbids him to do what

---

* *"Seneca." "Medea,"* 579–82.

† *"Contra Iouinianum." This treatise was written* 392–93.

he wishes, so that he cannot and dare not deny her anything that she asks? I should call him not only a slave, but the vilest of slaves, even if he comes of the noblest family. And Seneca, in the character of the raging Medea,* says: Why do you cease to follow your happy impulse; how great is that part of vengeance in which you rejoice? Where he adduces many proofs that a woman will not be governed, but will follow her own impulse even to her own destruction. In the same way we read of many women who have killed themselves either for love or sorrow because they were unable to work their vengeance.

S. Jerome, writing of Daniel, tells a story of Laodice, wife of Antiochus king of Syria; how, being jealous lest he should love his other wife, Berenice, more than her, she first caused Berenice and her daughter by Antiochus to be slain, and then poisoned herself. And why? Because she would not be governed, but would follow her own impulse. Therefore S. John Chrysostom says not without reason: O evil worse than all evil, a wicked woman, whether she be poor or rich. For if she be the wife of a rich man, she does not cease night and day to excite her husband with hot words, to use evil blandishments and violent importunations. And if she have a poor husband she does not cease to stir him also to anger and strife. And if she be a widow, she takes it upon herself everywhere to look down on everybody, and is inflamed to all boldness by the spirit of pride.

If we inquire, we find that nearly all the kingdoms of the world have been overthrown by women. Troy, which was a prosperous kingdom, was, for the rape of one woman, Helen, destroyed, and many thousands of Greeks slain. The kingdom of the Jews suffered much misfortune and destruction through the accursed Jezebel, and her daughter Athaliah, queen of Judah, who caused her son's sons to be killed, that on their death she might reign herself; yet each of them was slain. The kingdom of the Romans endured much evil through Cleopatra, Queen of Egypt, that worst of women. And so with others. Therefore it is no wonder if the world now suffers through the malice of women.

And now let us examine the carnal desires of the body itself, whence has arisen unconscionable harm to human life. Justly may we say with Cato of Utica: If the world could be rid of women, we should not be without God in our intercourse. For truly, without the wickedness of women, to say nothing of witchcraft, the world would still remain proof against innumerable dangers. Hear what Valerius said to Rufinus: You do not know that woman is the Chimaera, but it is good that you should know it; for that monster was of three forms; its face was that of a radiant and noble lion, it had the filthy belly of a goat, and it was armed with the virulent tail of a viper. And he means that a woman is beautiful to look upon, contaminating to the touch, and deadly to keep.

Let us consider another property of hers, the voice. For as she is a liar by nature, so in her speech she stings while she delights us. Wherefore her voice is like the song of the Sirens, who with their sweet melody entice the passers-by and kill them. For they kill them by emptying their purses, consuming their strength, and causing them to forsake God. Again Valerius says to Rufinus: When she speaks it is a delight which flavours the sin; the flower of love is a rose, because under its blossom there are hidden many thorns. See *Proverbs* v, 3-4: Her mouth is smoother than oil; that is, her speech is afterwards as bitter as absinthium. [Her throat is smoother than oil. But her end is as bitter as wormwood.]

Let us consider also her gait, posture, and habit, in which is vanity of vanities. There is no man in the world who studies so hard to please the good God as even an ordinary woman studies by her vanities to please men. An example of this is to be found in the life of Pelagia,* a worldly woman who was

---

* "Medea." V, 895-6:
Quid, anime, cessas sequere felicem impetum?
Pars ultionis ista, qua gaudes, quota est?

* "Pelagia." "Pelagia meretrix" or "Pelagia mima," a beautiful actress who led the life of a prostitute at Antioch. She was converted by the holy bishop Nonnus, and disguised as a man went on pilgrimage to Jerusalem, where for many years she led a life of extremest mortification and penance in a grotto on the Mount of Olives. This "bienheureuse pécheresse" attained to such heights of sanctity that she was canonized, and in the East, where her cult was long very popular, her festival is kept on 8 October, which is also the day of her commemoration in the Roman Martyrology.

wont to go about Antioch tired and adorned most extravagantly. A holy father, named Nonnus, saw her and began to weep, saying to his companions, that never in all his life had he used such diligence to please God; and much more he added to this effect, which is preserved in his orations.

It is this which is lamented in *Ecclesiastes* vii, and which the Church even now laments on account of the great multitude of witches. And I have found a woman more bitter than death, who is the hunter's snare, and her heart is a net, and her hands are bands. He that pleaseth God shall escape from her; but he that is a sinner shall be caught by her. More bitter than death, that is, than the devil: *Apocalypse* vi, 8, His name was Death. For though the devil tempted Eve to sin, yet Eve seduced Adam. And as the sin of Eve would not have brought death to our soul and body unless the sin had afterwards passed on to Adam, to which he was tempted by Eve, not by the devil, therefore she is more bitter than death.

More bitter than death, again, because that is natural and destroys only the body; but the sin which arose from woman destroys the soul by depriving it of grace, and delivers the body up to the punishment for sin.

More bitter than death, again, because bodily death is an open and terrible enemy, but woman is a wheedling and secret enemy.

And that she is more perilous than a snare does not speak of the snare of hunters, but of devils. For men are caught not only through their carnal desires, when they see and hear women: for S. Bernard says: Their face is a burning wind, and their voice the hissing of serpents: but they also cast wicked spells on countless men and animals. And when it is said that her heart is a net, it speaks of the inscrutable malice which reigns in their hearts. And her hands are as bands for binding; for when they place their hands on a creature to bewitch it, then with the help of the devil they perform their design.

To conclude. All witchcraft comes from carnal lust, which is in women insatiable. See *Proverbs* xxx: There are three things that are never satisfied, yea, a fourth thing which says not, It is enough; that is, the mouth of the womb. Wherefore for the sake of fulfilling their lusts they consort even with devils.

More such reasons could be brought forward, but to the understanding it is sufficiently clear that it is no matter for wonder that there are more women than men found infected with the heresy of witchcraft. And in consequence of this, it is better called the heresy of witches than of wizards, since the name is taken from the more powerful party. And blessed be the Highest Who has so far preserved the male sex from so great a crime: for since He was willing to be born and to suffer for us, therefore He has granted to men this privilege.

What sort of Women are found to be above all Others Superstitious and Witches.

As to our second inquiry, what sort of women more than others are found to be superstitious and infected with witchcraft; it must be said, as was shown in the preceding inquiry, that three general vices appear to have special dominion over wicked women, namely, infidelity, ambition, and lust. Therefore they are more than others inclined towards witchcraft, who more than others are given to these vices. Again, since of these three vices the last chiefly predominates, women being insatiable, etc., it follows that those among ambitious women are more deeply infected who are more hot to satisfy their filthy lusts; and such are adulteresses, fornicatresses, and the concubines of the Great.

Now there are, as it is said in the Papal Bull, seven methods by which they infect with witchcraft the venereal act and the conception of the womb: First, by inclining the minds of men to inordinate passion; second, by obstructing their generative force; third, by removing the members accommodated to that act; fourth, by changing men into beasts by their magic art; fifth, by destroying the generative force in women; sixth, by procuring abortion; seventh, by offering children to devils, besides other animals and fruits of the earth with which they work much harm. And all these will be considered later; but for the present let us give our minds to the injuries towards men.

And first concerning those who are bewitched into an inordinate love or hatred, this is a matter of a sort that it is difficult to discuss before the general intelligence. Yet it must be granted that it is a fact. For S. Thomas (IV,

34), treating of obstructions caused by witches, shows that God allows the devil greater power against men's venereal acts than against their other actions; and gives this reason, that this is likely to be so, since those women are chiefly apt to be witches who are most disposed to such acts.

For he says that, since the first corruption of sin by which man became the slave of the devil came to us through the act of generation, therefore greater power is allowed by God to the devil in this act than in all others. Also the power of witches is more apparent in serpents, as it is said, than in other animals, because through the means of a serpent the devil tempted woman. For this reason also, as is shown afterwards, although matrimony is a work of God, as being instituted by Him, yet it is sometimes wrecked by the work of the devil: not indeed through main force, since then he might be thought stronger than God, but with the permission of God, by causing some temporary or permanent impediment in the conjugal act.

And touching this we may say what is known by experience; that these women satisfy their filthy lusts not only in themselves, but even in the mighty ones of the age, of whatever state and condition; causing by all sorts of witchcraft the death of their souls through the excessive infatuation of carnal love, in such a way that for no shame or persuasion can they desist from such acts. And through such men, since the witches will not permit any harm to come to either from themselves or from others once they have them in their power, there arises the great danger of the time, namely, the extermination of the Faith. And in this way do witches every day increase.

And would that this were not true according to experience. But indeed such hatred is aroused by witchcraft between those joined in the sacrament of matrimony, and such freezing up of the generative forces, that men are unable to perform the necessary action for begetting offspring. But since love and hate exist in the soul, which even the devil cannot enter, lest these things should seem incredible to anyone, they must be inquired into; and by meeting argument with argument the matter will be made clear.

☆

QUESTION VII

Whether Witches can Sway the Minds of Men to Love or Hatred.

IT is asked whether devils, through the medium of witches, can change or incite the minds of men to inordinate love or hatred; and it is argued that, following the previous conclusions, they cannot do so. For there are three things in man: will, understanding, and body. The first is ruled by God Himself (for, The heart of the king is in the hand of the Lord); the second is enlightened by an Angel; and the body is governed by the motions of the stars. And as the devils cannot effect changes in the body, even less have they power to incite love or hatred in the soul. The consequence is clear; that though they have more power over things corporeal than over things spiritual, they cannot change even the body, as has been often proved. For they cannot induce any substantial or accidental form, except by the help of some other agent, which is as it were their artificer. In this connexion is quoted what has been said before; that whoever believes that any creature can be changed for the better or the worse or transformed into another kind or likeness, except by the Creator of all things, is worse than a pagan and a heretic.

Besides, everything that acts with design knows its own effect. If, therefore, the devil could change the minds of men to hatred or love, he would also be able to see the inner thoughts of the heart; but this is contrary to what is said in the Book of Ecclesiastic Dogma: The devil cannot see our inner thoughts. And again in the same place: Not all our evil thoughts are from the devil, but sometimes they arise from our own choice.

Besides, love and hatred are a matter of the will, which is rooted in the soul; therefore they cannot by any cunning be caused by the devil. The conclusion holds that He alone (as S. Augustine says) is able to enter into the soul, Who created it.

Besides, it is not valid to argue that because he can influence the inner emotions, therefore he can govern the will. For the emotions are stronger than physical strength; and the devil can effect nothing in a physical way, such as the formation of flesh and blood;

therefore he can effect nothing through the emotions.

But against this. The devil is said to tempt men not only visibly but also invisibly; but this would not be true unless he were able to exert some influence over the inner mind. Besides, S. John Damascene says: All evil and all filthiness is devised by the devil. And Dionysius, *de Divin. Nom.* IV: The multitude of devils is the cause of all evil, etc.

Answer. First, one sort of cause is to be distinguished from another: secondly, we shall show how the devil can affect the inner powers of the mind, that is the emotions; and thirdly, we shall draw the fit conclusion. And as to the first, it is to be considered that the cause of anything can be understood in two ways; either as direct, or as indirect. For when something causes a disposition to some effect, it is said to be an occasional and indirect cause of that effect. In this way it may be said that he who chops wood is the cause of the actual fire. And similarly we may say that the devil is the cause of all our sins; for he incited the first man to sin, from whose sin it has been handed down to the whole human race to have an inclination towards all sin. And in this way are to be understood the words of S. John Damascene and Dionysius.

But a direct cause is one that directly causes an effect; and in this sense the devil is not the cause of all sin. For all sins are not committed at the instigation of the devil, but some are of our own choosing. For Origen says: Even if the devil were not, men would still lust after food and venery and such things. And from these inordinate lusts much may result, unless such appetites be reasonably restrained. But to restrain such ungoverned desire is the part of man's free-will, over which even the devil has no power.

And because this distinction is not sufficient to explain how the devil at times produces a frantic infatuation of love, it is further to be noted that though he cannot cause that inordinate love by directly compelling a man's will, yet he can do so by means of persuasion. And this again in two ways, either visibly or invisibly. Visibly, when he appears to witches in the visible form of a man, and speaks to them materially, persuading them to sin. So he tempted our first parents in Paradise in the form of a serpent; and so he tempted Christ in the wilderness, appearing to Him in visible form.

But it is not to be thought that this is the only way he influences a man; for in that case no sin would proceed from the devil's instruction, except such as were suggested by him in visible form. Therefore it must be said that even invisibly he instigates man to sin. And this he does in two ways, either by persuasion or by disposition. By persuasion, he presents something to the understanding as being a good thing. And this he can do in three ways; for he presents it either to the intellect, or to the inner perceptions, or to the outer. And as for the intellect; the human intellect can be helped by a good Angel to understand a thing by means of enlightenment, as Dionysius says; and to understand a thing, according to Aristotle, is to suffer something: therefore the devil can impress some form upon the intellect, by which the act of understanding is called forth.

And it may be argued that the devil can do this by his natural power, which is not, as has been shown, diminished. *It is to be said,* however, that he cannot do this by means of enlightenment, but by persuasion. For the intellect of man is of that condition that, the more it is enlightened, the more it knows the truth, and the more it can defend itself from deception. And because the devil intends his deception to be permanent, therefore no persuasion that he uses can be called enlightenment: although it may be called revelation, in that when he invisibly uses persuasion, by means of some impression he plants something on the inner or outer senses. And by this the reasoning intellect is persuaded to perform some action.

But as to how he is enabled to create an impression on the inner senses, *it is to be noted* that the bodily nature is naturally born to be moved locally by the spiritual; which is clear from the case of our own bodies, which are moved by our souls; and the same is the case with the stars. But it is not by nature adapted to be directly subject to influences, by which we mean outside influences, not those with which it is informed. Wherefore the concurrence of some bodily agent is necessary, as is proved in the 7th book of the *Metaphysics.* Corporeal matter naturally obeys a good or bad angel as to local motion; and it is due to this that devils can through local motion collect semen, and employ it for the production of wonderful results. This was how it happened that Pharao's magicians produced serpents and actual animals, when corresponding active and passive agents were brought together. Therefore there is nothing to prevent the devils from effecting anything that appertains to the local motion of corporeal matter, unless God prevent it.

And now let us examine how the devil can through local motion excite the fancy and inner sensory perceptions of a man by apparitions and impulsive actions. It is to be noted that Aristotle (*De Somno et Uigilia*) assigns the cause of apparitions in dreams through local motion to the fact that, when an animal sleeps the blood flows to the inmost seat of the senses, from which descend motions or impressions which remain from past impressions preserved in the mind or inner perception; and these are Fancy or Imagination, which are the same thing according to S. Thomas, as will be shown.

For fancy or imagination is as it were the treasury of ideas received through the senses. And through this it happens that devils so stir up the inner perceptions, that is the power of conserving images, that they appear to be a new impression at that moment received from exterior things.

It is true that all do not agree to this; but if anyone wishes to occupy himself with this question, he must consider the number and the office of the inner perceptions. According to Avicenna, in his book *On the Mind*, these are five: namely, Common Sense, Fancy, Imagination, Thought, and Memory. But S. Thomas, in the First Part of Question 79, says that they are only four, since Fancy and Imagination are the same thing. For fear of prolixity I omit much more that has variously been said on this subject.

Only this must be said; that fancy is the treasury of ideas, but memory appears to be something different. For fancy is the treasury or repository of ideas received through the senses; but memory is the treasury of instincts, which are not received through the senses. For when a man sees a wolf, he runs away, not because of its ugly colour or appearance, which are ideas received through the outer senses and conserved in his fancy; but he runs

away because the wolf is his natural enemy. And this he knows through some instinct or fear, which is apart from thought, which recognizes the wolf as hostile, but a dog as friendly. But the repository of those instincts is memory. And reception and retention are two different things in animal nature; for those who are of a humid disposition receive readily, but retain badly; and the contrary is the case with those of a dry humour.

To return to the question. The apparitions that come in dreams to sleepers proceed from the ideas retained in the repository of their mind, through a natural local motion caused by the flow of blood to the first and inmost seat of their faculties of perception; and we speak of an intrinsic local motion in the head and the cells of the brain.

And this can also happen through a similar local motion created by devils. Also such things happen not only to the sleeping, but even to those who are awake. For in these also the devils can stir up and excite the inner perceptions and humours, so that ideas retained in the repositories of their minds are drawn out and made apparent to the faculties of fancy and imagination, so that such men imagine these things to be true. And this is called interior temptation.

And it is no wonder that the devil can do this by his own natural power; since any man by himself, being awake and having the use of his reason, can voluntarily draw from his repositories the images he has retained in them; in such a way that he can summon to himself the images of whatsoever things he pleases. And this being granted, it is easy to understand the matter of excessive infatuation in love.

Now there are two ways in which devils can, as has been said, raise up this kind of images. Sometimes they work without enchaining the human reason, as has been said in the matter of temptation, and the example of voluntary imagination. But sometimes the use of reason is entirely chained up; and this may be exemplified by certain naturally defective persons, and by madmen and drunkards. Therefore it is no wonder that devils can, with God's permission, chain up the reason; and such men are called delirious, because their senses have been snatched away by the devil. And this they do in two ways, either with or without the help of witches.

For Aristotle, in the work we have quoted, says that anyone who lives in passion is moved by only a little thing, as a lover by the remotest likeness of his love, and similarly with one who feels hatred. Therefore devils, who have learned from men's acts to which passions they are chiefly subject, incite them to this sort of inordinate love or hatred, impressing their purpose on men's imagination the more strongly and effectively, as they can do so the more easily. And this is the more easy for them, just as it is more easy for a lover to summon up the image of his love from his memory, and retain it pleasurably in his thoughts.

But they work by witchcraft when they do these things through and at the instance of witches, by reason of a pact entered into with them. But it is not possible to treat of such matters in detail, on account of the great number of instances both among the clergy and among the laity. For how many adulterers have put away the most beautiful wives to lust after the vilest of women!

We know of an old woman who, according to the common account of the brothers in that monastery even up to this day, in this manner not only bewitched three successive Abbots, but even killed them, and in the same way drove the fourth out of his mind. For she herself publicly confessed it, and does not fear to say: I did so and I do so, and they are not able to keep from loving me because they have eaten so much of my dung—measuring off a certain length on her arm. I confess, moreover, that since we had no case to prosecute her or bring her to trial, she survives to this day.

It will be remembered that it was said that the devil invisibly lures a man to sin, not only by means of persuasion, as has been said, but also by the means of disposition. Although this is not very pertinent, yet be it said that by a similar admonition of the disposition and humours of men, he renders some more disposed to anger, or concupiscence, or other passions. For it is manifest that a man who has a body so disposed is more prone to concupiscence and anger and such passions; and when they are aroused, he is more apt to surrender to them. But because it is difficult to quote precedents, therefore an easier method must be found of declaring them for the admonition of the people. And in the

Second Part of this book we treat of the remedies by which men so bewitched can be set free.

The Method of Preaching to the People about Infatuate Love.

Concerning what has been said above, a preacher asks this question: Is it a Catholic view to maintain that witches can infect the minds of men with an inordinate love of strange women, and so inflame their hearts that by no shame or punishment, by no words or actions can they be forced to desist from such love; and that similarly they can stir up such hatred between married couples that they are unable in any way to perform the procreant functions of marriage; so that, indeed, in the untimely silence of night, they cover great distances in search of mistresses and irregular lovers?

As to this matter, he may, if he wishes, find some arguments in the preceding question. Otherwise, it need only be said that there are difficulties in those questions on account of love and hate. For these passions invade the will, which is in its own act always free, and not to be coerced by any creature except God, Who can govern it. From which it is clear that neither the devil nor a witch working by his power can force a man's will to love or to hate. Again, since the will, like the understanding, exists subjectively in the soul, and He alone can enter into the soul Who created it, therefore this question presents many difficulties in the matter of unravelling the truth of it.

But notwithstanding this, we must speak first of infatuation and hatred, and secondly about the bewitching of the generative power. And as to the first, although the devil cannot directly operate upon the understanding and will of man, yet, according to all the learned Theologians in the 2nd *Book of Sentences*, on the subject of the power of the devil, he can act upon the body, or upon the faculties belonging to or allied to the body, whether they be the inner or outer perceptions. This is authoritatively and reasonably proved in the preceding question, if one cares to look; but if not, there is the authority of Job ii: The Lord said unto Satan, Behold, he is in thine hand. That is, Job is in his power. But this was only in regard to the body, for He would not give his soul into his power. Wherefore He said: Only save thou his life; that is, keep it unharmed. And that power that He gave him over his body, He gave also over all the faculties allied to the body, which are the four or five outer and inner perceptions, namely Common Sense, Fancy or Imagination, Thought, and Memory.

If no other instance can be given, let us take an example from pigs and sheep. For pigs know by instinct their way home. And by natural instinct sheep distinguish a wolf from a dog, knowing one to be the enemy and the other the friend of their nature.

Consequently, since all our reasoned knowledge comes from the senses (for Aristotle in the 2nd book *On the Mind* says that an intelligent man must take notice of phantasms), therefore the devil can affect the inner fancy, and darken the understanding. And this is not to act immediately upon the mind, but through the medium of phantasms. Because, also, nothing is loved until it is known.

As many examples as are needed could be taken from gold, which the miser loves because he knows its power, etc. Therefore when the understanding is darkened, the will also is darkened in its affections. Moreover, the devil can effect this either with or without the help of a witch; and such things can even happen through mere want of foresight. But we shall give examples of each kind. For, as it is said in *S. James* i: Every man is tempted when he is drawn away of his own lust, and enticed. Then when lust hath conceived, it bringeth forth sin: and sin, when it is finished, bringeth forth death. Again, when Shechem saw Dinah going out to see the daughters of the land, he loved her, and seized her, and lay with her, and his soul clave unto her (*Genesis* xxxiv). And according to the gloss: When the infirm mind forsakes its own business, and takes heed, like Dinah, of that of other people, it is led astray by habit, and becomes one with the sinners.

Secondly, that this lust can arise apart from witchcraft, and simply through the temptation of the devil, is shown as follows. For we read in II. *Samuel* xiii that Ammon desperately loved his own sister Tamar, and yearned greatly for her, so that he grew ill for love of her. But no one would fall

into so great and foul a crime unless he were totally corrupt, and grievously tempted by the devil. Wherefore the gloss says: This is a warning to us, and was permitted by God that we should always be on our guard lest vice should get the mastery over us, and the prince of sin, who promises a false peace to those who are in danger, finding us ready should slay us unaware.

Mention is made of this sort of passion in the Book of the Holy Fathers, where it says that, however far they withdrew themselves from all carnal lusts, yet they were sometimes tempted by the love of women more than could possibly be believed. Wherefore in II. *Corinthians* xii the Apostle says: There was given to me a thorn in the flesh, the messenger of Satan to buffet me. On which the gloss says: It was given to me to be tempted by lust. But he who is tempted and does not yield is no sinner, but it is a matter for the exercise of virtue. And by temptation is understood that of the devil, not that of the flesh, which is always venial in a little sin. The preacher could find many examples if he pleased.

The third point, that infatuate love proceeds from the evil works of the devil, has been discussed above; and we speak of this temptation.

It may be asked how it is possible to tell whether such inordinate love proceeds not from the devil but only from a witch. And the answer is that there are many ways. First, if the man tempted has a beautiful and honest wife, or the converse in the case of a woman, etc. Secondly, if the judgement of the reason is so chained up that by no blows or words or deeds, or even by shame, can he be made to desist from that lust. And thirdly, in especial, when he cannot contain himself, but that he is at times unexpectedly, and in spite of the roughness of the journey, forced to be carried through great distances (as anyone can learn from the confessions of such men), both by day and by night. For as S. John Chrysostom says on *Matthew* xx concerning the ass upon which Christ rode: When the devil possesses the will of a man with sin, he carries him at his will where he pleases. Giving the example of a ship in the sea without a rudder, which the winds carry about at their pleasure; and of a man firmly sitting a horse; and a King having dominion over a tyrant. And fourthly, it is shown by the fact that they are sometimes suddenly and unexpectedly carried away, and at times transformed, so that nothing can prevent it. It is shown also by the hideousness of their very appearance.

And before we proceed to the further question of witches, touching the powers of generation, which follows, we must first resolve the arguments.

Here Follow the Resolutions of the Arguments.

But for the answer to the arguments: for the first, that the will of man is ruled by God, just as his understanding is by a good Angel, the solution is clear. For the intellect is enlightened by a good Angel only to the knowledge of the truth, from which proceeds the love of that which is good, for the True and the Actual are the same thing. So also the intellect can be darkened by a bad angel in the knowledge of what appears to be true; and this through a confusion of the ideas and images received and stored by the perceptions, from which comes an inordinate love of the apparently good, such as bodily delectation, which such men seek after.

As to the second argument, that the devil cannot effect physical changes in the body; this is in part true, and in part not, and this is with reference to three sorts of mutation. For the devil cannot change the body in such a way that its whole shape and appearance is altered (which is rather to be called a new production than a change) without the help of some agent, or with the permission of God. But if we speak of a change in quality, as in the matter of sickness and health, as has been shown before, he can inflict upon the body various diseases, even to taking away the reason, and so can cause inordinate hatred and love.

And a third kind of mutation can be added, which is when a good or bad angel enters into the body, in the same way that we say that God alone is able to enter into the soul, that is, the essence of life. But when we speak of an angel, especially a bad angel, entering the body, as in the case of an obsession, he does not enter beyond the limits of the essence of the body; for in this way only God the Creator can enter, Who gave it to be as it were the intrinsic operation of life. But the devil is said to enter the body when he effects something about the body: for where he works, there he is, as S. John Damascene says. And then he works within the bounds of corporeal matter, but not within the very essence of the body.

From this it appears that the body has two properties, matter and spirit. And this is like the distinction between the apparent and the real. Therefore when devils enter the body, they enter the powers belonging to the bodily organs, and can so create impressions on those powers. And so it happens that through such operations and impressions a phantasm is projected before the understanding, such as the seeing of colours, as it is said in the 3rd book de Anima. And so this impression penetrates also to the will. For the will takes its conception of what is good from the intellect, according as the intellect accepts something as good either in truth or in appearance.

As for the third argument: a knowledge of the thoughts of the heart may come about in two ways, either from seeing their effects or by reading them actually in the intellect. In the first way they can be known not only by an angel, but even by man, although it will be shown that an angel has more skill in this matter. For sometimes the thoughts are made evident, not only by some external action, but even by a change in the countenance. And doctors also can discern some affections of the mind through the pulse. Wherefore S. Augustine says (de Diuin. Daem.) that sometimes it is very easy to tell a man's disposition, not only from his words, but from his very thoughts, which are signs of the soul expressed in the body; although in his book of Retractations he says that no definite rule can be laid down how this can be done; and I think that he is reluctant to admit that the devil can know the inner thoughts of the heart.

From another point of view, the thoughts of the intellect and the affections of the will can be known only by God. For the will of a rational creature is subject only to God, and He alone can work in it Who is its first cause and ultimate end. Therefore that which is in the will, or depends only on the will, is known only to God. Moreover, it is manifest what depends only on the will, if one considers things by their resultant actions. For when a man has the quality of knowledge, and the understanding that comes from it, he uses it when he wills.

It is proved, then, from what has been said, that a spirit cannot enter the soul, therefore he cannot, naturally, see what is in the mind, especially what is in the inner depths of the soul. Wherefore, when it is argued that the devil cannot see the thoughts of the heart, and therefore cannot move the hearts of men to love or hatred, it is answered that he does learn men's thoughts through their visible effects, and is more skilful in this matter than man; and so by subtle ways he can move men to love and hatred, by creating phantasms and darkening the intellect.

And this must be said by way of comfort to relieve the apprehensions of the virtuous: that when the sensible exterior and bodily change which accompanied men's thoughts is so vague and indeterminate that the devil cannot by it arrive at any certain knowledge of the thoughts, especially when the virtuous at times take a little leisure from study and good works, he molests them then chiefly in dreams; as is known by experience. But when the physical effect of thought is strong and determinate, the devil can know by a man's appearance whether his thoughts are turned towards envy or luxury. But we find that it must be left an open question whether he can by this means have certain knowledge in respect of all circumstances, as such and such; although it is true that he can know such circumstances from their subsequent results.

And fourthly: although to enter the soul belongs only to God, yet it is possible for a good or bad angel to enter the body and the faculties allied to the body, in the manner which has been shown above. And in this way hatred and love can be aroused in such a man. For the other argument, that the powers of the spirit are greater than the physical powers, which themselves cannot be changed by the devil, it is answered that the physical powers can be altered by the devil, in so far as they can be hastened or retarded in the flesh and bone. But he does this, not for the sake of impeding or stimulating the inner or outer perceptions, but for his own gain; since he derives his chief benefit by the deception of the senses and the delusion of the intellect.

☆

QUESTION VIII

Whether Witches can hebetate the Powers of Generation or obstruct the Venereal Act.

NOW the fact that adulterous drabs and whores are chiefly given to witchcraft is substantiated by the spells which are cast by witches upon the act of generation. And to make the truth more clear, we will consider the arguments of those who are in disagreement with us on this matter. And first it is argued that such a bewitching is not possible, because if it were it would apply equally to those who are married; and if this were conceded, then, since matrimony is God's work and witchcraft is the devil's, the devil's work would be stronger than God's. But if it is allowed that it can only affect fornicators and the unmarried, this involves a return to the opinion that witchcraft does not really exist, but only in men's imagination; and this was refuted in the First Question. Or else some reason will be found why it should affect the unmarried and not the married; and the only possible reason is that matrimony is God's work. And since, according to the Theologians, this reason is not valid, there still remains the argument that it would make the devil's work stronger than God's; and since it would be unseemly to make such an assertion, it is also unseemly to maintain that the venereal act can be obstructed by witchcraft.

Again, the devil cannot obstruct the other natural actions, such as eating, walking and standing, as is apparent from the fact that, if he could, he could destroy the whole world.

Besides, since the venereal act is common to all women, if it were obstructed it would be so with reference to all women; but this is not so, and therefore the first argument is good. For the facts prove that it is not so; for when a man says that he has been bewitched, he is still quite capable as regards other women, though not with her with whom he is unable to copulate; and the reason for this is that he does not wish to, and therefore cannot effect anything in the matter.

On the contrary and true side is the chapter in the Decretals (If by sortilege, etc.): as is also the opinion of all the Theologians and Canonists, where they treat of the obstruction to marriage caused by witchcraft.

There is also another reason: that since the devil is more powerful than man, and a man can obstruct the generative powers by means of frigid herbs or anything else that can be thought of, therefore much more can the devil do this, since he has greater knowledge and cunning.

Answer. The truth is sufficiently evident from two matters which have already been argued, although the method of obstruction has not been specifically declared. For it has been shown that witchcraft does not exist only in men's imaginations, and not in fact; but that truly and actually innumerable bewitchments can happen, with the permission of God. It has been shown, too, that God permits it more in the case of the generative powers, because of their greater corruption, than in the case of other human actions. But concerning the method by which such obstruction is procured, it is to be noted that it does not affect only the generative powers, but also the powers of the imagination or fancy.

And as to this, Peter of Palude (III, 34) notes five methods. For he says that the devil, being a spirit, has power over a corporeal creature to cause or prevent a local motion. Therefore he can prevent bodies from approaching each other, either directly or indirectly, by interposing himself in some bodily shape. In this way it happened to the young man who was betrothed to an idol and nevertheless married a young maiden, and was consequently unable to copulate with her. Secondly, he can excite a man to that act, or freeze his desire for it, by the virtue of secret things of which he best knows the power. Thirdly, he can so disturb a man's perception and imagination as to make the woman appear loathsome to him: since he can, as has been said, influence the imagination. Fourthly, he can directly prevent the erection of that member which is adapted to fructification, just as he can prevent a local motion. Fifthly, he can prevent the flow of the vital essence to the members in which lies the motive power; by closing as it were the seminary ducts, so that it does not descend to the generative channels, or falls back from them, or does not project from them, or in any of many ways fails in its function.

And he continues in agreement with what has been treated of above by other Doctors. For God allows the devil more latitude in respect of this act, through which sin was first spread abroad, than of other human acts. Similarly, serpents are more subject to magic spells than are other animals. And a little later he says: It is the same in the case of a woman, for the devil can so darken her understanding that she considers her husband so loathsome that not for all the world would she allow him to lie with her.

Later he wishes to find the reason why more men than women are bewitched in respect of that action; and he says that such obstruction generally occurs in the seminal duct, or in an inability in the matter of erection, which can more easily happen to men; and therefore more men than women are bewitched. It might also be said that, the greater part of witches being women, they lust more for men than for women. Also they act in the despite of married women, finding every opportunity for adultery when the husband is able to copulate with other women but not with his own wife; and similarly the wife also has to seek other lovers.

He adds also that God allows the devil to afflict sinners more bitterly than the just. Wherefore the Angel said to Tobias: He gives the devil power over those who are given up to lust. But he has power also against the just sometimes, as in the case of Job, but not in respect of the genital functions. Wherefore they ought to devote themselves to confession and other good works, lest the iron remain in the wound, and it be in vain to apply remedies. So much for Peter. But the method of removing such effects will be shown in the Second Part of this work.

Some Incidental Doubts on the subject of Copulation prevented by Evil Spells are made Clear.

But incidentally, if it is asked why this function is sometimes obstructed in respect of one woman but not of another, the answer, according to S. Bonaventura, is this. Either the enchantress or witch afflicts in this way those persons upon whom the devil has determined; or it is because God will not permit it to be inflicted on certain persons. For the hidden purpose of God in this is obscure, as is shown in the case of the wife of Tobias. And he adds:

If it is asked how the devil does this, it is to be said that he obstructs the genital power, not intrinsically by harming the organ, but extrinsically by rendering it useless. Therefore, since it is an artificial and not a natural obstruction, he can make a man impotent towards one woman but not towards others: by taking away the inflammation of his lust for her, but not for other women, either through his own power, or through some herb or stone, or some occult natural means. And this agrees with the words of Peter of Palude.

Besides, since impotency in this act is sometimes due to coldness of nature, or some natural defect, it is asked how it is possible to distinguish whether it is due to witchcraft or not. Hostiensis gives the answer in his *Summa* (but this must not be publicly preached): When the member is in no way stirred, and can never perform the act of coition, this is a sign of frigidity of nature; but when it is stirred and becomes erect, but yet cannot perform, it is a sign of witchcraft.

It is to be noted also that impotence of the member to perform the act is not the only bewitchment; but sometimes the woman is caused to be unable to conceive, or else she miscarries.

Note, moreover, that according to what is laid down by the Canons, whoever through desire of vengeance or for hatred does anything to a man or a woman to prevent them from begetting or conceiving must be considered a homicide. And note, further, that the Canon speaks of loose lovers who, to save their mistresses from shame, use contraceptives, such as potions, or herbs that contravene nature, without any help from devils. And such penitents are to be punished as homicides. But witches who do such things by witchcraft are by law punishable by the extreme penalty, as has been touched on above in the First Question.

And for a solution of the arguments; when it is objected that these things cannot happen to those joined together in matrimony, it is further to be noted that, even if the truth in this matter has not already been made sufficiently plain, yet these things can truly and actually happen just as much to those who are married as to those who are not. And the prudent reader,

who has plenty of books, will refer to the Theologians and the Canonists, especially where they speak of the impotent and bewitched. He will find them in agreement in condemning two errors: especially with regard to married people who seem to think that such bewitchment cannot happen to those who are joined in matrimony, advancing the reason that the devil cannot destroy the works of God.

And the first error which they condemn is that of those who say that there is no witchcraft in the world, but only in the imagination of men who, through their ignorance of hidden causes which no man yet understands, ascribe certain natural effects to witchcraft, as though they were effected not by hidden causes, but by devils working either by themselves or in conjunction with witches. And although all the other Doctors condemn this error as a pure falsehood, yet S. Thomas impugns it more vigorously and stigmatizes it as actual heresy, saying that this error proceeds from the root of infidelity. And since infidelity in a Christian is accounted heresy, therefore such deserve to be suspected as heretics. And this matter was touched on in the First Question, though it was not there declared so plainly. For if anyone considers the other sayings of S. Thomas in other places, he will find the reasons why he affirms that such an error proceeds from the root of infidelity.

For in his questions concerning Sin, where he treats of devils, and in his first question, whether devils have bodies that naturally belong to them, among many other matters he makes mention of those who referred every physical effect to the virtue of the stars; to which they said that the hidden causes of terrestrial effects were subject. And he says: It must be considered that the Peripatetics, the followers of Aristotle, held that devils did not really exist; but that those things which are attributed to devils proceeded from the power of the stars and other natural phenomena. Wherefore S. Augustine says (*de Ciuitate Dei*, X), that it was the opinion of Porphyry that from herbs and animals, and certain sounds and voices, and from figures and figments observed in the motion of the stars, powers corresponding to the stars were fabricated on earth by men in order to explain various natural effects. And the error of these is plain, since they referred everything to hidden causes in the stars, holding that devils were only fabricated by the imagination of men.

But this opinion is clearly proved to be false by S. Thomas in the same work; for some works of devils are found which can in no way proceed from any natural cause. For example, when one who is possessed by a devil speaks in an unknown language; and many other devils' works are found, both in the Rhapsodic and the Necromantic arts, which can in no way proceed except from some Intelligence, which may be naturally good but is evil in its intention. And therefore, because of these incongruities, other Philosophers were compelled to admit that there were devils. Yet they afterwards fell into various errors, some thinking that the souls of men, when they left their bodies, became devils. For this reason many Soothsayers have killed children, that they might have their souls as their co-operators; and many other errors are recounted.

From this it is clear that not without reason does the Holy Doctor say that such an opinion proceeds from the root of infidelity. And anyone who wishes may read S. Augustine (de Ciuitate Dei, VIII, IX) on the various errors of infidels concerning the nature of devils. And indeed the common opinion of all Doctors, quoted in the above-mentioned work, against those who err in this way by denying that there are any witches, is very weighty in its meaning, even if it is expressed in few words. For they say that they who maintain that there is no witchcraft in the world go contrary to the opinion of all the Doctors, and of the Holy Scripture; and declare that there are devils, and that devils have power over the bodies and imaginations of men, with the permission of God. Wherefore, those who are the instruments of the devils, at whose instance the devils at times do mischief to a creature, they call witches.

Now in the Doctors' condemnation of this first error nothing is said concerning those joined together in matrimony; but this is made clear in their condemnation of the second error. For they say that others fall into the error of believing that, though witchcraft exists and abounds in the world, even against carnal copulation, yet, since no such bewitchment can be considered to be permanent, it never annuls a marriage that has already been contracted. Here is where they speak of those joined in matrimony. Now in refuting this error (for we do so, even though it is little to the point, for the sake of those who have not many books), it is to be noted that they refute it by maintaining that it is against all precedent, and contrary to all laws both ancient and modern.

Wherefore the Catholic Doctors make the following distinction, that impotence caused by witchcraft is either temporary or permanent. And if it is temporary, then it does not annul the marriage. Moreover, it is presumed to be temporary if they are able to be healed of the impediment within three years from their cohabitation, having taken all possible pains, either through the sacraments of the Church, or through other remedies, to be cured. But if they are not then cured by any remedy, from that time it is presumed to be permanent. And in that case it either precedes both the contract and the consummation of marriage, and then it prevents the contracting of a marriage, and annuls one that is not yet contracted; or else it follows the contract of marriage but precedes its consummation, and then also, according to some, it annuls the previous contract. (For it is said in Book XXXIII, quest. 1, cap. 1 that the confirmation of a marriage consists in its carnal office.) Or else it is subsequent to the consummation of the marriage, and then the matrimonial bond is not annulled. Much is noted there concerning impotence by Hostiensis, and Godfrey, and the Doctors and Theologians.

To the arguments. As to the first, it is made sufficiently clear from what has been said. For as to the argument that God's works can be destroyed by the devil's works, if witchcraft has power against those who are married, it has no force; rather does the opposite appear, since the devil can do nothing without God's permission. For he does not destroy by main force like a tyrant, but through some extrinsic art, as is proved above. And the second argument is also made quite clear, why God allows this obstruction more in the case of the venereal act that of other acts. But the devil has power also over other acts, when God permits. Wherefore it is not sound to argue that he could destroy the whole world. And the third objection is similarly answered by what has been said.

☆

QUESTION IX

Whether Witches may work some Prestidigitatory Illusion so that the Male Organ appears to be entirely removed and separate from the Body.

HERE is declared the truth about diabolic operations with regard to the male organ. And to make plain the facts in this matter, it is asked whether witches can with the help of devils really and actually remove the member, or whether they only do so apparently by some glamour or illusion. And that they can actually do so is argued *a fortiori*; for since devils can do greater things than this, as killing them or carrying them from place to place—as was shown above in the cases of Job and Tobias—therefore they can also truly and actually remove men's members.

Again, an argument is taken from the gloss on the visitations of bad Angels, in the Psalms: God punishes by means of bad Angels, as He often punished the People of Israel with various diseases, truly and actually visited upon their bodies. Therefore the member is equally subject to such visitations.

It may be said that this is done with the Divine permission. And in that case, as it has already been said that God allows more power of witchcraft over the genital functions, on account of the first corruption of sin which came to us from the act of generation, so also He allows greater power over the actual genital organ, even to its total removal.

And again, it was a greater thing to turn Lot's wife into a pillar of salt than it is to take away the male organ; and that (*Genesis* xix) was a real and actual, not an apparent, metamorphosis (for it is said that that pillar is still to be seen). And this was done by a bad Angel; just as the good Angels struck the men of Sodom with blindness, so that they could not find the door of the house. And so it was with the other punishments of the men of Gomorrah. The gloss, indeed, affirms that Lot's wife was herself tainted with that vice, and therefore was she punished.

And again, whoever can create a natural shape can also take it away.

But devils have created many natural shapes, as is clear from Pharao's magicians, who with the help of devils made frogs and serpents. Also S. Augustine, in Book LXXXIII, says that those things which are visibly done by the lower powers of the air cannot be considered to be mere illusions; but even men are able, by some skilful incision, to remove the male organ; therefore devils can do invisibly what others do visibly.

But on the contrary side, S. Augustine (*de Ciuitate Dei*, XVIII) says: It is not to be believed that, through the art or power of devils, man's body can be changed into the likeness of a beast; therefore it is equally impossible that that should be removed which is essential to the truth of the human body. Also he says (*de Trinitate*, III): It must not be thought that this substance of visible matter is subject to the will of those fallen angels; for it is subject only to God.

Answer. There is no doubt that certain witches can do marvellous things with regard to male organs, for this agrees with what has been seen and heard by many, and with the general account of what has been known concerning that member through the senses of sight and touch. And as to how this thing is possible, it is to be said that it can be done in two ways, either actually and in fact, as the first arguments have said, or through some prestige or glamour. But when it is performed by witches, it is only a matter of glamour; although it is no illusion in the opinion of the sufferer. For his imagination can really and actually believe that something is not present, since by none of his exterior senses, such as sight or touch, can he perceive that it is present.

From this it may be said that there is a true abstraction of the member in imagination, although not in fact; and several things are to be noted as to how this happens. And first as to two methods by which it can be done. It is no wonder that the devil can deceive the outer human senses, since, as has been treated of above, he can illude the inner senses, by bringing to actual perception ideas that are stored in the imagination. Moreover, he deceives men in their natural functions, causing that which is visible to be invisible to them, and that which is tangible to be intangible, and the audible inaudible, and so with the other senses. But such things are not true in actual fact, since they are caused through some defect introduced in the senses, such as the eyes or the ears, or the touch, by reason of which defect a man's judgement is deceived.

And we can illustrate this from certain natural phenomena. For sweet wine appears bitter on the tongue of the fevered, his taste being deceived not by the actual fact, but through his disease. So also in the case under consideration, the deception is not due to fact, since the member is still actually in its place; but it is an illusion of the senses with regard to it.

Again, as has been said above concerning the generative powers, the devil can obstruct that action by imposing some other body of the same colour and appearance, in such a way that some smoothly fashioned body in the colour of flesh is interposed between the sight and touch, and between the true body of the sufferer, so that it seems to him that he can see and feel nothing but a smooth body with its surface interrupted by no genital organ. See the sayings of S. Thomas (2 dist. 8. artic. 5) concerning glamours and illusions, and also in the second of the second, 91, and in his questions concerning Sin; where he frequently quotes that of S. Augustine in Book LXXXIII : This evil of the devil creeps in through all the sensual approaches; he gives himself to figures, he adapts himself to colours, he abides in sounds, he lurks in smells, he infuses himself into flavours.

Besides, it is to be considered that such an illusion of the sight and touch can be caused not only by the interposition of some smooth unmembered body, but also by the summoning to the fancy or imagination of certain forms and ideas latent in the mind, in such a way that a thing is imagined as being perceived then for the first time. For, as was shown in the preceding question, devils can by their own power change bodies locally; and just as the disposition or humour can be affected in this way, so can the natural functions. I speak of things which appear natural to the imagination or senses. For Aristotle in the de Somno et Uigilia says, assigning the cause of apparitions in dreams, that when an animal sleeps much blood flows to the inner consciousness, and thence come ideas or impressions derived from actual previous experiences stored in the mind. It has already been defined how thus certain appearances convey the impression of new experiences. And since this can happen naturally, much more can the devil call to the imagination the appearance of a smooth body unprovided with the virile member, in such a way that the senses believe it to be an actual fact.

Secondly, some other methods are to be noted which are easier to understand and to explain. For, according to S. Isidore (Etym. VIII, 9), a glamour is nothing but a certain delusion of the senses, and especially of the eyes. And for this reason it is also called a prestige, from prestringo, since the sight of the eyes is so fettered that things seem to be other than they are. And Alexander of Hales,* Part 2, says that a prestige, properly understood, is an illusion of the devil, which is not caused by any change in matter, but only exists in the mind of him who is deluded, either as to his inner or outer perceptions.

Wherefore, in a manner of speaking, we may say even of human prestidigitatory art, that it can be effected in three ways. For the first, it can be done without devils, since it is artificially done by the agility of men who show things and conceal them, as in the case of the tricks of conjurers or ventriloquists. The second method is also without the help of devils; as when men can use some natural virtue in natural bodies or minerals so as to impart to such objects some other appearance quite different from their true appearance. Wherefore, according to S. Thomas (I, 114, 4), and several others, men, by the smoke of certain smouldering or lighted herbs, can make rods appear to be serpents. The third method of delusion is effected with the help of devils, the per-

---

* "Alexander." Alexander of Hales, the Franciscan theologian and philosopher, Doctor Irrefragabilis, was one of the greatest of the scholastics. He was born at Hales, or Hailles, in Gloucestershire towards the end of the twelfth century, and died at Paris at the convent of his Order in 1245. His principal work is the "Summa Uniuersae Theologiae," begun about the year 1231, and left unfinished. It has several times been published: Venice, 1475, 1576; Nuremburg, 1481, 1502; Pavia, 1481; Cologne, 1622. A critical edition, which is much needed, has been promised by the Quaracchi editors of the works of S. Bonaventura.

mission of God being granted. For it is clear that devils have, of their nature, some power over certain earthly matters, which they exercise upon them, when God permits, so that things appear to be other than they are.

And as to this third method, it is to be noted that the devil has five ways in which he can delude anyone so that he thinks a thing to be other than it is. First, by an artificial trick, as has been said; for that which a man can do by art, the devil can do even better. Second, by a natural method, by the application, as has been said, and interposition of some substance so as to hide the true body, or by confusing it in man's fancy. The third way is when in an assumed body he presents himself as being something which he is not; as witness the story which S. Gregory tells in his *First Dialogue* of a Nun, who ate a lettuce, which, however, as the devil himself confessed, was not a lettuce, but the devil in the form of a lettuce, or in the lettuce itself. Or as when he appeared to S. Antony in a lump of gold which he found in the desert. Or as when he touches a real man, and makes him appear like a brute animal, as will shortly be explained. The fourth method is when he confuses the organ of sight, so that a clear thing seems hazy, or the converse, or when an old woman appears to be a young girl. For even after weeping the light appears different from what it was before. His fifth method is by working in the imaginative power, and, by a disturbance of the humours, effecting a transmutation in the forms perceived by the senses, as has been treated of before, so that the senses then perceive as it were fresh and new images. And accordingly, by the last three of these methods, and even by the second, the devil can cast a glamour over the senses of a man. Wherefore there is no difficulty in his concealing the virile member by some prestige or glamour. And a manifest proof or example of this, which was revealed to us in our Inquisitorial capacity, will be set forth later, where more is recounted of these and other matters in the Second Part of this Treatise.

How a Bewitchment can be Distinguished from a Natural Defect.

An incidental question, with certain other difficulties, follows. Peter's member has been taken off, and he does not know whether it is by witchcraft or in some other way by the devil's power, with the permission of God. Are there any ways of determining or distinguishing between these? It can be answered as follows. First, that those to whom such things most commonly happen are adulterers or fornicators. For when they fail to respond to the demand of their mistress, or if they wish to desert them and attach themselves to other women, then their mistress, out of vengeance, causes such a thing to happen, or through some other power causes their members to be taken off. Secondly, it can be distinguished by the fact that it is not permanent. For if it is not due to witchcraft, then the loss is not permanent, but it will be restored some time.

But here there arises another doubt, whether it is due to the nature of the witchcraft that it is not permanent. It is answered that it can be permanent, and last until death, just as the Canonists and Theologians judge concerning the impediment of witchcraft in matrimony, that the temporary can become permanent. For Godfrey says in his *Summa*: A bewitchment cannot always be removed by him who caused it, either because he is dead, or because he does not know how to remove it, or because the charm has been lost. Wherefore we may say in the same way that the charm which has been worked on Peter will be permanent if the witch who did it cannot heal him.

For there are three degrees of witches. For some both heal and harm; some harm, but cannot heal; and some seem able only to heal, that is, to take away injuries, as will be shown later. For thus it happened to us : Two witches were quarrelling, and while they were taunting each other one said : I am not so wicked as you, for I know how to heal those whom I injure. The charm will also be permanent if, before it has been healed, the witch departs, either by changing her dwelling or by dying. For S. Thomas also says : Any charm may be permanent when it is such as can have no human remedy; or if it has a remedy, it is not known to men, or unlawful; although God can find a remedy through a holy Angel who can coerce the devil, if not the witch.

However, the chief remedy against witchcraft is the sacrament of Penitence. For bodily infirmity often pro-

ceeds from sin. And how the charms
of witches can be removed will be
shown in the Second Part of this
Treatise, and in the Second Question,
chapter VI, where other different
matters are treated of and explained.

Solutions of the Arguments.

For the first, it is clear that there is no
doubt but that, just as, with God's
permission, they can kill men, so also
can devils take off that member, as well
as others, truly and actually. But then
the devils do not work through the
medium of witches, concerning which
mention has already been made. And
from this the answer to the second
argument is also made clear. But this is
to be said: that God allows more power
of witchcraft over the genital forces because, etc.; and therefore even allows
that that member should be truly and
actually taken off. But it is not valid
to say that this always happens. For it
would not be after the manner of
witchcraft for it to happen so; and
even the witches, when they do such
works, do not pretend that they have
not the power to restore the member
when they wish to and know how to do
so. From which it is clear that it is not
actually taken off, but only by a
glamour. As for the third, concerning
the metamorphosis of Lot's wife, we
say that this was actual, and not a
glamour. And as to the fourth, that
devils can create certain substantial
shapes, and therefore can also remove
them: it is to be said with regard to
Pharaoh's magicians that they made
true serpents; and that devils can, with
the help of another agent, produce
certain effects on imperfect creatures
which they cannot on men, who are
God's chief care. For it is said: Does
God care for oxen? They can, nevertheless, with the permission of God, do
to men true and actual harm, as also they
can create a glamour of harm, and by
this the answer to the last argument is
made clear.

☆

QUESTION X

*Whether Witches can by some Glamour
Change Men into Beasts.*

HERE we declare the truth as to
whether and how witches transform men into beasts. And it is argued

that this is not possible, from the following passage of *Episcopus* (XXVI, 5):
Whoever believes that it is possible for
any creature to be changed for the
better or for the worse, or to be
transformed into any other shape or
likeness, except by the Creator Himself, Who made all things, and by
Whom all things are created, is without
doubt an infidel, and worse than a
pagan.

And we will quote the arguments of
S. Thomas in the *2nd Book of Sentences*, VIII: Whether devils can affect
the bodily senses by the delusion of a
glamour. There he argues first that
they cannot. For though that shape of a
beast which is seen must be somewhere,
it cannot exist only in the senses; for
the senses perceive no shape that is not
received from actual matter, and there is
no actual beast there; and he adduces
the authority of the Canon. And again,
that which seems to be, cannot really be;
as in the case of a woman who seems to
be a beast, for two substantial shapes
cannot exist at one and the same time
in the same matter. Therefore, since
that shape of a beast which appears
cannot exist anywhere, no glamour or
illusion can exist in the eye of the beholder; for the sight must have some
object in which it terminates.

And if it is argued that the shape
exists in the surrounding atmosphere,
this is not possible; both because the
atmosphere is not capable of taking any
shape or form, and also because the
air around that person is not always
constant, and cannot be so on account
of its fluid nature, especially when it
is moved. And again because in that
case such a transformation would be
visible to everyone; but this is not so,
because the devils seem to be unable to
deceive the sight of Holy Men in the
least.

Besides, the sense of sight, or the
faculty of vision, is a passive faculty, and
every passive faculty is set in motion
by the active agent that corresponds to
it. Now the active agent corresponding
to sight is twofold: one is the origin of
the act, or the object; the other is the
carrier, or medium. But that apparent
shape cannot be the object of the sense,
neither can it be the medium through
which it is carried. First, it cannot be
the object, since it cannot be taken hold
of by anything, as was shown in the
foregoing argument, since it does not

exist in the senses received from an object, neither is it in the actual object, nor even in the air, as in a carrying medium, as was treated of above in the third argument.

Besides, if the devil moves the inner consciousness, he does so either by projecting himself into the cognitive faculty, or by changing it. But he does not do so by projecting himself; for he would either have to assume a body, and even so could not penetrate into the inner organ of imagination; for two bodies cannot be at the same time in the same place; or he would assume a phantasmal body; and this again would be impossible, since no phantasm is quite without substance.

Similarly also he cannot do it by changing the cognition. For he would either change it by alteration, which he does not seem able to do, since all alteration is caused by active qualities, in which the devils are lacking; or he would change it by transformation or local motion; and this does not seem feasible for two reasons. First, because a transformation of an organ cannot be effected without a sense of pain. Secondly, because in this case the devil would only make things of a known shape appear; but S. Augustine says that he creates shapes of this sort, both known and unknown. Therefore it seems that the devils can in no way deceive the imagination or senses of a man.

But against this, S. Augustine says (de Ciuitate Dei, XVIII) that the transmutations of men into brute animals, said to be done by the art of devils, are not actual but only apparent. But this would not be possible if devils were not able to transmute the human senses. The authority of S. Augustine is again to the point in Book LXXXIII, which has already been quoted: This evil of the devil creeps in through all the sensual approaches, etc.

Answer. If the reader wishes to refer to the method of transmutation, he will find in the Second Part of this work, chapter VI, various methods. But proceeding for the present in a scholastic manner, let us say in agreement with the opinions of the three Doctors, that the devil can deceive the human fancy so that a man really seems to be an animal. The last of those opinions, which is that of S. Thomas, is more subtle than the rest. But the first is that of S.

Antoninus * in the first part of his Summa, V, 5, where he declares that the devil at times works to deceive a man's fancy, especially by an illusion of the senses; and he proves this by natural reasoning, by the authority of the Canon, and by a great number of examples.

And at first as follows: Our bodies naturally are subject to and obey the angelic nature as regards local motion. But the bad angels, although they have lost grace, have not lost their natural power, as has often been said before. And since the faculty of fancy or imagination is corporeal, that is, allied to a physical organ, it also is naturally subject to devils, so that they can transmute it, causing various phantasies, by the flow of the thoughts and perceptions to the original image received by them. So says S. Antoninus, and adds that it is proved by the following Canon (Episcopus, XXVI, 5): It must not be omitted that certain wicked women, perverted by Satan and seduced by the illusions and phantasms of devils, believe and profess that they ride in the night hours on certain beasts with Diana, the heathen goddess, or with Herodias, and with a countless number of women, and that in the untimely silence of night they travel over great distances of land. And later: Wherefore priests ought to preach to the people of God that they should know this to be altogether false, and that when such

---

* "S. Antoninus." The famous Dominican Archbishop of Florence, born at Florence, 1 March, 1389; died 2 May, 1459. His feast day is 10 May. His chief literary work is the "Summa Theologica Moralis, partibus IV distincta," written shortly before his death, and marking a very considerable development in moral theology. Crohns in his "Die Summa theologica des Antonin von Florenz und die Schätzung des Weibes im Hexenhammer," Helsingfors, 1903, has set out to show that the very pronounced misogyny which is apparent in the "Malleus Maleficarum" can be traced to the "Summa" of S. Antoninus. But Paulus, "Die Verachtung der Frau beim hl. Antonin," in "Historisch-Politische Blätter," 1904, pp. 812–30, has severely criticized this thesis, which he declares to be untenable.

Within fifty years after the first appearance of the "Summa" of S. Antoninus, fifteen editions were printed at various important centres of learning. Many other editions followed, and in 1740 it was issued at Verona in four volumes, folio, edited by P. Ballerini; in 1741 at Florence by two Dominicans, Mamachi and Remedelli.

phantasms afflict the minds of the faithful, it is not of God, but of an evil spirit. For Satan himself transforms himself into the shape and likeness of different persons, and in dreams deluding the mind which he holds captive, leads it through devious ways.

Indeed the meaning of this Canon has been treated of in the First Question, as to the four things which are to be preached. But it would be to misunderstand its meaning to maintain that witches cannot be so transported, when they wish and God does not prevent it; for very often men who are not witches are unwillingly transported bodily over great distances of land.

But that these transmutations can be effected in both ways will be shown by the aforesaid *Summa*, and in the chapter where S. Augustine relates that it is read in the books of the Gentiles that a certain sorceress named Circe changed the companions of Ulysses into beasts; but that this was due to some glamour or illusion, rather than an actual accomplishment, by altering the fancies of men; and this is clearly proved by several examples.

For we read in the *Lives of the Fathers*, that a certain girl would not consent to a young man who was begging her to commit a shameful act with him. And the young man, being angry because of this, caused a certain Jew to work a charm against her, by which she was changed into a filly. But this metamorphosis was not an actual fact, but an illusion of the devil, who changed the fancy and senses of the girl herself, and of those who looked at her, so that she seemed to be a filly, who was really a girl. For when she was led to the Blessed Macarius, the devil could not so work as to deceive his senses as he had those of other people, on account of his sanctity; for to him she seemed a true girl, not a filly. And at length by his prayer she was set free from that illusion, and it is said that this had happened to her because she did not give her mind to holy things, or attend the Sacraments as she ought; therefore the devil had power over her, although she was in other respects honest.

Therefore the devil can, by moving the inner perceptions and humours, effect changes in the actions and faculties, physical, mental, and emotional, working by means of any physical organ soever; and this accords

with S. Thomas, I, 91. And of this sort we may believe to have been the acts of Simon Magus in the incantations which are narrated of him. But the devil can do none of these things without the permission of God, Who with His good Angels often restrains the wickedness of him who seeks to deceive and hurt us. Wherefore S. Augustine, speaking of witches, says: These are they who, with the permission of God, stir up the elements, and confuse the minds of those who do not trust in God (XXVI, 5).

Also devils can by witchcraft cause a man to be unable to see his wife rightly, and the converse. And this comes from an affectation of the fancy, so that she is represented to him as an odious and horrible thing. The devil also suggests representations of loathsome things to the fancy of both the waking and the sleeping, to deceive them and lead them to sin. But because sin does not consist in the imagination but in the will, therefore man does not sin in these fancies suggested by the devil, and these various transformations, unless of his own will he consents to sin.

The second opinion of the modern Doctors is to the same effect, when they declare what is glamour, and in how many ways the devil can cause such illusions. Here we refer to what has already been said concerning the arguments of S. Antoninus, which there is no need to repeat.

The third opinion is that of S. Thomas, and is an answer to the argument where it is asked, Wherein lies the existence of the shape of a beast that is seen; in the senses, or in reality, or in the surrounding air? And his opinion is that the apparent shape of a beast only exists in the inner perception, which, through the force of imagination, sees it in some way as an exterior object. And the devil has two ways of effecting such a result.

In one way we may say that the forms of animals which are conserved in the treasury of the imagination pass by the operation of the devil into the organs of inner senses; and in this way it happens in dreams, as has been declared above. And so, when these forms are impressed on the organs of the outer senses, such as sight, they appear as if they were present as outer objects, and could actually be touched.

The other way results from a change

in the inner organs of perception, through which the judgement is deceived; as is shown in the case of him who has his taste corrupted, so that everything sweet seems bitter; and this is not very different from the first method. Moreover, even men can accomplish this by the virtue of certain natural things, as when in the vapour of a certain smoke the beams of a house appear to be serpents; and many other instances of this are found, as has been mentioned above.

Solutions of the Arguments.

As to the first argument, that text is often quoted, but is badly understood. For as to where it speaks of transformation into another shape or likeness, it has been made clear how this can be done by prestidigitatory art. And as to where it says that no creature can be made by the power of the devil, this is manifestly true if Made is understood to mean Created. But if the word Made is taken to refer to natural production, it is certain that devils can make some imperfect creatures. And S. Thomas shows how this may be done. For he says that all transmutations of bodily matters which can be effected by the forces of nature, in which the essential thing is the semen which is found in the elements of this world, on land or in the waters (as serpents and frogs and such things deposit their semen), can be effected by the work of devils who have acquired such semen. So also it is when anything is changed into serpents or frogs, which can be generated by putrefaction.

But those transmutations of bodily matters which cannot be effected by the forces of nature can in no way be truly effected by the work of the devils. For when the body of a man is changed into the body of a beast, or a dead body is brought to life, such things only seem to happen, and are a glamour or illusion; or else the devil appears before men in an assumed body.

These arguments are substantiated. For Blessed Albertus in his book *On Animals*, where he examines whether devils, or let us even say witches, can really make animals, says that they can, with God's permission, make imperfect animals. But they cannot do so in an instant, as God does, but by means of some motion, however sudden, as is clear

in the case of witches. And touching the passage in *Exodus* vii, where Pharao called his wise men, he says: The devils run throughout the world and collect various germs, and by using them can evolve various species. And the gloss thereon says: When witches attempt to effect anything by the invocation of devils, they run about the world and bring the semen of those things which are in question, and by its means, with the permission of God, they produce new species. But this has been spoken of above.

Another difficulty may arise, whether such devils' works are to be deemed miraculous. The answer was made clear in the preceding arguments, that even the devils can perform certain miracles to which their natural powers are adapted. And although such things are true in fact, they are not done with a view to the knowledge of the truth; and in this sense the works of Antichrist may be said to be deceptions, since they are done with a view to the seduction of men.

The answer to the other argument, that concerning the shape, is also clear. The shape of a beast which is seen does not exist in the air, or in actual fact, as has been shown, but only in the perception of the senses, as has been demonstrated above from the opinion of S. Thomas.

For the argument that every passive is set in motion by its corresponding active, this is granted. But when it is inferred that the shape which is seen cannot be the original object which sets in motion the act of sight, since it arises from none of the senses, it is answered that it does not arise, since it originates from some sensible image conserved in the imagination, which the devil can draw out and present to the imagination or powers of perception, as has been said above.

For the last argument, it is to be said that the devil does not, as has been shown, change the perceptive and imaginative powers by projecting himself into them, but by transmuting them; not indeed by altering them, except in respect of local motion. For he cannot of himself induce new appearances, as has been said. But he changes them by transmutation, that is, local motion. And this again he does, not by dividing the substance of the organ of perception, since that would result in a sense of pain, but by a movement of the perceptions and humours.

But it may be further objected as follows: that according to this the devil cannot present to a man the appearance of anything new in respect of things seen. It is to be said that a new thing can be understood in two ways. In one way it may be entirely new both in itself and in its beginnings; and in this sense the devil cannot present anything new to a man's sense of vision: for he cannot cause one who is born blind to imagine colours, or a deaf man to imagine sounds. In another sense, a thing may be new as to the composition of its whole; as we may say that it is an imaginatively new thing if a man imagines that he sees mountains of gold, which he never saw; for he has seen gold, and he has seen a mountain, and can by some natural operation imagine the phantasm of a mountain of gold. And in this way the devil can present a new thing to the imagination.

What is to be Thought of Wolves which sometimes Seize and Eat Men and Children out of their Cradles : whether this also is a Glamour caused by Witches.

There is incidentally a question concerning wolves, which sometimes snatch men and children out of their houses and eat them, and run about with such astuteness that by no skill or strength can they be hurt or captured. It is to be said that this sometimes has a natural cause, but is sometimes due to a glamour, when it is effected by witches. And as to the first, Blessed Albertus in his book *On Animals* says that it can arise from five causes. Sometimes on account of great famine, when stags and other beasts have come near to men. Sometimes on account of the fierceness of their strength, as in the case of dogs in cold regions. But this is nothing to the point; and we say that such things are caused by an illusion of devils, when God punishes some nation for sin. See *Leviticus* xxvi: If ye do not my commandments, I will send the beasts of the field against you, who shall consume you and your flocks. And again *Deuteronomy* xxxii: I will also send the teeth of beasts upon them, etc.

As to the question whether they are true wolves, or devils appearing in that shape, we say that they are true wolves, but are possessed by devils; and they

are so roused up in two ways. It may happen without the operation of witches: and so it was in the case of the two-and-forty boys who were devoured by two bears coming out of the woods, because they mocked the prophet Elisaus, saying, Go up, thou bald head, etc. Also in the case of the lion which slew the prophet who would not perform the commandment of God (III. *Kings* xiii). And it is told that a Bishop of Vienna ordered the minor Litanies to be solemnly chanted on certain days before the Feast of the Ascension, because wolves were entering the city and publicly devouring men.

But in another way it may be an illusion caused by witches. For William of Paris tells of a certain man who thought that he was turned into a wolf,* and at certain times went hiding among the caves. For there he went at a certain time, and though he remained there all the time stationary, he believed that he was a wolf which went about devouring children; and though the devil, having possessed a wolf, was really doing this, he erroneously thought that he was prowling about in his sleep. And he was for so long thus out of his senses that he was at last found lying in the wood raving. The devil delights in such things, and caused the illusion of the pagans who believed that men and old women were changed into beasts. From this it is seen that such things only happen by the permission of God alone and through the operation of devils, and not through any natural defect; since by no art or strength can such wolves be injured or captured. In this connexion also Vincent of Beauvais (*in Spec. Hist.*, VI, 40) tells that in Gaul, before the Incarnation of Christ, and before the Punic War, a wolf snatched a sentry's sword out of its sheath.

---

* "*A wolf.*" *There are two kinds of werwolves, voluntary and involuntary. The voluntary were, of course, wizards, such as Gilles Garnier, who on 18 January, 1573, was condemned by the court of Dôle, Lyons, to be burned alive for "the abominable crimes of lycanthropy and witchcraft." More than fifty witnesses deposed that he had attacked and killed children in the fields and vineyards, devouring their raw flesh. He was sometimes seen in human shape, sometimes as a "loup-garou." During the sixteenth century in France lycanthropy was very prevalent, and numerous trials clearly show that murder and cannibalism were rife in many country districts.*

QUESTION XI

That Witches who are Midwives in Various Ways Kill the Child Conceived in the Womb, and Procure an Abortion; or if they do not this Offer New-born Children to Devils.

HERE is set forth the truth concerning four horrible crimes which devils commit against infants, both in the mother's womb and afterwards. And since the devils do these things through the medium of women, and not men, this form of homicide is associated rather with women than with men. And the following are the methods by which it is done.

The Canonists treat more fully than the Theologians of the obstructions due to witchcraft; and they say that it is witchcraft, not only when anyone is unable to perform the carnal act, of which we have spoken above; but also when a woman is prevented from conceiving, or is made to miscarry after she has conceived. A third and fourth method of witchcraft is when they have failed to procure an abortion, and then either devour the child or offer it to a devil.

There is no doubt concerning the first two methods, since, without the help of devils, a man can by natural means, such as herbs, savin for example, or other emmenagogues, procure that a woman cannot generate or conceive, as has been mentioned above. But with the other two methods it is different; for they are effected by witches. And there is no need to bring forward the arguments, since very evident instances and examples will more readily show the truth of this matter.

The former of these two abominations is the fact that certain witches, against the instinct of human nature, and indeed against the nature of all beasts, with the possible exception of wolves, are in the habit of devouring and eating infant children. And concerning this, the Inquisitor of Como, who has been mentioned before, has told us the following: that he was summoned by the inhabitants of the County of Barby to hold an inquisition, because a certain man had missed his child from its cradle, and finding a congress of women in the night-time, swore that he saw them kill his child and drink its blood and devour it.

Also, in one single year, which is the year now last passed, he says that forty-one witches were burned, certain others taking flight to the Lord Archduke of Austria, Sigismund. For confirmation of this there are certain writings of John Nider in his *Formicarius,*[*] of whom, as of those events which he recounts, the memory is still fresh in men's minds; wherefore it is apparent that such things are not incredible. We must add that in all these matters witch midwives cause yet greater injuries, as penitent witches have often told to us and to others, saying: No one does more harm to the Catholic Faith than midwives. For when they do not kill children, then, as if for some other purpose, they take them out of the room and, raising them up in the air, offer them to devils. But the method which they observe in crimes of this sort will be shown in the Second Part, which we must soon approach. But first one more question must be inquired into, namely, that of the Divine permission. For it was said at the beginning that three things are necessary for the effecting of witchcraft: the devil, a witch, and the Divine permission.

☆

QUESTION XII

Whether the Permission of Almighty God is an Accompaniment of Witchcraft.

NOW we must consider the Divine permission itself, touching which four things are asked. First, whether it is necessary that this permission should accompany a work of witchcraft. Secondly, that God in His justice permits a creature naturally sinful to perpetrate witchcraft and other horrid crimes, the other two necessary concomitants being presupposed. Thirdly,

---

* *"Nider." John Nider, O.P., was born 1380 in Swabia; and died at Colmar, 13 August, 1438. He gained a wide reputation as a preacher and was active at the Council of Constance. An advocate of the strictest reforms, he became eminent in the annals of his Order by his energy and example. The most important among his many works is the "Formicarius," a treatise upon the theological, philosophical, and social questions of the day. A complete edition was published at Douai, 5 vols., 1602. The tractate "De Maleficis" has often been printed separately.*

that the crime of witchcraft exceeds all other evils which God permits to be done. Fourthly, in what way this matter should be preached to the people.

Concerning the third postulate of this First Part, namely, the Divine permission, it is asked: Whether it is as Catholic to affirm the Divine permission in these works of witches, as it is quite heretical to contradict such an affirmation? And it is argued that it is not heretical to maintain that God does not permit so great power to the devil in this sort of witchcraft. For it is Catholic, and not heretical, to refute such things as appear to be to the disparagement of the Creator. And it is submitted that it is Catholic to maintain that the devil is not allowed such power of injuring men, since to hold the opposite opinion seems to be a disparagement of the Creator. For it would then follow that not everything is subject to the Divine providence, since the all-wise Provider keeps away, as far as possible, all defect and evil from those for whom He cares. And if the works of witchcraft are permitted by God, they are not kept away by Him: and if He does not keep them away, then God Himself is not a wise Provider, and all things are not subject to His providence. But since this is false, therefore it is false that God permits witchcraft.

And again, to permit a thing to happen presupposes in him who permits it that either he can prevent it from happening if he wishes, or he cannot prevent it even if he wishes; and neither of these suppositions can apply to God. For in the first case, such a man would be thought spiteful, and in the second case impotent. Then it is incidentally asked: As to that bewitchment that happened to Peter, if God could have prevented it, and did not do so, then God is either despiteful or He does not care for all; but if He could not have prevented it even if He wished, then He is not omnipotent. But since it is not possible to maintain the opinion that God does not care for all, and the rest, therefore it cannot be said that witchcraft is done with the permission of God.

Besides, he who is responsible to himself and is the master of his own actions is not subject to the permission or providence of any governor. But men were made responsible to themselves by God, according to *Ecclesiasticus* xv: God made man from the beginning, and left him in the hand of his counsel. In particular, the sins which men do are left in their own counsel, according to the text: He gave to them according to their hearts' desire. Therefore not all evils are subject to Divine permission.

Yet again, S. Augustine says in the *Enchiridion*, as does also Aristotle in the ninth book of *Metaphysics:* It is better not to know certain vile things than to know them, but all that is good is to be ascribed to God. Therefore God does not prevent the very vile works of witchcraft, whether He permits or not. See also S. Paul in I. *Corinthians* ix: Doth God take care for oxen? And the same holds good of the other irrational beasts. Wherefore God takes no care whether they are bewitched or not, since they are not subject to His permission, which proceeds from His providence.

Again, that which happens of necessity has no need of provident permission or prudence. This is clearly shown in Aristotle's *Ethics*, Book II: Prudence is a right reasoning concerning things which happen and are subject to counsel and choice. But several effects of witchcraft happen of necessity; as when for some reason, or owing to the influence of the stars, diseases come, or any other things which we judge to be witchcraft. Therefore they are not always subject to Divine permission.

And again, if men are bewitched by Divine permission, then it is asked: Why does this happen to one more than to another? If it be said that it is because of sin, which abounds more in one than in another, this does not seem valid; for then the greater sinners would be the more bewitched, but this is manifestly not so, since they are less punished in this world. As it is said: Well is it for the liars. But, if this argument were good, they also would be bewitched. Finally, it is clear from the fact that innocent children and other just men suffer most from witchcraft.

But against these arguments: it is submitted that God permits evil to be done, though He does not wish it; and this is for the perfecting of the universe. See Dionysius, *de Diuin. Nom.* III: Evil will be for all time, even to the perfecting of the universe. And S.

Augustine in the *Enchiridion:* In all things good and evil consists the admirable beauty of the universe. So that what is said to be evil is well ordained, and kept in its due place commends more highly that which is good; for good things are more pleasing and laudable when compared with bad. S. Thomas also refutes the opinion of those who say that, although God has no wish for evil (since no creature seeks for evil, either in its natural, or its animal, or in its intellectual appetite, which is the will, whose object is good), yet He is willing that evil should exist and be done. This he says to be false; since God neither wishes evil to be done, nor wishes it not to be done, but is willing to allow evil to be done; and this is good for the perfecting of the universe.

And why it is erroneous to say that God wishes evil to be and to be done, for the good of the universe, he says is for the following reason. Nothing is to be judged good except what is good in itself and not by accident. As the virtuous man is judged good in his intellectual nature, not in his animal nature. But evil is not of itself ordained for good, but by accident. For against the intention of those who do evil, good results. In this way, against the intention of witches, or against the intention of tyrants, was it that through their persecutions the patience of the martyrs shone out clearly.

Answer. This question is as difficult to understand as it is profitable to elucidate. For there is among the arguments, not so much of Laymen as of certain Wise men, this in common; that they do not believe that such horrible witchcraft as has been spoken of is permitted by God; being ignorant of the causes of this Divine permission. And by reason of this ignorance, since witches are not put down with the vengeance that is due to them, they seem now to be depopulating the whole of Christianity. Therefore that both learned and unlearned may be satisfied in each way, according to the opinion of the Theologians, we make our answer by the discussion of two difficulties. And first, that the world is so subject to the Divine providence that He Himself provides for all. Secondly, that in His justice He permits the prevalence of sin, which consists of guilt, punishment, and loss, by reason of His two

first permissions, namely, the fall of the Angels and that of our first parents. From which also it will be clear that obstinately to disbelieve this smacks of heresy, since such a man implicates himself in the errors of the infidels.

And as for the first, it is to be noted that, presupposing that which pertains to the providence of God (see *Wisdom* xiv: Thy providence, O Father, governeth all things), we ought also to maintain that all things are subject to His providence, and that also He immediately provides for all things. And to make this clear, let us first refute a certain contrary error. For taking the text in *Job* xxii: Thick clouds are a covering to him that He seeth not us; and He walketh in the circuit of heaven: some have thought that the doctrine of S. Thomas, I, 22, means that only incorruptible things are subject to Divine providence, such as the separate Essences, and the stars, with also the species of lower things, which are also incorruptible; but they said that the individuals of the species, being corruptible, were not so subject. Wherefore they said that all lower things which are in the world are subject to Divine providence in the universal, but not in the particular or individual sense. But to others this opinion did not seem tenable, since God cares for the other animals just as He does for men. Therefore the Rabbi Moses, wishing to hold a middle course, agreed with their opinion in saying that all corruptible things are not individually entirely subject to Divine governance, but only in a universal sense, as has been said before; but he excepted men from the generality of corruptible things, because of the splendid nature of their intellect, which is comparable with that of the separate Essences. And so, according to his opinion, whatever witchcraft happens to men comes from the Divine permission; but not such as happens to the animals or to the other fruits of the earth.

Now though this opinion is nearer to the truth than that which altogether denies the providence of God in worldly matters, maintaining that the world was made by chance, as did Democritus and the Epicureans, yet it is not without great fallacy. For it must be said that everything is subject to Divine providence, not only in the general, but also in the particular sense; and that the bewitching not only of men, but also of animals and the fruits of the earth, comes from Divine and provident permission. And this is plainly true; the providence and ordinance of things to some end extend just so far as the causality of them itself extends. To take an example from things that are subject to some master; they are so far subject to his providence as they are themselves under his control. But the causality which is of God is the original agent, and extends itself to all beings, not only in a general but also in an individual sense, and not only to things incorruptible. Therefore, since all things must be of God, so all things are cared for by Him, that is, are ordained to some end.

This point is touched by S. Paul in *Romans* xiii: All things which are from God were ordained by Him. Which is to say that, just as all things come from God, so also are all things ordained by Him, and are consequently subject to His providence. For the providence of God is to be understood as nothing else than the reason, that is, the cause of the ordering of things to a purpose. Therefore, in so far as all things are a part of one purpose, so also are they subject to the providence of God. And God knows all things, not only in the mass generally, but also in the individual particularly. Now the knowledge which God has of things created is to be compared with a craftsman's knowledge of his work: therefore, just as all his work is subject to the order and providence of a craftsman, so are all things subject to the order and providence of God.

But this does not provide a satisfactory explanation of the fact that God in justice permits evil and witchcraft to be in the world, although He is Himself the provider and governor of all things; for it would seem that, if this is conceded, He ought to keep away all evil from those for whom He cares. For we see among men that a wise provider does all that he can to keep away all defect and harm from those who are his care; therefore why does not God, in the same way, keep away all evil? It must be noted that a particular and an universal controller or provider are two very different matters. For the particular controller must of necessity keep away all the harm he can, since he is not able to

extract good out of evil. But God is the universal controller of the whole world, and can extract much good from particular evils; as through the persecution of the tyrants came the patience of the martyrs, and through the works of witches comes the purgation or proving of the faith of the just, as will be shown. Therefore it is not God's purpose to prevent all evil, lest the universe should lack the cause of much good. Wherefore S. Augustine says in the *Enchiridion:* So merciful is Almighty God, that He would not allow any evil to be in His works unless He were so omnipotent and good that He can bring good even out of evil.

And we have an example of this in the actions of natural things. For although the corruptions and defects which occur in natural things are contrary to the purpose of that particular thing (as when a thief is hanged, or when animals are killed for human food), they are yet in accordance with the universal purpose of nature (as that man's life and property should be kept intact); and thus the universal good is preserved. For it is necessary for the conservation of the species that the death of one should be the preservation of another. For lions are kept alive by the slaughter of other animals.

*It is Explained with regard to the Divine Permission, that God would not make a Creature to be Naturally without Sin.**

Secondly, God in His justice permits the prevalence of evil, both that of sin and that of pain, and especially now that the world is cooling and declining to its end; and this we shall prove from two propositions which must be postulated. First, that God would not—or let us rather say, with the fear of God, that (humanly speaking) it is impossible that any creature, man or Angel, can be of such a nature that it cannot sin. And secondly, that it is just in God to permit man to sin, or to be tempted. These two proposi-

---

* "*Naturally without sin.*" *The theology here is very intricate and must be followed with the utmost caution. All have free-will, and therefore might sin. But Our Lord and Our Lady did not sin; and the thought that they might have sinned is blasphemy. And S. John says (I. iii. 9): "Whosoever is born of God, committeth not sin: for his seed abideth in him, and he cannot sin, because he is born of God."*

tions being granted, and since it is a part of the Divine providence that every creature shall be left to its own nature, it must be said that, according to the premisses, it is impossible that God does not permit witchcraft to be committed with the help of devils.

. And that it was not possible to communicate to a creature a natural incapacity for sin, is shown by S. Thomas (II, 23, art. 1). For if this quality were communicable to any creature, God would have communicated it; for He has, at least in kind, communicated all other graces and perfections to His creatures that are communicable. Such is the personal union of two natures in Christ, the Maternity and Virginity of Immaculate MARY, the free fellowship of travellers, the blessed companionship of the elect, and many other things. But we read that this quality was not given to any creature, either man or Angel; for it is said: Even in His Angels He found sin. Therefore it is certain that God will not communicate to man a natural incapacity for sin, although man may win to this through grace.

Again, if this were communicable, and were not communicated, the universe would not be perfect. And its perfection consists in the fact that all communicable good qualities of creatures are communicated in kind.

Neither is it valid to argue that God, being omnipotent, and having made men and Angels in His likeness, could also have caused his creatures to be by nature impeccable: or even that He would make that condition of Grace, which is the cause of confirmation in goodness, an essential part of the nature of Angels and men, so that through their natural origin and natural condition they would be so confirmed in goodness that they would not be able to sin.

For the first argument will not hold. Since, although God is all-powerful and all-good, yet he will not bestow this quality of impeccability; not because of any imperfection in His power, but because of the imperfection of the creature; and this imperfection lies chiefly in the fact that no creature, man or Angel, is capable of receiving this quality. And for this reason: that, being a creature, its being depends upon its Creator, just as an effect depends on the cause of its being. And to create is

to make something out of nothing; and this, if left to itself, perishes, but endures so long as it preserves the influence of its cause. You may take, if you wish, an example from a candle, which burns only so long as it has wax. This being so, it is to be noted that God created man, and left him in the hand of his own counsel (*Ecclesiasticus* xvii). And so also He created the Angels in the beginning of Creation. And this was done for the sake of Free-will, the property of which is to do or to omit doing, to recede or not to recede from its cause. And since to recede from God, from free-will, is to sin, therefore it was impossible for man or Angel to receive, and God did not will to give, such a natural quality that he should at the same time be endowed with free-will and also be incapable of sin.

Another imperfection by reason of which this quality cannot be communicated to man or Angel is that it implies a contradiction; and since a contradiction is by its nature impossible, we say that God will not do this thing. Or rather we should say that His creatures cannot receive such a quality. For example, it is impossible that anything can be at one and the same time alive and dead. And so it would imply this contradiction: that a man should have free-will, by which he would be able to depart from his Creator, and that he should also be unable to sin. But if he were unable to sin, he would be unable to depart from his Creator. For this is sin: to despise the incommutable good and cleave to things that are variable. But to despise or not to despise is a matter of free-will.

The second argument also is not valid. For if the confirmation of grace were so essential a part of the original creation that it became a natural quality of the creature to be unable to sin, then his inability to sin would arise, not from any exterior cause or from grace, but from his own very nature; and then he would be God, which is absurd. S. Thomas treats of this in his above solution of the last argument, when he says that whenever there happens to any creature something that can only be caused by a superior influence, the lower nature cannot of itself cause that effect without the co-operation of the higher nature. For example, a gas becomes ignited by fire; but it could not of its own nature light itself without fire.

I say, therefore, that since the confirmation of a rational creature comes only through grace, which is a sort of spiritual light or image of the light of Creation, it is impossible for any creature to have, of its own nature, that confirmation or grace, unless it be made one with the Divine nature; that is, unless it be of the same nature as God, which is altogether impossible. Let us conclude by saying that the inability to sin belongs by nature to God alone. For He does not depart from His nature, Who gives to all things their being, neither can He depart from the righteousness of His goodness; for this belongs to Him through the character of His nature. But for all others who have this quality that they cannot sin, it is conferred upon them through the confirmation in goodness by grace; by which the sons of God are made free from sin, and they who in any way consort with the Divine nature.

☆

QUESTION XIII

Herein is set forth the Question concerning the Two Divine Permissions which God justly allows, namely, that the Devil, the Author of all Evil, should Sin, and that our First Parents should Fall, from which Origins the Works of Witches are justly suffered to take place.

THE second question and proposition is that God justly permitted certain Angels to sin in deed, which He could not have allowed unless they were capable of sin; and that in like manner He preserved certain creatures through grace, without their having previously suffered temptation; and that He justly allows man both to be tempted and to sin. And all this is clearly shown as follows. For it is a part of Divine providence that each single thing should be left to its own nature, and not be altogether impeded in its natural works. For, as Dionysius says (*de Diuin. Nom.*, IV), Providence is not a destroyer, but a preserver of nature. This being so, it is manifest that, just as the good of the race is better than the good of the individual (Aristotle, *Ethics*, I), so also the good

of the universe takes precedence over the good of any particular creature. Therefore we must add that, if men were prevented from sinning, many steps to perfection would be removed. For that nature would be removed which has it in its power to sin or not to sin; but it has already been shown that this is a natural property of man's nature.

And let it be answered that, if there had been no sin, but immediate confirmation, then there would never have appeared what debt of grace in good works is due to God, and what the power of sin has been able to effect, and many other things without which the universe would suffer great loss. For it behoved that Satan should sin, not through some outside suggestion, but that he should find in himself the occasion of sin. And this he did when he wished to be equal to God. Now this is to be understood neither simply and directly, nor indirectly, but only with a reservation; and this is declared according to the authority of *Esaias* xiv: I will ascend above the heights of the clouds; I will be like the Most High. For it must not be understood simply and directly, because in that case he would have had a limited and erring understanding, in seeking something which was impossible for him. For he knew that he was a creature created by God, and therefore he knew that it was impossible for him to become equal to his Creator. Neither, again, must it be understood indirectly; for since the whole good of an Angel and a creature lies in its subjection to God, just as the whole transparence of the air consists in its subjection to the sun's rays; therefore nothing which would be contrary to the good of its nature could be sought for by an Angel. But he sought for equality with God, not absolutely, but with a reservation, which was as follows. The nature of God has two qualities, that of blessedness and goodness, and the fact that all the blessedness and goodness of His creatures issues from Him. Therefore the Angel, seeing that the dignity of his own nature transcended that of the other creatures, wished and asked that the blessedness and goodness of all the inferior creatures should be derived from him. And he sought this in his own natural capacity, that just as he was the first to be endowed in nature with those qualities, so the other creatures should receive them from the nobility of his nature. And he sought this of God, in perfect willingness to remain subject to God so long as he had that power granted to him. Therefore he did not wish to be made equal with God absolutely, but only with a reservation.

It is further to be noted that, wishing to bring his desire to the point of action, he suddenly made it known to others; and the understanding of the other Angels of his desire, and their perverse consenting to it, was also sudden. Therefore the sin of the First Angel exceeded and preceded the sins of the others in respect of the magnitude of his guilt and causality, but not in respect of duration. See *Apocalypse* xii. The dragon falling from heaven drew with him the third part of the stars. And he lives in the form of Leviathan, and is king over all the children of pride. And, according to Aristotle (*Metaph.*, V), he is called king of princes, inasmuch as he moves those who are subject to him according to his will and command. Therefore his sin was the occasion of sin in others, since he first, not having been tempted from outside, was the external temptation of others.

And that all these things happened instantaneously may be exemplified by physical things; for the ignition of a gas, the sight of the flame, and the impression formed by that sight all happen at one and the same time. I have put this matter at some length; for in the consideration of that stupendous Divine permission in the case of the most noble creatures with regard to the one sin of ambition, it will be easier to admit particular permissions in the case of the works of witches, which are in some circumstances even greater sins. For in certain circumstances the sins of witches are greater than that of the Angel or of our first parents, as will be shown in the Second Part.

Now the fact that the providence of God permitted the first man to be tempted and to sin is sufficiently clear from what has been said concerning the transgression of the Angels. For both man and the Angel were created to the same end, and left with free-will, in order that they might receive the reward of blessedness not without merit.

Therefore, just as the Angel was not preserved from his fall, in order that the power of sin on the one side and the power of the confirmation of grace on the other side might work together for the glory of the universe, so also ought it to be considered in the case of man.

Wherefore S. Thomas (II, 23, art. 2) says: That by which God is glorified ought not to be hindered from within. But God is glorified in sin, when He pardons in mercy and when He punishes in justice; therefore it behoves Him not to hinder sin. Let us, then, return to a brief recapitulation of our proposition, namely, that by the just providence of God man is permitted to sin for many reasons. First, that the power of God may be shown, Who alone is unchanging while every creature is variable. Secondly, that the wisdom of God may be declared, Who can bring good out of evil, which could not be unless God had allowed the creature to sin. Thirdly, that the mercy of God may be made manifest, by which Christ through His death liberated man who was lost. Fourthly, that the justice of God may be shown, which not only rewards the good, but also punishes the wicked. Fifthly, that the condition of man may not be worse than that of other creatures, all of whom God so governs that He allows them to act after their own nature; wherefore it behoved Him to leave man to his own judgement. Sixthly, for the glory of men; that is, the glory of the just man who could transgress but has not. And seventhly, for the adorning of the universe; for as there is a threefold evil in sin, namely, guilt, pain, and loss, so is the universe adorned by the corresponding threefold good, namely, righteousness, pleasure, and usefulness. For righteousness is adorned by guilt, pleasure by pain, and all usefulness by loss. And by this the answer to the arguments is made plain.

Solutions of the Arguments.

According to the first argument it is heretical to maintain that the devil is allowed power to injure men. But the opposite appears rather to be true; for it is heretical to assert that God does not permit man, of his own free-will, to sin when he wishes. And God permits much sin, by reason of His power to hurt men in the punishment of the wicked for the adorning of the universe. For it is said by S. Augustine in his *Book of Soliloquies:* Thou, Lord, hast commanded, and it is so, that the shame of guilt should never be without the glory of punishment.

And that is not a valid proof of the argument which is taken from the wise ruler who keeps away all defect and evil as far as he can. For it is quite different with God, Who has an universal care, from one who has only a particular care. For God, Whose care is universal, can bring good out of evil, as is shown by what has been said.

For the second argument, it is clear that God's power as well as His goodness and justice are manifest in His permission of sin. So when it is argued that God either can or cannot prevent evil, the answer is that He can prevent it, but that for the reasons already shown it does not behove Him to do so.

Neither is it valid to object that He therefore wishes evil to be, since He can prevent it but will not; for, as has been shown in the arguments for the truth, God cannot wish evil to be. He neither wishes nor does not wish it, but He permits it for the perfecting of the universe.

In the third argument S. Augustine and Aristotle are quoted on the subject of human knowledge, saying that it is better for a man not to have knowledge of that which is evil and vile for two reasons: first, that then he will have less opportunity to think of evil, since we cannot understand many things at the same time. And secondly, because knowledge of evil sometimes perverts the will towards evil. But these arguments do not concern God, Who without any detriment understands all the deeds of men and of witches.

For the fourth argument: S. Paul excepts the care of God from oxen, to show that a rational creature has through free-will command over its actions, as has been said. Therefore God has a special providence over him, that either blame or merit may be imputed to him, and he may receive either punishment or reward; but that God does not in this way care for the irrational beasts.

But to argue from that authority that the individuals of irrational creation have no part in Divine providence would be heretical; for it would be to maintain that all things are not subject to Divine providence, and would be contrary to the praise which is spoken in Holy Scripture concerning the Divine wisdom, which stretches mightily from end to end and disposes all things well; and it would be the error of the Rabbi Moses, as was shown in the arguments for the truth.

For the fifth argument, man did not institute nature, but puts the works of nature to the greatest use known to his skill and strength. Therefore human providence does not extend to the inevitable phenomena of nature, as that the sun will rise to-morrow. But God's providence does extend to these things, since He is Himself the author of nature. Wherefore also defects in nature, even if they arise out of the natural course of things, are subject to Divine providence. And therefore Democritus and the other natural philosophers were in error when they ascribed whatever happened to the inferior creation to the mere chance of matter.

For the last argument: although every punishment is inflicted by God for sin, yet the greatest sinners are not always afflicted with witchcraft. And this may be because the devil does not wish to afflict and tempt those whom he sees to belong to him by just title, or because he does not wish them to be turned back to God. As it is said: Their plagues were multiplied, and they turned them to God, etc. And that all punishment is inflicted by God for sin is shown by what follows; for according to S. Jerome: Whatever we suffer, we deserve for our sins.

Now it is declared that the sins of witches are more grievous than those of the bad angels and our first parents. Wherefore, just as the innocent are punished for the sins of their fathers, so are many blameless people damned and bewitched for the sins of witches.

☆

QUESTION XIV

The Enormity of Witches is Considered, and it is shown that the Whole Matter should be rightly Set Forth and Declared.

CONCERNING the enormity of crimes, it is asked whether the crimes of witches exceed, both in guilt, in pain, and in loss, all the evils which

God allows and has permitted from the beginning of the world up till now. And it seems that they do not, especially as regards guilt. For the sin which a man commits when he could easily avoid it is greater than the sin which another man commits when he could not so easily avoid it. This is shown by S. Augustine, *de Ciuit. Dei:* There is great wickedness in sinning when it is so easy not to sin. But Adam, and others who have sinned when in a state of perfection or even of grace, could more easily because of the help of grace have avoided their sins—especially Adam who was created in grace—than many witches, who have not shared in such gifts. Therefore the sins of such are greater than all the crimes of witches.

And again in respect of punishment: the greater punishment is due to the greater blame. But Adam's sin was the most heavily punished, as is plainly proved by the fact that both his guilt and his punishment are shown in all his posterity by the inheritance of original sin. Therefore his sin is greater than all other sins.

And again, the same is argued in respect of loss. For according to S. Augustine: A thing is evil in that it takes away from the good; therefore where there is the more good lost, there the greater evil has gone before. But the sin of our first parent brought the greatest loss both to nature and to grace, since it deprived us of innocence and immortality; and no subsequent sin has brought such loss, therefore, etc.

But on the contrary side: that which includes the most causes of evil is the greater evil, and such are the sins of witches. For they can, with God's permission, bring every evil upon that which is good by nature and in form, as is declared in the Papal Bull. Besides, Adam sinned only in doing that which was wrong in one of two ways; for it was forbidden, but was not wrong in itself: but witches and other sinners sin in doing that which is wrong in both ways, wrong in itself, and forbidden, such as murders and many other forbidden things. Therefore their sins are heavier than other sins.

Besides, sin which comes from definite malice is heavier than sin which comes from ignorance. But witches, out of great malice, despise the Faith and the sacraments of the Faith, as many of them have confessed.

Answer. The evils which are perpetrated by modern witches exceed all other sin which God has ever permitted to be done, as was said in the title of this Question. And this can be shown in three ways, in so far as they are sins involving perversity of character, though it is different with the sins that contravene the other Theological virtues. First in general, by comparing their works indifferently with any other worldly crimes. Secondly in particular, by considering the species of the superstition and into what pact they have entered with the devil. And thirdly, by comparing their sins with the sins of the bad Angels and even with that of our first parents.

And first, sin is threefold, involving guilt, punishment, and loss. Good also is correspondingly threefold, involving righteousness, felicity, and use. And righteousness corresponds with guilt, felicity with punishment, and use with loss.

That the guilt of witches exceeds all other sins is apparent in this way. For according to the teaching of S. Thomas (II, 22, art. 2), there is in the matter of sin much that may be considered whereby the gravity or lightness of the sin may be deduced; and the same sin may be found heavy in one and light in another. For example, we can say that in fornication a young man sins, but an old man is mad. Yet those sins are, simply speaking, the heavier which are not only attended by the more extensive and more powerful circumstances, but are in their nature and quantity of a more essentially serious sort.

And so we can say that, though the sin of Adam was in some respects heavier than all other sins, inasmuch as he fell to the instigation of a smaller temptation, since it came only from within; and also because he could more easily have resisted on account of the original justice in which he was created: nevertheless in the form and quantity of sin, and in other respects which aggravate the sin the more in that it is the cause of many yet heavier sins, the sins of witches exceed all other sins. And this will be made still clearer in two ways.

For one sin is said to be greater than another in one or other of the following respects: in causality, as was the sin of Lucifer; in generality, as Adam's sin; in hideousness, as was the sin of Judas; in the difficulty of forgiving it, as is the sin against the Holy Ghost; in danger, as is the sin of ignorance; in inseparability, as is the sin of covetousness; in inclination, as is the sin of the flesh; in the offending of the Divine Majesty, as is the sin of idolatry and infidelity; in the difficulty of combating it, as the sin of pride; in blindness of mind, as the sin of anger. Accordingly, after the sin of Lucifer, the works of witches exceed all other sins, in hideousness since they deny Him crucified, in inclination since they commit nastiness of the flesh with devils, in blindness of mind since in a pure spirit of malignity they rage and bring every injury upon the souls and bodies of men and beasts, as has been shown from what has been said before.

And this, indeed, is indicated, according to S. Isidore, by the word. For they are called witches (*maleficae*) on account of the enormity of their crimes, as has been said above.

Our contention is also deduced from the following. There are two gradations in sin, a turning away, and a change of heart. See our quotation from S. Augustine: Sin is to reject the incommutable good, and to cleave to things that are variable. And the turning away from God is as it were formal, just as the change of heart is as it were material. Therefore the more a man is separated from God by it, the heavier is the sin. And since infidelity is the chief cause of man's separation from God, the infidelity of witches stands out as the greatest of sins. And this is given the name of Heresy, which is Apostasy from the Faith; and in this witches sin throughout their whole lives.

For the sin of infidelity consists in opposing the Faith; and this may come about in two ways, by opposing a faith which has not yet been received, or by opposing it after it has been received. Of the first sort is the infidelity of the Pagans or Gentiles. In the second way, the Christian Faith may be denied in two ways: either by denying the prophecies concerning it, or by denying the actual manifestation of its truth. And the first of these is the infidelity of the Jews, and the second the infidelity of Heretics.

It is clear from this that the heresy of witches is the most heinous of the three degrees of infidelity; and this fact is proved both by reason and authority. For it is said in II. *S. Peter* ii: It had been better for them not to have known the way of righteousness, than, after they have known it, to turn from it. And it is reasonable to suppose that, just as he who does not perform what he has promised commits a greater sin than he who does not perform what he never promised, so the infidelity of heretics, who while professing the faith of the Gospel fight against it by corrupting it, is a greater sin than that of the Jews and Pagans.

And again, the Jews sin more greatly than the Pagans; for they received the prophecy of the Christian Faith in the Old Law, which they corrupt through badly interpreting it, which is not the case with the Pagans. Therefore their infidelity is a greater sin than that of the Gentiles, who never received the Faith of the Gospel. But concerning Apostasy, S. Thomas says in the *Second of the Second*, question 12: Apostasy means a turning away from God and religion, and this may happen according to the different ways by which man is joined to God; that is, by faith, or by the subjection of the will to obedience, or by religion and Holy Orders. S. Raymund and Hostiensis say that Apostasy is a rash departure from the state of faith or obedience or Religion. Now if that which precedes is removed, that which follows from it is also removed; but the converse proposition is not true. Therefore Apostasy from the Faith is a greater sin than the other two forms of infidelity, since in its case a precedent Religion has been removed.

But according to S. Raymund, a man is not to be judged an Apostate or deserter, however far and long he may have strayed, unless he shows by his subsequent life that he has no thought of returning to the Faith. And this would be shown in the case of a cleric if he were to marry a wife, or commit some similar crime. In the same way it is an Apostasy of disobedience when a man wilfully spurns the teaching of the Church and the Bishops. And such a man must be convicted of his infamy, and be excommunicated.

Now when we speak of the Apostasy of witches, we mean the Apostasy of perfidy; and this is so much the more heinous, in that it springs from a pact made with the enemy of the Faith and the way of salvation. For witches are bound to make this pact, which is exacted by that enemy either in part or wholly. For we Inquisitors have found some witches who have denied all the articles of Faith, and others who have denied only a certain number of them; but they are all bound to deny true and sacramental confession. And so, even the Apostasy of Julian does not seem to have been so great, although in other respects he did more harm against the Church; but we cannot speak of that here.

But it may be incidentally objected that it is possible that they may keep the Faith in the thoughts of their hearts, which God alone, and not even any Angel, can see into; but do reverence and obedience to the devil only in outward form. The answer to this seems to be that there are two degrees of the Apostasy of perfidy. One consists in outward acts of infidelity, without the formation of any pact with the devil, as when one lives in the lands of the infidels and conforms his life to that of the Mohammedans. The other consists in a pact made with the devil by one who lives in Christian lands. In the first case, men who keep the Faith in their hearts but deny it in their outward acts, though they are not Apostates or Heretics, are guilty of deadly sin. For in this way Solomon showed reverence to the gods of his wives. And no one can be excused on the ground that he does this through fear; for S. Augustine says: It is better to die of hunger than to be fed by Idolaters. But however much witches may retain the Faith in their hearts while denying it with their lips, they are still to be judged Apostates, since they have made a treaty with death and a compact with hell. Wherefore S. Thomas (II, 4), speaking of such magic works, and of those who in any way seek help from devils, says: They are all Apostates from the Faith, by reason of a pact made with the Devil, either in word, when some invocation is used, or by some deed, even if there is no actual sacrifice. For no man can serve two masters.

To the same effect writes Blessed Albertus Magnus, where he asks whether the sin of Magicians and Astrologers is an Apostasy from the Faith. And he answers: In such there is always Apostasy either of word or of deed. For if invocations are made, then there is an open pact made with the devil, and it is plainly Apostasy in word. But if their magic is simply a matter of action, then it is Apostasy in deed. And since in all these there is abuse of the Faith, seeing that they look for from the devil what they ought to look for from God, therefore they are always to be judged Apostates. See how clearly they set forth two degrees of Apostasy, understanding a third, namely, that of thought. And even if this last is lacking, yet witches are judged to be Apostates in word and deed. Therefore, as will be shown, they must be subject to the punishment of Heretics and Apostates.

And there is in them a third enormity of crime, exceeding all other heresies. For S. Augustine (XXVIII, 1 and 2) tells us that the whole life of infidels is a sin; and the gloss on *Romans* xiv says that everything which comes not of faith is sin. What then is to be thought of the whole life of witches, that is, of all their other actions which are not pleasing to the devil, such as fasting, attending church, communicating, and other things? For in all these things they commit deadly sin, as is shown as follows. So far have they fallen in sin that, although they have not lost all power of amendment (since sin does not corrupt the whole good of their nature, and a natural light yet remains in them); yet, because of their homage given to the devil, and unless they be absolved from it, all their works, even when they appear to be good, are rather of an evil nature. And this is not seen to be the case with other infidels.

For according to S. Thomas in the *Second of the Second*, question 10, Whether every action of an infidel is a sin; he says that the deeds of the unfaithful which are, of themselves, good, such as fasting, almsgiving, and deeds of that sort, are no merit to them because of their infidelity, which is a most grievous sin. Yet sin does not corrupt the whole good of their nature, and there remains in them a natural light. Therefore not every deed of theirs is mortal sin, but only those which proceed from their very infidelity, or are related to it. For example, a Saracen fasts, to observe the law of Mohammed as to fasting, and a Jew observes his Feast days; but in such things he is guilty of mortal sin. And in this way is to be understood the above dictum of S. Augustine, that the whole life of infidels is sin.

That Witches Deserve the heaviest Punishment above All the Criminals of the World.

The crimes of witches, then, exceed the sins of all others; and we now declare what punishment they deserve, whether as Heretics or as Apostates. Now Heretics, according to S. Raymund, are punished in various ways, as by excommunication, deposition, confiscation of their goods, and death. The reader can be fully informed concerning all these by consulting the law relating to the sentence of excommunication. Indeed even their followers, protectors, patrons and defenders incur the heaviest penalties. For, besides the punishment of excommunication inflicted on them, Heretics, together with their patrons, protectors and defenders, and with their children to the second generation on the father's side, and to the first degree on the mother's side, are admitted to no benefit or office of the Church. And if a Heretic have Catholic children, for the heinousness of his crime they are deprived of their paternal inheritance. And if a man be convicted, and refuse to be converted and abjure his heresy, he must at once be burned, if he is a layman. For if they who counterfeit money are summarily put to death, how much more must they who counterfeit the Faith? But if he is a cleric, after solemn degradation he is handed over to the secular Court to be put to death. But if they return to the Faith, they are to be imprisoned for life. But in practice they are treated more leniently after recantation than they should be according to the judgement of the Bishops and the Inquisition, as will be shown in the Third Part, where the various methods of sentencing such are treated of; that is to say, those who are arrested and convicted and have recanted their error.

But to punish witches in these ways does not seem sufficient, since they are not simple Heretics, but Apostates. More than this, in their very apostasy they do not deny the Faith for any fear of men or for any delight of the flesh, as has been said before; but, apart from their abnegation, even give homage to the very devils by offering them their bodies and souls. It is clear enough from this that, however much they are penitent and return to the Faith, they must not be punished like other Heretics with lifelong imprisonment, but must suffer the extreme penalty. And because of the temporal injury which they do to men and beasts in various ways, the laws demand this. It is even equally culpable to learn as it is to teach such iniquities, say the laws concerning Soothsayers. Then how much more emphatically do they speak concerning witches, where they say that the penalty for them is the confiscation of their goods and decapitation. The laws also say much concerning those who by witchcraft provoke a woman to lust, or, conversely, cohabit with beasts. But these matters were touched upon in the First Question.

☆

QUESTION XV

It is Shown that, on account of the Sins of Witches, the Innocent are often Bewitched, yea, Sometimes even for their Own Sins.

IT is a fact that, by Divine permission, many innocent people suffer loss and are punished by the aforesaid plagues, not for their own sins, but for those of witches. And lest this should seem to any a paradox, S. Thomas shows in the *Second of the Second*, quest. 8, that this is just in God. For he divides the punishments of this life into three classes. First, one man belongs to another; therefore, if a man be punished in his possessions, it may be that another man suffers for his punishment. For, bodily speaking, sons are a property of the father, and slaves and animals are the property of their masters; and so the sons are sometimes punished for their parents. Thus the son born to David from adultery quickly died; and the animals of the Amalekites were bidden to be killed. Yet the reason for these things remains a mystery.

Secondly, the sin of one may be passed on to another; and this in two ways. By imitation, as children imitate the sins of their parents, and slaves and dependents the sins of their masters, that they may sin more boldly. In this way the sons inherit ill-gotten gain, and slaves share in robberies and unjust feuds, in which they are often killed. And they who are subject to Governors sin the more boldly when they see them sin, even if they do not commit the same sins; wherefore they are justly punished.

Also the sin of one is passed on to another in the way of desert, as when the sins of wicked subjects are passed on to a bad Governor, because the sins of the subjects deserve a bad Governor. See *Job*: He makes Hypocrites to reign on account of the sins of the people.

Sin, and consequently punishment, can also be passed on through some consent or dissimulation. For when those in authority neglect to reprove sin, then very often the good are punished with the wicked, as S. Augustine says in the first book *de Ciuitate Dei*. An example was brought to our notice as Inquisitors. A town once was rendered almost destitute by the death of its citizens; and there was a rumour that a certain buried woman was gradually eating the shroud in which she had been buried, and that the plague could not cease until she had eaten the whole shroud and absorbed it into her stomach. A council was held, and the Podesta with the Governor of the city dug up the grave, and found half the shroud absorbed through the mouth and throat into the stomach, and consumed. In horror at this sight, the Podesta drew his sword and cut off her head and threw it out of the grave, and at once the plague ceased. Now the sins of that old woman were, by Divine permission, visited upon the innocent on account of the dissimulation of what had happened before. For when an Inquisition was held it was found that during a long time of her life she had been a Sorceress and Enchantress. Another example is the punishment of a pestilence because David numbered the people.

Thirdly, sin is passed on by Divine permission in commendation of the unity of human society, that one man should take care for another by refraining from sin; and also to make sin appear the more detestable, in that the sin of one redounds upon all, as though all were one body. An example is the sin of Achan in *Joshua* vii.

We can add to these two other methods: that the wicked are punished sometimes by the good, and sometimes by other wicked men. For as Gratianus says (XXIII, 5), sometimes God punishes the wicked through those who are exercising their legitimate power at His command; and this in two ways: sometimes with merit on the part of the punishers, as when He punished the sins of the Canaanites through His people; sometimes with no merit on the part of the punishers, but even to their own punishment, as when He punished the tribe of Benjamin and destroyed it except for a few men. And sometimes He punishes by His nations being aroused, either by command or permission, but with no intention of obeying God, but rather greedy for their own gain, and therefore to their own damnation; as He now punishes His people by the Turks, and did so more often by strange nations in the Old Law.

But it must be noted that for whatever cause a man be punished, if he does not bear his pains patiently, then it becomes a scourge, not of correction, but only of vengeance, that is, of punishment. See *Deuteronomy* xxxii: A fire is kindled in mine anger (that is, my punishment; for there is no other anger in God), and shall burn unto the lowest hell (that is, vengeance shall begin here and burn unto the last damnation, as S. Augustine explains). And there is further authority concerning punishment in his Fourth Distinction. But if men patiently bear their scourges, and are patient in the state of grace, they take the place of a correction, as S. Thomas says in his Fourth Book. And this is true even of one punished for committing witchcraft, or of a witch, to a greater or less degree according to the devotion of the sufferer and the quality of his crime.

But the natural death of the body, being the last terror, is not a correction, since of its nature it partakes in the punishment for original sin. Nevertheless, according to Scotus, when it is awaited with resignation and devotion, and offered in its bitterness to God, it can in some way become a correction. But violent death, whether a man deserves it or not, is always a correction, if it is borne patiently and in grace. So much for punishments inflicted on account of the sins of others.

But God also punishes men in this life for their own sins, especially in the matter of bewitchment. For see *Tobias* vii: The devil has power over those who follow their lusts. And this is clear from what we have already said concerning the member and the genital powers, which God chiefly allows to be bewitched.

However, for the purpose of preaching to the public it is to be noted that, notwithstanding the aforesaid punishments which God inflicts on men for their own and others' sins, the preacher should keep as his basic principle and preach to the people this ruling of the law; which says, No one must be punished without guilt, unless there is some cause for doing so. And this ruling holds good in the Court of Heaven, that is, of God, just as it does in the human Courts of Justice, whether secular or ecclesiastic.

The preacher may predicate this of the Court of Heaven. For the punishment of God is of two kinds, spiritual and temporal. In the former, punishment is never found without guilt. In the latter it is sometimes found quite without guilt, but not without cause. The first, or spiritual punishment, is of three kinds; the first being forfeiture of grace and a consequent hardening in sin, which is never inflicted except for the sufferer's own guilt. The second is the punishment of loss, that is, deprivation of glory, which is never inflicted without personal guilt in adults, or contracted guilt in children born from their parents' sin. The third is the punishment of pain, that is, the torture of hell fire, and is plainly due to guilt. Wherefore when it is said in *Exodus* xx: I am a jealous God, visiting the sins of the fathers upon the children unto the third and fourth generation: it is understood as speaking of the imitators of their fathers' crimes, as Gratian has explained, Book I, quest. 4; where he also gives other expositions.

Now with regard to God's second, or temporal punishment: first, it may be, as has been said before, for the sin of another, or even without personal sin or that of another (but not without cause), or for personal guilt only, without any other's sin. But if you wish to know the causes for which God punishes, and even without any guilt

of the sufferer or of another man, you may refer to the five methods which the Master expounds in Book IV, dist. 15, cap. 2. And you must take the three first causes, for the other two refer to personal guilt.

For he says that for five causes God scourges man in this life, or inflicts punishment. First, that God may be glorified; and this is when some punishment or affliction is miraculously removed, as in the case of the man born blind (*S. John* ix), or of the raising of Lazarus (*S. John* xi).

Secondly, if the first cause is absent, it is sent that merit may be acquired through the exercise of patience, and also that inner hidden virtue may be made manifest to others. Examples are *Job* i and *Tobias* ii.

Thirdly, that virtue may be preserved through the humiliation of castigation. S. Paul is an example, who says of himself in II. *Corinthians* xii: There was given unto me a thorn in the flesh, the messenger of Satan. And according to Remigius this thorn was the infirmity of carnal desire. These are the causes that are without guilt in the sufferer.

Fourthly, that eternal damnation should begin in this life, that it might be in some way shown what will be suffered in hell. Examples are Herod (*Acts* xii) and Antiochus (II. *Maccabees* ix).

Fifthly, that man may be purified, by the expulsion and obliteration of his guilt through scourges. Examples may be taken from Miriam, Aaron's sister, who was stricken with leprosy, and from the Israelites wandering in the wilderness, according to S. Jerome, XXIII, 4. Or it may be for the correction of sin, as is exemplified by the case of David, who, after being pardoned for his adultery, was driven from his kingdom, as is shown in II. *Kings*, and is commented on by S. Gregory in his discourse on sin. It may, in fact, be said that every punishment that we suffer proceeds from our own sin, or at least from the original sin in which we were born, which is itself the cause of all causes.

But as to the punishment of loss, meaning by that eternal damnation which they will suffer in the future, no one doubts that all the damned will be tortured with grievous pains. For just as grace is followed by the blessed vision of the Kingdom of Heaven, so is mortal sin followed by punishment in hell. And just as the degrees of blessedness in Heaven are measured in accordance with the degrees of charity and grace in life, so the degrees of punishment in hell are measured according to the degree of crime in this life. See *Deuteronomy* xxv : The measure of punishment will be according to the measure of sin. And this is so with all other sins, but applies especially to witches. See *Hebrews* x : Of how much sorer punishment, suppose ye, shall he be thought worthy, who hath trodden underfoot the Son of God, and hath counted the blood of the covenant, wherewith he was sanctified, an unholy thing?

And such are the sins of witches, who deny the Faith, and work many evil bewitchments through the most Holy Sacrament, as will be shown in the Second Part.

☆

QUESTION XVI

The Foregoing Truths are Set out in Particular, by a Comparison of the Works of Witches with Other Baleful Superstitions.

NOW the foregoing truth concerning the enormity of witches' crimes is proved by comparing them with the other practices of Magicians and Diviners. For there are fourteen species of magic, springing from the three kinds of Divination. The first of these three is open invocation of devils. The second is no more than a silent consideration of the disposition and movement of some thing, as of the stars, or the days, or the hours, and such things. The third is the consideration of some human act for the purpose of finding out something that is hidden, and is called by the name of Sortilege.

And the species of the first form of Divination, that is, an open invocation of devils, are the following : Sorcery, Oneiromancy, Necromancy, Oracles, Geomancy, Hydromancy, Aeromancy, Pyromancy, and Soothsaying (see S. Thomas, *Second of the Second*, quest. 95, 26, and 5). The species of the second kind are Horoscopy, Haruspicy, Augury, Observation of Omens, Cheiromancy and Spatulamancy.

The species of the third kind vary according to all those things which are classed as Sortilege for the finding out of something hidden, such as the consideration of pricks and straws, and figures in molten lead. And S. Thomas speaks also of these in the above-quoted reference.

Now the sins of witches exceed all these crimes, as will be proved in respect of the foregoing species. There can then be no question concerning smaller crimes.

For let us consider the first species, in which those who are skilled in sorcery and glamour deceive the human senses with certain apparitions, so that corporeal matter seems to become different to the sight and the touch, as was treated of above in the matter of the methods of creating illusions. Witches are not content with such practices in respect of the genital member, causing some prestidigitatory illusion of its disappearance (although this disappearance is not an actual fact); but they even frequently take away the generative power itself, so that a woman cannot conceive, and a man cannot perform the act even when he still retains his member. And without any illusion, they also cause abortion after conception, often accompanied with many other ills. And they even appear in various forms of beasts, as has been shown above.

Necromancy is the summoning of and speech with the dead, as is shown by its etymology; for it is derived from the Greek word *Nekros*, meaning a corpse, and *Manteia*, meaning divination. And they accomplish this by working some spell over the blood of a man or some animal, knowing that the devil delights in such sin, and loves blood and the pouring out of blood. Wherefore, when they think that they call the dead from hell to answer their questions, it is the devils in the likeness of the dead who appear and give such answers. And of this sort was the art of that great Pythoness spoken of in I. *Kings* xxviii, who raised up Samuel at the instance of Saul.

But let no one think that such practices are lawful because the Scripture records that the soul of the just Prophet, summoned from Hades to predict the event of Saul's coming war, appeared through the means of a woman who was a witch. For, as S. Augustine says to Simplicianus : It is not absurd to believe that it was permitted by some dispensation, not by the potency of any magic art, but by some hidden dispensation unknown to the Pythoness or to Saul, that the spirit of that just man should appear before the sight of the king, to deliver the Divine sentence against him. Or else it was not really the spirit of Samuel aroused from its rest, but some phantasm and imaginary illusion of devils caused by the machinations of the devil; and the Scripture calls that phantasm by the name of Samuel, just as the images of things are called by the names of the things they represent.* This he says in his answer to the question whether divination by the invocation of devils is lawful. In the same *Summa* the reader will find the answer to the question whether there are degrees of prophecy among the Blessed; and he may refer to S. Augustine, XXVI, 5. But this has little to do with the deeds of witches, which retain in themselves no vestige of piety, as is apparent from a consideration of their works; for they do not cease to shed innocent blood, to bring hidden things to light under the guidance of devils, and by destroying the soul with the body spare neither the living nor the dead.

Oneiromancy may be practised in two ways. The first is when a person uses dreams so that he may dip into the occult with the help of the revelation of devils invoked by him, with whom he has entered into an open pact. The second is when a man uses dreams for knowing the future, in so far as there is such virtue in dreams proceeding from Divine revelation, from a natural intrinsic or extrinsic cause; and such divination would not be unlawful. So says S. Thomas.

And that preachers may have at least the nucleus of an understanding of this matter, we must first speak about the Angels. An Angel is of limited power, and can more effectively reveal the future when the mind is adapted to such revelations than when it is not. Now the mind is chiefly so adapted after the relaxation of exterior and interior movement, as when nights are silent and the fumes of motion are quieted; and these conditions are fulfilled round

about the dawn, when digestion is completed. And I say this of us who are sinners, to whom the Angels in their Divine piety, and in the execution of their offices, reveal certain things, so that when we study at the time of the dawn we are given an understanding of certain occult matters in the Scriptures. For a good Angel presides over our understanding, just as God does over our will, and the stars over our bodies. But to certain more perfect men the Angel can at any hour reveal things, whether they are awake or asleep. However, according to Aristotle, *de Somno et Uigilia*, such men are more apt to receive revelations at one time than at another; and this is the case in all matters of Magic.

Secondly, it is to be noted that it happens through Nature's care for and regulation of the body, that certain future events have their natural cause in a man's dreams. And then those dreams or visions are not causes, as was said in the case of Angels, but only signs of that which is coming to a man in the future, such as health or sickness or danger. And this is the opinion of Aristotle. For in the dreams of the spirit Nature images the disposition of the heart, by which sickness or some other thing naturally comes to a man in the future. For if a man dreams of fires, it is a sign of a choleric disposition; if of flying or some such thing, it is a sign of a sanguine disposition; if he dreams of water or some other liquid, it is a sign of a phlegmatic, and if he dreams of terrene matters, it is a sign of a melancholy disposition. And therefore doctors are very often helped by dreams in their diagnosis (as Aristotle says in the same book).

But these are slight matters in comparison with the unholy dreams of witches. For when they do not wish, as has been mentioned above, to be bodily transferred to a place, but desire to see what their fellow-witches are doing, it is their practice to lie down on their left side in the name of their own and of all devils; and these things are revealed to their vision in images. And if they seek to know some secret, either for themselves or for others, they learn it in dreams from the devil, by reason of an open, not a tacit, pact entered into with him. And this pact, again, is not a symbolical one, accomplished by the sacrifice of some animal, or some act

---

* "*Represent.*" *For a full discussion of the appearance of Samuel at Endor, see my "History of Witchcraft," c.v.: "The Witch in Holy Writ," pp. 176–81.*

of sacrilege, or by embracing the worship of some strange cult; but it is an actual offering of themselves, body and soul, to the devil, by a sacrilegiously uttered and inwardly purposed abnegation of the Faith. And not content with this, they even kill, or offer to devils, their own and others' children.

Another species of divination is practised by Pythons, so called from Pythian Apollo, who is said to have been the originator of this kind of divination, according to S. Isidore. This is not effected by dreams or by converse with the dead, but by means of living men, as in the case of those who are lashed into a frenzy by the devil, either willingly or unwillingly, only for the purpose of foretelling the future, and not for the perpetration of any other monstrosities. Of this sort was the girl mentioned in *Acts* xvi, who cried after the Apostles that they were the servants of the true God; and S. Paul, being angered by this, commanded the spirit to come out of her. But it is clear that there is no comparison between such things and the deeds of witches, who, according to S. Isidore, are so called for the magnitude of their sins and the enormity of their crimes.

Wherefore, for the sake of brevity, there is no need to continue this argument in respect of the minor forms of divination, since it has been proved in respect of the major forms. For the preacher may, if he wishes, apply these arguments to the other forms of divination: to Geomancy, which is concerned with terrene matters, such as iron or polished stone; Hydromancy, which deals with water and crystals; Aeromancy, which is concerned with the air; Pyromancy, which is concerned with fire; Soothsaying, which has to do with the entrails of animals sacrificed on the devil's altars. For although all these are done by means of open invocation of devils, they cannot be compared with the crimes of witches, since they are not directly purposed for the harming of men or animals or the fruits of the earth, but only for the foreknowledge of the future. The other species of divination, which are performed with a tacit, but not an open, invocation of devils, are Horoscopy, or Astrology, so called from the consideration of the stars at birth; Haruspicy, which observes the days and hours; Augury, which observes the behaviour

and cries of birds; Omens, which observe the words of men; and Cheiromancy, which observes the lines of the hand, or of the paws of animals. Anyone who wishes may refer to the teaching of Nider, and he will find much as to when such things are lawful and when they are not. But the works of witches are never lawful.

☆

QUESTION XVII

A Comparison of their Crimes under Fourteen Heads, with the Sins of the Devils of all and every Kind.

SO heinous are the crimes of witches that they even exceed the sins and the fall of the bad Angels; and if this is true as to their guilt, how should it not also be true of their punishments in hell? And it is not difficult to prove this by various arguments with regard to their guilt. And first, although the sin of Satan is unpardonable, this is not on account of the greatness of his crime, having regard to the nature of the Angels, with particular attention to the opinion of those who say that the Angels were created only in a state of nature, and never in a state of grace. And since the good of grace exceeds the good of nature, therefore the sins of those who fall from a state of grace, as do the witches by denying the faith which they received in baptism, exceed the sins of the Angels. And even if we say that the Angels were created, but not confirmed, in grace; so also witches, though they are not created in grace, have yet of their own will fallen from grace; just as Satan sinned of his own will.

Secondly, it is granted that Satan's sin is unpardonable for various other reasons. For S. Augustine says that he sinned at the instigation of none, therefore his sin is justly remediable by none. And S. John Damascene says that he sinned in his understanding against the character of God; and that his sin was the greater by reason of the nobility of his understanding. For the servant who knows the will of his master, etc. The same authority says that, since Satan is incapable of repentance, therefore he is incapable of pardon; and this is due to his very nature, which, being spiritual, could only be changed once, when he changed it for ever; but this is not so with men, in whom the flesh is always warring against the spirit. Or because he sinned in the high places of heaven, whereas man sins in the earth.

But notwithstanding all this, his sin is in many respects small in comparison with the crimes of witches. First, as S. Anselm* showed in one of his *Sermons*, he sinned in his pride while there was yet no punishment for sin. But witches continue to sin after great punishments have been often inflicted upon many other witches, and after the punishments which the Church teaches them have been inflicted by reason of the devil and his fall; and they make light of all these, and hasten to commit, not the least deadly of sins, as do other sinners who sin through infirmity or wickedness yet not from habitual malice, but rather the most horrible crimes from the deep malice of their hearts.

Secondly, although the Bad Angel fell from innocence to guilt, and thence to misery and punishment; yet he fell from innocence once only, in such a way that he was never restored. But the sinner who is restored to innocence by baptism, and again falls from it, falls very deep. And this is especially true of witches, as is proved by their crimes.

Thirdly, he sinned against the Creator; but we, and especially witches, sin against the Creator and the Redeemer.

Fourthly, he forsook God, who permitted him to sin but accorded him no pity; whereas we, and witches above all, withdraw ourselves from God by our sins, while, in spite of his permission of our sins, He continually pities us and prevents us with His countless benefits.

Fifthly, when he sinned, God rejected him without showing him any grace; whereas we wretches run into sin although God is continually calling us back.

Sixthly, he keeps his heart hardened against a punisher; but we against a merciful persuader. Both sin against God; but he against a commanding God, and we against One who dies for us, Whom, as we have said, wicked witches offend above all.

The Solutions of the Arguments again Declare the Truth by Comparison.

To the arguments. The answer to the first is clear from what was said in the beginning of this whole question. It was submitted that one sin ought to be thought heavier than another; and that the sins of witches are heavier than all others in respect of guilt, but not in respect of the penalties that they entail. To this it must be said that the punishment of Adam, just as his guilt, may be considered in two ways; either as touching him personally, or as touching the whole of nature, that is, the posterity which came after him. As to the first, greater sins have been committed after Adam; for he sinned only in doing that which was evil, not in itself, but because it was forbidden: but fornication, adultery, and murder are in both senses sins in themselves, and because they are forbidden. Therefore such sins deserve the heavier punishment.

As to the second, it is true that the greatest punishment resulted from the first sin; but this is only indirectly true, in that through Adam all posterity was infected with original sin, and he was the first father of all those for whom the Only Son of God was able to atone by the power which was ordained. Moreover, Adam in his own person, with the mediation of Divine grace, repented, and was afterwards saved through the Sacrifice of Christ. But the sins of witches are incomparably greater, since they are not content with their own sins and perdition, but ever draw countless others after them.

And thirdly, it follows from what has been said that it was by accident that

* *"S. Anselm." Doctor of the Church; Archbishop of Canterbury, born at Aosta, a Burgundian town in the borders of Lombardy, 1033-34; died 21 April, 1109. High praise is given him in the Breviary Office for his Feast, 21 April, Second Nocturn of Matins, Lection VI: "Obdormiuit in Domino, famam non solum miraculorum et sanctitatis (praecipue ob insignem deuotionem erga Domini nostri passionem, et beatam Uirginem eius Matrem) assecutus, sed etiam doctrinae, quam ad defensionem Christianae religionis, animarum profectum, et omnium theologorum, qui sacras litteras scholastica methodo tradiderunt, normam coelitus hausisse ex eius omnibus apparet." There are several collections of the works of S. Anselm, but of these few, if any, can claim to be critical, and none are adapted for modern requirements. At the same time there are very numerous separate editions, and even translations of the more important treatises, in particular the "Cur Deus Homo."*

Adam's sin involved the greater injury. For he found nature uncorrupted, and it was inevitable, and not of his own will, that he left it defiled; therefore it does not follow that his sin was intrinsically greater than others. And again, posterity would have committed the same sin if it had found nature in the same state. Similarly, he who has not found grace does not commit so deadly a sin as he who has found it and lost it. This is the solution of S. Thomas (II, 21, art. 2), in his solution of the second argument. And if anyone wishes fully to understand this solution, he must consider that even if Adam had kept his original innocence, he would not have passed it down to all posterity; for, as S. Anselm says, anyone coming after him could still have sinned. See also S. Thomas, dist. 20, where he considers whether new-born children would have been confirmed in grace; and in dist. 101, whether men who are now saved would have been saved if Adam had not sinned.

☆

QUESTION XVIII

Here follows the Method of Preaching against and Controverting Five Arguments of Laymen and Lewd Folk, which seem to be Variously Approved, that God does not Allow so Great Power to the Devil and Witches as is Involved in the Performance of such Mighty Works of Witchcraft.

FINALLY, let the preacher be armed against certain arguments of laymen, and even of some learned men, who deny, up to a certain point, that there are witches. For, although they concede the malice and power of the devil to inflict such evils at his will, they deny that the Divine permission is granted to him, and will not admit that God allows such things to be done. And although they have no method in their argument, groping blindly now this way and now that, it is yet necessary to reduce their assertions to five arguments, from which all their cavillings proceed. And the first is, that God does not permit the devil to rage against men with such great power.

The question put is whether the Divine permission must always accompany an infliction caused by the devil through a witch. And five arguments are submitted to prove that God does not permit it, and that therefore there is no witchcraft in the world. And the first argument is taken from God; the second from the devil; the third from the witch; the fourth from the affliction ascribed to witchcraft; and the fifth from preachers and judges, on the assumption that they have so preached against and punished witches that they would have no security in life.

And first as follows: God can punish men for their sins, and He punishes with the sword, famine, and pestilence; as well as with various and countless other infirmities to which human nature is subject. Wherefore, there being no need for Him to add further punishments, He does not permit witchcraft.

Secondly, if that which is said of the devil were true, namely, that he can obstruct the generative forces so that a woman cannot conceive, or that if she does conceive, he can cause an abortion; or, if there is no abortion, he can cause the children to be killed after birth; in that case he would be able to destroy the whole world; and it could also be said that the devil's works were stronger than God's, since the Sacrament of matrimony is a work of God.

Thirdly, they argue from man himself, that if there were any witchcraft in the world, then some men would be more bewitched than others; and that it is a false argument to say that men are bewitched for a punishment of their sins, and therefore false to maintain that there is witchcraft in the world. And they prove that it is false by arguing that, if it were true, then the greater sinners would receive the greater punishment, and that this is not the case; for sinners are less punished sometimes than the just, as is seen in the case of innocent children who are alleged to be bewitched.

Their fourth argument can be added to that which they adduce concerning God; namely, that a thing which a man can prevent and does not prevent, but allows it to be done, may be judged to proceed from his will. But since God is All-Good, He cannot wish evil, and therefore cannot permit evil to be done which He is able to prevent.

Again, taking their argument from the infliction itself, which is alleged to be due to witchcraft; they submit that they are similar to natural infirmities and defects, and may therefore be caused by a natural defect, For it may happen through some natural defect that a man becomes lame, or blind, or loses his reason, or even dies; wherefore such things cannot confidently be ascribed to witches.

Lastly, they argue that preachers and judges have preached and practised against witches in such a way that, if there were witches, their lives would never be safe from them on account of the great hatred that witches would have for them.

But the contrary arguments may be taken from the First Question, where it treats of the third postulate of the First Part; and those points may be propounded to the people which are most fitting. How God permits evil to be, even though He does not wish it; but He permits it for the wonderful perfecting of the universe, which may be considered in the fact that good things are more highly commendable, are more pleasing and laudable, when they are compared with bad things; and authority can be quoted in support of this. Also that the depth of God's Divine wisdom, justice, and goodness should be shown forth, whereas it would otherwise remain hidden.

For a brief settlement of this question there are various treatises available on this subject for the information of the people, to the effect, namely, that God justly permitted two Falls, that of the Angels and that of our first parents; and since these were the greatest of all falls, it is no matter for wonder if other smaller ones are permitted. But it is in their consequences that those two Falls were the greatest, not in their circumstances, in which last respect, as was shown in the last Question, the sins of witches exceed those of the bad angels and our first parents. In the same place it is shown how God justly permitted those first Falls, and anyone is at liberty to collect and enlarge upon what is there said as much as he wishes.

But we must answer their arguments. As to the first, that God punishes quite enough by means of natural diseases, and by sword and famine, we make a threefold answer. First, that God did not limit His power to the processes of nature, or even to the influences of the stars, in such a way that He cannot go beyond those limits; for He has often exceeded them in the punishment of

sins, by sending plagues and other afflictions beyond all the influence of the stars; as when He punished the sin of pride in David, when he numbered the people, by sending a pestilence upon the people.

Secondly, it agrees with the Divine wisdom that He should so govern all things that He allows them to act at their own instigation. Consequently, it is not His purpose to prevent altogether the malice of the devil, but rather to permit it as far as He sees it to be for the ultimate good of the universe; although it is true that the devil is continually held in check by the good Angels, so that he may not do all the harm that he wishes. Similarly He does not propose to restrain the human sins which are possible to man through his free-will, such as the abnegation of the Faith and the devotion of himself to the devil, which things are in the power of the human will. From these two premisses it follows that, when God is most offended, He justly permits those evils which are chiefly sought for by witches, and for which they deny the Faith, up to the extent of the devil's power; and such is the ability to injure men, animals, and the fruits of the earth.

Thirdly, God justly permits those evils which indirectly cause the greatest uneasiness and torment to the devil; and of such a sort are those evils which are done by witches through the power of devils. For the devil is indirectly tormented very greatly when he sees that, against his will, God uses all evil for the glory of His name, for the commendation of the Faith, for the purgation of the elect, and for the acquisition of merit. For it is certain that nothing can be more galling to the pride of the devil, which he always rears up against God (as it is said: The pride of them that hate Thee increases ever), than that God should convert his evil machinations to His own glory. Therefore God justly permits all these things.

Their second argument has been answered before; but there are two points in it which must be answered in detail. In the first place, far from its being true that the devil, or his works, are stronger than God, it is apparent that his power is small, since he can do nothing without the Divine permission. Therefore it may be said that the devil's power is small in comparison with the Divine permission, although it is very great in comparison with earthly powers, which it naturally excels, as is shown in the often quoted text in *Job* xi : There is no power on earth to be compared with him.

In the second place, we must answer the question why God permits witchcraft to affect the generative powers more than any other human function. This has been dealt with above, under the title, How witches can obstruct the generative powers and the venereal act. For it is on account of the shamefulness of that act, and because the original sin due to the guilt of our first parents is inherited by means of that act. It is symbolized also by the serpent, who was the first instrument of the devil.

To their third argument we answer that the devil has more intention and desire to tempt the good than the wicked; although he does in fact tempt the wicked more than the good, for the reason that the wicked have more aptitude than the good to respond to his temptation. In the same way, he is more eager to injure the good than the bad, but he finds it easier to injure the wicked. And the reason for this is, according to S. Gregory, that the more often a man gives way to the devil, the harder he makes it for himself to struggle against him. But since it is the wicked who most often give way to the devil, their temptations are the hardest and most frequent, as they have not the shield of Faith with which to protect themselves. Concerning this shield S. Paul speaks in *Ephesians* vi. Above all, taking the shield of faith, wherewith ye shall be able to quench all the fiery darts of the wicked. But on the other hand, he assails the good more bitterly than the wicked. And the reason for this is that he already possesses the wicked, but not the good; and therefore he tries the harder to draw into his power through tribulation the just, who are not his, than the wicked, who are already his. In the same way, an earthly prince more severely chastises those who disobey his laws, or injure his kingdom, than those who do not set themselves against him.

In answer to their fourth argument, in addition to what has already been written on this subject, the preacher

can expound the truth that God permits evil to be done, but does not wish it to be done, by the five signs of the Divine will, which are Precept, Prohibition, Advice, Operation, and Permission. See S. Thomas, especially in his First Part, quest. 19, art. 12, where this is very plainly set forth. For although there is only one will in God, which is God Himself, just as His Essence is One; yet in respect of its fulfilment, His will is shown and signified to us in many ways, as the *Psalm* says: The mighty works of the Lord are fulfilled in all His wishes. Wherefore there is a distinction between the actual essential Will of God and its visible effects; even as the will, properly so called, is the will of a man's good pleasure, but in a metaphorical sense it is the will expressed by outward signs. For it is by signs and metaphors that we are shown that God wishes this to be.

We may take an example from a human father who, while he has only one will in himself, expresses that will in five ways, either by his own agency, or through that of someone else. Through his own agency he expresses it in two ways, either directly or indirectly. Directly, when he himself does a thing; and then it is Operation. Indirectly, when he does not hinder someone else from acting (see Aristotle's *Physics*, IV : Prohibition is indirect causation), and this is called the sign of Permission. And the human father signifies his will through the agency of someone else in three ways. Either he orders someone to do something, or conversely forbids something; and these are the signs of Precept and Prohibition. Or he persuades and advises someone to do something; and this is the sign of Advice. And just as the human will is manifested in these five ways, so is God's will. For that God's will is shown by Precept, Prohibition, and Advice is seen in *S. Matthew* vi : Thy will be done in earth as it is in heaven: that is to say, may we on earth fulfil His Precepts, avoid His Prohibitions, and follow His Advice. And in the same way, S. Augustine shows that Permission and Operation are signs of God's will, where he says in the *Enchiridion :* Nothing is done unless Almighty God wishes it to be done, either by permitting it or by Himself doing it.

To return to the argument; it is perfectly true that when a man can prevent a thing, and does not, that thing may be said to proceed from his will. And the inference that God, being All-Good, cannot wish evil to be done, is also true in respect of the actual Good Pleasure of God's Will, and also in respect of four of the signs of His Will; for it is needless to say that He cannot operate evil, or command evil to be done, or fail to be opposed to evil, or advise evil; but He can, however, permit evil to be done.

And if it is asked how it is possible to distinguish whether an illness is caused by witchcraft or by some natural physical defect, we answer that there are various methods. And the first is by means of the judgement of doctors. See the words of S. Augustine *On the Christian Doctrine:* To this class of superstition belong all charms and amulets suspended or bound about the person, which the School of Medicine despises. For example, doctors may perceive from the circumstances, such as the patient's age, healthy complexion, and the reaction of his eyes, that his disease does not result from any defect of the blood or the stomach, or any other infirmity; and they therefore judge that it is not due to any natural defect, but to some extrinsic cause. And since that extrinsic cause cannot be any poisonous infection, which would be accompanied by ill humours in the blood and stomach, they have sufficient reason to judge that it is due to witchcraft.

And secondly, when the disease is incurable, so that the patient can be relieved by no drugs, but rather seems to be aggravated by them.

Thirdly, the evil may come so suddenly upon a man that it can only be ascribed to witchcraft. An example of how this happened to one man has been made known to us. A certain well-born citizen of Spires had a wife who was of such an obstinate disposition that, though he tried to please her in every way, yet she refused in nearly every way to comply with his wishes, and was always plaguing him with abusive taunts. It happened that, on going into his house one day, and his wife railing against him as usual with opprobrious words, he wished to go out of the house to escape from quarrelling. But she quickly ran before him and locked the door by which he

wished to go out; and loudly swore that, unless he beat her, there was no honesty or faithfulness in him. At these heavy words he stretched out his hand, not intending to hurt her, and struck her lightly with his open palm on the buttock; whereupon he suddenly fell to the ground and lost all his senses, and lay in bed for many weeks afflicted with a most grievous illness. Now it is obvious that this was not a natural illness, but was caused by some witchcraft of the woman. And very many similar cases have happened, and been made known to many.

There are some who can distinguish such illnesses by means of a certain practice, which is as follows. They hold molten lead over the sick man, and pour it into a bowl of water. And if the lead condenses into some image, they judge that the sickness is due to witchcraft. And when such men are asked whether the image so formed is caused by the work of devils, or is due to some natural cause, they answer that it is due to the power of Saturn over lead, the influence of that planet being in other respects evil, and that the sun has a similar power over gold. But what should be thought of this practice, and whether it is lawful or not, will be discussed in the Second Part of this treatise. For the Canonists say that it is lawful that vanity may be confounded by vanity; but the Theologians hold a directly opposite view, saying that it is not right to do evil that good may come.

In their last argument they advance several objections. First, why do not witches become rich? Secondly, why, having the favour of princes, do they not co-operate for the destruction of all their enemies? Thirdly, why are they unable to injure Preachers and others who persecute them?

For the first, it is to be said that witches are not generally rich for this reason: that the devils like to show their contempt for the Creator by buying witches for the lowest possible price. And also, lest they should be conspicuous by their riches.

Secondly, they do not injure princes because they wish to retain, as far as possible, their friendship. And if it is asked why they do not hurt their enemies, it is answered that a good Angel, working on the other side, prevents such witchcraft. Compare the passage in *Daniel:** The Prince of the Persians withstood me for twenty-one days. See S. Thomas in the *Second Book of Sentences*, where he debates whether there is any contest among the good Angels, and of what sort.

Thirdly, it is said that they cannot injure Inquisitors and other officials, because they dispense public justice. Many examples could be adduced to prove this, but time does not permit it.

* *"Daniel" x, 13: "But the prince of the kingdom of the Persians resisted me one-and-twenty days: And behold Michael, one of the chief princes, came to help me, and I remained there by the King of the Persians." The Prince of the Persians is the angel guardian of Persia: who, according to his office, seeking the spiritual good of the Persians, was desirous that many of the Jews should remain among them.*

THE SECOND PART, TREATING OF THE METHODS BY WHICH WITCHCRAFT IS INFLICTED, AND HOW IT MAY BE AUSPICIOUSLY REMOVED

RESOLVED IN TWO ONLY QUESTIONS, BUT DIVIDED INTO MANY CHAPTERS

☆

QUESTION I

Of those against whom the Power of Witches availeth not at all.

THE second main part of this work deals with the method of procedure adopted by witches for the performance of their witchcraft; and these are distinguished under eighteen heads, proceeding from two chief difficulties. The first of these two, dealt with in the beginning, concerns protective remedies, by which a man is rendered immune from witchcraft: the second, dealt with at the end, concerns curative remedies, by which those who are bewitched can be cured. For, as Aristotle says (*Physics*, IV), prevention and cure are related to one another, and are, accidentally, matters of causation. In this way the whole foundation of this horrible heresy may be made clear.

In the above two divisions, the following points will be principally emphasized. First, the initiation of witches, and their profession of sacrilege. Second, the progress of their method of working, and of their horrible observances. Third, the preventive protections against their witchcrafts. And because we are now dealing with matters relating to morals and behaviour, and there is no need for a variety of arguments and disquisitions, since those matters which now follow under their headings are sufficiently discussed in the foregoing Questions; therefore we pray God that the reader will not look for proofs in every case, since it is enough to adduce examples that have been personally seen or heard, or are accepted at the word of credible witnesses.

In the first of the points mentioned, two matters will be chiefly examined: first, the various methods of enticement adopted by the devil himself; second, the various ways in which witches profess their heresy. And in the second of the main points, six matters will be examined in order, relating to the procedure of witchcraft, and its cure. First, the practices of witches with regard to themselves and their own bodies. Second, their practices with regard to other men. Third, those relating to beasts. Fourth, the mischief they do to the fruits of the earth. Fifth, those kinds of witchcraft which are practised by men only and not by women. Sixth, the question of removing witchcraft, and how those who are bewitched may be cured. The First Question, therefore, is divided into eighteen heads, since in so many ways are their observances varied and multiplied.

It is asked whether a man can be so blessed by the good Angels that he cannot be bewitched by witches in any of the ways that follow. And it seems that he cannot, for it has already been proved that even the blameless and innocent and the just are often afflicted by devils, as was Job; and many innocent children, as well as countless other just men, are seen to be bewitched, although not to the same extent as sinners; for they are not afflicted in the perdition of their souls, but only in their worldly goods and their bodies. But the contrary is indicated by the confessions of witches, namely, that they cannot injure everybody, but only those whom they learn, through the information of devils, to be destitute of Divine help.

Answer. There are three classes of men blessed by God, whom that detestable race cannot injure with their witchcraft. And the first are those who administer public justice against them, or prosecute them in any public official capacity. The second are those who, according to the traditional and holy rites of the Church, make lawful use of the power and virtue which the Church by her exorcisms furnishes in the aspersion of Holy Water, the taking of consecrated salt, the carrying of blessed candles on the Day of the Purification of Our Lady, of palm leaves upon Palm Sunday, and men who thus fortify themselves are acting so that the powers of devils are diminished; and of these we shall speak later. The third class are those who, in various and infinite ways, are blessed by the Holy Angels.

The reason for this in the first class will be given and proved by various examples. For since, as S. Paul says, all power is from God, and a sword for the avenging of the wicked and the retribution of the good, it is no wonder that devils are kept at bay when justice is being done to avenge that horrible crime.

To the same effect the Doctors note that there are five ways in which the devil's power is hindered, either wholly or in part. First, by a limit fixed by God to his power, as is seen in *Job* i and ii. Another example is the case of the man we read of in the *Formicarius* of Nider, who had confessed to a judge that he had invoked the devil in order that he might kill an enemy of his, or do him bodily harm, or strike him dead with lightning. And he said: "When I had invoked the devil that I might commit such a deed with his help, he answered me that he was unable to do any of those things, because the man had good faith and diligently defended himself with the sign of the cross; and that therefore he could not harm him in his body, but the most he could do was to destroy an eleventh part of the fruits of his lands."

Secondly, it is hindered by the application of some exterior force, as in the case of Balaam's ass, *Numbers* xxii. Thirdly, by some externally performed miracle of power. And there are some who are blessed with an unique privilege, as will be shown later in the case of the third class of men who cannot be bewitched. Fourthly, by the good providence of God, Who disposes each thing severally, and causes a good Angel to stand in the devil's way, as when Asmodeus killed the seven husbands of the virgin Sara, but did not kill Tobias.

Fifthly, it is sometimes due to the caution of the devil himself, for at times he does not wish to do hurt, in order that worse may follow from it. As, for example, when he could molest the excommunicated but does not do so, as in the case of the excommunicated Corinthian (I. *Corinthians* v), in order that he may weaken the faith of the Church in the power of such banishment. Therefore we may similarly say that, even if the administrators of public justice were not protected by Divine power, yet the devils often of their own accord withdraw their support and

guardianship from witches, either because they fear their conversion, or because they desire and hasten their damnation.

This fact is proved also by actual experience. For the aforesaid Doctor affirms that witches have borne witness that it is a fact of their own experience that, merely because they have been taken by officials of public justice, they have immediately lost all their power of witchcraft. For example, a judge named Peter, whom we have mentioned before, wished his officials to arrest a certain witch called Stadlin;* but their hands were seized with so great a trembling, and such a nauseous stench came into their nostrils, that they gave up hope of daring to touch the witch. And the judge commanded them, saying: "You may safely arrest the wretch, for when he is touched by the hand of public justice, he will lose all the power of his iniquity." And so the event proved; for he was taken and burned for many witchcrafts perpetrated by him, which are mentioned here and there in this work in their appropriate places.

And many more such experiences have happened to us Inquisitors in the exercise of our inquisitorial office, which would turn the mind of the reader to wonder if it were expedient to relate them. But since self-praise is sordid and mean, it is better to pass them over in silence than to incur the stigma of boastfulness and conceit. But we must except those which have become so well known that they cannot be concealed.

Not long ago in the town of Ratisbon the magistrates had condemned a witch to be burned, and were asked why it was that we Inquisitors were not afflicted like other men with witchcraft. They answered that witches had often tried to injure them, but could not. And, being asked the reason for this, they answered that they did not know, unless it was because the devils had warned them against doing so. For, they said, it would be impossible to tell how many times they have pestered us by day and by night, now in the form of

---

* "*Stadlin.*" *Stadelein, who is described as* "*grandis maleficus,*" "*a most notorious warlock,*" *lived at Boltingen, a town in the duchy and diocese of Lausanne. John Nider sat as assessor at his trial. See the "Formicarius," c. III.*

apes, now of dogs or goats, disturbing us with their cries and insults; fetching us from our beds at their blasphemous prayers, so that we have stood outside the window of their prison, which was so high that no one could reach it without the longest of ladders; and then they have seemed to stick the pins with which their head-cloth was fastened violently into their heads, and so they were found by us when we had risen, as if they had wished to stick them into our own heads. But praise be to Almighty God, Who in His pity, and for no merit of our own, has preserved us as unworthy public servants of the justice of the Faith.

The reason in the case of the second class of men is self-evident. For the exorcisms of the Church are for this very purpose, and are entirely efficacious remedies for preserving oneself from the injuries of witches.

But if it is asked in what manner a man ought to use such protections, we must speak first of those that are used without the uttering of sacred words, and then of the actual sacred invocations. For in the first place it is lawful in any decent habitation of men or beasts to sprinkle Holy Water for the safety and securing of men and beasts, with the invocation of the Most Holy Trinity and a Paternoster. For it is said in the Office of Exorcism, that wherever it is sprinkled, all uncleanness is purified, all harm is repelled, and no pestilent spirit can abide there, etc. For the Lord saves both man and beast, according to the Prophet, each in his degree.

Secondly, just as the first must necessarily be sprinkled, so in the case of a Blessed Candle, although it is more appropriate to light it, the wax of it may with advantage be sprinkled about dwelling-houses. And thirdly, it is expedient to place or to burn consecrated herbs in those rooms where they can best be consumed in some convenient place.

Now it happened in the city of Spires, in the same year that this book was begun, that a certain devout woman held conversation with a suspected witch, and, after the manner of women, they used abusive words to each other. But in the night she wished to put her little suckling child in its cradle, and remembered her encounter that day with the suspected witch. So, fearing

some danger to the child, she placed consecrated herbs under it, sprinkled it with Holy Water, put a little Blessed Salt to its lips, signed it with the Sign of the Cross, and diligently secured the cradle. About the middle of the night she heard the child crying, and, as women do, wished to embrace the child, and lift the cradle on to her bed. She lifted the cradle, indeed, but could not embrace the child, because he was not there. The poor woman, in terror, and bitterly weeping for the loss of her child, lit a light, and found the child in a corner under a chair, crying but unhurt.

In this it may be seen what virtue there is in the exorcisms of the Church against the snares of the devil. It is manifest that Almighty God, in His mercy and wisdom which extend from end to end, watches over the deeds of those wicked men; and that he gently directs the witchcraft of devils, so that when they try to diminish and weaken the Faith, they on the contrary strengthen it and make it more firmly rooted in the hearts of many. For the faithful may derive much profit from these evils; when, by reason of devils' works, the faith is made strong, God's mercy is seen, and His power manifested, and men are led into His keeping and to the reverence of Christ's Passion, and are enlightened by the ceremonies of the Church.

There lived in a town of Wiesenthal a certain Mayor who was bewitched with the most terrible pains and bodily contortions; and he discovered, not by means of other witches, but from his own experience, how that witchcraft had been practised on him. For he said he was in the habit of fortifying himself every Sunday with Blessed Salt and Holy Water, but that he had neglected to do so on one occasion owing to the celebration of somebody's marriage; and on that same day he was bewitched.

In Ratisbon a man was being tempted by the devil in the form of a woman to copulate, and became greatly disturbed when the devil would not desist. But it came into the poor man's mind that he ought to defend himself by taking Blessed Salt, as he had heard in a sermon. So, he took some Blessed Salt on entering the bath-room; and the woman looked fiercely at him, and, cursing whatever devil had taught him to do this, suddenly disappeared. For the devil can, with God's permission, present himself either in the form of a witch, or by possessing the body of an actual witch.

There were also three companions walking along a road, and two of them were struck by lightning. The third was terrified, when he heard voices speaking in the air, "Let us strike him too." But another voice answered, "We cannot, for to-day he has heard the words 'The Word was made Flesh.'" And he understood that he had been saved because he had that day heard Mass, and, at the end of the Mass, the Gospel of S. John: In the beginning was the Word, etc.

Also sacred words bound to the body are marvellously protective, if seven conditions for their use are observed. But these will be mentioned in the last Question of this Second Part, where we speak of curative, as here we speak of preventive measures. And those sacred words help not only to protect, but also to cure those who are bewitched.

But the surest protection for places, men, or animals are the words of the triumphal title of our Saviour, if they be written in four places in the form of a cross: IESUS † NAZARENUS † REX † IUDAEORUM †. There may also be added the name of the Virgin MARY and of the Evangelists, or the words of S. John: The Word was made Flesh.

But the third class of men which cannot be hurt by witches is the most remarkable; for they are protected by a special Angelic guardianship, both within and without. Within, by the inpouring of grace; without, by the virtue of the stars, that is, by the protection of the Powers which move the stars. And this class is divided into two sections of the Elect: for some are protected against all sorts of witchcrafts, so that they can be hurt in no way; and others are particularly rendered chaste by the good Angels with regard to the generative functions, just as evil spirits by their witchcrafts inflame the lusts of certain wicked men towards one woman, while they make them cold towards another.

And their interior and exterior protection, by grace and by the influence of the stars, is explained as follows. For though it is God Himself Who pours grace into our souls, and no other creature has so great power as to do this (as it is said: The Lord will give grace and glory); yet, when God wishes to bestow some especial grace, He does so in a dispositive way through the agency of a good Angel, as S. Thomas teaches us in a certain place in the *Third Book of Sentences*.

And this is the doctrine put forward by Dionysius in the fourth chapter *de Diuinis Nominibus:* This is the fixed and unalterable law of Divinity, that the High proceeds to the Low through a Medium; so that whatever of good emanates to us from the fountain of all goodness, comes through the ministry of the good Angels. And this is proved both by examples and by argument. For although only the Divine power was the cause of the Conception of the Word of God in the Most Blessed Virgin, through whom God was made man; yet the mind of the Virgin was by the ministry of an Angel much stimulated by the Salutation, and by the strengthening and information of her understanding, and was thus predisposed to goodness. This truth can also be reasoned as follows: It is the opinion of the above-mentioned Doctor that there are three properties in man, the will, the understanding, and the inner and outer powers belonging to the bodily members and organs. The first God alone can influence: For the heart of the king is in the hand of the Lord. A good Angel can influence the understanding towards a clearer knowledge of the true and the good, so that in the second of his properties both God and a good Angel can enlighten a man. Similarly in the third, a good Angel can endow a man with good qualities, and a bad Angel can, with God's permission, afflict him with evil temptations. However, it is in the power of the human will either to accept such evil influences or to reject them; and this a man can always do by invoking the grace of God.

As to the exterior protection which comes from God through the Movers of the stars, the tradition is widespread, and conforms equally with the Sacred Writings and with natural philosophy. For all the heavenly bodies are moved by angelic powers which are called by Christ the Movers of the stars, and by the Church the Powers of the heavens; and consequently all the corporeal substances of this world are governed by the celestial influences, as witness Aristotle, *Metaphysics* I. Therefore we can say that the providence of God overlooks each one of His elect, but He subjects some of them to the ills of this life for their correction, while He so protects others that they can in no way be injured. And this gift they receive either from the good Angels deputed by God for their protection, or from the influence of the heavenly bodies or the Powers which move them.

It is further to be noted that some are protected against all witchcrafts, and some against only a part of them. For some are particularly purified by the good Angels in their genital functions, so that witches can in no way bewitch them in respect of those functions. But it is in one sense superfluous to write of these, although in another sense it is needful for this reason: for those who are bewitched in their generative function are so deprived of the guardianship of Angels that they are either in mortal sin always, or practise those impurities with too lustful a zest. In this connexion it has been shown in the First Part of this work that God permits greater powers of witchcraft against that function, not so much because of its nastiness, as because it was this act that caused the corruption of our first parents and, by its contagion, brought the inheritance of original sin upon the whole human race.

But let us give a few examples of how a good Angel sometimes blesses just and holy men, especially in the matter of the genital instincts. For the following was the experience of the Abbot S. Serenus, as it is told by Cassian* in his

---

* "Cassian." John Cassian, monk and ascetic writer of Southern Gaul, and the first to introduce the rules of Eastern monasticism into the West, was born probably in Provence about 360; and died near Marseilles about 435. The two principal works of Cassian are the "Institutes; De institutis coenobiorum et de octo principalium uitiorum remediis libri XII"; and the "Collations" or "Conferences," "Collationes XXIV." The author has himself remarked upon the relation between the two works: "These books ('the Institutes') . . . are mainly taken up with what belongs to the outer man and the customs of the coenobia; the others (the 'Conferences') deal rather with the training of the inner man and the perfection of the heart." The best edition of the works of Cassian is that by Petschenig, Vienna, 1885–88.

Although never formally canonized, from very early days Cassian was regarded as a saint. At Marseilles his feast (with an octave) is celebrated 23 July, and his name is found in the Greek Calendar.

Collations of the Fathers, in the first conference of the Abbot Serenus. This man, he says, laboured to achieve an inward chastity of heart and soul, by prayers both by night and day, by fasting and by vigils, till he at last perceived that, by Divine grace, he had extinguished all the surgings of carnal concupiscence. Finally, stirred by an even greater zeal for chastity, he used all the above holy practices to pray the Almighty and All-Good God to grant him that, by God's gift, the chastity which he felt in his heart should be visibly conferred upon his body. Then an Angel of the Lord came to him in a vision in the night, and seemed to open his belly and take from his entrails a burning tumour of flesh, and then to replace all his intestines as they had been; and said: Lo! the provocation of your flesh is cut out, and know that this day you have obtained perpetual purity of your body, according to the prayer which you prayed, so that you will never again be pricked with that natural desire which is aroused even in babes and sucklings.

Similarly S. Gregory, in the first book of his Dialogues, tells of the Blessed Abbot Equitius. This man, he says, was in his youth greatly troubled by the provocation of the flesh; but the very distress of his temptation made him all the more zealous in his application to prayer. And when he continuously prayed Almighty God for a remedy against this affliction, an Angel appeared to him one night and seemed to make him an eunuch, and it seemed to him in his vision that all feeling was taken away from his genital organs; and from that time he was such a stranger to temptation as if he had no sex in his body. Behold what benefit there was in that purification; for he was so filled with virtue that, with the help of Almighty God, just as he was before pre-eminent among men, so he afterwards became pre-eminent over women.

Again, in the Lives of the Fathers collected by that very holy man S. Heraclides,† in the book which he calls Paradise, he tells of a certain holy Father, a monk named Helias. This man was

---

† "S. Heraclides." Episcopus Tamasi in Cypro, cuius Festum agitur die xvii Septembris. See "Analecta Bollandiana," XXVI, 238–9; and Fr. Nau, "Revue de l'Orient chrétien," XII (197), 125–38.

moved by pity to collect thirty women in a monastery, and began to rule over them. But after two years, when he was thirty years old, he fled from the temptation of the flesh into a hermitage, and fasting there for two days, prayed to God, saying: "O Lord God, either slay me, or deliver me from this temptation." And in the evening a dream came to him, and he saw three Angels approach him; and they asked him why he had fled from that monastery of virgins. But when he did not dare to answer, for shame, the Angels said: If you are set free from temptation, will you return to your cure of those women? And he answered that he would willingly. They then exacted an oath to that effect from him, and made him an eunuch. For one seemed to hold his hands, another his feet, and the third to cut out his testicles with a knife; though this was not really so, but only seemed to be. And when they asked if he felt himself remedied, he answered that he was entirely delivered. So, on the fifth day, he returned to the sorrowing women, and ruled over them for the forty years that he continued to live, and never again felt a spark of that first temptation.

No less a benefit do we read to have been conferred upon the Blessed Thomas,* a Doctor of our Order, whom his brothers imprisoned for entering that Order; and, wishing to tempt him, they sent in to him a seductive and sumptuously adorned harlot. But when the Doctor had looked at her, he ran to the material fire, and snatching up a lighted torch, drove the engine of the fire of lust out of his prison; and, prostrating himself in a prayer for the

gift of chastity, went to sleep. Two Angels then appeared to him, saying: Behold, at the bidding of God we gird you with a girdle of chastity, which cannot be loosed by any other such temptation; neither can it be acquired by the merits of human virtue, but is given as a gift by God alone. And he felt himself girded, and was aware of the touch of the girdle, and cried out and awaked. And thereafter he felt himself endowed with so great a gift of chastity, that from that time he abhorred all the delights of the flesh, so that he could not even speak to a woman except under compulsion, but was strong in his perfect chastity. This we take from the *Formicarius* of Nider.

With the exception, therefore, of these three classes of men, no one is secure from witches. For all others are liable to be bewitched, or to be tempted and incited by some witchery, in the eighteen ways that are now to be considered. For we must first describe these methods in their order, that we may afterwards discuss more clearly the remedies by which those who are bewitched can be relieved. And that the eighteen methods may be more clearly shown, they are set forth under as many chapters as follows. First, we show the various methods of initiation of witches, and how they entice innocent girls to swell the numbers of their perfidious company. Second, how witches profess their sacrilege, and the oath of allegiance to the devil which they take. Third, how they are transported from place to place, either bodily or in the spirit. Fourth, how they subject themselves to Incubi, who are devils. Fifth, their general method of practising witchcraft through the Sacraments of the Church, and in particular how, with the permission of God, they can afflict all creatures except the Celestial Bodies. Sixth, their method of obstructing the generative function. Seventh, how they can take off the virile member by some art of illusion. Eighth, how they change men into the shapes of beasts. Ninth, how devils can enter the mind without hurting it, when they work some glamour or illusion. Tenth, how devils, through the operation of witches, sometimes substantially inhabit men. Eleventh, how they cause every sort of infirmity, and this in general. Twelfth, of certain infirmities in particular. Thirteenth, how witch mid-

---

* "Blessed Thomas." At the instance of his mother Theodora, Countess of Teano, S. Thomas, who had received the Dominican habit some time between 1240 and August 1243, was whilst on his way to Rome from Naples captured near Aquapendente by his two brothers, Landolfo and Rinaldo, officers in the army of the Emperor Frederick. They confined him for nearly two years in the fortress of San Giovanni at Rocca Secca. He revealed this vision of Holy Angels who endowed him with the white girdle of chastity to his faithful friend, Reginald of Piperno. One of the particular devotions of the Dominican Order consists in wearing, as a devout memorial of this event, a white girdle for which a special form of blessing is prescribed: "Benedictio Cinguli S. Thomae Aquinatis Ad Seruandam Castitatem."

wives cause the greatest damage, either killing children or sacrilegiously offering them to devils. Fourteenth, how they cause various plagues to afflict animals. Fifteenth, how they raise hailstorms and tempests, and thunder and lightning, to fall upon men and animals. Sixteenth, seventeenth, and eighteenth, the three ways in which men only, and not women, are addicted to witchcraft. After these will follow the question of the methods by which these sorts of witchcraft may be removed.

But let no one think that, because we have enumerated the various methods by which various forms of witchcraft are inflicted, he will arrive at a complete knowledge of these practices; for such knowledge would be of little use, and might even be harmful. Not even the forbidden books of Necromancy contain such knowledge; for witchcraft is not taught in books, nor is it practised by the learned, but by the altogether uneducated; having only one foundation, without the acknowledgement or practice of which it is impossible for anyone to work witchcraft as a witch.

Moreover, the methods are enumerated here at the beginning, that their deeds may not seem incredible, as they have often been thought hitherto, to the great damage of the Faith, and the increase of witches themselves. But if anyone maintains that, since (as has been proved above) some men are protected by the influence of the stars so that they can be hurt by no witchcraft, it should also be attributed to the stars when anyone is bewitched, as if it were a matter of predestination whether a man be immune from or subject to witchcraft, such a man does not rightly understand the meaning of the Doctors; and this in various respects.

And first, because there are three human qualities which may be said to be ruled by three celestial causes, namely, the act of volition, the act of understanding, and bodily acts. And the first, as has been said, is governed directly and only by God; the second by an Angel; and the third is governed, but not compelled, by a celestial body.

Secondly, it is clear from what has been said that choice and volition are governed directly by God, as S. Paul says: It is God Who causeth us to will and to perform, according to His good pleasure: and the understanding of the human intellect is ordered by God through the mediation of the Angels. Accordingly also all things corporeal, whether they be interior as are the powers and knowledge acquired through the inner bodily faculties, or exterior as are sickness and health, are dispensed by the celestial bodies, through the mediation of Angels. And when Dionysius, in the fourth chapter de Diuinis Nominibus, says that the celestial bodies are the cause of that which happens in this world, this is to be understood as to natural health and sickness. But the sicknesses we are considering are supernatural, since they are inflicted by the power of the devil, with God's permission. Therefore we cannot say that it is due to the influence of the stars that a man is bewitched; although it can truly be said that it is due to the influence of the stars that some men cannot be bewitched.

But if it is objected that these two opposite effects must spring from the same cause, and that the pendulum must swing both ways, it is answered that, when a man is preserved by the influence of the stars from these supernatural ills, this is not due directly to the influence of the stars, but to an angelic power, which can strengthen that influence so that the enemy with his malice cannot prevail against it; and that angelic power can be passed on through the virtue of the stars. For a man may be at the point of death, having reached the natural term of life, and God in His power, which in such matters always works indirectly, may alter this by sending some power of preservation instead of the natural defect in the man and in his dominating influence. Accordingly we may say of a man who is subject to witchcraft, that he can in just the same way be preserved from witchcraft, or that this preservation comes of an Angel deputed to guard him; and this is the chief of all means of protection.

And when it is said in Jeremias xxii: Write ye this man childless, a man that shall not prosper in his days: this is to be understood with regard to the choices of the will, in which one man prospers and another does not; and this also can be ascribed to the influence of the stars. For example: one man may be influenced by his stars to make a useful choice, such as to enter some religious Order. And when his understanding is enlightened to consider such a step, and by Divine operation his will is inclined to put it into execution, such a man is said to prosper well. Or similarly when a man is inclined to some trade, or anything that is useful. On the other hand, he will be called unfortunate when his choice is inclined by the higher Powers to unprofitable things.

S. Thomas, in his third book of the *Summa* against the Gentiles, and in several other places, speaks of these and many other opinions, when he discusses in what lies the difference that one man should be well born and another unfortunately born, that a man should be lucky or unlucky, or well or badly governed and guarded. For according to the disposition of his stars a man is said to be well or badly born, and so fortunate or unfortunate; and according as he is enlightened by an Angel, and follows such enlightenment, he is said to be well or badly guarded. And according as he is directed by God towards good, and follows it, he is said to be well governed. But these choices have no place here, since we are not concerned with them but with the preservation from witchcraft; and we have said enough for the present on this subject. We proceed to the rites practised by witches, and first to a consideration of how they lure the innocent into becoming partakers of their perfidies.

☆

CHAPTER I

Of the several Methods by which Devils through Witches Entice and Allure the Innocent to the Increase of that Horrid Craft and Company.

THERE are three methods above all by which devils, through the agency of witches, subvert the innocent, and by which that perfidy is continually being increased. And the first is through weariness, through inflicting grievous losses in their temporal possessions. For, as S. Gregory says: The devil often tempts us to give way from very weariness. And it is to be understood that it is within the power of a man to resist such temptation; but that God permits it as a warning to us not to give way to sloth. And in this sense is *Judges* ii to be understood, where it says that God did not destroy those

nations, that through them He might prove the people of Israel; and it speaks of the neighbouring nations of the Canaanites, Jebusites, and others. And in our time the Hussites and other Heretics are permitted, so that they cannot be destroyed. Devils, therefore, by means of witches, so afflict their innocent neighbours with temporal losses, that they are as it were compelled, first to beg the suffrages of witches, and at length to submit themselves to their counsels; as many experiences have taught us.

We know a stranger in the diocese of Augsburg, who before he was forty-four years old lost all his horses in succession through witchcraft. His wife, being afflicted with weariness by reason of this, consulted with witches, and after following their counsels, unwholesome as they were, all the horses which he bought after that (for he was a carrier) were preserved from witchcraft.

And how many women have complained to us in our capacity of Inquisitors, that when their cows have been injured by being deprived of their milk, or in any other way, they have consulted with suspected witches, and even been given remedies by them, on condition that they would promise something to some spirit; and when they asked what they would have to promise, the witches answered that it was only a small thing, that they should agree to execute the instructions of that master with regard to certain observances during the Holy Offices of the Church, or to observe some silent reservations in their confessions to priests.

Here it is to be noted that, as has already been hinted, this iniquity has small and scant beginnings, as that at the time of the elevation of the Body of Christ they spit on the ground, or shut their eyes, or mutter some vain words. We know a woman who yet lives, protected by the secular law, who, when the priest at the celebration of the Mass blesses the people, saying, *Dominus uobiscum*, always adds to herself these words in the vulgar tongue, "Kehr mir die Zung im Arss umb." Or they even say some such thing at confession after they have received absolution, or do not confess everything, especially mortal sins, and so by slow degrees are led to a total abnegation of the Faith, and to the abominable profession of sacrilege.

This, or something like it, is the method which witches use towards honest matrons who are little given to carnal vices but concerned for worldly profit. But towards young girls, more given to bodily lusts and pleasures, they observe a different method, working through their carnal desires and the pleasures of the flesh.

Here it is to be noted that the devil is more eager and keen to tempt the good than the wicked, although in actual practice he tempts the wicked more than the good, because more aptitude for being tempted is found in the wicked than in the good. Therefore the devil tries all the harder to seduce all the more saintly virgins and girls; and there is reason in this, besides many examples of it.

For since he already possesses the wicked, but not the good, he tries the harder to seduce into his power the good whom he does not, than the wicked whom he does, possess. Similarly any earthly prince takes up arms against those who do not acknowledge his rule rather than against those who do not oppose him.

And here is an example. Two witches were burned in Ratisbon, as we shall tell later where we treat of their methods of raising tempests. And one of them, who was a bath-woman, had confessed among other things the following: that she had suffered much injury from the devil for this reason. There was a certain devout virgin, the daughter of a very rich man whom there is no need to name, since the girl is now dead in the disposition of Divine mercy, and we would not that his thoughts should be perverted by evil; and the witch was ordered to seduce her by inviting her to her house on some Feast Day, in order that the devil himself, in the form of a young man, might speak with her. And although she had tried very often to accomplish this, yet whenever she had spoken to the young girl, she had protected herself with the sign of the Holy Cross. And no one can doubt that she did this at the instigation of a holy Angel, to repel the works of the devil.

Another virgin living in the diocese of Strasburg confessed to one of us that she was alone on a certain Sunday in her father's house, when an old woman of that town came to visit her and, among other scurrilous words, made the following proposition; that, if she liked, she would take her to a place where there were some young men unknown to all the townsmen. And when, said the virgin, I consented, and followed her to her house, the old woman said, " See, we go upstairs to an upper room where the young men are; but take care not to make the sign of the Cross." I gave my promise not to do so, and as she was going before me and I was going up the stairs, I secretly crossed myself. At the top of the stairs, when we were both standing outside the room, the hag turned angrily upon me with a horrible countenance, and looking at me said, " Curse you! Why did you cross yourself? Go away from here. Depart in the name of the devil." And so I returned unharmed to my home.

It can be seen from this how craftily that old enemy labours in the seduction of souls. For it was in this way that the bath-woman whom we have mentioned, and who was burned, confessed that she had been seduced by some old woman. A different method, however, was used in the case of her companion witch, who had met the devil in human form on the road while she herself was going to visit her lover for the purpose of fornication. And when the Incubus devil had seen her, and had asked her whether she recognized him, and she had said that she did not, he had answered: " I am the devil; and if you wish, I will always be ready at your pleasure, and will not fail you in any necessity." And when she had consented, she continued for eighteen years, up to the end of her life, to practise diabolical filthiness with him, together with a total abnegation of the Faith as a necessary condition.

There is also a third method of temptation through the way of sadness and poverty. For when girls have been corrupted, and have been scorned by their lovers after they have immodestly copulated with them in the hope and promise of marriage with them, and have found themselves disappointed in all their hopes and everywhere despised, they turn to the help and protection of devils; either for the sake of vengeance by bewitching those lovers or the wives they have married, or for the sake of giving themselves up to every sort of lechery. Alas! experience tells us that there is no number to such girls, and consequently the witches that spring from this class are innumerable. Let us give a few out of many examples.

There is a place in the diocese of Brixen where a young man deposed the following facts concerning the bewitchment of his wife.

" In the time of my youth I loved a girl who importuned me to marry her; but I refused her and married another girl from another country. But wishing for friendship's sake to please her, I invited her to the wedding. She came, and while the other honest women were wishing us luck and offering gifts, she raised her hand and, in the hearing of the other women who were standing round, said, You will have few days of health after to-day. My bride was frightened, since she did not know her (for, as I have said, I had married her from another country), and asked the bystanders who she was who had threatened her in that way; and they said that she was a loose and vagrom woman. None the less, it happened just as she had said. For after a few days my wife was so bewitched that she lost the use of all her limbs, and even now, after ten years, the effects of witchcraft can be seen on her body."

If we were to collect all the similar instances which have occurred in one town of that diocese, it would take a whole book; but they are written and preserved at the house of the Bishop of Brixen, who still lives to testify to their truth, astounding and unheard-of though they are.

But we must not pass over in silence one unheard-of and astonishing instance. A certain high-born Count in the ward of Westerich, in the diocese of Strasburg, married a noble girl of equal birth; but after he had celebrated the wedding, he was for three years unable to know her carnally, on account, as the event proved, of a certain charm which prevented him. In great anxiety, and not knowing what to do, he called loudly on the Saints of God. It happened that he went to the State of Metz to negotiate some business; and while he was walking about the streets and squares of the city, attended by his servants and domestics, he met a certain woman who had formerly been

his mistress. Seeing her, and not at all thinking of the spell that was on him, he spontaneously addressed her kindly for the sake of their old friendship, asking her how she did, and whether she was well. And she, seeing the Count's gentleness, in her turn asked very particularly after his health and affairs; and when he answered that he was well, and that everything prospered with him, she was astonished and was silent for a time. The Count, seeing her thus astonished, again spoke kindly to her, inviting her to converse with him. So she inquired after his wife, and received a similar reply, that she was in all respects well. Then she asked if he had any children; and the Count said he had three sons, one born in each year. At that she was more astonished, and was again silent for a while. And the Count asked her, Why, my dear, do you make such careful inquiries? I am sure that you congratulate me on my happiness. Then she answered, Certainly I congratulate you; but curse that old woman who said she would bewitch your body so that you could not have connexion with your wife! And in proof of this, there is a pot in the well in the middle of your yard containing certain objects evilly bewitched, and this was placed there in order that, as long as its contents were preserved intact, for so long you would be unable to cohabit. But see! it is all in vain, and I am glad, etc. On his return home the Count did not delay to have the well drained; and, finding the pot, burned its contents and all, whereupon he immediately recovered the virility which he had lost. Wherefore the Countess again invited all the nobility to a fresh wedding celebration, saying that she was now the Lady of that castle and estate, after having for so long remained a virgin. For the sake of the Count's reputation it is not expedient to name that castle and estate; but we have related this story in order that the truth of the matter may be known, to bring so great a crime into open detestation.

From this it is clear that witches use various methods to increase their numbers. For the above-mentioned woman, because she had been supplanted by the Count's wife, cast that spell upon the Count with the help of another witch; and this is how one witchcraft brings innumerable others in its train.

☆

CHAPTER II

Of the Way whereby a Formal Pact with Evil is made.

THE method by which they profess their sacrilege through an open pact of fidelity to devils varies according to the several practices to which different witches are addicted. And to understand this it first must be noted that there are, as was shown in the First Part of this treatise, three kinds of witches; namely, those who injure but cannot cure; those who cure but, through some strange pact with the devil, cannot injure; and those who both injure and cure. And among those who injure, one class in particular stands out, which can perform every sort of witchcraft and spell, comprehending all that all the others individually can do. Wherefore, if we describe the method of profession in their case, it will suffice also for all the other kinds. And this class is made up of those who, against every instinct of human or animal nature, are in the habit of eating and devouring the children of their own species.

And this is the most powerful class of witches, who practise innumerable other harms also. For they raise hailstorms and hurtful tempests and lightnings; cause sterility in men and animals; offer to devils, or otherwise kill, the children whom they do not devour. But these are only the children who have not been re-born by baptism at the font, for they cannot devour those who have been baptized, nor any without God's permission. They can also, before the eyes of their parents, and when no one is in sight, throw into the water children walking by the water side; they make horses go mad under their riders; they can transport themselves from place to place through the air, either in body or in imagination; they can affect Judges and Magistrates so that they cannot hurt them; they can cause themselves and others to keep silence under torture; they can bring about a great trembling in the hands and horror in the minds of those who would arrest them; they can show to others occult things and certain future events, by the information of devils, though this may sometimes have a natural cause (see the question: *Whether devils can foretell the future,* in the *Second Book of Sentences*); they can see absent things as if they were present; they can turn the minds of men to inordinate love or hatred; they can at times strike whom they will with lightning, and even kill some men and animals; they can make of no effect the generative desires, and even the power of copulation, cause abortion, kill infants in the mother's womb by a mere exterior touch; they can at times bewitch men and animals with a mere look, without touching them, and cause death; they dedicate their own children to devils; and in short, as has been said, they can cause all the plagues which other witches can only cause in part, that is, when the Justice of God permits such things to be. All these things this most powerful of all classes of witches can do, but they cannot undo them.

But it is common to all of them to practise carnal copulation with devils; therefore, if we show the method used by this chief class in their profession of their sacrilege, anyone may easily understand the method of the other classes.

There were such witches lately, thirty years ago, in the district of Savoy, towards the State of Berne, as Nider tells in his *Formicarius.* And there are now some in the country of Lombardy, in the domains of the Duke of Austria, where the Inquisitor of Como, as we told in the former Part, caused forty-one witches to be burned in one year; and he was fifty-five years old, and still continues to labour in the Inquisition.

Now the method of profession is twofold. One is a solemn ceremony, like a solemn vow. The other is private, and can be made to the devil at any hour alone. The first method is when witches meet together in conclave on a set day, and the devil appears to them in the assumed body of a man, and urges them to keep faith with him, promising them worldly prosperity and length of life; and they recommend a novice to his acceptance. And the devil asks whether she will abjure the Faith, and forsake the holy Christian religion and the worship of the Anomalous Woman (for so they call the Most Blessed Virgin MARY), and never venerate the Sacraments; and if he finds the novice or disciple willing, then the devil stretches out his hand, and so does the novice, and she swears with upraised hand to keep that covenant. And when this is done, the devil at once adds that this is not enough; and when the disciple asks what more must be done, the devil demands the following oath of homage to himself: that she give herself to him, body and soul, for ever, and do her utmost to bring others of both sexes into his power. He adds, finally, that she is to make certain unguents from the bones and limbs of children, especially those who have been baptized; by all which means she will be able to fulfil all her wishes with his help.

We Inquisitors had credible experience of this method in the town of Breisach in the diocese of Basel, receiving full information from a young girl witch who had been converted, whose aunt also had been burned in the diocese of Strasburg. And she added that she had become a witch by the method in which her aunt had first tried to seduce her.

For one day her aunt ordered her to go upstairs with her, and at her command to go into a room where she found fifteen young men clothed in green garments after the manner of German knights. And her aunt said to her: Choose whom you wish from these young men, and I will give him to you, and he will take you for his wife. And when she said she did not wish for any of them, she was sorely beaten and at last consented, and was initiated according to the aforesaid ceremony. She said also that she was often transported by night with her aunt over vast distances, even from Strasburg to Cologne.

This is she who occasioned our inquiry in the First Part into the question whether witches are truly and bodily transported by devils from place to place: and this was on account of the words of the Canon (6, q. 5, *Episcopi*), which seem to imply that they are only so carried in imagination; whereas they are at times actually and bodily transported.

For when she was asked whether it was only in imagination and phantastically that they so rode, through an illusion of devils, she answered that they did so in both ways; according to the truth which we shall declare later of the manner in which they are transferred from place to place. She said also that the greatest injuries were inflicted by midwives, because they were under an obligation to kill or offer to devils as many children as possible; and that she had been severely beaten by her aunt because she had opened a secret pot and found the heads of a great many children. And much more she told us, having first, as was proper, taken an oath to speak the truth.

And her account of the method of professing the devil's faith undoubtedly agrees with what has been written by that most eminent Doctor, John Nider, who even in our times has written very illuminatingly; and it may be especially remarked that he tells us the following, which he had from an Inquisitor of the diocese of Edua, who held many inquisitions on witches in that diocese, and caused many to be burned.

For he says that this Inquisitor told him that in the Duchy of Lausanne certain witches had cooked and eaten their own children, and that the following was the method in which they became initiated into such practices. The witches met together and, by their art, summoned a devil in the form of a man, to whom the novice was compelled to swear to deny the Christian religion, never to adore the Eucharist, and to tread the Cross underfoot whenever she could do so secretly.

Here is another example from the same source. There was lately a general report, brought to the notice of Peter the Judge in Boltingen, that thirteen infants had been devoured in the State of Berne; and public justice exacted full vengeance on the murderers. And when Peter asked one of the captive witches in what manner they ate children, she replied: "This is the manner of it. We set our snares chiefly for unbaptized children, and even for those that have been baptized, especially when they have not been protected by the sign of the Cross and prayers" (Reader, notice that, at the devil's command, they take the unbaptized chiefly, in order that they may not be baptized), "and with our spells we kill them in their cradles or even when they are sleeping by their parents' side, in such a way that they afterwards are thought to have been overlain or to have died some other natural death. Then we secretly take them from their graves, and cook them in a cauldron, until the whole flesh comes away from the bones to make a soup which may easily be drunk. Of the more solid matter we make an unguent which is of virtue to help us in our arts and pleasures and our transportations; and with the liquid we fill a flask or skin, whoever drinks from which, with the addition of a few other ceremonies, immediately acquires much knowledge and becomes a leader in our sect."

Here is another very clear and distinct example. A young man and his wife, both witches, were imprisoned in Berne; and the man, shut up by himself apart from her in a separate tower, said: "If I could obtain pardon for my sins, I would willingly declare all that I know about witchcraft; for I see that I ought to die." And when he was told by the learned clerks who were there that he could obtain complete pardon if he truly repented, he joyfully resigned himself to death, and laid bare the method by which he had first been infected with his heresy. "The following," he said, "is the manner in which I was seduced. It is first necessary that, on a Sunday before the consecration of Holy Water, the novice should enter the church with the masters, and there in their presence deny Christ, his Faith, baptism, and the whole Church. And then he must pay homage to the Little Master, for so and not otherwise do they call the devil." Here it is to be noted that this method agrees with those that have been recounted; for it is immaterial whether the devil is himself present or not, when homage is offered to him. For this he does in his cunning, perceiving the temperament of the novice, who might be frightened by his actual presence into retracting his vows, whereas he would be more easily persuaded to consent by those who are known to him. And therefore they call him the Little Master when he is absent, that through seeming disparagement of his Master the novice may feel less fear. "And then he drinks from the skin, which has been mentioned, and immediately feels within himself a knowledge of all our arts and an understanding of our rites and ceremonies. And in this manner was I

seduced. But I believe my wife to be so obstinate that she would rather go straight to the fire than confess the smallest part of the truth; but, alas! we are both guilty." And as the young man said, so it happened in every respect. For the young man confessed and was seen to die in the greatest contrition; but the wife, though convicted by witnesses, would not confess any of the truth, either under torture or in death itself; but when the fire had been prepared by the gaoler, cursed him in the most terrible words, and so was burned. And from these examples their method of initiation in solemn conclave is made clear.

The other private method is variously performed. For sometimes when men or women have been involved in some bodily or temporal affliction, the devil comes to them, at times in person, and at times speaking to them through the mouth of someone else; and he promises that, if they will agree to his counsels, he will do for them whatever they wish. But he starts from small things, as was said in the first chapter, and leads gradually to the bigger things. We could mention many examples which have come to our knowledge in the Inquisition, but, since this matter presents no difficulty, it can briefly be included with the previous matter.

A Few Points are to be Noticed in the Explanation of their Oath of Homage.

Now there are certain points to be noted concerning the homage which the devil exacts, as, namely, for what reason and in what different ways he does this. It is obvious that his principal motive is to offer the greater offence to the Divine Majesty by usurping to himself a creature dedicated to God, and thus more certainly to ensure his disciple's future damnation, which is his chief object. Nevertheless, it is often found by us that he has received such homage for a fixed term of years at the time of the profession of perfidy; and sometimes he exacts the profession only, postponing the homage to a later day.

And let us declare that the profession consists in a total or partial abnegation of the Faith: total, as has been said before, when the Faith is entirely abjured; partial, when the original pact makes it incumbent on the witch to observe certain ceremonies in opposition to the decrees of the Church, such as fasting on Sundays, eating meat on Fridays, concealing certain crimes at confession, or some such profane thing. But let us declare that homage consists in the surrender of body and soul.

And we can assign four reasons why the devil requires the practice of such things. For we showed in the First Part of this treatise, when we examined whether devils could turn the minds of men to love or hatred, that they cannot enter the inner thoughts of the heart, since this belongs to God alone. But the devil can arrive at a knowledge of men's thoughts by conjecture, as will be shown later. Therefore, if that cunning enemy sees that a novice will be hard to persuade, he approaches her gently, exacting only small things that he may gradually lead her to greater things.

Secondly, it must be believed that there is some diversity among those who deny the Faith, since some do so with their lips but not in their heart, and some both with their lips and in their heart. Therefore the devil, wishing to know whether their profession comes from the heart as well as from the lips, sets them a certain period, so that he may understand their minds from their works and behaviour.

Thirdly, if after the lapse of a set time he find that she is less willing to perform certain practices, and is bound to him only by word but not in her heart, he presumes that the Divine Mercy has given her the guardianship of a good Angel, which he knows to be of great power. Then he casts her off, and tries to expose her to temporal afflictions, so that he gain some profit from her despair.

The truth of this is clear. For if it is asked why some witches will not confess the truth under even the greatest tortures, while others readily confess their crimes when they are questioned (and some of them, after they have confessed, try to kill themselves by hanging), the reason is as follows. It may truly be said that, when it is not due to a Divine impulse conveyed through a holy Angel that a witch is made to confess the truth and abandon the spell of silence, then it is due to the devil whether she preserves silence or confesses her crimes. The

former is the case with those whom he knows to have denied the Faith both with their lips and in their hearts, and also to have given him their homage; for he is sure of their constancy. But in the latter case he withdraws his protection, since he knows that they are of no profit to him.

We have often learned from the confessions of those whom we have caused to be burned, that they have not been willing agents of witchcraft. And they have not said this in the hope of escaping damnation, for its truth is witnessed by the blows and stripes which they have received from devils when they have been unwilling to perform their orders, and we have often seen their swollen and livid faces. Similarly, after they have confessed their crimes under torture they always try to hang themselves; and this we know for a fact; for after the confession of their crimes, guards are deputed to watch them all the time, and even then, when the guards have been negligent, they have been found hanged with their shoe-laces or garments. For, as we have said, the devil causes this, lest they should obtain pardon through contrition or sacramental confession; and those whose hearts he cannot seduce from finding grace with God, he tries to lead into despair through worldly loss and a horrible death. However, through the great grace of God, as it is pious to believe, they can obtain forgiveness by true contrition and pure confession, when they have not been willing participators in those foul and filthy practices.

This is exemplified by certain events which took place hardly three years ago in the dioceses of Strasburg and Constance, and in the towns of Hagenau and Ratisbon. For in the first town one hanged herself with a trifling and flimsy garment. Another, named Walpurgis, was notorious for her power of preserving silence, and used to teach other women how to achieve a like quality of silence by cooking their first-born sons in an oven. Many such examples are to our hand, as they are also in the case of others burned in the second town, some of which will be related.

And there is a fourth reason why the devil exacts a varying degree of homage, making it relatively small in some cases because he is more skilful than Astronomers in knowing the length of human life, and so can easily fix a term which he knows will be preceded by death, or can, in the manner already told, forestall natural death with some accident.

All this, in short, can be shown by the actions and behaviour of witches. But first we can deduce the astuteness of the devil in such things. For according to S. Augustine in the *de Natura Daemonis**seven reasons are assigned why devils can conjecture probable future events, though they cannot know them certainly. The first is that they have a natural subtlety in their understanding, by which they arrive at their knowledge without the process of reasoning which is necessary for us. Secondly, by their long experience and by revelation of supernal spirits, they know more than we do. For S. Isidore says that the Doctors have often affirmed that devils derive their marvellous cunning from three sources, their natural subtlety, their long experience, and the revelation of supernal spirits. The third reason is their rapidity of motion, by which they can with miraculous speed anticipate in the West things which are happening in the East. Fourthly, just as they are able, with God's permission, to cause diseases and famines, so also they can predict them. Fifthly, they can more cunningly read the signs of death than a physician can by looking at the urine or feeling the pulse. For just as a physician sees signs in a sick man which a layman would not notice, so the devil sees what no man can naturally see. Sixthly, they can by signs which proceed from a man's mind conjecture more astutely than the wisest men what is or will be in that man's mind. For they know what impulses, and therefore what actions, will probably follow. Seventhly, they understand better than men the acts and writings of the Prophets, and, since on these much of the future depends, they can foretell from them much that will happen. Therefore it is not wonderful that they can know the natural term of a man's life; though it is different in the case of the accidental

term when a witch is burned; for this the devil ultimately causes when, as has been said, he finds a witch reluctant, and fears for her conversion; whereas he protects even up to their natural death others whom he knows to be his willing agents.

Let us give examples of both these cases, which are known to us. There was in the diocese of Basel, in a town called Oberweiler situated on the Rhine, an honest parish priest, who fondly held the opinion, or rather error, that there was no witchcraft in the world, but that it only existed in the imagination of men who attributed such things to witches. And God wished so to purge him of this error that he might even be made aware of the practice of devils in setting a term to the lives of witches. For as he was hastening to cross a bridge, on some business that he had to do, he met a certain old woman in his hurry, and would not give way to her, but pressed on so that he thrust the old woman into the mud. She indignantly broke into a flood of abuse, and said to him, "Father, you will not cross with impunity." And though he took small notice of those words, in the night, when he wished to get out of his bed, he felt himself bewitched below the waist, so that he always had to be supported by the arms of other men when he wished to go to the church; and so he remained for three years, under the care of his own mother. After that time the old woman fell sick, the hag whom he had always suspected as being the cause of his witchcraft, owing to the abusive words with which she had threatened him; and it happened that she sent to him to hear her confession. And though the priest angrily said, "Let her confess to the devil her master," yet, at the instance of his mother, he went to the house supported by two servants, and sat at the head of the bed where the witch lay. And the two servants listened outside the window, so eager were they to know whether she would confess that she had bewitched the priest. Now it happened that, though she made no mention in her confession of having been the cause of his malady, after the confession was finished, she said, "Father, do you know who bewitched you?" And when he gently answered that he did not, she added,

---

* "*De Natura Daemonis.*" "*De Diuinatione Daemonum,*" *written 406–11. Migne, "Patres Latini," XL, pp. 581–92.*

"You suspect me, and with reason; for know that I brought it upon you for this reason," explaining as we have already told. And when he begged to be liberated, she said, "Lo! the set time has come, and I must die; but I will so cause it that in a few days, after my death, you will be healed." And so it happened. For she died at the time fixed by the devil, and within thirty days the priest found himself completely healed one night. The name of that priest is Father Hässlin, and he lives yet in the diocese of Strasburg.

Similarly in the diocese of Basel, in the village called Buchel, near the town of Gewyll, this happened. A certain woman was taken, and finally burned, who for six years had had an Incubus devil, even when she was lying in bed by the side of her husband. And this she did three times a week, on Sundays, Tuesdays, and Thursdays, and on some of the other more holy nights.* But the homage she had given to the devil was of such a sort that she was bound to dedicate herself body and soul to him for ever, after seven years. But God provided mercifully: for she was taken in the sixth year and condemned to the fire, and having truly and completely confessed, is believed to have obtained pardon from God. For she went most willingly to her death, saying that she would gladly suffer an even more terrible death, if only she could be set free from and escape the power of the devil.

☆

CHAPTER III

How they are Transported from Place to Place.

AND now we must consider their ceremonies and in what manner they proceed in their operations, first in respect of their actions towards themselves and in their own persons. And among their chief operations are being bodily transported from place to place, and to practise carnal connexion with Incubus devils, which we shall treat of separately, beginning with their

bodily vectitation. But here it must be noted that this transvection offers a difficulty, which has often been mentioned, arising from one single authority, where it is said: It cannot be admitted as true that certain wicked women, perverted by Satan and seduced by the illusions and phantasms of devils, do actually, as they believe and profess, ride in the night-time on certain beasts with Diana, a goddess of the Pagans, or with Herodias and an innumerable multitude of women, and in the untimely silence of night pass over immense tracts of land, and have to obey her in all things as their Mistress, etc. Wherefore the priests of God ought to preach to the people that this is altogether false, and that such phantasms are sent not by God, but by an evil Spirit to confuse the minds of the faithful. For Satan himself transforms himself into various shapes and forms; and by deluding in dreams the mind which he holds captive, leads it through devious ways, etc.

And there are those who, taking their example from S. Germain and a certain other man who kept watch over his daughter to determine this matter, sometimes preach that this is an altogether impossible thing; and that it is indiscreet to ascribe to witches and their operations such levitations, as well as the injuries which happen to men, animals, and the fruits of the earth; since just as they are the victims of phantasy in their transvections, so also are they deluded in the matter of the harm they wreak on living creatures.

But this opinion was refuted as heretical in the First Question; for it leaves out of account the Divine permission with regard to the devil's power, which extends to even greater things than this: and it is contrary to the meaning of Sacred Scripture, and has caused intolerable damage to Holy Church, since now for many years, thanks to this pestiferous doctrine, witches have remained unpunished, because the secular courts have lost their power to punish them. Therefore the diligent reader will consider what was there set down for the stamping out of that opinion, and will for the present note how they are transported, and in what ways this is possible, of which some examples will be adduced.

It is shown in various ways that they can be bodily transported; and first,

---

* "Holy Nights." Saturday, however, was always particularly avoided as being the day sacred to the Immaculate Mother of God. See my "History of Witchcraft," c. IV, pp. 115-16.

from the operations of other Magicians. For if they could not be transported, it would either be because God does not permit it, or because the devil cannot do this since it is contrary to nature. It cannot be for the first reason, for both greater and less things can be done by the permission of God; and greater things are very often done both to children and men, even to just men confirmed in grace.

For when it is asked whether substitutions of children can be effected by the work of devils, and whether the devil can carry a man from place to place even against his will; to the first question the answer is, Yes. For William of Paris says in the last part of his *De Uniuerso:* Substitutions of children are, with God's permission, possible, so that the devil can effect a change of the child or even a transformation. For such children are always miserable and crying; and although four or five mothers could hardly supply enough milk for them, they never grow fat, yet are heavy beyond the ordinary. But this should neither be affirmed nor denied to women, on account of the great fear which it may cause them, but they should be instructed to ask the opinion of learned men. For God permits this on account of the sins of the parents, in that sometimes men curse their pregnant wives, saying, May you be carrying a devil! or some such thing. In the same way impatient women often say something of the sort. And many examples have been given by other men, some of them pious men.

For Vincent of Beauvais (*Spec. Hist.*, XXVI, 43) relates a story told by S. Peter Damian* of a five-year-old son of a nobleman, who was for the time living in a monastery; and one night he was carried out of the monastery into a locked mill, where he was found in the morning. And when he was questioned, he said that he had been carried by some men to a great feast and bidden to eat; and afterwards he was put into the mill, through the roof.

And what of those Magicians whom we generally call Necromancers, who

are often carried through the air by devils for long distances? And sometimes they even persuade others to go with them on a horse, which is not really a horse but a devil in that form, and, as they say, thus warn their companions not to make the sign of the Cross.

And though we are two who write this book, one of us has very often seen and known such men. For there is a man who was once a scholar, and is now believed to be a priest in the diocese of Freising, who used to say that at one time he had been bodily carried through the air by a devil, and taken to the most remote parts.

There lives another priest in Oberdorf, a town near Landshut, who was at that time a friend of that one of us, who saw with his own eyes such a transportation, and tells how the man was borne on high with arms stretched out, shouting but not whimpering. And the cause, as he tells it, was as follows. A number of scholars had met together to drink beer, and they all agreed that the one who fetched the beer should not have to pay anything. And so one of them was going to fetch the beer, and on opening the door saw a thick cloud before the grunsel, and returning in terror told his companions why he would not go for the drink. Then that one of them who was carried away said angrily: "Even if the devil were there, I shall fetch the drink." And, going out, he was carried through the air in the sight of all the others.

And indeed it must be confessed that such things can happen not only to those who are awake, but also to men who are asleep; namely, they can be bodily transported through the air while they are fast asleep.

This is clear in the case of certain men who walk in their sleep on the roofs of houses and over the highest buildings, and no one can oppose their progress either on high or below. And if they are called by their own names by the other bystanders, they immediately fall crashing to the ground.

Many think, and not without reason, that this is devils' work. For devils are of many different kinds, and some, who fell from the lower choir of Angels, are tortured as if for smaller sins with lighter punishments as well as the punishment of damnation which they must suffer eternally. And these cannot hurt anybody, at least not seri-

---

* "*S. Peter Damian.*" *Doctor of the Church, Cardinal-Bishop of Ostia, born at Ravenna 1007; died at Faenza, 21 February, 1072. His works, which have been more than once collected, may be conveniently found in Migne, "Patres Latini," CXLIV–CXLV.*

ously, but for the most part carry out only practical jokes. And others are Incubi or Succubi, who punish men in the night, defiling them in the sin of lechery. It is not wonderful if they are given also to horse-play such as this.

The truth can be deduced from the words of Cassian, *Collationes* I, where he says that there is no doubt that there are as many different unclean spirits as there are different desires in men. For it is manifest that some of them, which the common people call Fauns, and we call Trolls, which abound in Norway, are such buffoons and jokers that they haunt certain places and roads and, without being able to do any hurt to those who pass by, are content with mocking and deluding them, and try to weary them rather than hurt them. And some of them only visit men with harmless nightmares. But others are so furious and truculent that they are not content to afflict with an atrocious dilation the bodies of those whom they inflate, but even come rushing from on high and hasten to strike them with the most savage blows. Our author means that they do not only possess men, but torture them horribly, as did those which are described in *S. Matthew* viii.

From this we can conclude, first that it must not be said that witches cannot be locally transported because God does not permit it. For if He permits it in the case of the just and innocent, and of other Magicians, how should He not in the case of those who are totally dedicated to the devil? And we say with all reverence: Did not the devil take our Saviour, and carry Him up to a high place, as the Gospel testifies?

Neither can the second argument of our opponents be conceded, that the devil cannot do this thing. For it has already been shown that he has so great natural power, exceeding all corporeal power, that there is no earthly power that can be compared with him; as it is said: "There is no power on earth that can be compared with him," etc. Indeed the natural power or virtue which is in Lucifer is so great that there is none greater among the good Angels in Heaven. For just as he excelled all the Angels in his nature, and not his nature, but only his grace, was diminished by his Fall, so that nature still remains in him, although it is darkened and bound. Wherefore the gloss on that "There is no power on earth" says:

Although he excels all things, yet he is subject to the merits of the Saints.

Two objections which someone may bring forward are not valid. First, that man's soul could resist him, and that the text seems to speak of one devil in particular, since it speaks in the singular, namely Lucifer. And because it was he who tempted Christ in the wilderness, and seduced the first man, he is now bound in chains. And the other Angels are not so powerful, since he excels them all. Therefore the other spirits cannot transport wicked men through the air from place to place.

These arguments have no force. For, to consider the Angels first, even the least Angel is incomparably superior to all human power, as can be proved in many ways. First, a spiritual is stronger than a corporeal power, and so is the power of an Angel, or even of the soul, greater than that of the body. Secondly, as to the soul; every bodily shape owes its individuality to matter, and, in the case of human beings, to the fact that a soul informs it; but immaterial forms are absolute intelligences, and therefore have an absolute and more universal power. For this reason, the soul when joined to the body cannot in this way suddenly transfer its body locally or raise it up in the air; although it could easily do so, with God's permission, if it were separate from its body. Much more, then, is this possible to an entirely immaterial spirit, such as a good or bad Angel. For a good Angel transported Habacuc* in a moment from Judaea

---

* "*Habacuc.*" "*Daniel*" xiv, 32–38: 32. *Now there was in Judea a prophet called Habacuc, and he had boiled pottage, and had broken bread in a bowl: and was going into the field, to carry it to the reapers.*

33. *And the angel of the Lord said to Habacuc: Carry the dinner which thou hast into Babylon to Daniel, who is in the lions' den.*

34. *And Habacuc said: Lord, I never saw Babylon, nor do I know the den.*

35. *And the angel of the Lord took him by the top of his head, and carried him by the hair on his head, and set him in Babylon over the den in the force of his spirit.*

36. *And Habacuc cried, saying: O Daniel, thou servant of God, take the dinner that God hath sent thee.*

37. *And Daniel said: Thou hast remembered me, O God, and thou hast not forsaken them that love thee.*

38. *And Daniel arose and ate. And the angel of the Lord presently set Habacuc again in his own place.*

to Chaldaea. And for this reason it is concluded that those who by night are carried in their sleep over high buildings are not carried by their own souls, nor by the influence of the stars, but by some mightier power, as was shown above.

Thirdly, it is the nature of the body to be moved, as to place, directly by a spiritual nature; and, as Aristotle says, *Physics*, VIII, local motion is the first of motions, being the most perfect of all bodily motions; and he proves this by saying that local motion is not intrinsically in the power of any body as such, but is due to some exterior force.

Wherefore it is concluded, not so much from the holy Doctors as from the Philosophers, that the highest bodies, that is, the stars, are moved by spiritual essences, and by separate Intelligences which are good both by nature and in intention. For we see that the soul is the prime and chief cause of local motion in the body.

It must be said, therefore, that neither in its physical capacity nor in that of its soul can the human body resist being suddenly transported from place to place, with God's permission, by a spiritual essence good both in intention and by nature, when the good, who are confirmed in grace, are transported; or by an essence good by nature, but not good in intention, when the wicked are transported. Any who wish may refer to S. Thomas in three articles in Part I, question 90, and again in his question concerning Sin, and also in the *Second Book of Sentences*, dist. 7, on the power of devils over bodily effects.

Now the following is their method of being transported. They take the unguent* which, as we have said, they make at the devil's instruction from the limbs of children, particularly of those whom they have killed before baptism, and anoint with it a chair or a broomstick; whereupon they are immediately carried up into the air, either by day or by night, and either visibly or, if they wish, invisibly; for the devil can conceal a body by the interposition of some other substance, as was shown in the First Part of the treatise where we spoke of the glamours and illusions caused by the devil. And although the devil for the most part performs this by means of this unguent, to the end that children should be deprived of the grace of baptism and of salvation, yet he often seems to effect the same transvection without its use. For at times he transports the witches on animals, which are not true animals but devils in that form; and sometimes even without any exterior help they are visibly carried solely by the operation of the devil's power.

Here is an instance of a visible transvection in the day-time. In the town of Waldshut on the Rhine, in the diocese of Constance, there was a certain witch who was so detested by the townsfolk that she was not invited to the celebration of a wedding at which, however, nearly all the other townsfolk were present. Being indignant because of this, and wishing to be revenged, she summoned a devil and, telling him the cause of her vexation, asked him to raise a hailstorm and drive all the wedding guests from their dancing; and the devil agreed, and raising her up, carried her through the air to a hill near the town, in the sight of some shepherds. And since, as she afterwards confessed, she had no water to pour into the trench (for this, as we shall show, is the method they use to raise hailstorms), she made a small trench and filled it with her urine instead of water, and stirred it with her finger, after their custom, with the devil standing by. Then the devil suddenly raised that liquid up and sent a violent storm of hailstones which fell only on the dancers and townsfolk. And when they had dispersed and were discussing among themselves the cause of that storm, the witch shortly afterwards entered the town; and this greatly aroused their suspicions. But when the shepherds had told what they had seen, their suspicions became almost a certainty. So she was arrested, and confessed that she had done this thing because she had not been invited to the wedding: and for this, and for many other witchcrafts which she had perpetrated, she was burned.

And since the public report of this sort of transvection is continually being

---

* *Henry Boguet, "Discours des Sorciers," Lyons, 1590, XVI, 4, points out that this flying ointment is of itself useless. The actual formulae for its confection have been preserved and the employment thereof is to be considered, say most demonologists, as a piece of vain and empty ceremony of Satan, yet more to delude his votaries.*

spread even among the common people, it is unnecessary to add further proof of it here. But we hope that this will suffice to refute those who either deny altogether that there are such transvections, or try to maintain that they are only imaginary or phantastical. And, indeed, it would be a matter of small importance if such men were left in their error, were it not that this error tends to the damage of the Faith. For notice that, not content with that error, they do not fear to maintain and publish others also, to the increase of witches and the detriment of the Faith. For they assert that all the witchcraft which is truly and actually ascribed to witches as instruments of the devil is only so ascribed in imagination and illusion, as if they were really harmless, just as their transvection is only phantastic. And for this reason many witches remain unpunished, to the great dispraise of the Creator, and to their own most heavy increase.

The arguments on which they base their fallacy cannot be conceded. For first they advance the chapter of the Canon (*Episcopi*, 26, q. 5), where it is said that witches are only transported in imagination; but who is so foolish as to conclude from this that they cannot also be bodily transported? Similarly at the end of that chapter it is set down that whoever believes that a man can be changed for the better or the worse, or can be transformed into another shape, is to be thought worse than an infidel or a pagan; but who could conclude from this that men cannot be transformed into beasts by a glamour, or that they cannot be changed from health to sickness and from better to worse? They who so scratch at the surface of the words of the Canon hold an opinion which is contrary to that of all the holy Doctors, and, indeed, against the teaching of Holy Scripture.

For the contrary opinion is abundantly proved by what has been written in various places in the First Part of this treatise; and it is necessary to study the inner meaning of the words of the Canon. And this was examined in the First Question of the First Part of the treatise, in refuting the second of three errors which are there condemned, and where it is said that four things are to be preached to the people. For they are transported both bodily and phantastically, as is proved by their

own confessions, not only of those who have been burned, but also of others who have returned to penitence and the Faith.

Among such there was the woman in the town of Breisach whom we asked whether they could be transported only in imagination, or actually in the body; and she answered that it was possible in both ways. For if they do not wish to be bodily transferred, but want to know all that is being done in a meeting of their companions, then they observe the following procedure. In the name of all the devils they lie down to sleep on their left side, and then a sort of bluish vapour comes from their mouth, through which they can clearly see what is happening. But if they wish to be bodily transported, they must observe the method which has been told.

Besides, even if that Canon be understood in its bare meaning without any explanation, who is so dense as to maintain on that account that all their witchcraft and injuries are phantastic and imaginary, when the contrary is evident to the senses of everybody? Especially since there are many species of superstition, namely, fourteen; among which the species of witches holds the highest degree in spells and injuries, and the species of Pythonesses, to which they can be reduced, which is only able to be transported in imagination, holds the lowest degree.

And we do not concede that their error can be substantiated by the Legends of S. Germain* and certain others. For it was possible for the devils to lie down themselves by the side of the sleeping husbands, during the time when a watch was being kept on the wives, just as if they were sleeping with their husbands. And we do not say that this was done for any reverence felt for the Saint; but the case is put that the opposite of what is set down in the Legend may not be believed to be impossible.

In the same way all other objections can be answered: that it is found that some witches are transported only in imagination, but that it is also found in the writings of the Doctors that many

---

* "*S. Germain.*" *Bishop of Auxerre, born circa 380; died at Ravenna, 31 July, 448. His body was brought back to Auxerre, and later there arose the celebrated Benedictine Abbey known as St. Germain's.*

have been bodily transported. Whoever wishes may refer to Thomas of
Brabant in his book about *Bees*, and he
will find many wonderful things concerning both the imaginary and the
bodily transvection of men.

☆

CHAPTER IV

Here follows the Way whereby Witches
copulate with those Devils known as
Incubi.

AS to the method in which witches
copulate with Incubus devils, six
points are to be noted. First, as to the
devil and the body which he assumes,
of what element it is formed. Second,
as to the act, whether it is always accompanied with the injection of semen received from some other man. Third, as
to the time and place, whether one time
is more favourable than another for this
practice. Fourth, whether the act is
visible to the women, and whether only
those who were begotten in this way are
so visited by devils. Fifth, whether it
applies only to those who were offered
to the devil at birth by midwives. Sixth,
whether the actual venereal pleasure is
greater or less in this act. And we will
speak first of the matter and quality of
the body which the devil assumes.

It must be said that he assumes an
aerial body, and that it is in some
respects terrestrial, in so far as it has an
earthly property through condensation;
and this is explained as follows. The air
cannot of itself take definite shape, except the shape of some other body in
which it is included. And in that case
it is not bound by its own limits, but by
those of something else; and one part
of the air continues into the next part.
Therefore he cannot simply assume an
aerial body as such.

Know, moreover, that the air is in
every way a most changeable and fluid
matter: and a sign of this is the fact that
when any have tried to cut or pierce
with a sword the body assumed by a
devil, they have not been able to; for
the divided parts of the air at once join
together again. From this it follows
that air is in itself a very competent
matter, but because it cannot take shape
unless some other terrestrial matter is
joined with it, therefore it is necessary
that the air which forms the devil's

assumed body should be in some way
inspissated, and approach the property
of the earth, while still retaining its true
property as air. And devils and disembodied spirits can effect this condensation by means of gross vapours
raised from the earth, and by collecting
them together into shapes in which they
abide, not as defilers of them, but only
as their motive power which gives to
that body the formal appearance of life,
in very much the same way as the soul
informs the body to which it is joined.
They are, moreover, in these assumed
and shaped bodies like a sailor in a ship
which the wind moves.

So when it is asked of what sort is the
body assumed by the devil, it is to be
said that with regard to its material, it
is one thing to speak of the beginning of
its assumption, and another thing to
speak of its end. For in the beginning
it is just air; but in the end it is inspissated air, partaking of some of the
properties of earth. And all this the
devils, with God's permission, can do
of their own nature; for the spiritual
nature is superior to the bodily. Therefore the bodily nature must obey the
devils in respect of local motion, though
not in respect of the assumption of
natural shapes, either accidental or substantial, except in the case of some small
creatures (and then only with the help
of some other agent, as has been hinted
before). But as to local motion, no
shape is beyond their power; thus they
can move them as they wish, in such
circumstances as they will.

From this there may arise an incidental question as to what should be
thought when a good or bad Angel performs some of the functions of life by
means of true natural bodies, and not in
aerial bodies; as in the case of Balaam's
ass, through which the Angel spoke,
and when devils take possession of
bodies. It is to be said that those bodies
are not called assumed, but occupied.
See S. Thomas, II. 8, Whether Angels
assume bodies. But let us keep strictly
to our argument.

In what way is it to be understood
that devils talk with witches, see them,
hear them, eat with them, and copulate
with them? And this is the second part
of this first difficulty.

For the first, it is to be said that three
things are required for true conversation: namely, lungs to draw in the air;
and this is not only for the sake of pro-

ducing sound, but also to cool the heart; and even mutes have this necessary quality.

Secondly, it is necessary that some percussion be made of a body in the air, as a greater or less sound is made when one beats wood in the air, or rings a bell. For when a substance that is susceptible to sound is struck by a sound-producing instrument, it gives out a sound according to its size, which is received in the air and multiplied to the ears of the hearer, to whom, if he is far off, it seems to come through space.

Thirdly, a voice is required; and it may be said that what is called Sound in inanimate bodies is called Voice in living bodies. And here the tongue strikes the respirations of air against an instrument or living natural organ provided by God. And this is not a bell, which is called a sound, whereas this is a voice. And this third requisite may clearly be exemplified by the second; and I have set this down that preachers may have a method of teaching the people.

And fourthly, it is necessary that he who forms the voice should mean to express by means of that voice some concept of the mind to someone else, and that he should himself understand what he is saying; and so manage his voice by successively striking his teeth with his tongue in his mouth, by opening and shutting his lips, and by sending the air struck in his mouth into the outer air, that in this way the sound is reproduced in order in the ears of the hearer, who then understands his meaning.

To return to the point. Devils have no lungs or tongue, though they can show the latter, as well as teeth and lips, artificially made according to the condition of their body; therefore they cannot truly and properly speak. But since they have understanding, and when they wish to express their meaning, then, by some disturbance of the air included in their assumed body, not of air breathed in and out as in the case of men, they produce, not voices, but sounds which have some likeness to voices, and send them articulately through the outside air to the ears of the hearer. And that the likeness of a voice can be made without the respiration of air is clear from the case of other animals which do not breathe, but are said to make a sound, as do also

certain other instruments, as Aristotle says in the *de Anima*. For certain fishes, when they are caught, suddenly utter a cry outside the water, and die.

All this is applicable to what follows, so far as the point where we treat of the generative function, but not as regards good Angels. If anyone wishes to inquire further into the matter of devils speaking in possessed bodies, he may refer to S. Thomas in the *Second Book of Sentences*, dist. 8, art. 5. For in that case they use the bodily organs of the possessed body; since they occupy those bodies in respect of the limits of their corporeal quantity, but not in respect of the limits of their essence, either of the body or of the soul. Observe a distinction between substance and quantity, or accident. But this is impertinent.

For now we must say in what manner they see and hear. Now sight is of two kinds, spiritual and corporeal, and the former infinitely excels the latter; for it can penetrate, and is not hindered by distance, owing to the faculty of light of which it makes use. Therefore it must be said that in no way does an Angel, either good or bad, see with the eyes of its assumed body, nor does it use any bodily property as it does in speaking, when it uses the air and the vibration of the air to produce sound which becomes reproduced in the ears of the hearer. Wherefore their eyes are painted eyes. And they freely appear to men in these likenesses that they may manifest to them their natural properties and converse with them spiritually by these means.

For with this purpose the holy Angels have often appeared to the Fathers at the command of God and with His permission. And the bad angels manifest themselves to wicked men in order that men, recognizing their qualities, may associate themselves with them, here in sin, and elsewhere in punishment.

S. Dionysius, at the end of his *Celestial Hierarchy*, says: In all parts of the human body the Angel teaches us to consider their properties: concluding that since corporeal vision is an operation of the living body through a bodily organ, which devils lack, therefore in their assumed bodies, just as they have the likeness of limbs, so they have the likeness of their functions.

And we can speak in the same way of their hearing, which is far finer than that of the body; for it can know the concept of the mind and the conversation of the soul more subtly than can a man by hearing the mental concept through the medium of spoken words. See S. Thomas, the *Second Book of Sentences*, dist. 8. For if the secret wishes of a man are read in his face, and physicians can tell the thoughts of the heart from the heart-beats and the state of the pulse, all the more can such things be known by devils.

And we may say as to eating, that in the complete act of eating there are four processes. Mastication in the mouth, swallowing into the stomach, digestion in the stomach, and fourthly, metabolism of the necessary nutriment and ejection of what is superfluous. All Angels can perform the first two processes of eating in their assumed bodies, but not the third and fourth; but instead of digesting and ejecting they have another power by which the food is suddenly dissolved in the surrounding matter. In Christ the process of eating was in all respects complete, since He had the nutritive and metabolistic powers; not, be it said, for the purpose of converting the food into His own body, for those powers were, like His body, glorified; so that the food was suddenly dissolved in His body, as when one throws water on to fire.

How in Modern Times Witches perform the Carnal Act with Incubus Devils, and how they are Multiplied by this Means.

But no difficulty arises out of what has been said, with regard to our principal subject, which is the carnal act which Incubi in an assumed body perform with witches: unless perhaps anyone doubts whether modern witches practise such abominable coitus; and whether witches had their origin in this abomination.

In answering these two doubts we shall say, as to the former of them, something of the activities of the witches who lived in olden times, about 1400 years before the Incarnation of Our Lord. It is, for example, unknown whether they were addicted to these filthy practices as modern witches have been since that time; for so far as we know history tells us nothing on this subject. But no one who reads the histories can doubt that there have always been witches, and that by their evil works much harm has been done to

men, animals, and the fruits of the earth, and that Incubus and Succubus devils have always existed; for the traditions of the Canons and the holy Doctors have left and handed down to posterity many things concerning them through many hundreds of years. Yet there is this difference, that in times long past the Incubus devils used to infest women against their wills, as is often shown by Nider in his *Formicarius*, and by Thomas of Brabant in his book on the *Universal Good*, or on *Bees*.

But the theory that modern witches are tainted with this sort of diabolic filthiness is not substantiated only in our opinion, since the expert testimony of the witches themselves has made all these things credible; and that they do not now, as in times past, subject themselves unwillingly, but willingly embrace this most foul and miserable servitude. For how many women have we left to be punished by secular law in various dioceses, especially in Constance and the town of Ratisbon, who have been for many years addicted to these abominations, some from their twentieth and some from their twelfth or thirteenth year, and always with a total or partial abnegation of the Faith? All the inhabitants of those places are witnesses of it. For without reckoning those who secretly repented, and those who returned to the Faith, no less than forty-eight have been burned in five years. And there was no question of credulity in accepting their stories because they turned to free repentance; for they all agreed in this, namely, that they were bound to indulge in these lewd practices in order that the ranks of their perfidy might be increased. But we shall treat of these individually in the Second Part of this work, where their particular deeds are described; omitting those which came under the notice of our colleague the Inquisitor of Como in the County of Burbia, who in the space of one year, which was the year of grace 1485, caused forty-one witches to be burned; who all publicly affirmed, as it is said, that they had practised these abominations with devils. Therefore this matter is fully substantiated by eye-witnesses, by hearsay, and the testimony of credible witnesses.

As for the second doubt, whether witches had their origin from these abominations, we may say with S. Augustine that it is true that all the superstitious arts had their origin in a pestilent association of men with devils. For he says so in his work *On the Christian Doctrine:* All this sort of practices, whether of trifling or of noxious superstition, arose from some pestilent association of men with devils, as though some pact of infidel and guileful friendship had been formed, and they are all utterly to be repudiated. Notice here that it is manifest that, as there are various kinds of superstition or magic arts, and various societies of those who practise them; and as among the fourteen kinds of that art the species of witches is the worst, since they have not a tacit but an overt and expressed pact with the devil, and more than this, have to acknowledge a form of devil-worship through abjuring the Faith; therefore it follows that witches hold the worst kind of association with devils, with especial reference to the behaviour of women, who always delight in vain things.

Notice also S. Thomas, the *Second Book of Sentences* (dist. 4, art. 4), in the solution of an argument, where he asks whether those begotten in this way by devils are more powerful than other men. He answers that this is the truth, basing his belief not only on the text of Scripture in *Genesis* vi: And the same became the mighty men which were of old; but also on the following reason. Devils know how to ascertain the virtue in semen: first, by the temperament of him from whom the semen is obtained; secondly, by knowing what woman is most fitted for the reception of that semen; thirdly, by knowing what constellation is favourable to that corporeal effect; and we may add, fourthly, from their own words we learn that those whom they beget have the best sort of disposition for devils' work. When all these causes so concur, it is concluded that men born in this way are powerful and big in body.

Therefore, to return to the question whether witches had their origin in these abominations, we shall say that they originated from some pestilent mutual association with devils, as is clear from our first knowledge of them. But no one can affirm with certainty that they did not increase and multiply by means of these fouls practices, althoug devils commit this deed for the

sake not of pleasure but of corruption. And this appears to be the order of the process. A Succubus devil draws the semen from a wicked man; and if he is that man's own particular devil, and does not wish to make himself an Incubus to a witch, he passes that semen on to the devil deputed to a woman or witch; and this last, under some constellation that favours his purpose that the man or woman so born should be strong in the practice of witchcraft, becomes the Incubus to the witch.

And it is no objection that those of whom the text speaks were not witches but only giants and famous and powerful men; for, as was said before, witchcraft was not perpetrated in the time of the law of Nature, because of the recent memory of the Creation of the world, which left no room for Idolatry. But when the wickedness of man began to increase, the devil found more opportunity to disseminate this kind of perfidy. Nevertheless, it is not to be understood that those who were said to be famous men were necessarily so called by reason of their good virtues.

Whether the Relations of an Incubus Devil with a Witch are always accompanied by the Injection of Semen.

To this question it is answered that the devil has a thousand ways and means of inflicting injury, and from the time of his first Fall has tried to destroy the unity of the Church, and in every way to subvert the human race. Therefore no infallible rule can be stated as to this matter, but there is this probable distinction: that a witch is either old and sterile, or she is not. And if she is, then he naturally associates with the witch without the injection of semen, since it would be of no use, and the devil avoids superfluity in his operations as far as he can. But if she is not sterile, he approaches her in the way of carnal delectation which is procured for the witch. And should she be disposed to pregnancy, then if he can conveniently possess the semen extracted from some man, he does not delay to approach her with it for the sake of infecting her progeny.

But if it is asked whether he is able to collect the semen emitted in some nocturnal pollution in sleep, just as he collects that which is spent in the carnal act, the answer is that it is probable that he cannot, though others hold a contrary opinion. For it must be noted that, as has been said, the devils pay attention to the generative virtue of the semen, and such virtue is more abundant and better preserved in semen obtained by the carnal act, being wasted in the semen that is due to nocturnal pollutions in sleep, which arises only from the superfluity of the humours and is not emitted with so great generative virtue. Therefore it is believed that he does not make use of such semen for the generation of progeny, unless perhaps he knows that the necessary virtue is present in that semen.

But this also cannot altogether be denied, that even in the case of a married witch who has been impregnated by her husband, the devil can, by the commixture of another semen, infect that which has been conceived.

Whether the Incubus operates more at one Time than another: and similarly of the Place.

To the question whether the devil observes times and places it is to be said that, apart from his observation of certain times and constellations when his purpose is to effect the pollution of the progeny, he also observes certain times when his object is not pollution, but the causing of venereal pleasure on the part of the witch; and these are the most sacred times of the whole year, such as Christmas, Easter, Pentecost, and other Feast Days.

And the devils do this for three reasons. First, that in this way witches may become imbued not only with the vice of perfidy through apostasy from the Faith, but also with that of Sacrilege, and that the greater offence may be done to the Creator, and the heavier damnation rest upon the souls of the witches.

The second reason is that when God is so heavily offended, He allows them greater power of injuring even innocent men by punishing them either in their affairs or their bodies. For when it is said: "The son shall not bear the iniquity of the father," etc., this refers only to eternal punishment, for very often the innocent are punished with temporal afflictions on account of the sins of others. Wherefore in another place God says: "I am a mighty and jealous God, visiting the sins of the fathers unto the third and fourth generation."* Such punishment was exemplified in the children of the men of Sodom, who were destroyed for their fathers' sins.

The third reason is that they have greater opportunity to observe many people, especially young girls, who on Feast Days are more intent on idleness and curiosity, and are therefore more easily seduced by old witches. And the following happened in the native country of one of us Inquisitors (for there are two of us collaborating in this work).

A certain young girl, a devout virgin, was solicited one Feast Day by an old woman to go with her upstairs to a room where there were some very beautiful young men. And when she consented, and as they were going upstairs with the old woman leading the way, she warned the girl not to make the sign of the Cross. And though she agreed to this, yet she secretly crossed herself. Consequently it happened that, when they had gone up, the virgin saw no one, because the devils who were there were unable to show themselves in assumed bodies to that virgin. And the old woman cursed her, saying: Depart in the name of all the devils; why did you cross yourself? This I had from the frank relation of that good and honest maiden.

A fourth reason can be added, namely, that they can in this way more easily seduce men, by causing them to think that if God permits such things to be done at the most holy times, it cannot be such a heavy sin as if He did not permit them at such times.

With regard to the question whether they favour one place more than another, it is to be said that it is proved by the words and actions of witches that they are quite unable to commit these abominations in sacred places. And in this can be seen the efficacy of the Guardian Angels, that such places are reverenced. And further, witches assert that they never have any peace except at the time of Divine Service when they are present in the church; and therefore they are the first to enter and the last to leave the church. Nevertheless, they are bound to observe cer-

---

* "*Generation.*" "*Exodus*" xx, 5: xxxiv, 7.

tain other abominable ceremonies at the command of the devils, such as to spit on the ground at the Elevation of the Host, or to utter, either verbally or otherwise, the filthiest thoughts, as: I wish you were in such or such a place. This matter is touched upon in the Second Part.

Whether Incubi and Succubi Commit this Act Visibly on the part of the Witch, or on the part of Bystanders.

As to whether they commit these abominations together visibly or invisibly, it is to be said that, in all the cases of which we have had knowledge, the devil has always operated in a form visible to the witch; for there is no need for him to approach her invisibly, because of the pact of federation with him that has been expressed. But with regard to any bystanders, the witches themselves have often been seen lying on their backs in the fields or the woods, naked up to the very navel, and it has been apparent from the disposition of those limbs and members which pertain to the venereal act and orgasm, as also from the agitation of their legs and thighs, that, all invisibly to the bystanders, they have been copulating with Incubus devils; yet sometimes, howbeit this is rare, at the end of the act a very black vapour, of about the stature of a man, rises up into the air from the witch. And the reason is that that Schemer knows that he can in this way seduce or pervert the minds of girls or other men who are standing by. But of these matters, and how they have been performed in many places, in the town of Ratisbon and on the estate of the nobles of Rappolstein, and in certain other countries, we will treat in the Second Part.

It is certain also that the following has happened. Husbands have actually seen Incubus devils swiving their wives, although they have thought that they were not devils but men. And when they have taken up a weapon and tried to run them through, the devil has suddenly disappeared, making himself invisible. And then their wives have thrown their arms about them, although they have sometimes been hurt, and railed at their husbands, mocking them, and asking them if they had eyes, or whether they were possessed of devils.

That Incubus Devils do not Infest only those Women who have been Begotten by their Filthy Deeds or those who have been Offered to them by Midwives, but All Indifferently with Greater or Less Venereal Delectation.

In conclusion, finally, it can be said that these Incubus devils will not only infest those women who have been generated by means of such abominations, or those who have been offered to them by midwives, but that they try with all their might, by means of witches who are bawds or hot whores, to seduce all the devout and chaste maidens in that whole district or town. For this is well known by the constant experience of Magistrates; and in the town of Ratisbon, when certain witches were burned, these wretches affirmed, before their final sentence, that they had been commanded by their Masters to use every endeavour to effect the subversion of pious maids and widows.

If it be asked: Whether the venereal delectation is greater or less with Incubus devils in assumed bodies than it is in like circumstances with men in a true physical body, we may say this: It seems that, although the pleasure should naturally be greater when like disports with like, yet that cunning Enemy can so bring together the active and passive elements, not indeed naturally, but in such qualities of warmth and temperament, that he seems to excite no less degree of concupiscence. But this matter will be discussed more fully later with reference to the qualities of the feminine sex.

☆

CHAPTER V

Witches commonly perform their Spells through the Sacraments of the Church. And how they Impair the Powers of Generation, and how they may Cause other Ills to happen to God's Creatures of all kinds. But herein we except the Question of the Influence of the Stars.

BUT now there are several things to be noted concerning their methods of bringing injury upon other creatures of both sexes, and upon the fruits of the earth: first with regard to men, then with regard to beasts, and thirdly with regard to the fruits of the earth. And as to men, first, how they can cast an obstructive spell on the procreant forces, and even on the venereal act, so that a woman cannot conceive, or a man cannot perform the act. Secondly, how that act is obstructed sometimes with regard to one woman but not another. Thirdly, how they take away the virile member as though it were altogether torn away from the body. Fourthly, if it is possible to distinguish whether any of the above injuries have been caused by a devil on his own account, or if it has been through the agency of a witch. Fifthly, how witches change men and women into beasts by some prestige or glamour. Sixthly, how witch midwives in various ways kill that which has been conceived in the mother's womb; and when they do not do this, offer the children to devils. And lest these things should seem incredible, they have been proved in the First Part of this work by questions and answers to arguments; to which, if necessary, the doubtful reader may turn back for the purpose of investigating the truth.

For the present our object is only to adduce actual facts and examples which have been found by us, or have been written by others in detestation of so great a crime, to substantiate those former arguments in case they should be difficult for anyone to understand; and, by those things that are related in this Second Part, to bring back to the Faith and away from their error those who think there are no witches, and that no witchcraft can be done in the world.

And with regard to the first class of injuries with which they afflict the human race, it is to be noted that, apart from the methods by which they injure other creatures, they have six ways of injuring humanity. And one is, to induce an evil love in a man for a woman, or in a woman for a man. The second is to plant hatred or jealousy in anyone. The third is to bewitch them so that a man cannot perform the genital act with a woman, or conversely a woman with a man; or by various means to procure an abortion, as has been said before. The fourth is to cause some disease in any of the human organs. The fifth, to take away life. The sixth, to deprive them of reason.

In this connexion it should be said that, saving the influence of the stars, the devils can by their natural power in every way cause real defects and infirmities, and this by their natural spiritual power, which is superior to any bodily power. For no one infirmity is quite like another, and this is equally true of natural defects in which there is no physical infirmity. Therefore they proceed by different methods to cause each different infirmity or defect. And of these we shall give instances in the body of this work as the necessity arises.

But first, lest the reader's mind should be kept in any doubt as to why they have no power to alter the influence of the stars, we shall say that there is a threefold reason. First, the stars are above them even in the region of punishment, which is the region of the lower mists; and this by reason of the duty which is assigned to them. See the First Part, Question II, where we dealt with Incubus and Succubus devils.

The second reason is that the stars are governed by the good Angels. See many places concerning the Powers which move the stars, and especially S. Thomas, part 1, quest. 90. And in this matter the Philosophers agree with the Theologians.

Thirdly, it is on account of the general order and common good of the Universe, which would suffer general detriment if evil spirits were allowed to cause any alteration in the influence of the stars. Wherefore those changes which were miraculously caused in the Old or New Testament were done by God through the good Angels; as, for example, when the sun stood still for Joshua, or when it went backward for Hezekiah, or when it was supernaturally darkened at the Passion of Christ. But in all other matters, with God's permission, they can work their spells, either the devils by themselves, or devils through the agency of witches; and, in fact, it is evident that they do so.

Secondly, it is to be noted that in all their methods of working injury they nearly always instruct witches to make their instruments of witchcraft by means of the Sacraments or sacramental things of the Church, or some holy thing consecrated to God: as when they sometimes place a waxen image under the Altar-cloth, or draw a thread through the Holy Chrism, or use some other consecrated thing in such a way. And there are three reasons for this.

For a similar reason they are wont to practise their witchcraft at the more sacred times of the year, especially at the Advent of Our Lord, and at Christmas. First, that by such means they may make men guilty of not only perfidy, but also sacrilege, by contaminating whatever is divine in them; and that so they may the more deeply offend God their Creator, damn their own souls, and cause many more to rush into sin.

Secondly, that God, being so heavily offended by men, may grant the devil greater power of tormenting men. For so says S. Gregory, that in His anger He sometimes grants the wicked their prayers and petitions, which He mercifully denies to others. And the third reason is that, by the seeming appearance of good, he may more easily deceive certain simple men, who think that they have performed some pious act and obtained grace from God, whereas they have only sinned the more heavily.

A fourth reason also can be added touching the more sacred seasons and the New Year. For, according to S. Augustine, there are other mortal sins besides adultery by which the observance of the Festivals may be infringed. Superstition, moreover, and witchcraft arising from the most servile operations of the devil are contrary to the reverence that is due to God. Therefore, as has been said, he causes a man to fall more deeply, and the Creator is the more offended.

And of the New Year we may say, according to S. Isidore, *Etym.* VIII. 2, that Janus, from whom the month of January is named, which also begins on the Day of Circumcision, was an idol with two faces, as if one were the end of the old year and the other the beginning of the new, and, as it were, the protector and auspicious author of the coming year. And in honour of him, or rather of the devil in the form of that idol, the Pagans made much boisterous revelry, and were very merry among themselves, holding various dances and feasts. And concerning these Blessed Augustine makes mention in many places, and gives a very ample description of them in his Twenty-sixth Book.

And now bad Christians imitate these corruptions, turning them to lasciviousness when they run about at the time of Carnival * with masks and jests and other superstitions. Similarly witches use these revelries of the devil for their own advantage, and work their spells about the time of the New Year in respect of the Divine Offices and Worship; as on S. Andrew's Day and at Christmas.

And now, as to how they work their witchcraft, first by means of the Sacraments, and then by means of sacramental objects, we will refer to a few known facts, discovered by us in the Inquisition.

In a town which it is better not to name, for the sake of charity and expediency, when a certain witch received the Body of Our Lord, she suddenly lowered her head, as is the detestable habit of women, placed her garment near her mouth, and taking the Body of the Lord out of her mouth, wrapped it in a handkerchief; and afterwards, at the suggestion of the devil, placed it in a pot in which there was a toad, and hid it in the ground near her house by the storehouse, together with several other things, by means of which she had to work her witchcraft.† But with the help

* *"Carnival." These Pagan practices are sternly reprobated in the "Liber Poenitentialis" of S. Theodore, seventh Archbishop of Canterbury. In Book XXXVII is written: "If anyone at the Kalends of January goeth about as a stag or a bull-calf, that is, making himself into a wild animal, and dressing in the skins of a herd animal, and putting on the heads of beasts; those who in such wise transform themselves into the appearance of a wild animal, let them do penance for three years, because this is devilish." See my "Geography of Witchcraft," Chap. II, pp. 65–73. The Council of Auxerre in 578 (or 585) forbade anyone "to masquerade as a bull-calf or a stag on the first of January or to distribute devilish charms."*

† *"Witchcraft." It is not unusual for Satanists to go to Holy Communion in various churches of a town, and instead of consuming the Host they spit God's Body from their mouths into a handkerchief or cloth and take it away to abuse in their horrid worship. In the notorious case of the Lancashire witches, at the first trial, 1612, James Device confessed "that vpon Sheare Thursday was two yeares, his Grand-Mother Elizabeth Southernes alias Demdike, did bid him this Examinate goe to the Church to receive the Communion (the next day after being Good Friday), and then not to eate the Bread the Minister gave him, but to bring it and deliver it to such a thing as should meet him in his way homewards; Notwithstanding her perswasions*

of God's mercy this great crime was detected and brought to light. For on the following day a workman was going on his business near that house, and heard a sound like a child crying; and when he had come near to the stone under which the pot had been hidden, he heard it much more clearly, and thinking that some child had been buried there by the woman, went to the Mayor or chief magistrate, and told him what had been done, as he thought, by the infanticide. And the Mayor quickly sent his servants and found it to be as he had said. But they were unwilling to exhume the child, thinking it wiser to place a watch and wait to see if any woman came near the place; for they did not know that it was the Lord's Body that was hidden there. And so it happened that the same witch came to the place, and secretly hid the pot under her garment before their eyes. And when she was taken and questioned, she discovered her crime, saying that the Lord's Body had been hidden in the pot with a toad, so that by means of their dust she might be able to cause injuries at her will to men and other creatures.

It is also to be noted that when witches communicate they observe this custom, that, when they can do so without being noticed, they receive the Lord's Body under their tongue instead of on the top. And as far as can be seen, the reason is that they never wish to receive any remedy that might counteract their abjuration of the

Faith, either by Confession or by receiving the Sacrament of the Eucharist; and secondly, because in this way it is easier for them to take the Lord's Body out of their mouths so that they can apply it, as has been said, to their own uses, to the greater offence of the Creator.

For this reason all rectors of the Church and those who communicate the people are enjoined to take the utmost care when they communicate women that the mouth shall be well open and the tongue thrust well out, and their garments be kept quite clear. And the more care is taken in this respect, the more witches become known by this means.

Numberless other superstitions they practise by means of sacramental objects. Sometimes they place a waxen image or some aromatic substance under the altar-cloth,* as we said before, and then hide it under the threshold of a house, so that the person for whom it is placed there may be bewitched on crossing over it. Countless instances could be brought forward, but these minor sorts of spells are proved by the greater.

☆

CHAPTER VI

How Witches Impede and Prevent the Power of Procreation.

CONCERNING the method by which they obstruct the procreant function both in men and animals, and in both sexes, the reader may consult that which has been written already on the question, Whether devils can through witches turn the minds of men to love or hatred. There, after the solutions of the arguments, a specific declaration is made relating to the method by which, with God's permission, they can obstruct the procreant function.

But it must be noted that such obstruction is caused both intrinsically and extrinsically. Intrinsically they cause it in two ways. First, when they directly prevent the erection of the member which is accommodated to fructification. And this need not seem impossible, when it is considered that they are

---

this Examinate did eate the Bread: and so in his comming homeward some fortie roodes off the said Church, there met him a thing in the shape of a Hare, who spoke vnto this Examinate, and asked him whether he had brought the Bread."

The toad constantly appears as a familiar. In 1579 at Windsor "one Mother Dutton dwellyng in Cleworthe Parishe keepeth a Spirite or Feende in the likenesse of a Toade, and fedeth the same Feende liyng in a border of greene Hearbes, within her garden, with blood whiche she causeth to issue from her owne flancke." Ursley Kemp, a S. Osyth witch (1582), had a familiar, Pygine, "black like a Toad." Ales Hunt of the same coven nourished two familiars, "the which she kept in a little lowe earthern pot." Margerie Sammon, another S. Osyth's witch, "hath also two spirites like Toades, the one called 'Tom,' and the other 'Robbyn.' " When Ursley Kemp peeped through Mother Hunt's window she "espied a spirite to looke out of a porcharde from vnder a clothe, the nose thereof being browne like vnto a Ferret."

---

* "Altar-Cloth." These practices still survive.

able to vitiate the natural use of any member. Secondly, when they prevent the flow of the vital essences to the members in which resides the motive force, closing up the seminal ducts so that it does not reach the generative vessels, or so that it cannot be ejaculated, or is fruitlessly spilled.

Extrinsically they cause it at times by means of images, or by the eating of herbs; sometimes by other external means, such as cocks' testicles. But it must not be thought that it is by the virtue of these things that a man is made impotent, but by the occult power of devils' illusions witches by this means procure such impotence, namely, that they cause a man to be unable to copulate, or a woman to conceive.

And the reason for this is that God allows them more power over this act, by which the first sin was disseminated, than over other human actions. Similarly they have more power over serpents, which are the most subject to the influence of incantations, than over other animals. Wherefore it has often been found by us and other Inquisitors that they have caused this obstruction by means of serpents or some such things.

For a certain wizard who had been arrested confessed that for many years he had by witchcraft brought sterility upon all the men and animals which inhabited a certain house. Moreover, Nider tells of a wizard named Stadlin * who was taken in the diocese of Lausanne, and confessed that in a certain house where a man and his wife were living, he had by his witchcraft successively killed in the woman's womb seven children, so that for many years the woman always miscarried. And that, in the same way, he had caused that all the pregnant cattle and animals of the house were during those years unable to give birth to any live issue. And when he was questioned as to how he had done this, and what manner of charge should be preferred against him, he discovered his crime, saying: I put a serpent under the threshold of the outer door of the house; and if this is removed, fecundity will be restored to the inhabitants. And it was as he said; for though the serpent was not found, having been reduced to dust, the whole piece of ground was removed, and in the

same year fecundity was restored to the wife and to all the animals.

Another instance occurred hardly four years ago in Reichshofen. There was a most notorious witch, who could at all times and by a mere touch bewitch women and cause an abortion. Now the wife of a certain nobleman in that place had become pregnant and had engaged a midwife to take care of her, and had been warned by the midwife not to go out of the castle, and above all to be careful not to hold any speech or conversation with that witch. After some weeks, unmindful of that warning, she went out of the castle to visit some women who were met together on some festive occasion; and when she had sat down for a little, the witch came, and, as if for the purpose of saluting her, placed both her hands on her stomach; and suddenly she felt the child moving in pain. Frightened by this, she returned home and told the midwife what had happened. Then the midwife exclaimed: "Alas! you have already lost your child." And so it proved when her time came; for she gave birth, not to an entire abortion, but little by little to separate fragments of its head and feet and hands. And this great affliction was permitted by God to punish her husband, whose duty it was to bring witches to justice and avenge their injuries to the Creator.

And there was in the town of Mersburg in the diocese of Constance a certain young man who was bewitched in such a way that he could never perform the carnal act with any woman except one. And many have heard him tell that he had often wished to refuse that woman, and take flight to other lands; but that hitherto he had been compelled to rise up in the night and to come very quickly back, sometimes over land, and sometimes through the air as if he were flying.

☆

CHAPTER VII

How, as it were, they Deprive Man of his Virile Member.

WE have already shown that they can take away the male organ, not indeed by actually despoiling the human body of it, but by concealing it with some glamour, in the manner which we

---

* "Stadlin." "Formicarius," c. III.

have already declared. And of this we shall instance a few examples.

In the town of Ratisbon a certain young man who had an intrigue with a girl, wishing to leave her, lost his member; that is to say, some glamour was cast over it so that he could see or touch nothing but his smooth body. In his worry over this he went to a tavern to drink wine; and after he had sat there for a while he got into conversation with another woman who was there, and told her the cause of his sadness, explaining everything, and demonstrating in his body that it was so. The woman was astute, and asked whether he suspected anyone; and when he named such a one, unfolding the whole matter, she said: "If persuasion is not enough, you must use some violence, to induce her to restore to you your health." So in the evening the young man watched the way by which the witch was in the habit of going, and finding her, prayed her to restore to him the health of his body. And when she maintained that she was innocent and knew nothing about it, he fell upon her, and winding a towel tightly round her neck, choked her, saying: "Unless you give me back my health, you shall die at my hands." Then she, being unable to cry out, and with her face already swelling and growing black, said: "Let me go, and I will heal you." The young man then relaxed the pressure of the towel, and the witch touched him with her hand between the thighs, saying: "Now you have what you desire." And the young man, as he afterwards said, plainly felt, before he had verified it by looking or touching, that his member had been restored to him by the mere touch of the witch.

A similar experience is narrated by a certain venerable Father from the Dominican House of Spires, well known in the Order for the honesty of his life and for his learning. "One day," he says, "while I was hearing confessions, a young man came to me and, in the course of his confession, woefully said that he had lost his member. Being astonished at this, and not being willing to give it easy credence, since in the opinion of the wise it is a mark of light-heartedness to believe too easily, I obtained proof of it when I saw nothing on the young man's removing his clothes and showing the place. Then, using the wisest counsel I could, I asked whether he sus-

pected anyone of having so bewitched him. And the young man said that he did suspect someone, but that she was absent and living in Worms. Then I said: 'I advise you to go to her as soon as possible and try your utmost to soften her with gentle words and promises'; and he did so. For he came back after a few days and thanked me, saying that he was whole and had recovered everything. And I believed his words, but again proved them by the evidence of my eyes."

But there are some points to be noted for the clearer understanding of what has already been written concerning this matter. First, it must in no way be believed that such members are really torn away from the body, but that they are hidden by the devil through some prestidigitatory art so that they can be neither seen nor felt. And this is proved by the authorities and by argument; although it has been treated of before, where Alexander of Hales says that a Prestige, properly understood, is an illusion of the devil, which is not caused by any material change, but exists only in the perceptions of him who is deluded, either in his interior or exterior senses.

With reference to these words it is to be noted that, in the case we are considering, two of the exterior senses, namely, those of sight and touch, are deluded, and not the interior senses, namely, common-sense, fancy, imagination, thought, and memory. (But S. Thomas says they are only four, as has been told before, reckoning fancy and imagination as one; and with some reason, for there is little difference between imagining and fancying. See S. Thomas, I, 79.) And these senses, and not only the exterior senses, are affected when it is not a case of hiding something, but of causing something to appear to a man either when he is awake or asleep.

As when a man who is awake sees things otherwise than as they are; such as seeing someone devour a horse with its rider, or thinking he sees a man transformed into a beast, or thinking that he is himself a beast and must associate with beasts. For then the exterior senses are deluded and are employed by the interior senses. For by the power of devils, with God's permission, mental images long retained in the treasury of such images, which is the memory, are drawn out, not from the intellectual understanding in which such images are stored, but from the memory, which is the repository of mental images, and is situated at the back of the head, and are presented to the imaginative faculty. And so strongly are they impressed on that faculty that a man has an inevitable impulse to imagine a horse or a beast, when the devil draws from the memory an image of a horse or a beast; and so he is compelled to think that he sees with his external eyes such a beast when there is actually no such beast to see; but it seems to be so by reason of the impulsive force of the devil working by means of those images.

And it need not seem wonderful that devils can do this, when even a natural defect is able to effect the same result, as is shown in the case of frantic and melancholy men, and in maniacs and some drunkards, who are unable to discern truly. For frantic men think they see marvellous things, such as beasts and other horrors, when in actual fact they see nothing. See above, in the question, Whether witches can turn the minds of men to love and hatred; where many things are noted.

And, finally, the reason is self-evident. For since the devil has power over inferior things, except only the soul, therefore he is able to effect certain changes in those things, when God allows, so that things appear to be otherwise than they are. And this he does, as I have said, either by confusing and deluding the organ of sight so that a clear thing appears cloudy: just as after weeping, owing to the collected humours, the light appears different from what it was before. Or by operating on the imaginative faculty by a transmutation of mental images, as has been said. Or by some agitation of various humours, so that matters which are earthy and dry seem to be fire or water: as some people make everyone in the house strip themselves naked under the impression that they are swimming in water.

It may be asked further with reference to the above method of devils, whether this sort of illusions can happen indifferently to the good and to the wicked: just as other bodily infirmities can, as will be shown later, be brought by witches even upon those who are in a state of grace. To this question, following the words of Cassian in his

Second Collation of the Abbot Sirenus, we must answer that they cannot. And from this it follows that all who are deluded in this way are presumed to be in deadly sin. For he says, as is clear from the words of S. Antony: The devil can in no way enter the mind or body of any man, nor has the power to penetrate into the thoughts of anybody, unless such a person has first become destitute of all holy thoughts, and is quite bereft and denuded of spiritual contemplation.

This agrees with Boethius where he says in the *Consolation of Philosophy:* * We had given you such arms that, if you had not thrown them away, you would have been preserved from infirmity.

Also Cassian tells in the same place of two Pagan witches, each in his own way malicious, who by their witchcraft sent a succession of devils into the cell of S. Antony for the purpose of driving him from there by their temptations; being infected with hatred for the holy man because a great number of people visited him every day. And though these devils assailed him with the keenest of spurs to his thoughts, yet he drove them away by crossing himself on the forehead and breast, and by prostrating himself in earnest prayer.

Therefore we may say that all who are so deluded by devils, not reckoning any other bodily infirmities, are lacking in the gift of divine grace. And so it is said in *Tobias* vi: The devil has power against those who are subject to their lusts.

This is also substantiated by what we told in the First Part in the question, Whether witches can change men into the shapes of beasts. For we told of a girl who was turned into a filly, as she herself and, except S. Macharius, all who looked at her were persuaded. But the devil could not deceive the senses of the holy man; and when she was brought to him to be healed, he saw a true woman and not a horse, while on the other hand everyone else exclaimed that she seemed to be a horse. And the Saint, by his prayers, freed her and the others from that illusion, saying that this had happened to her because she had not attended sufficiently to holy things,

---

* "Boethius." "De Consolatione Philosophiae." Liber I, Prosa ii. "Atqui talia contuleramus arma, quae nisi prius abiecisses, inuicta te firmitate tuerentur."

nor used as she should Holy Confession and the Eucharist. And for this reason, because in her honesty she would not consent to the shameful proposal of a young man, he had caused a Jew who was a witch to bewitch the girl so that, by the power of the devil, he turned her into a filly.

We may summarize our conclusions as follows:—Devils can, for their profit and probation, injure the good in their fortunes, that is, in such exterior things as riches, fame, and bodily health. This is clear from the case of the Blessed Job, who was afflicted by the devil in such matters. But such injuries are not of their own causing, so that they cannot be led or driven into any sin, although they can be tempted both inwardly and outwardly in the flesh. But the devils cannot afflict the good with this sort of illusions, either actively or passively.

Not actively, by deluding their senses as they do those of others who are not in a state of grace. And not passively, by taking away their male organs by some glamour. For in these two respects they could never injure Job, especially the passive injury with regard to the venereal act; for he was of such continence that he was able to say: I have vowed a vow with my eyes that I shall never think about a virgin, and still less about another man's wife. Nevertheless the devil knows that he has great power over sinners (see *S. Luke* xi: When a strong man armed keepeth his palace, his goods are in peace).

But it may be asked, as to illusions in respect of the male organ, whether, granted that the devil cannot impose this illusion on those in a state of grace in a passive way, he cannot still do so in an active sense: the argument being that the man in a state of grace is deluded because he ought to see the member in its right place, when he who thinks it has been taken away from him, as well as other bystanders, does not see it in its place; but if this is conceded, it seems to be contrary to what has been said. It can be said that there is not so much force in the active as in the passive loss; meaning by active loss, not his who bears the loss, but his who sees the loss from without, as is self-evident. Therefore, although a man in a state of grace can see the loss of another, and to that extent the devil can delude his senses; yet he cannot passively suffer such loss in his own body, as, for ex-

ample, to be deprived of his member, since he is not subject to lust. In the same way the converse is true, as the Angel said to Tobias: Those who are given to lust, the devil has power over them.

And what, then, is to be thought of those witches who in this way sometimes collect male organs in great numbers, as many as twenty or thirty members together, and put them in a bird's nest, or shut them up in a box, where they move themselves like living members, and eat oats and corn, as has been seen by many and is a matter of common report? It is to be said that it is all done by devil's work and illusion, for the senses of those who see them are deluded in the way we have said. For a certain man tells that, when he had lost his member, he approached a known witch to ask her to restore it to him. She told the afflicted man to climb a certain tree, and that he might take which he liked out of a nest in which there were several members. And when he tried to take a big one, the witch said: You must not take that one; adding, because it belonged to a parish priest.

All these things are caused by devils through an illusion or glamour, in the manner we have said, by confusing the organ of vision by transmuting the mental images in the imaginative faculty. And it must not be said that these members which are shown are devils in assumed members, just as they sometimes appear to witches and men in assumed aerial bodies, and converse with them. And the reason is that they effect this thing by an easier method, namely, by drawing out an inner mental image from the repository of the memory, and impressing it on the imagination.

And if anyone wishes to say that they could go to work in a similar way, when they are said to converse with witches and other men in assumed bodies; that is, that they could cause such apparitions by changing the mental images in the imaginative faculty, so that when men thought the devils were present in assumed bodies, they were really nothing but an illusion caused by such a change of the mental images in the inner perceptions.

It is to be said that, if the devil had no other purpose than merely to show himself in human form, then there would be no need for him to appear in an assumed body, since he could effect his purpose well enough by the aforesaid illusion. But this is not so; for he has another purpose, namely, to speak and eat with them, and to commit other abominations. Therefore it is necessary that he should himself be present, placing himself actually in sight in an assumed body. For, as S. Thomas says, Where the Angel's power is, there he operates.

And it may be asked, if the devil by himself and without any witch takes away anyone's virile member, whether there is any difference between one sort of deprivation and the other. In addition to what has been said in the First Part of this work on the question, Whether witches can take away the male organ, it can be said that, when the devil by himself takes away a member, he does actually take it away, and it is actually restored when it has to be restored. Secondly, as it is not taken away without injury, so it is not without pain. Thirdly, that he never does this unless compelled by a good Angel, for by so doing he cuts off a great source of profit to him; for he knows that he can work more witchcraft on that act than on other human acts. For God permits him to do more injury to that than to other human acts, as has been said. But none of the above points apply when he works through the agency of a witch, with God's permission.

And if it is asked whether the devil is more apt to injure men and creatures by himself than through a witch, it can be said that there is no comparison between the two cases. For he is infinitely more apt to do harm through the agency of witches. First, because he thus gives greater offence to God, by usurping to himself a creature dedicated to Him. Secondly, because when God is the more offended, He allows him the more power of injuring men. And thirdly, for his own gain, which he places in the perdition of souls.

✫

CHAPTER VIII

Of the Manner whereby they Change Men into the Shapes of Beasts.

BUT that witches, by the power of devils, change men into the shapes of beasts (for this is their chief manner of transmutation), although it has been sufficiently proved in the First Part of the work, Question 10, Whether witches can do such things: nevertheless, since that question with its arguments and solutions may be rather obscure to some; especially since no actual examples are adduced to prove them, and even the method by which they so transform themselves is not explained; therefore we add the present exposition by the resolution of several doubts.

And first, that Canon (26, Q. 5, Episcopi) is not to be understood in this matter in the way in which even many learned men (but would that their learning were good!) are deceived; who do not fear to affirm publicly in their sermons that such prestidigitatory transmutations are in no way possible even by the power of devils. And we have often said that this doctrine is greatly to the detriment of the Faith, and strengthens the witches, who rejoice very much in such sermons.

But such preachers, as has been noted, touch only the outer surface, and fail to reach the inner meaning of the words of the Canon. For when it says: Whoever believes that any creature can be made, or can be changed for the better or the worse, or be transformed into any other shape or likeness except by the Creator Himself Who made all, is without doubt an infidel. . . .

The reader must here remark two chief things. First, concerning the words "be made"; and secondly, concerning the words "be transformed into another likeness." And as to the first, it is answered that "be made" can be understood in two ways: namely, as meaning "be created," or as in the sense of the natural production of anything. Now in the first sense it belongs only to God, as is well known, Who in His infinite might can make something out of nothing.

But in the second sense there is a distinction to be drawn between creatures; for some are perfect creatures, like a man, and an ass, etc. And others are imperfect, such as serpents, frogs, mice, etc., for they can also be generated from putrefaction. Now the Canon obviously speaks only of the former sort, not of the second; for in the case of the second it can be proved from what Blessed Albert says in his book *On*

Animals, where he asks: whether devils can make true animals; and he answers that they can; but only imperfect animals; and still with this difference, that they cannot do so in an instant, as God does, but by some motion, however sudden, as is shown in the case of the Magicians in *Exodus* vii. The reader may, if he likes, refer to some of the remarks in the question we have quoted in the First Part of the work, and in the solution of the first argument.

Secondly, it is said that they cannot transmute any creature. You may say that transmutation is of two sorts, substantial and accidental; and this accidental is again of two kinds, consisting either in the natural form belonging to the thing which is seen, or in a form which does not belong to the thing which is seen, but exists only in the organs and perceptions of him who sees. The Canon speaks of the former, and especially of formal and actual transmutation, in which one substance is transmuted into another; and this sort only God can effect, Who is the Creator of such actual substances. And it speaks also of the second, although the devil can effect that, in so far as, with God's permission, he causes certain diseases and induces some appearance on the accidental body. As when a face appears to be leprous, or some such thing.

But properly speaking it is not such matters that are in question, but apparitions and glamours, by which things seem to be transmuted into other likenesses; and we say that the words of the Canon cannot exclude such transmutations; for their existence is proved by authority, by reason, and by experience; namely, by certain experiences related by S. Augustine in Book XVIII, chapter 17, of the *De Ciuitate Dei*, and by the arguments in explanation of them. For among other prestidigitatory transformations, he mentions that the very famous Sorceress, Circe, changed the companions of Ulysses into beasts; and that certain innkeepers' wives had turned their guests into beasts of burden. He mentions also that the companions of Diomedes were changed into birds, and for a long time flew about the temple of Diomedes; and that Praestantius tells it for a fact that his father said that he had been a packhorse, and had carried corn with other animals.

Now when the companions of Ulysses were changed into beasts, it was only an appearance, or deception of the eyes; for the animal shapes were drawn out of the repository or memory of images, and impressed on the imaginative faculty. And so imaginary vision was caused, and through the strong impression on the other senses and organs, the beholder thought that he saw animals, in the manner of which we have already treated. But how these things can be done by the devil's power without any injury will be shown later.

But when the guests were changed into beasts of burden by the innkeepers' wives; and when the father of Praestantius thought he was a packhorse and carried corn; it is to be noted that in these cases there were three deceptions.

First, that those men were caused by a glamour to seem to be changed into beasts of burden, and this change was caused in the way we have said. Second, that devils invisibly bore those burdens up when they were too heavy to be carried. Third, that those who seemed to others to be changed in shape seemed also to themselves to be changed into beasts; as it happened to Nabuchodonosor, who lived for seven years eating straw like an ox.*

And as to the comrades of Diomedes being changed into birds and flying round his temple, it is to be said that this Diomedes was one of the Greeks who went to the siege of Troy; and when he wished to return home, he was drowned with his comrades in the sea; and then, at the suggestion of some idol, a temple was built to him that he might be numbered among the gods; and for a long time, to keep that error alive, devils in the shape of birds flew about in place of his companions. Therefore that superstition was one of the glamours we have spoken of; for it was not caused by the impression of mental images on the imaginative faculty, but by their flying in the sight of men in the assumed bodies of birds.

But if it is asked whether the devils

---

* "*An Ox.*" "*Daniel*" iv, 30: "*The same hour the word was fulfilled upon Nabuchodonosor, and he was driven away from among men, and did eat grass like an ox, and his body was wet with the dew of heaven: till his hairs grew like the feathers of eagles and his nails like birds' claws.*"

could have deluded the onlookers by the above-mentioned method of working upon their mental images, and not by assuming aerial bodies like flying birds, the answer is that they could have done so.

For it was the opinion of some (as S. Thomas tells in the *Second Book of Sentences*, dist. 8, art. 2) that no Angel, good or bad, ever assumed a body'; but that all that we read in the Scriptures about their appearances was caused by a glamour, or by imaginary vision.

And here the learned Saint notes a difference between a glamour and imaginary vision. For in a glamour there may be an exterior object which is seen, but it seems other than it is. But imaginary vision does not necessarily require an exterior object, but can be caused without that and only by those inner mental images impressed on the imagination.

So, following their opinion, the comrades of Diomedes were not represented by devils in the assumed bodies and likeness of birds, but only by a fantastic and imaginary vision caused by working upon those mental images, etc.

But the learned Saint condemns this as an erroneous and not a simple opinion (though, it is piously believed, it is not actually heretical), although such appearances of good and bad Angels may at times have been imaginary, with no assumed body. But, as he says, the saints are agreed that the Angels also appeared to the actual sight, and such appearance was in an assumed body. And the scriptural text reads more as if it speaks of bodily appearances than imaginary or prestidigitatory ones. Therefore we can say for the present concerning any visions like that of the comrades of Diomedes: that although those comrades could by the devil's work have appeared in the imaginary vision of the beholders in the manner we have said, yet it is rather presumed that they were caused to be seen by devils in assumed aerial bodies like flying birds; or else that other natural birds were caused by devils to represent them,

☆

CHAPTER IX

How Devils may enter the Human Body and the Head without doing any Hurt, when they cause such Metamorphosis by Means of Prestidigitation.

CONCERNING the method of causing these illusory transmutations it may further be asked: whether the devils are then inside the bodies and heads of those who are deceived, and whether the latter are to be considered as possessed by devils; how it can happen without injury to the inner perceptions and faculties that a mental image is transferred from one inner faculty to another; and whether or not such work ought to be considered miraculous.

First we must again refer to a distinction between such illusory glamours; for sometimes the outer perceptions only are affected, and sometimes the inner perceptions are deluded and so affect the outer perceptions.

In the former case the glamour can be caused without the devils' entering into the outer perceptions, and merely by an exterior illusion; as when the devil wishes to hide some body by the interposition of some other body, or in some other way; or when he himself assumes a body and imposes himself on the vision.

But in the latter case it is necessary that he must first occupy the head and the faculties. And this is proved by authority and by reason.

And it is not a valid objection to say that two created spirits cannot be in one and the same place, and that the soul pervades the whole of the body. For on this question there is the authority of S. John Damascene, when he says: Where the Angel is, there he operates. And S. Thomas, in the *Second Book of Sentences*, dist. 7, art. 5, says: All Angels, good and bad, by their natural power, which is superior to all bodily power, are able to transmute our bodies.

And this is clearly true, not only by reason of the superior nobility of their nature, but because the whole mechanism of the world and all corporeal creatures are administrated by Angels; as S. Gregory says in the 4th Dialogue: In this visible world nothing can be disposed except by an invisible creature. Therefore all corporeal matters are governed by the Angels, who are also called, not only by the Holy Doctors but also by all the Philosophers, the Powers which move the stars. It is clear also from the fact that all human bodies are moved by their souls, just as all other matter is moved by the stars and the Powers which move them. Any who wish may refer to S. Thomas in the First Part, Quest. 90, art. 1.

From this it is concluded that, since devils operate there where they are, therefore when they confuse the fancy and the inner perceptions they are existing in them.

Again, although to enter the soul is possible only to God Who created it, yet devils can, with God's permission, enter our bodies; and they can then make impressions on the inner faculties corresponding to the bodily organs. And by those impressions the organs are affected in proportion as the inner perceptions are affected in the way which has been shown: that the devil can draw out some image retained in a faculty corresponding to one of the senses; as he draws from the memory, which is in the back part of the head, an image of a horse, and locally moves that phantasm to the middle part of the head, where are the cells of imaginative power; and finally to the sense of reason, which is in the front of the head. And he causes such a sudden change and confusion, that such objects are necessarily thought to be actual things seen with the eyes. This can be clearly exemplified by the natural defect in frantic men and other maniacs.

But if it is asked how he can do this without causing pain in the head, the answer is easy. For in the first place he does not cause any actual physical change in the organs, but only moves the mental images. And secondly, he does not effect these changes by injecting any active quality which would necessarily cause pain, since the devil is himself without any corporeal quality, and can therefore operate without the use of any such quality. Thirdly, as has been said, he effects these transmutations only by a local movement from one organ to another, and not by other movements through which painful transformations are sometimes caused.

And as for the objection that two spirits cannot separately exist in the same place, and that, since the soul exists in the head, how can a devil be there also? It is to be said that the soul is thought to reside in the centre of the heart, in which it communicates with all the members by an outpouring of life. An example can be taken from a spider, which feels in the middle of its web when any part of the web is touched.

However, S. Augustine says in his book *On the Spirit and the Soul,** that it is all in all, and all in every part of the body. Granting that the soul is in the head, still the devil can work there; for his work is different from the work of the soul. The work of the soul is in the body, to inform it and fill it with life; so that it exists not merely locally, but in the whole matter. But the devil works in such a part and such a place of the body, effecting his changes in respect of the mental images. Therefore, since there is no confusion between their respective operations, they can both exist together in the same part of the body.

There is also the question whether such men are to be considered obsessed or frenzied, that is, possessed of devils. But this is considered separately; namely, whether it is possible through the work of witches for a man to be obsessed with a devil, that is, that the devil should actually and bodily possess him. And this question is specially discussed in the following chapter, since it has this special difficulty, namely, whether this can be caused through the operations of witches.

But as to the question whether the temporal works of witches and devils are to be considered as miracles or of a miraculous nature; it is to be said that they are so, in so far as they are beyond the order of created nature as known to us, and are done by creatures unknown to us. But they are not properly speaking miracles as are those which are outside the whole of created nature; as are the miracles of God and the Saints. (See what was written in the First Part of this work, in the Fifth Question, in the refutation of the third error.)

---

* *"On the Spirit." The treatise "De Natura et Origine Animae" was written towards the end of the year 419.*

But there are those who object that this sort of works must not be considered miracles, but simply works of the devil; since the purpose of miracles is the strengthening of the Faith, and they must not be conceded to the adversary of the Faith. And also because the signs of Antichrist are called lying signs by the Apostle.*

First it is to be said that to work miracles is the gift of freely given grace. And they can be done by bad men and bad spirits, up to the limits of the power which is in them.

Wherefore the miracles wrought by the good can be distinguished from those wrought by the wicked in at least three ways. First, the signs which are given by the good are done by Divine power in such matters as are beyond the capacity of their own natural power, such as raising the dead, and things of that sort, which the devils are not able to accomplish in truth, but only by an illusion: so Simon Magus moved the head of a dead man; but such manifestations cannot last long. Secondly, they can be distinguished by their utility; for the miracles of the good are of a useful nature, as the healing of sickness, and such things. But the miracles done by witches are concerned with harmful and idle things; as when they fly in the air, or benumb the limbs of men, or such things. And S. Peter assigns this difference in the *Itinerarium* † of Clement.

The third difference relates to the Faith. For the miracles of the good are ordained for the edification of the Faith and of good living; whereas the miracles of the wicked are manifestly detrimental to the Faith and to righteousness.

They are distinguished also by the way in which they are done. For the good do miracles by a pious and reverent invocation of the Divine Name. But witches and wicked men work them by certain ravings and invocations of devils.

And there is no difficulty in the fact that the Apostle called the works of the devil and Antichrist lying wonders;‡

for the marvels so done by Divine permission are true in some respects and false in others. They are true in so far as they are within the limits of the devil's power. But they are false when he appears to do things which are beyond his power, such as raising the dead, or making the blind to see. For when he appears to do the former, he either enters into the dead body or else removes it, and himself takes its place in an assumed aerial body; and in the latter case he takes away the sight by a glamour, and then suddenly restores it by taking away the disability he has caused, not by bringing light to the inner perceptions, as is told in the legend of Bartholomew. Indeed all the marvellous works of Antichrist and of witches can be said to be lying signs, inasmuch as their only purpose is to deceive. See S. Thomas, dist. 8, *de Uirtute Daemonum.*

We may also quote here the distinction which is drawn in the Compendium of Theological Truth between a wonder and a miracle. For in a miracle four conditions are required: that it should be done by God; that it should be beyond the existing order of nature; thirdly, that it should be manifest; and fourthly, that it should be for the corroboration of the Faith. But since the works of witches fail to fulfil at least the first and last conditions, therefore they may be called wonderful works, but not miracles.

It can also be argued in this way. Although witches' works can in a sense be said to be miraculous, yet some miracles are supernatural, some unnatural, and some preternatural. And they are supernatural when they can be compared with nothing in nature, or in natural power, as when a virgin gives birth. They are unnatural when they are against the normal course of nature but do not overstep the limits of nature, such as causing the blind to see. And they are preternatural when they are done in a manner parallel to that of nature, as when rods are changed into serpents; for this can be done naturally also, through long putrefaction on account of seminal reasons; and thus the works of magicians may be said to be marvellous.

It is expedient to recount an actual example, and then to explain it step by step. There is a town in the diocese of Strasburg, the name of

---

* "*Apostle.*" S. Paul, "*II. Thessalonians*" ii, 8, 9.

† "*Itinerarium.*" *Pseudo-Clementines.*

‡ "*Lying Wonders.*" "*II. Thessalonians*" ii, 8–9: "*That wicked one . . . whose coming is according to the working of Satan, in all power, and signs, and lying wonders.*"

which it is charitable and honourable to withhold, in which a workman was one day chopping some wood to burn in his house. A large cat suddenly appeared and began to attack him; and when he was driving it off, another even larger one came and attacked him with the first more fiercely. And when he again tried to drive them away, behold, three of them together attacked him, jumping up at his face, and biting and scratching his legs. In great fright and, as he said, more panic-stricken than he had ever been, he crossed himself and, leaving his work, fell upon the cats, which were swarming over the wood and again leaping at his face and throat, and with difficulty drove them away by beating one on the head, another on the legs, and another on the back. After the space of an hour, while he was again engaged upon his task, two servants of the town magistrates came and took him as a malefactor and led him into the presence of the bailiff or judge. And the judge, looking at him from a distance, and refusing to hear him, ordered him to be thrown into the deepest dungeon of a certain tower or prison, where those who were under sentence of death were placed. The man cried out, and for three days bitterly complained to the prison guards that he should suffer in that way, when he was conscious of no crime; but the more the guards tried to procure him a hearing, the more furious the judge became, expressing in the strongest terms his indignation that so great a malefactor had not yet acknowledged his crime, but dared to proclaim his innocence when the evidence of the facts proved his horrible crime. But although these could not prevail upon him, yet the judge was induced by the advice of the other magistrates to grant the man a hearing. So when he was brought out of prison into the presence of the judge, and the judge refused to look at him, the poor man threw himself before the knees of the other magistrates, pleading that he might know the reason for his misfortune; and the judge broke into these words: You most wicked of men, how can you not acknowledge your crime? At such a time on such a day you beat three respected matrons of this town, so that they lie in their beds unable to rise or to move. The poor man cast

his mind back to the events of that day and that hour, and said: Never in all my life have I struck or beaten a woman, and I can prove by credible witnesses that at that time on that day I was busy chopping wood; and an hour afterwards your servants found me still engaged on that task. Then the judge again exclaimed in a fury: See how he tries to conceal his crime! The women are bewailing their blows, they exhibit the marks, and publicly testify that he struck them. Then the poor man considered more closely on that event, and said: I remember that I struck some creatures at that time, but they were not women. The magistrates in astonishment asked him to relate what sort of creatures he had struck; and he told, to their great amazement, all that had happened, as we have related it. So, understanding that it was the work of the devil, they released the poor man and let him go away unharmed, telling him not to speak of this matter to anyone. But it could not be hidden from those devout persons present who were zealous for the Faith.

Now concerning this it may be asked, whether the devils appeared thus in assumed shapes without the presence of the witches, or whether the witches were actually present, converted by some glamour into the shapes of those beasts. And in answering this it should be said that, although it was equally possible for the devils to act in either way, it is rather presumed that it was done in the second manner. For when the devils attacked the workman in the shapes of cats, they could suddenly, by local motion through the air, transfer the women to their houses with the blows which they received as cats from the workman; and no one doubts that this was because of a mutual pact formerly made between them. For in the same way they can cause an injury or wound in a person whom they wish to bewitch, by means of puncturing a painted or molten image which represents the person whom they wish to injure. Many examples of this could be adduced.

And it cannot be validly objected that perhaps those women who were so injured were innocent, because according to previously quoted examples it is shown that injuries may happen even to the innocent, when someone is unknowingly hurt by a witch by means of an artificial image. The example is not apposite; for it is one thing to be hurt by a devil through a witch, and another thing to be hurt by the devil himself without any witch. For the devil receives blows in the form of an animal, and transfers them to one who is bound to him by a pact, when it is with such an one's consent that he acts in this manner in such a shape. Therefore he can in this way hurt only the guilty who are bound to him by a pact, and never the innocent. But when devils seek to do injury by means of witches, then, with the permission of God for the avenging of so great a crime, they often afflict even the innocent.

Nevertheless, devils at times, with God's permission, in their own persons hurt even the innocent; and formerly they injured the Blessed Job, although they were not personally present, nor did the devils make use of any such illusory apparition as in the example we have quoted, when they used the phantasm of a cat, an animal which is, in the Scriptures, an appropriate symbol of the perfidious, just as a dog is the symbol of preachers; for cats are always setting snares for each other. And the Order of Preaching Friars was represented in its first Founder by a dog barking against heresy.

Therefore it is presumed that those three witches attacked the workman in the second manner, either because the first manner did not please them so much, or because the second suited more with their curiosity.

And this was the order which they observed. First, they were urged to do this at the instance of the devils, and not the devils at the instance of the witches. For so we have often found in their confessions, that at the instance of devils who constantly spur them on to commit evil, they have to do more than they would. And it is likely that the witches would not, on their own account, have thought of attacking the poor man.

And there is no doubt that the reason why the devils urged them to do this is that they knew well that, when a manifest crime remains unpunished, God is the more offended, the Catholic Faith is brought into disrepute, and the number of witches is the more increased. Secondly, having gained

their consent, the devils transported their bodies with that ease which belongs to a spiritual power over a bodily power. Thirdly, having in the way which has been told been turned into the forms of beasts by some glamour, they had to attack the workman; and the devils did not defend them from the blows, although they could have done so just as easily as they had transported them; but they permitted them to be beaten, and the one who beat them to be known, in the knowledge that those crimes would, for the reasons we have mentioned, remain unpunished by faint-hearted men who had no zeal for the Faith.

We read also of a certain holy man, who once found the devil in the form of a devout priest preaching in a church, and knowing in his spirit that it was the devil, observed his words, whether he was teaching the people well or ill. And finding him irreproachable and inveighing against sin, he went up to him at the end of the sermon and asked him the reason for this. And the devil answered: I preach the truth, knowing that, because they are hearers of the word only, and not doers, God is the more offended and my gain is increased.

☆

CHAPTER X

Of the Method by which Devils through the Operations of Witches sometimes actually possess Men.

IT has been shown in the previous chapter how devils can enter the heads and other parts of the body of men, and can move the inner mental images from place to place. But someone may doubt whether they are able at the instance of witches to obsess men entirely; or feel some uncertainty about their various methods of causing such obsession without the instance of witches. And to clear up these doubts we must undertake three explanations. First, as to the various methods of possession. Secondly, how at the instance of witches and with God's permission devils at times possess men in all those ways. Thirdly, we must substantiate our arguments with facts and examples.

With reference to the first, we must

make an exception of that general method by which the devil inhabits a man in any mortal sin. S. Thomas, in Book 3, quest. 3, speaks of this method where he considers the doubt whether the devil always substantially possesses a man when he commits mortal sin; and the reason for the doubt is that the indwelling Holy Ghost always forms a man with grace, according to I. *Corinthians*, iii: Ye are the temple of God, and the spirit of God dwelleth in you. And, since guilt is opposed to grace, it would seem that there were opposing forces in the same place.

And there he proves that to possess a man can be understood in two ways: either with regard to the soul, or with regard to the body. And in the first way it is not possible for the devil to possess the soul, since God alone can enter that; therefore the devil is not in this way the cause of sin, which the Holy Spirit permits the soul itself to commit; so there is no similitude between the two.

But as to the body, we may say that the devil can possess a man in two ways, just as there are two classes of men: those who are in sin, and those who are in grace. In the first way, we may say that, since a man is by any mortal sin brought into the devil's service, in so far as the devil provides the outer suggestion of sin either to the senses or to the imagination, to that extent he is said to inhabit the character of a man when he is moved by every stirring of temptation, like a ship in the sea without a rudder.

The devil can also essentially possess a man, as is clear in the case of frantic men. But this rather belongs to the question of punishment than that of sin, as will be shown; and bodily punishments are not always the consequence of sin, but are inflicted now upon sinners and now upon the innocent. Therefore both those who are and those who are not in a state of grace can, in the depth of the incomprehensible judgement of God, be essentially possessed by devils. And though this method of possession is not quite pertinent to our inquiry, we have set it down lest it should seem impossible to anyone that, with God's permission, men should at times be substantially inhabited by devils at the instance of witches.

We may say, therefore, that just as there are five ways in which devils by themselves, without witches, can injure and possess men, so they can also do so in all those ways at the instance of witches; since then God is the more offended, and greater power of molesting men is allowed to the devil through witches. And the methods are briefly the following, excepting the fact that they sometimes plague a man through his external possessions: sometimes they injure men only in their own bodies; sometimes in their bodies and in their inner faculties; sometimes they only tempt them inwardly and outwardly; others they at times deprive of the use of their reason; others they change into the appearance of irrational beasts. We shall speak of these methods singly.

But first we shall rehearse five reasons why God allows men to be possessed, for the sake of preserving a due order in our matter. For sometimes a man is possessed for his own greater advantage; sometimes for a slight sin of another; sometimes for his own venial sin; sometimes for another's heavy sin; and sometimes for his own heavy sin. For all these reasons let no one doubt that God allows such things to be done by devils at the instance of witches; and it is better to prove each of them by the Scriptures, rather than by recent examples, since new things are always strengthened by old examples.

For an example of the first is clearly shown in the *Dialogue* of Severus,* a very dear disciple of S. Martin, where he tells that a certain Father of very holy life was so gifted by grace with the power of expelling devils, that they were put to flight not only by his words, but even by his letters or his hair-shirt. And since the Father became very famous in the world, and felt himself tempted with vainglory, although he manfully resisted that vice, yet, that he might be the more humiliated, he prayed with his whole heart to God that he might be for five months

---

* "*Severus.*" *Sulpicius Severus, who has been styled the Christian Sallust, was born in Aquitaine about 360; and died* circa *420–25. He became a personal friend and enthusiastic disciple of S. Martin, and lived near Eauze, at Toulouse and Luz in Southern France. His* "*Life of S. Martin*" *was very popular during the Middle Ages, as also were his* "*Two Dialogues,*" *formerly divided into three. His works are to be found in Migne,* "*Patres Latini,*" *XX, 95–248.*

possessed by a devil; and this was done. For he was at once possessed and had to be put in chains, and everything had to be applied to him which is customary in the case of demoniacs. But at the end of the fifth month he was immediately delivered both from all vainglory and from the devil. But we do not read, nor is it for the present maintained, that for this reason a man can be possessed by a devil through the witchcraft of another man; although, as we have said, the judgements of God are incomprehensible.

For the second reason, when someone is possessed because of the light sin of another, S. Gregory gives an example. The Blessed Abbot Eleutherius, a most devout man, was spending the night near a convent of virgins, who unknown to him ordered to be put by his cell a young boy who used to be tormented all night by the devil. But on that same night the boy was delivered from the devil by the presence of the Father. When the Abbot learned of this, and the boy now being placed in the holy man's monastery, after many days he began to exult rather immoderately over the boy's liberation, and said to his brother monks: The devil was playing his pranks with those Sisters, but he has not presumed to approach this boy since he came to the servants of God. And behold! the devil at once began to torment the boy. And by the tears and fasting of the holy man and his brethren he was with difficulty delivered, but on the same day. And indeed that an innocent person should be possessed for the slight fault of another is not surprising when men are possessed by devils for their own light fault, or for another's heavy sin, or for their own heavy sin, and some also at the instance of witches.

Cassia, in his First Collation of the Abbot Serenus, gives an example of how one Moses was possessed for his own venial sin. This Moses, he says, was a hermit of upright and pious life; but because on one occasion he engaged in a dispute with the Abbot Macharius, and went a little too far in the expression of a certain opinion, he was immediately delivered up to a terrible devil, who caused him to void his natural excrements through his mouth. And that this scourge was inflicted by God for the sake of purgation, lest any stain of his momentary

fault should remain in him, is clear from his miraculous cure. For by continual prayers and submission to the Abbot Macharius, the vile spirit was quickly driven away and departed from him.

A similar case is that related by S. Gregory in his First Dialogue of the nun who ate a lettuce without having first made the sign of the Cross, and was set free by the Blessed Father Equitius.*

In the same Dialogue St. Gregory tells an example of the fourth case, where someone is possessed because of the heavy sin of another. The Blessed Bishop Fortunatus had driven the devil from a possessed man, and the devil began to walk about the streets of the city in the guise of a pilgrim, crying out: Oh, the holy man Bishop Fortunatus! See, he has cast me, a pilgrim, out of my lodging, and I can find no rest anywhere. Then a certain man sitting with his wife and son invited the pilgrim to lodge with him, and asking why he had been turned out, was delighted with the derogatory story of the holy man which the pilgrim had invented. And thereupon the devil entered his son, and cast him upon the fire, and killed him. And then for the first time did the unhappy father understand whom he had received as a guest.

And fifthly, we read many examples of men being possessed for their own heavy sin, both in the Holy Scripture and in the passions of the Saints. For in I. Kings xv, Saul was possessed for disobedience to God. And, as we have said, we have mentioned all these so that it need not seem to anyone impossible that men should also be possessed because of the crimes of, and at the instance of, witches. And we shall be able to understand the various methods of such possession by quoting actual examples.

In the time of Pope Pius II † the following was the experience of one of us two Inquisitors before he entered upon his office in the Inquisition. A

* "Equitius." In 487 Equitius was Bishop of Matelica, a diocese now joined to Fabriano. Only one other Bishop (Florentius) of the ancient see is known.

† "Pius II." Enea Silvio de' Piccolomini was born at Corsignano, near Siena, 18 October, 1405; and elected to the Chair of S. Peter, 19 August, 1458. He died at Ancona, 14 August, 1464.

certain Bohemian from the town of Dachov brought his only son, a secular priest, to Rome to be delivered, because he was possessed. It happened that I, one of us Inquisitors, went into a refectory, and that priest and his father came and sat down at the same table with me. We saluted each other, and talked together, as is customary; and the father kept sighing and praying Almighty God that his journey might prove to have been successful. I felt great pity for him, and began to ask what was the reason of his journey and of his sorrow. Then he, in the hearing of his son who was sitting next to me at the table, answered: "Alas! I have a son possessed by a devil, and with great trouble and expense I have brought him here to be delivered." And when I asked where the son was, he showed me him sitting by my side. I was a little frightened, and looked at him closely; and because he took his food with such modesty, and answered piously to all questions, I began to doubt that he was not possessed, but that some infirmity had happened to him. Then the son himself told what had happened, showing how and for how long he had been possessed, and saying: "A certain witch brought this evil upon me. For I was rebuking her on some matter concerned with the discipline of the Church, upbraiding her rather strongly since she was of an obstinate disposition, when she said that after a few days that would happen to me which has happened. And the devil which possesses me has told me that a charm was placed by the witch under a certain tree, and that until it was removed I could not be delivered; but he would not tell me which was the tree." But I would not in the least have believed his words if he had not at once informed me of the facts of the case. For when I asked him about the length of the intervals during which he had the use of his reason more than is usual in the case of persons possessed, he answered: "I am only deprived of the use of my reason when I wish to contemplate holy things or to visit sacred places. For the devil specifically told me in his own words uttered through my mouth that, because he had up to that time been much offended by my sermons to the people, he would in no way allow me to preach." For according to his father, he was a preacher full of grace, and loved by all. But I, the Inquisitor, wishing for proofs, had him taken for a fortnight and more to various holy places, and especially to the Church of S. Praxedes the Virgin,* where there is part of the marble pillar to which Our Saviour was bound when He was scourged, and to the place where S. Peter the Apostle was crucified; and in all these places he uttered horrible cries while he was being exorcised, now saying that he wished to come forth, and after a little maintaining the contrary. And as we have said before, in all his behaviour he remained a sober priest without any eccentricity, except during the process of any exorcisms; and when these were finished, and the stole was taken from his neck, he showed no sign of madness or any immoderate action. But when he passed any church, and genuflected in honour of the Glorious Virgin, the devil made him thrust his tongue far out of his mouth; and when he was asked whether he could not restrain himself from doing this, he answered: "I cannot help myself at all, for so he uses all my limbs and organs, my neck, my tongue, and my lungs, whenever he pleases, causing me to speak or

---

* "S. Praxedes." Praxedes and Pudentiana were the daughters of the Senator Pudens, a pupil of S. Peter. There was an old title-church of Rome, "titulus Pudentis," called also the "ecclesia Pudentiana." The two female figures in the mosaic of the apse of S. Pudenziana, via Urbana, are Pudentiana and Praxedes. In the fourth century a new church, "titulus Praxedis," was built near Santa Maria Maggiore, and when Paschal I in 822 rebuilt the church in its present form (the basilica and title-church S. Prassede all' Esquilino) he translated to it the bodies of S. Praxedes, S. Pudentiana, and of many other martyrs. Under the High Altar are the chief Relics of the Saints. In the Chapel of S. Zeno, which dates from the ninth century, is the Holy Pillar of the Scourging brought in 1223 from Jerusalem by Cardinal Giovanni Colonna. Another portion of the Holy Pillar is preserved in the Church of the Holy Sepulchre at Jerusalem, where it is publicly venerated each year on Easter Eve. S. Prassede is one of the richest churches in Rome in Relics. It contains the Bodies of S. Zoe, S. Feldian, S. Candid, S. Basil, S. Celestine I, S. Nicomedius; important Relics of S. Matthew, S. Luke, S. Bartholomew, S. Philip, S. Andrew, S. Peter, S. Paul, and S. John Baptist; some of the garments of Our Lady; a piece of the seamless robe of Our Lord; three Thorns from the Crown of Thorns; and four fragments of wood from the True Cross.

to cry out; and I hear the words as if they were spoken by myself, but I am altogether unable to restrain them; and when I try to engage in prayer he attacks me more violently, thrusting out my tongue." And there was in the Church of S. Peter a column brought from Solomon's Temple, by virtue of which many who are obsessed with devils are liberated, because Christ had stood near it when He preached in the Temple; but even here he could not be delivered, owing to the hidden purpose of God which reserved another method for his liberation. For though he remained shut in by the column for a whole day and night, yet on the following day, after various exorcisms had been performed upon him, with a great concourse of people standing round, he was asked by which part of the column Christ had stood; and he bit the column with his teeth, and, crying out, showed the place, saying: "Here He stood! Here He stood!" And at last he said, "I will not go forth." And when he was asked why, he answered, Because of the Lombards. And being asked why he would not go forth because of the Lombards, he answered in the Italian tongue (although the poor priest did not understand that language), They all practise such and such things, naming the worst vice of lustfulness. And afterwards the priest asked me, saying, "Father, what did those Italian words mean which came from my mouth?" And when I told him, he answered, "I heard the words, but I could not understand them." Eventually it proved that this demoniac was of that sort of which the Saviour spoke in the Gospel, saying: This sort goeth not out save by prayer and fasting. For a venerable Bishop, who had been driven from his see by the Turks, piously took compassion on him, and by fasting on bread and water for forty days, and by prayers and exorcisms, at last through the grace of God delivered him and sent him back to his home rejoicing.

Now it would be a miracle if anyone in this life could thoroughly explain in what and in how many ways the devil possesses or injures men: yet we can say that, leaving out of account his method of injuring men in their temporal fortunes, there are five ways. For some are affected only in their own bodies; some both in their bodies and in their inner perceptions; some only in their inner perceptions; some are so punished as to be at times only deprived of their reason; and others are turned into the semblance of irrational beasts. Now the priest we have just mentioned was possessed in the fourth manner. For he was not touched in his worldly fortunes or in his own body, as it happened to the Blessed Job, over whom the Scripture clearly tells us that God gave the devil power, saying to Satan: Behold, all that he hath is in thy power; only upon himself put not forth thine hand. And this refers to exterior things. But afterwards He gave him power over his body, saying: Behold, he is in thine hand; but save his life.

And it can also be said that Job was tormented in the third manner, that is, in the inner perceptions of his soul as well as his body; for it is said in *Job* xii: If it is said to the Lord, My bed will console me, and I will take comfort to myself on my couch, then Thou wilt terrify me with dreams, and shake me with the horror of visions: though these dreams were caused by the devil, according to Nicolas of Lyra* and S. Thomas: Thou wilt terrify me with dreams, which appear to me in sleep, and with visions which come to me waking by a distortion of my inner perceptions. For the phantasms which occur to the thoughts in the day-time can become the terror of sleepers, and such were visited upon Job through the infirmity of his body. Therefore he was so shut off from all comfort that he saw no remedy or way of escaping from his misery except in death, and said that he was shaken with horror. And no one doubts that witches can injure men in these ways through devils, as will be shown in what follows, how they bring injuries upon the fortunes of men and upon the bodies of men and animals by means of hailstorms.

And there is a third way of injuring the body and the inner perceptions, without taking away the reason, which

---

* "*Nicolas of Lyra.*" "*Doctor planus et utilis,*" *the famous exegete, was born at Lyra in Normandy, 1270; and died at Paris, 1340. He is the author of numerous theological works, by far the most famous of which is his monumental "Postillae perpetuae in uniuersam S. Scripturam," which was so popular that it gained the distinction of being the first biblical commentary to be printed.*

is shown when witches, as has been said, so inflame the minds of men with unlawful lust that they are compelled to travel long distances in the night to go to their mistresses, being too fast bound in the net of carnal desire.

We may mention an example which is said to have happened in Hesse, in the diocese of Marburg. A certain priest was possessed, and during an exorcism the devil was asked for how long he had inhabited that priest. He answered, For seven years. And when the exorcist objected, But you have tormented him for hardly three years; where were you for the rest of the time? He answered, I was hiding in his body. And when he asked in what part of the body, he answered, Generally in his head. And when he was again asked where he was when the priest was celebrating the Sacrament, he said, I hid myself under his tongue. And the other said: Wretch! How were you so bold as not to flee from the presence of your Creator? Then the devil said: Anyone may hide under a bridge while a holy man is crossing, as long as he does not pause in his walk. But with the help of Divine grace the priest was delivered, whether he told the truth or not; for both he and his father are liars.

The fourth method applies to the case of the priest who was liberated in Rome, under the proposition that the devil can enter the body, but not the soul, which only God can enter. But when I say that the devil can enter the body, I do not mean that he can occupy the essential limits of the body.

I will explain this further; and in doing so it will be shown how devils sometimes substantially occupy a man, and at times deprive him of his reason. For we may say that the limits of the body can be considered in two ways: they may be physical or essential limits. Whenever any Angel, good or bad, works within the physical limits of the body, he enters the body in such a way as to influence its physical capacities. And in this way the good Angels cause imaginary visions in the good. But they are never said to enter into the essence of the body, since they cannot do so, either as a part of it or as a quality of it. Not as a part, for the angelic and the human essence are entirely different from each other; and not as a quality, as if giving it its

character, for it has its character by creation from God. Wherefore He alone is able to influence its inner essence, and to preserve it when He is pleased in His mercy to preserve it.

So we conclude that, speaking of all other perfections in the good or defects in the wicked, when these are caused by a spirit operating in the head and its attributes, such a spirit enters into the head within the physical limits of the physical capacities of the body.

But if the spirit is working upon the soul, then again it works from the outside, but in various ways. And they are said to work on the soul when they represent phantasms or shapes to the intellect, and not only to the common understanding and the outer perceptions. And when bad Angels so operate, there follow temptations and evil thoughts and affections, caused by an indirect influence upon the intellect. But good Angels cause phantasms of revelation which enlighten the understanding. And there is this difference between them; that good Angels can even directly impress enlightening fancies upon the intellect; but bad Angels are said not to enlighten but rather to darken by means of their phantasms, and they cannot influence the intellect directly, but only indirectly, in so far as the intellect is bound to take such phantasms into consideration.

But even a good Angel is not said to enter into the soul, although he enlightens it: similarly a superior Angel is not said to enter into an inferior, although he enlightens it; but he works only from the outside, and co-operates in the way we have said. Therefore far less can a bad Angel enter the soul.

And so the devil occupied the body of the priest in three ways. First, as he could enter his body within its physical limits, so he occupied his head by substantially inhabiting it. Secondly, he could extrinsically work upon his soul so as to darken his understanding and deprive him of the use of his reason. And he could have so tormented him without any intermission or respite; but we may say that the priest had this gift from God, that he should not be tormented by the devil without intermission. Thirdly, that although he was deprived of the power of the sane use of words, yet he was always conscious of his words, though not of their meaning. And this differs from the other methods of obsession, for we generally read that those who are possessed are afflicted by devils without intermission; as is clear in the case of the lunatic in the Gospel, whose father said to Jesus: Lord, have mercy on my son, for he is lunatic, and sore vexed (*S. Matthew* xvii); and of the woman whom Satan had crippled for eighteen years, who was bowed together and could in no wise lift herself up (*S. Luke* xiii). And in these ways devils can without doubt at the instance of witches and with God's permission inflict torments.

☆

CHAPTER XI

Of the Method by which they can Inflict Every Sort of Infirmity, generally Ills of the Graver Kind.

BUT there is no bodily infirmity, not even leprosy or epilepsy, which cannot be caused by witches, with God's permission. And this is proved by the fact that no sort of infirmity is excepted by the Doctors. For a careful consideration of what has already been written concerning the power of devils and the wickedness of witches will show that this statement offers no difficulty. Nider also deals with this subject both in his *Book of Precepts** and in his *Formicarius*, where he asks: Whether witches can actually injure men by their witchcraft. And the question makes no exception of any infirmity, however incurable. And he there answers that they can do so, and proceeds to ask in what way and by what means.

And as to the first, he answers, as has been shown in the First Question of the First Part of this treatise. And it is proved also by S. Isidore where he describes the operations of witches (*Etym.* 8, cap. 9), and says that they are called witches on account of the magnitude of their crimes; for they disturb the elements by raising up storms with the help of devils, they confuse the minds of men in the ways already mentioned, by either entirely obstructing or gravely impeding the use of their reason. He adds also that, without the use of any poison, but by the mere virulence of their incantations, they can deprive men of their lives.

It is proved also by S. Thomas in the *Second Book of Sentences*, dist. 7 and 8, and in Book IV, dist. 34, and in general all the Theologians write that witches can with the help of the devil bring harm upon men and their affairs in all the ways in which the devil alone can injure or deceive, namely, in their affairs, their reputation, their body, their reason, and their life; which means that those injuries which are caused by the devil without any witch, can also be caused by a witch; and even more readily so, on account of the greater offence which is given to the Divine Majesty, as has been shown above.

In *Job* i and ii is found a clear case of the injury in temporal affairs. The injury to reputation is shown in the history of the Blessed Jerome, that the devil transformed himself into the appearance of S. Silvanus, Bishop of Nazareth, a friend of S. Jerome. And this devil approached a noble woman by night in her bed and began first to provoke and entice her with lewd words, and then invited her to perform the sinful act. And when she called out, the devil in the form of the saintly Bishop hid under the woman's bed, and being sought for and found there, he in lickerish language declared lyingly that he was the Bishop Silvanus. On the morrow therefore, when the devil had disappeared, the holy man was scandalously defamed; but his good name was cleared when the devil confessed at the tomb of S. Jerome that he had done this in an assumed body.

The injury to the body is shown in the case of the Blessed Job, who was stricken by the devil with terrible sores, which are explained as a form of leprosy. And Sigisbert† and Vincent

---

* "*Book of Precepts*." "*Praeceptorum diuinae legis Liber*," of which there were seventeen editions before 1500. I have used that of Douai, 1612.

† "*Sigisbert*." *Sigebert of Gembloux, the celebrated Benedictine historian, was born at Gembloux (pr. Namur) about 1035, and died at the same place, 5 November, 1112. He was a prolific author, and his most famous work, "Chronicon siue Chronographia," is the basis of many other histories. It has frequently been reprinted. The works of Sigebert may be conveniently found in Migne, "Patres Latini," CLX. There is a study by Hirsch, "De uita et scriptis Sigeberti Monachi Gemblacensis," Berlin, 1841.*

of Beauvais (*Spec. Hist.* XXV. 37) both tell that in the time of the Emperor Louis II,* in the diocese of Mainz, a certain devil began to throw stones and to beat at the houses as if with a hammer. And then by public statements, and secret insinuations, he spread discord and troubled the minds of many. Then he excited the anger of all against one man, whose lodging, wherever he was resting, he set on fire, and said that they were all suffering for his sins. So at last that man had to find his lodging in the fields. And when the priests were saying a litany on this account, the devil stoned many of the people with stones till he hurt them to bleeding; and sometimes he would desist, and sometimes rage; and this continued for three years, until all the houses there were burned down.

Examples of the injury to the use of the reason, and of the tormenting of the inner perceptions, are seen in those possessed and frenzied men of whom the Gospels tell. And as for death, and that they deprive some of their lives, it is proved in *Tobias* vi, in the case of the seven husbands of the virgin Sara, who were killed because of their lecherous lust and unbridled desire for the virgin Sara, of whom they were not worthy to be the husbands. Therefore it is concluded that both by themselves, and all the more with the help of witches, devils can injure men in every way without exception.

But if it is asked whether injuries of this sort are to be ascribed rather to devils than to witches, it is answered that, when the devils cause injuries by their own direct action, then they are principally to be ascribed to them. But when they work through the agency of witches for the disparagement and offending of God and the perdition of souls, knowing that by this means God is made more angry and allows them greater power of doing evil; and because they do indeed perpetrate countless witchcrafts which the devil would not be allowed to bring upon men if he wished to injure men alone by himself, but are permitted, in the just and hidden purpose of God, through the agency of witches, on

account of their perfidy and abjuration of the Catholic Faith; therefore such injuries are justly ascribed to witches secondarily, however much the devil may be the principal actor.

Therefore when a woman dips a twig in water and sprinkles the water in the air to make it rain, although she does not herself cause the rain, and could not be blamed on that account, yet, because she has entered into a pact with the devil by which she can do this as a witch, although it is the devil who causes the rain, she herself nevertheless deservedly bears the blame, because she is an infidel and does the devil's work, surrendering herself to his service.

So also when a witch makes a waxen image or some such thing in order to bewitch somebody; or when an image of someone appears by pouring molten lead into water, and some injury is done upon the image, such as piercing it or hurting it in any other way, when it is the bewitched man who is in imagination being so hurt; although the injury is actually done to the image by the witch or some other man, and the devil in the same manner invisibly injures the bewitched man, yet it is deservedly ascribed to the witch. For, without her, God would never allow the devil to inflict the injury, nor would the devil on his own account try to injure the man.

But because it has been said that in the matter of their good name the devils can injure men on their own account and without the co-operation of witches, there may arise a doubt whether the devils cannot also defame honest women so that they are reputed to be witches, when they appear in their likeness to bewitch someone; from which it would happen that such a woman would be defamed without cause.

In answering this we must premise a few remarks. First, it has been said that the devil can do nothing without the Divine permission, as is shown in the First Part of this work in the last Question. It has also been shown that God does not allow so great power of evil against the just and those who live in grace, as against sinners; and as the devils have more power against sinners (see the text: When a strong man† armed, etc.), so they are per-

---

* "*Louis II.*" Son of Lothaire I, was born about 822. He became associated with his father in the Empire in 849, and succeeded to the Imperial Crown in 855. He died in 875.

† "*Strong Man.*" "*S. Luke*" xi, 21.

mitted by God to afflict them more than the just. Finally, although they can, with God's permission, injure the just in their affairs, their reputation, and their bodily health, yet, because they know that this power is granted them chiefly for the increase of the merits of the just, they are the less eager to injure them.

Therefore it can be said that in this difficulty there are several points to be considered. First, the Divine permission. Secondly, the man who is thought to be righteous, for they who are so reputed are not always actually in a state of grace. Thirdly, the crime of which an innocent man would be suspected; for that crime in its very origin exceeds all the crimes of the world. Therefore it is to be said that it is granted that, with God's permission, an innocent person, whether or not he is in a state of grace, may be injured in his affairs or reputation; but, having respect to this particular crime and the gravity of the accusation (for we have often quoted S. Isidore's saying that they are called witches from the magnitude of their crimes), it can be said that for an innocent person to be defamed by the devil in the way that has been suggested does not seem at all possible, for many reasons.

In the first place, it is one thing to be defamed in respect of vices which are committed without any expressed or tacit contract with the devil, such as theft, robbery, or fornication; but quite another matter to be defamed in respect of vices which it is impossible to accuse a man of having perpetrated unless he has entered upon an expressed contract with the devil; and such are the works of witches, which cannot be laid at their door unless it is by the power of devils that they bewitch men, animals and the fruits of the earth. Therefore, although the devil can blacken men's reputations in respect of other vices, yet it does not seem possible for him to do so in respect of this vice which cannot be perpetrated without his co-operation.

Besides, it has never hitherto been known to have happened that an innocent person has been defamed by the devil to such an extent that he was condemned to death for this particular crime. Furthermore, when a person is only under suspicion, he suffers no punishment except that which the

Canon prescribes for his purgation, as will be shown in the Third Part of this work in the second method of sentencing witches.

And it is set down there that, if such a man fails in his purgation, he is to be considered guilty, but that he should be solemnly adjured before the punishment due to his sin is proceeded with and enforced. But here we are dealing with actual events; and it has never yet been known that an innocent person has been punished on suspicion of witchcraft, and there is no doubt that God will never permit such a thing to happen.

Besides, He does not suffer the innocent who are under Angelic protection to be suspected of smaller crimes, such as robbery and such things; then all the more will He preserve those who are under that protection from suspicion of the crime of witchcraft.

And it is no valid objection to quote the legend of S. Germanus, when devils assumed the bodies of other women and sat down at table and slept with the husbands, deluding the latter into the belief that those women were in their own bodies eating and drinking with them, as we have mentioned before. For the women in this case are not to be held guiltless. For in the Canon (*Episcopi* 26, q. 2) such women are condemned for thinking that they are really and actually transported, when they are so only in imagination; although, as we have shown above, they are at times bodily transported by devils.

But our present proposition is that they can, with God's permission, cause all other infirmities, with no exception; and it is to be concluded from what we have said that this is so. Fo no exception is made by the Doctors, and there is no reason why there should be any, since, as we have often said, the natural power of devils is superior to all corporeal power. And we have found in our experience that this is true. For although greater difficulty may be felt in believing that witches are able to cause leprosy or epilepsy, since these diseases generally arise from some longstanding physical predisposition or defect, none the less it has sometimes been found that even these have been caused by witchcraft. For in the diocese of Basel, in the district of Alsace and Lorraine, a certain honest labourer spoke roughly to a certain quarrelsome woman, and she angrily threatened him that she would soon avenge herself on him. He took little notice of her; but on the same night he felt a pustule grow upon his neck, and he rubbed it a little, and found his whole face and neck puffed up and swollen, and a horrible form of leprosy appeared all over his body. He immediately went to his friends for advice, and told them of the woman's threat, and said that he would stake his life on the suspicion that this had been done to him by the magic art of that same witch. In short, the woman was taken, questioned, and confessed her crime. But when the judge asked her particularly about the reason for it, and how she had done it, she answered: "When that man used abusive words to me, I was angry and went home; and my familiar began to ask the reason for my ill humour. I told him, and begged him to avenge me on the man. And he asked what I wanted him to do to him; and I answered that I wished he would always have a swollen face. And the devil went away and afflicted the man even beyond my asking; for I had not hoped that he would infect him with such sore leprosy." And so the woman was burned.

And in the diocese of Constance, between Breisach and Freiburg, there is a leprous woman (unless she has paid the debt of all flesh within these two years) who used to tell to many people how the same thing had happened to her by reason of a similar quarrel which took place between her and another woman. For one night when she went out of the house to do something in front of the door, a warm wind came from the house of the other woman, which was opposite, and suddenly struck her face; and from that time she had been afflicted with the leprosy which she now suffered.

And lastly, in the same diocese, in the territory of the Black Forest, a witch was being lifted by a gaoler on to the pile of wood prepared for her burning, and said: "I will pay you"; and blew into his face. And he was at once afflicted with a horrible leprosy all over his body, and did not survive many days. For the sake of brevity, the fearful crimes of this witch, and many more instances which could be recounted, are omitted. For we have

often found that certain people have been visited with epilepsy or the falling sickness by means of eggs which have been buried with dead bodies, especially the dead bodies of witches, together with other ceremonies of which we cannot speak, particularly when these eggs have been given to a person either in food or drink.

☆

CHAPTER XII

Of the Way how in Particular they Afflict Men with Other Like Infirmities.

BUT who can reckon the number of the other infirmities which they have inflicted upon men, such as blindness, the sharpest pains, and contortions of the body? Yet we shall set down a few examples which we have seen with our eyes, or have been related to one of us Inquisitors.

When an inquisition was being held on some witches in the town of Innsbruck, the following case, among others, was brought to light. A certain honest woman who had been legally married to one of the household of the Archduke formally deposed the following. In the time of her maidenhood she had been in the service of one of the citizens, whose wife became afflicted with grievous pains in the head; and a woman came who said she could cure her, and so began certain incantations and rites which she said would assuage the pains. And I carefully watched (said this woman) what she did, and saw that, against the nature of water poured into a vase, she caused water to rise in its vessel, together with other ceremonies which there is no need to mention. And considering that the pains in my mistress's head were not assuaged by these means, I addressed the witch in some indignation with these words: "I do not know what you are doing, but whatever it is, it is witchcraft, and you are doing it for your own profit." Then the witch at once replied: "You will know in three days whether I am a witch or not." And so it proved; for on the third day when I sat down and took up a spindle, I suddenly felt a terrible pain in my body. First it was inside me, so that it seemed that there was no part of my body in which I did not feel horrible shooting pains; then it seemed to me just as if burning coals were being continually heaped upon my head; thirdly, from the crown of my head to the soles of my feet there was no place large enough for a pin-prick that was not covered with a rash of white pustules; and so I remained in these pains, crying out and wishing only for death, until the fourth day. At last my mistress's husband told me to go to a certain tavern; and with great difficulty I went, whilst he walked before, until we were in front of the tavern. "See!" he said to me; "there is a loaf of white bread over the tavern door." "I see," said I. Then he said: "Take it down, if you possibly can; for it may do you good." And I, holding on to the door with one hand as much as I could, got hold of the loaf with the other. "Open it" (said my master) "and look carefully at what is inside." Then, when I had broken open the loaf, I found many things inside it, especially some white grains very like the pustules on my body; and I saw also some seeds and herbs such as I could not eat or even look at, with the bones of serpents and other animals. In my astonishment I asked my master what was to be done; and he told me to throw it all into the fire. I did so; and behold! suddenly, not in an hour or even a few minutes, but at the moment when that matter was thrown into the fire, I regained all my former health.

And much more was deposed against the wife of the citizen in whose service this woman had been, by reason of which she was not lightly but very strongly suspected, and especially because she had used great familiarity with known witches. It is presumed that, having knowledge of the spell of witchcraft hidden in the loaf, she had told it to her husband; and then, in the way described, the maid-servant recovered her health.

To bring so great a crime into detestation, it is well that we should tell how another person, also a woman, was bewitched in the same town. An honest married woman deposed the following on oath.

Behind my house (she said) I have a greenhouse, and my neighbour's garden borders on it. One day I noticed that a passage had been made from my neighbour's garden to my greenhouse, not without some damage being caused; and as I was standing in the door of my greenhouse reckoning to myself and bemoaning both the passage and the damage, my neighbour suddenly came up and asked if I suspected her. But I was frightened because of her bad reputation, and only answered, "The footprints on the grass are a proof of the damage." Then she was indignant because I had not, as she hoped, accused her with action-able words, and went away murmuring; and though I could hear her words, I could not understand them. After a few days I became very ill with pains in the stomach, and the sharpest twinges shooting from my left side to my right, and conversely, as if two swords or knives were thrust through my breast; whence day and night I disturbed all the neighbours with my cries. And when they came from all sides to console me, it happened that a certain clay-worker, who was engaged in an adulterous intrigue with that witch, my neighbour, coming to visit me, took pity on my illness, and after a few words of comfort went away. But the next day he returned in a hurry, and, after consoling me, added: "I am going to test whether your illness is due to witchcraft, and if I find that it is, I shall restore your health." So he took some molten lead, and while I was lying in bed, poured it into a bowl of water which he placed on my body. And when the lead solidified into a certain image and various shapes, he said: "See! your illness has been caused by witchcraft; and one of the instru-ments of that witchcraft is hidden under the threshold of your house door. Let us go, then, and remove it, and you will feel better." So my husband and he went to remove the charm; and the clay-worker, taking up the threshold, told my husband to put his hand into the hole which then appeared, and take out whatever he found; and he did so. And first he brought out a waxen image about a palm long, perforated all over, and pierced through the sides with two needles, just in the same way that I felt the stabbing pains from side to side; and then little bags con-taining all sorts of things, such as grains and seeds and bones. And when all these things were burned, I became better, but not entirely well. For although the shootings and twinges stopped, and I quite regained my appetite for food, yet even now I am by no means fully restored to health.— And when we asked her why it was that she had not been completely restored, she answered: There are some other instruments of witchcraft hidden away which I cannot find. And when I asked the man how he knew where the first instruments were hidden, he answered: "I knew this through the love which prompts a friend to tell things to a friend; for your neighbour revealed this to me when she was coaxing me to commit adultery with her." This is the story of the sick woman.

But if I were to tell all the instances that were found in that one town I should need to make a book of them. For countless men and women who were blind, or lame, or withered, or plagued with various infirmities, severally took their oath that they had strong suspicions that their illnesses, both in general and in particular, were caused by witches, and that they were bound to endure those ills either for a period or right up to their deaths. And all that they said and testified was true, either as regards a specified illness or as regards the death of others. For that country abounds in henchmen and knights who have leisure for vice, and seduce women, and then wish to cast them off when they desire to marry an honest woman. But they can rarely do this without incurring the vengeance of some witchcraft upon themselves or their wives. For when those women see themselves despised, they persist in tormenting not so much the husband as the wife, in the fond hope that, if the wife should die, the husband would return to his former mistress.

For when a cook of the Archduke had married an honest girl from a foreign country, a witch, who had been his mistress, met them in the public road and, in the hearing of other honest people, foretold the bewitching and death of the girl, stretching out her hand and saying: "Not for long will you rejoice in your husband." And at once, on the following day, she took to her bed, and after a few days paid the debt of all flesh, exclaiming just as she expired: Lo! thus I die, because that woman, with God's permission, has killed me by her witchcraft; yet verily I go to another and better marriage with God.

In the same way, according to the evidence of public report, a certain soldier was slain by witchcraft, and many others whom I omit to mention.

But among them there was a well-known gentleman, whom his mistress wished to come to her on one occasion to pass the night; but he sent his servant to tell her that he could not visit her that night because he was busy. She promptly flew into a rage, and said to the servant: Go and tell your master that he will not trouble me for long. On the very next day he was taken ill, and was buried within a week.

And there are witches who can bewitch their judges by a mere look or glance from their eyes, and publicly boast that they cannot be punished; and when malefactors have been imprisoned for their crimes, and exposed to the severest torture to make them tell the truth, these witches can endow them with such an obstinacy of preserving silence that they are unable to lay bare their crimes.

And there are some who, in order to accomplish their evil charms and spells, beat and stab the Crucifix, and utter the filthiest words against the Purity of the Most Glorious Virgin MARY, casting the foulest aspersions on the Nativity of Our Saviour from Her inviolate womb. It is not expedient to repeat those vile words, nor yet to describe their detestable crimes, as the narrative would give too great offence to the ears of the pious; but they are all kept and preserved in writing, detailing the manner in which a certain baptized Jewess had instructed other young girls. And one of them, named Walpurgis, being in the same year at the point of death, and being urged by those who stood round her to confess her sins, exclaimed: I have given myself body and soul to the devil; there is no hope of forgiveness for me; and so died.

These particulars have not been written to the shame, but rather to the praise and glory of the most illustrious Archduke. For he was truly a Catholic Prince, and laboured very zealously with the Church at Brixen to exterminate witches. But they are written rather in hate and loathing of so great a crime, and that men may not cease to avenge their wrongs, and the insults and offences these wretches offer to the Creator and our Holy Faith, to say nothing of the temporal losses which they cause. For this is their greatest and gravest crime, namely, that they abjure the Faith.

☆

CHAPTER XIII

How Witch Midwives commit most Horrid Crimes when they either Kill Children or Offer them to Devils in most Accursed Wise.

WE must not omit to mention the injuries done to children by witch midwives, first by killing them, and secondly by blasphemously offering them to devils. In the diocese of Strasburg and in the town of Zabern there is an honest woman very devoted to the Blessed Virgin MARY, who tells the following experience of hers to all the guests that come to the tavern which she keeps, known by the sign of the Black Eagle.

I was, she says, pregnant by my lawful husband, now dead, and as my time approached, a certain midwife importuned me to engage her to assist at the birth of my child. But I knew her bad reputation, and although I had decided to engage another woman, pretended with conciliatory words to agree to her request. But when the pains came upon me, and I had brought in another midwife, the first one was very angry, and hardly a week later came into my room one night with two other women, and approached the bed where I was lying. And when I tried to call my husband, who was sleeping in another room, all the use was taken away from my limbs and tongue, so that except for seeing and hearing I could not move a muscle. And the witch, standing between the other two, said: "See! this vile woman, who would not take me for her mid-wife, shall not win through unpunished." The other two standing by her pleaded for me, saying: "She has never harmed any of us." But the witch added: "Because she has offended me I am going to put something into her entrails; but, to please you, she shall not feel any pain for half a year, but after that time she shall be tortured enough." So she came up and touched my belly with her hands; and it seemed to me

that she took out my entrails, and put in something which, however, I could not see. And when they had gone away, and I had recovered my power of speech, I called my husband as soon as possible, and told him what had happened. But he put it down to pregnancy, and said: "You pregnant women are always suffering from fancies and delusions." And when he would by no means believe me, I replied: "I have been given six months' grace, and if, after that time, no torment comes to me, I shall believe you."

She related this to her son, a cleric who was then Archdeacon of the district, and who came to visit her on the same day. And what happened? When exactly six months had passed, such a terrible pain came into her belly that she could not help disturbing everybody with her cries day and night. And because, as has been said, she was most devout to the Virgin, the Queen of Mercy, she fasted with bread and water every Saturday, so that she believed that she was delivered by Her intercession. For one day, when she wanted to perform an action of nature, all those unclean things fell from her body; and she called her husband and her son, and said: "Are those fancies? Did I not say that after half a year the truth would be known? Or who ever saw me eat thorns, bones, and even bits of wood?" For there were brambles as long as a palm, as well as a quantity of other things.

Moreover (as was said in the First Part of the work), it was shown by the confession of the servant, who was brought to judgement at Breisach, that the greatest injuries to the Faith as regards the heresy of witches are done by midwives; and this is made clearer than daylight itself by the confessions of some who were afterwards burned.

For in the diocese of Basel at the town of Dann, a witch who was burned confessed that she had killed more than forty children, by sticking a needle through the crowns of their heads into their brains, as they came out from the womb.

Finally, another woman in the diocese of Strasburg confessed that she had killed more children than she could count. And she was caught in this way. She had been called from one town to another to act as midwife to a certain woman, and, having performed her office, was going back home. But as she went out of the town gate, the arm of a newly-born child fell out of the cloak she had wrapped round her, in whose folds the arm had been concealed. This was seen by those who were sitting in the gateway, and when she had gone on, they picked up from the ground what they took to be a piece of meat; but when they looked more closely and saw that it was not a piece of meat, but recognized it by its fingers as a child's arm, they reported it to the magistrates, and it was found that a child had died before baptism, lacking an arm. So the witch was taken and questioned, and confessed the crime, and that she had, as has been said, killed more children than she could count.

Now the reason for such practices is as follows: It is to be presumed that witches are compelled to do such things at the command of evil spirits, and sometimes against their own wills. For the devil knows that, because of the pain of loss,* or original sin, such children are debarred from entering the Kingdom of Heaven. And by this means the Last Judgement is delayed, when the devils will be condemned to eternal torture; since the number of the elect is more slowly completed, on the fulfilment of which the world will be consumed. And also, as has already been shown, witches are taught by the devil to confect from the limbs of such children an unguent which is very useful for their spells.

But in order to bring so great a sin into utter detestation, we must not pass over in silence the following horrible crime. For when they do not kill the child, they blasphemously offer it to the devil in this manner. As soon as the child is born, the midwife, if the mother herself is not a witch, carries it out of the room on the pretext of warming it, raises it up, and offers it to the Prince of Devils, that is Lucifer, and to all the devils. And this is done by the kitchen fire.

A certain man relates that he noticed that his wife, when her time came to give birth, against the usual custom of women in childbirth, did not allow any woman to approach the bed except her own daughter, who acted as midwife. Wishing to know the reason for

this, he hid himself in the house and saw the whole order of the sacrilege and dedication to the devil, as it has been described. He saw also, as it seemed to him, that without any human support, but by the power of the devil, the child was climbing up the chain by which the cooking-pots were suspended. In great consternation both at the terrible words of the invocation of the devils, and at the other iniquitous ceremonies, he strongly insisted that the child should be baptized immediately. While it was being carried to the next village, where there was a church, and when they had to cross a bridge over a certain river, he drew his sword and ran at his daughter, who was carrying the child, saying in the hearing of two others who were with them: "You shall not carry the child over the bridge; for either it must cross the bridge by itself, or you shall be drowned in the river." The daughter was terrified and, together with the other women in company, asked him if he were in his right mind (for he had hidden what had happened from all the others except the two men who were with him). Then he answered: "You vile drab, by your magic arts you made the child climb the chain in the kitchen; now make it cross the bridge with no one carrying it, or I shall drown you in the river." And so, being compelled, she put the child down on the bridge, and invoked the devil by her art; and suddenly the child was seen on the other side of the bridge. And when the child had been baptized, and he had returned home, since he now had witnesses to convict his daughter of witchcraft (for he could not prove the former crime of the oblation to the devil, inasmuch as he had been the only witness of that sacrilegious ritual), he accused both daughter and mother before the judge after their period of purgation; and they were both burned, and the crime of midwives of making that sacrilegious offering was discovered.

But here the doubt arises: to what end or purpose is this sacrilegious offering of children, and how does it benefit the devils? To this it can be said that the devils do this for three reasons, which serve three most wicked purposes. The first reason arises from their pride, which always increases; as it is said: "They that hate Thee have

---

* "Pain of loss." Poena damni.

lifted up the head."* For they try as far as possible to conform with divine rites and ceremonies. Secondly, they can more easily deceive men under the mask of an outwardly seeming pious action. For in the same way they entice young virgins and boys into their power; for though they might solicit such by means of evil and corrupt men, yet they rather deceive them by magic mirrors and the reflections seen in witches' finger-nails, and lure them on in the belief that they love chastity, whereas they hate it. For the devil hates above all the Blessed Virgin, because she bruised his head (Genesis iii. 15).† Just so in this oblation of children they deceive the minds of witches into the vice of infidelity under the appearance of a virtuous act. And the third reason is, that the perfidy of witches may grow, to the devils' own gain, when they have witches dedicated to them from their very cradles.

And this sacrilege affects the child in three ways. In the first place, visible offerings to God are made of visible things, such as wine or bread or the fruits of the earth, as a sign of honour and subjection to Him, as it is said in Ecclesiasticus xxv : Thou shalt not appear empty before the Lord. And such offerings cannot and must not afterwards be put to profane uses. Therefore the holy Father, S. John Damascene, says: The oblations which are offered in church belong only to the priests, but not that they should divert them to their own uses, but that they should faithfully distribute them, partly in the observance of divine worship, and partly for the use of the poor. From this it follows that a child who has been offered to the devil in sign of subjection and homage to him cannot possibly be dedicated by Catholics to a holy life, in worthy and fruitful service to God for the benefit of himself and others.

For who can say that the sins of the mothers and of others do not redound in punishment upon the children? Perhaps someone will quote that saying of the prophet: "The son shall not bear the iniquity of the father." But there is that other passage in Exodus xx: I am a jealous God, visiting the sins of the fathers upon the children unto the third and fourth generation. Now the meaning of these two sayings is as follows. The first speaks of spiritual punishment in the judgement of Heaven or God, and not in the judgement of men. And this is the punishment of the soul, such as loss or the forfeiture of glory, or the punishment of pain, that is, of the torment of eternal fire. And with such punishments no one is punished except for his own sin, either inherited as original sin or committed as actual sin.

The second text speaks of those who imitate the sins of their fathers, as Gratian* has explained (I, q. 4, etc.); and there he gives other explanations as to how the judgement of God inflicts other punishments on a man, not only for his own sins which he has committed, or which he might commit (but is prevented by punishment from committing), but also for the sins of others.

And it cannot be argued that then a man is punished without cause, and without sin, which should be the cause of punishment. For according to the rule of the law, no one must be punished without sin, unless there is some cause for it. And we can say that there is always a most just cause, though it may not be known to us: see S. Augustine, XXIV, 4. And if we cannot in the result penetrate the depth of God's judgement, yet we know that what He has said is true, and what He has done is just.

But there is this distinction to be observed in innocent children who are offered to devils not by their mothers when they are witches, but by midwives who, as we have said, secretly take from the embrace and the womb of an honest mother. Such children are not

---

* "Head." "Psalm" lxxxii, 2.

† "Genesis." Inimicitias ponam inter te et mulierem, et semen tuum et semen illius: ipsa conteret caput tuum, et tu insidiaberis calcaneo eius.

* "Gratian." The little that is known concerning the author of the "Concordantia discordantium canonum," more generally called the "Decretum Gratiani," must be gathered from the work itself. Gratian was born in Italy, perhaps at Chiusi. He became a Camaldolese monk and taught at Bologna. It is uncertain at what time he compiled the "Decretum," but it was commonly held to have been completed in 1151. More recent authorities, however, are inclined to suggest 1140. Gratian died before 1179, some think as early as 1160. He is regarded as the true founder of the science of canon law.

so cut off from grace that they must necessarily become prone to such crimes; but it is piously to be believed that they may rather cultivate their mothers' virtues.

The second result to the children of this sacrilege is as follows. When a man offers himself as a sacrifice to God, he recognizes God as his Beginning and his End; and this sacrifice is more worthy than all the external sacrifices which he makes, having its beginning in his creation and its end in his glorification, as it is said: A sacrifice to God is an afflicted spirit,* etc. In the same way, when a witch offers a child to the devil, she commends it body and soul to him as its beginning and its end in eternal damnation; wherefore not without some miracle can the child be set free from the payment of so great a debt.

And we read often in history of children whom their mothers, in some passion or mental disturbance, have unthinkingly offered to the devil from the very womb, and how it is only with the very greatest difficulty that they can, when they have grown to adult age, be delivered from that bondage which the devil has, with God's permission, usurped to himself. And of this the *Book of Examples, Most Blessed Virgin MARY,* affords many illustrations; a notable instance being that of the man whom the Supreme Pontiff was unable to deliver from the torments of the devil, but at last he was sent to a holy man living in the East, and finally with great difficulty was delivered from his bondage through the intercession of the Most Glorious Virgin Herself.

And if God so severely punishes even such a thoughtless, I will not say sacrifice, but commendation used angrily by a mother when her husband, after copulating with her, says, I hope a child will come of it; and she answers, May the child go to the devil! How much greater must be the punishment when the Divine Majesty is offended in the way we have described!

The third effect of this sacrilegious oblation is to inculcate an habitual inclination to cast spells upon men, animals, and the fruits of the earth. This is shown by S. Thomas in the 2nd Book, quest. 108, where he speaks

of temporal punishment, how some are punished for the sins of others. For he says that, bodily speaking, sons are part of their fathers' possessions, and servants and animals belong to their masters; therefore when a man is punished in all his possessions, it follows that often the sons suffer for the fathers.

And this is quite a different matter from what has been said about God visiting the sins of the fathers upon the children unto the third and fourth generation. For there it is a question of those who imitate their fathers' sins; but here we speak of those who suffer instead of their fathers, when they do not imitate their sins by committing them in fact, but only inherit the results of their sins. For in this way the son born to David in adultery died very soon; and the animals of the Amalekites were ordered to be killed. Nevertheless, there is much mystery in all this.

Taking into consideration all that we have said, we may well conclude that such children are always, up to the end of their lives, predisposed to the perpetration of witchcraft. For just as God sanctifies that which is dedicated to Him, as is proved by the deeds of the Saints, when parents offer to God the fruit which they have generated; so also the devil does not cease to infect with evil that which is offered to him. Many examples can be found in the Old and New Testaments. For so were many of the Patriarchs and Prophets, such as Isaac, Samuel, and Samson; and so were Alexis and Nicolas,† and many more, guided by much grace to a holy life.

---

† *"Alexis."* S. Alexis, Confessor. Feast, 17 July. The Basilica and title-church of SS. Bonifacio ed Alessio all' Aventino, Rome, contains the bodies of S. Boniface and S. Alexis under the High Altar. S. Aglae is buried in the confessional.

S. Nicolas of Tolentino, O.S.A., circa 1246–1306, was born of gentlefolk, Compagnonus de Guarutti and Amata de Guidiani, pious and devout, living in great seclusion on very moderate means. He was the child of prayer, his mother being advanced in years and vowing her son, should she bare one, to God from the womb. His parents joyfully consented to his joining the Order of Augustinian Hermits, of which he is one of the greatest glories. S. Nicolas was distinguished by angelic meekness and celestial purity. He died 10 September, and his feast is celebrated on that day.

---

* *"Spirit."* *"Psalm"* l, 19.

Finally, we know from experience that the daughters of witches are always suspected of similar practices, as imitators of their mothers' crimes; and that indeed the whole of a witch's progeny is infected. And the reason for this and for all that has been said before is, that according to their pact with the devil, they always have to leave behind them and carefully instruct a survivor, so that they may fulfil their vow to do all they can to increase the number of witches.* For how else could it happen, as it has very often been found, that tender girls of eight or ten years have raised up tempests and hailstorms, unless they had been dedicated to the devil under such a pact by their mothers. For the children could not do such things of themselves by abjuring the Faith, which is how all adult witches have to begin, since they have no knowledge of any single article of the Faith. We will recount an example of such a child.

In the duchy of Swabia a certain farmer went to his fields with his little daughter, hardly eight years old, to look at his crops, and began complaining about the drought, saying: Alas! when will it rain? The girl heard him, and in the simplicity of her heart said: Father, if you want it to rain, I can soon make it come. And her father said to her: What? Do you know how to make it rain? And the girl answered: I can make it rain, and I can make hailstorms and tempests too. And the father asked: Who taught you? And she answered: My mother did, but she told me not to tell anybody. Then the father asked: How did she teach you? And she answered: She sent me to a master who will do anything I ask at any time. But her father said: Have you ever seen him?

And she said: I have sometimes seen men coming in and out to my mother; and when I asked her who they were, she told me that they were our masters to whom she had given me, and that they were powerful and rich patrons. The father was terrified, and asked her if she could raise a hailstorm then. And the girl said: Yes, if I had a little water. Then he led the girl by the hand to a stream, and said: Do it, but only on our land. Then the girl put her hand in the water and stirred it in the name of her master, as her mother had taught her; and behold! the rain fell only on that land. Seeing this, the father said: Make it hail now, but only on one of our fields. And when the girl had done this, the father was convinced by the evidence, and accused his wife before the judge. And the wife was taken and convicted and burned; but the daughter was reconciled and solemnly dedicated to God, since which hour she could no more work these spells and charms.

☆

CHAPTER XIV

Here followeth how Witches Injure Cattle in Various Ways.

WHEN S. Paul said, Doth God care for oxen? † he meant that, though all things are subject to Divine providence, both man and beast each in its degree, as the Psalmist says,‡ yet the sons of men are especially in His governance and under the protection of His wings. I say, therefore, if men are injured by witches, with God's permission, both the innocent and just as well as sinners, and if parents are bewitched in their children, as being part of their possessions, who can then presume to doubt that, with God's permission, various injuries can be brought by witches upon cattle and the fruits of the earth, which are also part of men's possessions? For so was Job stricken by the devil and lost all his cattle. So also there is not even the smallest farm where women do not injure each other's cows, by drying up their milk, and very often killing them.

But let us first consider the smallest

---

* *"Number of Witches." Francesco Maria Guazzo, "Compendium Maleficarum," Milan, 1608, tells us that the witches promise the devil "to strive with all their power and to use every inducement and endeavour to draw other men and women to their detestable practices and the worship of Satan." So in the case of Janet Breadheid of Auldearne it was her husband who "enticed her into that craft."* (Pitcairn, *"Criminal Trials," Edinburgh, 1833.) At Salem, George Burroughs, a minister, was accused by a large number of women as "the person who had Seduc'd and Compell'd them into the snares of Witchcraft." See my "History of Witchcraft," Chap. III, pp. 83–84.*

† "Oxen." "I. Corinthians," ix. 9.
‡ "Psalmist." "Psalmist" xxxv, 7, 8.

of these injuries, that of drying up the milk. If it is asked how they can do this, it can be answered that, according to Blessed Albert in his *Book on Animals*, milk is naturally menstrual in any animal; and, like another flux in women, when it is not stopped by some natural infirmity, it is due to witchcraft that it is stopped. Now the flow of milk is naturally stopped when the animal becomes pregnant; and it is stopped by an accidental infirmity when the animal eats some herb the nature of which is to dry up the milk and make the cow ill.

But they can cause this in various ways by witchcraft. For on the more holy nights according to the instructions of the devil and for the greater offence to the Divine Majesty of God, a witch will sit down in a corner of her house with a pail between her legs, stick a knife or some instrument in the wall or a post, and make as if to milk it with her hands. Then she summons her familiar who always works with her in everything, and tells him that she wishes to milk a certain cow from a certain house, which is healthy and abounding in milk. And suddenly the devil takes the milk from the udder of that cow, and brings it to where the witch is sitting, as if it were flowing from the knife.

But when this is publicly preached to the people they get no bad information by it; for however much anyone may invoke the devil, and think that by this means alone he can do this thing, he deceives himself, because he is without the foundation of that perfidy, not having rendered homage to the devil or abjured the Faith. I have set this down because some have thought that several of the matters of which I have written ought not to be preached to the people, on account of the danger of giving them evil knowledge; whereas it is impossible for anyone to learn from a preacher how to perform any of the things that have been mentioned. But they have been written rather to bring so great a crime into detestation, and should be preached from the pulpit, so that judges may be more eager to punish the horrible crime of the abnegation of the Faith. Yet they should not always be preached in this way; for the secular mind pays more attention to temporal losses, being more concerned with earthly than

spiritual matters; therefore when witches can be accused of inflicting temporal loss, judges are more zealous to punish them. But who can fathom the cunning of the devil?

I know of some men in a certain city who wished to eat some May butter one May time. And as they were walking along they came to a meadow and sat down by a stream; and one of them, who had formed some open or tacit pact with the devil, said: I will get you the best May butter. And at once he took off his clothes and went into the stream, not standing up but sitting with his back against the current; and while the others looked on, he uttered certain words, and moved the water with his hands behind his back; and in a short time he brought out a great quantity of butter of the sort that the country women sell in the market in May. And the others tasted it, and declared it was the very best butter.

From this we can deduce first the following fact concerning their practices. They are either true witches, by reason of an expressed pact formed with the devil, or they know by some tacit understanding that the devil will do what they ask. In the first case there is no need for any discussion, for such are true witches. But in the second case, then they owe the devil's help to the fact that they were blasphemously offered to the devil by a midwife or by their own mothers.

But it may be objected that the devil perhaps brought the butter without any compact, expressed or tacit, and without any previous dedication to himself. It is answered that no one can ever use the devil's help in such matters without invoking him; and that by that very act of seeking help from the devil he is an apostate from the Faith. This is the decision of S. Thomas in the *Second Book of Sentences*, dist. 8, on the question, Whether it is apostasy from the Faith to use the devil's help. And although Blessed Albert the Great agrees with the other Doctors, yet he says more expressly that in such matters there is always apostasy either in word or in deed. For if invocations, conjurations, fumigations and adorations are used, then an open pact is formed with the devil, even if there has been no surrender of body and soul together with explicit abjuration of the Faith either wholly or in part. For by the mere invocation of the devil a man commits open verbal apostasy. But if there is no spoken invocation, but only a bare action from which follows something that could not be done without the devil's help, then whether a man does it by beginning in the name of the devil, or with some other unknown words, or without any words but with that intention; then, says Blessed Albert, it is apostasy of deed, because that action is looked for from the devil. But since to expect or receive anything from the devil is always a disparagement of the Faith, it is also apostasy.

So it is concluded that, by whatever means that sorcerer procured the butter, it was done with either a tacit or an expressed pact with the devil; and since, if it had been with an expressed pact, he would have behaved after the usual manner of witches, it is probable that there was a tacit or secret pact, originating either from himself or from his mother or a midwife. And I say that it arose from himself, since he only went through certain motions, and expected the devil to produce the effect.

The second conclusion we can draw from this and similar practices is this. The devil cannot create new species of things; therefore when natural butter suddenly came out of the water, the devil did not do this by changing the water into milk, but by taking butter from some place where it was kept and bringing it to the man's hand. Or else he took natural milk from a natural cow and suddenly churned it into natural butter; for while the art of women takes a little time to make butter, the devil could do it in the shortest space of time and bring it to the man.

It is in the same way that certain dealers in magic, when they find themselves in need of wine or some such necessity, merely go out in the night into a village with a flask or vessel, and bring it back suddenly filled with wine. For then the devil takes natural wine from some vessel and fills their flasks for them.

And with regard to the manner whereby witches kill animals and cattle, it should be said that they act very much as they do in the case of men. They can bewitch them by a touch and a look, or by a look only; or by placing under the threshold of the stable door, or near the place where they go to water, some charm or periapt of witchcraft.

For in this way those witches who were burned at Ratisbon, of whom we shall say more later on, were always incited by the devil to bewitch the best horses and the fattest cattle. And when they were asked how they did so, one of them named Agnes said that they hid certain things under the threshold of the stable door. And, asked what sort of things, she said: The bones of different kinds of animals. She was further asked in whose name they did this, and answered, In the name of the devil and all the other devils. And there was another of them, named Anna, who had killed twenty-three horses in succession belonging to one of the citizens who was a carrier. This man at last, when he had bought his twenty-fourth horse and was reduced to extreme poverty, stood in his stable and said to the witch, who was standing in the door of her house: "See, I have bought a horse, and I swear to God and His Holy Mother that if this horse dies I shall kill you with my own hands." At that the witch was frightened, and left the horse alone. But when she was taken and asked how she had done these things, she answered that she had done nothing but dig a little hole, after which the devil had put in it certain things unknown to her. From this it is concluded that the witch co-operates sufficiently if it is only by a touch or a look; for the devil is permitted no power of injuring creatures without some co-operation on the part of the witch, as has been shown before. And this is for the great offence to the Divine Majesty.

For shepherds have often seen animals in the fields give three or four jumps into the air, and then suddenly fall to the ground and die; and this is caused by the power of witches at the instance of the devil.

In the diocese of Strasburg, between the town of Fiessen and Mount Ferrer, a certain very rich man affirmed that more than forty oxen and cows belonging to him and others had been bewitched in the Alps within the space of one year, and that there had been no natural plague or sickness to cause it. To prove this, he said that when cattle die from some chance plague or disease, they do not do so all at once, but by degrees; but that this witchcraft had suddenly taken all the strength from them, and therefore everyone judged that they had been killed by witchcraft. I have said forty head of cattle, but I believe he put the number higher than that. However, it is very true that many cattle are said to have been bewitched in some districts, especially in the Alps; and it is known that this form of witchcraft is unhappily most widespread. We shall consider some similar cases later, in the chapter where we discuss the remedies for cattle that have been bewitched.

☆

CHAPTER XV

How they Raise and Stir up Hailstorms and Tempests, and Cause Lightning to Blast both Men and Beasts.

THAT devils and their disciples can by witchcraft cause lightnings and hailstorms and tempests, and that the devils have power from God to do this, and their disciples do so with God's permission, is proved by Holy Scripture in *Job* i and ii. For the devil received power from God, and immediately caused it to happen that the Sabeans took away from Job fifty yoke of oxen and five hundred asses, and then fire came from heaven and consumed seven thousand camels, and a great wind came and smote down the house, killing his seven sons and his three daughters, and all the young men, that is to say, the servants, except him who brought the news, were killed; and finally the devil smote the body of the holy man with the most terrible sores, and caused his wife and his three friends to vex him grievously.

S. Thomas in his commentary on Job says as follows: It must be confessed that, with God's permission, the devils can disturb the air, raise up winds, and make the fire fall from heaven. For although, in the matter of taking various shapes, corporeal nature is not at the command of any Angel, either good or bad, but only at that of God the Creator, yet in the matter of local motion corporeal nature has to obey the spiritual nature. And

this truth is clearly exemplified in man himself; for at the mere command of the will, which exists subjectively in the soul, the limbs are moved to perform that which they have been willed to do. Therefore whatever can be accomplished by mere local motion, this not only good but also bad spirits can by their natural power accomplish, unless God should forbid it. But winds and rain and other similar disturbances of the air can be caused by the mere movement of vapours released from the earth or the water; therefore the natural power of devils is sufficient to cause such things. So says S. Thomas.

For God in His justice using the devils as his agents of punishment inflicts the evils which come to us who live in this world. Therefore, with reference to that in the Psalms: "He called a famine on the land, and wasted all their substance of bread"; the gloss says: God allowed this evil to be caused by the bad Angels who are in charge of such matters; and by famine is meant the Angel in charge of famine.

We refer the reader also to what has been written above on the question as to whether witches must always have the devil's help to aid them in their works, and concerning the three kinds of harm which the devils at times inflict without the agency of a witch. But the devils are more eager to injure men with the help of a witch, since in this way God is the more offended, and greater power is given to them to torment and punish.

And relevant to this subject is what the Doctors have written in the *Second Book of Sentences*, dist. 6, on the question whether there is a special place assigned to the bad Angels in the clouds of the air. For in devils there are three things to be considered—their nature, their duty and their sin; and by nature they belong to the empyrean of heaven, through sin to the lower hell, but by reason of the duty assigned to them, as we have said, as ministers of punishment to the wicked and trial to the good, their place is in the clouds of the air. For they do not dwell here with us on the earth lest they should plague us too much; but in the air and around the fiery sphere they can so bring together the active and passive agents that, when God permits, they can bring down fire and lightning from heaven.

A story is told in the *Formicarius** of a certain man who had been taken, and was asked by the judge how they went about to raise up hailstorms and tempests, and whether it was easy for them to do so. He answered: We can easily cause hailstorms, but we cannot do all the harm that we wish, because of the guardianship of good Angels. And he added: We can only injure those who are deprived of God's help; but we cannot hurt those who make the sign of the Cross. And this is how we go to work: first we use certain words in the fields to implore the chief of the devils to send one of his servants to strike the man whom we name. Then, when the devil has come, we sacrifice to him a black cock at two cross-roads,† throwing it up into the air; and when the devil has received this, he performs our wish and stirs up the air, but not always in the places which we have named, and, according to the permission of the living God, sends down hailstorms and lightnings.

In the same work we hear of a certain leader or heresiarch of witches named Staufer,‡ who lived in Berne and the adjacent country, and used publicly to boast that, whenever he liked, he could change himself into a mouse in the sight of his rivals and slip through the hands of his deadly enemies; and that he had often escaped from the hands of his mortal foes in this manner. But when the Divine justice wished to put an end to his wickedness, some of his enemies lay in wait for him cautiously and saw him sitting in a basket near a window,

and suddenly pierced him through with swords and spears, so that he miserably died for his crimes. Yet he left behind him a disciple, named Hoppo, who had also for his master that Stadlin whom we have mentioned before in the sixth chapter.

These two could, whenever they pleased, cause the third part of the manure or straw or corn to pass invisibly from a neighbour's field to their own; they could raise the most violent hailstorms and destructive winds and lightning; could cast into the water in the sight of their parents children walking by the water-side, when there was no one else in sight; could cause barrenness in men and animals; could reveal hidden things to others; could in many ways injure men in their affairs or their bodies; could at times kill whom they would by lightning; and could cause many other plagues, when and where the justice of God permitted such things to be done.

It is better to add an instance which came within our own experience. For in the diocese of Constance, twenty-eight German miles from the town of Ratisbon in the direction of Salzburg, a violent hailstorm destroyed all the fruit, crops and vineyards in a belt one mile wide, so that the vines hardly bore fruit for three years. This was brought to the notice of the Inquisition, since the people clamoured for an inquiry to be held; many beside all the townsmen being of the opinion that it was caused by witchcraft. Accordingly it was agreed after fifteen days' formal deliberation that it was a case of witch-craft for us to consider; and among a large number of suspects, we particularly examined two women, one named Agnes, a bath-woman, and the other Anna von Mindelheim. These two were taken and shut up separately in different prisons, neither of them know-ing in the least what had happened to the other. On the following day the bath-woman was very gently questioned in the presence of a notary by the chief magistrate, a justice named Gelre very zealous for the Faith, and by the other magistrates with him; and although she was undoubtedly well provided with that evil gift of silence which is the constant bane of judges, and at the first trial affirmed that she was innocent of any crime against man or woman;

---

* *"Formicarius,"* Chap. iii.

† *"Cross-Roads."* In the trial of Dame Alice Kyteler of Kilkenny, *1324, it was shown that she had sacrificed at the cross-roads live animals (Holinshed says nine red cocks) to her familiar, Robert Artisson, "qui se facit appellari Artis Filium."* In Greek tradition the χερκώπις, a poltergeist, haunted the cross-ways. Lemoine, VI, p. 109, tells us: "Celui qui veut devenir sorcier doit aller à un ' quatre chemins' avec une ' poule noire,' ou bien encore au 'cimetière,' sur une ' tombe' et toujours à ' minuit.' Il vient alors quel-qu'un qui demande: 'Que venez-vous faire ici?' 'J'ai une poule à vendre,' répond-on. Ce quel-qu'un (est) le Méchant."

‡ *"Staufer." Staufus. "Formicarius,"* Chap. iii. The edition Frankfort, 1588, Vol. I, p. 722, reads *"Scavius"* and in the margin *"Schasius."* (Marginal note: *"De Schasio in murem se conuertente."*)

yet, in the Divine mercy that so great a crime should not pass unpunished, suddenly, when she had been freed from her chains, although it was in the torture chamber, she fully laid bare all the crimes which she had committed. For when she was questioned by the Notary of the Inquisition upon the accusations which had been brought against her of harm done to men and cattle, by reason of which she had been gravely suspected of being a witch, although there had been no witness to prove that she had abjured the Faith or performed coitus with an Incubus devil (for she had been most secret); nevertheless, after she had confessed to the harm which she had caused to animals and men, she acknowledged also all that she was asked concerning the abjuration of the Faith, and copulation committed with an Incubus devil; saying that for more than eighteen years she had given her body to an Incubus devil, with a complete abnegation of the Faith.

After this she was asked whether she knew anything about the hailstorm which we have mentioned, and answered that she did. And, being asked how and in what way, she answered: "I was in my house, and at midday a familiar came to me and told me to go with a little water on to the field or plain of Kuppel (for so is it named). And when I asked what he wanted to do with the water, he said that he wanted to make it rain. So I went out at the town gate, and found the devil standing under a tree." The judge asked her, under which tree; and she said, "Under that one opposite that tower," pointing it out. Asked what she did under the tree, she said, "The devil told me to dig a little hole and pour the water into it." Asked whether they sat down together, she said, "I sat down, but the devil stood up." Then she was asked, with what words and in what manner she had stirred the water; and she answered, "I stirred it with my finger, and called on the name of the devil himself and all the other devils." Again the judge asked what was done with the water, and she answered: "It disappeared, and the devil took it up into the air." Then she was asked if she had any associate, and answered: "Under another tree opposite I had a companion (naming the other captured witch, Anna von

Mindelheim), but I do not know what she did." Finally, the bath-woman was asked how long it was between the taking up of the water and the hailstorm; and she answered: "There was just sufficient interval of time to allow me to get back to my house."

But (and this is remarkable) when on the next day the other witch had at first been exposed to the very gentlest questions, being suspended hardly clear of the ground by her thumbs, after she had been set quite free, she disclosed the whole matter without the slightest discrepancy from what the other had told; agreeing as to the place, that it was under such a tree and the other had been under another; as to the time, that it was at midday; as to the method, namely, of stirring water poured into a hole in the name of the devil and all the devils; and as to the interval of time, that the hailstorm had come after her devil had taken the water up into the air and she had returned home. Accordingly, on the third day they were burned. And the bath-woman was contrite and confessed, and commended herself to God, saying that she would die with a willing heart if she could escape the tortures of the devil, and held in her hand a cross which she kissed. But the other witch scorned her for doing so. And this one had consorted with an Incubus devil for more than twenty years with a complete abjuration of the Faith, and had done far more harm than the former witch to men, cattle and the fruits of the earth, as is shown in the preserved record of their trial.

These instances must serve, since indeed countless examples of this sort of mischief could be recounted. But very often men and beasts and store-houses are struck by lightning by the power of devils; and the cause of this seems to be more hidden and ambiguous, since it often appears to happen by Divine permission without the co-operation of any witch. However, it has been found that witches have freely confessed that they have done such things, and there are various known instances of it, which could be mentioned, in addition to what has already been said. Therefore it is reasonable to conclude that, just as easily as they raise hailstorms, so can they cause lightning and storms at sea; and so no doubt at all remains on these points.

CHAPTER XVI

Of Three Ways in which Men and not Women may be Discovered to be Addicted to Witchcraft : Divided into Three Heads : and First of the Witchcraft of Archers.

FOR our present purpose the last class of witchcraft is that which is practised in three forms by men; and first we must consider the seven deadly and horrible crimes which are committed by wizards who are archers. For first, on the Sacred Day of the Passion of Our Lord, that is to say, on Good Friday, as it is called, during the solemnization of the Mass of the Presanctified they shoot with arrows, as at a target, at the most sacred image of the Crucifix. Oh, the cruelty and injury to the Saviour! Secondly, though there is some doubt whether they have to utter a verbal form of apostasy to the devil in addition to that apostasy of deed, yet whether it be so or not, no greater injury to the Faith can be done by a Christian. For it is certain that, if such things were done by an infidel, they would be of no efficacy; for no such easy method of gratifying their hostility to the Faith is granted to them. Therefore these wretches ought to consider the truth and power of the Catholic Faith, for the confirmation of which God justly permits such crimes.

Thirdly, such an archer has to shoot three or four arrows in this way, and as a consequence he is able to kill on any day just the same number of men. Fourthly, they have the following assurance from the devil; that though they must first actually set eyes on the man they wish to kill, and must bend their whole will on killing him, yet it matters not where the man may shut himself up, for he cannot be protected, but the arrows which have been shot will be carried and struck into him by the devil.

Fifthly, they can shoot an arrow* with such precision as to shoot a penny

from a person's head without hurting his head, and they can continue to do this indefinitely. Sixthly, in order to gain this power they have to offer homage of body and soul to the devil. We shall give some instances of this sort of practice.

For a certain prince of the Rhineland, named Eberhard Longbeard because he let his beard grow, had, before he was sixty years old, acquired for himself some of the Imperial territory, and was besieging a certain castle named Lendenbrunnen because of the raids which were made by the men of the castle. And he had in his company a wizard of this sort, named Puncker, who so molested the men of the castle that he killed them all in succession with his arrows, except one. And this is how he proceeded. Whenever he had looked at a man, it did not matter where that man went to or hid himself, he had only to loose an arrow and that man was mortally wounded and killed; and he was able to shoot three such arrows every day because he had shot three arrows at the image of the Saviour. It is probable that the devil favours the number three more than any other, because it represents an effective denial of the Holy Trinity. But after he had shot those three arrows, he could only shoot with the same uncertainty as other men. At last one of the men of the castle called out to him mockingly, "Puncker, will you not at least spare the ring which hangs in the gate?" And he answered from outside in the night, "No; I shall take it away on the day that the castle is captured." And he fulfilled his promise : for when, as has been said, all were killed except one, and the castle had been taken, he took that ring and hung it in his own house at Rorbach in the diocese of Worms, where it can be seen hanging to this day. But afterwards he was one night killed with their spades by some peasants whom he had injured, and he perished in his sins.

It is told also of this man, that a very eminent person wished to have proof of his skill, and for a test placed his little son before the target with a penny on his cap, and ordered him to shoot the penny away without removing the cap. The wizard said that he would do it, but with reluctance; for he would rather have refrained, not being sure whether the devil was seducing him

---

* *"Shoot an Arrow." This old tradition was made the subject of the celebrated opera "Der Freischutz," the libretto of which is by Kind, the music by Weber. It was originally produced at Berlin in 1821, and on 22 July, 1824, first performed in England at the Lyceum Theatre, London, as "Der Freischutz; or, The Seventh Bullet."*

to his death. But, yielding to the persuasions of the prince, he placed one arrow in readiness in the cord which was slung over his shoulder, fitted another to his bow, and shot the penny from the cap without hurting the boy. Seeing this, the prince asked him why he had placed the arrow in that cord; and he answered: "If I had been deceived by the devil and had killed my son, since I should have had to die I would quickly have shot you with the other arrow to avenge my death."

And though such wickedness is permitted by God for the proving and chastisement of the faithful, nevertheless more powerful miracles are performed by the Saviour's mercy for the strengthening and glory of the Faith.

For in the diocese of Constance, near the castle of Hohenzorn and a convent of nuns, there is a newly-built church where may be seen an image of Our Saviour pierced with an arrow and bleeding. And the truth of this miracle is shown as follows. A miserable wretch who wished to be assured by the devil of having three or four arrows with which he could, in the manner we have told, kill whom he pleased, shot and pierced with an arrow (just as it is still seen) a certain Crucifix at a cross-road; and when it miraculously began to bleed,* the wretch was struck motion-

less in his steps by Divine power. And when he was asked by a passer-by why he stood fixed there, he shook his head, and trembling in his arms and his hands, in which he held the bow, and all over his body, could answer nothing. So the other looked about him, and saw the Crucifix with the arrow and the blood, and said: "You villain, you have pierced the image of Our Lord!" And calling some others, he told them to see that he did not escape (although, as has been said, he could not move), and ran to the castle and told what had happened. And they came down and found the wretched man in the same place; and when they had questioned him, and he had confessed his crime, he was removed from that district by public justice, and suffered a miserable death in merited expiation of his deeds.

But, alas! how horrible it is to think that human perversity is not afraid to countenance such crimes. For it is said that in the halls of the great such men are maintained to glory in their crimes in open contempt of the Faith, to the heavy offence of the Divine Majesty, and in scorn of Our Redeemer; and are permitted to boast of their deeds.

Wherefore such protectors, defenders and patrons are to be judged not only heretics, but even apostates from the Faith, and are to be punished in the manner that will be told. And this is the seventh deadly sin of these wizards. For first they are by very law excommunicated; and if the patrons are clerics they are degraded and deprived of all office and benefit, nor can they be restored except by a special indulgence from the Apostolic See. Also, if after their proscription such protectors remain obstinate in their excommunication for the period of a year, they are to be condemned as heretics.

This is in accordance with the Canon Law; for, in Book VI, it touches on the question of direct or indirect interference with the proceedings of Diocesans and Inquisitors in the cause

---

* "*Began to Bleed.*" On 29 May, 1187, a number of mercenaries and bandits were playing with dice before the door of the church at Déols. One of these fellows, who had lost a throw, cursing and swearing, took up a stone, which he flung at the figure of Our Lady with the Child over the sacred portal. The arm of the Infant JESUS was snapped in twain. "A stream of blood poured from the arm of the broken image and made a pool on the earth below. The wretch who flung the stone was seized with madness, and dropped down dead upon the spot." The blood was carefully collected in a phial which was deposited in an Oratory dedicated to Our Lady. Numberless cures were effected, and a Confraternity which was founded in honour of the miracle flourished until the Revolution. It was reorganized in 1830, and on 31 May there is a solemn Commemoration of the Blood-shedding of Notre Dame de Déols.

After S. Paul of the Cross (1694–1775) had preached for the last time in the church of Piagaro, a Crucifix over one of the side-altars was seen to be oozing with blood. Hundreds witnessed the miracle, and later a chapel was built to enshrine the Miraculous Cross. In 1630 at Spoleto, drops of blood flowed from the head of a figure of Our Lord Crowned with Thorns. Even in this unbelieving age the Most Holy Crucifix of Limpias, El Santo Cristo de la Agonia, sweats blood, whilst tears have been observed in the eyes, which turn from side to side, and the head sometimes moves as in all the weariness of bitter pain. Very many other instances of similar miracles might be cited.

of the Faith, and mentions the aforesaid punishment to be inflicted after a year. For it says: We forbid any interference from Potentates, temporal Lords and Rulers, and their Officials, etc. Anyone may refer to the chapter.

And further, that witches and their protectors are by very law to be excommunicated is shown in the Canon of the suppressing of the heresy of witchcraft; especially where it says: We excommunicate and anathematize all heretics, Catharists, Sectaries . . . and others, by whatever names they are known, etc. And with these it includes all their sympathizers and protectors, and others; saying later on: Also we excommunicate all followers, protectors, defenders and patrons of such heretics.

The Canon Law prescribes various penalties which are incurred within the space of a year by such heretics, whether laymen or clerics, where it says: We place under the ban of excommunication all their protectors, patrons and defenders, so that when any such has been so sentenced and has scorned to recant his heresy, within a year from that time he shall be considered an outlaw, and shall not be admitted to any office or council, nor be able to vote in the election of such officers, nor be allowed to give evidence; he is not to be called as a witness, or to be allowed free opportunity of giving evidence; he shall not succeed to any inheritance, and no one shall be held responsible for any business transaction with him. If he be a judge, his judgement shall not stand, nor shall any case be brought to his hearing. If he be an advocate, he shall not be allowed to plead. If he be a notary, no instrument drawn up by him shall have any weight, but is to be condemned together with its condemned author; and similar penalties are decreed for the holders of other offices. But if he be a cleric, he is to be degraded from all office and benefice; for, his guilt being the greater, it is more heavily avenged. And if any such, after they have been marked down by the Church, contemptuously try to ignore their punishment, the sentence of excommunication is to be rigorously applied to them to the extreme limits of vengeance. And the clergy shall not administer the Sacraments of the Church to such heretics, nor presume to give them Christian burial, nor accept their alms and

oblations, on pain of being deprived of their office, to which they can in no way be restored without a special indulgence from the Apostolic See.

There are, finally, many other penalties incurred by such heretics even when they do not persist in their obstinacy for a year, and also by their children and grandchildren: for they can be degraded by a Bishop or by an Inquisitor, declared deprived of all titles, possessions, honours and ecclesiastical benefits, in fine of all public offices whatsoever. But this is only when they are persistently and obstinately impenitent. Also their sons to the second generation may be disqualified and unable to obtain either ecclesiastical preferment or public office; but this is to be understood only of the descendants on the father's side, and not on the mother's, and only of those who are impenitent. Also all their followers, protectors, fautors and patrons shall be denied all right of petition or appeal; and this is explained as meaning that, after a verdict has been returned that they are such heretics, then can they make no appeal before their sentence, however much they may have been in any respect ill-used or treated with undue severity. Much more could be adduced in support of our standpoint, but this is sufficient.

Now for the better understanding of what has been said, some few points are to be discussed. And first, if a prince or secular potentate employ such a wizard as we have described for the destruction of some castle in a just war, and with his help crushes the tyranny of wicked men; is his whole army to be considered as protectors and patrons of that wizard, and to be subjected to the penalties we have mentioned? The answer seems to be that 'the rigour of justice must be tempered on account of their numbers. For the leader, with his counsellors and advisers, must be considered to have aided and abetted such witchcraft, and they are by law implicated in the aforesaid penalties when, after being warned by their spiritual advisers, they have persisted in their bad course; and then they are to be judged protectors and patrons, and are to be punished. But the rest of the army, since they have no part in their leaders' council, but are simply prepared to risk their lives in defence of their country, although they may view with approval the feats of the wizard, nevertheless escape the sentence of excommunication; but they must in their confession acknowledge the guilt of the wizard, and in their absolution by the confessor must receive a solemn warning to hold all such practices for ever in detestation, and as far as they are able drive from their land all such wizards.

It may be asked by whom such princes are to be absolved when they come to their senses, whether by their own spiritual advisers or by the Inquisitors? We answer that, if they repent, they may be absolved either by their spiritual advisers, or by the Inquisitors. This is provided in the Canon Law concerning the proceedings to be taken, in the fear of God and as a warning to men, against heretics, their followers, protectors, patrons and fautors, as also against those who are accused or suspected of heresy. But if any of the above, forswearing his former lapse into heresy, wish to return to the unity of the Church, he may receive the benefit of absolution provided by Holy Church.

A prince, or any other, may be said to have returned to his senses when he has delivered up the wizard to be punished for his offences against the Creator; when he has banished from his dominions all who have been found guilty of witchcraft or heresy; when he is truly penitent for the past; and when, as becomes a Catholic prince, he is firmly determined in his mind not to show any favour to any other such wizard.

But it may be asked to whom should such a man be surrendered, in what court he should be tried, and whether he is to be judged as one openly apprehended in heresy? The first difficulty is specially dealt with at the beginning of the Third Part; namely, whether it is the business of a secular or of an ecclesiastical judge to punish such men. It is manifestly stated in the Canon Law that no temporal magistrate or judge is competent to try a case of heresy without a licence from the Bishops and Inquisitors, or at least under the hand of someone who has authority from them. But when it says that the secular courts have no jurisdiction in this matter because the crime of heresy is exclusively

ecclesiastical, this does not seem to apply to the case of witches; for the crimes of witches are not exclusively ecclesiastical, but are also civil on account of the temporal damage which they do. Nevertheless, as will be shown later, although the ecclesiastical judge must try and judge the case, yet it is for the secular judge to carry out the sentence and inflict punishment, as is shown in the chapters of the Canon on the abolition of heresy, and on excommunication. Wherefore, even if he does surrender the witch to the Ordinary to be judged, the secular judge has still the power of punishing him after he has been delivered back by the Bishop; and with the consent of the Bishop, the secular judge can even perform both offices, that is, he can both sentence and punish.

And it is no valid objection to say that such wizards are rather apostates than heretics; for both these are offenders against the Faith; but whereas a heretic is only in some partial or total doubt with regard to the Faith, witchcraft in its very essence implies apostasy intent from the Faith. For it is a heavier sin to corrupt the Faith, which is the life of the soul, than to falsify money, which is a prop to the life of the body. And if counterfeiters of money, and other malefactors, are immediately sentenced to death by the secular courts, how much more just and equitable it is that such heretics and apostates should be immediately put to death when they are convicted.

Here we have also answered the second difficulty, namely, by what court and judge such men are to be punished. But this will be more fully considered in the Third Part of this work, where we treat of the methods of sentencing the offenders, and how one taken in open heresy is to be sentenced (see the eighth and twelfth methods), and of the question whether one who becomes penitent is still to be put to death.

For if a simple heretic constantly backslides as often as he repents, he is to be put to death according to the Canon Law; and this is reasonable according to S. Thomas, as being for the general good. For if relapsed heretics are often and often received back and allowed to live and keep their temporal goods, it might prejudice the salvation of others, both because they might infect others if they fell again, and because, if they were to escape without punishment, others would have less fear in being infected with heresy. And their very relapse argues that they are not constant in the Faith, and they are therefore justly to be put to death. And so we ought to say here that, if a mere suspicion of inconstancy is sufficient warrant for an ecclesiastical judge to hand over such a backslider to the secular court to be put to death, much more must he do so in the case of one who refuses to prove his penitence and change of heart by handing over to the secular court an apostate or any witch, but rather leaves free and unchecked one whom the secular judge wishes to put to death as a witch according to the law, on account of the temporal injuries of which he has been guilty. But if the witch is penitent, the ecclesiastical judge must first absolve him from the excommunication which he has incurred because of the heresy of witchcraft. Also when a heretic is penitent, he can be received back into the bosom of the Church for the salvation of his soul. This matter is further discussed in the First Question of the Third Part, and this is ample for the present. Only let all Rulers consider how strictly and minutely they will be called to account by that terrible Judge; for indeed there will be a very severe judgement on those in authority who allow such wizards to live and work their injuries against the Creator.

The other two classes of wizards belong to the general category of those who can use incantations and sacrilegious charms so as to render certain weapons incapable of harming or wounding them; and these are divided into two kinds. For the first class resemble the archer-wizards of whom we have just spoken, in that they also mutilate the image of Christ crucified. For example, if they wish their head to be immune from any wound from a weapon or from any blow, they take off the head of the Crucifix; if they wish their neck to be invulnerable, they take off its neck; if their arm, they take off, or at least shorten, the arm, and so on. And sometimes they take away all above the waist, or below it. And in proof of this, hardly one in ten of the Crucifixes set up at cross-roads or in the fields can be found whole and

intact. And some carry the limbs thus broken off about with them, and others procure their invulnerability by means of sacred or unknown words: therefore there is this difference between them. The first sort resemble the archer-wizards in their contempt of the Faith and their mutilation of the image of the Saviour, and are therefore to be considered as true apostates, and so must be judged when they are taken; but not to the same degree as the archers, for it is manifest that they do not approach them in wickedness. For they seem only to act for the protection of their own bodies, either above the waist or below it, or of the whole body. Therefore they are to be judged as penitent heretics and not relapsed, when they have been convicted as wizards and have repented; and they are to be imposed a penance according to the eighth manner, with solemn adjuration and incarceration, as is shown in the Third Part of this work.

The second sort can magically enchant weapons so that they can walk on them with bare feet, and similar strange feats do they perform (for according to S. Isidore, *Etym.* VIII, enchanters are those who have some skill to perform wonders by means of words). And there is a distinction to be made between them; for some perform their incantations by means of sacred words, or charms written up over the sick, and these are lawful provided that seven conditions are observed, as will be shown later where we deal with the methods of curing those who are bewitched. But incantations made over weapons by certain secret words, or cases where the charms written for the sick have been taken down, are matters for the judge's attention. For when they use words of which they do not themselves know the meaning, or characters and signs which are not the sign of the Cross, such practices are altogether to be repudiated, and good men should beware of the cruel arts of these warlocks. And if they will not desist from such deeds, they must be judged as suspects although lightly, and the manner of sentencing such after the second method will be shown later. For they are not untainted with the sin of heresy; for deeds of this kind can only be done with the help of the devil, and, as we have shown, he who uses such help is judged to be an apostate from the Faith. Yet on the plea of ignorance or of mending their ways they may be dealt with more leniently than the archer-wizards.

It is most commonly found that traders and merchants are in the habit of carrying about them such charms and runes; and since they partake of the nature of incantations, a complete riddance must be made of them, either by the father confessor in the box, or in open court by the ecclesiastical judge. For these unknown words and characters imply a tacit compact with the devil, who secretly uses such things for his own purpose, granting their wearers their wishes, that he may lure them on to worse things. Therefore in the court of law such men must be warned and sentenced after the second method. In the box, the confessor must examine the charm, and if he is unwilling to throw it away altogether, he must delete the unknown words and signs, but may keep any Gospel words or the sign of the Cross.

Now with regard to all these classes of wizards, and especially the archers, it must be noted, as has been declared above, whether they are to be judged as heretics openly taken in that sin; and we have touched on this matter even before in the First Question of the First Part. And there it is shown that S. Bernard says that there are three ways by which a man can be convicted of heresy: either by the evidence of the fact when in simple heresy he publicly preaches his errors, or by the credible evidence of witnesses, or by a man's own confession. S. Bernard also explains the meaning of some of the words of the Canon Law in this connexion, as was shown in the First Question of the First Part of this work.

It is clear, therefore, that archer-wizards, and those mages who enchant other weapons, are to be considered as manifestly guilty of flagrant heresy, through some expressed pact with the devil, since it is obvious that their feats would not be possible without the devil's help.

Secondly, it is equally clear that the patrons, protectors and defenders of such men are manifestly to be judged in the same way, and subjected to the prescribed punishments. For there is not in their case, as there may be in that of several others, any doubt as to whether they are to be regarded as lightly or strongly or gravely suspected; but they are always very grave sinners against the Faith, and are always visited by God with a miserable death.

For it is told that a certain prince used to keep such wizards in his favour, and by their help unduly oppressed a certain city in matters of commerce. And when one of his retainers remonstrated with him over this, he threw away all fear of God and exclaimed, "God grant that I may die in this place if I am oppressing them unjustly." Divine vengeance quickly followed these words, and he was stricken down with sudden death. And this vengeance was not so much on account of his unjust oppression as because of his patronage of heresy.

Thirdly, it is clear that all Bishops and Rulers who do not essay their utmost to suppress crimes of this sort, with their authors and patrons, are themselves to be judged as evident abettors of the crime, and are manifestly to be punished in the prescribed manner.

☆

QUESTION II

The Methods of Destroying and Curing Witchcraft.

Introduction, wherein is set Forth the Difficulty of this Question.

IS it lawful to remove witchcraft by means of further witchcraft, or by any other forbidden means?

It is argued that it is not; for it has already been shown that in the *Second Book of Sentences*, and the 8th Distinction, all the Doctors agree that it is unlawful to use the help of devils, since to do so involves apostasy from the Faith. And, it is argued, no witchcraft can be removed without the help of devils. For it is submitted that it must be cured either by human power, or by diabolic, or by Divine power. It cannot be by the first; for the lower power cannot counteract the higher, having no control over that which is outside its own natural capacity. Neither can it be by Divine power; for this would be a miracle, which God performs only at His own will, and not at the instance of men. For when His

Mother besought Christ to perform a miracle to supply the need for wine, He answered: Woman, what have I to do with thee? And the Doctors explain this as meaning, "What association is there between you and me in the working of a miracle?"* Also it appears that it is very rarely that men are delivered from a bewitchment by calling on God's help or the prayers of the Saints. Therefore it follows that they can only be delivered by the help of devils; and it is unlawful to seek such help.

Again it is pointed out that the common method in practice of taking off a bewitchment, although it is quite unlawful, is for the bewitched persons to resort to wise women, by whom they are very frequently cured, and not by priests or exorcists. So experience shows that such cures are effected by the help of devils, which it is unlawful to seek; therefore it cannot be lawful thus to cure a bewitchment, but it must patiently be borne.

It is further argued that S. Thomas and S. Bonaventura, in Book IV, dist. 34, have said that a bewitchment must be permanent because it can have no human remedy; for if there is a remedy, it is either unknown to men or unlawful. And these words are taken to mean that this infirmity is incurable and must be regarded as permanent; and they add that, even if God should provide a remedy by coercing the devil, and the devil should remove his plague from a man, and the man should be cured, that cure would not be a human one. Therefore, unless God should cure it, it is not lawful for a man himself to try in any way to look for a cure.

In the same place these two Doctors add that it is unlawful even to seek a remedy by the superadding of another bewitchment. For they say that, granting this to be possible, and that the original spell be removed, yet the witchcraft is none the less to be considered permanent; for it is in no way lawful to invoke the devil's help through witchcraft.

Further, it is submitted that the exorcisms of the Church are not always effective in the repression of devils† in the matter of bodily afflictions, since such are cured only at the discretion of God; but they are effective always against those molestations of devils against which they are chiefly instituted, as, for example, against men who are possessed, or in the matter of exorcising children.

Again, it does not follow that, because the devil has been given power over someone on account of his sins, that power must come to an end on the cessation of the sin. For very often a man may cease from sinning, but his sins still remain. So it seems from these sayings that the two Doctors we have cited were of the opinion that it is unlawful to remove a bewitchment, but that it must be suffered, just as it is permitted by the Lord God, Who can remove it when it seems good to Him.

Against this opinion it is argued that just as God and Nature do not abound in superfluities, so also they are not deficient in necessities; and it is a necessity that there should be given to the faithful against such devils' work not only a means of protection (of which we treat in the beginning of this Second Part), but also curative remedies. For otherwise the faithful would not be sufficiently provided for by God, and the works of the devil would seem to be stronger than God's works.

Also there is the gloss on that text in *Job*. There is no power on earth, etc. The gloss says that, although the devil has power over all things human, he is nevertheless subject to the merits of the Saints, and even to the merits of saintly men in this life.

Again, S. Augustine (*De moribus Ecclesiae*)‡ says: No Angel is more powerful than our mind, when we hold fast to God. For if power is a virtue in this world, then the mind that keeps close to God is more sublime than the

* "*Miracle.*" *The sense is completely mistaken here. It should rather be,* "*Lady, what is it to Me and to Thee*" *if these people lack wine? Our Lord marvels at the supreme charity of Our Lady. The first miracle was wrought at the request of MARY. Quod Deus imperio tu prece, Virgo, potes. It may be argued that all miracles are performed at the request of Our Lady, since, as S. Bernard says, God wishes us to obtain everything through Her. Totum nos uoluit habere per MARIAM.*

† "*Devils.*" *If the exorcism is not effective it is owing to lack of faith.*

‡ "*De Moribus.*" "*De Moribus ecclesiae catholicae et de moribus Manichaeorum*" *was written 388-89.*

whole world. Therefore such minds can undo the works of the devil.

Answer. Here are two weighty opinions which, it seems, are at complete variance with each other.

For there are certain Theologians and Canonists who agree that it is lawful to remove witchcraft even by superstitious and vain means. And of this opinion are Duns Scotus,* Henry of Segusio, and Godfrey, and all the Canonists. But it is the opinion of the other Theologians, especially the ancient ones, and of some of the modern ones, such as S. Thomas, S. Bonaventura, Blessed Albert, Peter a Palude, and many others, that in no case must evil be done that good may result, and that a man ought rather to die than consent to be cured by superstitious and vain means.

Let us now examine their opinions, with a view to bringing them as far as possible into agreement. Scotus, in his Fourth Book, dist. 34, on obstructions and impotence caused by witchcraft, says that it is foolish to maintain that it is unlawful to remove a bewitchment even by superstitious and vain means, and that to do so is in no way contrary to the Faith; for he who destroys the work of the devil is not an accessory to such works, but believes that the devil has the power and inclination to help in the infliction of an injury only so long as the outward token or sign of that injury endures. Therefore when that token is destroyed he puts an end to the injury. And he adds that it is meritorious to destroy the works of the devil. But, as he speaks of tokens, we will give an example.

There are women who discover a witch by the following token. When a cow's supply of milk has been diminished by witchcraft, they hang a pail of milk over the fire, and uttering certain superstitious words, beat the pail with a stick. And though it is the pail that the women beat, yet the devil carries all those blows to the back of the witch; and in this way are both the witch and the devil made weary.

But the devil does this in order that he may lead on the woman who beats the pail to worse practices. And so, if it were not for the risk which it entails, there would be no difficulty in accepting the opinion of this learned Doctor. Many other examples could be given.

Henry of Segusio, in his eloquent *Summa* on genital impotence caused by witchcraft, says that in such cases recourse must be had to the remedies of physicians; and although some of these remedies seem to be vain and superstitious cantrips and charms, yet everyone must be trusted in his own profession, and the Church may well tolerate the suppression of vanities by means of other vanities.

Ubertinus† also, in his Fourth Book, uses these words: A bewitchment can be removed either by prayer or by the same art by which it was inflicted.

Godfrey says in his *Summa:* A bewitchment cannot always be removed by him who caused it, either because he is dead, or because he does not know how to cure it, or because the necessary charm is lost. But if he knows how to effect relief, it is lawful for him to cure it. Our author is speaking against those who said that an obstruction of the carnal act could not be caused by witchcraft, and that it could never be permanent, and therefore did not annul a marriage already contracted.

Besides, those who maintained that no spell is permanent were moved by the following reasons: they thought that every bewitchment could be removed either by another magic spell, or by the exorcisms of the Church which are ordained for the suppression of the devil's power, or by true penitence, since the devil has power only over sinners. So in the first respect they agree with the opinion of the others, namely, that a spell can be removed by superstitious means.

But S. Thomas is of the contrary opinion when he says: If a spell cannot be revoked except by some unlaw-

---

* *"Duns Scotus." John Duns Scotus, Doctor Subtilis, the famous Franciscan scholastic, died 8 November, 1308. He lived and taught at Oxford, and for a time at Paris. His complete work with commentaries appeared at Paris, 1891–95, in twenty-six volumes, quarto, being a reprint of the twelve folio volumes which were issued by Luke Wadding in 1639 at Lyons.*

† *"Ubertinus." Ubertino of Casale, leader of the Spiritual Franciscans, who expressed extreme views regarding evangelical poverty. He was born in 1259, and died about 1330. Owing to his warm advocacy of the strictest ideas he was severely condemned by the authorities, and his history is a matter of considerable difficulty. His chief work is generally considered to be "Arbor uitae crucifixae JESU Christi."*

ful means, such as the devil's help or anything of that sort, even if it is known that it can be revoked in that way, it is nevertheless to be considered permanent; for the remedy is not lawful.

Of the same opinion are S. Bonaventura, Peter a Palude, Blessed Albert, and all the Theologians. For, touching briefly on the question of invoking the help of the devil either tacitly or expressedly, they seem to hold that such spells may only be removed by lawful exorcism or true penitence (as is set down in the Canon Law concerning sortilege), being moved, as it seems, by the considerations mentioned in the beginning of this Question.

But it is expedient to bring these various opinions of the learned Doctors as far as possible into agreement, and this can be done in one respect. For this purpose it is to be noted that the methods by which a spell of witchcraft can be removed are as follows:—either by the agency of another witch and another spell; or without the agency of a witch, but by means of magic and unlawful ceremonies. And this last method may be divided into two; namely, the use of ceremonies which are both unlawful and vain, or the use of ceremonies which are vain but not unlawful.

The first remedy is altogether unlawful, in respect both of the agent and of the remedy itself. But it may be accomplished in two ways; either with some injury to him who worked the spell, or without any injury, but with magic and unlawful ceremonies. In the latter case it can be included with the second method, namely, that by which the spell is removed not by the agency of a witch, but by magic and unlawful ceremonies; and in this case it is still to be judged unlawful, though not to the same extent as the first method.

We may summarize the position as follows. There are three conditions by which a remedy is rendered unlawful. First, when the spell is removed through the agency of another witch, and by further witchcraft, that is, by the power of some devil. Secondly, when it is not removed by a witch, but by some honest person, in such a way, however, that the spell is by some magical remedy transferred from one person to another; and this again is unlawful. Thirdly, when the spell is removed without imposing it on another person, but

some open or tacit invocation of devils is used; and then again it is unlawful.

And it is with reference to these methods that the Theologians say that it is better to die than to consent to them. But there are two other methods by which, according to the Canonists, it is lawful, or not idle and vain, to remove a spell; and that such methods may be used when all the remedies of the Church, such as exorcisms and the prayers of the Saints and true penitence, have been tried and have failed. But for a clearer understanding of these remedies we will recount some examples known to our experience.

In the time of Pope Nicolas there had come to Rome on some business a certain Bishop from Germany, whom it is charitable not to name although he has now paid the debt of all nature. There he fell in love with a girl, and sent her to his diocese in charge of two servants and certain other of his possessions, including some rich jewels. While this girl was on her way, with the usual greed of women, she grew covetous of these jewels, which were indeed very valuable, and began to think in her heart that, if only the Bishop were to die through some witchcraft, she would be able to take possession of the rings, the pendants and carcanets. The next night the Bishop suddenly fell ill, and the physicians and his servants gravely suspected that he had been poisoned; for there was such a fire in his breast that he had to take continual draughts of cold water to assuage it. On the third day, when there seemed no hope of his life, an old woman came and begged that she might see him, saying that she had come to heal him. So they let her in, and she promised the Bishop that she could heal him if he would agree to her proposals. When the Bishop asked what it was to which he had to agree in order to regain his health, as he so greatly desired, the old woman answered: Your illness has been caused by a spell of witchcraft, and you can only be healed by another spell, which will transfer the illness from you to the witch who caused it, so that she will die. The Bishop was astounded; and seeing that he could be healed in no other way, and not wishing to come to a rash decision, decided to ask the advice of the Pope. Now the Holy

Father loved him very dearly, and when he learned that he could only be healed by the death of the witch, he agreed to permit the lesser of two evils, and signed this permission with his seal. So the old woman was again approached and told that both he and the Pope had agreed to the death of the witch, on condition that he was restored to his former health; and the old woman went away, promising him that he would be healed on the following night. And behold! when about the middle of the night he felt himself cured and free from all illness, he sent a messenger to learn what had happened to the girl; and he came back and reported that she had suddenly been taken ill in the middle of the night while sleeping by her mother's side.

It is to be understood that at the very same hour and moment the illness left the Bishop and afflicted the girl witch, through the agency of the old witch; and so the evil spirit, by ceasing to plague the Bishop, appeared to restore him to health by chance, whereas it was not he but God Who permitted him to afflict him, and it was God Who properly speaking restored him; and the devil, by reason of his compact with the second witch, who envied the fortune of the girl, had to afflict the Bishop's mistress. And it must be thought that those two evil spells were not worked by one devil serving two persons, but by two devils serving two separate witches. For the devils do not work against themselves,* but work as much as possible in agreement for the perdition of souls.

Finally, the Bishop went out of compassion to visit the girl; but when he entered the room, she received him with horrible execrations, crying out: May you and she who wrought your cure be damned for ever! And the Bishop tried to soften her mind to penitence, and told her that he forgave her all her wrongs; but she turned her face away and said: I have no hope of pardon, but commend my soul to all the devils in hell; and died miserably. But the Bishop returned home with joy and thankfulness.

Here it is to be noted that a privilege

granted to one does not constitute a precedent for all, and the dispensation of the Pope in this case does not argue that it is lawful in all cases.

Nider in his *Formicarius* refers to the same matter, for he says: The following method is sometimes employed for removing or taking vengeance for a spell of witchcraft. Someone who has been bewitched either in himself or in his possessions comes to a witch desiring to know who has injured him. Then the witch pours molten lead into water until, by the work of the devil, some image is formed by the solidified lead. On this, the witch asks in which part of the body he wishes his enemy to be hurt, so that he may recognize him by that hurt. And when he has chosen, the witch immediately pierces or wounds with a knife the leaden image in the same part, and shows him the place by which he can recognize the guilty person. And it is found by experience that, just in the same way as the leaden image is hurt, so is the witch hurt who cast the spell.

But of this sort of remedy I say, and of others like it, that generally they are unlawful; although human weakness, in the hope of obtaining pardon from God, is very often ensnared in such practices, being more careful for the health of the body than for that of the soul.

The second kind of cure which is wrought by witches who remove a spell again requires an expressed pact with the devil, but is not accompanied by any injury to another person. And in what light such witches should be considered, and how they are to be recognized, will be shown later in the fifteenth method of sentencing witches. There are very many such witches, for they are always to be found at intervals of one or two German miles, and these seem to be able to cure any who have been bewitched by another witch in their own district. Some of them claim to be able to effect such cures at all times; some that they can only cure those bewitched in the neighbouring signiory; others that they can only perform their cures with the consent of the witch who cast the original spell.

And it is known that these women have entered into an open pact with the devil, because they reveal secret matters to those who come to them to

---

* "*Against themselves.*" "*S. Matthew*" xii, 26: "*Et si Satanas Satanam eiicit, aduersus se diuisus est: quomodo ergo stabit regnum eius?*"

be cured. For they suddenly disclose to such a person the cause of his calamity, telling him that he has been bewitched either in his own person or in his possessions because of some quarrel he has had with a neighbour or with some other woman or man; and at times, in order to keep their criminal practices secret, they enjoin upon their clients some pilgrimage or other pious work. But to approach such women in order to be cured is all the more pernicious because they seem to bring greater contempt upon the Faith than others who effect their cures by means of a merely tacit compact with the devil.

For they who resort to such witches are thinking more of their bodily health than of God, and besides that, God cuts short their lives to punish them for taking into their own hands the vengeance for their wrongs. For so the Divine vengeance overtook Saul, because he first cast out of the land all magicians and wizards, and afterwards consulted a witch; wherefore he was slain in battle with his sons, I. *Samuel* xxviii, and I. *Paralipomenon* x. And for the same reason the sick Ochozias* had to die, IV. *Kings* i (Ahaziah; II. *Kings* i. *A.V.*).

Also they who consult such witches are regarded as defamed, and cannot be allowed to bring an accusation, as will be shown in the Third Part; and they are by law to be sentenced to capital punishment, as was said in the First Question of this work.

But alas! O Lord God, Who art just in all Thy judgements, who shall deliver the poor who are bewitched and cry out in their ceaseless pains? For our sins are so great, and the enemy is so strong; and where are they who can undo the works of the devil by lawful exorcisms? This one remedy appears to be left; that judges should, by various penalties, keep such wickedness as far as possible in check by punishing the witches who are the cause of it; that so they may deprive the sick of the opportunity of consulting witches. But, alas! no one understands this in his heart; but they all seek for their own gain instead of that of JESUS Christ.

For so many people used to go to be freed from spells to that witch in Reichshofen, whom we have already mentioned, that the Count of the castle set up a toll-booth, and all who were bewitched in their own persons or in their possessions had to pay a penny before they could visit her house; and he boasted that he made a substantial profit by this means.

We know from experience that there are many such witches in the diocese of Constance: not that this diocese is more infected than others, since this form of infidelity is general in all dioceses; but this diocese has been more thoroughly sifted. It was found that daily resort was being made to a man named Hengst by a very large concourse of poor folk who had been bewitched, and with our own eyes we saw such crowds in the village of Eningen, that certainly the poor never flocked to any shrine of the Blessed Virgin, or to a Holy Well or a Hermitage, in such numbers as they went to that sorcerer. For in the very coldest winter weather, when all the highways and byways were snow-bound, they came to him from two or three miles round in spite of the greatest difficulties; and some were cured, but others not. For I suppose that all spells are not equally easy to remove, on account of various obstacles, as has been said before. And these witches remove spells by means of an open invocation of devils after the manner of the second kind of remedies, which are unlawful, but not to the same extent as the first kind.

The third kind of remedy is that which is wrought by means of certain superstitious ceremonies, but without any injury to anyone, and not by an overt witch. An example of this method is as follows:

A certain market merchant in the town of Spires deposed that the following experience had happened to him. I was staying, he said, in Swabia in a well-known nobleman's castle, and one day after dinner I was strolling at my ease with two of the servants in the

---

* "*Ochozias*," *who when sick "sent messengers, saying to them: Go, consult Beelzebub, the god of Hecaron, whether I shall recover of this my illness. And an angel of the Lord spoke to Elias the Thesbite, saying: Arise, and go up to meet the messengers of the king of Samaria, and say to them: Is there not a God in Israel, that ye go to consult Beelzebub, the god of Hecaron? Wherefore thus saith the Lord: From the bed on which thou art gone up thou shalt not come down, but thou shalt surely die.*"

fields, when a woman met us. But while she was still a long way off my companions recognized her, and one of them said to me, "Cross yourself quickly," and the other one urged me in like manner. I asked them what they feared, and they answered, "The most dangerous witch in the whole Province is coming to meet us, and she can cast a spell on men by only looking at them." But I obstinately boasted that I had never been afraid of such; and hardly had I uttered the words before I felt myself grievously hurt in the left foot, so that I could not move it from the ground or take a step without the greatest pain. Whereupon they quickly sent to the castle for a horse for me, and thus led me back. But the pains went on increasing for three days.

The people of the castle, understanding that I had been bewitched, related what had happened to a certain peasant who lived about a mile away, whom they knew to have skill in removing spells. This man quickly came and, after examining my foot, said, "I will test whether these pains are due to a natural cause; and if I find that they are due to witchcraft, I will cure you with the help of God; but if they are not, you must have recourse to natural remedies." Whereupon I made reply, "If I can be cured without any magic, and with the help of God, I will gladly agree; but I will have nothing to do with the devil, nor do I wish for his help." And the peasant promised that he would use none except lawful means, and that he would cure me by the help of God, provided that he could make certain that my pains were due to witchcraft. So I consented to his proposals. Then he took molten lead (in the manner of another witch whom we have mentioned), and held it in an iron ladle over my foot, and poured it into a bowl of water; and immediately there appeared the shapes of various things, as if thorns and hairs and bones and such things had been put into the bowl. "Now," he said, "I see that this infirmity is not natural, but certainly due to witchcraft." And when I asked him how he could tell this from the molten lead, he answered, "There are seven metals belonging to the seven planets; and since Saturn is the Lord of lead, when lead is poured out over anyone who has been bewitched, it is his property to discover the witchcraft by

his power. And so it has surely proved, and you will soon be cured; yet I must visit you for as many days as you have been under this spell." And he asked me how many days had passed; and when I told him that was the third day, he came to see me on each of the next three days, and merely by examining and touching my foot and by saying over to himself certain words, he dissolved the charm and restored me to complete health.

In this case it is clear that the healer is not a witch, although his method is something superstitious. For in that he promised a cure by the help of God, and not by devils' work, and that he alleged the influence of Saturn over lead, he was irreproachable and rather to be commended. But there remains some small doubt as to the power by which the witch's spell was removed, and the figures caused in the lead. For no witchcraft can be removed by any natural power, although it may be assuaged, as will be proved later where we speak of the remedies for those who are possessed: therefore it seems that he performed this cure by means of at least some tacit pact with a devil. And we call such a pact tacit when the practitioner agrees tacitly, at any rate, to employ the devil's aid. And in this way many superstitious works are done, but with a varying degree of offence to the Creator, since there may be far more offence to Him in one operation than in another.

Yet because this peasant was certain of effecting a cure, and because he had to visit the patient for as many days as he had been ill, and although he used no natural remedies, yet cured him according to the promise made; for these reasons, although he had entered into no open pact with the devil, he is to be judged not only as a suspect, but as one plainly guilty of heresy, and must be considered as convicted and subject at least to the penalties set out below in the second method of sentencing; but his punishment must be accompanied with a solemn adjuration, unless he is protected by other laws which seem to be of a contrary intention; and what the Ordinary should do in such a case will be shown later in the solution of the arguments.

The fourth class of remedies, concerning which the Canonists are in partial agreement with some of the Theologians, is said to be no worse than idle and vain; since it is superstitious only, and there is no pact either open or tacit with the devil as regards the intention or purpose of the practitioner. And I say that the Canonists and some Theologians are only partially agreed that this sort of remedy is to be tolerated; for their agreement or non-agreement depends upon whether or not they class this sort of remedies together with the third sort. But this sort of vain remedy is exemplified above in the case of the women who beat a pail hung over the fire in order that the witch may be beaten who has caused a cow to be drained of milk; although this may be done either in the name of the devil or without any reference to him.

We may adduce other examples of the same kind. For sometimes when a cow has been injured in this way, and they wish to discover who has bewitched it, they drive it out into the fields with a man's trousers, or some such unclean thing, upon its head or back. And this they do chiefly on Feast Days and Holy Days, and possibly with some sort of invocation of the devil; and they beat the cow with a stick and drive it away. Then the cow runs straight to the house of the witch, and beats vehemently upon the door with its horns, lowing loudly all the while; and the devil causes the cow to go on doing this until it is pacified by some other witchcraft.

Actually, and according to the aforesaid Doctors, such remedies can be tolerated, but they are not meritorious, as some try to maintain. For S. Paul says that everything which we do, in word or deed, must be done in the name of Our Lord JESUS Christ. Now in this sort of remedy there may be no direct invocation of the devil, and yet the devil's name may be mentioned: and again there may be no intention to do such things by means of any open or tacit pact with the devil, yet a man may say, "I wish to do this, whether the devil has any part in it or not"; and that very temerity, by putting aside the fear of God, offends God, Who therefore grants the devil power to accomplish such cures. Therefore they who use such practices must be led into the way of penitence, and urged to leave such things and turn

rather to the remedies of which we shall speak later, though we have touched upon them before, namely, the use of Holy Water and Blessed Salt and exorcisms, etc.

In the same light should be regarded those who use the following method. When an animal has been killed by witchcraft, and they wish to find out the witch, or to make certain whether its death was natural or due to witchcraft, they go to the place where dead animals are skinned, and drag its intestines along the ground up to their house; not into the house through the main door, but over the threshold of the back entrance into the kitchen; and then they make a fire and put the intestines over it on a hurdle. Then, according to what we have very often been told, just as the intestines get hot and burn, so are the intestines of the witch afflicted with burning pains.*

---

* *"Burning pains."* The following quotation is from an article *"Witchcraft, Past and Present,"* by Lady Peirse, that appeared in *"Word-Lore,"* Vol. I, No. 3 (pp. 122-28), May-June, 1926. The district to which reference is made is "a south-country village in England." "A local farmer, whose cows and sheep ailed mysteriously, and showed all the usual signs of being 'overlooked' or bewitched, whilst things in general went wrong with him, consulted the witch doctor, and was told to repeat a certain charm last thing at night, to nail a sheep's heart to his front door, to bolt and bar up the house, to sit up alone, and on no account to open the door till morning, no matter what happened.

"This the farmer did, and when his family had repaired to bed, he commenced his lonely vigil by the kitchen fire. After a while there came a thunderous knocking on the door, and a voice crying 'Open and let me in.' The voice was very urgent, but the farmer, though he trembled exceedingly, kept firm grip of himself and never moved from his chair. Then came the knocking a second time and a deplorable voice begging to be allowed in, but the farmer remained obdurate. Lastly came a feeble knocking and moaning. The farmer, who was greatly alarmed, remained at his post till the sun was up next morning. When he opened his door a neighbour lay stretched across his threshold dead.

"The doctor, so my friend was told, believed it to be a case of heart failure. We can only imagine that the farmer and his family remained silent about the voice and the knocking at the door; perhaps no one but the farmer had heard. To the doctor, a simple though regrettable episode; to the farmer, an awesome case of retribution. To the world at large, a story that may be interpreted in many different ways; but

But when they perform this experiment they take great care that the door is securely locked; because the witch is compelled by her pains to try to enter the house, and if she can take a coal from the fire, all her pains will disappear. And we have often been told that, when she is unable to enter the house, she surrounds it inside and out with the densest fog, with such horrible shrieks and commotions that at last all those in the house think the roof is verily going to fall down and crush them unless they open the door.

Certain other experiments are of the same nature. For sometimes people pick out the witches from a number of women in church by causing the witches to be unable to leave the church without their permission, even after the service is finished. And they do it in this way. On a Sunday they smear the shoes of the young men with grease, lard or pigs' fat, as is their wont when they wish to repair and renew the freshness of the leather, and thus the juvenals enter the church, whence it is impossible for any witches who are present to make their way out or depart until those who are anxious to espy them either go away themselves or give them express leave to make their way to their homes.†

It is the same with certain words, which it is not expedient to mention lest anyone should be seduced by the devil to use them. For judges and magistrates should not attach too much weight to the evidence of those who pretend to discover witches by this means, for fear lest the devil, that wily enemy, should induce them under this pretext to defame innocent women. Therefore such persons must be enjoined to seek the remedy of penitence. However, practices of this kind are on occasion to be tolerated and allowed.

In this way we have answered the arguments that no spell of witchcraft must be removed. For the first two remedies are altogether unlawful. The third remedy is tolerated by the law, but needs very careful examination on the part of the ecclesiastical judge. And what the civil law tolerates is shown in the chapter on witches, where it is said that those who have skill to prevent men's labours from being vitiated by tempests and hailstorms are worthy, not of punishment, but of reward. S. Antoninus also, in his *Summa*, points out this discrepancy between the Canon Law and civil law. Therefore it seems

---

with a lesson for all who run to read, namely, that it does not pay to practise witchcraft or the indulgence of personal spite if there happens to be a witch doctor in the neighbourhood, since it is apparently quite an easy thing, with a little occult knowledge, to do the witch to death! Throughout many centuries witches in the long run always seem to come off second best. Faith and fear in their victims seem to lend them strength, just as faith and love help righteousness."

Not very many years ago a farmer and his wife who lived in the country just outside Milan came to the conclusion that their daughter, who had long been suffering from a mysterious ailment, which the best doctors in Milan seemed unable to diagnose and cure, was bewitched by an old woman dwelling in their village, a wretch of notoriously bad reputation, whom the girl had unwittingly offended in some small way. Accordingly they resorted to a "wise man," who lived in a small town a good many miles distant. He gave them a bundle of herbs, telling them to boil these in water and at the same time to recite a certain rune or rhyme which he taught them. He told them that if their daughter was indeed plagued by the malice of some individual, as the water boiled the witch who had cast the spell would be so tormented that she would hasten to their house and betray herself by begging them to take the cauldron from the fire. They could then refuse to do so unless she at once relieved the girl from her sickness. They precisely obeyed the directions which had been given, and hardly had the water begun to bubble with the heat than there came running the hag whom they had suspected, imploring them with every symptom of intense agony to throw away the contents of the pot. This they would not do unless the charm was broken. In her despair the old woman promised to restore their daughter to health, and from that time the child rapidly began to mend until she was as stout and sturdy as any lass in the whole country-side.

---

† The text of this passage seems corrupt and varies considerably in the later editions. The earliest edition of the "Malleus" in the British Museum reads: "Nam die d̄nico sotularia iuuenū fungia seu pinguedī̄ porci vt moris e p̄ restauratōe fieri p̄ungūt et sic vbi ecclesiā intrāt tādiu malefice exire ecc̄ias non poterūt quo adusq: exploratores aut exeunt aut illis licentiā sub exp̄ssione ut sup̄ exeundi p̄eedāt." "Die d̄nico" was almost immediately altered to "die dominica." The usual reading is "die Dominica Sotularia, iuuenum fungia . . ." Venice, 1576, introduces a fresh error: "die dominica Solutaria iuuenum fungia. . . ." The Lyons text of 1669 has an excellent emendation, which is, no doubt, correct: "die Dominica Sotularia iuuenum axungia. . . ."

that the civil law concedes the legality of such practices for the preservation of crops and cattle, and that in any event certain men who use such arts are not only to be tolerated but even rewarded. Wherefore the ecclesiastical judge must take particular note whether the methods used in counteraction of hailstorms and tempests are within the spirit of the law, or whether they are in any way superstitious; and then, if no scandal to the Faith is involved, they can be tolerated. But actually this does not belong to the third method, but to the fourth, and also to the fifth, of which we shall speak later in the following chapters, where we deal with the ecclesiastical and lawful remedies, with which are sometimes included certain superstitious practices belonging to the fourth method.

☆

CHAPTER I

The Remedies prescribed by Holy Church against Incubus and Succubus Devils.

IN the foregoing chapters on the First Question we have treated of the methods of bewitching men, animals and the fruits of the earth, and especially of the behaviour of witches in their own persons; how they seduce young girls in order to increase their evil numbers; what is their method of profession and of offering homage; how they offer to devils their own children and the children of others; and how they are transported from place to place. Now I say that there is no remedy for such practices, unless witches be entirely eradicated by the judges, or at least punished as an example to all who may wish to imitate them; but we are not immediately treating of this point, which will be dealt with in the last Part of this work, where we set forth the twenty ways of proceeding against and sentencing witches.

For the present we are concerned only with the remedies against the injuries which they inflict; and first how men who are bewitched can be cured; secondly, beasts, and thirdly, how the fruits of the earth may be secured from blight or phylloxera.

With regard to the bewitchment of

human beings by means of Incubus and Succubus devils, it is to be noted that this can happen in three ways. First, as in the case of witches themselves, when women voluntarily prostitute themselves to Incubus devils. Secondly, when men have connexion with Succubus devils; yet it does not appear that men thus devilishly fornicate with the same full degree of culpability; for men, being by nature intellectually stronger than women, are more apt to abhor such practices. Thirdly, it may happen that men or women are by witchcraft entangled with Incubi or Succubi against their will. This chiefly happens in the case of certain virgins who are molested by Incubus devils wholly against their will; and it would seem that such are bewitched by witches who, just as they very often cause other infirmities, cause devils to molest such virgins in the form of Incubi for the purpose of seducing them into joining their vile company. Let us give an example.

There is in the town of Coblenz a poor man who is bewitched in this way. In the presence of his wife he is in the habit of acting after the manner of men with women, that is to say, of practising coition, as it were, and he continues to do this repeatedly, nor have the cries and urgent appeals of his wife any effect in making him desist. And after he has fornicated thus two or three times, he bawls out, "We are going to start all over again"; when actually there is no person visible to mortal sight lying with him. And after an incredible number of such bouts, the poor man at last sinks to the floor utterly exhausted. When he has recovered his strength a little and is asked how this has happened to him, and whether he has had any woman with him, he answers that he saw nothing, but that his mind is in some way possessed so that he can by no means refrain from such priapism. And indeed he harbours a great suspicion that a certain woman bewitched him in this way, because he had offended her, and she had cursed him with threatening words, telling him what she would like to happen to him.

But there are no laws or ministers of justice which can proceed to the avenging of so great a crime with no other warrant than a vague charge or a grave suspicion; for it is held that no one ought to be condemned unless he has been convicted by his own confession, or by the evidence of three trustworthy witnesses; since the mere fact of the crime coupled with even the gravest suspicions against some person is not sufficient to warrant the punishment of that person. But this matter will be dealt with later.

As for instances where young maidens are molested by Incubus devils in this way, it would take too long to mention even those that have been known to happen in our own time, for there are very many well-attested stories of such bewitchments. But the great difficulty of finding a remedy for such afflictions can be illustrated from a story told by Thomas of Brabant in his *Book on Bees.*

I saw, he writes, and heard the confession of a virgin in a religious habit, who said at first that she had never been a consenting party to fornication, but at the same time gave me to understand that she had been known in this way. This I could not believe, but narrowly charged and exhorted her, with the most solemn adjurations, to speak the truth on peril of her very soul. At last, weeping bitterly, she acknowledged that she had been corrupted rather in mind than in body; and that though she had afterwards grieved almost to death, and had daily confessed with tears, yet by no device or study or art could she be delivered from an Incubus* devil, nor yet by the sign of the Cross, nor by Holy Water, which are specially ordained for the expulsion of devils, nor even by the Sacrament of the Body of Our Lord, which even the Angels fear. But at last after many years of prayer and fasting she was delivered.

It may be believed (saving a better judgement) that, after she repented and confessed her sin, the Incubus devil should be regarded rather in the light of a punishment for sin than as a sin in itself.

A devout nun, named Christina, in the Low Country of the Duchy of Brabant, told me the following concerning this same woman. On the vigil of one Pentecost the woman came to her complaining that she dared not take the Sacrament because of the importunate molestation of a devil. Christina, pitying her, said: "Go, and rest assured that you will receive the Body of Our Lord to-morrow; for I will take your punishment upon myself." So she went away joyfully, and after praying that night slept in peace, and rose up in the morning and communicated in all tranquillity of soul. But Christina, not thinking of the punishment she had taken upon herself, went to her rest in the evening, and as she lay in bed heard, as it were, a violent attack being made upon her; and, seizing whatever it was by the throat, tried to throw it off. She lay down again, but was again molested, and rose up in terror; and this happened many times, whilst all the straw of her bed was turned over and thrown about everywhere, so at length she perceived that she was being persecuted by the malice of a devil. Thereupon she left her pallet, and passed a sleepless night; and when she wished to pray, she was so tormented by the devil that she said she had never suffered so much before. In the morning, therefore, saying to the other woman, "I renounce your punishment, and I am hardly alive to renounce it," she escaped from the violence of that wicked tempter. From this it can be seen how difficult it is to cure this sort of evil, whether or not it is due to witchcraft.

However, there are still some means by which these devils may be driven away, of which Nider writes in his *Formicarius.* He says that there are five ways by which girls or men can be delivered: first, by Sacramental Confession; second, by the Sacred Sign of the Cross, or by the recital of the Angelic Salutation; third, by the use of exorcisms; fourth, by moving to another place; and fifth, by means of excommunication prudently employed by holy men. It is evident from what has been said that the first two methods did not avail the nun; but they are not on that account to be neglected, for that which cures one person does not necessarily cure another, and conversely. And it is a recorded fact that Incubus devils have often been driven away by the Lord's Prayer, or by the sprinkling

---

* "*Incubus.*" *Sinistrari tells of a case which came under his own notice when a deacon, a monk of the Certosa at Pavia, was sorely vexed by an Incubus. Exorcisms seemed unavailing; the Incubus himself in the shape of Father Prior blessed the place with Holy Water. However, the demon was at last banished. See my translation, "Demoniality," pp. 57–59, and passim.*

of Holy Water, and also especially by the Angelic Salutation.

For S. Caesarius* tells in his *Dialogue* that, after a certain priest had hanged himself, his concubine entered a convent, where she was carnally solicited by an Incubus. She drove him away by crossing herself and using Holy Water, yet he immediately returned. But when she recited the Angelic Salutation, he vanished like an arrow shot from a bow; still he came back, although he did not dare to come near her, because of that Ave MARIA.

S. Caesarius also refers to the remedy of Sacramental Confession. For he says that the aforesaid concubine was entirely abandoned by the Incubus after she was clean confessed. He tells also of a man in Leyden who was plagued by a Succubus, and was entirely delivered after Sacramental Confession.

He adds yet another example, of an enclosed nun, a contemplative, whom an Incubus would not leave in spite of prayers and confession and other religious exercises. For he persisted in forcing his way to her bed. But when, acting on the advice of a certain religious man, she uttered the word Benedicite, the devil at once left her.

Of the fourth method, that of moving to another place, he says that a certain priest's daughter had been defiled by an Incubus and driven frantic with grief; but when she went far away across the Rhine, she was left in peace by the Incubus. Her father, however, because he had sent her away, was so afflicted by the devil that he died within three days.

He also mentions a woman who was often molested by an Incubus in her own bed, and asked a devout friend of hers to come and sleep with her. She did so, and was troubled all night with the utmost uneasiness and disquiet, and then the first woman was left in peace.

William of Paris notes also that Incubi seem chiefly to molest women and girls with beautiful hair; either because they devote themselves too much to the care and adornment of their hair, or because they are wont to try to excite men by means of their hair, or because they are boastfully vain about it, or because God in His goodness permits this so that women may be afraid to entice men by the very means by which the devils wish them to entice men.

The fifth method, that of excommunication, which is perhaps the same as exorcism, is exemplified in a history of S. Bernard. In Aquitaine a woman had for six years been molested by an Incubus with incredible carnal abuse and lechery; and she heard the Incubus threaten her that she must not go near the holy man, who was coming that way, saying: "It will avail you nothing: for when he has gone away, I, who have till now been your lover, will become the cruellest of tyrants to you." None the less she went to S. Bernard, and he said to her: "Take my staff and set it in your bed, and may the devil do what he can." When she had done this, the devil did not dare to enter the woman's room, but threatened her terribly from outside, saying that he would persecute her when S. Bernard had gone away. When S. Bernard heard this from the woman, he called the people together, bidding them carry lighted candles in their hands, and, with the whole assembly which was gathered, excommunicated the devil, forbidding him evermore to approach that woman or any other. And so she was delivered from that punishment.

Here it is to be noted that the power of the Keys granted to S. Peter and his successors, which resounds on the earth, is really a power of healing granted to the Church on behalf of travellers who are subject to the jurisdiction of the Papal power; therefore it seems wonderful that even the Powers of the air can be warded off by this virtue. But it must be remembered that persons who are molested by devils are under the jurisdiction of the Pope and his Keys; and therefore it is not surprising if such Powers are indirectly kept at bay by the virtue of the Keys, just as by the same virtue the souls in purgatory can indirectly be delivered from the pains of the fire; inasmuch as

* "*Caesarius.*" A learned monk of the Cistercian monastery of Heisterbach near Bonn, born about 1170 at Cologne, died about 1240 as Prior of Heisterbach. Abbot Henry requested Caesarius to draw up an abstract of his teaching, and this resulted in the famous "*Dialogus magnus uisionum atque miraculorum, Libri XII*," which it is no exaggeration to say was probably the most popular book in Germany of its period. More than fifty MSS. are extant, and seven printed editions are known. The latest, two volumes, was edited by Strange, Cologne, 1851; an index to this followed, Coblenz, 1857.

this Power availeth upon the earth, ay, and to the relief of souls that are under the earth.

But it is not seemly to discuss the Power of the Keys granted to the Head of the Church as Christ's Vicar; since it is known that, for the use of the Church, Christ granted to the Church and His Vicar as much power as it is possible for God to grant to mere man.

And it is piously to be believed that, when infirmities inflicted by witches through the power of devils, together with the witches and devils themselves, are excommunicated, those who were afflicted will no longer be tormented; and that they will be delivered all the sooner by the use of other lawful exorcisms in addition.

There is a common report current in the districts of the river Etsch, as also in other places, that by the permission of God a swarm of locusts came and devoured all the vines, green leaves and crops; and that they were suddenly put to flight and dispersed by means of this kind of excommunication and cursing. Now if any wish that this should be ascribed to some holy man, and not to the virtue of the Keys, let it be so, in the name of the Lord; but of one thing we are certain, that both the power to perform miracles and the power of the Keys necessarily presuppose a condition of grace in him who performs that act of grace, since both these powers proceed from grace granted to men who are in a state of grace.

Again, it is to be noted that, if none of the aforesaid remedies are of any avail, then recourse must be had to the usual exorcisms, of which we shall treat later. And if even these are not sufficient to banish the iniquity of the devil, then that affliction must be considered to be an expiatory punishment for sin, which should be borne in all meekness, as are other ills of this sort which oppress us that they may, as it were, drive us to seek God.

But it must also be remarked that sometimes persons only think that they are molested by an Incubus when they are not so actually; and this is more apt to be the case with women than with men, for they are more timid and liable to imagine extraordinary things.

In this connexion William of Paris is often quoted. He says: Many phantastical apparitions occur to persons suffering from a melancholy disease, especially to women, as is shown by their dreams and visions. And the reason for this, as physicians know, is that women's souls are by nature far more easily and lightly impressionable than men's souls. And he adds: I know that I have seen a woman who thought that a devil copulated with her from inside, and said she was physically conscious of such incredible things.

At times also women think they have been made pregnant by an Incubus, and their bellies grow to an enormous size; but when the time of parturition comes, their swelling is relieved by no more than the expulsion of a great quantity of wind. For by taking ants' eggs in drink, or the seeds of spurge or of the black pine, an incredible amount of wind and flatulence is generated in the human stomach. And it is very easy for the devil to cause these and even greater disorders in the stomach. This has been set down in order that too easy credence should not be given to women, but only to those whom experience has shown to be trustworthy, and to those who, by sleeping in their beds or near by them, know for a fact that such things as we have spoken of are true.

✶

CHAPTER II

Remedies prescribed for Those who are Bewitched by the Limitation of the Generative Power.

ALTHOUGH far more women are witches than men, as was shown in the First Part of the work, yet men are more often bewitched than women. And the reason for this lies in the fact that God allows the devil more power over the venereal act, by which the original sin is handed down, than over other human actions. In the same way He allows more witchcraft to be performed by means of serpents, which are more subject to incantations than other animals, because that was the first instrument of the devil. And the venereal act can be more readily and easily bewitched in a man than in a woman, as has been clearly shown. For there are five ways in which the devil can impede the act of generation, and they are more easily operated against men.

As far as possible we shall set out the remedies which can be applied in each separate kind of obstruction; and let him who is bewitched in this faculty take note to which class of obstruction his belongs. For there are five classes, according to Peter a Palude in his Fourth Book, dist. 34, of the trial of this sort of bewitchment.

For the devil, being a spirit, has by his very nature power, with God's permission, over a bodily creature, especially to promote or to prevent local motion. So by this power they can prevent the bodies of men and women from approaching each other; and this either directly or indirectly. Directly, when they remove one to a distance from another, and do not allow him to approach the other. Indirectly, when they cause some obstruction, or when they interpose themselves in an assumed body. So it happened to that young Pagan who had married an idol, but none the less contracted a marriage with a girl; but because of this he was unable to copulate with her, as has been shown above.

Secondly, the devil can inflame a man towards one woman and render him impotent towards another; and this he can secretly cause by the application of certain herbs or other matters of which he well knows the virtue for this purpose.

Thirdly, he can disturb the apperception of a man or a woman, so that he makes one appear hideous to the other; for, as has been shown, he can influence the imagination.

Fourthly, he can suppress the vigour of that member which is necessary for procreation; just as he can deprive any organ of the power of local motion.

Fifthly, he can prevent the flow of the semen to the members in which is the motive power, by as it were closing the seminal duct so that it does not descend to the genital vessels, or does not ascend again from them, or cannot come forth, or is spent vainly.

But if a man should say: I do not know by which of these different methods I have been bewitched; all I know is that I cannot do anything with my wife: he should be answered in this way. If he is active and able with regard to other women, but not with his wife, then he is bewitched in the second way; for he can be certified as to the first way, that he is being deluded by

Succubus or Incubus devils. Moreover, if he does not find his wife repellent, and yet cannot know her, but can know other women, then again it is the second way; but if he finds her repellent and cannot copulate with her, then it is the second and the third way. If he does not find her repellent and wishes to have connexion with her, but has no power in his member, then it is the fourth way. But if he has power in his member, yet cannot emit his semen, then it is the fifth way. The method of curing these will be shown where we consider whether those who live in grace and those who do not are equally liable to be bewitched in these manners; and we answer that they are not, with the exception of the fourth manner, and even then very rarely. For such an affliction can happen to a man living in grace and righteousness; but the reader must understand that in this case we speak of the conjugal act between married people; for in any other case they are all liable to bewitchment; for every venereal act outside wedlock is a mortal sin, and is only committed by those who are not in a state of grace.

We have, indeed, the authority of the whole of Scriptural teaching that God allows the devil to afflict sinners more than the just. For although that most just man, Job, was stricken, yet he was not so particularly or directly in respect of the procreant function. And it may be said that, when a married couple are afflicted in this way, either both the parties or one of them is not living in a state of grace; and this opinion is substantiated in the Scriptures both by authority and by reason. For the Angel said to Tobias:* The devil receives power against those who are given over to lust: and he proved it in the slaying of the seven husbands of the virgin Sara.

Cassian, in his *Collation of the Fathers*, quotes S. Antony as saying that the devil can in no way enter our mind or body unless he has first de-

---

* "Tobias." "Tobias" vi, 16 and 17: Then the angel Raphael said to him: Hear me, and I will show thee who they are, over whom the devil can prevail. For they who in such manner receive matrimony as to shut out God from themselves, and from their mind, and to give themselves to their lust, as the horse and mule, which have not understanding, over them the devil hath power.

prived it of all holy thoughts and made it empty and bare of spiritual contemplation. These words should not be applied to an evil affliction over the whole of the body, for when Job was so afflicted he was not denuded of Divine grace; but they have particular reference to a particular infirmity inflicted upon the body for some sin. And the infirmity we are considering can only be due to the sin of incontinence. For, as we have said, God allows the devil more power over that act than over other human acts, because of its natural nastiness, and because by it the first sin was handed down to posterity. Therefore when people joined in matrimony have for some sin been deprived of Divine help, God allows them to be bewitched chiefly in their procreant functions.

But if it is asked of what sort are those sins, it can be said, according to S. Jerome, that even in a state of matrimony it is possible to commit the sin of incontinence in various ways. See the text: He who loves his wife to excess is an adulterer. And they who love in this way are more liable to be bewitched after the manner we have said.

The remedies of the Church, then, are twofold: one applicable in the public court, the other in the tribunal of the confessional. As for the first, when it has been publicly found that the impotence is due to witchcraft, then it must be distinguished whether it is temporary or permanent. If it is only temporary, it does not annul the marriage. And it is assumed to be temporary if, within the space of three years, by using every possible expedient of the Sacraments of the Church and other remedies, a cure can be caused. But if, after that time, they cannot be cured by any remedy, then it is assumed to be permanent.

Now the disability either precedes both the contract and the consummation of marriage; and in this case it impedes the contract: or it follows the contract but precedes the consummation; and in this case it annuls the contract. For men are very often bewitched in this way because they have cast off their former mistresses, who, hoping that they were to be married and being disappointed, so bewitch the men that they cannot copulate with another woman. And in such a case, according to the opinion of many, the marriage

already contracted is annulled, unless, like Our Blessed Lady and S. Joseph, they are willing to live together in holy continence. This opinion is supported by the Canon where it says (23, q. 1) that a marriage is confirmed by the carnal act. And a little later it says that impotence before such confirmation dissolves the ties of marriage.

Or else the disability follows the consummation of a marriage, and then it does not dissolve the bonds of matrimony. Much more to this effect is noted by the Doctors, where in various writings they treat of the obstruction due to witchcraft; but since it is not precisely relevant to the present inquiry, it is here omitted.

But some may find it difficult to understand how this function can be obstructed in respect of one woman but not of another. S. Bonaventura answers that this may be because some witch has persuaded the devil to effect this only with respect to one woman, or because God will not allow the obstruction to apply save to some particular woman. The judgement of God in this matter is a mystery, as in the case of the wife of Tobias. But how the devil procures this disability is plainly shown by what has already been said. And S. Bonaventura says that he obstructs the procreant function, not intrinsically by harming the organ, but extrinsically by impeding its use; and it is an artificial, not a natural impediment; and so he can cause it to apply to one woman and not to another. Or else he takes away all desire for one or another woman; and this he does by his own power, or else by means of some herb or stone or some occult creature. And in this he is in substantial agreement with Peter a Palude.

The ecclesiastical remedy in the tribunal of God is set forth in the Canon where it says: If with the permission of the just and secret judgement of God, through the arts of sorceresses and witches and the preparation of the devil, men are bewitched in their procreant function, they are to be urged to make clean confession to God and His priest of all their sins with a contrite heart and a humble spirit; and to make satisfaction to God with many tears and large offerings and prayers and fasting.

From these words it is clear that such afflictions are only on account of sin, and occur only to those who do not live in a state of grace. It proceeds to tell how the ministers of the Church can effect a cure by means of exorcisms and the other protections and cures provided by the Church. In this way, with the help of God, Abraham cured by his prayers Abimelech and his house.*

In conclusion we may say that there are five remedies which may lawfully be applied to those who are bewitched in this way: namely, a pilgrimage to some holy and venerable shrine; true confession of their sins with contrition; the plentiful use of the sign of the Cross and devout prayer; lawful exorcism by solemn words, the nature of which will be explained later; and lastly, a remedy can be effected by prudently approaching the witch, as was shown in the case of the Count who for three years was unable to cohabit carnally with a virgin whom he had married.

☆

CHAPTER III

Remedies prescribed for those who are Bewitched by being Inflamed with Inordinate Love or Extraordinary Hatred.

JUST as the generative faculty can be bewitched, so can inordinate love or hatred be caused in the human mind. First we shall consider the cause of this, and then, as far as possible, the remedies.

Philocaption, or inordinate love of one person for another, can be caused in three ways. Sometimes it is due merely to a lack of control over the eyes; sometimes to the temptation of devils; sometimes to the spells of necromancers and witches, with the help of devils.

The first is spoken of in *S. James* i. 14, 15: Every man is tempted by his own concupiscence, being drawn away and allured. Then when concupiscence hath conceived, it bringeth forth sin: but sin, when it is completed, begetteth death. And so, when Shechem saw Dinah going out to see the daughters of the land, he loved her, and ravished her, and lay with her, and his soul clave unto her (*Genesis* xxxiv). And here the gloss says that this happened to an infirm spirit because she left her

* "Abimelech." "Genesis" xx.

own concerns to inquire into those of other people; and such a soul is seduced by bad habits, and is led to consent to unlawful practices.

The second cause arises from the temptation of devils. In this way Amnon loved his beautiful sister Tamar, and was so vexed that he fell sick for love of her (II. *Samuel* xiii). For he could not have been so totally corrupt in his mind as to fall into so great a crime of incest unless he had been grievously tempted by the devil. The book of the Holy Fathers refers to this kind of love, where it says that even in their hermitages they were exposed to every temptation, including that of carnal desire; for some of them were at times tempted with the love of women more than it is possible to believe. S. Paul also says, in II. *Corinthians* xii: There was given to me a thorn in the flesh, the messenger of Satan to buffet me: and the gloss explains this as referring to the temptation of lust.

But it is said that when a man does not give way to temptation he does not sin, but it is an exercise for his virtue; but this is to be understood of the temptation of the devil, not of that of the flesh; for this is a venial sin even if a man does not yield to it. Many examples of this are to be read.

As for the third cause, by which inordinate love proceeds from devils' and witches' works, the possibility of this sort of witchcraft has been exhaustively considered in the Questions of the First Part as to whether devils through the agency of witches can turn the minds of men to inordinate love or hatred, and it was proved by examples which had fallen within our own experience. Indeed this is the best known and most general form of witchcraft.

But the following question may be asked: Peter has been seized with an inordinate love of this description, but he does not know whether it is due to the first or the second or the third cause. It must be answered that it can be by the work of the devil that hatred is stirred up between married people so as to cause the crime of adultery. But when a man is so bound in the meshes of carnal lust and desire that he can be made to desist from it by no shame, words, blows or action; and when a man often puts away his beautiful wife to cleave to the most hideous of women, and when he cannot rest in the night, but is so demented that he must go by devious ways to his mistress; and when it is found that those of noblest birth, Governors, and other rich men, are the most miserably involved in this sin (for this age is dominated by women, and was foretold by S. Hildegard,* as Vincent of Beauvais records in the *Mirror of History*, although he said it would not endure for as long as it already has); and when the world is now full of adultery, especially among the most highly born; when all this is considered, I say, of what use is it to speak of remedies to those who desire no remedy? Nevertheless, for the satisfaction of the pious reader, we will set down briefly some of the remedies for *Philocaption* when it is not due to witchcraft.

Avicenna mentions seven remedies which may be used when a man is made physically ill by this sort of love; but they are hardly relevant to our inquiry except in so far as they may be of service to the sickness of the soul. For he says, in Book III, that the root of the sickness may be discovered by feeling the pulse and uttering the name of the object of the patient's love; and then, if the law permits, he may be married to her, and so be cured by yielding to nature. Or certain medi-

cines may be applied, concerning which he gives instructions. Or the sick man may be turned from his love by lawful remedies which will cause him to direct his love to a more worthy object. Or he may avoid her presence, and so distract his mind from her. Or, if he is open to correction, he may be admonished and expostulated with, to the effect that such love is the greatest misery. Or he may be directed to someone who, as far as he may with God's truth, will vilify the body and disposition of his love, and so blacken her character that she may appear to him altogether base and deformed. Or, finally, he is to be set to arduous duties which may distract his thoughts.

Indeed, just as the animal nature of a man may be cured by such remedies, so may they all be of use in reforming his inner spirit. Let a man obey the law of his intellect rather than that of nature, let him turn his love to safe pleasures, let him remember how momentary is the fruition of lust and how eternal the punishment, let him seek his pleasure in that life where joys begin never to end, and let him consider that if he cleaves to his earthly love, that will be his sole reward, but he will lose the bliss of Heaven, and be condemned to eternal fire: behold! the three irrecoverable losses which proceed from inordinate lust.

With regard to *Philocaption* caused by witchcraft, the remedies detailed in the preceding chapter may not inconveniently be applied here also; especially the exorcisms by sacred words which the bewitched person can himself use. Let him daily invoke the Guardian Angel deputed to him by God, let him use confession and frequent the shrines of the Saints, especially of the Blessed Virgin, and without doubt he will be delivered.

But how abject are those strong men who, discarding their natural gifts and the armour of virtue, cease to defend themselves; whereas the girls themselves in their invincible frailty use those very rejected weapons to repel this kind of witchcraft. We give one out of many examples in their praise.

There was in a country village near Lindau in the diocese of Constance a grown maid fair to see and of even more elegant behaviour, at sight of whom a certain man of loose principles, a cleric in sooth, but not a priest,

---

* "*S. Hildegard.*" *Born at Böckelheim on the Nahe, 1098; died on the Rupertsberg near Bingen, 1179. This great Benedictine seeress and prophetess has been called the Sibyl of the Rhine. From her earliest years she was favoured with visions, and when she was aged about forty she received a Divine command to publish to the world what she had seen and heard. After much hesitation owing to her humility she obeyed, and in 1141 she commenced her profound treatise "Scivias" ("scire uias Domini"), which occupied her for ten years. It is ecstatic and prophetic throughout, and demands profoundest study. Herwegen, "Kirchl. Handlexikon" (1908), remarks that in order fully to appreciate this marvellous writer a new and critical edition of her writings must be prepared, a task entailing immense labour and research. No formal canonization of S. Hildegard has taken place, but many miracles were wrought at her intercession, and her name is in the Roman Martyrology. The feast is celebrated on 17 September in the dioceses of Speyer, Mainz, Trier and Limburg, and by the Solesmes monks on 18 September with a proper Office. The Relics of the Saint are at Eibingen, of which town she is patron. The convent of S. Hildegard there was formally constituted on 17 September, 1904.*

was smitten with violent pangs of love. And being unable to conceal the wound in his heart any longer, he went to the place where the girl was working, and with fair words showed that he was in the net of the devil, beginning by venturing in words only to persuade the girl to grant him her love. She, perceiving by Divine instinct his meaning, and being chaste in mind and body, bravely answered him: Master, do not come to my house with such words, for modesty itself forbids. To this he replied: Although you will not be persuaded by gentle words to love me, yet I promise you that soon you will be compelled by my deeds to love me. Now that man was a suspected enchanter and wizard. The maiden considered his words as but empty air, and until then felt in herself no spark of carnal love for him; but after a short time she began to have amorous thoughts. Perceiving this, and being inspired by God, she sought the protection of the Mother of Mercy, and devoutly implored Her to intercede with Her Son to help her. Anxious, moreover, to enjoy the society of pious folk, she went on a pilgrimage to a hermitage,* where there was a church

---

* "*Hermitage.*" *The famous shrine of Our Lady of the Hermits, at the Benedictine Abbey of Einsiedeln, in the Canton of Schwyz, Switzerland. S. Meinrad, who was assassinated by bandits in 861, had embraced the solitary life and established his hermitage on the slopes of Mount Etzel, when he built a small oratory for the wonder-working statue of Our Lady which had been given him by Abbess Hildegard of Zurich. Several anchorites succeeded him, and one of these, by name Eberhard, erected a monastery and church there. This fane was miraculously consecrated in 948 by Christ Himself, assisted by the Four Evangelists, S. Peter and S. Gregory the Great. Even the rationalistic Father Thurston, S.J., will be unable to impugn this holy marvel, as it was investigated and confirmed by Pope Leo VIII, and subsequently ratified by many a Pontiff, the last being Pius VI, who in 1793 confirmed the acts of all his predecessors. The miraculous statue is enthroned in a little chapel which stands within the great abbey church in much the same way as the Holy House at Loreto, encased in marbles and elaborate wood-work, the goal of ten thousand pilgrimages. The two chief days are the fourteenth of September and the thirteenth of October, the first being the anniversary of the Divine consecration of Eberhard's basilica, the second that of the translation of the Relics of S. Meinrad from Reichenau to Einsiedeln in 1039.*

miraculously consecrated in that diocese to the Mother of God. There she confessed her sins, so that no evil spirit could enter her, and after her prayers to the Mother of Pity all the devil's machinations against her ceased, so that these evil crafts thenceforth never afflicted her.

None the less there are still some strong men cruelly enticed by witches to this sort of love, so that it would seem that they could never restrain themselves from their inordinate lust for them, yet these often most manfully resist the temptation of lewd and filthy enticements, and by the aforesaid defences overcome all the wiles of the devil.

A rich young man in the town of Innsbruck provides us with a notable pattern of this sort of struggle. He was so importuned by witches that it is hardly possible for pen to describe his strivings, but he always kept a brave heart, and escaped by means of the remedies we have mentioned. Therefore it may justly be concluded that these remedies are infallible against this disease, and that they who use such weapons will most surely be delivered.

And it must be understood that what we have said concerning inordinate love applies also to inordinate hatred, since the same discipline is of benefit for the two opposite extremes. But though the degree of witchcraft is equal in each, yet there is this difference in the case of hatred; the person who is hated must seek another remedy. For the man who hates his wife and puts her out of his heart will not easily, if he is an adulterer, be turned back again to his wife, even though he go on many a pilgrimage.

Now it has been learned from witches that they cause this spell of hatred by means of serpents; for the serpent was the first instrument of the devil, and by reason of its curse inherits a hatred of women; therefore they cause such spells by placing the skin or head of a serpent under the threshold of a room or house. For this reason all the nooks and corners of the house where such a woman lives are to be closely examined and reconstructed as far as possible; or else she must be lodged in the houses of others.

And when it is said that bewitched men can exorcise themselves, it is to be understood that they can wear the sacred words or benedictions or incantations round their necks, if they are unable to read or pronounce the benedictions; but it will be shown later in what way this should be done.

☆

CHAPTER IV

Remedies prescribed for those who by Prestidigitatory Art have lost their Virile Members or have seemingly been Transformed into the Shapes of Beasts.

IN what has already been written it has clearly enough been shown the remedies which are available for the relief of those who are deluded by a glamour, and think that they have lost their virile member, or have been metamorphosed into animals. For since such men are entirely destitute of Divine grace, according to the essential condition of those who are so bewitched, it is not possible to apply a healing salve while the weapon still remains in the wound. Therefore before all things they must be reconciled to God by a good confession. Again, as was shown in the seventh chapter of the First Question of the Second Part, such members are never actually taken away from the body, but are only hidden by a glamour from the senses of sight and touch. It is clear, too, that those who live in grace are not so easily deluded in this way, either actively or passively, in such a manner, that is, that they seem to lose their members, or that those of others should appear to them to be missing. Therefore the remedy as well as the disease is explained in that chapter, namely, that they should as far as possible come to an amicable agreement with the witch herself.

As to those who think that they have been changed into beasts, it must be known that this kind of witchcraft is more practised in Eastern countries than in the West; that is to say, in the East witches more often bewitch other people in this way, but it appears that the witches so transform themselves more frequently in our part of the world; namely, when they change themselves, in full sight, into the shapes of animals, as was told in the eighth chapter. Therefore in their case the remedies to be used are those set out in the Third Part of this work, where we deal with the extermination of witches by the secular arm of the law.

But in the East the following remedy is used for such delusions. For we have learned much of this matter from the Knights of the Order of S. John of Jerusalem in Rhodes; and especially this case which happened in the city of Salamis in the kingdom of Cyprus. For that is a seaport, and once when a vessel was being laden with merchandise suitable for a ship which is sailing into foreign parts, and all her company were providing themselves with victuals, one of them, a strong young man, went to the house of a woman standing outside the city on the seashore, and asked her if she had any eggs to sell. The woman, seeing that he was a strong young man, and a merchant far away from his own country, thought that on that account the people of the city would feel less suspicion if he were to be lost, and said to him: "Wait a little, and I will get you all that you want." And when she went in and shut the door and kept him waiting, the young man outside began to call out to her to hurry, lest he should miss the ship. Then the woman brought some eggs and gave them to the young man, and told him to hurry back to the ship in case he should miss it. So he hastened back to the ship, which was anchored by the shore, and before going on board, since the full company of his companions was not yet returned, he decided to eat the eggs there and refresh himself. And behold! an hour later he was made dumb as if he had no power of speech; and, as he afterwards said, he wondered what could have happened to him, but was unable to find out. Yet when he wished to go on board, he was driven off with sticks by those who yet remained ashore, and who all cried out: "Look what this ass is doing! Curse the beast, you are not coming on board." The young man being thus driven away, and understanding from their words that they thought he was an ass, reflected and began to suspect that he had been bewitched by the woman, especially since he could utter no word, although he understood all that was said. And when, on again trying to board the ship, he was driven off with heavier blows, he was in bitterness of heart compelled to remain and watch the ship sail away. And so, as he ran here and there, since everybody thought he was an ass, he was necessarily treated as such. At last, under compulsion, he went back to the woman's house, and to keep himself alive served her at her pleasure for three years, doing no work but to bring to the house such necessities as wood and corn, and to carry away what had to be carried away like a beast of burden: the only consolation that was left to him being that although everyone else took him for an ass, the witches themselves, severally and in company, who frequented the house, recognized him as a man, and he could talk and behave with them as a man should.

Now if it is asked how burdens were placed upon him as if he were a beast, we must say that this case is analogous to that of which S. Augustine speaks in his *De Ciuitate Dei*, Book XVIII, chapter 17, where he tells of the tavern women who changed their guests into beasts of burden; and to that of the father of Praestantius, who thought he was a pack-horse and carried corn with other animals. For the delusion caused by this glamour was threefold.

First in its effect on the men who saw the young man not as a man but as an ass; and it is shown above in Chapter VIII how devils can easily cause this. Secondly, those burdens were no illusion; but when they were beyond the strength of the young man, the devil invisibly carried them. Thirdly, that when he was consorting with others, the young man himself considered in his imagination and perceptive faculties at least, which are faculties belonging to the bodily organs, that he was an ass; but not in his reason: for he was not so bound but that he knew himself to be a man, although he was magically deluded into imagining himself a beast. Nabuchodonosor provides an example of the same delusion.

After three years had passed in this way, in the fourth year it happened that the young man went one morning into the city, with the woman following a long way behind; and he passed by a church where Holy Mass was being celebrated, and heard the sacring-bell ring at the elevation of the Host (for in that kingdom the Mass is celebrated according to the Latin, and not according to the Greek rite). And he turned towards the church, and, not daring to enter for

fear of being driven off with blows, knelt down outside by bending the knees of his hind legs, and lifted his forelegs, that is, his hands, joined together over his ass's head, as it was thought to be, and looked upon the elevation of the Sacrament.* And when some Genoese merchants saw this prodigy, they followed the ass in astonishment, discussing this marvel among themselves; and behold! the witch came and belaboured the ass with her stick. And because, as we have said, this sort of witchcraft is better known in those parts, at the instance of the merchants the ass and the witch were taken before the judge; where, being questioned and tortured, she confessed her crime and promised to restore the young man to his true shape if she might be allowed to return to her house. So she was dismissed and went back to her house, where the young man was restored to his former shape; and being again arrested, she

---

* *"Sacrament." One of the most famous of the miracles of S. Antony of Padua, wrought for the conversion of heretics, was that of a mule, belonging to one Bovidilla, a blasphemer of the Sacrament. The animal, although it had been, as agreed, kept fasting for three days, refused to turn to a sieve of oats held out by its master, but fell down upon its knees and adored the Host which the Saint was carrying in the ostensory. Some narratives of the fourteenth century say this happened at Toulouse, and some name Bruges, but the actual place was Rimini. In the basilica Il Santo, at Padua, this miracle is depicted more than once. There is a bronze bas-relief by Donatello in the Chapel of the Sacrament, and a fresco by Campagnola. The same subject was painted by Van Dyck for the Recollects at Malines.*

Animals have been known to distinguish Our Lord's Body in the Host, a fact which, when one considers their sense and intelligence, is not at all surprising.

At the trial of the Satanist Louis Gaufridi it was proved that upon one occasion during their accursed rites a dog was led in to devour the consecrated Species, but he stretched out his paws in adoration before the Body of Christ and bowed down his head, nor could kicks nor blows compel him to stir. Several of the devotees broke down into tears and began loudly to bewail their sins, after which it was decreed in future that the Host should be defiled, but that no animals must be admitted. See my "Geography of Witchcraft," pp. 410– 411.

S. Optatus tells us that certain Donatists once threw the Host to some hungry dogs, who suddenly turned on the heretics and tore them to pieces.

paid the debt which her crimes merited. And the young man returned joyfully to his own country.

☆

CHAPTER V

Prescribed Remedies for those who are Obsessed owing to some Spell.

WE have shown in Chapter X of the preceding Question that sometimes devils, through witchcraft, substantially inhabit certain men, and why they do this: namely, that it may be for some grave crime of the man himself, and for his own ultimate benefit; or sometimes for the slight fault of another man; sometimes for a man's own venial sin; and sometimes for another man's grave sin. For any of these reasons a man may in varying degrees be possessed by a devil. Nider in his *Formicarius* states that there is no cause for wonder if devils, at the instance of witches and with God's permission, substantially take possession of men.

It is clear also from the details given in that chapter what are the remedies by which such men can be liberated; namely, by the exorcisms of the Church; and by true contrition and confession, when a man is possessed for some mortal sin. An example is the manner in which that Bohemian priest was set free. But there are three other remedies besides, which are of virtue; namely, the Holy Communion of the Eucharist, the visitation of shrines and the prayers of holy men, and by lifting the sentence of excommunication. Of these we shall speak, although they are plainly set out in the discourses of the Doctors, since all have not easy access to the necessary treatises.

Cassian, in his *Collation of the Abbots*, speaks in these words of the Eucharist: We do not remember that our elders ever forbade the administration of the Holy Communion to those possessed by evil spirits; it should even be given to them every day if possible.* For it must be believed that It is of great virtue in the purgation and protection of both soul and body; and that when a man receives It, the evil spirit which afflicts his members or lurks hidden in them is driven away as if it were burned with fire. And lately we saw the Abbot Andronicus healed in this way; and the devil will rage with mad fury when he feels himself shut out by the heavenly medicine, and he will try the harder and the oftener to inflict his tortures, as he feels himself driven farther off by this spiritual remedy. So says S. John Cassian.

And again he adds: Two things must be steadfastly believed. First, that without the permission of God no one is altogether possessed by these spirits. Second, that everything which God permits to happen to us, whether it seem to be sorrow or gladness, is sent for our good as from a pitying Father and a merciful Physician. For the devils are, as it were, schoolmasters of humility, so that they who descend from this world may either be purged for the eternal life or be sentenced to the pain of their punishment; and such, according to S. Paul, are in the present life delivered unto Satan for the destruction of the flesh, that the spirit may be saved in the day of the Lord Jesus Christ.

But here there arises a doubt. For S. Paul says: Let a man examine himself, and so eat of that Bread: then how can a man who is possessed communicate, since he has not the use of his reason? S. Thomas answers this in his Third Part, Question 80, saying that there are distinct degrees in madness. For to say that a man has not the use of his reason may mean two things. In one case he has some feeble power of reason; as a man is said to be blind when he can nevertheless see imperfectly. And since such men can to some extent join in the devotion of this Sacrament, it is not to be denied to them.

But others are said to be mad because they have been so from birth; and such may not partake of the Sacrament,

---

* *"Every day."* Since the Sacrament is *"medicina animae"*. In *"En Route,"* Chap. V, the Abbé Gévresin says: *"Je comprends très bien le système du père Milleriot qui forçait à communier des gens qu'il appréhendait de voir retomber dans leur péchés, après. Pour toute pénitence, il les obligeait à recommunier encore et* il finissait par les épurer avec les Saintes Espèces prises à de hautes doses. C'est une doctrine tout à la fois réaliste et surélevée."* Père Milleriot, S.J., was largely concerned in the conversion (1879–80) of Paul-Maximilien-Émile Littré, who died at Paris, 2 June, 1881.

since they are in no way able to engage in devout preparation for it.

Or perhaps they have not always been without the use of their reason; and then, if when they were sane they appeared to appreciate the devotion due to the Sacrament, It should be administered to them when they are at the point of death, unless it is feared that they may vomit or spew It out.

The following decision is recorded by the Council of Carthage (26, q. 6).* When a sick man wishes to confess, and if on the arrival of the priest he is rendered dumb by his infirmity, or falls into a frenzy, those who have heard him speak must give their testimony. And if he is thought to be at the point of death, let him be reconciled with God by the laying on of hands and the placing of the Sacrament in his mouth. S. Thomas also says that the same procedure may be used with baptized people who are bodily tormented by unclean spirits, and with other mentally distracted persons. And he adds, in Book IV, dist. 9, that the Communion must not be denied to demoniacs unless it is certain that they are being tortured by the devil for some crime. To this Peter a Palude adds: In this case they are to be considered as persons to be excommunicated and delivered up to Satan.

From this it is clear that, even if a man be possessed by a devil for his own crimes, yet if he has lucid intervals and, while he has the use of his reason, is contrite and confesses his sins, since he is absolved in the sight of God, he must in no way be deprived of the Communion of the Divine Sacrament of the Eucharist.

How those who are possessed may be delivered by the intercessions and prayers of the Saints is found in the Legends of the Saints. For by the merits of Saints, Martyrs, Confessors and Virgins the unclean spirits are subdued by their prayers in the land where they live, just as the Saints in their earthly journey subdued them.

Likewise we read that the devout prayers of wayfarers have often obtained the deliverance of those possessed. And Cassian urges them to pray for them, saying: If we hold the opinion or rather faith of which I have written above, that everything is sent by the Lord for the good of our souls and the betterment of the universe, we shall in no way despise those who are possessed; but we shall incessantly pray for them as for our own selves, and pity them with our whole heart.

As for the last method, that of releasing the sufferer from excommunication, it must be known that this is rare, and only lawfully practised by such as have authority and are informed by revelation that the man has become possessed on account of the excommunication of the Church: such was the case of the Corinthian fornicator (I. *Corinthians* v) who was excommunicated by S. Paul and the Church, and delivered unto Satan for the destruction of the flesh, that his spirit might be saved in the day of our Lord JESUS Christ; that is, as the gloss says, either for the illumination of grace by contrition or for judgement.

And he delivered to Satan false teachers who had lost the faith, such as Hymenaeus and Alexander, that they might learn not to blaspheme (I. *Timothy* i). For so great was the power and the grace of S. Paul, says the gloss, that by the mere words of his mouth he could deliver to Satan those who fell away from the faith.

S. Thomas (IV. 18) teaches concerning the three effects of excommunication as follows. If a man, he says, is deprived of the prayers of the Church, he suffers a threefold loss corresponding with the benefits which accrue to one who is in communion with the Church. For those who are excommunicated are bereft of the source from which flows an increase of grace to those who have it, and a means to obtain grace for those who have it not; and, being deprived of grace, they lose also the power of preserving their uprightness; although it must not be thought that they are altogether shut out from God's providence, but only from that special providence which watches over the sons of the Church; and they lose also a strong source of protection against the Enemy,

---

* "Carthage." *The earliest Council of Carthage of which we know was held about* A.D. *198, when seventy bishops, presided over by the Bishop of Carthage, Agrippinus, were present. After this date more than twenty Councils were held at Carthage, of which the most important were those under S. Cyprian, relative to the "lapsi," Novatianism, and the re-baptism of heretics, and the synods of 412, 416 and 418 which condemned the doctrines of Pelagius.*

for greater power is granted to the devil to injure such men, both bodily and spiritually.

For in the primitive Church, when men had to be drawn into the faith by signs, just as the Holy Spirit was made manifest by a visible sign, so also a bodily affliction by the devil was the visible sign of a man who was excommunicated. And it is not unfitting that a man whose case is not quite desperate should be delivered to Satan; for he is not given to the devil as one to be damned, but to be corrected, since it is in the power of the Church, when she pleases, to deliver him again from the hands of the devil. So says S. Thomas. Therefore the lifting of the ban of excommunication, when prudently used by a discreet exorcist, is a fitting remedy for those who are possessed.

But Nider adds that the exorcist must particularly beware of making too presumptive a use of his powers, or of mingling any ribaldry or jesting with the serious work of God, or adding to it anything that smacks of superstition or witchcraft; for otherwise he will hardly escape punishment, as he shows by an example.

For Blessed Gregory, in his First Dialogue, tells of a certain woman who, against her conscience, yielded to her husband's persuasions to take part in the ceremonies at the vigil of the dedication of the Church of S. Sebastian. And because she joined in the Church's procession against her conscience, she became possessed and raged publicly. When the priest of that church saw this, he took the cloth from the altar and covered her with it; and the devil suddenly entered into that priest. And because he had presumed beyond his strength, he was constrained by his torments to reveal who he was. So says S. Gregory.

And to show that no spirit of ribaldry * must be allowed to enter into the holy office of exorcism, Nider tells

that he saw in a monastery at Cologne a brother who was given to speaking jestingly, but was a very famous expeller of devils. This man was casting a devil out of a man possessed in the monastery, and the devil asked him to give him some place to which he could go. This pleased the Brother, and he jokingly said, "Go to my privy." So the devil went out; and when in the night the Brother wished to go and purge his belly, the devil attacked him so savagely in the privy that he with difficulty escaped with his life.

But especial care is to be taken that those who are obsessed through witchcraft should not be induced to go to witches to be healed. For S. Gregory goes on to say of the woman we have just mentioned: Her kindred and those who loved her in the flesh took her to some witches to be healed, by whom she was taken to a river and dipped in the water with many incantations; and upon this she was violently shaken, and instead of one devil being cast out, a legion entered into her, and she began to cry out in their several voices. Therefore her kindred confessed what they had done, and in great grief brought her to the holy Bishop Fortunatus,† who by daily prayers and fasting‡ entirely restored her to health.

But since it has been said that exorcists must beware lest they make use of anything savouring of superstition or witchcraft, some exorcist may doubt whether it is lawful to use certain unconsecrated herbs and stones. In answer we say that it is so much the better if the herbs are consecrated; but that if they are not, then it is not superstitious to use a certain herb called Demonifuge, § or even the natural properties of stones. But he must not think that he is casting out devils by the power of these; for then he would fall into the error of believing that he could use other herbs and incantations in the same way; and this is the error of necromancers, who think that they can perform this kind of work through the

---

* "Ribaldry." A rubric of the "De exorcizandis Obsessis a Daemonio" prescribes: "Necessarie uero interrogationes sunt, ut de numero et nomine spirituum obsidentium, de tempore quo ingressi sunt, de causa, et aliis huiusmodi. Ceteras autem daemoniis nugas, risus, et ineptias Exorcista cohibeat, aut contemnat, et circumstantes, qui pauci esse debent, admoneat, ne haec curent, neque ipsi interrogent obsessum: sed potius humiliter et enixe Deum pro eo precentur."

† "Fortunatus." Bishop of Naples, who was appointed to that see by S. Gregory the Great in 593 upon the deposition of Demetrius.

‡ "Fasting." "S. Matthew" xvii, 20: Hoc autem genus non eiicitur nisi per orationem et ieiunium.

§ "Demonifuge." See Sinistrari, "De Daemonialitate," LXVIII, in my translation "Demoniality," pp. 52–53.

natural and unknown virtues of such objects.

Therefore S. Thomas says, Book IV. dist. 7, art. the last: It must not be believed that devils are subject to any corporeal powers; and therefore they are not to be influenced by invocations or any acts of sorcery, except in so far as they have entered into a pact with a witch. Of this Esaias (xxviii) speaks: We have made a covenant with death, and with hell are we at agreement. And he thus explains the passage in *Job* xli: Canst thou draw out Leviathan with an hook? and the following words. For he says: If one rightly considers all that has been said before, it will seem that it belongs to the heretical presumption of necromancers when anyone tries to make an agreement with devils, or to subject them in any way to his own will.

Having, then, shown that man cannot of his own power overcome the devil, he concludes by saying: Place your hand upon him; but understand that, if you have any power, it is yet by Divine virtue that he is overcome. And he adds: Remember the battle which I wage against him; that is to say, the present being put for the future, I shall fight against him on the Cross, where Leviathan will be taken with an hook, that is, by the divinity hidden under the bait of humanity, since he will think our Saviour to be only a man. And afterwards it says: There is no power on earth to be compared with him: by which it is meant that no bodily power can equal the power of the devil, which is a purely spiritual power. So says S. Thomas.

But a man possessed by a devil can indirectly be relieved by the power of music, as was Saul by David's harp, or of a herb, or of any other bodily matter in which there lies some natural virtue. Therefore such remedies may be used, as can be argued both from authority and by reason. For S. Thomas, XXVI. 7, says that stones and herbs may be used for the relief of a man possessed by a devil. And there are the words of S. Jerome.

And as for the passage in *Tobias*, where the Angel says: Touching the heart and the liver (which you took from the fish), if a devil or an evil spirit trouble any, we must make a smoke thereof before the man or the woman, and the party shall be no more vexed; S. Thomas says: We ought not to marvel

at this, for the smoke of a certain tree when it is burned seems to have the same virtue, as if it had in it some spiritual sense, or power of spiritual prayer for the future.

Of the same opinion are Blessed Albert, in his commentary on *S. Luke* ix, and Nicolas of Lyra and Paul of Burgos,* on I. *Samuel* xvi. The last-named homilist comes to this conclusion: that it must be allowed that those possessed by a devil can not only be relieved, but even entirely delivered by means of material things, understanding that in the latter case they are not very fiercely molested. And he proves this by reasoning as follows: Devils cannot alter corporeal matter just at their will, but only by bringing together complementary active and passive agents, as Nicolas says. In the same way some material object can cause in the human body a disposition which makes it susceptible to the operations of the devil. For example, according to physicians, mania very much predisposes a man to dementia, and consequently to demoniac obsession: therefore if, in such a case, the predisposing passive agent be removed, it will follow that the active affliction of the devil will be cured.

In this light we may consider the fish's liver; and the music of David, by which Saul was at first relieved and then entirely delivered of the evil spirit; for it says: And the evil spirit departed from him. But it is not consonant with the meaning of the Scripture to say that this was done by the merits or prayers of David; for the Scripture says nothing of any such matter, whereas it would have spoken notably in his praise if this had been so. This reasoning we take from Paul of Burgos. There is also the reason which we gave in Question V of the First Part: that Saul was liber-

---

* *"Paul of Burgos." Paul de Santa Maria, a Spanish Archbishop, Lord Chancellor, and exegete, born at Burgos about 1351; died 29 August, 1435. The most wealthy and influential Jew of Burgos (Jewish name Solomon-Ha-Levi), and a scholar of the first rank in Talmudic and Rabbinical literature, a Rabbi of the Hebraic community, he was converted to Christianity by the irrefutable logic of the "Summa" of S. Thomas. He received baptism 21 July, 1390. His reputation as a Biblical writer chiefly rests upon his "Additiones" to the "Postilla" of Nicolas of Lyra, Nuremberg, 1481; Venice, 1481; and many other editions.*

ated because by the harp was pre-figured the virtue of the Cross on which were stretched the Sacred Limbs of Christ's Body. And more is written there which may be considered to-gether with the present inquiry. But we shall only conclude by saying that the use of material things in lawful exorcisms is not superstitious. And now it is expedient that we should speak about the exorcisms themselves.

☆

CHAPTER VI

Prescribed Remedies; to wit, the Lawful Exorcisms of the Church, for all Sorts of Infirmities and Ills due to Witchcraft; and the Method of Exorcising those who are Bewitched.

IT has already been stated that witches can afflict men with every kind of physical infirmity; therefore it can be taken as a general rule that the various verbal or practical remedies which can be applied in the case of those infirmi-ties which we have just been discussing are equally applicable to all other in-firmities, such as epilepsy or leprosy, for example. And as lawful exorcisms are reckoned among the verbal remedies and have been most often considered by us, they may be taken as a general type of such remedies; and there are three matters to be considered regarding them.

First, we must judge whether a per-son who has not been ordained as an exorcist, such as a layman or a secular cleric, may lawfully exorcise devils and their works. Bound up with this ques-tion are three others: namely; first, what constitutes the legality of this practice; secondly, the seven conditions which must be observed when one wishes to make private use of charms and benedictions; and thirdly, in what way the disease is to be exorcised and the devil conjured.

Secondly, we must consider what is to be done when no healing grace results from the exorcism.

Thirdly, we must consider practical and not verbal remedies; together with the solution of certain arguments.

For the first, we have the opinion of S. Thomas in Book IV, dist. 23. He says: When a man is ordained as an exorcist, or into any of the other minor Orders, he has conferred upon him the power of exorcism in his official ca-pacity; and this power may even law-fully be used by those who belong to no Order, but such do not exercise it in their official capacity. Similarly the Mass can be said in an unconsecrated house, although the very purpose of consecrating a church is that the Mass may be said there; but this is more on account of the grace which is in the righteous than of the grace of the Sacrament.

From these words we may conclude that, although it is good that in the liberation of a bewitched person re-course should be had to an exorcist having authority to exorcise such be-witchments, yet at times other devout persons may, either with or without any exorcism, cast out this sort of diseases.

For we hear of a certain poor and very devout virgin, one of whose friends had been grievously bewitched in his foot, so that it was clear to the phy-sicians that he could be cured by no medicines. But it happened that the virgin went to visit the sick man, and he at once begged her to apply some benediction to his foot. She consented, and did no more than silently say the Lord's Prayer and the Apostles' Creed, at the same time making use of the sign of the life-giving Cross. The sick man then felt himself at once cured, and, that he might have a remedy for the future, asked the virgin what charms she had used. But she answered: You are of little faith and do not hold to the holy and lawful practices of the Church, and you often apply forbidden charms and remedies for your infirmities; therefore are you rarely healthy in your body, because you are always sick in your soul. But if you would put your trust in prayer and in the efficacy of lawful symbols, you will often be very easily cured. For I did nothing but repeat the Lord's Prayer and the Apostles' Creed, and you are now cured.

This example gives rise to the ques-tion, whether there is not any efficacy in other benedictions and charms, and even conjurations by way of exorcism; for they seem to be condemned in this story. We answer that the virgin con-demned only unlawful charms and un-lawful conjurations and exorcisms.

To understand these last we must consider how they originated, and how they came to be abused. For they were in their origin entirely sacred; but just as by the means of devils and wicked men all things can be defiled, so also were these sacred words. For it is said in the last chapter of S. Mark, of the Apostles and holy men: In My Name shall they cast out devils; and they visited the sick, and prayed over them with sacred words; and in after times priests devoutly used similar rites; and therefore there are to be found to-day in ancient Churches devout prayers and holy exorcisms which men can use or undergo, when they are applied by pious men as they used to be, without any superstition; even as there are now to be found learned men and Doctors of holy Theology who visit the sick and use such words for the healing not only of demoniacs, but of other diseases as well.

But, alas! superstitious men have, on the pattern of these, found for themselves many vain and unlawful remedies which they employ in these days for sick men and animals; and the clergy have become too slothful to use any more the lawful words when they visit the sick. On this account Gulielmus Durandus,* the commentator on S. Raymond, says that such lawful exorcisms may be used by a religious and discreet priest, or by a layman, or even by a woman of good life and proved discretion; by the offering of lawful prayers over the sick: not over fruits or animals, but over the sick. For the Gospel says: They shall place their hands upon the sick, etc. And such persons are not to be prevented from practising in this way; unless perhaps it is feared that, following their example, other indiscreet and superstitious persons should make improper use of incantations. It is these superstitious diviners whom that virgin we have mentioned condemned, when

she said that they who consulted with such had weak, that is to say bad, faith.

Now for the elucidation of this matter it is asked how it is possible to know whether the words of such charms and benedictions are lawful or superstitious, and how they ought to be used; and whether the devil can be conjured and diseases exorcised.

In the first place, that is said to be lawful in the Christian religion which is not superstitious; and that is said to be superstitious which is over and above the prescribed form of religion. See *Colossians* ii: Which things indeed have a show of wisdom in superstition: on which the gloss says: Superstition is undisciplined religion, that is, religion observed with defective methods in evil circumstances.

Anything, also, is superstition which human tradition without higher authority has caused to usurp the name of religion; such as the interpolation of hymns at Holy Mass, the alteration of the Preface for Requiems, the abbreviation of the Creed which is to be sung at Mass, the reliance upon an organ rather than upon the choir for the music, neglect to have a Server on the Altar, and such practices. But to return to our point, when a work is done by virtue of the Christian religion, as when someone wishes to heal the sick by means of prayer and benediction and sacred words (which is the matter we are considering), such a person must observe seven conditions by which such benedictions are rendered lawful. And even if he uses adjurations, through the virtue of the Divine Name, and by the virtue of the works of Christ, His Birth, Passion and Precious Death, by which the devil was conquered and cast out; such benedictions and charms and exorcisms shall be called lawful, and they who practise them are exorcists or lawful enchanters. See S. Isidore, *Etym.* VIII, Enchanters are they whose art and skill lies in the use of words.

And the first of these conditions, as we learn from S. Thomas, is that there must be nothing in the words which hints at any expressed or tacit invocation of devils. If such were expressed, it would be obviously unlawful. If it were tacit, it might be considered in the light of intention, or in that of fact: in that of intention, when the operator has no care whether it is God or the devil who is helping him, so long as he attains his

---

* *"Durandus." William Duranti, canonist and one of the most important mediaeval liturgical writers, born about 1237 at Puimisson, Provence; died at Rome 1 November, 1296. His career was most noble and distinguished. A long epitaph upon his monument in Santa Maria sopra Minerva tells the story of his life and gives a list of his works. The most important of these is the "Rationale diuinorum officiorum," the first edition of which by Fust and Schoeffer was issued at Mainz in 1459. It has been frequently reprinted, the last complete edition being Naples, 1839. The "Speculum Iudiciale" and the "Commentarius in canones Concilii Lugdunensis II" are valuable treatises upon the canons and canonical processes.*

desired result; in that of fact, when a person has no natural aptitude for such work, but creates some artificial means. And of such not only must physicians and astronomers be the judges, but especially Theologians. For in this way do necromancers work, making images and rings and stones by artificial means; which have no natural virtue to effect the results which they very often expect: therefore the devil must be concerned in their works.

Secondly, the benedictions or charms must contain no unknown names; for according to S. John Chrysostom such are to be regarded with fear, lest they should conceal some matter of superstition.

Thirdly, there must be nothing in the words that is untrue; for if there is, the effect of them cannot be from God, Who is not a witness to a lie. But some old women in their incantations use some such jingling doggerel as the following:

Blessed MARY went a-walking
Over Jordan river.
Stephen met her, and fell a-talking, etc.

Fourthly, there must be no vanities, or written characters beyond the sign of the Cross. Therefore the charms which soldiers are wont to carry are condemned.

Fifthly, no faith must be placed in the method of writing or reading or binding the charm about a person, or in any such vanity, which has nothing to do with the reverence of God, without which a charm is altogether superstitious.

Sixthly, in the citing and uttering of Divine words and of Holy Scripture attention must only be paid to the sacred words themselves and their meaning, and to the reverence of God; whether the effect be looked for from the Divine virtue, or from the relics of Saints, which are a secondary power, since their virtue springs originally from God.

Seventhly, the looked-for effect must be left to the Divine Will; for He knows whether it is best for a man to be healed or to be plagued, or to die. This condition was set down by S. Thomas.

So we may conclude that if none of these conditions be broken, the incantation will be lawful. And S. Thomas writes in this connexion on the last chapter of *S. Mark:* And these signs shall follow them that believe; in my name shall they cast out devils; they shall take up serpents. From this it is clear that, provided the above conditions are observed, it is lawful by means of sacred words to keep serpents away.

S. Thomas says further: The words of God are not less holy than the Relics of the Saints. As S. Augustine says: The word of God is not less than the Body of Christ. But all are agreed that it is lawful to carry reverently about the person the Relics of the Saints: therefore let us by all means invoke the name of God by duly using the Lord's Prayer and the Angelic Salutation, by His Birth and Passion, by His Five Wounds, and by the Seven Words which He spoke on the Cross, by the Triumphant Inscription, by the three nails, and by the other weapons of Christ's army against the devil and his works. By all these means it is lawful to work, and our trust may be placed in them, leaving the issue to God's will.

And what has been said about the keeping off of serpents applies also to other animals, provided that the attention is fixed only on the sacred words and the Divine virtue. But great care is to be used in incantations of this nature. For S. Thomas says: Such diviners often use unlawful observances, and obtain magic effects by means of devils, especially in the case of serpents; for the serpent was the devil's first instrument by which he deceived mankind.

For in the town of Salzburg there was a certain mage who one day, in open view of all, wanted to charm all the snakes into a particular pit, and kill them all within an area of a mile. So he gathered all the snakes together, and was himself standing over the pit, when last of all there came a huge and horrible serpent which would not go into the pit. This serpent kept making signs to the man to let it go away and crawl where it would; but he would not cease from his incantation, but insisted that, as all the other snakes had entered the pit and there died, so also must this horrible serpent. But it stood on the opposite side to the warlock, and suddenly leapt over the pit and fell upon the man, wrapping itself round his belly, and dragged him with itself into the pit, where they both died. From this it may be seen that only for a useful purpose, such as driving them away from men's houses, are such incantations to be practised, and they are to be done by the Divine virtue, and in the fear of God, and with reverence.

In the second place we have to consider how exorcisms or charms of this kind ought to be used, and whether they should be worn round the neck or sewn into the clothing. It may seem that such practices are unlawful; for S. Augustine says, in the *Second Book on the Christian Doctrine* : There are a thousand magic devices and amulets and charms which are all superstitious, and the School of Medicine utterly condemns them all, whether they are incantations, or certain marks which are called characters, or engraved charms to be hung round the neck.

Also S. John Chrysostom, commenting on *S. Matthew*, says: Some persons wear round their neck some written portion of the Gospel; but is not the Gospel every day read in the church and heard by all? How then shall a man be helped by wearing the Gospel round his neck, when he has reaped no benefit from hearing it with his ears? For in what does the virtue of the Gospel consist; in the characters of its letters, or in the meaning of its words? If in the characters, you do well to hang it round your neck; but if in the meaning, surely it is of more benefit when planted in the heart than when worn round the neck.

But, on the other hand, the Doctors answer as follows, especially S. Thomas where he asks whether it is unlawful to hang sacred words round the neck. Their opinion is that, in all charms and writings so worn, there are two things to be avoided.

First, in whatever is written there must be nothing that savours of an invocation of devils; for then it is manifestly superstitious and unlawful, and must be judged as an apostasy from the faith, as has often been said before.

Similarly, in accordance with the above seven conditions, it must not contain any unknown names. But if these two snares be avoided, it is lawful both to place such charms on the lips of the sick, and for the sick to carry them with them. But the Doctors condemn their use in one respect, that is, when a man pays greater attention to and has more reliance upon the mere signs of the written letters than upon their meaning.

It may be said that a layman who does not understand the words cannot pay any attention to their meaning. But it is enough if such a man fixes his thoughts on the Divine virtue, and leaves it to the Divine will to do what seems good to His mercy.

In the third place we have to consider whether the devil is to be conjured and the disease exorcised at the same time, or whether a different order should be observed, or whether one of these operations can take place without the other. Here there are several points to be considered. First, whether the devil is always present when the sick man is afflicted. Second, what sort of things are capable of being exorcised or remedied. Third, the method of exorcising.

For the first point, it would seem, following that pronouncement of S. John Damascene that where the devil operates there he is, that the devil is always present in the sick man when he afflicts him. Also in the history of S. Bartholomew it seems that a man is only delivered from the devil when he is cured of his sickness.

But this can be answered as follows. When it is said that the devil is present in a sick man, this can be understood in two ways: either that he is personally present, or that he is present in the effect which he has caused. In the first sense he is present when he first causes the sickness; in the second sense he is said to be present not personally but in the effect. In this way, when the Doctors ask whether the devil substantially inhabits a man who commits mortal sin, they say that he is not personally present, but only in effect; just as a master is said to dwell in his servants in respect of his mastership. But the case is quite otherwise with men who are possessed by a devil.

For the second point, as to what sort of things can be exorcised, the opinion of S. Thomas, Book IV, dist. 6, should be noted, where he says that on account of man's sin the devil receives power over a man and over everything which a man uses, to hurt him with them; and since there can be no compromise of Christ with Belial, therefore whenever anything is to be sanctified for Divine worship, it is first exorcised that it may be consecrated to God freed from the power of the devil, by which it might be turned to the hurt of men.

This is shown in the blessing of water, the consecration of a church, and in all matters of this sort. Therefore, since the first act of reconciliation by which a man is consecrated to God is in baptism, it is necessary that a man should be exorcised before he is baptized; indeed in this it is more imperative than in any other circumstance. For in man himself lies the cause by reason of which the devil receives his power in other matters which are brought about by man, namely, sin, either original or actual. This then is the significance of the words that are used in exorcism, as when it is said, "Depart, O Satan, from him"; and likewise of the things that are then done.

To return, then, to the actual point. When it is asked whether the disease is to be exorcised and the devil adjured, and which of these should be done first; it is answered that not the disease, but the sick and bewitched man himself is exorcised: just as in the case of a child, it is not the infection of the *fomes* which is exorcised, but the child itself. Also, just as the child is first exorcised, and then the devil is adjured to depart; so also is the bewitched person first exorcised, and afterwards the devil and his works are bidden to depart. Again, just as salt and water are exorcised, so are all things which can be used by the sick man, so that it is expedient to exorcise and bless chiefly his food and drink. In the case of baptism the following ceremony of exorcism is observed: the exsufflation towards the West and the renunciation of the devil; secondly, the raising of the hands with a solemn confession of the faith of the Christian religion; thirdly, prayer, benediction, and the laying on of hands; fourthly, the stripping and anointing with Holy Oil; and after baptism, the communion and the putting on of the chrisom. But all this is not necessary in the exorcism of one who is bewitched; but that he should first have made a good confession, and if possible he is to hold a lighted candle, and receive the Holy Communion; and instead of putting on a chrisom, he is to remain bound naked to a Holy Candle of the length of Christ's body or of the Cross. And then may be said the following:

I exorcise thee, Peter, or thee, Barbara, being weak but reborn in Holy Baptism, by the living God, by the true God, by God Who redeemed thee with His Precious Blood, that thou mayest be exorcised, that all the illusions and wickedness of the devil's deceits may depart and flee from thee together with every unclean spirit, adjured by Him Who will come to judge both the quick and the dead, and who will purge the earth with fire. Amen.

Let us pray.

O God of mercy and pity, Who according to Thy tender lovingkindness chastenest those whom Thou dost cherish, and dost gently compel those whom Thou receivest to turn their hearts, we invoke Thee, O Lord, that Thou wilt vouchsafe to bestow Thy grace upon Thy servant who suffereth from a weakness in the limbs of his body, that whatever is corrupt by earthly frailty, whatever is made violate by the deceit of the devil, may find redemption in the unity of the body of the Church. Have mercy, O Lord, on his groaning, have mercy upon his tears; and as he putteth his trust only in Thy mercy, receive him in the sacrament of Thy reconciliation, through Jesus Christ Our Lord. Amen.

Therefore, accursed devil, hear thy doom, and give honour to the true and living God, give honour to the Lord Jesus Christ, that thou depart with thy works from this servant whom our Lord Jesus Christ hath redeemed with His Precious Blood.

Then let him exorcise him a second and yet a third time, with the prayers as above.

Let us pray.

God, Who dost ever mercifully govern all things that Thou hast made, incline Thine ear to our prayers, and look in mercy upon Thy servant labouring under the sickness of the body; visit him, and grant him Thy salvation and the healing virtue of Thy heavenly grace, through Christ our Lord. Amen.

Therefore, accursed devil, etc.

The prayer for the third exorcism.

O God, the only protection of human frailty, show forth the mighty power of Thy strong aid upon our sick brother (or sister), that being holpen by Thy mercy he (she) may be worthy to enter Thy Holy Church in safety, through Christ our Lord. Amen.

And let the exorcist continually sprinkle him with Holy Water. And note that this method is recommended, not because it must be rigidly observed, or that other exorcisms are not of greater efficacy, but that there should be some regular system of exorcism and adjuration. For in the old histories and books of the Church there are sometimes found more devout and powerful exorcisms; but since before all things the reverence of God is necessary, let each proceed in this matter as he finds it best.

In conclusion, and for the sake of clearness, we may recommend this form of exorcism for a person who is bewitched. Let him first make a good confession (according to the often-quoted Canon: If by sortilege, etc.). Then let a diligent search be made in all corners and in the beds and mattresses and under the threshold of the door, in case some instrument of witchcraft may be found. The bodies of animals bewitched to death are at once to be burned. And it is expedient that all bed-clothes and garments should be renewed, and even that he should change his house and dwelling. But in case nothing is found, then he who is to to be exorcised should if possible go into the church in the morning, especially on the Holier Days, such as the Feasts of Our Lady, or on some Vigil; and the better if the priest also has confessed and is in a state of grace, for then the stronger will he be. And let him who is to be exorcised hold in his hand a Holy Candle as well as he can, either sitting or kneeling; and let those who are present offer up devout prayers for his deliverance. And let him begin the Litany at "Our help is in the Name of the Lord," and let one be appointed to make the responses: let him sprinkle him with Holy Water, and place a stole round his neck, and recite the Psalm "Haste thee, O God, to deliver me"; and let him continue the Litany for the Sick, saying at the Invocation of the Saints, "Pray for him and be favourable; deliver him, O Lord," continuing thus to the end. But where the prayers are to be said, then in the place of the prayers let him begin the exorcism, and continue in the way we have declared, or in any other better way, as seems good to him. And this sort of exorcism may be continued at least three times a week, that so through many intercessions the grace of health may be obtained.

Finally, he must receive the Sacrament of the Eucharist; although some think that this should be done before the exorcism. And at his confession the confessor must inquire whether he is under any bond of excommunication, and if he is, whether he has rashly omitted to obtain absolution from his Judge; for then, although he may at his discretion absolve him, yet when he has regained his health, he must seek absolution also from the Judge who excommunicated him.

It should further be noted that, when the exorcist is not ordained to the Order of Exorcist, then he may proceed with prayers; and if he can read the Scriptures, let him read the beginnings of the four Gospels of the Evangelists, and the Gospel beginning, "There was an Angel sent"; and the Passion of our Lord; all of which have great power to expel the works of the devil. Also let the Gospel of S. John, "In the beginning was the Word," be written and hung round the sick man's neck, and so let the grace of healing be looked for from God.

But if anyone asks what is the difference between the aspersion of Holy Water and exorcism, since both are ordained against the plagues of the devil, the answer is supplied by S. Thomas, who says: The devil attacks us from without and from within. Therefore Holy Water is ordained against his attacks from without; but exorcism against those from within. For this reason those for whom exorcism is necessary are called Energoumenoi, from En, meaning In, and Ergon, meaning Work, since they labour within themselves. But in exorcising a bewitched person both methods are to be used, because he is tormented both within and without.

Our second main consideration is what is to be done when no healing grace results from exorcisms. Now this may happen for six reasons; and there is a seventh about which we suspend any definite judgement. For when a person is not healed, it is due either to want of faith in the bystanders or in those who present the sick man, or to the sins of them who suffer from the bewitchment, or to a neglect of the due and fitting remedies, or to some flaw in the faith of the exorcist, or to the lack of a greater trust in the powers of another exorcist, or to the need of purgation and for the increased merit of the bewitched person.

Concerning the first four of these the Gospel teaches us in the incident of the only son of his father, who was a lunatic, and of the disciples of Christ being there present (*S. Matthew* xvii. and *S. Mark* ix.). For in the first place He said that the multitude were without faith; whereupon the father prayed Him, saying: Lord, I believe: help Thou mine unbelief. And JESUS said to the multitude: O faithless and perverse generation, how long shall I be with you?

Secondly, with regard to him who endured the devil, JESUS rebuked him, that is, the son; for, as Saint Jerome says, he had been tormented by the devil because of his sins.

Thirdly, this illustrates the neglect of the rightful remedies, because good and perfect men were not at first present. For S. John Chrysostom says: The pillars of the faith, namely, Peter and James and John, were not present, for they were at the Transfiguration of Christ: neither were there prayer and fasting, without which Christ said that this sort of devil goeth not out. Therefore Origen, writing on this passage, says: If at any time a man be not cured after prayer, let us not wonder or ask questions or speak, as if the unclean spirit were listening to us; but let us cast out our evil spirits by prayer and fasting. And the gloss says: This sort of devil, that is, the variability of carnal desires induced by that spirit, is not conquered except by strengthening the soul with prayer, and subduing the flesh with fasting.

Fourthly, the flaw in the faith of the exorcist is exemplified in the disciples of Christ who were present. For when they afterwards asked Him privately the cause of their failure, He answered: Because of your unbelief: for verily I say unto you, If ye have faith as a grain of mustard seed, ye shall say unto this mountain, Remove hence,* etc. And

S. Hilary says: The Apostles believed, indeed, but they were not yet perfect in faith: for while the Lord was away in the mountain with the other three, and they remained with the multitude, their faith became lukewarm.

The fifth reason is illustrated in the Lives of the Fathers, where we read that certain possessed persons could not be delivered by S. Antony, but were delivered by his disciple, Paul.

The sixth reason has already been made clear; for not always when a man is freed from sin is he also freed from punishment, but sometimes the penalty remains as a punishment and atonement for the previous sin.

There is yet another remedy by which many have been said to be delivered, namely, the re-baptizing of those who are bewitched; but this is a matter on which, as we have said, we can make no definite pronouncement. Nevertheless it is most true that when a person has not been duly exorcised before baptism, the devil, with God's permission, has always more power against such a person. And it is clearly shown without any doubt in what has just been written, that much negligence is committed by improperly instructed priests (in which case it pertains to the fourth of the above-noted impediments, namely, a flaw in the exorcist), or else by old women who do not observe the proper method of baptism at the necessary time.

However, God forbid that I should maintain that the Sacraments cannot be administered by wicked men, or that when baptism is performed by a wicked man it is not valid, provided that he observes the proper forms and words. Similarly in the exorcism let him proceed with due care, not timidly and not rashly. And let no one meddle with such sacred offices by any accidental or habitual omission of any necessary forms or words; for there are four matters to be observed in the right performance of

---

* "*Remove hence.*" *The miracle of the removal of a mountain was actually performed by S. Gregory Thaumaturgus, Bishop of Neocaesarea (d. circa 270-275), as the Venerable Bede tells us in his Commentary upon* "*S. Mark*" *xi:* "Hoc quoque fieri potuisset, ut mons ablatus de terra mitteretur in mare, si necessitas id fieri poscisset. Quomodo legimus factum precibus beati patris Gregorii Neocaesareae Ponti Antistitis, uiri mentis et uirtutibus eximii, ut mons in terra tantum loco cederet, quantum incolae ciuitatis opus habebant. Cum enim uolens aedificare ecclesiam in loco apto, uident eum angustiorem esse quam res exigebat, eo quod ex una parte rupe maris, ex alia monte proximo coarctaretur; uenit nocte ad locum, et genibus flexis admonuit Dominum promissionis suae, ut montem longius iuxta fidem petentis ageret. Et mane facto reuersus inuenit montem tantum spatii reliquisse structoribus ecclesiae, quantum opus habuerant.*"

exorcism, namely, the matter, the form, the intention and the order, as we have set them out above; and when one of these is lacking it cannot be complete.

And it is not valid to object that in the primitive Church persons were baptized without exorcism, and that even now a person is truly baptized without any exorcism; for in that case S. Gregory would have instituted exorcism in vain, and the Church would be in error in its ceremonies.* Therefore I have not dared altogether to condemn the re-baptism under certain conditions of bewitched persons, that they may recover that which was at first omitted.

It is said, also, of those who walk in their sleep during the night over high buildings without any harm, that it is the work of evil spirits who thus lead them; and many affirm that when such people are re-baptized they are much benefited. And it is wonderful that, when they are called by their own names, they suddenly fall to the earth, as if that name had not been given to them in proper form at their baptism.

Let the reader pay attention to those six impediments mentioned above, although they refer to *Energoumenoi*, or men possessed, rather than to men bewitched; for though equal virtue is required in both cases, yet it may be said that it is more difficult to cure a bewitched person than one possessed. Therefore those impediments apply even more pertinently to the case of those who are bewitched; as is proved by the following reasoning.

It was shown in Chapter X of the First Question of the Second Part that some men are at times possessed for no sin of their own, but for the venial sin of another man, and for various other causes. But in witchcraft, when adults are bewitched, it generally happens to them that the devil grievously possesses them from within for the destruction of their souls. Therefore the labour required in the case of the bewitched is twofold, whereas it is only single in the case of the possessed. Of this most grievous possession John Cassian speaks in his *Collation* of the Abbot Serenus: They are truly to be judged unhappy and miserable who, although they pollute themselves with every crime and wickedness, yet show no outward sign of being filled with the devil, nor does there seem to be any temptation commensurate with their deeds, nor any punishment sufficient to restrain them. For they do not deserve even the healing medicine of purgatory, who in their hardness of heart and impenitence are beyond the reach of any earthly correction, and lay up to themselves anger and vengeance in that day of wrath and revelation of the Just Judgement, when their worm shall not die.

And a little earlier, comparing the possession of the body with the binding of the soul in sin, he says: Far more grievous and violent is the torment of those who show no sign of being bodily possessed by devils, but are most terribly possessed in their souls, being fast bound by their sins and vices. For according to the Apostle, a man becomes the slave of him by whom he is conquered. And in this respect their case is the most desperate, since they are the servants of devils, and can neither resist nor tolerate that domination. It is clear then that, not they who are possessed by the devil from without, but they who are bewitched in their bodies and possessed from within to the perdition of their souls, are, by reason of many impediments, the more difficult to heal.

Our third main consideration is that of curative charms, and it is to be noted that these are of two sorts. They are either quite lawful and free from suspicion, or they are to be suspected and are not altogether lawful. We have dealt with the first sort in Chapter V, towards the end, where we disposed of a doubt as to the legality of using herbs and stones to drive away a bewitchment.

Now we must treat of the second sort which are under suspicion of not being altogether lawful; and we must draw attention to what was said in the Intro-

---

* "*Ceremonies.*" *Actually baptismal exorcism is earlier than S. Gregory. From the very first catechumens were exorcised as a preparation for the Sacrament of Baptism. In this connexion exorcism is a symbolical anticipation of one of the chief effects of the Sacrament of Regeneration, and since it was used in the case of children who had no personal sins, S. Augustine, writing against the Pelagians, appeals to it as clearly implying the doctrine of original sin. S. Cyril of Jerusalem in his "Catecheses," A.D. 347, gives a detailed description of baptismal exorcism, by which it appears that anointing with exorcised oil formed a part of this function in the East. The earliest Western witness which explicitly treats unction as part of the baptismal exorcism is that of the Arabic Canons of Hippolytus.*

duction to the Second Question of the Second Part of this work as to the four remedies, of which three are judged to be unlawful, and the fourth not altogether so, but vain, being that of which the Canonists say that it is lawful to oppose vanity to vanity. But we Inquisitors are of the same opinion as the Holy Doctors, that when, owing to the six or seven impediments which we have detailed, the remedies of sacred words and lawful exorcism are not sufficient, then those who are so bewitched are to be exhorted to bear with a patient spirit the evils of this present life for the purgation of their crimes, and not to seek further in any way for superstitious and vain remedies. Therefore, if anyone is not content with the aforesaid lawful exorcisms, and wishes to have recourse to remedies which are, at least, vain, of which we have spoken before, let him know that he does not do this with our consent or permission. But the reason why we have so carefully explained and detailed such remedies is that we might bring into some sort of agreement the opinions of such Doctors as Duns Scotus and Henry of Segusio on the one hand, and those of the other Theologians on the other hand. Yet we are in agreement with S. Augustine in his *Sermon against Fortune-tellers and Diviners*, which is called the *Sermon on Auguries*,* where he says: Brethren, you know that I have often entreated you that you should not follow the customs of Pagans and sorcerers, but this has had little effect on some of you. Yet, if I do not speak out to you, I shall be answerable for you in the Day of Judgement, and both you and I must suffer eternal damnation. Therefore I absolve myself before God, that again and again I admonish and adjure you, that none of you seek out diviners or fortune-tellers, and that you consult with them for no cause or infirmity; for whosoever commits this sin, the sacrament of baptism is immediately lost in him, and he at once becomes a sacrilegious and a Pagan, and unless he repents will perish in eternity.

And afterwards he adds: Let no one observe days for going out and coming back; for God hath made all things well, and He Who ordained one day

* *"Auguries." The "De Auguriis," which is often ascribed to another writer, may be found in the Migne S. Augustine, Ap. V, 2268.*

ordained also another. But as often as you have to do anything or to go out, cross yourselves in the name of Christ, and saying faithfully the Creed or the Lord's Prayer you may go about your business secure in the help of God.

But certain superstitious sons of our times, not content with the above securities and accumulating error upon error, and going beyond the meaning or intention of Scotus and the Canonists, try to justify themselves with the following arguments. That natural objects have certain hidden virtues the cause of which cannot be explained by men; as a lodestone attracts iron, and many other such things which are enumerated by S. Augustine in the *City of God*, xxi. Therefore, they say, to seek for the recovery of one's health by the virtue of such things, when exorcisms and natural medicines have failed, will not be unlawful, although it may seem to be vain. This would be the case if a man tried to procure his own or another's health by means of images, not necromantic but astrological, or by rings and such devices. They argue also that, just as natural matter is subject to the influence of the stars, so also are artificial objects such as images, which receive some hidden virtue from the stars by which they can cause certain effects: therefore it is not unlawful to make use of such things.

Besides, the devils can in very many ways change bodies, as S. Augustine says, *de Trinitate*, 3, and as is evident in the case of those who are bewitched: therefore it is lawful to use the virtues of such bodies for the removing of witchcraft.

But actually all the Holy Doctors are of an entirely contrary opinion to this, as has been shown here and there in the course of this work.

Therefore we can answer their first argument in this way: that if natural objects are used in a simple way to produce certain effects for which they are thought to have some natural virtue, this is not unlawful. But if there are joined to this certain characters and unknown signs and vain observations, which manifestly cannot have any natural efficacy, then it is superstitious and unlawful. Wherefore S. Thomas, II, q. 96, art. 2, speaking of this matter, says that when any object is used for the purpose of causing some bodily effect, such as curing the sick, notice must be taken whether such objects appear to have any natural quality which could cause such an effect; and if so, then it is not unlawful, since it is lawful to apply natural causes to their effects. But if it does not appear that they can naturally cause such effects, it follows that they are not applied as causes of those effects, but as signs or symbols; and so they pertain to some pact symbolically formed with devils. Also S. Augustine says, in the *City of God*, xxi: The devils ensnare us by means of creatures formed not by themselves, but by God, and with various delights consonant with their own versatility; not as animals with food, but as spirits with signs, by various kinds of stones and herbs and trees, animals and charms and ceremonies.

Secondly, S. Thomas says: The natural virtues of natural objects follow their material forms which they obtain from the influence of the stars, and from the same influence they derive certain active virtues. But the forms of artificial objects proceed from the conception of the craftsman; and since, as Aristotle says in his *Physics*, I, they are nothing but an artificial composition, they can have no natural virtue to cause any effect. It follows then that the virtue received from the influence of the stars can only reside in natural and not in artificial objects. Therefore, as S. Augustine says in the *City of God*, x, Porphyry was in error when he thought that from herbs and stones and animals, and from certain sounds and voices and figures, and from certain configurations in the revolutions of the stars and their motions, men fabricated on earth certain Powers corresponding to the various effects of the stars; as if the effects of magicians proceeded from the virtue of the stars. But, as S. Augustine adds, all such matters belong to the devils, the deceivers of souls which are subject to them. So also are those images which are called astronomical the work of devils, the sign of which is that they have inscribed upon them certain characters which can have no natural power to effect anything; for a figure or sign is no cause of natural action. But there is this difference between the images of astronomers and those of necromancers; that in the case of the latter there is an open invocation, and therefore an open and expressed pact

with devils; whereas the signs and characters on astronomical images imply only a tacit pact.

Thirdly, there is no power given to men over devils, whereby a man may lawfully use them for his own purposes; but there is war declared between man and the devils, therefore by no means may he use the help of devils, by either a tacit or an expressed pact with them. So says S. Thomas.

To return to the point: he says, "By no means"; therefore not even by means of any vain things in which the devil may in any way be involved. But if they are merely vain, and man in his frailty has recourse to them for the recovery of his health, let him repent for the past and take care for the future, and let him pray that his sins may be forgiven and that he be no more led into temptation; as S. Augustine says at the end of his Rule.

☆

CHAPTER VII

Remedies prescribed against Hailstorms, and for Animals that are Bewitched.

WITH regard to the remedies for bewitched animals, and charms against tempests, we must first note some unlawful remedies which are practised by certain people. For these are done by means of superstitious words or actions; as when men cure the worms in the fingers or limbs by means of certain words or charms,* the method of deciding the legality of which has been explained in the preceding chapter. There are others who do not sprinkle Holy Water over bewitched cattle, but pour it into their mouths.

Beside the proofs we have already given that the remedy of words is unlawful, William of Paris, whom we have often quoted, gives the following reason. If there were any virtue in words as words, then it would be due to one of three things: either their material, which is air; or their form, which is sound; or their meaning; or else to all three

---

* "Charms." Cf. Shirley's comedy "The Sisters," licensed April 1642, where Antonio says to one of the supposed astrologers, III, 1:

"You are one of the knaves that stroll the country,
And live by picking worms out of fools' fingers."

together. Now it cannot be due to air, which has no power to kill unless it be poisonous; neither can it be due to sound, the power of which is broken by a more solid object; neither can it be due to the meaning, for in that case the words Devil or Death or Hell would always be harmful, and the words Health and Goodness always beneficial. Also it cannot be due to all these three together; for when the parts of a whole are invalid, the whole itself is also invalid.

And it cannot validly be objected that God gave virtue to words just as He did to herbs and stones. For whatever virtue there is in certain sacramental words and benedictions and lawful incantations belongs to them, not as words, but by Divine institution and ordinance according to God's promise. It is, as it were, a promise from God that whoever does such and such a thing will receive such and such a grace. And so the words of the sacraments are effective because of their meaning; although some hold that they have an intrinsic virtue; but these two opinions are not mutually inconsistent. But the case of other words and incantations is clear from what has already been said; for the mere composing or uttering or writing of words, as such, can have no effect; but the invocation of the Divine Name, and public prayer, which is a sacred protestation committing the effect to the Divine Will, are beneficial.

We have treated above of remedies performed by actions which seem to be unlawful. The following is a common practice in parts of Swabia. On the first of May before sunrise the women of the village go out and gather from the woods leaves and branches from willow trees, and weave them into a wreath which they hang over the stable door, affirming that all the cattle will then remain unhurt and safe from witchcraft for a whole year. And in the opinion of those who hold that vanity may be opposed by vanity, this remedy would not be unlawful; and neither would be the driving away of diseases by unknown cantrips and incantations. But without meaning any offence, we say that a woman or anyone else may go out on the first or any other day of the month, without considering the rising or the setting of the sun, and collect herbs or leaves and branches, saying the Lord's Prayer or the Creed, and hang them over the stable door in good faith,

trusting to the will of God for their protective efficacy; yet even so the practice is not above reproach, as was shown in the preceding chapter in the words of S. Jerome; for even if he is not invoked, the devil has some part in the efficacy of herbs and stones.

It is the same with those who make the sign of the Cross with leaves and consecrated flowers on Palm Sunday, and set it up among their vines or crops; asserting that, although the crops all round should be destroyed by hail, yet they will remain unharmed in their own fields. Such matters should be decided upon according to the distinction of which we have already treated.

Similarly there are women who, for the preservation of milk and that cows should not be deprived of their milk by witchcraft, give freely to the poor in God's name the whole of a Sunday's yield of milk; and say that, by this sort of alms, the cows yield even more milk and are preserved from witchcraft. This need not be regarded as superstitious, provided that it is done out of pity for the poor, and that they implore the Divine mercy for the protection of their cattle, leaving the effect to the good pleasure of Divine providence.

Again, Nider in the First chapter of his *Præceptorium* says that it is lawful to bless cattle, in the same way as sick men, by means of written charms and sacred words, even if they have the appearance of incantations, as long as the seven conditions we have mentioned are observed. For he says that devout persons and virgins have been known to sign a cow with the sign of the Cross, together with the Lord's Prayer and the Angelic Salutation, upon which the devil's work has been driven off, if it is due to witchcraft.

And in his *Formicarius* he tells that witches confess that their witchcraft is obstructed by the reverent observation of the ceremonies of the Church; as by the aspersion of Holy Water, or the consumption of consecrated salt, by the lawful use of candles on the Day of Purification and of blessed palms, and such things. For this reason the Church uses these in her exorcisms, that they may lessen the power of the devil.

Also, because when witches wish to deprive a cow of milk they are in the habit of begging a little of the milk or butter which comes from that cow, so that they may afterwards by their art bewitch the cow; therefore women should take care, when they are asked by persons suspected of this crime, not to give away the least thing to them.

Again, there are women who, when they have been turning a churn for a long while to no purpose, and if they suspect that this is due to some witch, procure if possible a little butter from the house of that witch. Then they make that butter into three pieces and throw them into the churn, invoking the Holy Trinity, the Father, the Son, and the Holy Ghost; and so all witchcraft is put to flight. Here again it is a case of opposing vanity to vanity, for the simple reason that the butter must be borrowed from the suspected witch. But if it were done without this; if with the invocation of the Holy Trinity and the Lord's Prayer the woman were to throw in three pieces of her own butter, or of that belonging to someone else if she have none of her own, and were to commit the effect to the Divine Will, she would remain beyond reproach. Nevertheless it is not a commendable practice to throw in the three pieces of butter; for it would be better to banish the witchcraft by means of sprinkling Holy Water or putting in some exorcised salt, always with the prayers we have mentioned.

Again, since often the whole of a person's cattle are destroyed by witchcraft, those who have suffered in this way ought to take care to remove the soil under the threshold of the stable or stall, and where the cattle go to water, and replace it with fresh soil sprinkled with Holy Water. For witches have often confessed that they have placed some instrument of witchcraft in such places; and that sometimes, at the instance of devils, they have only had to make a hole in which the devil has placed the instrument of witchcraft; and that this was a visible object, such as a stone or a piece of wood or a mouse or some serpent. For it is agreed that the devil can perform such things by himself without the need of any partner; but usually, for the perdition of her soul, he compels a witch to co-operate with him.

In addition to the setting up of the sign of the Cross which we have mentioned, the following procedure is practised against hailstorms and tempests. Three of the hailstones are thrown into the fire with an invocation of the Most Holy Trinity, and the Lord's Prayer and the Angelic Salutation are repeated twice or three times, together with the Gospel of S. John, *In the beginning was the Word.* And the sign of the Cross is made in every direction towards each quarter of the world. Finally, *The Word was made Flesh* is repeated three times, and three times, "By the words of this Gospel may this tempest be dispersed." And suddenly, if the tempest is due to witchcraft, it will cease. This is most true and need not be regarded with any suspicion. For if the hailstones were thrown into the fire without the invocation of the Divine Name, then it would be considered superstitious.

But it may be asked whether the tempest could not be stilled without the use of those hailstones. We answer that it is the other sacred words that are chiefly effective; but by throwing in the hailstones a man means to torment the devil, and tries to destroy his works by the invocation of the Holy Trinity. And he throws them into the fire rather than into water, because the more quickly they are dissolved the sooner is the devil's work destroyed. But he must commit to the Divine Will the effect which is hoped for.

Relevant to this is the reply given by a witch to a Judge who asked her if there were any means of stilling a tempest raised by witchcraft. She answered: Yes, by this means. I adjure you, hailstorms and winds, by the five wounds of Christ, and by the three nails which pierced His hands and feet, and by the four Holy Evangelists, Matthew, Mark, Luke and John, that you be dissolved and fall as rain.

Many also confess, some freely and some under stress of torture, that there are five things by which they are much hindered, sometimes entirely, sometimes in part, sometimes so that they cannot harm a certain man himself, and sometimes so that they cannot harm his friends. And these are, that a man should have a pure faith and keep the commandments of God; that he should protect himself with the sign of the Cross and with prayer; that he should reverence the rites and ceremonies of the Church; that he should be diligent in the performance of public justice; and that he should meditate aloud or in his heart on the Passion of Christ. And of these things Nider also speaks. And for this reason it is a general practice of the Church to ring bells as a protection against storms, both that the devils may flee from them as being consecrated to God and refrain from their wickedness, and also that the people may be roused up to invoke God against tempests. And for the same reason it is common to proceed against tempests with the Sacrament of the Altar and sacred words, following the very ancient custom of the Church in France and Germany.

But since this method of carrying out the Sacrament to still a storm seems to many a little superstitious, because they do not understand the rules by which it is possible to distinguish between that which is superstitious and that which is not; therefore it must be considered that five rules are given by which anyone may know whether an action is superstitious, that is, outside the observances of the Christian religion, or whether it is in accordance with the due and proper worship and honour of God, proceeding from the true virtue of religion both in the thoughts of the heart and in the actions of the body. For these are explained in the gloss on *Colossians* ii, where S. Paul says: Which things have a show of wisdom in superstition; and the gloss says: Superstition is religion observed without due discipline; as was said before.

The first of these is, that in all our works the glory of God ought to be our chief aim; as it is said: Whether ye eat or drink, or whatsoever else ye do, do all in the glory of God.* Therefore in every work relating to the Christian religion let care be taken that it is to the glory of God, and that in it man should give the glory chiefly to God, so that by that very work the mind of man may be put in subjection to God. And although, according to this rule, the ceremonies and legal procedures of the Old Testament are not now observed, since they are to be understood figuratively, whereas the truth is made known in the New Testament, yet the carrying out of the Sacrament or of Relics to still a storm does not seem to militate against this rule.

The second rule is that care should be taken that the work is a discipline to restrain concupiscence, or a bodily abstinence, but in the way that is owed

to virtue, that is, according to the rites of the Church and moral doctrine. For S. Paul says, *Romans* xii : Let your service be reasonable. And because of this rule, they are foolish who make a vow not to comb their hair on the Sabbath, or who fast on Sunday, saying, The better the day the better the deed, and such like. But again it does not seem that it is superstitious to carry out the Sacrament, etc.

The third rule is to be sure that what is done is in accordance with the statutes of the Catholic Church, or with the witness of Holy Scripture, or according at least to the rites of some particular Church, or in accordance with universal use, which S. Augustine says may be taken as a law. Accordingly when the Bishops of the English were in doubt because the Mass was celebrated in different manners in different Churches, S. Gregory wrote to them that they might use whatever methods they found most pleasing to God, whether they followed the rites of the Roman or of the Gallican or of any other Church. For the fact that different Churches have different methods in Divine worship does not militate against the truth, and therefore such customs are to be preserved, and it is unlawful to neglect them. And so, as we said in the beginning, it is a very ancient custom in the Churches of France and some parts of Germany, after the consecration of the Eucharist to carry It out into the open; and this cannot be unlawful, provided that It is not carried exposed to the air, but enclosed and contained in a Pyx.

The fourth rule is to take care that what is done bears some natural relation to the effect which is expected; for if it does not, it is judged to be superstitious. On this account unknown characters and suspected names, and the images or charts of necromancers and astronomers, are altogether to be condemned as suspect. But we cannot say that on this account it is superstitious to carry out Holy Relics or the Eucharist as a protection against the plagues of the devil; for it is rather a most religious and salutary practice, since in that Sacrament lies all our help against the Adversary.

The fifth rule is to be careful that what is done should give no occasion for scandal or stumbling; for in that case, although it be not superstitious, yet because of the scandal it should be

---

* *"Glory of God."* *"I. Corinthians"* x, 31.

forgone or postponed, or done secretly without scandal. Therefore if this carrying of the Sacrament can be done without scandal, or even secretly, then it should not be neglected. For by this rule many secular priests neglect the use of benedictions by means of devout words either uttered over the sick or bound round their necks. I say that nothing should be done, at least publicly, if it can give any occasion of stumbling to other simple folk.

Let this be enough on the subject of the remedies against hailstorms, either by words or lawful actions.

☆

CHAPTER VIII

Certain Remedies prescribed against those Dark and Horrid Harms with which Devils may Afflict Men.

YET again we reserve our judgement in discussing the remedies against certain injuries to the fruits of the earth, which are caused by cankerworms, or by huge flights of locusts and other insects which cover vast areas of land, and seem to hide the surface of the ground, eating up everything to the very roots in the vineyards and devouring fields of ripe crops. In the same light too we consider the remedies against the stealing of children by the work of devils.

But with regard to the former kind of injury we may quote S. Thomas, the *Second of the Second*, Question 90, where he asks whether it is lawful to adjure an irrational creature. He answers that it is; but only in the way of compulsion, by which it is sent back to the devil, who uses irrational creatures to harm us. And such is the method of adjuration in the exorcisms of the Church by which the power of the devil is kept away from irrational creatures. But if the adjuration is addressed to the irrational creature itself, which understands nothing, then it would be nugatory and vain. From this it can be understood that they can be driven off by lawful exorcisms and adjurations, the help of the Divine mercy being granted; but first the people should be bidden to fast and to go in procession and practise other devotions. For this sort of evil is sent on account of adulteries and the multiplication of crimes;

wherefore men must be urged to confess their sins.

In some provinces even solemn excommunications are pronounced; but then they obtain power of adjuration over devils.

Another terrible thing which God permits to happen to men is when their own children are taken away from women, and strange children are put in their place by devils. And these children, which are commonly called changelings, or in the German tongue *Wechselkinder*, are of three kinds. For some are always ailing and crying, and yet the milk of four women is not enough to satisfy them. Some are generated by the operation of Incubus devils, of whom, however, they are not the sons, but of that man from whom the devil has received the semen as a Succubus, or whose semen he has collected from some nocturnal pollution in sleep. For these children are sometimes, by Divine permission, substituted for the real children.

And there is a third kind, when the devils at times appear in the form of young children and attach themselves to the nurses. But all three kinds have this in common, that though they are very heavy, they are always ailing and do not grow, and cannot receive enough milk to satisfy them, and are often reported to have vanished away.

And it can be said that the Divine pity permits such things for two reasons. First, when the parents dote upon their children too much, and this is a punishment for their own good. Secondly, it is to be presumed that the women to whom such things happen are very superstitious, and are in many other ways seduced by devils. But God is truly jealous in the right sense of the word, which means a strong love for a man's own wife, which not only does not allow another man to approach her, but like a jealous husband will not suffer the hint or suspicion of adultery. In the same way is God jealous of the soul which He bought with His Precious Blood and espoused in the Faith; and cannot suffer it to be touched by, to converse with, or in any way to approach or have dealings with the devil, the enemy and adversary of salvation. And if a jealous husband cannot suffer even a hint of adultery, how much more will he be disturbed when adultery is actually committed! Therefore it is no wonder if their own children are taken away and adulterous children substituted.

And indeed that it may be more strongly impressed how God is jealous of the soul, and will not suffer anything which might cause a suspicion, it is shown in the Old Law where, that He might drive His people farther from idolatry, He not only forbade idolatry, but also many other things which might give occasion to idolatry, and seemed to have no use in themselves, although in some marvellous way they retain some use in a mystical sense. For He not only says in *Exodus* xxii: Thou shalt not suffer a witch to live on the earth; but He adds this: She shall not dwell in thy land, lest perchance she cause thee to sin. Similarly common bawds and bulkers are put to death, and not allowed to company with men.

Note the jealousy of God, Who says as follows in *Deuteronomy* xxii: If thou find a bird's nest, and the dam sitting upon the eggs or upon the young ones, thou shalt not take the dam with the young, but thou shalt let the dam fly away; because the Gentiles used these to procure sterility. The jealous God would not suffer in His people this sign of adultery. In like manner in our days when old women find a penny, they think it a sign of great fortune; and conversely, when they dream of money it is an unlucky sign. Also God taught that all vessels should be covered, and that when a vessel had no cover it should be considered unclean.

There was an erroneous belief that when devils came in the night (or the Good People * as old women call them, though they are witches, or devils in their forms) they must eat up everything, that afterwards they may bring greater abundance of stores. Some people give colour to the story, and call them Screech Owls; but this is against the opinion of the Doctors, who say that there are no rational creatures except men and Angels; therefore they can only be devils.

Again, in *Leviticus* xix: Ye shall not round the corners of your heads, neither shalt thou mar the corners of thy beard; because they did this idolatrously in veneration of idols.

Again in *Deuteronomy* xxii: God says that men shall not put on the garments of women, or conversely; because they did this in honour of the goddess Venus, and others in honour of Mars or Priapus.

And for the same reason He commanded the altars of idols to be destroyed; and Hezechias destroyed the Brazen Serpent when the people wanted to sacrifice to it, saying: It is brass. For the same reason He forbade the observance of visions and auguries, and commanded that the man or woman in whom there was a familiar spirit should be put to death. Such are now called soothsayers. All these things, because they give rise to suspicion of spiritual adultery, therefore, as has been said, from the jealousy which God has for the souls He has espoused, as a husband espouses a wife, they were all forbidden by Him.

And so we preachers also ought to bear in mind that no sacrifice is more acceptable to God than a jealousy of souls, as S. Jerome says in his commentaries upon Ezekiel.

Therefore in the Third Part of this work we shall treat of the extermination of witches, which is the ultimate remedy. For this is the last recourse of the Church, to which she is bound by Divine commandment. For it has been said: Ye shall not suffer witches to live upon the earth. And with this will be included the remedies against archerwizards; since this kind can only be exterminated by secular law.

A remedy. When certain persons for the sake of temporal gain have devoted themselves entirely to the devil, it has often been found that, though they may be freed from the devil's power by true confession, yet they have been long and grievously tormented, especially in the night. And God allows this for their punishment. But a sign that they have been delivered is that, after confession, all the money in their purses or coffers vanishes. Many examples of this could be adduced, but for the sake of brevity they are passed over and omitted.

---

* *"Good People."* So in Ireland the fairies are called "good people," and traditionally seem to be of a benevolent but capricious and even mischievous disposition. In some parts of Highland Scotland fairies are called "daoine sithe" or "men of peace," and it is believed that every year the devil carries off a tenth part of them.

It will be readily remembered that to the Greeks the Fairies were αἱ Εὐμενίδες, the gracious goddesses.

THE THIRD PART RELATING TO THE JUDICIAL PROCEEDINGS IN BOTH THE ECCLESIASTICAL AND CIVIL COURTS AGAINST WITCHES AND INDEED ALL HERETICS

CONTAINING XXXV QUESTIONS IN WHICH IS MOST CLEARLY SET OUT THE FORMAL RULES FOR INITIATING A PROCESS OF JUSTICE, HOW IT SHOULD BE CONDUCTED, AND THE METHOD OF PRONOUNCING SENTENCE

☆

GENERAL
&
INTRODUCTORY

Who are the Fit and Proper Judges in the Trial of Witches?

THE question is whether witches, together with their patrons and protectors and defenders, are so entirely subject to the jurisdiction of the Diocesan Ecclesiastical Court and the Civil Court so that the Inquisitors of the crime of heresy can be altogether relieved from the duty of sitting in judgement upon them. And it is argued that this is so. For the Canon (c. *accusatus*, § *sane*, lib. VI) says: Certainly those whose high privilege it is to judge concerning matters of the faith ought not to be distracted by other business; and Inquisitors deputed by the Apostolic See to inquire into the pest of heresy should manifestly not have to concern themselves with diviners and soothsayers, unless these are also heretics, nor should it be their business to punish such, but they may leave them to be punished by their own judges.

Nor does there seem any difficulty in the fact that the heresy of witches is not mentioned in that Canon.. For these are subject to the same punishment as the others in the court of conscience, as the Canon goes on to say (dist. 1, *pro dilectione*). If the sin of diviners and witches is secret, a penance of forty days shall be imposed upon them: if it is notorious, they shall be refused the Eucharist. And those whose punishment is identical should receive it from the same Court. Then, again, the guilt of both being the same, since just as

soothsayers obtain their results by curious means, so do witches look for and obtain from the devil the injuries which they do to creatures, unlawfully seeking from His creatures that which should be sought from God alone; therefore both are guilty of the sin of idolatry.

This is the sense of *Ezechiel* xxi, 23; that the King of Babylon stood at the cross-roads, shuffling his arrows * and interrogating idols.

Again it may be said that, when the Canon says "Unless these are also heretics," it allows that some diviners and soothsayers are heretics, and should therefore be subject to trial by the Inquisitors; but in that case artificial diviners would also be so subject, and no written authority for that can be found.

Again, if witches are to be tried by the Inquisitors, it must be for the crime of heresy; but it is clear that the deeds of witches can be committed without any heresy. For when they stamp into the mud the Body of Christ, although this is a most horrible crime, yet it may be done without any error in the understanding, and therefore without heresy. For it is entirely possible for a

---

* *"Arrows." Esarhaddon is employing a mode of sortilege by arrows, belomancy, which was extensively practised among the Chaldeans, as also among the Arabs. Upon this text S. Jerome comments: "He shall stand in the highway, and consult the oracle after the manner of his nation, that he may cast arrows into a quiver, and mix them together, being written upon or marked with the names of each people, that he may see whose arrow will come forth, and which city he ought first to attack." The arrows employed by the Arabs were often three in number, upon the first of which was inscribed, "My Lord hath commanded me"; upon the second, "My Lord hath forbidden me"; and the third was blank. If the inquirer drew the first it was an augury of success; the second gave an omen of failure; if the third were drawn, all three were mixed again and another trial was made. In some countries divining rods were employed instead of arrows. These were drawn from a vessel, or, it might be, cast into the air, the position in which they fell being carefully noted. This practice is rhabdomancy. The LXX, "Ezechiel" xxi, 21, reads ῥαβδομαντεία, not βελομαντεία, and rhabdomancy is mentioned by S. Cyril of Alexandria. The "Koran," V, forbids prognostication by divining arrows, which are there denounced as "an abomination of the work of Satan." See my "History of Witchcraft," Chap. V, pp. 182–83.*

person to believe that It is the Lord's Body, and yet throw It into the mud to satisfy the devil, and this by reason of some pact with him, that he may obtain some desired end, such as the finding of a treasure or anything of that sort. Therefore the deeds of witches need involve no error in faith, however great the sin may be; in which case they are not liable to the Court of the Inquisition, but are left to their own judges.

Again, Solomon showed reverence to the gods of his wives out of complaisance, and was not on that account guilty of apostasy from the Faith; for in his heart he was faithful and kept the true Faith. So also when witches give homage to devils by reason of the pact they have entered into, but keep the Faith in their hearts, they are not on that account to be reckoned as heretics.

But it may be said that all witches have to deny the Faith, and therefore must be judged heretics. On the contrary, even if they were to deny the Faith in their hearts and minds, still they could not be reckoned as heretics, but as apostates. But a heretic is different from an apostate, and it is heretics who are subject to the Court of the Inquisition; therefore witches are not so subject.

Again it is said, in c. 26, quest. 5: Let the Bishops and their representatives strive by every means to rid their parishes entirely of the pernicious art of soothsaying and magic derived from Zoroaster; and if they find any man or woman addicted to this crime, let him be shamefully cast out of their parishes in disgrace. So when it says at the end of c. 348, Let them leave them to their own Judges; and since it speaks in the plural, both of the Ecclesiastic and the Civil Court; therefore, according to this Canon they are subject to no more than the Diocesan Court.

But if, just as these arguments seem to show it to be reasonable in the case of Inquisitors, the Diocesans also wish to be relieved of this responsibility, and to leave the punishment of witches to the secular Courts, such a claim could be made good by the following arguments. For the Canon says, c. *ut inquisitionis:* We strictly forbid the temporal lords and rulers and their officers in any way to try or judge this crime, since it is purely an ecclesiastical matter: and it speaks of the crime of heresy. It follows therefore that, when the crime is not purely ecclesiastical, as is the case with witches because of the temporal injuries which they commit, it must be punished by the Civil and not by the Ecclesiastical Court.

Besides, in the last Canon Law concerning Jews it says: His goods are to be confiscated, and he is to be condemned to death, because with perverse doctrine he opposed the Faith of Christ. But if it is said that this law refers to Jews who have been converted, and have afterwards returned to the worship of the Jews, this is not a valid objection. Rather is the argument strengthened by it; because the civil Judge has to punish such Jews as apostates from the Faith; and therefore witches who abjure the Faith ought to be treated in the same way; for abjuration of the Faith, either wholly or in part, is the essential principle of witches.

And although it says that apostasy and heresy are to be judged in the same way, yet it is not the part of the ecclesiastical but of the civil Judge to concern himself with witches. For no one must cause a commotion among the people by reason of a trial for heresy; but the Governor himself must make provision for such cases.

The *Authentics* of Justinian, speaking of ruling princes, says: You shall not permit anyone to stir up your Province by reason of a judicial inquiry into matters concerning religions or heresies, or in any way allow an injunction to be put upon the Province over which you govern; but you shall yourself provide, making use of such monies and other means of investigation as are competent, and not allow anything to be done in matters of religion except in accordance with our precepts. It is clear from this that no one must meddle with a rebellion against the Faith except the Governor himself.

Besides, if the trial and punishment of such witches were not entirely a matter for the civil Judge, what would be the purpose of the laws which provide as follows? All those who are commonly called witches are to be condemned to death. And again: Those who harm innocent lives by magic arts are to be thrown to the beasts. Again, it is laid down that they are to be subjected to questions and tortures; and that none of the faithful are to associate with them, under pain of exile and the confiscation of all their goods. And many other penalties are added, which anyone may read in those laws.

But in contradiction of all these arguments, the truth of the matter is that such witches may be tried and punished conjointly by the Civil and the Ecclesiastical Courts. For a canonical crime must be tried by the Governor and the Metropolitan of the Province; not by the Metropolitan alone, but together with the Governor. This is clear in the *Authentics*, where ruling princes are enjoined as follows: If it is a canonical matter which is to be tried, you shall inquire into it together with the Metropolitan of the Province. And to remove all doubt on this subject, the gloss says: If it is a simple matter of the observance of the faith, the Governor alone may try it; but if the matter is more complicated, then it must be tried by a Bishop and the Governor; and the matter must be kept within decent limits by someone who has found favour with God, who shall protect the orthodox faith, and impose suitable indemnities of money, and keep our subjects inviolate, that is, shall not corrupt the faith in them.

And again, although a secular prince may impose the capital sentence, yet this does not exclude the judgement of the Church, whose part it is to try and judge the case. Indeed this is perfectly clear from the Canon Law in the chapters *de summa trin.* and *fid. cath.*, and again in the Law concerning heresy, c. *ad abolendam* and c. *uergentis* and c. *excommunicamus*, 1 and 2. For the same penalties are provided by both the Civil and the Canon Laws, as is shown by the Canon Laws concerning the Manichaean* and Arian heresies. Therefore the punishment of witches belongs to both Courts together, and not to one separately.

Again, the laws decree that clerics shall be corrected by their own Judges, and not by the temporal or secular Courts, because their crimes are considered to be purely ecclesiastical. But the crime of witches is partly civil and partly ecclesiastical, because they commit temporal harm and violate the faith; therefore it belongs to the Judges of both Courts to try, sentence, and punish them.

This opinion is substantiated by the *Authentics*, where it is said: If it is an ecclesiastical crime needing ecclesiastical punishment and fine, it shall be tried by a Bishop who stands in favour with God, and not even the most illustrious Judges of the Province shall have any hand in it. And we do not wish the civil Judges to have any knowledge of such proceedings; for such matters must be examined ecclesiastically and the souls of the offenders must be corrected by ecclesiastical penalties, according to the sacred and divine rules which our laws worthily follow. So it is said. Therefore it follows that on the other hand a crime which is of a mixed nature must be tried and punished by both Courts.

We make our answer to all the above as follows. Our main object here is to show how, with God's pleasure, we Inquisitors of Upper Germany may be relieved of the duty of trying witches, and leave them to be punished by their own provincial Judges; and this because of the arduousness of the work: provided always that such a course shall in no way endanger the preservation of the faith and the salvation of souls. And therefore we engaged upon this work, that we might leave to the Judges themselves the methods of trying, judging and sentencing in such cases.

Therefore in order to show that the Bishops can in many cases proceed against witches without the Inquisitors; although they cannot so proceed without the temporal and civil Judges in cases involving capital punishment; it is expedient that we set down the opinions of certain other Inquisitors in parts of Spain, and (saving always the reverence due to them), since we all belong to one and the same Order of Preachers, to refute them, so that each detail may be more clearly understood.

Their opinion is, then, that all witches, diviners, necromancers, and in short all who practise any kind of divination, if they have once embraced and professed the Holy Faith, are liable to the Inquisitorial Court, as in the three cases noted in the beginning of the chapter, *Multorum querela*, in the

---

* "*Manichaean.*" *For the close connexion between the Manichees and witches see my "History of Witchcraft," Chap. I.*

decretals of Pope Clement * concerning heresy; in which it says that neither must the Inquisitor proceed without the Bishop, nor the Bishop without the Inquisitor: although there are five other cases in which one may proceed without the other, as anyone who reads the chapter may see. But in one case it is definitively stated that one must not proceed without the other, and that is when the above diviners are to be considered as heretics.

In the same category they place blasphemers, and those who in any way invoke devils, and those who are excommunicated and have contumaciously remained under the ban of excommunication for a whole year, either because of some matter concerning faith or, in certain circumstances, not on account of the faith; and they further include several other such offences. And by reason of this the authority of the Ordinary is weakened, since so many more burdens are placed upon us Inquisitors which we cannot safely bear in the sight of the terrible Judge who will demand from us a strict account of the duties imposed upon us.

And because their opinion cannot be refuted unless the fundamental thesis upon which it is founded is proved unsound, it is to be noted that it is based upon the commentators on the Canon, especially on the chapter *accusatus*, and § *sane*, and on the words "savour of heresy." Also they rely upon the sayings of the Theologians, S. Thomas, Blessed Albert, and S. Bonaventura, in the *Second Book of Sentences*, dist. 7.

It is best to consider some of these in detail. For when the Canon says, as was shown in the first argument, that the Inquisitors of heresy should not concern themselves with soothsayers and diviners unless they manifestly savour of heresy, they say that soothsayers and diviners are of two sorts, either artificial or heretical. And the first sort are called diviners pure and simple, since they work merely by art; and such are referred to in the chapter *de sortilegiis*, where it says that the presbyter Udalricus went to a secret place with a certain infamous person, that is, a diviner, says the gloss, not with the intention of invoking the devil, which would have been heresy, but that, by inspecting the astrolabe, he might find out some hidden thing. And this, they say, is pure divination or sortilege.

But the second sort are called heretical diviners, whose art involves some worship of or subjection to devils, and who essay by divination to predict the future or something of that nature, which manifestly savours of heresy; and such are, like other heretics, liable to the Inquisitorial Court.

And that this is the meaning of the Canon they prove from commentaries of the Canonists on the word "savour." For Giovanni d'Andrea, writing on this Canon *accusatus*, and on the word "savour," says: They savour of heresy in this way, that they utter nefarious prayers and offer sacrifices at the altars of idols, and they consult with devils and receive answers from them; or they meet together to practise heretical sortes, or make predictions by means of blood or by the Lord's Body; or in their sortes, that they may have an answer, re-baptize a child, and practise other such matters.

Many others also they quote in support of their opinion, including John Modestus; S. Raymund, and William de Laudun, O.P. And they refer to the decision of the Church at the Council of Aquitaine, c. 26, q. 5, Episcopi, where such superstitious women are called infidels, saying, Would that these had perished alone in their perfidy. And perfidy in a Christian is called heresy; therefore they are subject to the Court of the Inquisitors of heresy.

They quote also the Theologians, especially S. Thomas, the *Second Book of Sentences*, dist. 7, where he considers whether it is a sin to use the help of devils. For speaking of that passage in

---

* "*Pope Clement.*" *Pope Clement V, born at Villandraut, 1264; elected to the Chair of S. Peter, 5 June, 1305; died at Roquemare, 20 April, 1314; completed the mediaeval "Corpus Iuris Canonici" by the publication of a collection of papal decretals known as "Clementinae" or "Liber Clementinarum," sometimes as "Liber Septimus" in reference to the "Liber Sextus" of Boniface VIII. It contains decretals of this latter Pontiff, of Benedict XI, and of Clement himself. Together with the decrees of the Council of Vienne it was promulgated, 21 March, 1314, at the Papal residence of Monteaux near Carpentras. It is divided into five books with subdivisions of titles and chapters. As Clement V died before the collection had been generally published, John XXII promulgated it anew, 25 October, 1317, and sent it to the University of Bologna as the authoritative Corpus of decretals to be used in the courts and schools.*

Esaias viii: Should not a people seek unto their God? he says among other things: In everything the fulfilment of which is looked for from the power of the devil, because of a pact entered into with him, there is apostasy from the faith, either in word, if there is some invocation, or in deed, even if there be no sacrifice offered.

To the same effect they quote Albertus, and Peter of Tarentaise, and Giovanni Bonaventura,* who has lately been canonized, not under the name of Giovanni, although that was his true name. Also they quote Alexander of Hales and Guido the Carmelite.† All these say that those who invoke devils are apostates, and consequently heretics, and therefore subject to the Court of the Inquisitors of heretics.

But the said Inquisitors of Spain have not, by the above or any other arguments, made out a sufficient case to prove that such soothsayers etc. may not be tried by the Ordinary or the Bishops without the Inquisitors; and that the Inquisitors may not be relieved from the duty of trying such diviners and necromancers, and even witches: not that the Inquisitors are not rather to be praised than blamed when they do try such cases, when the Bishops fail to do so. And this is the reason that they have not proved their case. The Inquisitors need only concern themselves with matters of heresy, and the heresy must be manifest; as is shown by the frequently quoted Canon *accusatus,* § *sane.*

---

* "*Bonaventura.*" *The parents of S. Bonaventura were Giovanni di Fidanza and Maria Ritella. He was born at Bagnorea, near Viterbo, in 1221, and baptized Giovanni. This was changed to Bonaventura owing to the exclamation of S. Francis, "O buona ventura," when the child was brought to him to be cured of a dangerous illness. (This account has been doubted, and it is true that others bore the name before S. Bonaventura.) S. Bonaventura was canonized by Sixtus IV, 14 April, 1482. This formal enrolment in the catalogue of the Saints was thus long delayed mainly owing to the unfortunate dissensions concerning Franciscan affairs after the Saint's death, 15 July, 1274. He was inscribed among the principal Doctors of the Church by Sixtus V, 14 March, 1587. His feast is celebrated 14 July.*

† "*Guido the Carmelite.*" *Guy de Perpignan, "Doctor Parisiensis," d. 1342; General of the Carmelite Order from 1318–20. His chief work was the "Summa de Haeresibus."*

This being the case, it follows that, however serious and grave may be the sin which a person commits, if it does not necessarily imply heresy, then he must not be judged as a heretic, although he is to be punished. Consequently an Inquisitor need not interfere in the case of a man who is to be punished as a malefactor, but not as a heretic, but may leave him to be tried by the Judges of his own Province.

It follows again that all the crimes of invoking devils and sacrificing to them, of which the Commentators and Canonists and Theologians speak, are no concern of the Inquisitors, but can be left to the secular or episcopal Courts, unless they also imply heresy. This being so, and it being the case that the crimes we are considering are very often committed without any heresy, those who are guilty of such crimes are not to be judged or condemned as heretics, as is proved by the following authorities and arguments.

For a person rightly to be adjudged a heretic he must fulfil five conditions. First, there must be an error in his reasoning. Secondly, that error must be in matters concerning the faith, either being contrary to the teaching of the Church as to the true faith, or against sound morality and therefore not leading to the attainment of eternal life. Thirdly, the error must lie in one who has professed the Catholic faith, for otherwise he would be a Jew or a Pagan, not a heretic. Fourthly, the error must be of such a nature that he who holds it must still confess some of the truth of Christ as touching either His Godhead or His Manhood; for if a man wholly denies the faith, he is an apostate. Fifthly, he must pertinaciously and obstinately hold to and follow that error. And that this is the sense of the Canon where it speaks of heresy and heretics is proved as follows (not by way of refuting, but of substantiating the gloss of the Canonists).

For it is well known to all through common practice that the first essential of a heretic is an error in the understanding; but two conditions are necessary before a man can be called a heretic; the first material, that is, an error in reasoning, and the second formal, that is, an obstinate mind. S. Augustine shows this when he says: A heretic is one who either initiates or follows new and false opinions. It can also be proved by the following reasoning: heresy is a form of infidelity, and infidelity exists subjectively in the intellect, in such a way that a man believes something which is quite contrary to the true faith.

This being so, whatever crime a man commits, if he acts without an error in his understanding he is not a heretic. For example, if a man commits fornication or adultery, although he is disobeying the command *Thou shalt not commit adultery*, yet he is not a heretic unless he holds the opinion that it is lawful to commit adultery. The point can be argued in this way: When the nature of a thing is such that two constituent parts are necessary to its existence, if one of those two parts is wanting the thing itself cannot exist; for if it could, then it would not be true that that part is necessary to its existence. For in the constitution of a house it is necessary that there should be a foundation, walls, and a roof; and if one of these is missing, there is no house. Similarly, since an error in the understanding is a necessary condition of heresy, no action which is done entirely without any such error can make a man a heretic.

Therefore we Inquisitors of Germany are in agreement with Blessed Antoninus where he treats of this matter in the second part of his *Summa;* saying that to baptize images, to worship devils, to sacrifice to them, to tread underfoot the Body of Christ, and all such terrible crimes, do not make a man a heretic unless there is an error in his understanding. Therefore a man is not a heretic who, for example, baptizes an image, not holding any erroneous belief about the Sacrament of Baptism or its effect, nor thinking that the baptism of the image can have any effect of its own virtue; but does this in order that he may more easily obtain some desire from the devil whom he seeks to please by this means, acting with either an implied or an expressed pact that the devil will fulfil the desires either of himself or of someone else. In this way men who, with either a tacit or an expressed pact, invoke devils with characters and figures in accordance with magic practice to perform their desires are not necessarily heretics. But they must not ask from the devil anything which is beyond the power or the knowledge of the devil, having a wrong

understanding of his power and knowledge. Such would be the case with any who believed that the devil could coerce a man's free will; or that, by reason of their pact with him, the devil could do anything which they desired, however much it were forbidden by God; or that the devil can know the whole of the future; or that he can effect anything which only God can do. For there is no doubt that men with such beliefs have an error in their understanding, holding a wrong opinion of the power of the devil; and therefore, granting the other conditions necessary for heresy, they would be heretics, and would be subject at once to the Ordinary and to the Inquisitorial Court.

But if they act for the reasons we have said, not out of any wrong belief concerning baptism or the other matters we have mentioned, as they very commonly do; for since witches and necromancers know that the devil is the enemy of the faith and the adversary of salvation, it must follow that they are compelled to believe in their hearts that there is great might in the faith and that there is no false doctrine of which the father of lies is not known to be the origin; then, although they sin most grievously, yet they are not heretics. And the reason is that they have no wrong belief concerning the sacrament, although they use it wrongly and sacrilegiously. Therefore they are rather sorcerers than heretics, and are to be classed with those whom the above Canon *accusatus* declares are not properly subject to the Inquisitorial Court, since they do not manifestly savour of heresy; their heresy being hidden, if indeed it exists at all.

It is the same with those who worship and sacrifice to the devil. For if they do this in the belief that there is any divinity in devils, or that they ought to be worshipped and that, by reason of such worship, they can obtain from the devil what they desire in spite of the prohibition or permission of God, then they are heretics. But if they act in such a way not out of any such belief concerning the devil, but so that they may the more easily obtain their desires because of some pact formed with the devil, then they are not necessarily heretics, although they sin most grievously.

For greater clearness, some objections are to be disposed of and refuted. For it appears to be against our argument that, according to the laws, a simonist is not a heretic (1, q. 1 : "Whoever by means of money, but not having an error of the understanding"). For a simonist is not in the narrow and exact sense of the word a heretic; but broadly speaking and by comparison he is so, according to S. Thomas, when he buys or sells holy things in the belief that the gift of grace can be had for money. But if, as is often the case, he does not act in this belief, he is not a heretic. Yet he truly would be if he did believe that the gift of grace could be had for money.

Again we are apparently in opposition to what is said of heretics in the Canon; namely, that he who reveres a heretic is himself a heretic, but he who worships the devil sins more heavily than he who reveres a heretic, therefore, etc.

Also, a man must be obviously a heretic in order that he may be judged as such. For the Church is competent to judge only of those things which are obvious, God alone having knowledge and being the Judge of that which is hidden (dist. 33, *erubescant*). But the inner understanding can only be made apparent by intrinsic actions, either seen or proved; therefore a man who commits such actions as we are considering is to be judged a heretic.

Also, it seems impossible that anyone should commit such an action as the treading underfoot of the Body of Christ unless he held a wrong opinion concerning the Body of Christ; for it is impossible for evil to exist in the will unless there is error in the understanding. For according to Aristotle every wicked man is either ignorant or in error. Therefore, since they who do such things have evil in their wills, they must have an error in their understandings.

To these three objections we answer as follows; and the first and third may be considered together. There are two kinds of judgement, that of God and that of men. God judges the inner man; whereas man can only judge of the inner thoughts as they are reflected by outer actions, as is admitted in the third of these arguments. Now he who is a heretic in the judgement of God is truly and actually a heretic; for God judges no one as a heretic unless he has some wrong belief concerning the faith in his understanding. But when a man is a heretic in the judgement of men, he need not necessarily be actually a heretic; but because his deeds give an appearance of a wrong understanding of the faith he is, by legal presumption, considered to be a heretic.

And if it be asked whether the Church should stigmatize at once as heretics those who worship devils or baptize images, note these answers. First, it belongs rather to the Canonists than to the Theologians to discriminate in this matter. The Canonists will say that they are by legal presumption to be considered as heretics, and to be punished as such. A Theologian will say that it is in the first instance a matter for the Apostolic See to judge whether a heresy actually exists or is only to be presumed in law. And this may be because whenever an effect can proceed from a twofold cause, no precise judgement can be formed of the actual nature of the cause merely on the basis of the effect.

Therefore, since such effects as the worship of the devil or asking his help in the working of witchcraft, by baptizing an image, or offering to him a living child, or killing an infant, and other matters of this sort, can proceed from two separate causes, namely, a belief that it is right to worship the devil and sacrifice to him, and that images can receive sacraments; or because a man has formed some pact with the devil, so that he may obtain the more easily from the devil that which he desires in those matters which are not beyond the capacity of the devil, as we have explained above; it follows that no one ought hastily to form a definite judgement merely on the basis of the effect as to what is its cause, that is, whether a man does such things out of a wrong opinion concerning the faith. So when there is no doubt about the effect, still it is necessary to inquire farther into the cause; and if it be found that a man has acted out of a perverse and erroneous opinion concerning the faith, then he is to be judged a heretic and will be subject to trial by the Inquisitors together with the Ordinary. But if he has not acted for these reasons, he is to be considered a sorcerer, and a very vile sinner.

Another answer which touches the matter nearly is that, whatever may be said and alleged, it is agreed that all diviners and witches who are judged as heretics by legal presumption and not by actual fact are subject to the Court of the Ordinary, not of the Inquisitors. And the aforesaid Inquisitors of other countries cannot defend their opinions by quoting the Canon and its commentators, because they who sacrifice to and worship devils are judged to be heretics by legal presumption, and not because the facts obviously show that they are such. For the text says that they must savour of heresy manifestly, that is, intrinsically and by their very nature. And it is enough for us Inquisitors to concern ourselves with those who are manifestly from the intrinsic nature of the case heretics, leaving others to their own judges.

It has been said that the cause must be inquired into, to know whether or not a man acts out of an error of faith; and this is easy. For the spirit of faith is known by the act of faith, which is to believe and confess the faith; as the spirit of chastity is shown by a chaste life: similarly the Church must judge a man a heretic if his actions show that he disputes any article of the faith. In this way even a witch, who has wholly or in part denied the faith, or used vilely the Body of Christ, and offered homage to the devil, may have done this merely to propitiate the devil; and even if she has totally denied the faith in her heart, she is to be judged as an apostate, for the fourth condition, which is necessary before anyone can rightly be said to be a heretic, will be wanting.

But if against this conclusion be set the Bull and commission given to us by our Holy Father Innocent VIII, that witches should be tried by the Inquisitors, we answer in this way. That this is not to say that the Diocesans also cannot proceed to a definite sentence against witches, in accordance with those ancient laws, as has been said. For that Bull was rather given to us because of the great care with which we have wrought to the utmost of our ability with the help of God.

Therefore we cannot concede to those other Inquisitors their first argument, since the contrary conclusion is rather the true one; for simonists are thought to be heretics only by legal presumption, and the Ordinaries themselves without the Inquisitors can try them. Indeed, the Inquisitors have no need to concern themselves with various simonists, or similarly with any others who are judged to be heretics only by legal presumption. For they cannot proceed against schismatic Bishops and other high Dignitaries, as is shown by the chapter of the Inquisition *Concerning Heretics*, Book VI, where it says: The Inquisitors of the sin of heresy deputed by the Apostolic See or by any other authority have no power to try such offenders on this sort of charge, or to proceed against them under pretext of their office, unless it is expressly stated in the letters of commission from the Apostolic See that they are empowered to do so.

But if the Inquisitors know or discover that Bishops or other high Dignitaries have been charged with heresy, or have been denounced or suspected of that crime, it is their duty to report the fact to the Apostolic See.

Similarly the answer to their second argument is clear from what has been said. For he who cherishes and comforts a heretic is himself a heretic if he does this in the belief that he is worthy to be cherished or honoured on account of his doctrine or opinion. But if he honours him for some temporal reason, without any error of faith in his understanding, he is not rightly speaking a heretic, though he is so by a legal fiction or presumption or comparison, because he acts as if he held a wrong belief concerning the faith like him whom he cherishes: so in this case he is not subject to the Inquisitorial Court.

The third argument is similarly answered. For though a man should be judged by the Church as a heretic on account of his outward actions, visible and proved, yet it does not always follow that he is actually a heretic, but is only so reputed by legal presumption. Therefore in this case he is not liable to be tried by the Inquisitorial Court, because he does not manifestly savour of heresy.

For their fourth argument, it is a false assumption to say that it is not possible for anyone to tread underfoot the Body of Christ unless he has some perverse and wrong belief concerning the Body of Christ. For a man may do this with a full knowledge of his sin, and with a firm belief that the Body of Christ is truly there. But he does it to please the devil, and that he may more easily obtain his desire from him. And though in every sin there is error, it need not necessarily be an error of the understanding, which is heresy or a wrong belief concerning the faith; for it may be an erroneous use of some power which turns it to vicious purposes; and then it will only be the first of those five conditions which are necessary constituents of heresy, in accordance with which a heretic is rightly liable to the Inquisitorial Court.

And it is not a valid objection to say that an Inquisitor may, nevertheless, proceed against those who are denounced as heretics, or are under a light or a strong or a grave suspicion of heresy, although they do not appear to savour manifestly of heresy. For we answer that an Inquisitor may proceed against such in so far as they are denounced or suspected for heresy rightly so called; and this is the sort of heresy of which we are speaking (as we have often said), in which there is an error in the understanding, and the other four conditions are superadded. And the second of these conditions is that such error should consist in matters concerning the faith, or should be contrary to the true decisions of the Church in matters of faith and good behaviour and that which is necessary for the attainment of eternal life. For if the error be in some matter which does not concern the faith, as, for example, a belief that the sun is not greater than the earth, or something of that sort, then it is not a dangerous error. But an error against Holy Scripture, against the articles of the faith, or against the decision of the Church, as has been said above, is heresy (art. 24, q. 1, *haec est fides*).

Again, the determination of doubts respecting the faith belongs chiefly to the Church, and especially to the Supreme Pontiff, Christ's Vicar, the successor of S. Peter, as is expressly stated (art. 24, q. 1, *quotiens*). And against the determination of the Church, as S. Thomas says, art. 2, q. 2, no Doctor or Saint maintains his own opinion; not S. Jerome nor S. Augustine nor any other. For just as he who obstinately argues against the faith is a heretic, so also is he who stubbornly maintains his opinion against the determination of the Church in matters concerning the faith and that which is necessary for salvation. For the Church herself has never been proved to be in error over matters of faith (as it is said in art. 24, q. 1, *a recta*,

and in other chapters). And it is expressly said, that he who maintains anything against the determination of the Church, not in an open and honest manner, but in matters which concern faith and salvation, is a heretic. For he need not be a heretic because he disagrees over other matters, such as the separability of law from use in matters which are affected by use: this matter has been settled by Pope John XXII in his *Extrauagantes*,* where he says that they who contradict this opinion are stubborn and rebellious against the Church, but not heretics.

The third condition required is that he who holds the error should be one who has professed the Catholic faith. For if a man has never professed the Christian faith, he is not a heretic but simply an infidel, like the Jews or the Gentiles who are outside the faith. Therefore S. Augustine says in the *City of God:* The devil, seeing the human race to be delivered from the worship of idols and devils, stirred up heretics who, under the guise of Christians, should oppose Christian doctrine. So for a man to be a heretic it is necessary that he should have received the Christian faith in baptism.

Fourthly, it is necessary that the man who so errs should retain some of the true belief concerning Christ, pertaining either to His divinity or to His humanity. For if he retains no part of the faith, he is more rightly to be considered an apostate than a heretic. In this way Julian was an apostate. For

---

* "*Extrauagantes.*" *This word designates some Papal decretals not contained in certain canonical collections which possess a special authority, that is, they are not found in (but "wander outside," "extra uagari") the Decree of Gratian, or the three great official collections of the "Corpus Iuris" (the Decretals of Gregory IX; the Sixth Book of the Decretals; and the Clementines). The term is now applied to the collections known as the "Extrauagantes Ioannis XXII" and the "Extrauagantes Communes." When John XXII (1316–34) published the Decretals already known as "Clementines," there also existed various pontifical documents, obligatory upon the whole Church indeed, but not included in the "Corpus Iuris," and these were called "Extrauagantes." In 1325 Zenselinus de Cassanis added glosses to twenty constitutions of John XXII, and named this collection "Uiginti Extrauagantes papae Ioannis XXII." Chappuis also classified these under fourteen titles containing in all twenty chapters.*

the two are quite distinct, though sometimes they are confused. For in this manner there are found to be men who, driven by poverty and various afflictions, surrender themselves body and soul to the devil, and deny the faith, on condition that the devil will help them in their need to the attainment of riches and honours.

For we Inquisitors have known some, of whom a few afterwards repented, who have behaved in this way merely for the sake of temporal gain, and not through any error in the understanding; wherefore they are not rightly heretics, nor even apostates in their hearts, as was Julian, though they must be reckoned as apostates.

They who are apostates in their heart and refuse to return to the faith are, like impenitent heretics, to be delivered to the secular Court. But if they are desirous of reconciliation, they are received back into the Church, like penitent heretics. See the chapter *ad abolendam,*§ *praesenti, de haeretic.,* lib. 6. Of the same opinion is S. Raymund in his work *de Apostolica,* cap. *reuertentes,* where he says that they who return from the perfidy of apostasy, though they were heretics, are to be received back like penitent heretics. And here the two are confused, as we have said. And he adds: Those who deny the faith through fear of death (that is, who deny the faith for the sake of temporal gain from the devil, but do not believe their error) are heretics in the sight of the law, but are not, properly speaking, heretics. And he adds: Although they have no erroneous belief, yet since the Church must judge by outward signs they are to be considered as heretics (note this fiction of the law); and if they return, they are to be received as penitent heretics. For the fear of death, or the desire for temporal gain, is not sufficient to cause a constant man to deny the faith of Christ. Wherefore he concludes that it is more holy to die than to deny the faith or to be fed by idolatrous means, as S. Augustine says.

The judgement of witches who deny the faith would be the same; that when they wish to return they should be received as penitents, but otherwise they should be left to the secular Court. But they are by all means to be received back into the bosom of the Church when they repent; and are left to the secular Court if they will not return;

and this is because of the temporal injuries which they cause, as will be shown in the methods of passing sentence. And all this may be done by the Ordinary, so that the Inquisitor can leave his duties to him, at least in a case of apostasy; for it is otherwise in other cases of sorcerers.

The fifth condition necessary for a man to be rightly thought a heretic is that he should obstinately and stubbornly persist in his error. Hence, according to S. Jerome, the etymological meaning of heresy is Choice. And again S. Augustine says: Not he who initiates or follows false doctrines, but he who obstinately defends them, is to be considered a heretic. Therefore if anyone does not evilly persist in believing some false doctrine, but errs through ignorance and is prepared to be corrected and to be shown that his opinion is false and contrary to Holy Scripture and the determination of the Church, he is not a heretic. S. Paul also confirms this opinion. And S. Augustine himself used to say: I may err, but I shall not be a heretic. For he was ready to be corrected when his error was pointed out to him. And it is agreed that every day the Doctors have various opinions concerning Divine matters, and sometimes they are contradictory, so that one of them must be false; and yet none of them are reputed to be false until the Church has come to a decision concerning them. See art. 24, q. 3, *qui in ecclesia.*

From all this it is concluded that the sayings of the Canonists on the words "savour manifestly of heresy" in the chapter *accusatus* do not sufficiently prove that witches and others who in any way invoke devils are subject to trial by the Inquisitorial Court; for it is only by a legal fiction that they judge such to be heretics. Neither is it proved by the words of the Theologians; for they call such persons apostates either in word or in deed, but not in their thoughts and their hearts; and it is of this last error that the words "savour of heresy" speak.

And though such persons should be judged to be heretics, it does not follow from this that a Bishop cannot proceed against them without an Inquisitor to a definite sentence, or punish them with imprisonment or torture. More than this, even when this decision does not seem enough to warrant the exemption of us Inquisitors from the duty of trying witches, still we are unwilling to consider that we are legally compelled to perform such duties ourselves, since we can depute the Diocesans to our office, at least in respect of arriving at a judgement.

For this provision is made in the Canon Law (c. *multorum in prin. de haeret. in Clem.*). There it says: As a result of a general complaint, and that this sort of Inquisition may proceed more fortunately and the inquiry into this crime be conducted more skilfully, diligently, and carefully, we order that this kind of case may be tried by the Diocesan Bishops as well as by the Inquisitors deputed by the Apostolic See, all carnal hatred or fear or any temporal affection of this sort being put aside; and so either of the above may move without the other, and arrest or seize a witch, placing her in safe custody in fetters and iron chains, if it seems good to him; and in this matter we leave the conduct of the affair to his own conscience; but there must be no negligence in inquiring into such matters in a manner agreeable to God and justice; but such witches must be thrust into prison rather as a matter of punishment than custody, or be exposed to torture, or be sentenced to some punishment. And a Bishop can proceed without an Inquisitor, or an Inquisitor without a Bishop; or, if either of their offices be vacant, their deputies may act independently of each other, provided that it is impossible for them to meet together for joint action within eight days of the time when the inquiry is due to commence; but if there be no valid reason for their not meeting together, the action shall be null and void in law.

The chapter proceeds to support our contention as follows: But if the Bishop or the Inquisitor, or either of their deputies, are unable or unwilling, for any of the reasons which we have mentioned, to meet together personally, they can severally depute their duties to each other, or else signify their advice and approval by letters.

From this it is clear that even in those cases where the Bishop is not entirely independent of the Inquisitor, the Inquisitor can depute the Bishop to act in his stead, especially in the matter of passing sentence: therefore we ourselves have decided to act according to this decision, leaving other Inquisitors in other districts to act as seems good to them.

Therefore in answer to the arguments, it is clear that witches and sorcerers have not necessarily to be tried by the Inquisitors. But as for the other arguments which seek to make it possible for the Bishops in their turn to be relieved from the trial of witches, and leave this to the Civil Court, it is clear that this is not so easy in their case as it is in that of the Inquisitors. For the Canon Law (c. *ad abolendam*, c. *uergentis*, and c. *excommunicamus utrumque*) says that in a case of heresy it is for the ecclesiastical judge to try and to judge, but for the secular judge to carry out the sentence and to punish; that is, when a capital punishment is in question, though it is otherwise with other penitential punishments.

It seems also that in the heresy of witches, though not in the case of other heresies, the Diocesans also can hand over to the Civil Courts the duty of trying and judging, and this for two reasons: first because, as we have mentioned in our arguments, the crime of witches is not purely ecclesiastical, being rather civil on account of the temporal injuries which they commit; and also because special laws are provided for dealing with witches.

Finally, it seems that in this way it is easiest to proceed with the extermination of witches, and that the greatest help is thus given to the Ordinary in the sight of that terrible Judge who, as the Scriptures testify, will exact the strictest account from and will most hardly judge those who have been placed in authority. Accordingly we will proceed on this understanding, namely, that the secular Judge can try and judge such cases, himself proceeding to the capital punishment, but leaving the imposition of any other penitential punishment to the Ordinary.

A Summary or Classification of the Matters Treated of in this Third Part.

In order, then, that the Judges both ecclesiastical and civil may have a ready knowledge of the methods of trying, judging and sentencing in these cases, we shall proceed under three main heads. First, the method of initiating a process concerning matters of the faith; second, the method of proceeding with the trial; and third, the method of bringing it to a conclusion and passing sentence on witches.

The first head deals with five difficulties. First, which of the three methods of procedure provided by the law is the most suitable. Second, the number of witnesses. Third, whether these can be compelled to take the oath. Fourth, the condition of the witnesses. Fifth, whether mortal enemies may be allowed to give evidence.

The second head contains eleven Questions. I. How witnesses are to be examined, and that there should always be five persons present. Also how witches are to be interrogated, generally and particularly. (This will be numbered the Sixth Question of the whole Part; but we alter the numeration here to facilitate reference by the reader.) II. Various doubts are cleared up as to negative answers, and when a witch is to be imprisoned, and when she is to be considered as manifestly guilty of the heresy of witchcraft. III. The method of arresting witches. IV. Of two duties which devolve upon the Judge after the arrest, and whether the names of the deponents should be made known to the accused. V. Of the conditions under which an Advocate shall be allowed to plead for the defence. VI. What measures the Advocate shall take when the names of the witnesses are not made known to him, and when he wishes to protest to the Judge that the witnesses are mortal enemies of the prisoner. VII. How the Judge ought to investigate the suspicion of such mortal enmity. VIII. Of the points which the Judge must consider before consigning the prisoner to torture. IX. Of the method of sentencing the prisoner to examination by torture. X. Of the method of proceeding with the torture, and how they are to be tortured; and of the provisions against silence on the part of the witch. XI. Of the final interrogations and precautions to be observed by the Judge.

The third head contains first of all three Questions dealing with matters which the Judge must take into consideration, on which depends the whole method of passing sentence. First, whether a prisoner can be convicted by a trial of red-hot iron. Second, of the method in which all sentences should be passed. Third, what degrees of suspicion can justify a trial, and what sort of sentence ought to be passed in respect of each degree of suspicion. Finally, we treat of twenty methods of delivering sentence, thirteen of which are common to all kinds of heresy, and the remainder particular to the heresy of witches. But since these will appear in their own places, for the sake of brevity they are not detailed here.

☆

THE FIRST HEAD

QUESTION I

The Method of Initiating a Process.

THE first question, then, is what is the suitable method of instituting a process on behalf of the faith against witches. In answer to this it must be said that there are three methods allowed by Canon Law. The first is when someone accuses a person before a judge of the crime of heresy, or of protecting heretics, offering to prove it, and to submit himself to the penalty of talion if he fails to prove it. The second method is when someone denounces a person, but does not offer to prove it and is not willing to embroil himself in the matter; but says that he lays information out of zeal for the faith, or because of a sentence of excommunication inflicted by the Ordinary or his Vicar; or because of the temporal punishment exacted by the secular Judge upon those who fail to lay information.

The third method involves an inquisition, that is, when there is no accuser or informer, but a general report that there are witches in some town or place; and then the Judge must proceed, not at the instance of any party, but simply by virtue of his office.

Here it is to be noted that a judge should not readily admit the first method of procedure. For one thing, it is not actuated by motives of faith, nor is it very applicable to the case of witches, since they commit their deeds in secret. Then, again, it is full of danger to the accuser, because of the penalty of talion which he will incur if he fails to prove his case. Then, again, it is very litigious.

Let the process begin with a general citation affixed to the walls of the

Parish Church or the Town Hall, in the following manner.

WHEREAS we, the Vicar of such and such Ordinary (or the Judge of such and such county), do endeavour with all our might and strive with our whole heart to preserve the Christian people entrusted to us in unity and the happiness of the Catholic faith and to keep them far removed from every plague of abominable heresy: Therefore we the aforesaid Judge to whose office it belongs, to the glory and honour of the worshipful name of JESUS Christ and for the exaltation of the Holy Orthodox Faith, and for the putting down of the abomination of heresy, especially in all witches in general and in each one severally of whatever condition or estate: (Here, if he is an ecclesiastical Judge, let him add a summons to all priests and dignitaries of the Church in that town and for a distance of two miles about it, who have knowledge of this notice. And he shall add) By the authority which we exercise in this district, and in virtue of holy obedience and under pain of excommunication, we direct, command, require, and admonish that within the space of twelve days (Here the secular Judge shall command in his own manner under pain of penalties suitable to his office), the first four of which shall stand for the first warning, the second for the second, and the third for the third warning; and we give this treble canonical warning that they should reveal it unto us if anyone know, see, or have heard that any person is reported to be a heretic or a witch, or if any is suspected especially of such practices as cause injury to men, cattle, or the fruits of the earth, to the loss of the State. But if any do not obey these aforesaid commands and admonitions by revealing such matters within the term fixed, let him know (Here the ecclesiastical Judge shall add) that he is cut off by the sword of excommunication (The secular Judge shall add the temporal punishments). Which sentence of excommunication we impose as from this time by this writing upon all and several who thus stubbornly set at naught these our canonical warnings aforesaid, and our requirement of their obedience, reserving to ourselves alone the absolution of such sentence (The secular Judge shall conclude in his manner). Given, etc.

Note also that in the case of the second method the following caution should be observed. For it has been said that the second method of procedure and of instituting a process on behalf of the faith is by means of an information, where the informer does not offer to prove his statement and is not ready to be embroiled in the case, but only speaks because of a sentence of excommunication, or out of zeal for the faith and for the good of the State. Therefore the secular Judge must specify in his general citation or warning aforesaid, that none should think that he will become liable to a penalty even if he fails to prove his words; since he comes forward not as an accuser but as an informer.

And then, since several will appear to lay information before the Judge, he ought to take care to proceed in the following manner. First, let him have a Notary and two honest persons, either clerics or laymen; or if a Notary is not to be procured, then let there be two suitable men in the place of the Notary. For this is dealt with in the c. *ut officium,* § *uerum,* lib. 6, where it is said: But because it is expedient to proceed with great caution in the trial of a grave crime, that no error may be committed in imposing upon the guilty a deservedly severe punishment; we desire and command that, in the examination of the witnesses necessary in such a charge, you shall have two religious and discreet persons, either clerics or laymen.

It goes on to say: In the presence of these persons the depositions of the witnesses shall be faithfully written down by a public official if one is obtainable, or, if not, by two suitable men. Note therefore that, having these persons, the Judge shall order the informer to lay his information in writing, or at least give it clearly by word of mouth. And then the Notary or the Judge shall begin the process in the following manner.

In the Name of the Lord. Amen.

In the year of Our Lord ——, on the —— day of the —— month, in the presence of me the Notary and of the witnesses subscribed, N. of the town of —— in the Diocese of ——, as above, appeared in person at —— before the honourable Judge, and offered him a schedule to the following effect.

(Here shall follow the schedule in its entirety. But if he has not deposed in writing but by word of mouth, it shall continue thus.)

He appeared, etc. and laid information to the Judge that N. of the town or parish of —— in the Diocese of —— had said and asserted that he knew how to perform or had actually done certain injuries to the deponent or to other persons.

After this, he shall immediately make the deponent take the oath in the usual manner, either on the four Gospels of God, or on the Cross, raising three fingers and depressing two in witness of the Holy Trinity and of the damnation of his soul and body, that he will speak the truth in his depositions. And when the oath has been sworn, he shall question him as to how he knows that his depositions are true, and whether he saw or heard that to which he swears. And if he says that he has seen anything, as, for example, that the accused was present at such a time of tempest, or that he had touched an animal, or had entered a stable, the Judge shall ask when he saw him, and where, and how often, and in what manner, and who were present. If he says that he did not see it, but heard of it, he shall ask him from whom he heard it, where, when, and how often, and in whose presence, making separate articles of each of the several points above mentioned. And the Notary or scribe shall set down a record of them immediately after the aforesaid denunciation; and it shall continue thus:

This denunciation, as we have said, having been made, the Inquisitor himself did at once cause him to swear as above on the four Gospels, etc. that he was speaking the truth in his depositions, and did ask him how and why he knew or suspected that what he said was true. He did make answer either that he saw, or that he heard. The Inquisitor did then ask him where he saw or heard this; and he answered on the —— day of the —— month in the year —— in the town or parish of ——. He asked him how often he saw or heard it, etc. And separate articles shall be made, and the whole set down in process, as has been said. And particularly he shall be asked who shared or could share in his knowledge of the case. When all this has been done, he shall finally be asked whether he lays his information out of ill-will, hatred, or rancour; or if he has omitted anything through favour or love; or if he has been requested or suborned to lay information.

Finally, he shall be enjoined, by virtue of his oath, to keep secret whatever he has said there, or whatever the Judge has said to him; and the whole process shall be set down in writing. And when all this is completed, it shall be set down a little lower as follows. This was done at such a place on the —— day of the —— month in the year ——, in the presence of me the Notary or scribe together with those associated with me in the duty of writing, and of such and such witnesses summoned and interrogated.

The third method of beginning a process is the commonest and most usual one, because it is secret, and no accuser or informer has to appear. But when there is a general report of witchcraft in some town or parish, because of this report the Judge may proceed without a general citation or admonition as above, since the noise of that report comes often to his ears; and then again he can begin a process in the presence of the persons, as we have said before.

In the Name of the Lord. Amen.

In the year of Our Lord ——, on the —— day of the —— month, or in —— months, to the ears of such and such official or judge there came a persistent public report and rumour that N. of the town or parish of —— did or said such and such a thing savouring of witchcraft, against the faith and the common good of the State.

And the whole shall be set down according to the common report. And a little lower:

The case was heard on the —— day of the —— month in the year ——, in the presence of me the Notary of such and such authority, or of such and such a scribe, and of such and such witnesses who were called and interrogated.

But before we proceed to the second Head, which deals with the method of conducting this sort of process, we must first say something of the witnesses who are to be examined, as to how many they should be, and what should be their condition.

☆

QUESTION II

Of the Number of the Witnesses.

SINCE we have said that in the second method the evidence of the witnesses is to be written down, it is necessary to know how many witnesses there should be, and of what condition. The question is whether a Judge may lawfully convict any person of the heresy of witchcraft on the evidence of two legitimate witnesses whose evidence is entirely concordant, or whether more than two are necessary. And we say that the evidence of witnesses is not entirely concordant when it is only partially so; that is, when two witnesses differ in their accounts, but agree in the substance or effect: as when one says, " She bewitched my cow," and the other says, " She bewitched my child," but they agree as to the fact of witchcraft.

But here we are concerned with the case of two witnesses being in entire, not partial, agreement. And the answer is that, although two witnesses seem to be enough to satisfy the rigour of the law (for the rule is that that which is sworn to by two or three is taken for the truth); yet in a charge of this kind two witnesses do not seem sufficient to ensure an equitable judgement, on account of the heinousness of the crime in question. For the proof of an accusation ought to be clearer than daylight; and especially ought this to be so in the case of the grave charge of heresy.

But it may be said that very little proof is required in a charge of this nature, since it takes very little argument to expose a person's guilt; for it is said in the Canon de Haereticis, lib. II, that a man makes himself a heretic if in the least of his opinions he wanders from the teaching and the path of the Catholic religion. We answer that this is true enough with reference to the presumption that a person is a heretic, but not as regards a condemnation. For in a charge of this sort the usual order of judicial procedure is cut short, since the defendant does not see the witnesses take the oath, nor are they made known to him, because this might expose them to grave danger; therefore, according to the statute, the prisoner is not permitted to know who are his accusers. But the Judge himself must, by virtue of his office, inquire into any personal enmity felt by the witnesses towards the prisoner; and such witnesses cannot be allowed, as will be shown later. And when the witnesses give confused evidence on account of something lying on their conscience, the Judge is empowered to put them through a second interrogatory. For the less opportunity the prisoner has to defend himself, the more carefully and diligently should the Judge conduct his inquiry.

Therefore, although there are two legitimate and concordant witnesses against a person, even so I do not allow that this would be sufficient warrant for a Judge to condemn a person on so great a charge; but if the prisoner is the subject of an evil report, a period should be set for his purgation; and if he is under strong suspicion on account of the evidence of two witnesses, the Judge should make him abjure the heresy, or question him, or defer his sentence. For it does not seem just to condemn a man of good name on so great a charge on the evidence of only two witnesses, though the case is otherwise with a person of bad reputation. This matter is fully dealt with in the Canon Law of heretics, where it is set down that the Bishop shall cause three or more men of good standing to give evidence on oath to speak the truth as to whether they have any knowledge of the existence of heretics in such a parish.

Again it may be asked whether the Judge can justly condemn a person of such heresy only on the evidence of witnesses who in some respects differ in their evidence, or merely on the strength of a general accusation. We answer that he cannot do so on either of the above grounds. Especially since the proofs of a charge ought, as we have said, to be clearer than daylight; and in this particular charge no one is to be condemned on merely presumptive evidence. Therefore in the case of a prisoner who is the subject of a general accusation, a period of purgation shall be set for him; and in the case of one who is under strong suspicion arising from the evidence of witnesses, he shall be made to abjure his heresy. But when, in spite of certain discrepancies, the witnesses agree in the main facts, then the matter shall rest with the Judge's discretion; and indirectly the question arises how often the witnesses can be examined.

☆

QUESTION III

Of the Solemn Adjuration and Re-examination of Witnesses.

BUT it may be asked whether the Judge can compel witnesses to swear on oath to tell the truth in a case concerning the Faith or witches, or if he can examine them many times. We answer that he can do so, especially an ecclesiastical Judge, and that in ecclesiastical cases witnesses can be compelled to speak the truth, and this on oath, since otherwise their evidence would not be valid. For the Canon Law says: The Archbishop or Bishop may make a circuit of the parish in which it is rumoured that there are heretics, and compel three or more men of good repute, or even, if it seems good to him, the whole neighbourhood, to give evidence. And if any through damnable obstinacy stubbornly refuse to take the oath, they shall on that account be considered as heretics.

And that the witnesses can be examined several times is shown by the Canon, where it says that, when the witnesses have given their evidence in a confused manner, or appear to have withheld part of their knowledge for some reason, the Judge must take care to examine them afresh; for he may legally do so.

☆

QUESTION IV

Of the Quality and Condition of Witnesses.

NOTE that persons under a sentence of excommunication, associates and accomplices in the crime, notorious evildoers and criminals, or servants giving evidence against their masters, are admitted as witnesses in a case concerning the Faith. And just as a heretic may give evidence against a heretic, so may a witch against a witch; but this only in default of other proofs, and such evidence can only be admitted for the prosecution and not for the defence: this is true also of the evidence of the prisoner's wife, sons and kindred; for the evidence of such has more weight in proving a charge than in disproving it.

This is made clear in the c. *in fidei de haer.*, where it says: As a protection of the faith we allow that in a case of inquiry into the sin of heresy, persons under excommunication and partners and accomplices in the crime shall be admitted as witnesses, in default of other proofs against heretics and their patrons, protectors and defenders; provided that it appears probable both from the number of the witnesses and of those against whom they give evidence, and from other circumstances, that they are not giving false testimony.

The case of evidence given by perjurers,* when it is presumed that they are speaking out of zeal for the faith, is dealt with in the Canon c. *accusatus*, § *licet*, where it says that the evidence of perjurers, after they have repented, is admissible; and it goes on to say: If it manifestly appears that they do not speak in a spirit of levity, or from motives of enmity, or by reason of a bribe, but purely out of zeal for the orthodox faith, wishing to correct what they have said, or to reveal something about which they had kept silence, in defence of the faith, their testimony shall be as valid as that of anyone else, provided that there is no other objection to it.

And it is clear from the same chapter of the Canon that the testimony of men of low repute and criminals, and of servants against their masters, is admitted; for it says: So great is the plague of heresy that, in an action involving this crime, even servants are admitted as witnesses against their masters, and any criminal evildoer may give evidence against any person soever.

☆

QUESTION V

Whether Mortal Enemies may be Admitted as Witnesses.

BUT if it is asked whether the Judge can admit the mortal enemies of the prisoner to give evidence against him in such a case, we answer that he cannot; for the same chapter of the Canon says: You must not understand that in this kind of charge a mortal personal enemy may be admitted to give evidence. Henry of Segusio also makes this quite clear. But it is mortal enemies that are spoken of; and it is to be noted that a witness is not necessarily to be disqualified because of every sort of enmity. And a mortal enmity is constituted by the following circumstances: when there is a death feud or vendetta between the parties, or when there has been an attempted homicide, or some serious wound or injury which manifestly shows that there is mortal hatred on the part of the witness against the prisoner. And in such a case it is presumed that, just as the witness has tried to inflict temporal death on the prisoner by wounding him, so he will also be willing to effect his object by accusing him of heresy; and just as he wished to take away his life, so he would be willing to take away his good name. Therefore the evidence of such mortal enemies is justly disqualified.

But there are other serious degrees of enmity (for women are easily provoked to hatred), which need not totally disqualify a witness, although they render his evidence very doubtful, so that full credence cannot be placed in his words unless they are substantiated by independent proofs, and other witnesses supply an indubitable proof of them. For the Judge must ask the prisoner whether he thinks that he has any enemy who would dare to accuse him of that crime out of hatred, so that he might compass his death; and if he says that he has, he shall ask who that person is; and then the Judge shall take note whether the person named as being likely to give evidence from motives of malice has actually done so. And if it is found that this is the case, and the Judge has learned from trustworthy men the cause of that enmity, and if the evidence in question is not substantiated by other proofs and the words of other witnesses, then he may safely reject such evidence. But if the prisoner says that he hopes he has no such enemy, but admits that he has had quarrels with women; or if he says that he has an enemy, but names someone who, perhaps, has not given evidence, in that case, even if other witnesses say that such a person has given evidence from motives of enmity, the Judge must not reject his evidence, but admit it together with the other proofs.

There are many who are not sufficiently careful and circumspect, and consider that the depositions of such quarrelsome women should be altogether rejected, saying that no faith can be placed in them, since they are nearly always actuated by motives of hatred. Such men are ignorant of the subtlety and precautions of magistrates, and speak and judge like men who are colour-blind. But these precautions are dealt with in Questions XI and XII.

☆

THE SECOND HEAD

QUESTION VI

How the Trial is to be Proceeded with and Continued. And how the Witnesses are to be Examined in the Presence of Four Other Persons, and how the Accused is to be Questioned in Two Ways.

IN considering the method of proceeding with a trial of a witch in the cause of the faith, it must first be noted that such cases must be conducted in the simplest and most summary manner, without the arguments and contentions of advocates.

This is explained in the Canon as follows: It often happens that we institute a criminal process, and order it to be conducted in a simple straightforward manner without the legal quibbles and contentions which are introduced in other cases. Now much doubt has been experienced as to the meaning of these words, and as to exactly in what manner such cases should be conducted; but we, desiring as far as possible to remove all doubt on the matter, sanction the following procedure once and for all as valid: The Judge to whom we commit such a case need not require any writ, or demand that the action should be contested; he may conduct the case on holidays for the sake of the convenience of the public; he should shorten the conduct of the case as much as he can by disallowing all dilatory exceptions, appeals and obstructions, the impertinent contentions of pleaders and advocates, and the quarrels of witnesses, and by restraining the superfluous number of witnesses; but not in such a way as to neglect the necessary proofs; and we do not mean by this that he should omit the citation of and swearing of witnesses to tell and not to hide the truth.

And since, as we have shown, the

process is to be conducted in a simple manner, and it is initiated either at the instance of an accuser, or of an informer actuated by zeal, or by reason of a general outcry and rumour; therefore the Judge should try to avoid the first method of beginning the action, namely, at the instance of an accusing party. For the deeds of witches in conjunction with devils are done in secret, and the accuser cannot in this case, as in others, have definite evidence by which he can make his statements good; therefore the Judge ought to advise the accuser to set aside his formal accusation and to speak rather as an informer, because of the grave danger that is incurred by an accuser. And so he can proceed in the second manner, which is commonly used, and likewise in the third manner, in which the process is begun not at the instance of any party.

It is to be noted that we have already said that the Judge ought particularly to ask the informer who shares or could share in his knowledge of the case. Accordingly the Judge should call as witnesses those whom the informer names, who seem to have most knowledge of the matter, and their names shall be entered by the scribe. After this the Judge, having regard to the fact that the aforesaid denunciation of heresy involves of its very nature such a grave charge that it cannot and must not be lightly passed over, since to do so would imply an offence to the Divine Majesty and an injury to the Catholic Faith and to the State, shall proceed to inform himself and examine the witnesses in the following manner.

Examination of Witnesses.

The witness N., of such a place, was called, sworn, and questioned whether he knew N. (naming the accused), and answered that he did. Asked how he knew him, he answered that he had seen and spoken with him on several occasions, or that they had been comrades (so explaining his reason for knowing him). Asked for how long he had known him, he answered, for ten or for so many years. Asked concerning his reputation, especially in matters concerning the faith, he answered that in his morals he was a good (or bad) man, but with regard to his faith, there was a report in such a place that he used certain practices contrary to the Faith,

as a witch. Asked what was the report, he made answer. Asked whether he had seen or heard him doing such things, he again answered accordingly. Asked where he had heard him use such words, he answered, in such a place. Asked in whose presence, he answered, in the presence of such and such.

Further, he was asked whether any of the accused's kindred had formerly been burned as witches, or had been suspected, and he answered. Asked whether he associated with suspected witches, he answered. Asked concerning the manner and reason of the accused's alleged words, he answered, for such a reason and in such a manner. Asked whether he thought that the prisoner had used those words carelessly, unmeaningly and thoughtlessly, or rather with deliberate intention, he answered that he had used them jokingly or in temper, or without meaning or believing what he said, or else with deliberate intention.

Asked further how he could distinguish the accused's motive, he answered that he knew it because he had spoken with a laugh.

This is a matter which must be inquired into very diligently; for very often people use words quoting someone else, or merely in temper, or as a test of the opinions of other people; although sometimes they are used assertively with definite intention.

He was further asked whether he made this deposition out of hatred or rancour, or whether he had suppressed anything out of favour or love, and he answered, etc. Following this, he was enjoined to preserve secrecy. This was done at such a place on such a day in the presence of such witnesses called and questioned, and of me the Notary or scribe.

Here it must always be noted that in such an examination at least five persons must be present, namely, the presiding Judge, the witness or informer, the respondent or accused, who appears afterwards, and the third is the Notary or scribe: where there is no Notary the scribe shall co-opt another honest man, and these two, as has been said, shall perform the duties of the Notary; and this is provided for by Apostolic authority, as was shown above, that in this kind of action two honest men should perform as it were the duty of witnesses of the depositions.

Also it must be noted that when a witness is called he must also be sworn, that is, he must take the oath in the manner we have shown; otherwise he would falsely be described as called and sworn.

In the same way the other witnesses are to be examined. And after this the Judge shall decide whether the fact is fully proven; and if not fully, whether there are great indications and strong suspicions of its truth. Observe that we do not speak of a light suspicion, arising from slight conjectures, but of a persistent report that the accused has worked witchcraft upon children or animals, etc. Then, if the Judge fears the escape of the accused, he shall cause him or her to be placed in custody; but if he does not fear his escape, he shall have him called for examination. But whether or not he places him in custody, he shall first cause his house to be searched unexpectedly, and all chests to be opened and all boxes in the corners, and all implements of witchcraft which are found to be taken away. And having done this, the Judge shall compare together everything of which he has been accused, and everything of which he has been convicted or suspected by the evidence of witnesses, and conduct an interrogatory on them, having with him a Notary, etc., as above, and having caused the accused to swear by the four Gospels of God to speak the truth concerning both himself and others. And they shall all be written down in this following manner.

The General Examination of a Witch or Wizard: and it is the First Action.

The accused N. of such a place was sworn by personally touching the four Gospels of God to speak the truth concerning both himself and others, and was then asked whence he was and from where he originated. And he answered, from such a place in such a Diocese. Asked who were his parents, and whether they were alive or dead, he answered that they were alive in such a place, or dead in such a place. Asked whether they died a natural death, or were burned, he answered in such a way. (Here note that this question is put because, as was shown in the Second Part of this work, witches generally offer or devote their own children to devils, and commonly their whole

progeny is infected; and when the informer has deposed to this effect, and the witch herself has denied it, it lays her open to suspicion.)

Asked where he was brought up, and where he chiefly lived, he answered, in such or such a place. And if it appears that he has changed his abode because, perhaps, his mother or any of his kindred was not suspected, and had lived in foreign districts, especially in such places as are most frequented by witches, he shall be questioned accordingly.

Asked why he had moved from his birthplace and gone to live in such or such a place, he answered, for such a reason. Asked whether in those said places or elsewhere he had heard any talk of witches, as, for example, the stirring up of tempests, the bewitching of cattle, the depriving of cows of their milk, or any such matter of which he was accused; if he should answer that he had, he must be asked what he had heard, and all that he says must be written down. But if he denies it, and says that he has heard nothing, then he must be asked whether he believes that there are such things as witches, and that such things as were mentioned could be done, as that tempests could be raised or men and animals bewitched.

Note that for the most part witches deny this at first; and therefore this engenders a greater suspicion than if they were to answer that they left it to a superior judgement to say whether there were such or not. So if they deny it, they must be questioned as follows: Then are they innocently condemned when they are burned? And he or she must answer.

The Particular Examination of the Same.

Let the Judge take care not to delay the following questions, but to proceed at once with them. Let her be asked why the common people fear her, and whether she knows that she is defamed and hated, and why she had threatened such a person, saying, "You shall not cross me with impunity," and let her answers be noted.

Then let her be asked what harm that person had done her, that she should have used such words to threaten him with injury. And note that this question is necessary in order to arrive at the cause of their enmity, for in the end the accused will allege that the informer has spoken out of enmity; but when this is not mortal, but only a womanish quarrel, it is no impediment. For this is a common custom of witches, to stir up enmity against themselves by some word or action, as, for example, to ask someone to lend them something or else they will damage his garden, or something of that sort, in order to make an occasion for deeds of witchcraft; and they manifest themselves either in word or in action, since they are compelled to do so at the instance of the devils, so that in this way the sins of Judges are aggravated while the witch remains unpunished.

For note that they do not do such things in the presence of others, so that if the informer wishes to produce witnesses he cannot do so. Note again that they are spurred on by the devils, as we have learned from many witches who have afterwards been burned; so that often they have to work witchcraft against their own wills.

Further, she was asked how the effect could follow from those threats, as that a child or animal should so quickly be bewitched, and she answered. Asked, "Why did you say that he would never know a day of health, and it was so?" she answered. And if she denies everything, let her be asked concerning other bewitchments, alleged by other witnesses, upon cattle or children. Asked why she was seen in the fields or in the stable with the cattle, and touching them, as is sometimes their custom, she answered.

Asked why she touched a child, and afterwards it fell sick, she answered. Also she was asked what she did in the fields at the time of a tempest, and so with many other matters. Again, why, having one or two cows, she had more milk than her neighbours who had four or six. Again, let her be asked why she persists in a state of adultery or concubinage; for although this is beside the point, yet such questions engender more suspicion than would be the case with a chaste and honest woman who stood accused.

And note that she is to be continually questioned as to the depositions which have been laid against her, to see whether she always returns the same answers or not. And when this examination has been completed, whether her answers have been negative, or affirmative, or ambiguous, let them be written down: Executed in such a place, etc., as above.

☆

QUESTION VII

In Which Various Doubts are Set Forth with Regard to the Foregoing Questions and Negative Answers. Whether the Accused is to be Imprisoned, and when she is to be considered as Manifestly Taken in the Foul Heresy of Witchcraft. This is the Second Action.

IT is asked first what is to be done when, as often happens, the accused denies everything. We answer that the Judge has three points to consider, namely, her bad reputation, the evidence of the fact, and the words of the witnesses; and he must see whether all these agree together. And if, as very often is the case, they do not altogether agree together, since witches are variously accused of different deeds committed in some village or town; but the evidences of the fact are visible to the eye, as that a child has been harmed by sorcery, or, more often, a beast has been bewitched or deprived of its milk; and if a number of witnesses have come forward whose evidence, even if it show certain discrepancies (as that one should say she had bewitched his child, another his beast, and a third should merely witness to her reputation, and so with the others), but nevertheless agree in the substance of the fact, that is, as to the witchcraft, and that she is suspected of being a witch; although those witnesses are not enough to warrant a conviction without the fact of the general report, or even with that fact, as was shown above at the end of Question III, yet, taken in conjunction with the visible and tangible evidence of the fact, the Judge may, in consideration of these three points together, decide that the accused is to be reputed, not as strongly or gravely under suspicion (which suspicions will be explained later), but as manifestly taken in the heresy of witchcraft; provided, that is, that the witnesses are of a suitable condition and have not given evidence out of enmity, and that a sufficient number of them, say six or eight or ten, have agreed together on oath. And then, according to the Canon Law, he must subject her to punishment, whether she has confessed her crime or not. And this is proved as follows.

For since it is said, that when all three of the above considerations are in agreement, then she should be thought to be manifestly taken in heresy, it must not be understood that it is necessary for all three to be in agreement, but only that if this is the case the proof is all the stronger. For either one instance by itself of the following two circumstances, namely, the evidence of the fact and the production of legitimate witnesses, is sufficient to cause a person to be reputed as manifestly taken in heresy; and all the more when both these considerations are in agreement.

For when the Jurists ask in how many ways a person may be considered as manifestly taken in heresy, we answer that there are three ways, as S. Bernard has explained. This matter was treated of above in the First Question at the beginning of this work, namely, the evidence of the fact, when a person has publicly preached heresy. But here we consider the evidence of the fact provided by public threats uttered by the accused, as when she said, "You shall have no healthy days," or some such thing, and the threatened effect has followed. The other two ways are the legitimate proof of the case by witnesses, and thirdly her own confession. Therefore, if each of these singly is sufficient to cause a person to be manifestly suspected, how much more is this the case when the reputation of the accused, the evidence of the fact, and the depositions of witnesses all together point to the same conclusion. It is true that S. Bernard speaks of an evident fact, and we here speak of the evidence of the fact; but this is because the devil does not work openly, but secretly. Therefore the injuries and the instruments of witchcraft which are found constitute the evidence of the fact. And whereas in other heresies an evident fact is alone sufficient, here we join three proofs together.

Secondly, it is thus proved that a person so taken is to be punished according to the law, even though she denies the accusation. For a person taken on the evidence of the fact, or on the depositions of witnesses, either confesses the crime or does not. If he confesses and is impenitent, he is to be handed over to the secular court to suffer the extreme

penalty, according to the chapter *ad abolendam*, or he is to be imprisoned for life, according to the chapter *excommunicamus*. But if he does not confess, and stoutly maintains his denial, he is to be delivered as an impenitent to the power of the Civil Court to be punished in a fitting manner, as Henry of Segusio shows in his *Summa*, where he treats of the manner of proceeding against heretics.

It is therefore concluded that it is most just if the Judge proceeds in that manner with his questions and the depositions of witnesses, since, as has been said, he can in a case concerning the Faith conduct matters quite plainly and in a short and summary manner; and it is meet that he should consign the accused to prison for a time, or for several years, in case perhaps, being depressed after a year of the squalor of prison, she may confess her crimes.

But, lest it should seem that he arrives at his sentence precipitately, and to show that he proceeds with all equity, let us inquire into what should next be done.

☆

QUESTION VIII

Which Follows from the Preceding Question, Whether the Witch is to be Imprisoned, and of the Method of Taking her. This is the Third Action of the Judge.

IT is asked whether, after she has denied the accusation, the witch ought to be kept in custody in prison, when the three aforesaid conditions, namely, her reputation, the evidence of the fact, and the depositions of witnesses, are in agreement; or whether she should be dismissed with the security of sureties, so that she may again be called and questioned. As to this question there are three opinions.

First, it is the opinion of some that she should be sent to prison, and that by no means ought she to be dismissed under bond; and they hold this opinion on the strength of the reasoning brought forward in the preceding question, namely, that she is to be considered as manifestly guilty when all those three considerations are in agreement.

Others, again, think that before she is imprisoned she may be dismissed with the safeguard of sureties; so that if she makes her escape, she can then be considered as convicted. But after she has been imprisoned because of her negative answers, she is not to be released under any safeguard or condition of bail, that is, when those three considerations noted above are in agreement; because in that case she could not subsequently be sentenced and punished by death; and this, they say, is the general custom.

The third opinion is that no definite rule can be given, but that it must be left to the Judge to act in accordance with the gravity of the matter as shown by the testimony of the witnesses, the reputation of the accused, and the evidence as to the fact, and the extent to which these three agree with each other; and that he should follow the custom of the country. And they who hold this opinion conclude by saying that if reputable and responsible sureties are not to be procured, and the accused is suspected of contemplating flight, she should then be cast into prison. And this third opinion seems to be the most reasonable, as long as the correct procedure is observed; and this consists in three things.

First, that her house should be searched* as thoroughly as possible, in all holes and corners and chests, top and bottom; and if she is a noted witch, then without doubt, unless she has previously hidden them, there will be found various instruments of witchcraft, as we have shown above.

Secondly, if she has a maid-servant or companions, that she or they should be shut up by themselves; for though they are not accused, yet it is presumed that none of the accused's secrets are hidden from them.

Thirdly, in taking her, if she be taken in her own house, let her not be given

time to go into her room; for they are wont to secure in this way, and bring away with them, some object or power of witchcraft which procures them the faculty of keeping silent under examination.

This gives rise to the question whether the method employed by some to capture a witch is lawful, namely, that she should be lifted from the ground by the officers, and carried out in a basket or on a plank of wood so that she cannot again touch the ground. This can be answered by the opinion of the Canonists and of certain Theologians, that this is lawful in three respects. First, because, as is shown in the introductory question of this Third Part, it is clear from the opinion of many authorities, and especially of such Doctors as no one would dare to dispute, as Duns Scotus, Henry of Segusio and Godfrey of Fontaines, that it is lawful to oppose vanity with vanity. Also we know from experience and the confessions of witches that when they are taken in this manner they more often lose the power of keeping silence under examination: indeed many who have been about to be burned have asked that they might be allowed at least to touch the ground with one foot; and when this has been denied them and they have been asked why they made such a request, they have answered that if they had touched the ground they would have liberated themselves, striking many other people dead with lightning.

The second reason is this. It was manifestly shown in the Second Part of this work that a witch loses all her power when she falls into the hands of public justice, that is, with regard to the past; but with regard to the future, unless she receives from the devil fresh powers of keeping silent, she will confess all her crimes. Therefore let us say with S. Paul:† Whatsoever we do in word or deed, let all be done in the name of the Lord JESUS Christ. And if the witch be innocent, this form of capture will not harm her.

Thirdly, according to the Doctors it is lawful to counteract witchcraft by vain means; for they all agree as to this, though they are at variance over the question as to when those vain means may also be unlawful. Therefore when Henry of Segusio says that it is lawful

---

* "*House should be searched.*" Thus in the famous witch trial of Dame Alice Kyteler and her coven before the Bishop of Ossory in 1324, John le Poer, the husband of Dame Alice, deposed that in her closet were discovered mysterious vials and elixirs, strange necromantic instruments and ghastly relics of mortality which she used in her horrid craft. Holinshed in his "Chronicle of Ireland" (London, 1587, p. 93), sub anno 1323, has: "In rifling the closet of the ladie, they found a wafer of sacramental bread, having the divels name stamped thereon in steed of JESUS Christ, and a pipe of ointment, wherewith she greased a staffe, upon which she ambled and gallopped thorough thicke and thin when and in what manner she listed." See my "Geography of Witchcraft," Chap. II, pp. 85-91.

† "S. Paul." "Colossians" iii, 17.

to oppose vanity with vanity, this is explained as meaning that he speaks of vain means, not of unlawful means. All the more, then, is it lawful to obstruct witchcraft; and it is this obstruction which is referred to here, and not any unlawful practice.

Let the Judge note also that there are two sorts of imprisonment; one being a punishment inflicted upon criminals, but the other only a matter of custody in the house of detention. And these two sorts are noted in the chapter *multorum querela;* therefore she ought at least to be placed in custody. But if it is only a slight matter of which she is accused, and she is not of bad reputation, and there is no evidence of her work upon children or animals, then she may be sent back to her house. But because she has certainly associated with witches and knows their secrets, she must give sureties; and if she cannot do so, she must be bound by oaths and penalties not to go out of her house unless she is summoned. But her servants and domestics, of whom we spoke above, must be kept in custody, yet not punished.

☆

QUESTION IX

What is to be done after the Arrest, and whether the Names of the Witnesses should be made Known to the Accused. This is the Fourth Action.

THERE are two matters to be attended to after the arrest, but it is left to the Judge which shall be taken first; namely, the question of allowing the accused to be defended, and whether she should be examined in the place of torture, though not necessarily in order that she should be tortured. The first is only allowed when a direct request is made; the second only when her servants and companions, if she has any, have first been examined in the house.

But let us proceed in the order as above. If the accused says that she is innocent and falsely accused, and that she wishes to see and hear her accusers, then it is a sign that she is asking to defend herself. But it is an open question whether the Judge is bound to make the deponents known to her and bring them to confront her face to face. For here let the Judge take note

that he is not bound either to publish the names of the deponents or to bring them before the accused, unless they themselves should freely and willingly offer to come before the accused and lay their depositions in her presence. And it is by reason of the danger incurred by the deponents that the Judge is not bound to do this. For although different Popes have had different opinions on this matter, none of them has ever said that in such a case the Judge is bound to make known to the accused the names of the informers or accusers (but here we are not dealing with the case of an accuser). On the contrary, some have thought that in no case ought he to do so, while others have thought that he should in certain circumstances.

But, finally, Boniface VIII* decreed as follows: If in a case of heresy it appears to the Bishop or Inquisitor that grave danger would be incurred by the witnesses or informers on account of the powers of the persons against whom they lay their depositions, should their names be published, he shall not publish them. But if there is no danger, their names shall be published just as in other cases.

Here it is to be noted that this refers not only to a Bishop or Inquisitor, but to any Judge conducting a case against witches with the consent of the Inquisitor or Bishop; for, as was shown in the introductory Question, they can depute their duties to a Judge. So that any such Judge, even if he be secular, has the authority of the Pope, and not only of the Emperor.

Also a careful Judge will take notice of the powers of the accused persons; for these are of three kinds, namely, the power of birth and family, the power of riches, and the power of malice. And the last of these is more to be feared than the other two, since it threatens more danger to the wit-

---

* *"Boniface VIII." Benedetto Gaetani, born at Anagni about 1235; elected Pope, 24 December, 1294; died at Rome, 11 October, 1303. He was one of the most eminent canonists of his age, and as Supreme Pontiff enriched legislation by the promulgation (Bull "Sacrosanctae," 1298) of a large number of his own constitutions and those of his predecessors since 1234, when Gregory IX issued his five books of Decretals. In reference to this, the collection of Boniface VIII is known as "Liber Sixtus," i.e. of Pontifical Constitutions.*

nesses if their names are made known to the accused. The reason for this is that it is more dangerous to make known the names of the witnesses to an accused person who is poor, because such a person has many evil accomplices, such as outlaws and homicides, associated with him, who venture nothing but their own persons, which is not the case with anyone who is nobly born or rich, and abounding in temporal possessions. And the kind of danger which is to be feared is explained by Pope John XXII as the death or cutting off of themselves or their children or kindred, or the wasting of their substance, or some such matter.

Further, let the Judge take notice that, as he acts in this matter with the authority of the Supreme Pontiff and the permission of the Ordinary, both he himself and all who are associated with him at the depositions, or afterwards at the pronouncing of the sentence, must keep the names of the witnesses secret, under pain of excommunication. And it is in the power of the Bishop thus to punish him or them if they do otherwise. Therefore he should very implicitly warn them not to reveal the names from the very beginning of the process.

Wherefore the above decree of Pope Boniface VIII goes on to say : And that the danger to those accusers and witnesses may be the more effectively met, and the inquiry conducted more cautiously, we permit, by the authority of this statute, that the Bishop or Inquisitors (or, as we have said, the Judge) shall forbid all those who are concerned in the inquiry to reveal without their permission any secrets which they have learned from the Bishop or Inquisitors, under pain of excommunication which they may incur by violating such secrets.

It is further to be noted that just as it is a punishable offence to publish the names of witnesses indiscreetly, so also it is to conceal them without good reason from, for instance, such people as have a right to know them, such as the lawyers and assessors whose opinion is to be sought in proceeding to the sentence; in the same way the names must not be concealed when it is possible to publish them without risk of any danger to the witnesses. On this subject the above decree speaks as follows, towards the end : We command that in all cases the Bishop or Inquisitors shall take especial care not to suppress the names of the witnesses as if there were danger to them when there is perfect security, nor conversely to decide to publish them when there is some danger threatened, the decision in this matter resting with their own conscience and discretion. And it has been written in comment on these words : Whoever you are who are a Judge in such a case, mark those words well, for they do not refer to a slight risk but to a grave danger; therefore do not deprive a prisoner of his legal rights without very good cause, for this cannot but be an offence to Almighty God.

The reader must note that all the process which we have already described, and all that we have yet to describe, up to the methods of passing sentence (except the death sentence), which it is in the province of the ecclesiastical Judge to conduct, can also, with the consent of the Diocesans, be conducted by a secular Judge. Therefore the reader need find no difficulty in the fact that the above Decree speaks of an ecclesiastical and not a secular Judge; for the latter can take his method of inflicting the death sentence from that of the Ordinary in passing sentence of penance.

☆

QUESTION X

What Kind of Defence may be Allowed, and of the Appointment of an Advocate. This is the Fifth Action.

IF, therefore, the accused asks to be defended, how can this be admitted when the names of the witnesses are kept altogether secret? It is to be said that three considerations are to be observed in admitting any defence. First, that an Advocate shall be allotted to the accused. Second, that the names of the witnesses shall not be made known to the Advocate, even under an oath of secrecy, but that he shall be informed of everything contained in the depositions. Third, the accused shall as far as possible be given the benefit of every doubt, provided that this involves no scandal to the faith nor is in any way detrimental to justice, as will be shown. And in like manner the prisoner's procurator shall have full access to the whole process, only the names of the witnesses and deponents being suppressed; and the Advocate can act also in the name of procurator.

As to the first of these points: it should be noted that an Advocate is not to be appointed at the desire of the accused, as if he may choose which Advocate he will have; but the Judge must take great care to appoint neither a litigious nor an evil-minded man, nor yet one who is easily bribed (as many are), but rather an honourable man to whom no sort of suspicion attaches.

And the Judge ought to note four points, and if the Advocate be found to conform to them, he shall be allowed to plead, but not otherwise. For first of all the Advocate must examine the nature of the case, and then if he finds it a just one he may undertake it, but if he finds it unjust he must refuse it; and he must be very careful not to undertake an unjust or desperate case. But if he has unwittingly accepted the brief, together with a fee, from someone who wishes to do him an injury, but discovers during the process that the case is hopeless, then he must signify to his client (that is, the accused) that he abandons the case, and must return the fee which he has received. This is the opinion of Godfrey of Fontaines, which is wholly in conformity with the Canon *de jud.* 1, *rem non novam.* But Henry of Segusio holds an opposite view concerning the return of the fee in a case in which the Advocate has worked very hard. Consequently if an Advocate has wittingly undertaken to defend a prisoner whom he knows to be guilty, he shall be liable for the costs and expenses (*de admin. tut.* 1, *non tamen est ignotum*).

The second point to be observed is that in his pleading he should conduct himself properly in three respects. First, his behaviour must be modest and free from prolixity or pretentious oratory. Secondly, he must abide by the truth, not bringing forward any fallacious arguments or reasoning, or calling false witnesses, or introducing legal quirks and quibbles if he be a skilled lawyer, or bringing counter-accusations; especially in cases of this sort, which must be conducted as simply and summarily as possible. Thirdly, his fee must be regulated by the usual practice of the district.

But to return to our point; the Judge must make the above conditions clear to the Advocate, and finally admonish him not to incur the charge of defending heresy, which would make him liable to excommunication.

And it is not a valid argument for him to say to the Judge that he is not defending the error, but the person. For he must not by any means so conduct his defence as to prevent the case from being conducted in a plain and summary manner, and he would be doing so if he introduced any complications or appeals into it; all which things are disallowed altogether. For it is granted that he does not defend the error; for in that case he would be more damnably guilty than the witches themselves, and rather a heresiarch than a heretical wizard. Nevertheless, if he unduly defends a person already suspect of heresy, he makes himself as it were a patron of that heresy, and lays himself under not only a light but a strong suspicion, in accordance with the manner of his defence; and ought publicly to abjure that heresy before the Bishop.

We have put this matter at some length, and it is not to be neglected by the Judge, because much danger may arise from an improper conducting of the defence by an Advocate or Procurator. Therefore, when there is any objection to the Advocate, the Judge must dispense with him and proceed in accordance with the facts and the proofs. But when the Advocate for the accused is not open to any objection, but is a zealous man and a lover of justice, then the Judge may reveal to him the names of the witnesses, under an oath of secrecy.

☆

QUESTION XI

What Course the Advocate should Adopt when the Names of the Witnesses are not Revealed to him. The Sixth Action.

BUT it may be asked: What, then, should the Advocate acting as Procurator for the accused do, when the names of the witnesses are withheld from both himself and his client, although the accused earnestly desires that they should be made known? We answer that he should obtain information from the Judge on every point of the accusation, which must be given to him at his request, only the names of the witnesses being suppressed; and with this information he should approach the accused and, if the matter involves a very grave charge, exhort him to exercise all the patience which he can.

And if the accused again and again insists that she should know the names of the witnesses against her, he can answer her as follows: You can guess from the charges which are made against you who are the witnesses. For the child or beast of so and so has been bewitched; or to such a woman or man, because they refused to lend you something for which you asked, you said, "You shall know that it would have been better to have agreed to my request," and they bear witness that in consequence of your words the person was suddenly taken ill; and facts are stronger evidence than words. And you know that you have a bad reputation, and have for a long time been suspected of casting spells upon and injuring many men. And talking in this manner, he may finally induce her to enter a plea that they had borne witness against her from motives of hatred; or to say, "I confess that I did say so, but not with any intent to do harm."

Therefore the Advocate must first lay before the Judge and his assessors this plea of personal enmity, and the Judge must inquire into it. And if it should be found to be a case of mortal enmity, as that there has been some attempted or accomplished murder committed by the husbands or kindred of the parties, or that someone of one party has been charged with a crime by someone of the other party, so that he fell into the hands of public justice, or that serious wounds have resulted from quarrels and brawls between them; then the upright and careful Judge will consult with his assessors whether the accused or the deponent was the aggravating party. For if, for example, the husband or friends of the accused have unjustly oppressed the friends of the deponent, then if there is no evidence of the fact that children or animals or men have been bewitched, and if there are no other witnesses, and the accused is not even commonly suspected of witchcraft, in that case it is presumed that the depositions were laid against her from motives of vengeance, and she is to be discharged as innocent and freely dismissed, after having been duly cautioned against seeking to avenge herself, in the manner which is usually used by Judges.

The following case may be put. Katharina's child, or she herself, is bewitched, or she has suffered much loss in her cattle; and she suspects the accused because her husband or brothers had previously brought an unjust accusation against her own husband or brother. Here the cause of enmity is twofold on the part of the deponent, having its root both in her own bewitchment and in the unjust accusation brought against her husband or brother. Then ought her deposition to be rejected or not? From one point of view it seems that it should, because she is actuated by enmity; from another point of view it should not, because there is the evidence of the fact in her bewitchment.

We answer that if in this case there are no other deponents, and the accused is not even under common suspicion, then her depositions cannot be allowed, but must be rejected; but if the accused is rendered suspect, and if the disease is not due to natural causes but to witchcraft (and we shall show later how this can be distinguished), she is to be subjected to a canonical purgation.

If it be asked further whether the other deponents must bear witness to the evidence of the fact as experienced by themselves or others, or only to the public reputation of the accused; we answer that, if they give evidence of the fact, so much the better. But if they only give evidence as to her general character, and the matter stands so, then, although the Judge must reject that deponent on the grounds of personal enmity, yet he shall take the evidence of the fact, and of her bad reputation given by the other witnesses, as proof that the accused must be strongly suspect, and on these grounds he can sentence her to a threefold punishment: namely, to a canonical purgation because of her reputation; or to an abjuration, because of the suspicion under which she rests, and there are various forms of abjuration for various degrees of suspicion, as will be shown in the fourth method of passing sentence; or, because of the evidence of the fact, and if she confesses her crime and is penitent, she shall not be handed over to the secular branch for capital punishment, but be sentenced by the ecclesiastical Judge to imprisonment for life. But notwithstanding the fact that she has been sentenced to imprisonment for life by the ecclesiastical Judge, the secular Judge can, on account of the temporal injuries which she has committed, deliver her to be burned. But all these matters will be made clear later when we deal with the sixth method of passing sentence.

To sum up: Let the Judge first take care not to lend too easy belief to the Advocate when he pleads mortal enmity on behalf of the accused; for in these cases it is very seldom that anyone bears witness without enmity, because witches are always hated by everybody. Secondly, let him take note that there are four ways by which a witch can be convicted, namely, by witnesses, by direct evidence of the fact, by indirect evidence of the fact, and by her own confession. And if she is detained on account of a general report, she can be convicted by the evidence of witnesses; if on account of a definite suspicion, the direct or indirect evidence of the facts can convict her, and by reason of these the suspicion may be judged to be either light or strong or grave. All this is when she does not confess; but when she does, the case can proceed as has been said.

Thirdly, let the Judge make use of all the foregoing circumstances to meet the plea of the Advocate, whether the accused is charged only by reason of a general report, or whether there are also certain evidences to support the charge by which she incurs slight or strong suspicion; and then he will be able to answer the Advocate's allegation of personal enmity, which is the first line of defence which he may assume.

But when the Advocate assumes the second line of defence, admitting that the accused has used such words against the deponent as, "You shall soon know what is going to happen to you," or "You will wish soon enough that you had lent or sold me what I asked for," or some such words; and submits that, although the deponent afterwards experienced some injury either to his person or his property, yet it does not follow from this that the accused was the cause of it as a witch, for illnesses may be due to various different causes. Also he submits that it is a common habit of women to quarrel together with such words, etc.

The Judge ought to answer such allegations in the following manner. If the illness is due to natural causes, then the excuse is good. But the evidence indicates the contrary; for it cannot be cured by any natural remedy; or in the opinion of the physicians the illness is due to witchcraft, or is what is in common speech called a Night-scathe. Again, perhaps other enchantresses are of the opinion that it is due to witchcraft. Or because it came suddenly, without any previous sickening, whereas natural diseases generally develop gradually. Or perhaps because the plaintiff had found certain instruments of witchcraft under his bed or in his clothes or elsewhere, and when these were removed he was suddenly restored to health, as often happens, as we showed in the Second Part of this work where we treated of remedies. And by some such answer as this the Judge can easily meet this allegation, and show that the illness was due rather to witchcraft than to any natural causes, and that the accused must be suspected of causing such witchcraft, by reason of her threatening words. In the same way, if someone said, "I wish your barn would be burned down," and this should afterwards happen, it would engender a grave suspicion that the person who had used that threat had caused the barn to be set on fire, even if another person, and not he himself, had actually set light to it.

☆

QUESTION XII

Of the Same Matter, Declaring more Particularly how the Question of Personal Enmity is to be Investigated. The Seventh Action.

TAKE notice that only mortal enemies are debarred from giving evidence, as was shown in the Fifth Question. But the Judge may consider that to come to a decision about such enmity by the means we have just explained is rather dubious and unsatisfactory; and the accused or her Procurator may not be willing to accept a decision arrived at on such grounds as to whether the enmity is mortal or not. Therefore the Judge must use other means to decide concerning the alleged enmity, so that he may not punish the innocent, but exact full justice from the guilty. And though these means may savour of cunning and even guile, yet the Judge may employ them for the good of the faith and the State; for even S. Paul says: But being crafty, I caught you by guile. And these means are especially to be employed in the case of a prisoner who has not been publicly defamed, and is not suspected because of the evidence of any fact; and the Judge may also employ them against prisoners who have alleged enmity on the part of the deponents, and wish to know all the names of the witnesses.

The first method is this. The accused or her Advocate is given a copy of the process with the names of the deponents or informers, but not in the order in which they deposed; but in such a way that the name of the witness who comes first in the copy is sixth or seventh in the schedule, and he who comes second is last or last but one. In this way the accused will be deceived as to which witness deposed this or that. And then she will either say that they are all her enemies, or not; and if she says that they all are, she will be the more easily detected in a lie when the cause of the enmity is investigated by the Judge; and if she names only certain ones, still the cause of the enmity will be more easily investigated.

The second method is similar, when the Advocate is given a copy of the process, and separately a list of the names of the deponents; but there are added other matters perpetrated elsewhere by witches, but not set down in writing by the witnesses or deponents. And so the accused will not be able to say definitely that this one or that one is her mortal enemy, because she does not know what they have deposed against her.

The third method was touched upon in the Fifth Question above. For when the accused is questioned at the end of her second examination, and before she has demanded to be defended or an Advocate has been allotted to her, let her be asked whether she thinks that she has any mortal enemies who, setting aside all fear of God, would falsely accuse her of the crime of heresy and witchcraft. And then perhaps without thinking, and not having seen the depositions of the witnesses, she will answer that she does not think that she has any such enemies. Or if she says, "I think I have," and names any of the witnesses who have laid information, and the reason for that enmity is known, then the Judge will be able to investigate it with more certainty afterwards, when the accused has been given separate copies of the process and of the names of the witnesses, in the manner we have explained.

The fourth method is this. At the end of her second examination and confession (as we showed in the Sixth Question), before she is granted any means of defence, let her be questioned as to the witnesses who have laid the more serious charges against her, in this manner. "Do you know So-and-so?" naming one of the witnesses; and then she will answer either Yes or No. If she says No, she will not be able, after she has been given means of defence and an Advocate, to plead that he is a mortal enemy, since she has said on oath that she does not know him. But if she says Yes, let her be asked whether she knows or has heard that he or she has acted in any way contrary to the Christian faith in the manner of a witch. Then if she says Yes, for he did such and such a thing; let her be asked whether he is her friend or enemy; and she will immediately answer that he is her friend, because the testimony of such is not of very great account; and consequently she will not be able afterwards to plead on oath through her Advocate that he is her enemy, for she has already said that he is her friend. But if she answers that she knows nothing about him, let her again be asked whether he is her friend or enemy, and she will at once answer that he is her friend; for it would be futile to allege enmity on the part of someone of whom she knows nothing. Therefore she says, "I am his friend, but if I knew anything about him I would not fail to reveal it." Therefore she will not be able afterwards to plead that he is her enemy. Or perhaps she will from the very beginning allege reasons for mortal enmity, and in that case some credence must be placed in the plea of the Advocate.

A fifth method is to give the Advocate or the accused a copy of the process, with the names of the informers suppressed. And then the accused will guess, and very often rightly, who has deposed such and such against her. And then if she says, "So-and-so is my mortal enemy, and I am willing to prove it by witnesses," then the Judge must consider whether the person named is the same person named in the schedule; and since she has said that she is willing to prove it by witnesses, he will examine those witnesses and inquire into the causes of the enmity, having secretly called into consultation learned and aged men of known prudence. And if he finds sufficient reasons for mortal enmity, he shall reject that evidence and dismiss the prisoner, unless there are other grave charges against her, sworn to by other witnesses.

And this fifth method is commonly used; and it is found in practice that witches quickly guess from the copy of the process who has laid information against them. And because in such cases mortal enmity is rarely found unless it arises from the wicked deeds of the witch, therefore the Judge can easily come to a decision by the above means. Also it is to be noted that often the informers desire to confront the witch personally, and to charge her to her face with the bewitchment which has befallen them.

There is still one more method whereunto the Judge may finally have recourse, when perhaps the other methods, and especially the first four, seem to some to savour too much of cunning and deceit. Accordingly, to satisfy and content the scrupulous, and that no fault may be found with the Judge, let him take care, after he has found by the above methods that there is no mortal enmity between the accused and the deponent, but wishes to remove all grounds for complaint by settling the question finally in consultation with his other assessors, to act as follows. Let him give to the accused or her Advocate a copy of the process, with the names of the deponents or informers suppressed. And since her defence is that she has mortal enemies, and perhaps she has alleged various reasons for the enmity, whether or not the facts are in agreement with her statements, let the Judge call into consultation learned men of every faculty (if such can be had), or at least some honest and reputable persons (for this is the purport of that statute we have so often quoted); and let him cause the whole process to be read through to them from end to end by the Notary or scribe, and let the names of the witnesses be made known to them, but under an oath of secrecy; and he shall first inquire whether or not they are willing to be bound by such an oath, for if not the names must by no means be declared to them.

Then let him tell how he has inquired in such and such a manner into the alleged enmity, and has not been able to find any testimony of fact. But he shall add that, if they please, one of two courses shall be pursued. Either they shall decide then and there in consultation whether the evidence of any of the witnesses shall be rejected on the grounds of mortal personal enmity; or let them choose three or four or five persons who have most knowledge in that town or village of any friendship or enmity between the accused and the informer, who are not present at the consultation, and let them be informed of the names only of the accused and the witness, but not of the information which has been deposed, and let the whole question be left to their judgement. If they follow the former of these courses, they cannot very well reject any witness, since the Judge has already used his own methods of investigation; but by the second course he protects himself perfectly, and clears himself of all ugly suspicions. And he ought to observe this last method when the accused has been taken in a foreign town or country. These methods will suffice for examining the question of personal enmity.

☆

QUESTION XIII

Of the Points to be Observed by the Judge before the Formal Examination in the Place of Detention and Torture. This is the Eighth Action.

THE next action of the Judge is quite clear. For common justice demands that a witch should not be condemned to death unless she is convicted by her own confession. But here we are considering the case of one who is judged to be taken in manifest heresy for one of the other two reasons set down in the First Question, namely, direct or indirect evidence of the fact, or the legitimate production of witnesses; and in this case she is to be exposed to questions and torture to extort a confession of her crimes.

And to make the matter clear we will quote a case which occurred at Spires and came to the knowledge of many. A certain honest man was bargaining with a woman, and would not come to terms with her about the price of some article; so she angrily called after him, "You will soon wish you had agreed." For witches generally use this manner of speaking, or something like it, when they wish to bewitch a person by looking at him. Then he, not unreasonably being angry with her, looked over his shoulder to see with what intention she had uttered those words; and behold! he was suddenly bewitched so that his mouth was stretched sideways as far as his ears in a horrible deformity, and he could not draw it back, but remained so deformed for a long time.

We put the case that this was submitted to the Judge as direct evidence of the fact; and it is asked whether the woman is to be considered as manifestly taken in the heresy of witchcraft. This should be answered from the words of S. Bernard which we have quoted above. For there are three ways in which a person may be judged to be so taken, and they not so closely conjoined as though it were necessary for all three to agree in one conclusion, but each one by itself, namely, the evidence of the fact, or the legitimate production of witnesses, or her own confession, is sufficient to prove a witch to be manifestly taken in that heresy.

But indirect evidence of the fact is different from direct evidence; yet though it is not so conclusive, it is still taken from the words and deeds of witches, as was shown in the Seventh Question, and it is judged from witchcraft which is not so immediate in its effect, but follows after some lapse of time from the utterance of the threatening words. Wherefore may we conclude that this is the case with such witches who have been accused and have not

made good their defence (or have failed to defend themselves because this privilege was not granted them; and it was not granted because they did not ask for it). But what we are to consider now is what action the Judge should take, and how he should proceed to question the accused with a view to extorting the truth from her so that sentence of death may finally be passed upon her.

And here, because of the great trouble caused by the stubborn silence of witches, there are several points which the Judge must notice, and these are dealt with under their several heads.

And the first is that he must not be too quick to subject a witch to examination, but must pay attention to certain signs which will follow. And he must not be too quick for this reason: unless God, through a holy Angel, compels the devil to withhold his help from the witch, she will be so insensible to the pains of torture that she will sooner be torn limb from limb than confess any of the truth.

But the torture is not to be neglected for this reason, for they are not all equally endowed with this power, and also the devil sometimes of his own will permits them to confess their crimes without being compelled by a holy Angel. And for the understanding of this the reader is referred to that which is written in the Second Part of this work concerning the homage which they offer to the devil.

For there are some who obtain from the devil a respite of six or eight or ten years before they have to offer him their homage, that is, devote themselves to him body and soul; whereas others, when they first profess their abjuration of the faith, at the same time offer their homage. And the reason why the devil allows that stipulated interval of time is that, during that time, he may find out whether the witch has denied the faith with her lips only but not in her heart, and would therefore offer him her homage in the same way.

For the devil cannot know the inner thoughts of the heart except conjecturally from outward indications, as we showed in the First Part of this work where we dealt with the question whether devils can turn the minds of men to hatred or love. And many have been found who, driven by some necessity or poverty, have been induced by other witches, in the hope of ultimate forgiveness in confession, to become either total or partial apostates from the faith. And it is such whom the devil deserts without any compulsion by a holy Angel; and therefore they readily confess their crimes, whereas others, who have from their hearts bound themselves to the devil, are protected by his power and preserve a stubborn silence.

And this provides a clear answer to the question how it comes about that some witches readily confess, and others will by no means do so. For in the case of the former, when the devil is not compelled by God, he still deserts them of his own will, in order that by temporal unhappiness and a horrible death he may lead to despair those over whose hearts he could never obtain the mastery. For it is evident from their sacramental confessions that they have never voluntarily obeyed the devil, but have been compelled by him to work witchcraft.

And some also are distinguished by the fact that, after they have admitted their crimes, they try to commit suicide by strangling or hanging * themselves.

And they are induced to do this by the Enemy, lest they should obtain pardon from God through sacramental confession. This chiefly happens in the case of those who have not been willing agents of the devil; although it may also happen in the case of willing agents, after they have confessed their crimes: but then it is because the devil has been compelled to desert the witch.

In conclusion we may say that it is as difficult, or more difficult, to compel a witch to tell the truth as it is to exorcise a person possessed of the devil.

---

* *"Hanging." There are recorded many instances of this. In 1597 the Scotch warlock Playfair, having killed Lord Lothian by witchcraft, was laid for, and "being soon apprehended, was made prisoner in Dalkeith steeple, and having confest that and much more wickedness to Mr. Archibald Simson, minister there, and that confession coming to the ears of Robert, Earl of Lothian, my lord's son, he had moyen to get some persons admitted to speak with the prisoner in the night, by which means he was found worried in the morning, and the point of his breeches knit about his neck, but never more inquiry was made who had done the deed."*

Alice Gooderidge, a Derbyshire witch, who was tried in 1597 and condemned, "should haue bin executed, but that her spirit killed her in the prison." John Stewart, a warlock of Irvine, in 1618, "for his better preferring to the day of the assys, was put in ane lockfast buith, . . . and for avoyding of putting violent handis on himself, was verie strictly gairdit and flitherit be the airms, as us is." He was visited by two ministers, who exhorted him to repentance, and seemed very contrite, confessing his witchcrafts. However, almost immediately after "he was fund be the burrow officers, quha went about him stranglit and hangit be the cruik of the dur, with ane tait of hemp (or a string maid of hemp, supposed to haif been his garters, or string of his

bonnet) not above the length of two span long, his kneyis not being from the grund half ane span, and was brocht out of the hous, his lyf not being so layt expellit: but notwithstanding of quhatsomever meines usit to the contrair for remeid of his lyf, he revievit not, but so endit his lyf miserable by the help of the devill his maister." In 1649 the lady of Pittahro, Mistress Henderson, *"being delated by many to be a witch, was apprehended and carried to Edenbroughe, wher she was keiped fast; and after her remaining in prison for a tyme, being in health all night, vpon the morne was found dead. It was thought, and spoken by many, that she wronged her selfe, either by strangling or by poyson."*

It is recorded of the Renfrewshire trials (1697) that John Reid, a notorious warlock of Bargarran, "after his Confession had called out of his prison Window, desiring Baily Scott to keep that old body Angus Forrester, who had been his fellow prisoner, close and secure; whereupon the company asked John when they were leaving him on Friday night the 21st of May, whether he desired company or would be afraid alone, he said he had no fear of anything: So being left till Saturday in the Forenoon, he was found in this posture, viz. sitting upon a stool which was on the Hearth of the Chimney, with his feet on the floor and his Body straight upward, his shoulders touching the lintel of the Chimney, but his Neck tied with his own neck-cloath (whereof the knot was behind) to a small stick thrust into a hole above the lintel of the Chimney, upon which the Company, especially John Campbel a Chyrurgeon who was called, thought at first in respect of his being in an ordinary posture of sitting, and the neck-cloath not having any drawn knot (or " run loup ") but an ordinary one which was not very strait, and the sticke not having the strength to bear the weight of his Body or the struggle, that he had not been quite dead; but finding it otherways, and that he was in such a Situation that he could not have been the Actor thereof himself, concluded that some extraordinary Agent had done it, especially considering that the Door of the Room was secured, and that there was a board set over the Window which was not there the night before when they left him."

Therefore the Judge ought not to be too willing or ready to proceed to such examination, unless, as has been said, the death penalty is involved. And in this case he must exercise great care, as we shall show; and first we shall speak of the method of sentencing a witch to such torture.

☆

QUESTION XIV

Of the Method of Sentencing the Accused to be Questioned: and How she must be Questioned on the First Day; and Whether she may be Promised her Life. The Ninth Action.

SECONDLY, the Judge must take care to frame his sentence in the following manner.

We, the Judge and assessors, having attended to and considered the details of the process enacted by us against you N. of such a place in such a Diocese, and having diligently examined the whole matter, find that you are equivocal in your admissions; as for example, when you say that you used such threats with no intention of doing an injury, but nevertheless there are various proofs which are sufficient warrant for exposing you to the question and torture. Wherefore, that the truth may be known from your own mouth, and that henceforth you may not offend the ears of the Judges, we declare, judge and sentence that on this present day at such an hour you be placed under the question and torture. This sentence was given, etc.

Alternatively, as has been said, the Judge may not be willing to deliver the accused up to be questioned, but may punish her with imprisonment with the following object in view. Let him summon her friends and put it to them that she may escape the death penalty, although she will be punished in another way, if she confesses the truth, and urge them to try to persuade her to do so. For very often meditation, and the misery of imprisonment, and the repeated advice of honest men, dispose the accused to discover the truth.

And we have found that witches have been so strengthened by this sort of advice that, as a sign of their rebel-lion, they have spat on the ground as if it were in the devil's face, saying, "Depart, cursed devil; I shall do what is just"; and afterwards they have confessed their crimes.

But if, after keeping the accused in a state of suspense, and continually postponing the day of examination, and frequently using verbal persuasions, the Judge should truly believe that the accused is denying the truth, let them question her lightly without shedding blood; knowing that such questioning is fallacious and often, as has been said, ineffective.

And it should be begun in this way. While the officers are preparing for the questioning, let the accused be stripped; or if she is a woman, let her first be led to the penal cells and there stripped by honest women of good reputation. And the reason for this is that they should search for any instrument of witchcraft sewn into her clothes; for they often make such instruments, at the instruction of devils, out of the limbs of unbaptized children, the purpose being that those children should be deprived of the beatific vision. And when such instruments have been disposed of, the Judge shall use his own persuasions and those of other honest men zealous for the faith to induce her to confess the truth voluntarily; and if she will not, let him order the officers to bind her with cords, and apply her to some engine of torture; and then let them obey at once but not joyfully, rather appearing to be disturbed by their duty. Then let her be released again at someone's earnest request, and taken on one side, and let her again be persuaded; and in persuading her, let her be told that she can escape the death penalty.

Here it is asked whether, in the case of a prisoner legally convicted by her general bad reputation, by witnesses, and by the evidence of the fact, so that the only thing lacking is a confession of the crime from her own mouth, the Judge can lawfully promise her her life, whereas if she were to confess the crime she would suffer the extreme penalty.

We answer that different people have various opinions on this question. For some hold that if the accused is of a notoriously bad reputation, and gravely suspected on unequivocal evidence of the crime; and if she is herself a great source of danger, as being the mistress of other witches, then she may be promised her life on the following conditions: that she be sentenced to imprisonment for life on bread and water, provided that she supply evidence which will lead to the conviction of other witches. And she is not to be told, when she is promised her life, that she is to be imprisoned in this way; but should be led to suppose that some other penance, such as exile, will be imposed on her as punishment. And without doubt notorious witches, especially such as use witches' medicines and cure the bewitched by superstitious means, should be kept in this way, both that they may help the bewitched, and that they may betray other witches. But such a betrayal by them must not be considered of itself sufficient ground for a conviction, since the devil is a liar, unless it is also substantiated by the evidence of the fact, and by witnesses.

Others think that, after she has been consigned to prison in this way, the promise to spare her life should be kept for a time, but that after a certain period she should be burned.

A third opinion is that the Judge may safely promise the accused her life, but in such a way that he should afterwards disclaim the duty of passing sentence on her, deputing another Judge in his place.

There seems to be some advantage in pursuing the first of these courses on account of the benefit which may accrue from it to those who are bewitched; yet it is not lawful to use witchcraft to cure witchcraft, although (as was shown in the First and Introductory Question to this Third Part) the general opinion is that it is lawful to use vain and superstitious means to remove a spell. But use and experience and the variety of such cases will be of more value to Judges than any art or text-book; therefore this is a matter which should be left to the Judges. But it has certainly been very often found by experience that many would confess the truth if they were not held back by the fear of death.

But if neither threats nor such promises will induce her to confess the truth, then the officers must proceed with the sentence, and she must be examined, not in any new or exquisite manner, but in the usual way, lightly or heavily according as the nature of her crimes demands. And while she is being questioned about each several point, let her be often and frequently exposed to torture, beginning with the more gentle of them; for the Judge should not be too hasty to proceed to the graver kind. And while this is being done, let the Notary write all down, how she is tortured and what questions are asked and how she answers.

And note that, if she confesses under torture, she should then be taken to another place and questioned anew, so that she does not confess only under the stress of torture.

The next step of the Judge should be that, if after being fittingly tortured she refuses to confess the truth, he should have other engines of torture brought before her, and tell her that she will have to endure these if she does not confess. If then she is not induced by terror to confess, the torture must be continued on the second or third day, but not repeated at that present time unless there should be some fresh indication of its probable success.

Let the sentence be pronounced in her presence in the following manner: We the aforesaid Judge, as above, assign to you N. such a day for the continuation of your questioning, that the truth may be heard from your own mouth. And the Notary shall write all down in the process.

And during the interval before that assigned time the Judge himself or other honest men shall do all in their power to persuade her to confess the truth in the manner we have said, giving her, if it seems expedient to them, a promise that her life will be spared.

The Judge should also take care that during that interval there should always be guards with her, so that she is never left alone, for fear lest the devil will cause her to kill herself. But the devil himself knows better than anyone can set down in writing whether he will desert her of his own will, or be compelled to do so by God.

☆

QUESTION XV

Of the Continuing of the Torture, and of the Devices and Signs by which the Judge can Recognize a Witch; and how he ought to Protect himself from their Spells. Also how they are to be Shaved in those Parts where they use to Conceal their Devil's Masks and Tokens together with the due Setting Forth of Various Means of Overcoming their Obstinacy in Keeping Silence and Refusal to Confess. And it is the Tenth Action.

THE Judge should act as follows in the continuation of the torture. First he should bear in mind that, just as the same medicine is not applicable to all the members, but there are various and distinct salves for each several member, so not all heretics or those accused of heresy are to be subjected to the same method of questioning, examination and torture as to the charges laid against them; but various and different means are to be employed according to their various natures and persons. Now a surgeon cuts off rotten limbs; and mangy sheep are isolated from the healthy; but a prudent Judge will not consider it safe to bind himself down to one invariable rule in his method of dealing with a prisoner who is endowed with a witch's power of taciturnity, and whose silence he is unable to overcome. For if the sons of darkness were to become accustomed to one general rule they would provide means of evading it as a well-known snare set for their destruction.

Therefore a prudent and zealous Judge should seize his opportunity and choose his method of conducting his examination according to the answers or depositions of the witnesses, or as his own previous experience or native wit indicates to him, using the following precautions.

If he wishes to find out whether she is endowed with a witch's power of preserving silence, let him take note whether she is able to shed tears when standing in his presence, or when being tortured. For we are taught both by the words of worthy men of old and by our own experience that this is a most certain sign, and it has been found that even if she be urged and exhorted by solemn conjurations to shed tears, if she be a witch she will not be able to weep: although she will assume a tearful aspect and smear her cheeks and eyes with spittle to make it appear that she is weeping; wherefore she must be closely watched by the attendants.

In passing sentence the Judge or priest may use some such method as the following in conjuring her to true tears if she be innocent, or in restraining false tears. Let him place his hand on the head of the accused and say: I conjure you by the bitter tears shed on the Cross by our Saviour the Lord JESUS Christ for the salvation of the world, and by the burning tears poured in the evening hour over His wounds by the most glorious Virgin MARY, His Mother, and by all the tears* which have been shed here in this world by the Saints and Elect of God, from whose eyes He has now wiped away all tears, that if you be innocent you do now shed tears, but if you be guilty that you shall by no means do so. In the name of the Father, and of the Son, and of the Holy Ghost, Amen.

And it is found by experience that the more they are conjured the less are they able to weep, however hard they may try to do so, or smear their cheeks with spittle. Nevertheless it is possible that afterwards, in the absence of the Judge and not at the time or in the place of torture, they may be able to weep in the presence of their gaolers.

And as for the reason for a witch's inability to weep, it can be said that the grace of tears is one of the chief gifts allowed to the penitent; for S. Bernard tells us that the tears of the humble can penetrate to heaven and conquer the unconquerable. Therefore there can be no doubt that they are

---

* "Tears." *The beautiful devotion to the Sacred Tears of Our Lord is well known. The Premonstratensians have a Mass, "De Lacryma Christi," proper to the Order.*

Our Lady of Tears, Santa Maria delle Lagrime, is the Patroness of Spoleto. A picture of Our Lady, painted upon the wall of the house belonging to Diotallevio d'Antonio, which stood on the road from Spoleto to Trevi, was seen to shed tears in great abundance. Many graces and favours were obtained before the miraculous picture. A small chapel was erected on the spot in August, 1485, and Mass was daily offered therein. On 27 March, 1487, the large basilica was begun, which on its completion, 8 March, 1489, was entrusted to the Olivetans.

displeasing to the devil, and that he uses all his endeavour to restrain them, to prevent a witch from finally attaining to penitence.

But it may be objected that it might suit with the devil's cunning, with God's permission, to allow even a witch to weep; since tearful grieving, weaving and deceiving are said to be proper to women. We may answer that in this case, since the judgements of God are a mystery, if there is no other way of convicting the accused, by legitimate witnesses or the evidence of the fact, and if she is not under a strong or grave suspicion, she is to be discharged; but because she rests under a slight suspicion by reason of her reputation to which the witnesses have testified, she must be required to abjure the heresy of witchcraft, as we shall show when we deal with the second method of pronouncing sentence.

A second precaution is to be observed, not only at this point but during the whole process, by the Judge and all his assessors; namely, that they must not allow themselves to be touched physically by the witch, especially in any contact of their bare arms or hands; but they must always carry about them some salt consecrated on Palm Sunday and some Blessed Herbs. For these can be enclosed together in Blessed Wax* and worn round the neck, as we showed in the Second Part when we discussed the remedies against illnesses and diseases caused by witchcraft; and that these have a wonderful protective virtue is known not only from the testimony of witches, but from the use and practice of the Church, which exorcizes and blesses such objects for this very purpose, as is shown in the ceremony of exorcism when it is said, For the banishing of all the power of the devil, etc.

But let it not be thought that physical contact of the joints or limbs is the only thing to be guarded against; for sometimes, with God's permission, they are able with the help of the devil to bewitch the Judge by the mere sound of the words which they utter, especially

at the time when they are exposed to torture.

And we know from experience that some witches, when detained in prison, have importunately begged their gaolers to grant them this one thing, that they should be allowed to look at the Judge before he looks at them; and by so getting the first sight of the Judge they have been able so to alter the minds of the Judge or his assessors that they have lost all their anger against them and have not presumed to molest them in any way, but have allowed them to go free. He who knows and has experienced it gives this true testimony; and would that they were not able to effect such things!

Let judges not despise such precautions and protections, for by holding them in little account after such warning they run the risk of eternal damnation. For our Saviour said: If I had not come, and spoken to them, they would not have sin; but now they have no excuse for their sin.† Therefore let the judges protect themselves in the above manner, according to the provisions of the Church.

And if it can conveniently be done, the witch should be led backward into the presence of the Judge and his assessors. And not only at the present point, but in all that has preceded or shall follow it, let him cross himself and approach her manfully, and with God's help the power of that old Serpent will be broken. And no one need think that it is superstitious to lead her in backwards; for, as we have often said, the Canonists allow even more than this to be done for the protection against witchcraft, and always say that it is lawful to oppose vanity with vanity.

The third precaution to be observed in this tenth action is that the hair should be shaved from every part of her body. The reason for this is the same as that for stripping her of her clothes, which we have already mentioned; for in order to preserve their power of silence they are in the habit of hiding some superstitious object in their clothes or in their hair, or even in the most secret parts of their bodies which must not be named.

But it may be objected that the devil might, without the use of such charms, so harden the heart of a witch

---

* *"Blessed Wax." The "Agnus Dei," which is a disc of wax, stamped with the figure of a Lamb, and on certain stated days blessed by the Holy Father. These Agnus Deis may either be worn suspended round the neck, or preserved as objects of devotion. They are to be regarded as Sacramentals.*

† *"Sin." "S. John" xv, 22.*

that she is unable to confess her crimes; just as it is often found in the case of other criminals, no matter how great the tortures to which they are exposed, or how much they are convicted by the evidence of the facts and of witnesses. We answer that it is true that the devil can effect such taciturnity without the use of such charms; but he prefers to use them for the perdition of souls and the greater offence to the Divine Majesty of God.

This can be made clear from the example of a certain witch in the town of Hagenau, whom we have mentioned in the Second Part of this work. She used to obtain this gift of silence* in the following manner: she killed a newly-born first-born male child who had not been baptized, and having roasted it in an oven together with other matters which it is not expedient to mention, ground it to powder and ashes; and if any witch or criminal carried about him some of this substance he would in no way be able to confess his crimes.

Here it is clear that a hundred thousand children so employed could not of their own virtue endow a person with such a power of keeping silence; but any intelligent person can understand that such means are used by the devil for the perdition of souls and to offend the Divine Majesty.

Again, it may be objected that very often criminals who are not witches exhibit the same power of keeping silence. In answer to this it must be said that this power of taciturnity can proceed from three causes. First, from a natural hardness of heart; for some are soft-hearted, or even feeble-minded, so that at the slightest torture they admit everything, even some things which are not true; whereas others are so hard that however much they are tortured the truth is not to be had from them; and this is especially the case with those who have been tortured before, even if their arms are suddenly stretched and twisted.

Secondly, it may proceed from some instrument of witchcraft carried about the person, as has been said, either in the clothes or in the hairs of the body. And thirdly, even if the prisoner has no such object secreted about her person, they are sometimes endowed with this power by other witches, however far they may be removed from them. For a certain witch at Issbrug used to boast that, if she had no more than a thread from the garments of any prisoner, she could so work that however much that prisoner were tortured, even to death, she would be unable to confess anything. So the answer to this objection is clear.

But what is to be said of a case that happened in the Diocese of Ratisbon? Certain heretics were convicted by their own confession not only as impenitent but as open advocates of that perfidy; and when they were condemned to death it happened that they remained unharmed in the fire. At length their sentence was altered to death by drowning, but this was no more effective. All were astonished, and some even began to say that their heresy must be true; and the Bishop, in great anxiety for his flock, ordered a three days' fast. When this had been devoutly fulfilled, it came to the knowledge of someone that those heretics had a magic charm sewed between the skin and the flesh under one arm; and when this was found and removed, they were delivered to the flames and immediately burned. Some say that a certain necromancer learned this secret during a consultation with a devil, and betrayed it; but however it became known, it is probable that the devil, who is always scheming for the subversion of the faith, was in some way compelled by Divine power to reveal the matter.

From this it may be seen what a Judge ought to do when such a case happens to him: namely, that he should rely upon the protection of God, and by the prayers and fasting of devout

---

* *"Gift of Silence."* De Lancre, *"Tableau de l'inconstance des mauvais anges et démons,"* Paris, 1612, has: *"Pour ne confesser iamais le secret de l'escole, on faict au sabbat vne paste de millet noir, auec de la poudre du foyer de quelque enfant non baptisé qu'on faict secher, puis meslant cette poudre auec ladicte paste, elle a cette vertu de taciturnité; si bien que qui en mange ne confesse iamais."* Five Forfar witches, of which one was Helen Guthrie, in 1661 dug up the body of an unbaptized infant, which was buried in the churchyard near the south-east door of the church "and took severall peices thereof, as the feet, hands, pairt of the head, and a pairt of the buttocks, and they made a py thereof, that they might eat of it, that by this meanes they might never make a confession (as they thought) of their witchcraft."

persons drive away this sort of devil's work from witches, in those cases where they cannot be made to confess under torture even after their clothes have been changed and all their hair has been shaved off and abraded.

Now in the parts of Germany such shaving, especially of the secret parts, is not generally considered delicate, and therefore wê Inquisitors do not use it; but we cause the hair of their head to be cut off, and placing a morsel of Blessed Wax in a cup of Holy Water and invoking the most Holy Trinity, we give it them to drink three times on a fasting stomach, and by the grace of God we have by this means caused many to break their silence. But in other countries the Inquisitors order the witch to be shaved all over her body. And the Inquisitor of Como has informed us that last year, that is, in 1485, he ordered forty-one witches to be burned, after they had been shaved all over. And this was in the district and county of Burbia, commonly called Wormserbad, in the territory of the Archduke of Austria, towards Milan.

But it may be asked whether, in a time of need, when all other means of breaking a witch's silence have failed, it would be lawful to ask the advice in this matter of sorceresses who are able to cure those who are bewitched. We answer that, whatever may have been done in that matter at Ratisbon, it is our earnest admonition in the Lord that no one, no matter how great may be the need, should consult with sorceresses on behalf of the State; and this because of the great offence which is thereby caused to the Divine Majesty, when there are so many other means open to us which we may use either in their own proper form or in some equivalent form, so that the truth will be had from their own mouths and they can be consigned to the flames; or failing this, God will in the meantime provide some other death for the witch.

For there remain to us the following remedies against this power of silence. First, let a man do all that lies in his own power by the exercise of his own qualities, persisting often with the methods we have already mentioned, and especially on certain days, as will be shown in the following Question. See II. Corinthians ix: That ye may abound in all good works.

Secondly, if this should fail, let him consult with other persons; for perhaps they may think of some means which has not occurred to him, since there are various methods of counteracting witchcraft.

Thirdly, if these two fail, let him have recourse to devout persons, as it is said in Ecclesiasticus xxxvii: Be continually with a godly man, whom thou knowest to keep the commandments of the Lord. Also let him invoke the Patron Saints of the country. But if all these fail, let the Judge and all the people at once put their trust in God with prayers and fasting, that the witchcraft may be removed by reason of their piety. For so Josaphat prayed in II. Paralipomenon xx: When we know not what we should do, we have this one refuge, that we should turn our eyes to Thee. And without doubt God will not fail us in our need.

To this effect also S. Augustine speaks (26, q. 7, non obseruabitis): Whosoever observes any divinations or auguries, or attends to or consents to such as observe them, or gives credit to such by following after their works, or goes into their houses, or introduces them into his own house, or asks questions of them, let him know that he has perverted the Christian faith and his baptism and is a pagan and apostate and enemy of God, and runs grave danger of the eternal wrath of God, unless he is corrected by ecclesiastical penances and is reconciled with God. Therefore let the Judge not fail always to use the lawful remedies, as we have said, together with these following final precautions.

✫

QUESTION XVI

Of the fit Time and of the Method of the Second Examination. And it is the Eleventh Action, concerning the Final Precautions to be Observed by the Judge.

THERE are one or two points to be noted with regard to what we have just written. First, that witches should be questioned on the more Holy Days and during the solemnization of the Mass, and that the people should be exhorted to pray for Divine help, not in any specific manner, but that they should invoke the prayers of the Saints against all the plagues of the devil.

Secondly, as we have said before, the Judge should wear round his neck Consecrated Salt and other matters, with the Seven Words which Christ uttered on the Cross written in a schedule, and all bound together. And he should, if he conveniently can, wear these made into the length of Christ's stature against his naked body, and bind other Holy things about him. For it is shown by experience that witches are greatly troubled by these things, and can hardly refrain from confessing the truth. The Relics of the Saints, too, are of especial virtue.

Having taken these precautions, and after giving her Holy Water to drink, let him again begin to question her, all the time exhorting her as before. And while she is raised from the ground, if she is being tortured in this way, let the Judge read or cause to be read to her the depositions of the witnesses with their names, saying: "See! You are convicted by the witnesses." Also, if the witnesses are willing to confront her face to face, the Judge shall ask her if she will confess if the witnesses are brought before her. And if she consents, let the witnesses be brought in and stand before her, so that she may be constrained or shamed into confessing some of her crimes.

Finally, if he sees that she will not admit her crimes, he shall ask her whether, to prove her innocence, she is ready to undergo the ordeal by red-hot iron. And they all desire this, knowing that the devil will prevent them from being hurt; therefore a true witch is exposed in this manner. The Judge shall ask her how she can be so rash as to run so great a risk, and all shall be written down; but it will be shown later that they are never to be allowed to undergo this ordeal by red-hot iron.

Let the Judge also note that when witches are questioned on a Friday, while the people are gathered together at Holy Mass to await our Saviour, they very often confess.

But we must proceed to the extreme case, when after every expedient has been tried the witch still maintains silence. The Judge shall then loose her and, using the precautions which follow, shall take her from the place of punishment to another place under a strong guard; but let him take particular care not to release her on any sort of security; for when that is done, they never

confess the truth, but always become worse.

But in the first place let him cause her to be well treated in the matter of food and drink, and meanwhile let honest persons who are under no suspicion enter to her and talk often with her on indifferent subjects, and finally advise her in confidence to confess the truth, promising that the Judge will be merciful to her and that they will intercede for her. And finally let the Judge come in and promise that he will be merciful, with the mental reservation that he means he will be merciful to himself or the State; for whatever is done for the safety of the State is merciful.

But if he promises her her life, as we showed in Question XIV that he can do in three ways, let it all be written down by the Notary in what words and with what intention mercy was promised. And if the accused begs for mercy in this way, and discovers her crime, let her be promised in a vague and general way that she will receive even more than she has petitioned for, so that she may speak with the greater confidence.

As a second precaution in this case, when she refuses altogether to reveal the truth, the Judge should, as we have said before, examine her friends and associates without her knowledge; and if these have deposed anything which might lead to her conviction, this must be diligently investigated. Also, if any instruments or unguents or boxes have been found in her house, they should be shown to her, and she should be asked for what purpose they have been used.

A third precaution can be taken when she still persists in her obstinacy after her associates have been examined and borne witness against her, and not for her. If she has no friends, let some other trustworthy man who is known to be congenial to the accused and to some extent a patron of hers, enter to the witch one evening and engage her in a protracted conversation. And then, if he is not an accomplice, let him pretend that it is too late for him to return, and stay in the prison with her, and continue talking during the night. And if he is an accomplice, let them eat and drink together, and talk to each other about the things they have done. And then let it be arranged that spies should stand outside in a convenient place, and listen to them and take note of their words, and if necessary let them have a scribe with them.

As a fourth precaution, if she then begins to tell the truth, let the Judge on no account postpone hearing her confession, even in the middle of the night, but proceed with it to the best of his ability. And if it is in the day-time, let him not care if he delays his luncheon or dinner, but persist until she has told the truth, at least in the main. For it is generally found that, after postponements and interruptions, they return* to their vomit and will not reveal the truth which they began to confess, having thought worse of it.

And let the Judge take note that, after she has confessed the injuries done to men and animals, he shall ask her for how many years she has had an Incubus devil, and how long it is since she abjured the faith. For they never confess to these matters unless they have first confessed their other deeds; therefore they must be asked concerning these last of all.

As a fifth precaution, when all the above have failed, let her, if possible, be led to some castle; and after she has been kept there under custody for some days, let the castellan pretend that he is going on a long journey. And then let some of his household, or even some honest women, visit her and promise that they will set her entirely at liberty if she will teach them how to conduct certain practices. And let the Judge take note that by this means they have very often confessed and been convicted.

Quite lately a witch was detained in the Castle of Königsheim near the town of Schlettstadt in the Diocese of Strasburg, and could not be induced by any tortures or questions to confess her crimes. But at last the castellan used the method we have just described. Although he was himself present in the castle, the witch thought he was away, and three of his household came in to her and promised they would set her free if she would teach them how to do certain things. At first she refused, saying that they were trying to entrap her; but at last she asked what it was that they wanted to know. And one asked how to raise a hailstorm, and another asked about carnal matters. When at length she agreed to show him how to raise a hailstorm, and a bowl of water had been brought in, the witch told him to stir the water a little with his finger, and herself uttered certain words; and suddenly the place which he had named, a wood near the castle, was visited by such a tempest and storm of hail as had not been seen for many years.

It yet remains to show how the Judge is to proceed in pronouncing sentence in a case where all these means have failed, or what is further to be done even when she has confessed her crimes, that the whole process may be brought to an end; and we shall complete this Last Part of this work with a consideration of these matters.

☆

THE THIRD HEAD

Which is the Last Part of the Work: How the Process is to be Concluded by the Pronouncement of a Definite and Just Sentence.

HAVING by the grace of God examined the proper means of arriving at a knowledge of the heresy of witchcraft, and having shown how the process on behalf of the faith should be initiated and proceeded with, it remains to discuss how that process is to be brought to a fitting termination with an appropriate sentence.

Here it is to be noted that this heresy, as was shown in the beginning of this Last Part, is not to be confused with other simple heresies, since it is obvious that it is not a pure and single crime, but partly ecclesiastical and partly civil. Therefore in dealing with the methods of passing sentence, we must first consider a certain kind of sentence to which witches are in the habit of appealing, in which the secular judge can act on his own account independently of the Ordinary. Secondly, we shall consider those in which he cannot act without the Ordinary. And so thirdly it will be shown how the Ordinaries can discharge themselves of their duties.

---

* *"They Return."* *"Proverbs"* xxvi, 11: "As a dog that returneth to his vomit, so is the fool that repeateth his folly." II. S. Peter, ii, 22: "For, that of the true proverb has happened to them: the dog is returned to his vomit: and, The sow that was washed, to her wallowing in the mire."

QUESTION XVII

Of Common Purgation, and especially of the Trial by Red-hot Iron, to which Witches Appeal.

THE question is now asked whether the secular judge may allow a witch to be submitted to a common purgation (concerning which see the Canon 2, q. 4, *consuluisti*, and cap. *monomachiam*), in the manner in which a civil defendant is allowed the trial by ordeal, as, for example, that by red-hot iron. And it may seem that he may do so.

For trial by combat is allowable in a criminal case for the protection of life, and in a civil case for the protection of property; then wherefore not the trial by red-hot iron or boiling water? S. Thomas allows that the former is permissible in some cases, when he says in the last article of the *Second of the Second*, q. 95, that a duel is lawful when it appears to be consonant with common-sense. Therefore the trial by red-hot iron should also be lawful in some cases.

Also it has been used by many Princes of saintly life who have availed themselves of the advice and counsel of good men; as, for example, the Sainted Emperor Henry* in the case of the virgin Cunegond whom he had married, who was suspected of adultery.

Again, a judge, who is responsible

for the safety of the community, may lawfully allow a smaller evil that a greater may be avoided; as he allows the existence of harlots in towns in order to avoid a general confusion of lust. For S. Augustine *On Free Will*† says: Take away the harlots, and you will create a general chaos and confusion of lust. So, when a person has been loaded with insults and injuries by any community, he can clear himself of any criminal or civil charge by means of a trial by ordeal.

Also, since less hurt is caused to the hands by the red-hot iron than is the loss of life in a duel, if a duel is permitted where such things are customary, much more should the trial by red-hot iron be allowed.

But the contrary view is argued where it says (2, q. 5, *monomachiam*) that they who practise such and similar things appear to be tempting God. And here the Doctors affirm it must be noted that, according to S. Paul (I. *Thessalonians* v), we must abstain, not only from evil, but from all appearance of evil. Therefore the Canon says in that chapter, not that they who use such practices tempt God, but that they appear to tempt Him, so that it may be understood that, even if a man engage in such a trial with none but good intentions, yet since it has the appearance of evil, it is to be avoided.

I answer that such tests or trials are unlawful for two reasons. First, because their purpose is to judge of hidden matters of which it belongs only to God to judge. Secondly, because there is no Divine authority for such trials, nor are they anywhere sanctioned in the writings of the Holy Fathers. And it says in the chapter *consuluisti*, 2, q. 5: That which is not sanctioned in the writings of the Sainted Fathers is to be presumed superstitious. And Pope Stephen‡ in the same chapter says: It is left to your judgement to try prisoners who are convicted by their own confession or the

---

* "*Henry.*" *S. Henry II, German King and Roman Emperor, was born 972, and died in his palace of Grona, at Göttingen, 13 July, 1024. He was canonized in 1146 by Eugenius III; and his wife Cunegond on 3 March, 1200, by Innocent III. Later writers are inclined to believe that the ascetic theme of his maiden marriage has no foundation in fact. Saint Henry on assuming the Imperial dignity took to wife Cunegond, daughter of Siegfried, Count of Luxemburg. It has been beautifully said that she shares her husband's celestial, as she shared his earthly crown. When scandalous reports were circulated concerning her honour, although her husband could not for a moment suspect her purity, she insisted upon an appeal to the trial by ordeal, and having walked unhurt over the red-hot plough-shares, publicly testified her innocence. The story is immensely popular in German poetry and German art. A print by Hans Burgkmair shows her stepping over the shares, one of which she holds in her hand. Upon her shrine in the Cathedral at Bamburg a bas-relief by Hans Thielmann of Warzburg depicts the same incident. Having already retired to a Benedictine cloister, upon the death of her husband S. Cunegond took the veil.*

† "*On Free Will.*" *S. Augustine's "De Gratia et libero Arbitrio" was written 426–27. It will be found in Migne, "Patres Latini," xliv, pp. 881–912.*

‡ "*Pope Stephen.*" *Stephen (IX) X, elected 3 August, 1057; died at Florence, 29 March, 1058. He was buried in the church of S. Reparata. He was distinguished for his learning and even during the few short months of his Pontificate he showed himself a zealous reformer.*

proofs of the evidence; but leave that which is hidden and unknown to Him Who alone knows the hearts of men.

There is, nevertheless, a difference between a duel and the trial by red-hot iron or boiling water. For a duel appears to be more humanly reasonable, the combatants being of similar strength and skill, than a trial by red-hot iron. For although the purpose of both is to search out something hidden by means of a human act; yet in the case of trial by red-hot iron a miraculous effect is looked for, whereas this is not so in the case of a duel, in which all that can happen is the death of either, or both, of the combatants. Therefore the trial by red-hot iron is altogether unlawful; though a duel is not illegal to the same extent. So much has been incidentally admitted in respect of duels, on account of Princes and secular Judges.

It is to be noted that, because of those words of S. Thomas which make the above distinction, Nicolas of Lyra, in his Commentary on the duel or combat between David and Goliath, I. *Regum* xvii, tries to prove that in some cases a duel is lawful. But Paul of Burgos proves that not this, but rather the opposite was the meaning of S. Thomas; and all Princes and secular Judges ought to pay particular attention to his proof.

His first point is that a duel, like the other trial by ordeal, has as its purpose the judgement of something hidden, which ought to be left to the judgement of God, as we have said. And it cannot be said that this combat of David is an authority for duelling; for it was revealed to him by the Lord through some inner instinct that he must engage in that combat and avenge upon the Philistine the injuries done against God, as is proved by David's words: I come against thee in the name of the living God. So he was not properly speaking a duellist, but he was an executor of Divine justice.

His second point is that Judges must especially note that in a duel power, or at least licence, is given to each of the parties to kill the other. But since one of them is innocent, that power or licence is given for the killing of an innocent man; and this is unlawful, as being contrary to the dictates of natural law and to the teaching of God. Therefore a duel is altogether unlawful, not only on the part of the appellant and

the respondent, but also on the part of the Judge and his advisers, who are all equally to be considered homicides or parties to manslaughter.

Thirdly, he points out that a duel is a single combat between two men, the purpose of which is that the justice of the case should be made clear by the victory of one party, as if by Divine judgement, notwithstanding the fact that one of the parties is fighting in an unjust cause; and in this way God is tempted. Therefore it is unlawful on the part both of the appellant and the respondent. But considering the fact that the judges have other means of arriving at an equitable and just termination of the dispute, when they do not use such means, but advise or even permit a duel when they could forbid it, they are consenting to the death of an innocent person.

But since it is unlikely that Nicolas the Commentator was unaware or ignorant of the above reasoning, it is concluded that, when he says that in some cases a duel can be fought without mortal sin, he is speaking on the part of the Judges or advisers, namely, in a case when such a trial is undertaken, not on their responsibility or advice, but purely on that of the appellant and respondent themselves.

But since it is not our purpose to linger over and debate such considerations, but to return to the question of witches, it is clear that, if this sort of trial is forbidden in the case of other criminal causes, such as theft or robbery, still more must it be forbidden in the case of witches, who, it is agreed, obtain all their power from the devil, whether it be for causing or curing an injury, for removing or for preventing an effect of witchcraft.

And it is not wonderful that witches are able to undergo this trial by ordeal unscathed with the help of devils; for we learn from naturalists that if the hands be anointed with the juice of a certain herb they are protected from burning. Now the devil has an exact knowledge of the virtues of such herbs: therefore, although he can cause the hand of the accused to be protected from the red-hot iron by invisibly interposing some other substance, yet he can procure the same effect by the use of natural objects. Hence even less than other criminals ought witches to be allowed this trial by ordeal, because of their intimate familiarity with the devil; and from the very fact of their appealing to this trial they are to be held as suspected witches.

An incident illustrative of our argument occurred hardly three years ago in the Diocese of Constance. For in the territory of the Counts of Fürstenberg and the Black Forest there was a notorious witch who had been the subject of much public complaint. At last, as the result of a general demand, she was seized by the Count and accused of various evil works of witchcraft. When she was being tortured and questioned, wishing to escape from their hands, she appealed to the trial by red-hot iron; and the Count, being young and inexperienced, allowed it. And she then carried the red-hot iron not only for the stipulated three paces, but for six, and offered to carry it even farther. Then, although they ought to have taken this as a manifest proof that she was a witch (since none of the Saints dared to tempt the help of God in this manner), she was released from her chains and lives to the present time, not without grave scandal to the Faith in those parts.

✫

QUESTION XVIII

Of the Manner of Pronouncing a Sentence which is Final and Definitive.

IN proceeding to treat of those cases in which the secular Judge by himself can arrive at a judgement and pronounce sentence without the co-operation of the Diocesan and Ordinaries, we necessarily presuppose that not only is it consistent with the protection of the faith and of justice that we Inquisitors should be relieved of the duty of passing sentence in these cases, but in the same sincerity of spirit we endeavour to relieve the Diocesans also from that duty; not in any desire to detract from their authority and jurisdiction, for if they should elect to exercise their authority in such matters, it would follow that we Inquisitors must also concur in it.

It must be remembered, also, that this crime of witches is not purely ecclesiastic; therefore the temporal potentates and Lords are not debarred from trying and judging it. At the same time

we shall show that in some cases they must not arrive at a definitive judgement without the authorisation of the Diocesans.

But first we must consider the sentence itself: secondly, the nature of its pronouncement; and thirdly, in how many ways it is to be pronounced.

With regard to the first of these questions, S. Augustine says that we must not pronounce sentence against any person unless he has been proved guilty, or has confessed. Now there are three kinds of sentence—interlocutory, definitive, and preceptive. These are explained as follows by S. Raymund. An interlocutory sentence is one which is given not on the main issue of the case but on some other side issues which emerge during the hearing of a case; such as a decision whether or not a witness is to be disallowed, or whether some digression is to be admitted, and such matters as that. Or it may perhaps be called interlocutory because it is delivered simply by word of mouth without the formality of putting it in writing.

A definitive sentence is one which pronounces a final decision as to the main issue of the case.

A preceptive sentence is one which is pronounced by a lower authority on the instruction of a higher. But we shall be concerned with the first two of these, and especially with the definitive sentence.

Now it is laid down by law that a definitive sentence which has been arrived at without a due observance of the proper legal procedure in trying a case is null and void in law; and the legal conduct of a case consists in two things. One concerns the basis of the judgement; for there must be a due provision for the hearing of arguments both for the prosecution and the defence, and a sentence arrived at without such a hearing cannot stand. The other is not concerned with the basis of the judgement, but provides that the sentence must not be conditional; for example, a claim for possession should not be decided conditionally upon some subsequent claim of property; but where there is no question of such an objection the sentence shall stand.

But in the case we are considering, which is a process on behalf of the faith against a charge of heresy (though the charge is a mixed one), the procedure is straightforward and summary. That is to say, the Judge need not require a writ, or demand that the case should be contested. But he must allow opportunity for the necessary proofs, and issue his citation, and exact the protestation of the oath concerning calumny, etc. Therefore there has lately been a new law made as to the method of procedure in such cases.

To proceed to our second consideration, namely, of the nature of the pronouncement of the sentence, it must be noted that it should be pronounced by the Judge and no one else, otherwise it is not valid. Also the Judge must be sitting in a public and honourable place; and he must pronounce it in the day-time and not in the darkness; and there are other conditions to be observed; for example, the sentence must not be promulgated upon a Holy Day, nor yet merely delivered in writing.

Yet it is to be noted that since, as we have said, this case is conducted in a simple and summary manner, it may lawfully be conducted on Holy Days for the sake of the convenience of the public, and the Judge may cut short any digressions. Therefore the Judge may, if he pleases, act in such a manner, and even pass sentence without putting it in writing. For we are authoritatively informed that there are cases in which a sentence is valid without its being put into writing, as, for example, when such is the custom of any particular locality or Court. Also there is excellent precedent for a Bishop, when he is the Judge, allowing the sentence to be pronounced by some other person.

Note again that, although in criminal actions the execution of the sentence is not to be delayed, this rule does not hold good in four cases, with two of which we are here concerned. First, when the prisoner is a pregnant woman; and then the sentence shall be delayed until she has given birth. Secondly, when the prisoner has confessed her crime, but has afterwards denied it again: that is to say, when the confession has not been repeated in the way which we explained in the Fourteenth Question.

Now before we proceed to our third consideration, namely, the different methods of passing sentence which we shall proceed to treat of up to the end of this work, we must first make some remarks about the various ways in which a prisoner is rendered suspect,

from which the various methods of passing sentence follow as a consequence.

✩

QUESTION XIX

Of the Various Degrees of Overt Suspicion which render the Accused liable to be Sentenced.

BOTH the old and the new legislature provide an answer to the question as to in how many and what ways a person can be held suspect of heresy or any other crime, and whether they can be judged and sentenced by reason of such suspicions. For the gloss on the chapter *nos in quemquam*, which we quoted in the last Question, says that there are four means of convicting a prisoner: either by the depositions of witnesses in Court, or by the evidence of the facts, or by reason of previous convictions · against the prisoner, or because of a grave suspicion.

And the Canonists note that suspicion is of three kinds. The first, of which the Canon says, "You shall not judge anyone because he is suspect in your own opinion." The second is Probable; and this, but not the first, leads to a purgation. The third is Grave, and leads to a conviction; and S. Jerome understands this kind of suspicion when he says that a wife may be divorced either for fornication or for a reasonably suspected fornication.

It must further be noted that the second, or highly probable and circumstantial, suspicion is admitted as a kind of half-proof; that is to say, it helps to substantiate other proofs. Therefore it can also lead to a judgement, and not only to a purgation. And as for the grave suspicion, which suffices for a conviction, note that it is of two kinds. One is of the law and by the law, as when the law fixes and determines some point against which no proof can be admitted. For example, if a man has given a woman a promise of matrimony, and copulation has ensued, then matrimony is presumed, and no proof to the contrary is admitted. The second is of the law but not by the law, as where the law presumes but does not determine a fact. For example, if a man has lived for a long time with a woman, she is presumed to have had connexion with him; but against this proofs are admitted.

Applying this to our discussion of the heresy of witches and to the modern laws, we say that in law there are three degrees of suspicion in the matter of heresy: the first slight, the second great, and the third very great.

The first is in law called a light suspicion. Of this it is said in the chapter *Accusatus, de Haeret.* lib. 6: If the accused has incurred only a light and small suspicion, and if she should again fall under that suspicion, although she is to be severely punished for this, she ought not to suffer the punishment of those who have relapsed into heresy. And this suspicion is called small or light, both because it can be removed by a small and light defence, and because it arises from small and light conjectures. Therefore it is called small, because of the small proofs of it; and light, because of the light conjectures.

As an example of simple heresy, if people are found to be meeting together secretly for the purpose of worship, or differing in their manner of life and behaviour from the usual habits of the faithful; or if they meet together in sheds and barns, or at the more Holy Seasons in the remoter fields or woods, by day or by night, or are in any way found to separate themselves and not to attend Mass at the usual times or in the usual manner, or form secret friendships with suspected witches: such people incur at least a light suspicion of heresy, because it is proved that heretics often act in this manner. And of this light suspicion the Canon says: They who are by a slight argument discovered to have deviated from the teaching and path of the Catholic religion are not to be classed as heretics, nor is a sentence to be pronounced against them.

Henry of Segusio agrees with this in his *Summa; de Praesumptione,* where he says: It is to be noted that although a heretic be convicted by a slight argument of that matter of which he is suspected, he is not on that account to be considered a heretic; and he proves it by the above reasoning.

The second or grave suspicion is in law called grave or vehement, and of this the above Canon (*Accusatus*) again says: One who is accused or suspected of heresy, against whom a grave or vehement suspicion of this crime has arisen, etc. And it goes on: And these

are not two kinds but the same kind of suspicion. Giovanni d'Andrea also says: Vehement is the same as strong, as the Archdeacon says speaking of this Canon. Also Bernardus Papiensis* and Huguccio† say that vehement is the same as strong or great. S. Gregory also, in the First Book of his *Morals,* says: A vehement wind sprang up. Therefore we say that anyone has a vehement case when he has a strong one. So much for this.

Therefore a great suspicion is called vehement or strong; and it is so called because it is dispelled only by a vehement and strong defence, and because it arises from great, vehement, and strong conjectures, arguments, and evidence. As, to take an example of simple heresy, when people are found to shelter known heretics, and show favour to them, or visit and associate with them and give gifts to them, receive them into their houses and protect them, and such like: such people are vehemently suspected of heresy. And similarly in the heresy of witches, they are brought under suspicion when they share in the crimes of witches.

And here are especially to be noted those men or women who cherish some inordinate love or excessive hatred, even if they do not use to work any

---

* "*Papiensis.*" Bernardus Papiensis, a famous and prolific Italian canonist of the thirteenth century, who died 18 September, 1213. He was born at Pavia, studied law and theology at Bologna, was provost of the Cathedral of Pavia until 1191, Bishop of Faenza until 1198, and then Bishop of Pavia until his death. The most celebrated of his many works is the "*Breuiarium extrauagantium*" (later called "*Compilatio prima antiqua*"), a collection of canonical texts comprising ancient canons not inserted in the "*Decretum*" of Gratian, as also various later documents. The work was compiled between 1187 and 1191, and was edited by Friedberg, "*Quinque compilationes antiquae,*" Leipzig, 1882.

† "*Huguccio.*" Hugh of Pisa, a distinguished Italian canonist, who died in 1210. He was born at Pisa, but the date is unknown. He studied at Bologna, where later he professed Canon Law. In 1190 he became Bishop of Ferrara. Among his works are a "*Liber deriuationum*" which treats of etymology. He also wrote a "*Summa*" on the "*Decretum*" of Gratian, which has been considered the most extensive and one of the most valuable commentaries of the time. There are, however, certain omissions, but these gaps were filled by the industry of Joannes de Deo.

harm against men or animals in other ways. For, as we have said, those who behave in this way in any heresy are strongly to be suspected. And this is shown by the Canon where it says that there is no doubt that such persons act in this way out of some heretical sympathy.

The third and greatest suspicion is in law called grave or violent: for the Canon and the glosses of the Archdeacon and Giovanni d'Andrea explain that the word vehement does not mean the same as the word violent. And of this suspicion the Canon says (dist. 34) : This presumption or suspicion is called violent because it violently constrains and compels a Judge to believe it, and cannot be cast off by any evasion; and also because it arises from violent and convincing conjectures.

For example, in simple heresy, if persons are found to show a reverent love for heretics, to receive consolation or communion from them, or perpetrate any other such matter in accordance with their rites and ceremonies: such persons would fall under and be convicted of a violent suspicion of heresy and heretical beliefs. (See many chapters on this subject in Book VI of the Canon.) For there is no doubt that such persons act in this way out of a belief in some heresy.

It is the same, as regards the heresy of witches, with those who perform and persist in performing any of the actions which pertain to the rites of witches. Now these are of various kinds. Sometimes it is only some threatening speech, such as "You shall soon feel what will happen to you," or something similar. Sometimes it is a touch, just laying their hands curiously on a man or a beast. Sometimes it is only a matter of being seen, when they show themselves by day or by night to others who are sleeping in their beds; and this they do when they wish to bewitch men or beasts. But for raising hailstorms they observe various other methods and ceremonies, and perform various ritual actions round about a river, as we have shown before where we discussed the manner and methods of working witchcraft. When such are found and are publicly notorious they are convicted of a violent suspicion of the heresy' of witchcraft; especially when some effect of witchcraft has followed upon their actions, either

immediately or after some interval. For then there is direct evidence of the fact, or indirect evidence when any instruments of witchcraft are found hidden in some place. And although when some interval of time has elapsed the evidence of the fact is not so strong, such a person still remains under strong suspicion of witchcraft, and therefore much more of simple heresy.

And if it be asked whether the devil cannot inflict injury upon men and beasts without the means of a woman being seen in a vision or by her touch, we answer that he can, when God permits it. But the permission of God is more readily granted in the case of a creature that was dedicated to God, but by denying the faith has consented to other horrible crimes; and therefore the devil more often uses such means to harm creatures. Further, we may say that, although the devil can work without a witch, he yet very much prefers to work with one, for the many reasons which we showed earlier in this work.

To sum up our conclusions on this matter, it is to be said that, following the above distinctions, those who are suspected of the heresy of witchcraft are separated into three categories, since some are lightly, some strongly, and some gravely suspected. And they are lightly suspected who act in such a way as to give rise to a small or light suspicion against them of this heresy. And although, as has been said, a person who is found to be suspected in this way is not to be branded as a heretic, yet he must undergo a canonical purgation, or he must be caused to pronounce a solemn abjuration as in the case of one convicted of a slight heresy.

For the Canon (cap. *excommunicamus*) says: Those who have been found to rest under a probable suspicion (that is, says Henry of Segusio, a light suspicion), unless, having respect to the nature of the suspicion and the quality of their persons, they should prove their innocence by a fitting purgation, they are to be stricken with the sword of anathema as a worthy satisfaction in the sight of all men. And if they continue obstinate in their excommunication for the period of a year, they are to be utterly condemned as heretics.

And note that, in the purgation imposed upon them, whether or not they consent to it, and whether or not they fail in it, they are throughout to be judged as reputed heretics on whom a canonical purgation is to be imposed.

And that a person under this light suspicion can and should be caused to pronounce a solemn abjuration is shown in the chapter *Accusatus*, where it says: A person accused or suspected of heresy, against whom there is a strong suspicion of this crime, if he abjures the heresy before the Judge and afterwards commits it, then, by a sort of legal fiction, he shall be judged to have relapsed into heresy, although the heresy was not proved against him before his abjuration. But if the suspicion was in the first place a small or light one, although such a relapse renders the accused liable to severe punishment, yet he is not to suffer the punishment of those who relapse into heresy.

But those who are strongly suspected, that is, those who have acted in such a way as to engender a great and strong suspicion; even these are not necessarily heretics or to be condemned as such. For it is expressly stated in the Canon that no one is to be condemned of so great a crime by reason of a strong suspicion. And it says:

Therefore we order that, when the accused is only under suspicion, even if it be a strong one, we do not wish him to be condemned of so grave a crime; but such a one so strongly suspected must be commanded to abjure all heresy in general, and in particular that of which he is strongly suspected.

But if he afterwards relapses either into his former heresy or into any other, or if he associates with those whom he knows to be witches or heretics, or visits them, receives, consults with, forgives, or favours them, he shall not escape the punishment of backsliders, according to the chapter *Accusatus*. For it says there: He who has been involved in one kind or sect of heresy, or has erred in one article of the faith or sacrament of the Church, and has afterwards specifically and generally abjured his heresy: if thereafter he follows another kind or sect of heresy, or errs in another article or sacrament of the Church, it is our will that he be judged a backslider. He, therefore, who is known to have lapsed into heresy before his abjuration, if after his abjuration he receives heretics, visits them, gives or sends them presents or

gifts, or shows favour to them, etc., he is worthily and truly to be judged a backslider; for by this proof there is no doubt that he was in the first place guilty. Such is the tenor of the Canon.

From these words it is clear that there are three cases in which a person under strong suspicion of heresy shall, after his abjuration, be punished as a backslider. The first is when he falls back into the same heresy of which he was strongly suspected. The second is when he has abjured all heresy in general, and yet lapses into another heresy, even if he has never before been suspected or accused of that heresy. The third is when he receives and shows favour to heretics. And this last comprises and embraces many cases.

But it is asked what should be done when a person who has fallen under so strong a suspicion steadily refuses to comply with his Judge's order to abjure his heresy: is he to be at once handed over to the secular Court to be punished? We answer that by no means must this be done; for the Canon (*ad abolendam*) expressly speaks, not of suspects, but of those who are manifestly taken in heresy. And more rigorous action is to be employed against those who are manifestly taken than against those who are only suspected.

And if it is asked, How then is such a one to be proceeded against? We answer that the Judge must proceed against him in accordance with the chapter *excommunicamus*, and he must be excommunicated. And if he continues obstinate after a year's excommunication, he is to be condemned as a heretic.

There are others again who are violently or gravely suspected, whose actions give rise to a violent suspicion against them; and such a one is to be considered as a heretic, and throughout he is to be treated as if he were taken in heresy, in accordance with the Canon Law. For these either confess their crime or not; and if they do, and wish to return to the faith and abjure their heresy, they are to be received back into penitence. But if they refuse to abjure, they are to be handed over to the secular Court for punishment.

But if he does not confess his crime after he has been convicted, and does not consent to abjure his heresy, he is to be condemned as an impenitent heretic. For a violent suspicion is sufficient to warrant a conviction, and admits no proof to the contrary.

Now this discussion deals with simple heresy, where there is no direct or indirect evidence of the fact, as will be shown in the sixth method of passing sentence, where a man is to be condemned as a heretic even though he may not actually be one: then how much more is it applicable to the heresy of witches, where there is always in addition either the direct evidence of bewitched children, men, or animals, or the indirect evidence of instruments of witchcraft which have been found.

And although in the case of simple heresy those who are penitent and abjure are, as has been said, admitted to penitence and imprisonment for life; yet in this heresy, although the ecclesiastic Judge may receive the prisoner into penitence, yet the civil Judge can, because of her temporal injuries, that is to say, the harm she has done to men, cattle, and goods, punish her with death; nor can the ecclesiastic Judge prevent this, for even if he does not hand her over to be punished, yet he is compelled to deliver her up at the request of the civil Judge.

☆

QUESTION XX

Of the First Method of Pronouncing Sentence.

SINCE, therefore, the accused is either found innocent and is to be altogether absolved, or is found only to be generally defamed as a heretic, or is found a proper subject for the questions and the torture on account of her reputation, or is found to be lightly suspected of heresy, or is found to be strongly or gravely suspected of heresy, or is found to be at the same time commonly defamed and suspected of heresy, or is found to have confessed her heresy and to be penitent and not to have relapsed truly, or is found to have confessed and to be penitent but probably to have relapsed, or is found to have confessed her heresy and to be impenitent but not really to have relapsed, or is found to have confessed and to be impenitent and certainly to have relapsed, or is found not to have confessed but by legitimate witnesses and otherwise legally to have been con-

victed of heresy, or is found to have been convicted of heresy but to have escaped or defiantly absented herself, or is found not to have done injury by witchcraft but to have removed bewitchments unfittingly and by unlawful means, or is found to be an archer-wizard or enchanter of weapons with the purpose of causing death, or is found to be a witch-midwife offering infants to the devil in the manner of an enemy, or is found to make frivolous and fraudulent appeals with a view to saving her life:

Therefore, if she is found to be entirely innocent, the final sentence shall be pronounced in the following manner:

Here it is first to be noted that the accused is found to be entirely innocent when, after the facts of the process have been diligently discussed in consultation with skilled lawyers, she cannot be convicted either by her own confession, or by the evidence of the fact, or by the production of legitimate witnesses (since they have disagreed upon the main issue); and when the accused has never before been suspected of or publicly defamed as regards that crime (but the case is different if she has been defamed as regards some other crime); and when there is no evidence of the fact against her. In such a case the following procedure is observed; for she is to be absolved by the Bishop or Judge by a sentence to the following effect:

We N., by the mercy of God Bishop of such a town (or Judge, etc.), considering that you N. of such a place and such a Diocese have been accused before us of the crime of heresy and namely of witchcraft; and considering that this accusation was such as we could not pass over with connivent eyes, have condescended to inquire whether the aforesaid accusation can be substantiated as true, by calling witnesses, by examining you, and by using other means which are fitting according to the canonical sanctions. Wherefore having diligently seen and examined all that has been done and said in this case, and having had the counsel of learned lawyers and Theologians, and having repeatedly examined and inquired into all; sitting as Judges on this tribunal and having only God before our eyes and the truth of the case, and the Holy Gospels being placed before us that our judgement may proceed from the countenance of God and our eyes behold equity, we proceed to our definitive sentence in this way, invoking the name of Christ. Since by that which we have seen and heard, and has been produced, offered, done, and executed before us in this present case, we have not found that anything has legally been proved against you of those things of which you were accused before us, we pronounce, declare, and give it as our final sentence that no act has legally been proved to us against you by which you can or ought to be judged a heretic or witch or be in any way suspected of the sin of heresy. Wherefore by this present declaration, inquiry, and judgement, we freely discharge you. This sentence was given, etc.

Let care be taken not to put anywhere in the sentence that the accused is innocent or immune, but that it was not legally proved against him; for if after a little time he should again be brought to trial, and it should be legally proved, he can, notwithstanding the previous sentence of absolution, then be condemned.

Note also that the same method of absolution may be used in the case of one who is accused of receiving, protecting, or otherwise comforting and favouring heretics, when nothing is legally proved against him.

A secular Judge commissioned by the Bishop shall use his own manner of pronouncement.

☆

QUESTION XXI

Of the Second Method of Pronouncing Sentence, when the Accused is no more than Defamed.

THE second method of delivering judgement is to be employed when he or she who is accused, after a diligent discussion of the merits of the case in consultation with learned lawyers, is found to be no more than defamed as a heretic in some village, town, or province. And this is when the accused does not stand convicted either by her own confession, or by the evidence of the facts, or by the legitimate production of witnesses; nor has there been anything proved against her except that she is the subject of common aspersion: so that no particular act of witchcraft can be proved by which she can be brought under strong or grave suspicion, as that she has uttered threatening words, for example, " You will soon feel what will happen to you," or something to that effect, and afterwards some injury has befallen the person or the cattle of the man she threatened.

The following procedure, therefore, is to be employed in the case of such a one against whom nothing has been proved except public obloquy. In this case judgement cannot be delivered for the accused, nor can she be absolved as in the first method; but a canonical purgation must be imposed upon her. Therefore let the Bishop or his deputy, or the Judge, first take note that, in a case of heresy, it is not necessary that a person should be defamed only by good and respected people; for the calumniation uttered by common and simple folk carries equal weight.

And the reason for this is, that the same persons who are admitted as accusers in a case of heresy are also admitted as detractors. Now any heretic can be accused by anybody, except his mortal enemies; therefore he can also be defamed by anybody.

Therefore let the Bishop or Judge pronounce his sentence of canonical purgation in this or some similar manner:

We N., by the mercy of God Bishop of such a city, or Judge of such a county, having diligently examined the merits of the process conducted by us against you N. of such a Diocese accused before us of the crime of heresy, etc. We have not found that you have confessed to or have been convicted of the aforesaid sin or that you are even lightly suspected of it, except that we find that truly and legitimately you are publicly defamed by both good and bad in such a village, town, or Diocese; and that you may be in good odour among the company of the faithful we impose upon you as by law a canonical purgation, assigning to you such a day of such a month at such hour of the day, upon which you shall appear in person before us with so many persons of equal station with you to purge you of your defamation. Which sponsors must be men of the Catholic faith and of good life who have known your habits and manner of living not only recently but in time past. And we signify that, if you should fail in this purgation, we shall hold you convicted, according to the canonical sanctions.

Here it is to be considered that, when a person is duly found to be publicly defamed of some heresy, and nothing is proved against him except that defamation, a canonical purgation shall be imposed upon him. That is, he must produce some seven, ten, twenty, or thirty men, according to the extent to which he has been defamed and the size and importance of the place concerned, and these must be men of his own station and condition. For example, if he who is defamed is a religious, they must be religious; if he is a secular, they must be seculars; if he be a soldier, they must be soldiers who purge him from the crime for which he is defamed. And these sponsors must be men professing the Catholic faith and of good life, who have known his habits and life both recently and for a long time.

But if he refuses this purgation, he must be excommunicated; and if he remains obstinate in that excommunication for a year, he is then to be condemned as a heretic.

And if he accepts the purgation and fails in it; that is, if he cannot find sponsors of the number and quality desired; he shall be considered as convicted, and is to be condemned as a heretic.

And it must here be remarked that, when it is said that he must purge himself by means of so many men of his own station in life, this is meant generically and not specifically. Thus, if a Bishop is to be purged, it is not necessary that all his sponsors should be Bishops; but Abbots and other religious who are priests are admitted; and similarly in other cases.

And the defamed person shall purge himself in the following manner. At the time assigned to him for his canonical purgation, he shall appear in person with his sponsors before the Bishop who is his Judge, in the place where he is known to be defamed; and, placing his hand upon the Book of the Gospels set before him, he shall say as follows:

I swear upon these four Holy Gospels of God that I never held, believed or taught, neither do I hold or believe such heresy (naming it) for which I am defamed.

That is to say, he shall deny on oath whatever it is for which he is defamed.

After this, all his sponsors shall place their hands on the Gospels; and each of them severally shall say: And I swear upon this Holy Gospel of God that I believe him to have sworn the truth. And then he is canonically purged.

It is also to be noted that a person defamed of heresy is to be purged in the place where he is known to be defamed. And if he has been defamed in many places, he must be required to profess the Catholic faith and deny the heresy in all the places in which he is known as defamed.

And let not such a person hold in light esteem this canonical purgation. For it is provided by the Canon Law that, if he afterwards falls into the heresy of which he has been purged, he is to be handed over as a backslider to the secular Court. But the case is somewhat different if he falls into some other heresy, of which he has not before been purged.

☆

QUESTION XXII

Of the Third kind of Sentence, to be Pronounced on one who is Defamed, and who is to be put to the Question.

THE third method of bringing a process on behalf of the faith to a conclusive termination is when the person accused of heresy, after a careful consideration of the merits of the process in consultation with learned lawyers, is found to be inconsistent in his statements, or it is found that there are sufficient grounds to warrant his exposure to the question and torture: so that if, after he has been thus questioned, he confesses nothing, he may be considered innocent. And this is when the prisoner has not been taken in heresy, nor has he been convicted by his own confession, or by the evidence of the facts, or by the legitimate production of witnesses, and there are no indications that he is under such a suspicion as to warrant his being made to abjure the heresy; but nevertheless he is inconsistent in his answers when interrogated. Or there may be other sufficient reasons for exposing him to torture. And in such a case the following procedure is to be observed.

And because such a judgement includes an interlocutory sentence which must be against and not for the prisoner, the Inquisitor must not divide it into two sentences, but include it all in one. And in the first place, if the accused remains firm in his denials and can in no way be induced by honest men to confess the truth, the following manner of sentence, which is in some respects definitive, shall be used.

We N., by the mercy of God Bishop of such a town, or Judge in the territory subject to the rule of such a Prince, having regard to the merits of the process conducted by us against you N., of such a place in such a Diocese, and after careful examination, find that you are not consistent in your answers, and that there are sufficient indications besides that you ought to be exposed to the question and torture. Therefore, that the truth may be known from your own mouth and that from henceforth you may not offend the ears of your Judges with your equivocations, we declare, pronounce, and give sentence that on this present day at such an hour you are to be subjected to an interrogatory under torture. This sentence was given, etc.

If the person to be questioned is both found to be equivocal and at the same time there are other indications sufficient to warrant his being tortured, let both these facts be included in the sentence, as they are above. But if only one or the other of these hold good, let that one only be put in the sentence. But let the sentence be soon put into execution, or let them make as if to execute it. Nevertheless let not the Judge be too willing to subject a person to torture, for this should only be resorted to in default of other proofs. Therefore let him seek for other proofs; and if he cannot find them, and thinks it probable that the accused is guilty but denies the truth out of fear, let him use other approved methods, always with due precautions, and by using the persuasions of the friends of the accused do his utmost to extract the truth from his own lips. And let him not hasten the business; for very often meditation, and the ordeal of imprisonment, and the repeated persuasion of honest men will induce the accused to discover the truth.

But if, after keeping the accused in suspense, and after due and decent postponements of the time, and many exhortations of the accused, the Bishop and the Judge are well persuaded that, all circumstances considered, the accused is denying the truth, let them torture him slightly, without shedding blood, bearing in mind that torture is often fallacious and ineffective. For some are so soft-hearted and feeble-minded that at the least torture they will confess anything, whether it be true or not. Others are so stubborn that, however much they are tortured, the truth is not to be had from them. There are others who, having been tortured before, are the better able to endure it a second time, since their arms have been accommodated to the stretchings and twistings involved; whereas the effect on others is to make them weaker, so that they can the less easily endure torture. Others are bewitched, and make use of the fact in their torture, so that they will die before they will confess anything; for they become, as it were, insensible to pain. Therefore there is need for much prudence in the matter of torture, and the greatest attention is to be given to the condition of the person who is to be tortured.

When, then, the sentence has been pronounced, the officers shall without delay prepare to torture the accused. And while they are making their preparations, the Bishop or Judge shall use his own persuasions and those of other honest men zealous for the faith to induce the accused to confess the truth freely, if necessary promising to spare his life, as we have shown above.

But if the accused cannot thus be terrified into telling the truth, a second or third day may be appointed for the continuation of the torture; but it must not be repeated then and there. For such a repetition is not permissible unless some further indications against the accused should transpire. But there is nothing to prevent a continuation of the torture on another day.

Let it then be said: We N. Bishop and N. Judge (if he is present) aforesaid, assign to you N. such a day for the continuation of the torture, that the truth may be known from your own mouth. And let all be set down in the process. And during the interval appointed to him, let them use their own persuasions and those of other honest men to induce him to confess the truth.

But if he has refused to confess, the torture can be continued on the day assigned, more or less severely according to the gravity of the offences in question. And the Judges will be able to observe many lawful precautions, both in word and deed, by which they may come at the truth: but these are more easily learned by use and experience and the variety of different cases than by the art or teaching of anyone.

But if, after having been fittingly questioned and tortured, he will not discover the truth, let him not be further molested, but be freely allowed to depart. If, however, he confesses, and abides by his confession, and uncovers the truth, acknowledging his guilt and asking the pardon of the Church; then according to the Canon *ad abolendam* he is to be treated as one taken in heresy on his own confession, but penitent, and he must abjure the heresy, and sentence must be pronounced against him as in the case of those who are convicted by their own confession as being taken in heresy. This will be explained in the eighth method of sentencing such, to which the reader may refer.

If, on the other hand, he confesses the truth, but is not penitent but obstinately persists in his heresy, but is not a relapsed heretic, then according to the Canon, after a decent interval and due warning, he is to be condemned as a heretic and handed over to the secular Court to suffer the extreme penalty, as we show later in the tenth method. But if he is a relapsed heretic, he is to be condemned in the way which is again explained in the tenth method, to which the reader may refer.

But here it must be particularly noted that in some instances he who is to be questioned confesses nothing against himself before the torture, nor is anything proved on the strength of which he can be required to abjure the heresy or be condemned as a heretic; and in such cases the above procedure should be adopted, as we have said, immediately. But in other cases the accused is taken in heresy, or there are other proved indications by reason of which he ought to be required to abjure the heresy, or he is to be considered either lightly or strongly suspected; and he is not to be tortured in respect of such matters; but if, apart from these, he denies some points which are not proved, but of which there is sufficient indication to warrant his being tortured; and

if, having been questioned as to these under torture, he confesses to none of them, he is not on that account to be absolved in accordance with the first method; but he must be proceeded against according to that which has been proved against him, and he or she must abjure the heresy as being one under suspicion of or taken in heresy, as the merits of the process may exact or require. And if, after torture, he confesses all or part of that for which he was tortured, then he must abjure both this and the former heresy which was proved against him, and sentence must be pronounced against him in respect of both of these.

☆

QUESTION XXIII

The Fourth Method of Sentencing, in the Case of one Accused upon a Light Suspicion.

THE fourth method of concluding the process on behalf of the faith is used when, after the merits of the process have been diligently examined in consultation with expert lawyers, the accused is found to rest under only a light suspicion of heresy. And this is when the accused is not taken in heresy, nor is convicted by her own confession or by the evidence of the facts or by the legitimate production of witnesses, and there are no other strong or vehement indications of heresy against her; but only small and light indications of such a sort as, in the opinion of the Court, to engender a light suspicion against her. And such a one must be required to abjure the heresy of which she is accused; and then, if she relapses into heresy, she is not liable to the punishment of backsliders, although she must be more severely punished than would be the case if she had not previously abjured the heresy (see the Canon c. *accusatus*). The following procedure shall be followed in such a case. For such an accused, if the matter be a public one, will publicly make the following abjuration in the Church:

I, N., of such a Diocese, a citizen of such a city or place, being on my trial, do swear before you the Lord Bishop of such a city, and upon the Holy Gospels placed before me and upon which I set my hand, that I believe in my heart and profess with my lips that Holy Catholic and Apostolic Faith which the Holy Roman Church believes, confesses, preaches, and observes. Also I swear that I believe in my heart and profess with my lips that the Lord JESUS Christ, in company with all the Saints, abominates the wicked heresy of witches; and that all who follow or adhere to it will with the devil and his Angels be punished in eternal fire unless they turn their hearts and are reconciled by the penitence of the Holy Church. And therefore I abjure, renounce, and revoke that heresy of which you, my Lord Bishop, and your Officers hold me suspected: namely, that I have been familiar with witches, have ignorantly defended their errors, have held in detestation their Inquisitors and prosecutors, or that I have failed to bring their crimes to light. Also I swear that I have never believed the aforesaid heresy, nor do I believe it, nor have I adhered, nor do I adhere to it, nor shall I ever believe, adhere to, or teach it, nor do I intend to teach it. And if I should hereafter be guilty of any of the aforesaid practices (which God forbid), I shall willingly submit myself to the punishment provided by law for such who are so forsworn; and I am ready to undergo any penance which you see fit to enjoin me for those words or deeds of mine for which you hold me deservedly suspect; and I swear to fulfil such penance to the best of my strength, and to omit no part of it, so help me God and these Holy Gospels.

The above abjuration shall be made in the common speech, so that all may understand it. And when it is done, the Judge, if he is present, or his deputy shall speak to her in the common speech to the following effect:

My son (or daughter), you have not unworthily abjured the suspicion which we entertained of you, and have purged yourself by the aforesaid abjuration. Beware then lest hereafter you fall into the heresy you have abjured. For although, if you should repent, you would not be delivered up to the secular Court, since you made your abjuration as one under a light, and not a strong, suspicion, yet you would then be far more severely punished than you would have been if you had not abjured, and you would then rest under a strong instead of a light suspicion. And when you should abjure as such, and afterwards should relapse, you would suffer the due punishment of a backslider, and would without mercy be delivered to the secular Court to endure the extreme penalty.

But if she makes her abjuration secretly in the chamber of the Bishop or Judge, which will be the case when the matter is not a public one, she shall abjure in the same manner. And afterwards sentence shall be pronounced as follows:

We, by the mercy of God Bishop of such a city, or (if he is present) Judge in the territory subject to such a Prince, having carefully seen and examined the merits of the process conducted by us against you N., accused before us of heresy, find that you have committed such and such (naming them) which render you lightly suspected of heresy, on account of which we have judged it proper to cause you to abjure that heresy as one lightly suspected of it. But not for that can you be dismissed unpunished. And that you may become more careful in the future, having consulted with many eminent persons learned in the law and with religious men, and having carefully weighed and digested the whole matter, having only God before our eyes, and the irrefragable truth of the Holy Catholic Faith, and with the Holy Gospels placed before us that our sentence may proceed as from God's countenance and that our eyes may see with equity, and sitting in tribunal as Judge, we condemn, sentence, or rather impose penance upon you N., standing in person here in our presence, in the following manner. Namely, that never hereafter shall you knowingly hold to, associate with, defend in your speech, read (if you are well learned), or hereafter, etc. And let there be set down that which she has committed, on account of which she was held suspected of the crime of heresy. This sentence and penance were given, etc.

And let the Notary take care that he sets it down in the process that such abjuration was made as by one under a light, not a strong, suspicion of heresy; for otherwise great danger might ensue.

☆

QUESTION XXIV

The Fifth Manner of Sentence, in the Case of one under Strong Suspicion.

THE fifth method of concluding a process on behalf of the faith is used when she who is accused of heresy, after a careful examination of the merits of the process in consultation with learned lawyers, is found to be strongly suspected of heresy. And this is when the accused is not legally taken in heresy, nor has been convicted by her own confession or by the evidence of the facts or by the legitimate production of witnesses; but strong and weighty indications have been proved against her by reason of which she is held to be under strong suspicion of heresy.

The procedure in such a case is as follows. For such a person should abjure that heresy as one strongly suspected of it, in such a manner that, if she should afterwards relapse, she must be delivered to the secular Court to suffer the extreme penalty. And she shall make her abjuration publicly or secretly according to whether she is publicly or secretly suspected, or by more or less, high or low, as was just said in the case of one under a light suspicion; and she must abjure that specific heresy.

And the preparations for such an abjuration should be as follows:—When the Sunday comes which has been fixed for the abjuration and the hearing of the sentence or the imposition of the penance, the preacher shall deliver a general sermon. After this, the Notary or clerk shall publicly read out the crimes of which the accused has been convicted, and those of which she is strongly suspected as a heretic.

Then the Judge or his deputy shall say to her: Behold! according to that which has been read you are strongly suspected by us of such heresy; wherefore it behoves you to purge yourself and abjure the aforesaid heresy. And then the Book of the Gospels shall be placed before her, and she shall set her hand upon it; and if she can read competently, she shall be given the following written abjuration, and shall read it in the presence of the whole congregation.

But if she cannot read competently, the Notary shall read it phrase by phrase, and the accused shall repeat it in a loud and audible voice in the following manner. The Notary or clerk shall say: I, N., of such a place, and the accused person shall repeat after him the same words, but always in the vulgar tongue. And so on up to the end of the abjuration. And she shall abjure in the following manner:

I, N., of such a place in such a Diocese, standing my trial in person in presence of you reverend Lords the Bishop of such city and the Judge of the territory subject to the rule of such a Lord, upon the Holy Gospels set before me and touched by my hands, I swear that I believe in my heart and profess with my lips that Holy Catholic and Apostolic Faith which the Holy Roman Church teaches, professes, preaches, and holds. Also I swear that I believe in my heart and profess with my lips that, etc. And let her pronounce the Catholic article of the faith against that heresy of which she is strongly suspected.

For example, if the heresy of witchcraft is in question, let her say as follows:

I swear that I believe that not only will simple heretics and schismatics be tortured in fire everlasting, but that those above all will be so punished who are infected with the heresy of witches, who deny before the devil that faith which they received in Holy Baptism at the font, and practise demoniac lewdness for the fulfilment of their evil desires, inflicting all sorts of injuries upon men and animals and the fruits of the earth. And consequently I abjure, renounce, and revoke that heresy, or rather infidelity, which falsely and mendaciously maintains that there are no witches in the world, and that no one ought to believe that those injuries can be caused with the help of devils; for such infidelity is, as I now recognize, expressly contrary to the decision of our Holy Mother the Church and of all the Catholic Doctors, as also against the Imperial laws which have decreed that witches are to be burned.

Also I swear that I have never persistently believed in the aforesaid h_ csy, neither do I believe nor adhere to it at the present, nor have I taught it, nor intend to teach it, nor shall teach it. Also I swear and promise that I will never do or cause to be done such and such (naming them) of which you hold me strongly suspected as a heretic.

And if hereafter (which God forbid) I should do any of the aforesaid, I am ready to undergo the punishment provided by law for backsliders; and I am ready to submit myself to any penance which you decide to impose upon me for those deeds and words of mine for which you hold me strongly suspected of the said heresy. And I swear and promise that I will perform it to the best of my strength, and will omit no part of it, so God and this Holy Gospel help me.

And the said abjuration shall be made in the vulgar tongue so that it may be understood by all, unless it be made only in the presence of Clerics with a competent knowledge of the Latin tongue. But if the abjuration be made secretly in the Bishop's palace or chamber, when it is not a public matter, it shall be made in a similar manner. And afterwards the Bishop shall admonish her as above to beware lest she relapse and incur the penalty of a backslider. And let the Notary take care that he set it down how such abjuration was made by such a person as one strongly suspected of heresy, so that, if she should relapse, she may be punished as is proper for a backslider.

And when this has been done, let the sentence or penance be pronounced in the following manner:

We, N., Bishop of such city, and Brother N. (if he is present), Inquisitor of the sin of heresy in the domains subject to the rule of such a Prince, especially deputed by the Holy Apostolic See: having in mind that you, N., of such a place in such a Diocese, have done such and such (naming them), as lawfully appears from the carefully examined merits of the process, wherefore we reasonably hold you strongly suspected of such heresy, and have caused you to abjure it as one so suspected, being persuaded to that course by considerations of justice and the advice of men skilled in the law. But that you may be more careful in the future nor become more prone to the like practices, and that your crimes may not remain unpunished, and that you may be an example to other sinners; having consulted with many eminent and learned lawyers and Masters or Doctors of the faculty of Theology, having carefully digested the whole matter, and having before our eyes only God and the truth of the Catholic and Apostolic Faith, having set before us the Holy Gospel that our judgement may proceed as from God's countenance and our eyes see with equity, and sitting in tribunal as Judges, we condemn, or rather impose penance in the following manner upon you, N., standing here in person before us: namely, that you shall never hereafter presume to do, say, or teach such and such things. And let there be set down those things of which she has been convicted, and by reason of which she was strongly suspected of the aforesaid heresy, as well as certain others which, if she were to commit them, would make her guilty of a slight relapse into heresy; but this must be as the particular nature of the case demands and requires. As, for example, that she should never wittingly follow such practices, nor receive those whom she knows to have denied the faith, etc. This sentence was given, etc.

But it must be noted that those who are suspected, but not taken in heresy, whether they be strongly or lightly suspected, must not be imprisoned or confined for life. For this is the punishment of those who have been heretics and afterwards repented. But they may, because of their deeds for which they have come under suspicion, be sent to prison for a time, and afterwards, as will be seen, released.

Neither are they to be branded with the sign of the Cross, for such is the sign of a penitent heretic; and they are not convicted heretics, but only suspected, therefore they are not to be marked in this way. But they can be ordered either to stand on certain solemn days within the doors of a church, or near the altar, while Holy Mass is being celebrated, bearing in their hands a lighted candle of a certain weight;* or else to go on some pilgrimage, or something of the kind, according to the nature and requirements of the case.

---

* "A Certain Weight." This was exactly specified when sentence was delivered. Thus Urbain Grandier on 18 August, 1634, at Loudun, was sentenced "to make honourable amends, with bare head, a rope round his neck, and with a burning torch of two pounds' weight in his hand, before the principal door of the church of Saint-Pierre du Marché, and before that of Sainte Ursule of this town, and there, upon his knees, to ask pardon of God and the King." His execution followed.

QUESTION XXV

The Sixth Kind of Sentence, in the Case of one who is Gravely Suspect.

THE sixth method of bringing to a conclusion a process on behalf of the faith is used when the person accused of heresy, after a careful examination of the merits of the process in consultation with learned lawyers, is found to be gravely suspected of heresy. And this is when the accused is not convicted of heresy by her own confession or by the evidence of the facts or by the legitimate production of witnesses, but there are indications, not only light or even strong, but very strong and grave, which render her gravely suspected of the said heresy, and by reason of which she must be judged as one gravely suspected of the said heresy.

And for a clearer understanding of this, we shall give examples both of a case of simple heresy and of the heresy of witches. For the case would fall under this head in simple heresy if the accused were not lawfully found convicted by his own confession, etc. as above, but for something which he had said or done. As, for example, he may have been summoned in a case not concerning the faith, and have been sentenced to excommunication; and if he should continue obstinate in excommunication for a year or more, he would come under a light suspicion of heresy; for such behaviour is not without some suspicion of heresy. But if he should then be summoned on a charge concerning the faith, and should not appear but contumaciously refuse to appear, and therefore be excommunicated, then he would be strongly suspected of heresy; for then the light suspicion would become a strong one. And if he remained obstinate in that excommunication for a year, then he would be gravely suspected of heresy; for then the strong suspicion would become a grave one, against which no defence is admitted. And from that time such a person would be condemned as a heretic, as is shown by the Canon, c. *cum contumacia*, lib. 6.

An example of a grave suspicion in the heresy of witches would be when the accused has said or done anything which is practised by witches when they wish to bewitch anyone. And it commonly happens that they are constrained to manifest themselves by threatening words, by deeds, by a look or a touch, and this is for three reasons. First that their sins may be aggravated and more manifest to their Judges; secondly, that they may the more easily seduce the simple; and thirdly, that God may be the more offended and they may be granted more power of injuring men. Therefore a witch must be gravely suspected when, after she has used such threatening words as "I shall soon make you feel," or the like, some injury has befallen the person so threatened or his cattle. For then she is not to be considered as lightly suspected, as was the case with those who are familiar with witches, or those who wish to provoke someone to inordinate love. See above where we deal with the three degrees of suspicion, light, strong, and grave.

Now we must consider what procedure is to be observed in such a case. For in the case of one gravely suspected of simple heresy, the following is the procedure. Although he may not in actual truth be a heretic, since there may not be any error in his understanding, or if there is, he may not cling obstinately to it in his will: nevertheless he is to be condemned as a heretic because of the said grave suspicion, against which no proof is admitted.

Such a heretic is condemned in this manner. If he refuses to return and abjure his heresy and give fitting satisfaction, he is delivered to the secular Court to be punished. But if he is willing and consents, he abjures his heresy and is imprisoned for life. And the same holds good in the case of one gravely suspected of the heresy of witches.

But although the same method in the main is to be observed in the case of one gravely suspected of the heresy of witches, there are some differences. It is to be noted that, if the witch maintains her denial, or claims that she uttered those words not with the implied intention but in a vehement and womanish passion; then the Judge has not sufficient warrant to sentence her to the flames, in spite of the grave suspicion. Therefore he must place her in prison, and cause inquiry to be made by proclamation whether she has been known to have done the like before. And if it is found that this is so, he must inquire whether she was then publicly defamed in respect of that heresy; and from this he can proceed further so that, before all else, she may be exposed to an interrogation under the question and torture. And then, if she shows signs of such heresy, or of the taciturnity of witches; as that she should be unable to shed tears, or remain insensible under torture and quickly recover her strength afterwards; then he may proceed with the various precautions which we have already explained where we dealt with such cases.

And in case all should fail, then let him take note that, if she has perpetrated the like before, she is not to be altogether released, but must be sent to the squalor of prison for a year, and be tortured, and be examined very often, especially on the more Holy Days. But if, in addition to this, she has been defamed, then the Judge may proceed in the manner already shown in the case of simple heresy, and condemn her to the fire, especially if there is a multitude of witnesses and she had often been detected in similar or other deeds of witchcraft. But if he wishes to be merciful, he may set her a canonical purgation, that she should find twenty or thirty sponsors, sentencing her in such a way that, if she should fail in her purgation, she shall be condemned to the fire as convicted. And the Judge can proceed in such a manner.

And if she should purge herself, then the Judge must sentence her to an abjuration of all heresy, on pain of the punishment for backsliders, together with a perpetual penance, in the following manner. The preparations for the abjuration will be the same as were explained in the fourth and fifth methods of concluding a process on behalf of the faith.

Note that in all the following methods of pronouncing sentence, when the Judge wishes to proceed in a merciful manner he can act in the way we have already explained. But since secular Judges use their own various methods, proceeding with rigour but not always with equity, no fixed rule or method can be given for them as it can for an ecclesiastical Judge, who can receive the abjuration and impose a perpetual penance in the following manner :

I, N., of such a place in such a Diocese, standing in person before you my venerable Lords the Bishop of such city and Judges, having touched with my hands the Holy Gospel placed before me, swear that I believe in my heart and profess with my lips the Holy Catholic and Apostolic Faith which the Holy Roman Church holds, professes, believes, preaches and teaches. And consequently I abjure all heresy, and renounce and revoke all who raise themselves against the Holy Roman and Apostolic Church, of whatever sect or error they be. Also I swear and promise that I shall never henceforward do, say, or cause to be done such and such (naming them) which I have done and said, and for which, in my guilt, you hold me gravely suspected of the said heresy. Also I swear and promise that I will perform every penance which you wish to impose upon me for the said crimes to the best of my strength, and that I will not omit any part of it, so help me God and the Holy Gospel. And if (which God forbid) I should hereafter act in contravention of this abjuration, I here and now bind and oblige myself to suffer the due punishments for backsliders, however severe they be.

Let the Notary take care to set it down that the said abjuration was made by one gravely suspected of heresy, so that if she should be proved to have relapsed, she should then be judged accordingly and delivered up to the secular Court.

After this let the Bishop absolve her from the sentence of excommunication which she has incurred as one gravely suspected of heresy. For when a heretic returns to the faith and abjures his heresy, he is to be released from the sentence of excommunication which is passed on all heretics. Similarly, such a one as we are considering was condemned as a heretic, as we have said; but after she has abjured her heresy she is to be released from excommunication; and after this absolution she is to be sentenced in the following manner :

We N., Bishop of such city, and, if he is present, Judge in the territory of such Lord, seeing that you N., of such a place in such a Diocese, have been accused before us of such and such touching the faith (naming them), and that we have proceeded to inform ourselves concerning them as justice demanded by a careful examination of the merits of the process and of all that has been done and said in the present case, have found that you have committed such and such (naming them). Wherefore, and not without reason holding you gravely suspect of such heresy (naming it), we have caused you as one so suspected publicly to abjure all heresy in general, as the canonical sanctions bid us. And since according to those same canonical institutions all such are to be condemned as heretics, but you holding to wiser counsel and returning to the bosom of our Holy Mother the Church have abjured, as we have said, all vile heresy, therefore we absolve you from the sentence of excommunication by which you were deservedly bound as one hateful to the Church of God. And if with true heart and faith unfeigned you have returned to the unity of the Church, you shall be reckoned from henceforth among the penitent, and as from now are received back into the merciful bosom of the Holy Church. But since it would be most scandalous to pass over with connivent eyes and leave unpunished your offences against God and your injuries to men, for it is a graver matter to offend the Divine Majesty than a human monarch, and that your crimes may not be an incentive for other sinners, and that you may become more careful in the future and less prone to commit again the aforesaid crimes, and may suffer the less punishment in the next world: We the aforesaid Bishop and Judge, having availed ourselves of the wise and considered advice of learned men in this matter, sitting in tribunal as Judges judging, having before our eyes only God and the irrefragable truth of the Holy Faith, with the Holy Gospels placed before us that our judgement may proceed as from the countenance of God and our eyes see with equity, sentence and condemn, or rather impose penance in the following manner upon you N., appearing in person before us on the day and at the hour which was before assigned to you. First, you shall put on over all the garments which you wear a grey-blue garment after the manner of a monk's scapulary, made without a hood either before or behind, and having upon it crosses of yellow cloth three palms long and two palms wide, and you shall wear

this garment over all others for such a length of time (setting a period of one or two years, more or less as the guilt of the person demands). And in the said garment and crosses you shall stand in the door of such a church at such a time for so long, or on the four major Feasts* of the Glorious Virgin, or in such and such cities in the doors of such and such churches; and we sentence and condemn you for life, or for such a period, to such a prison. (Let this be set down as seems most to the honour of the faith, and according to the greater or less guilt and obstinacy of the accused.) And we expressly, and in the sure knowledge that it is so ordained by canonical institution, reserve to ourselves the right to mitigate the said penance, to increase it, change it, or remove it, in whole or in part, as often as seems good to us. This sentence was given, etc.

And when this has been read, it shall at once be duly put into execution, and she shall be clothed with the aforesaid garment with the crosses as has been said.

☆

QUESTION XXVI

The Method of passing Sentence upon one who is both Suspect and Defamed.

THE seventh method of bringing to a conclusion a process on behalf of the faith is employed when the person accused of the sin of heresy, after a careful examination of the merits of the process in consultation with men learned in the law, is found to be both suspected and defamed of heresy. And this is when the accused is not legally convicted by his own confession or by the evidence of the facts or by the legitimate production of witnesses; but is found to be publicly

---

* *"Four Major Feasts."* Presumably the Annunciation, the Visitation, Assumption, and Nativity of Our Lady are intended. Candlemas, which in the Middle Ages had an octave in many dioceses, may be intended instead of the Visitation. The last Pope, Sixtus IV, had in 1470 published a work on the Immaculate Conception. By a decree of 28 February, 1476, this Pontiff adopted the Feast of Our Lady's Conception for the entire Latin Church and granted an indulgence to all who should assist at the Divine Office of this Solemnity.

defamed, and there are also other indications which render him lightly or strongly suspected of heresy: as that he has held much familiarity with heretics. And such a person must, because of his defamation, undergo a canonical purgation; and because of the suspicion against him he must abjure the heresy.

The procedure in such a case will be as follows. Such a person, being publicly defamed for heresy, and being in addition to this suspected of heresy by reason of certain other indications, shall first publicly purge himself in the manner which we explained in the second method. Having performed this purgation, he shall immediately, as one against whom there are other indications of the suspected heresy, abjure that heresy in the following manner, having before him, as before, the Book of the Gospels:

I, N., of such a place in such a Diocese, standing my trial in person before you my Lords, N., Bishop of such city and Judge in the territory of such Prince, having touched with my hands the Holy Gospels placed before me, swear that I believe in my heart and profess with my lips that Holy Apostolic Faith which the Roman Church believes, professes, preaches and observes. And consequently I abjure, detest, renounce and revoke every heresy which rears itself up against the Holy and Apostolic Church, of whatever sect or error it be, etc., as above.

Also I swear and promise that I will never hereafter do or say or cause to be done such and such (naming them), for which I am justly defamed as having committed them, and of which you hold me suspected. Also I swear and promise that I will perform to the best of my strength every penance which you impose upon me, nor will I omit any part of it, so help me God and this Holy Gospel. And if hereafter I should act in any way contrary to this oath and abjuration (which God forbid), I here and now freely submit, oblige, and bind myself to the legal punishment for such, to the limit of sufferance, when it shall have been proved that I have committed such things.

But it must be noted that when the indications are so strong as to render the accused, either with or without the aforesaid defamation, strongly suspected of heresy, then he shall, as above, abjure all heresy in general. And if he relapses into any heresy, he shall suffer the due punishment of a backslider. But if the indications are so small and slight as, even taken together with the said defamation, not to render him strongly, but only lightly, suspected of heresy, then it is enough if he makes not a general abjuration, but specifically abjures that heresy of which he is suspected; so that, if he were to relapse into another form of heresy, he would not be liable to the penalty for backsliders. And even if he were to relapse into the same heresy which he had abjured, he would still not be liable to the said penalty, although he would be more severely punished than would have been the case if he had not abjured.

But there is a doubt whether he would be liable to the penalty for backsliders if, after his canonical purgation, he should relapse into the same heresy of which he was canonically purged. And it would seem that this would be so, from the Canon Law, c. *excommunicamus* and c. *ad abolendam*. Therefore the Notary must take great care to set it down whether such a person has made his abjuration as one under a light or a strong suspicion of heresy; for, as we have often said, there is a great difference between these. And when this has been done, sentence or penance shall be pronounced in the following manner:

We, N., Bishop of such city or Judge in the territories of such Prince, having diligently in mind that you, N., of such a place in such a Diocese, have been accused before us of such heresy (naming it); and wishing to inquire judicially whether you have fallen into the said heresy, by examining witnesses, by summoning and questioning you upon oath, and by all convenient means in our power, we have acted and proceeded as it behoved.

Having digested, observed and diligently inspected all the facts, and having discussed the merits of the process of this case, examining all and singular which has been done and said, and having consulted with and obtained the mature opinion of many learned Theologians and lawyers, we find that you have been in such place or places publicly defamed by good and sober men for the said heresy;

wherefore, as we are bidden by the canonical institutions, we have imposed upon you a canonical purgation by which you and your sponsors have here publicly purged yourself before us. We find also that you have committed such and such (naming them), by reason of which we have just cause to hold you strongly or lightly (let it be said whether it is one or the other) suspected of the said heresy; and therefore we have caused you to abjure heresy as one under such suspicion (here, if he has abjured as one under strong suspicion, let them say "all heresy"; and if as one under light suspicion, "the said heresy").

But because we cannot and must not in any way tolerate that which you have done, but are in justice compelled to abominate it, that you may become more careful in the future, and that your crimes may not remain unpunished, and that others may not be encouraged to fall into the like sins, and that the injuries to the Creator may not easily be passed over: Therefore against you, N., having so purged yourself and abjured, standing personally in our presence in this place at the time which was assigned to you, We, the aforesaid Bishop or Judge, sitting in tribunal as Judges judging, having before us the Holy Gospels that our judgement may proceed as from the countenance of God and our eyes see with equity, pronounce sentence or penance in the following manner, namely, that you must, etc.

And let them pronounce sentence as shall seem most to the honour of the faith and the extermination of the sin of heresy: as that on certain Sundays and Festivals he must stand at the door of such a church, holding a candle of such a weight, during the solemnization of Holy Mass, with head uncovered and bare feet, and offer the said candle at the altar; and that he must fast on Fridays, and that for a certain period he must not dare to depart from that place, but present himself before the Bishop or Judge on certain days of the week; and any similar penance which seems to be demanded by the particular nature of his guilt; for it is impossible to give a hard-and-fast rule. This sentence was given, etc. And let it be put into execution after it has been pronounced; and it can be cancelled, mitigated or changed as may be

required by the condition of the penitent and for his correction and humiliation; for the Bishop has this power by law.

☆

QUESTION XXVII

The Method of passing Sentence upon one who hath Confessed to Heresy, but is not Penitent.

THE eighth method of terminating a process on behalf of the faith is used when the person accused of heresy, after a careful examination of the merits of the process in consultation with learned lawyers, is found to have confessed his heresy, but to be penitent, and not truly to have relapsed into heresy. And this is when the accused has himself confessed in a Court of law under oath before the Bishop and Inquisitor that he has for so long lived and persisted in that heresy of which he is accused, or in any other, and has believed in and adhered to it; but that afterwards, being persuaded by the Bishop and others, he wishes to be converted and to return to the bosom of the Church, and to abjure that and every heresy, and to make such satisfaction as they require of him; and it is found that he has made no previous abjuration of any other heresy, but is now willing and prepared to abjure.

In such a case the procedure will be as follows. Although such a person has for many years persisted in the said heresy and even in others, and has believed and practised them and led many others into error; yet if at last he has consented to abjure those heresies and to make such satisfaction as the Bishop and the ecclesiastical Judge shall decree, he is not to be delivered up to the secular Court to suffer the extreme penalty; nor, if he is a cleric, is he to be degraded. But he is to be admitted to mercy, according to the Canon *ad abolendam*. And after he has abjured his former heresy he is to be confined in prison for life (see the Canon *excommunicamus*, where it provides for the absolution of such). But great care must be taken that he has not simulated a false penitence in order to be received back into the Church. Also the secular Court is not at all bound by such a sentence as the above.

He shall make his abjuration in the manner already set out, with this difference. He shall with his own mouth confess his crimes before the congregation in church on a Feast Day, in the following manner. The clerk shall ask him, Have you for so many years persisted in the heresy of witches? And he shall answer, Yes. And then, Have you done this and this to which you have confessed? And he shall answer, Yes. And so on. And finally he shall make his abjuration kneeling on his knees. And since, having been convicted of heresy, he has been excommunicated, after he has by abjuration returned to the bosom of the Church, he is to be granted the grace of absolution, according to the manner used by the Bishops with Apostolic authority of absolving from the major excommunication. And sentence shall at once be pronounced in the following manner:

We, the Bishop of such city, or the Judge in the territories of such Prince, seeing that you, N., of such a place in such a Diocese, have been by public report and the information of credible persons accused before us of the sin of heresy; and since you had for many years been infected with that heresy to the great damage of your soul; and because this accusation against you has keenly wounded our hearts: we whose duty it is by reason of the office which we have received to plant the Holy Catholic Faith in the hearts of men and to keep away all heresy from their minds, wishing to be more certainly informed whether there was any truth in the report which had come to our ears, in order that, if it were true, we might provide a healthy and fitting remedy, proceeded in the best way which was open to us to question and examine witnesses and to interrogate you on oath concerning that of which you were accused, doing all and singular which was required of us by justice and the canonical sanctions.

And since we wished to bring your case to a suitable conclusion, and to have a clear understanding of your past state of mind, whether you were walking in the darkness or in the light, and whether or not you had fallen into the sin of heresy; having conducted the whole process, we summoned together in council before us learned men of the Theological faculty and men skilled in both the Canon and the Civil Law, knowing that, according to canonical institution, the judgement is sound which is confirmed by the opinion of many; and having on all details consulted the opinion of the said learned men, and having diligently and carefully examined all the circumstances of the process; we find that you are, by your own confession made on oath before us in the Court, convicted of many of the sins of witches. (Let them be expressed in detail.)

But since the Lord in His infinite mercy permits men at times to fall into heresies and errors, not only that learned Catholics may be exercised in sacred arguments, but that they who have fallen from the faith may become more humble thereafter and perform works of penitence: having carefully discussed the circumstances of this same process, we find that you, at our frequent instance and following the advice of us and other honest men, have with a healthy mind returned to the unity and bosom of the Holy Mother Church, detesting the said errors and heresies, and acknowledging the irrefragable truth of the Holy Catholic Faith, laying it to your inmost heart: wherefore, following in His footsteps Who wishes that no one should perish, we have admitted you to this adjuration and public abjuration of the said and all other heresies. And having done this, we absolve you from the sentence of major excommunication by which you were bound for your fall into heresy, and reconciling you to the Holy Mother Church we restore you to the sacraments of the Church; provided that with a true heart, and not with simulated faith, you return to the unity of the Church, as we believe and hope that you have done.

But because it would be a very scandalous thing to avenge the injuries done to temporal Lords and to tolerate the offences committed against God the Creator of all the Heavens, since it is a far greater sin to offend against the Eternal than against a temporal Majesty, and that God Who pities sinners may have mercy upon you, that you may be an example for others, and that your sins may not remain unpunished, and that you may become more careful in the future, and not more prone but less apt to commit the said and any other crimes: We the said Bishop and Judge, or Judges, on behalf of the faith, sitting in tribunal as Judges judging, etc., as above . . . that you put on a grey-blue garment, etc. Also we sentence and condemn you to perpetual imprisonment, there to be punished with the bread of affliction and the water of distress;* reserving to ourselves the right to mitigate, aggravate, change, or remit wholly or in part the said sentence if, when, and as often as it shall seem good to us to do so. This sentence was given, etc.

After this the Judge shall proceed point by point, pronouncing sentence in the following or some similar manner:

My son, your sentence or penance consists in this, that you bear this cross during the whole period of your life, that you stand so bearing it on the altar steps or in the door of such churches, and that you be imprisoned for life on bread and water. But, my son, lest this may seem too hard for you, I assure you that if you patiently bear your punishment you will find mercy with us; therefore doubt not nor despair, but hope strongly.

After this, let the sentence be duly executed, and let him put on the said garment and be placed on high upon the altar steps in full view of the people as they go out, surrounded by the officers of the secular Court. And at the dinner hour let him be led by the officers to prison, and the rest of the sentence be carried out and duly performed. And after he is led out through the door of the church, let the ecclesiastical Judge have no more to do with the matter; and if the secular Court be satisfied, it is well, but if not, let it do its pleasure.

☆

QUESTION XXVIII

The Method of passing Sentence upon one who hath Confessed to Heresy but is Relapsed, Albeit now Penitent.

THE ninth method of arriving at a conclusive sentence in a process on behalf of the faith is used when the person accused of heresy, after a careful

investigation of the circumstances of the process in consultation with men of good judgement, is found to have confessed her heresy and to be penitent, but that she has truly relapsed. And this is when the accused herself confesses in Court before the Bishop or Judges that she has at another time abjured all heresy, and this is legally proved, and that she has afterwards fallen into such a heresy or error: or that she has abjured some particular heresy, such as that of witches, and has afterwards returned to it; but that following better advice she is penitent, and believes the Catholic faith, and returns to the unity of the Church. Such a one is not, if she humbly ask for them, to be denied the sacraments of Penance and the Eucharist; but however much she may repent, she is nevertheless to be delivered up as a backslider to the secular Court to suffer the extreme penalty. But it must be understood that this refers to one who had made her abjuration as one manifestly taken in heresy, or as one strongly suspected of heresy, and not to one who has so done as being under only a light suspicion.

The following procedure must be observed in this case. When, after mature and careful and, if necessary, repeated investigation by learned men, it has been concluded that the said prisoner has actually and prepense relapsed into heresy, the Bishop or Judge shall send to the said prisoner in the place of detention two or three honest men, especially religious or clerics, who are zealous for the faith, of whom the prisoner has no suspicion, but rather places confidence in them; and they shall go in to her at a suitable time and speak to her sweetly of the contempt of this world and the miseries of this life, and of the joys and glory of Paradise. And leading up from this, they shall indicate to her on the part of the Bishop or Judge that she cannot escape temporal death, and that she should therefore take care for the safety of her soul, and prepare herself to confess her sins and receive the Sacrament of the Eucharist. And they shall visit her often, persuading her to penitence and patience, strengthening her as much as they can in the Catholic truth, and they shall diligently cause her to confess, so that she may receive the Sacrament of the Eucharist at her

---

* *"Distress." "III. Kings"* (A.V., *"I. Kings"*) *xxii, 27: Put this man in prison, and feed him with bread of affliction, and water of distress.*

humble petition. For these Sacraments are not to be denied to such offenders.

And when she has received these Sacraments, and been well disposed by these men to salvation; after two or three days during which they have strengthened her in the Catholic faith and induced her to repentance, the Bishop or Judge of that place shall notify the bailiff of the place or the authorities of the secular Court, that on such a day at such an hour (not a Feast Day) he should be with his attendants in such a square or place (but it must be outside a church) to receive from their Court a certain backslider whom the Bishop and Judge will hand over to him.

And on the morning of the day fixed, or on the day before, it shall be publicly proclaimed throughout the city or place in those towns and villages where such proclamations are customary, that on such a day at such an hour in such a place there will be a sermon preached in defence of the Faith, and that the Bishop and other Judges will condemn a certain person who has relapsed into the sin of heresy, delivering her up to secular justice.

But here it must be considered that, if he who has so relapsed should have been ordained in any Holy Orders, or should be a priest or a religious of any Order, before he is handed over he is to be degraded and stripped of the privileges of his ecclesiastic order. And so, when he has been degraded from all ecclesiastical office, let him be handed over to secular justice to receive his due punishment.

When, therefore, such a one is to be degraded from his orders and handed over to the secular Court, let the Bishop summon together all the prelates and religious men of his Diocese. For in this case, though not in others, only the Bishop together with the other prelates and religious and learned men of his Diocese can degrade one who has received Holy Orders when he is to be delivered to the secular Court, or is to be imprisoned for life for the sin of heresy.

On the day appointed for the degrading of the backslider and the handing of him over to the secular Court, if he be a cleric, or, if he be a layman, for leaving him to hear his definitive sentence, the people shall gather together in some square or open place

outside the church, and the Inquisitor shall preach a sermon, and the prisoner shall be set on a high place in the presence of the secular authorities. And if the prisoner be a cleric who is to be degraded, the Bishop shall don his Pontifical robes, together with the other prelates of his Diocese in their vestments and copes, and the prisoner shall be clothed and robed as if he were to minister his office; and the Bishop shall degrade him from his orders, beginning from the higher and proceeding to the lowest. And just as in conferring Holy Orders the Bishop uses the words ordained by the Church, so in degrading him he shall take off his chasuble and stole, and so with the other vestments, using words of a directly opposite meaning.

When this degradation has been accomplished, the proceedings must continue in the legal and accustomed manner, and the Notary or religious or clerk shall be bidden to read the sentence, which shall be after the following manner, whether the prisoner be a layman or a degraded cleric:

We, N, by the mercy of God Bishop of such city, and Judge in the territories of such Prince, seeing that we are legitimately informed that you, N., of such a place in such a Diocese, have been before us (or before such Bishop and Judges) accused of such heresy or heresies (naming them), of which you were lawfully convicted by your own confession and by witnesses, and that you had obstinately persisted in them for so long, but afterwards, listening to better advice, publicly in such a place abjured, renounced and revoked those heresies in the form provided by the Church, on which account the said Bishop and Inquisitor, believing that you had truly returned to the bosom of the Holy Church of God, did absolve you from the sentence of excommunication by which you were bound, enjoining upon you a salutary penance if with true heart and faith unfeigned you had returned to the unity of the Holy Church; but whereas after all the aforesaid and the lapse of so many years you are again accused before us and have again fallen into such heresies which you had abjured (naming them), and though it was sore grief to us to hear such things of you, yet we were by justice compelled to investigate the matter, to examine the witnesses, and to summon and question you on oath, proceeding in each and every way as we are bidden by the canonical institutions.

And since we wished to conclude this case without any doubt, we convened in solemn council learned men of the Theological faculty and men skilled in the Canon and the Civil Law, and in consultation with them maturely and carefully examined all and singular which had been done, said and seen in the process and diligently discussed each circumstance, weighing all equally in the balance as it behoved us; and we find both by the legitimate evidence of witnesses and by your own confession received in Court that you have fallen into the heresies which you had abjured. For we find that you have said or done such and such (let all be named), on account of which, with the concurrence of the said learned men, we have judged and now judge that you are a backslider, according to the canonical institutions, to which we refer in grief and grieve to refer.

But since it has come to the knowledge of Us and of many honest Catholic men that, by the inspiration of Divine grace, you have once more returned to the bosom of the Church and to the truth of the faith, detesting the aforesaid errors and heresies and with true orthodoxy unfeigned believing and protesting the Catholic faith, we have admitted you to receive the Church's Sacraments of Penance and the Holy Eucharist at your humble request. But since the Church of God has no more which it can do in respect of you, seeing that it has acted so mercifully towards you in the manner we have said, and you have abused that mercy by falling back into the heresies which you had abjured : therefore We the said Bishop and Judges, sitting in tribunal as Judges judging, having before us the Holy Gospels that our judgement may proceed as from the countenance of God and our eyes see with equity, and having before our eyes only God and the irrefragable truth of the Holy Faith and the extirpation of the plague of heresy; against you, N., in this place on the day and at the hour before assigned to you for the hearing of your definitive sentence, we pronounce in sentence that you have truly fallen back into the sin of heresy,

although you are penitent; and as one truly so relapsed we cast you forth from this our ecclesiastical Court, and leave you to be delivered to the secular arm. But we earnestly pray that the said secular Court may temper its justice with mercy, that there be no bloodshed or danger of death.

And here the Bishop and his assessors shall withdraw, and the secular Court shall perform its office.

It is to be noted that, although the Bishop and Inquisitor ought to use their utmost diligence, both by their own efforts and those of others, to induce the prisoner to repent and return to the Catholic faith; yet, after he has repented and it has been decided in council that, though he is penitent, he is nevertheless truly a backslider and as such to be handed over in person to the secular Court, they ought not to inform him of such sentence and punishment. For the face of his Judge terrifies the prisoner, and his words are more likely to cause one who is to be punished to be impenitent than penitent. Therefore from that time, neither before nor after the sentence should they present themselves before him, that he be not moved in his spirit against them, a thing which is very carefully to be avoided in death of this sort. But, as we have said, let them send to him some honest men, especially those in religious orders, or clerics, in whom he has confidence; and let them inform him of the sentence to come and of his death, and strengthen him in the faith, exhorting him to have patience; and let them visit him after the sentence, and console him and pray with him, and not leave him until he has rendered his spirit to his Creator.

Let them, therefore, beware and be on their guard not to do or say anything which may enable the prisoner to anticipate his death, or place themselves in an irregular position. And, as they have burdened themselves with the care of his soul, let them then share also in his punishment and guilt.

It must also be remarked that such a sentence which delivers up a person to the secular Court ought not to be pronounced on a Festival or Solemn Day, nor in a church, but outside in some open space. For it is a sentence which leads to death; and it is more decent that it should be delivered on an ordinary day and outside the church;

for a Feast Day and the church are dedicated to God.

☆

QUESTION XXIX

The Method of passing Sentence upon one who hath Confessed to Heresy but is Impenitent, although not Relapsed.

THE tenth method of completing a process on behalf of the Faith by a final sentence is used when the person accused of heresy, after a careful examination of the circumstances of the process in consultation with skilled lawyers, is found to have confessed his heresy and to be impenitent, though he has not relapsed into the heresy. Such a case is very rarely found, but yet it has come within the experience of us Inquisitors. In such a case, therefore, the Bishop and Judge must not be in haste to sentence the prisoner, but must keep him well guarded and fettered, and induce him to be converted, even to the extent of several months, showing him that, by remaining impenitent, he will be damned in body and soul.

But if neither by comforts nor hardships, nor by threatening nor persuasion, can he be brought to renounce his errors, and the appointed period of grace has expired, let the Bishop and Judges prepare to deliver or abandon him to the secular Court; and they shall give notice to the herald or bailiff or secular authorities that on such a day, not a Feast, and at such an hour they should be in such a place with their attendants outside a church, and that they will deliver to them a certain impenitent heretic. None the less they shall themselves make public proclamation in the customary places that on such a day at such a time in the aforesaid place a sermon will be preached in defence of the faith, and that they will hand over a certain heretic to secular justice; and that all should come and be present, being granted the customary Indulgences.

After this, the prisoner shall be delivered to the secular Court in the following manner. But let him first be often admonished to renounce his heresy and repent; but if he altogether refuses, let the sentence be pronounced. We, N., by the mercy of God Bishop of such city, or Judge in the territories of such Prince, seeing that you, N., of such a place in such a Diocese, have been accused before us by public report and the information of credible persons (naming them) of heresy, and that you have for many years persisted in those heresies to the great hurt of your immortal soul; and since we, whose duty it is to exterminate the plague of heresy, wishing to be more certainly informed of this matter and to see whether you walked in darkness or the light, have diligently inquired into the said accusation, summoning and duly examining you, we find that you are indeed infected with the said heresy.

But since it is the chief desire of our hearts to plant the Holy Catholic Faith in the hearts of our people, and to eradicate the pest of heresy, we have used diverse and various suitable methods, both by ourselves and by others, to persuade you to renounce your said errors and heresies in which you had stood, were standing, and even now defiantly and obstinately stand with stubborn heart. But since the Enemy of the human race is present in your heart, wrapping you up and entangling you in the said errors, and you have refused and yet refuse to abjure the said heresies, choosing rather the death of your soul in hell and of your body in this world than to renounce the said heresies and return to the bosom of the Church and cleanse your soul, and since you are determined to remain in your sin :

Therefore inasmuch as you are bound by the chain of excommunication from the Holy Church, and are justly cut off from the number of the Lord's flock, and are deprived of the benefits of the Church, the Church can do no more for you, having done all that was possible. We the said Bishop and Judges on behalf of the Faith, sitting in tribunal as Judges judging, and having before us the Holy Gospels that our judgement may proceed as from the countenance of God and our eyes see with equity, and having before our eyes only God and the truth of the Holy Faith and the extirpation of the plague of heresy, on this day and at this hour and place assigned to you for the hearing of your final sentence, we give it as our judgement and sentence that you are indeed an impenitent heretic, and as truly such to be delivered and abandoned to the secular Court: wherefore by this sentence we cast you away as an impenitent heretic from our ecclesiastical Court, and deliver or abandon you to the power of the secular Court: praying the said Court to moderate or temper its sentence of death against you. This sentence was given, etc.

☆

QUESTION XXX

Of one who has Confessed to Heresy, is Relapsed, and is also Impenitent.

THE eleventh method of concluding and terminating a process on behalf of the Faith is used when the person accused of heresy, after a diligent discussion of the circumstances of the process in consultation with learned men, is found to have confessed her heresy, and to be impenitent, and to have relapsed into it. And this is when the accused confesses with her own mouth in Court that she believes and has practised such and such. The procedure in such a case is the same as that above; and because she is manifestly a heretic, sentence shall be pronounced in the following manner in the presence of the Bishop and Judges:

We N., by the mercy of God Bishop of such city, or Judge in the territories of such Prince, seeing that you N., of such a place in such a Diocese, were formerly accused before us (or before such and such, our predecessors) of the crime of heresy (naming them), and that you were legally convicted of that crime by your own confession and the testimony of worthy men, and that you obstinately persisted in it for so many years; but that afterwards, having listened to better advice, you publicly abjured those heresies in such a place and in the form required by the Church, on which account the aforesaid Bishop and Judge, believing that you had truly renounced the said errors and had returned with Catholic faith to the bosom of the Church, granted you the benefit of absolution, releasing you from the sentence of excommunication by which you were formerly bound, and, setting you a salutary penance if

with true heart and faith unfeigned you remained converted to the unity of the Holy Church, received you back in mercy. For the Holy Church of God is not closed to such as return to her bosom.

But after all the aforesaid you have to our great grief been accused before us of having again fallen into those damnable heresies which you formerly abjured in public; yea, you have done so and so (naming them) in contravention of the said abjuration and to the damage of your soul; and although we are sore wounded and cut to the heart to have heard such things of you, yet we were in justice compelled to inquire into the matter, to examine the witnesses, and to summon and question you on oath as it behoved us, and in every particular to proceed as we are bidden by the canonical institutions. And as we wished to conclude this case beyond any doubt, we summoned a solemn council of men learned in the Theological faculty and of those skilled in the Canon and Civil Laws.

And having obtained the mature and considered judgement of the said learned men upon every single particular which had been brought to notice and done in this case, after repeated examination of the whole process and careful and diligent discussion of every circumstance, as law and justice demanded, we find that you are legally convicted both by the evidence of credible witnesses and by your own repeated confession, that you have fallen, and fallen again, into the heresies which you abjured. For we find that you have said or done such and such (naming them), wherefore we have reason, in the opinion of the said learned men, and compelled thereto by your own excesses, to judge you as a backslider according to the canonical decrees. And that we say this with grief, and grieve to say it, He knows from Whom nothing is hid and Who seeth into the secrets of all hearts. And with all our hearts we desired and still desire to lead you back to the unity of Holy Church and to drive out from your heart the said foul heresy, that so you may save your soul and preserve your body and soul from destruction in hell, and we have exerted our utmost endeavour by various fitting methods to convert you to salvation; but you have been given up to your sin and led away and seduced by an evil spirit, and have chosen to be tortured with fearful and eternal torment in hell, and that your temporal body should here be consumed in the flames, rather than to give ear to better counsels and renounce your damnable and pestilent errors, and to return to the merciful bosom of our Holy Mother Church.

Wherefore since the Church of God can do nothing more for you, having done all that was possible to convert you: We the Bishop and Judges named in this cause on behalf of the faith, sitting in tribunal as Judges judging, having before us the Holy Gospels that our judgement may proceed as from the countenance of God and our eyes see with equity, and having before our eyes only God and the honour of the Holy Catholic Faith, on this day at this hour and place before assigned to you for the hearing of your final sentence, we pronounce judgement upon you N., here present before us, and condemn and sentence you as a truly impenitent and relapsed heretic, and as such to be delivered or abandoned to secular justice; and by this our definitive sentence we cast you out as a truly impenitent and relapsed heretic from our ecclesiastical Court, and deliver and abandon you to the power of the secular Court; praying that the said secular Court will temper or moderate its sentence of death against you. This sentence was given, etc.

☆

QUESTION XXXI

Of one Taken and Convicted, but Denying Everything.

THE twelfth method of finishing and concluding a process on behalf of the faith is used when the person accused of heresy, after a diligent examination of the merits of the process in consultation with skilled lawyers, is found to be convicted of heresy by the evidence of the facts or by the legitimate production of witnesses, but not by his own confession. That is to say, he may be convicted by the evidence of the facts, in that he has publicly practised heresy; or by the evidence of witnesses against whom he can take no legitimate exception;

yet, though so taken and convicted, he firmly and constantly denies the charge. See Henry of Segusio *On Heresy*, question 34.

The procedure in such a case is as follows. The accused must be kept in strong durance fettered and chained, and must often be visited by the officers, both in a body and severally, who will use their own best endeavours and those of others to induce him to discover the truth; telling him that if he does so and confesses his error, and abjures that vile heresy, he will be admitted to mercy; but that if he refuses and persists in his denial, he will in the end be abandoned to the secular law, and will not be able to escape temporal death.

But if he continues for a long time in his denials, the Bishop and his officers, now in a body and now severally, now personally and now with the assistance of other honest and upright men, shall summon before them now one witness, now another, and warn him to attend strictly to what he has deposed, and to be sure whether or not he has told the truth; that he should beware lest in damning another temporally he damn himself eternally; that if he be afraid, let him at least tell them the truth in secret, that the accused should not die unjustly. And let them be careful to talk to him in such a way that they may see clearly whether or not his depositions have been true.

But if the witnesses, after this warning, adhere to their statements, and the accused maintains his denials, let not the Bishop and his officers on that account be in any haste to pronounce a definitive sentence and hand the prisoner over to secular law; but let them detain him still longer, now persuading him to confess, now yet again urging the witnesses (but one at a time) to examine their consciences well. And let the Bishop and his officers pay particular attention to that witness who seems to be of the best conscience and the most disposed to good, and let them more insistently charge him on his conscience to speak the truth whether or not the matter was as he had deposed. And if they see any witness vacillate, or there are any other indications that he has given false evidence, let them attest him according to the counsel of learned men, and proceed as justice shall require.

For it is very often found that after a person so convicted by credible witnesses has long persisted in his denials, he has at length relented, especially on being truly informed that he will not be delivered to the secular Court, but be admitted to mercy if he confesses his sin, and he has then freely confessed the truth which he had so long denied. And it is often found that the witnesses, actuated by malice and overcome by enmity, have conspired together to accuse an innocent person of the sin of heresy; but afterwards, at the frequent entreaty of the Bishop and his officers, their consciences have been stricken with remorse and, by Divine inspiration, they have revoked their evidence and confessed that they have out of malice put that crime upon the accused. Therefore the prisoner in such a case is not to be sentenced hastily, but must be kept for a year or more before he is delivered up to the secular Court.

When a sufficient time has elapsed, and after all possible care has been taken, if the accused who has been thus legally convicted has acknowledged his guilt and confessed in legal form that he hath been for the period stated ensnared in the crime of heresy, and has consented to abjure that and every heresy, and to perform such satisfaction as shall seem proper to the Bishop and Inquisitor for one convicted of heresy both by his own confession and the legitimate production of witnesses; then let him as a penitent heretic publicly abjure all heresy, in the manner which we have set down in the eighth method of concluding a process on behalf of the faith.

But if he has confessed that he hath fallen into such heresy, but nevertheless obstinately adheres to it, he must be delivered to the secular Court as an impenitent, after the manner of the tenth method which we have explained above.

But if the accused has remained firm and unmoved in his denial of the charges against him, but the witnesses have withdrawn their charges, revoking their evidence and acknowledging their guilt, confessing that they had put so great a crime upon an innocent man from motives of rancour and hatred, or had been suborned or bribed thereto; then the accused shall be freely discharged, but they shall be punished as false witnesses, accusers or informers. This is made clear by Paul of Burgos in his comment on the Canon c. *multorum*. And sentence or penance shall be pronounced against them as shall seem proper to the Bishop and Judges; but in any case such false witnesses must be condemned to perpetual imprisonment on a diet of bread and water, and to do penance for all the days of their life, being made to stand upon the steps before the church door, etc. However, the Bishops have power to mitigate or even to increase the sentence after a year or some other period, in the usual manner.

But if the accused, after a year or other longer period which has been deemed sufficient, continues to maintain his denials, and the legitimate witnesses abide by their evidence, the Bishop and Judges shall prepare to abandon him to the secular Court; sending to him certain honest men zealous for the faith, especially religious, to tell him that he cannot escape temporal death while he thus persists in his denial, but will be delivered up as an impenitent heretic to the power of the secular Court. And the Bishop and his officers shall give notice to the Bailiff or authority of the secular Court that on such a day at such an hour and in such a place (not inside a church) he should come with his attendants to receive an impenitent heretic whom they will deliver to him. And let him make public proclamation in the usual places that all should be present on such a day at such an hour and place to hear a sermon preached on behalf of the faith, and that the Bishop and his officer will hand over a certain obstinate heretic to the secular Court.

On the appointed day for the pronouncement of sentence the Bishop and his officer shall be in the place aforesaid, and the prisoner shall be placed on high before the assembled clergy and people so that he may be seen by all, and the secular authorities shall be present before the prisoner. Then sentence shall be pronounced in the following manner:

We, N., by the mercy of God Bishop of such city, or Judge in the territories of such Prince, seeing that you, N., of such a place in such a Diocese, have been accused before us of such heresy (naming it); and wishing to be more certainly informed whether the charges made against you were true, and whether you walked in darkness or in the light; we proceeded to inform ourselves by diligently examining the witnesses, by often summoning and questioning you on oath, and admitting an Advocate to plead in your defence, and by proceeding in every way as we were bound by the canonical decrees.

And wishing to conclude your trial in a manner beyond all doubt, we convened in solemn council men learned in the Theological faculty and in the Canon and Civil Laws. And having diligently examined and discussed each circumstance of the process and maturely and carefully considered with the said learned men everything which has been said and done in this present case, we find that you, N., have been legally convicted of having been infected with the sin of heresy for so long a time, and that you have said and done such and such (naming them) on account of which it manifestly appears that you are legitimately convicted of the said heresy.

But since we desired, and still desire, that you should confess the truth and renounce the said heresy, and be led back to the bosom of Holy Church and to the unity of the Holy Faith, that so you should save your soul and escape the destruction of both your body and soul in hell; we have by our own efforts and those of others, and by delaying your sentence for a long time, tried to induce you to repent; but you being obstinately given over to wickedness have scorned to agree to our wholesome advice, and have persisted and do persist with stubborn and defiant mind in your contumacious and dogged denials; and this we say with grief, and grieve and mourn in saying it. But since the Church of God has waited so long for you to repent and acknowledge your guilt, and you have refused and still refuse, her grace and mercy can go no farther.

Wherefore that you may be an example to others and that they may be kept from all such heresies, and that such crimes may not remain unpunished: We the Bishop and Judges named on behalf of the faith, sitting in tribunal as Judges judging, and having before us the Holy Gospels that our judgement may proceed as from the countenance of God and our eyes see with equity, and having before our eyes only God and the glory and honour of the Holy Faith, we judge, declare and pronounce sentence that you standing here in our presence on this day at the hour and place appointed for the hearing of your final sentence, are an impenitent heretic, and as such to be delivered or abandoned to secular justice; and as an obstinate and impenitent heretic we have by this sentence cast you off from the ecclesiastical Court and deliver and abandon you to secular justice and the power of the secular Court. And we pray that the said secular Court may moderate its sentence of death upon you. This sentence was given, etc.

The Bishop and Judges may, moreover, arrange that just men zealous for the faith, known to and in the confidence of the secular Court, shall have access to the prisoner while the secular Court is performing its office, in order to console him and even yet induce him to confess the truth, acknowledge his guilt, and renounce his errors.

But if it should happen that after the sentence, and when the prisoner is already at the place where he is to be burned, he should say that he wishes to confess the truth and acknowledge his guilt, and does so; and if he should be willing to abjure that and every heresy; although it may be presumed that he does this rather from fear of death than for love of the truth, yet I should be of the opinion that he may in mercy be received as a penitent heretic and be imprisoned for life. See the gloss on the chapters *ad abolendam* and *excommunicamus*. Nevertheless, according to the rigour of the law, the Judges ought not to place much faith in a conversion of this sort; and furthermore, they can always punish him on account of the temporal injuries which he has committed.

☆

QUESTION XXXII

Of one who is Convicted but who hath Fled or who Contumaciously Absents himself.

THE thirteenth and last method of arriving at a definite sentence in a process on behalf of the Faith is used when the person accused of heresy, after a diligent discussion of the merits of the process in consultation with learned lawyers, is found to be convicted of heresy, but has made his escape, or defiantly absents himself after the expiration of a set time. And this happens in three cases.

First, when the accused is convicted of heresy by his own confession, or by the evidence of the facts, or by the legitimate production of witnesses, but has fled, or has absented himself and refused to appear after being legally summoned.

Secondly, when a person has been accused and certain information has been laid against him on account of which he rests under some suspicion, even if it be only a light one, and he has been summoned to answer for his faith; and because he has defiantly refused to appear, he is excommunicated, and has stubbornly remained in that excommunication for a year, and always defiantly absents himself.

The third case is when someone directly obstructs the Bishop's or Judges' sentence or process on behalf of the Faith, or lends his help, advice or protection for that purpose, and such a person has been stricken with the sword of excommunication. And if he has obstinately endured that excommunication for a year, he is then to be condemned as a heretic who has defied the administration of justice.

In the first case, such a person is, according to the Canon *ad abolendam*, to be condemned as an impenitent heretic. In the second and third cases he is not to be judged as an impenitent heretic, but to be condemned as if he were a penitent heretic. And in any of these cases the following procedure should be observed. When such a person has been awaited for a sufficient time, let him be summoned by the Bishop and his officer in the Cathedral Church of that Diocese in which he has sinned, and in the other churches of that place where he had his dwelling, and especially from where he has fled; and let him be summoned in the following manner:

We, N., by the mercy of God Bishop of such city, etc., or Judge of such Diocese, having in our charge the welfare of souls, and having above all the desires of our heart this most earnest desire that in our time in the said Diocese the Church should flourish and that there should be a fruitful and abundant harvest in that vineyard of the Lord of Hosts, which the right hand of the Most High Father has planted in the bosom of the righteous, which the Son of that Father has plentifully watered with His own life-giving Blood, which the reviving Spirit the Paraclete has made fruitful within by His wonderful and ineffable gifts, which the whole incomprehensible and ineffable Blessed Trinity has endowed and enriched with many very great and holy privileges; but the wild boar out of the forest, by which is meant any sort of heretic, has devoured and despoiled it, laying waste the fair fruit of the faith and planting thorny briars among the vines; and that tortuous serpent, the evil enemy of our human race, who is Satan and the devil, has breathed out venom and poisoned the fruit of the vineyard with the plague of heresy: And this is the field of the Lord, the Catholic Church, to till and cultivate which the only first-born Son of God the Father descended from the heights of Heaven, and sowed it with miracles and Holy discourse, going through towns and villages and teaching not without great labour; and He chose as His Apostles honest labouring men, and showed them the way, endowing them with eternal rewards; and the Son of God Himself expects to gather from that field on the Day of the Last Judgement a plentiful harvest, and by the hands of His Holy Angels to store it in His Holy barn in Heaven: But the foxes of Samson,* two-faced like them who have fallen into the sin of heresy, having their faces looking both ways but tied together by their burning tails, run about with many torches amidst the fields of the Lord now white unto harvest and shining with the splendour of the faith, and bitterly despoil them, speeding most cunningly here and there, and with their strong attacks burning, dissipating, and devastating, and subtly and damnably subverting the truth of the Holy Catholic Faith.

Wherefore, since you, N., are fallen into the damned heresies of witches, practising them publicly in such place (naming it), and have been by legitimate witnesses convicted of the sin of heresy, or by your own confession received by us in Court; and after

---

* "*Samson*." "*Judges*" xv, 1–6.

your capture you have escaped, refusing the medicine of your salvation : therefore we have summoned you to answer for the said crimes in person before us, but you, led away and seduced by a wicked spirit, have refused to appear.

Or as follows :

Wherefore, since you, N., have been accused before us of the sin of heresy, and from information received against you we have judged that you are under a light suspicion of that sin, we have summoned you to appear personally before us to answer for the Catholic faith. And since, having been summoned, you have defiantly refused to appear, we excommunicated you and caused you to be proclaimed excommunicate. And in this state you have remained stubborn for a year, or so many years, hiding here and there, so that even now we do not know whither the evil spirit has led you; and though we awaited you kindly and mercifully, that you might return to the bosom and the unity of the Holy Faith, you being wholly given up to evil have scorned to do so. Yet we wish and are bound by justice to conclude this case beyond any question, nor can we pass over with connivent eyes your iniquitous crimes.

We the Bishop and Judges in the said cause on behalf of the faith require and strictly command by this our present public edict that you the aforesaid, at present in hiding and a runaway and fugitive, shall on such a day of such a month in such a year, in such Cathedral Church of such Diocese, at the hour of Terce appear personally before us to hear your final sentence : signifying that, whether you appear or not, we shall proceed to our definitive sentence against you as law and justice shall require. And that our summons may come to your knowledge beforehand and you may not be able to protect yourself with a plea of ignorance, we wish and command that our said present letters, requisition and summons be publicly affixed to the doors of the said Cathedral Church. In witness of all which we have ordered these our present letters to be authorized by the impressions of our seals. Given, etc.

On the appointed day assigned for the hearing of the final sentence, if the fugitive shall have appeared and consented to abjure publicly all heresy, humbly praying to be admitted to mercy, he is to be admitted if he has not been a backslider; and if he was convicted by his own confession or by the legitimate production of witnesses, he shall abjure and repent as a penitent heretic, according to the manner explained in the eighth method of concluding a process on behalf of the faith. If he was gravely suspected, and refused to appear when he was summoned to answer for his faith, and was therefore excommunicated and had endured that excommunication obstinately for a year, but becomes penitent, let him be admitted, and abjure all heresy, and repent as one gravely suspected of heresy, in the manner explained in the sixth method of pronouncing sentence. But if he shall appear, and not consent to abjure, let him be delivered as a truly impenitent heretic to the secular Court, as was explained in the tenth method. But if he still defiantly refuses to appear, let the sentence be pronounced in the following manner:

We, N., by the mercy of God Bishop of such city, seeing that you, N., of such a place in such a Diocese were accused before us by public report and the information of worthy men of the sin of heresy: We, whose duty it is, proceeded to examine and inquire whether there was any truth in the report which had come to our ears. And finding that you were convicted of heresy by the depositions of many credible witnesses, we commanded that you be brought before us in custody. (Here let it be said whether he had appeared and been questioned under oath or not.) But afterwards, led away and seduced by the advice of the evil spirit, and fearing to have your wounds wholesomely healed with wine and oil, you fled away (or, if it was the case, You broke from your prison and place of detention and fled away), hiding here and there, and we are altogether ignorant of whither the said evil spirit has led you.

Or after this manner :

And finding that against you, accused as aforesaid before us of the sin of heresy, there were many indications by reason of which we judged you to be lightly suspected of the said heresy, we summoned you by public edict in such and such churches of such Diocese within a certain time assigned to appear in person before us to answer to the said charges against you and otherwise on matters concerning the Faith. But you, following some mad advice, obstinately refused to appear. And when, as in justice bound, we excommunicated you and caused you to be publicly proclaimed as excommunicate, you stubbornly remained in that excommunication for more than a year, and kept hidden here and there, so that we do not know whither the evil spirit has led you.

And whereas the Holy Church of God has long awaited you up to this present day in kindness and mercy, that you might fly to the bosom of her mercy, renouncing your errors and professing the Catholic Faith, and be nourished by the bounty of her mercy; but you have refused to consent, persisting in your obstinacy; and since we wished and still wish, as we ought to do and as justice compels us, to bring your case to an equitable conclusion, we have summoned you to appear in person before us on this day at this hour and place, to hear your final sentence. And since you have stubbornly refused to appear, you are manifestly proved to abide permanently in your errors and heresies; and this we say with grief, and grieve in saying it.

But since we cannot and will not delay to do justice, nor may we tolerate so great disobedience and defiance of the Church of God; for the exaltation of the Catholic Faith and the extirpation of vile heresy, at the call of justice, and by reason of your disobedience and obstinacy, on this day and at the hour and place heretofore strictly and precisely assigned to you for the hearing of your final sentence, having diligently and carefully discussed each several circumstance of the process with men learned in the Theological faculty and in the Canon and Civil Laws, sitting in tribunal as Judges judging, having before us the Holy Gospels that our judgement may proceed as from the countenance of God and our eyes see with equity, and having before our eyes only God and the irrefragable truth of the Holy Faith, and following in the footsteps of the Blessed Apostle Paul, in these writings we pronounce final sentence against you, N., absent or present, as follows, invoking the Name of Christ.

We the Bishop and Judges named on behalf of the Faith, whereas the process of this cause on behalf of the Faith has in all things been conducted as the laws require; and whereas you, having been legally summoned, have not appeared, and have not by yourself or any other person excused yourself; and whereas you have for a long time persisted and still obstinately persist in the said heresies, and have endured excommunication in the cause of the Faith for so many years, and still stubbornly endure it; and whereas the Holy Church of God can do no more for you, since you have persisted and intend to persist in your excommunication and said heresies: Therefore, following in the footsteps of the Blessed Apostle Paul, we declare, judge and sentence you, absent or present, to be a stubborn heretic, and as such to be abandoned to secular justice. And by this our definitive sentence we drive you from the ecclesiastical Court, and abandon you to the power of the secular Court; earnestly praying the said Court that, if ever it should have you in its power, it will moderate its sentence of death against you. This sentence was given, etc.

Here it is to be considered that, if that stubborn fugitive had been convicted of heresy, either by his own confession or by credible witnesses, and had fled before his abjuration, he is by the sentence to be judged an impenitent heretic, and so it must be expressed in the sentence. But if, on the other hand, he had not been convicted, but had been summoned as one under suspicion to answer for his faith; and, because he has refused to appear, has been excommunicated, and has obstinately endured that excommunication for more than a year, and has finally refused to appear; then he is not to be judged a heretic, but as a heretic, and must be condemned as such; and so it must be expressed in the sentence, as it is said above.

☆

QUESTION XXXIII

Of the Method of passing Sentence upon one who has been Accused by another Witch, who has been or is to be Burned at the Stake.

THE fourteenth method of finally concluding a process on behalf of the Faith is used when the person accused of heresy, after a careful discussion of the circumstances of the process with reference to the informant in consultation with learned lawyers, is found to be accused of that heresy only by another witch who has been or is to be burned. And this can happen in thirteen ways in thirteen cases. For a person so accused is either found innocent and is to be freely discharged; or she is found to be generally defamed for that heresy; or it is found that, in addition to her defamation, she is to be to some degree exposed to torture; or she is found to be strongly suspected of heresy; or she is found to be gravely suspected of heresy; or she is found to be at the same time defamed and suspected; and so on up to thirteen different cases, as was shown in the Twentieth Question.

The first case is when she is accused only by a witch in custody, and is not convicted either by her own confession or by legitimate witnesses, and there are no other indications found by reason of which she can truly be regarded as suspect. In such a case she is to be entirely absolved, even by the secular Judge himself who has either burned the deponent or is about to burn her either on his own authority or on that commissioned to him by the Bishop and Judge of the Ordinary Court; and she shall be absolved in the manner explained in the Twentieth Question.

The second case is when, in addition to being accused by a witch in custody, she is also publicly defamed throughout the whole village or city; so that she has always laboured under that particular defamation, but, after the deposition of the witch, it has become aggravated.

In such a case the following should be the procedure. The Judge should consider that, apart from the general report, nothing particular has been proved against her by other credible witnesses in the village or town; and although, perhaps, that witch has deposed some serious charges against her, yet, since she has lost her faith by denying it to the devil, Judges should give no ready credence to her words, unless there should be other circumstances which aggravate that report; and then the case would fall under the third and following case. Therefore she should be enjoined a canonical purgation, and the sentence should be

pronounced as shown in the Twenty-first Question.

And if the civil Judge orders this purgation to be made before the Bishop, and ends with a solemn declaration that, if she should fail, then, as an example to others, she should be more severely sentenced by both the ecclesiastical and civil Judges, well and good. But if he wishes to conduct it himself, let him command her to find ten or twenty compurgators of her own class, and proceed in accordance with the second method of sentencing such: except that, if she has to be excommunicated, then he must have recourse to the Ordinary; and this would be the case if she refused to purge herself.

The third case, then, happens when the person so accused is not convicted by her own confession, nor by the evidence of the facts, nor by credible witnesses, nor are there any other indications as to any fact in which she had ever been marked by the other inhabitants of that town or village, except her general reputation among them. But the general report has become intensified by the detention of that witch in custody, as that it is said that she had been her companion in everything and had participated in her crimes. But even so, the accused firmly denies all this, and nothing of it is known to other inhabitants, or of anything save good behaviour on her part, though her companionship with the witch is admitted.

In such a case the following is the procedure. First they are to be brought face to face, and their mutual answers and recriminations noted, to see whether there is any inconsistency in their words by reason of which the Judge can decide from her admissions and denials whether he ought to expose her to torture; and if so, he can proceed as in the third manner of pronouncing sentence, explained in the Twenty-second Question, submitting her to light tortures: at the same time exercising every possible precaution, as we explained at length towards the beginning of this Third Part, to find out whether she is innocent or guilty.

The fourth case is when a person accused in this manner is found to be lightly suspected, either because of her own confession or because of the depositions of the other witch in custody. There are some who include among those who should be thus lightly suspected those who go and consult witches for any purpose, or have procured for themselves a lover by stirring up hatred between married folk, or have consorted with witches in order to obtain some temporal advantage. But such are to be excommunicated as followers of heretics, according to the Canon c. *excommunicamus*, where it says: Similarly we judge those to be heretics who believe in their errors. For the effect is presumed from the facts. Therefore it seems that such are to be more severely sentenced and punished than those who are under a light suspicion of heresy and are to be judged from light conjectures. For example, if they had performed services for witches or carried their letters to them, they need not on that account believe in their errors: yet they have not laid information against them, and they have received wages and vails from them. But whether or not such people are to be included in this case, according to the opinion of learned men the procedure must be as in the case of those under a light suspicion, and the Judge will act as follows. Such a person will either abjure heresy or will purge herself canonically, as was explained in the fourth method of pronouncing sentence in the Twenty-third Question.

However, it seems that the better course is for such a person to be ordered to abjure heresy, for this is more in accordance with the meaning of the Canon c. *excommunicamus*, where it speaks of those who are found to be only under some notable suspicion. And if such should relapse, they should not incur the penalty for backsliders. The procedure will be as above explained in the fourth method of sentencing.

The fifth case is when such person is found to be under a strong suspicion, by reason, as before, of her own confession or of the depositions of the other witch in custody. In this class some include those who directly or indirectly obstruct the Court in the process of trying a witch, provided that they do this wittingly.

Also they include all who give help, advice or protection to those who cause such obstructions. Also those who instruct summoned or captured heretics to conceal the truth or in some way falsify it. Also all those who wittingly receive, or visit those whom they know to be heretics, or associate with them, send them gifts, or show favour to them; for all such actions, when done with full knowledge, bespeak favour felt towards the sin, and not to the person. And therefore they say that, when the accused is guilty of any of the above actions, and has been proved so after trial, then she should be sentenced in the fifth method, explained in the Twenty-fourth Question; so that she must abjure all heresy, under pain of being punished as a backslider.

As to these contentions we may say that the Judge must take into consideration the household and family of each several witch who has been burned or is detained; for these are generally found to be infected.

For witches are instructed by devils to offer to them even their own children; therefore there can be no doubt that such children are instructed in all manner of crimes, as is shown in the First Part of this work.

Again, in a case of simple heresy it happens that, on account of the familiarity between heretics who are akin to each other, when one is convicted of heresy it follows that his kindred also are strongly suspected; and the same is true of the heresy of witches.

But this present case is made clear in the chapter of the Canon *inter sollicitudines*. For a certain Dean was, owing to his reputation as a heretic, enjoined a canonical purgation; on account of his familiarity with heretics, he had to make a public abjuration; and through the scandal he was deprived of his benefice, so that the scandal might be allayed.

The sixth case is when such a person is under a grave suspicion; but no simple and bare deposition by another witch in custody can cause this, for there must be in addition some indication of the facts, derived from certain words or deeds uttered or committed by the witch in custody, in which the accused is at least said to have taken some part, and shared in the evil deeds of the deponent.

To understand this, the reader should refer to what was written in the Nineteenth Question, especially concerning the grave degree of suspicion, how it arises from grave and convincing conjectures; and how the Judge is forced to believe, on mere suspicion, that a person is a heretic, although perhaps in his heart he is a true Catholic. The Canonists give an example of this by the case, in simple heresy, of a man summoned to answer in the cause of the faith, and defiantly refusing to appear, on which account he is excommunicated, and if he persists in that state for a year, becomes gravely suspected of heresy.

And so likewise in the case of a person accused in the way we are considering, the indications of the facts are to be examined by which she is rendered gravely suspect. Let us put the case that the witch in custody has asserted that the accused has taken part in her evil works of witchcraft, but the accused firmly denies it. What then is to be done? It will be necessary to consider whether there are any facts to engender a strong suspicion of her, and whether that strong suspicion can become a grave one. Thus, if a man has been summoned to answer some charge, and has obstinately refused to appear, he would come under a light suspicion of heresy, even if he had not been summoned in a cause concerning the Faith. But if he then refused to appear in a cause concerning the Faith and was excommunicated for his obstinacy, then he would be strongly suspected; for the light suspicion would become a strong one; and if then he remained obstinate in excommunication for a year, the strong suspicion would become a grave one. Therefore the Judge will consider whether, by reason of her familiarity with the witch in custody, the accused is under a strong suspicion, in the manner shown in the fifth case above; and then he must consider whether there is anything which may turn that strong suspicion into a grave one. For it is presumed that it is possible for this to be the case, on account of the accused having perhaps shared in the crimes of the detained witch, if she has had frequent intercourse with her. Therefore the Judge must proceed as in the sixth method of sentencing explained in the Twenty-fifth Question. But it may be asked what the Judge is to do if the person so accused by a witch in custody still altogether persists in her denials, in spite of all indications against her. We answer as follows:

First the Judge must consider whether those denials do or do not proceed from the vice or witchcraft of taciturnity: and, as was shown in the Fifteenth and Sixteenth Questions of this Third Part, the Judge can know this from her ability or inability to shed tears, or from her insensibility under torture and quick recovery of her strength afterwards. For then the grave suspicion would be aggravated; and in such a case she is by no means to be freely discharged, but, according to the sixth method of sentencing, she must be condemned to perpetual imprisonment and penance.

But if she is not infected with the taciturnity of witches, but feels the keenest pains in her torture (whereas others, as has been said, become insensible to pain owing to the witchcraft of taciturnity), then the Judge must fall back upon his last expedient of a canonical purgation. And if this should be ordered by a secular Judge, it is called a lawful vulgar purgation, since it cannot be classed with other vulgar purgations. And if she should fail in this purgation she will be judged guilty.

The seventh case is when the accused is not found guilty by his own confession, by the evidence of the facts, or by legitimate witnesses, but is only found to be accused by a witch in custody, and there are also some indications found which bring him under light or strong suspicion. As, for example, that he had had great familiarity with witches; in which case he would, according to the Canon, have to undergo a canonical purgation on account of the general report concerning him; and on account of the suspicion against him he must abjure heresy, under pain of being punished as a backslider if it was a strong suspicion, but not if it was a light one.

The eighth case occurs when the person so accused is found to have confessed that heresy, but to be penitent, and never to have relapsed. But here it is to be noted that in this and the other cases, where it is a question of those who have or have not relapsed, and who are or are not penitent, these distinctions are made only for the benefit of Judges who are not concerned with the infliction of the extreme penalty. Therefore the civil Judge may proceed in accordance with the Civil and Imperial Laws, as justice shall demand, in the case of one who has confessed, no matter whether or not she be penitent, or whether or not she have relapsed. Only he may have recourse to those thirteen methods of pronouncing sentence, and act in accordance with them, if any doubtful question should arise.

☆

QUESTION XXXIV

Of the Method of passing Sentence upon a Witch who Annuls Spells wrought by Witchcraft ; and of Witch Midwives and Archer-Wizards.

THe fifteenth method of bringing a process on behalf of the faith to a definitive sentence is employed when the person accused of heresy is not found to be one who casts injurious spells of witchcraft, but one who removes them; and in such a case the procedure will be as follows. The remedies which she uses will either be lawful or unlawful; and if they are lawful, she is not to be judged a witch but a good Christian. But we have already shown at length what sort of remedies are lawful.

Unlawful remedies, on the other hand, are to be distinguished as either absolutely unlawful, or in some respect unlawful. If they are absolutely unlawful, these again can be divided into two classes, according as they do or do not involve some injury to another party; but in either case they are always accompanied by an expressed invocation of devils. But if they are only in some respect unlawful, that is to say, if they are practised with only a tacit, and not an expressed, invocation of devils, such are to be judged rather vain than unlawful, according to the Canonists and some Theologians, as we have already shown.

Therefore the Judge, whether ecclesiastical or civil, must not punish the first and last of the above practices, having rather to commend the first and tolerate the last, since the Canonists maintain that it is lawful to oppose vanity with vanity. But he must by no means tolerate those who remove spells by an expressed invocation of devils, especially those who in doing so bring some injury upon a third party; and this last is said to happen

when the spell is taken off one person and transferred to another. And we have already made it clear in a former part of this work that it makes no difference whether the person to whom the spell is transferred be herself a witch or not, or whether or not she be the person who cast the original spell, or whether it be a man or any other creature.

It may be asked what the Judge should do when such a person maintains that she removes spells by lawful and not unlawful means; and how the Judge can arrive at the truth of such a case. We answer that he should summon her and ask her what remedies she uses; but he must not rely only upon her word, for the ecclesiastical Judge whose duty it is must make diligent inquiry, either himself or by means of some parish priest who shall examine all his parishioners after placing them upon oath, as to what remedies she uses. And if, as is usually the case, they are found to be superstitious remedies, they must in no way be tolerated, on account of the terrible penalties laid down by the Canon Law, as will be shown.

Again, it may be asked how the lawful remedies can be distinguished from the unlawful, since they always assert that they remove spells by certain prayers and the use of herbs. We answer that this will be easy, provided that a diligent inquiry be made. For although they must necessarily conceal their superstitious remedies, either that they may not be arrested, or that they may the more easily ensnare the minds of the simple, and therefore make great show of their use of prayers and herbs; yet they can be manifestly convicted by four superstitious actions as sorceresses and witches.

For there are some who can divine secrets, and are able to tell things which they could only know through the revelation of evil spirits. For example : when the injured come to them to be healed, they can discover and make known the cause of their injury; as that it arose from some quarrel with a neighbour or some other cause; and they can perfectly know this and tell it to those who consult them.

Secondly, they sometimes undertake to cure the injury or spell of one person, but will have nothing to do with that of another. For in the Diocese of Spires there is a witch in a certain place called Zunhofen who, although she seems to heal many persons, confesses that she can in no way heal certain others; and this is for no other reason than, as the inhabitants of the place assert, that the spells cast on such persons have been so potently wrought by other witches with the help of devils that the devils themselves cannot remove them. For one devil cannot or will not always yield to another.

Thirdly, it sometimes happens that they know that they must make some reservation or exception in their cure of such injuries. Such a case is known to have occurred in the town of Spires itself. An honest woman who had been bewitched in her shins sent for a diviner of this sort to come and heal her; and when the witch had entered her house and looked at her, she made such an exception. For she said: If there are no scales and hairs in the wound, I could take out all the other evil matter. And she revealed the cause of the injury, although she had come from the country from a distance of two miles, saying: You quarrelled with your neighbour on such a day, and therefore this has happened to you. Then, having extracted from the wound many other matters of various sorts, which were not scales or hairs, she restored her to health.

Fourthly, they sometimes themselves observe, or cause to be observed, certain superstitious ceremonies. For instance, they fix some such time as before sunrise for people to visit them; or say that they cannot heal injuries which were caused beyond the limits of the estate on which they live; or that they can only heal two or three persons in a year. Yet they do not heal them, but only seem to do so by ceasing to injure them.

We could add many other considerations as touching the condition of such persons: as that, after the lapse of a certain time they have incurred the reputation of leading a bad and sinful life, or that they are adulteresses, or the survivors from covens of other witches. Therefore their gift of healing is not derived from God on account of the sanctity of their lives.

Here we must refer incidentally to witch midwives, who surpass all other witches in their crimes, as we have shown in the First Part of this work.

And the number of them is so great that, as has been found from their confessions, it is thought that there is scarcely any tiny hamlet in which at least one is not to be found. And that the magistrates may in some degree meet this danger, they should allow no midwife to practise without having been first sworn as a good Catholic; at the same time observing the other safeguards mentioned in the Second Part of this work.

Here too we must consider archer-wizards, who constitute the graver danger to the Christian religion in that they have obtained protection on the estates of nobles and Princes who receive, patronize, and defend them. But that all such receivers and protectors are more damnable than all witches, especially in certain cases, is shown as follows. The Canonists and Theologians divide into two classes the patrons of such archer-wizards, according as they defend the error or the person. They who defend the error are more damnable than the wizards themselves, since they are judged to be not only heretics but heresiarchs (24, quest. 3). And the laws do not make much special mention of such patrons, because they do not distinguish them from other heretics.

But there are others who, while not excusing the sin, yet defend the sinner. These, for example, will do all in their power to protect such wizards (or other heretics) from trial and punishment at the hands of the Judge acting on behalf of the Faith.

Similarly there are those in public authority, that is to say, public persons such as temporal Lords, and also spiritual Lords who have temporal jurisdiction, who are, either by omission or commission, patrons of such wizards and heretics.

They are their patrons by omission when they neglect to perform their duty in regard to such wizards and suspects, or to their followers, receivers, defenders and patrons, when they are required by the Bishops or Inquisitors to do this: that is, by failing to arrest them, by not guarding them carefully when they are arrested, by not taking them to the place within their jurisdiction which has been appointed for them, by not promptly executing the sentence passed upon them, and by other such derelictions of their duty.

They are their patrons by commission when, after such heretics have been arrested, they liberate them from prison without the licence or order of the Bishop or Judge; or when they directly or indirectly obstruct the trial, judgement, and sentence of such, or act in some similar way. The penalties for this have been declared in the Second Part of this work, where we treated of archer-wizards and other enchanters of weapons.

It is enough now to say that all these are by law excommunicated, and incur the twelve great penalties. And if they continue obstinate in that excommunication for a year, they are then to be condemned as heretics.

Who, then, are to be called receivers of such; and are they to be reckoned as heretics? All they, we answer, who receive such archer-wizards, enchanters of weapons, necromancers, or heretic witches as are the subject of this whole work. And such receivers are of two classes, as was the case with the defenders and patrons of such.

For there are some who do not receive them only once or twice, but many times and often; and these are well called in Latin *receptatores*, from the frequentative form of the verb. And receivers of this class are sometimes blameless, since they act in ignorance and there is no sinister suspicion attaching to them. But sometimes they are to blame, as being well aware of the sins of those whom they receive; for the Church always denounces these wizards as the most cruel enemies of the faith. And if nevertheless temporal Lords receive, keep and defend them, etc., they are and are rightly called receivers of heretics. And with regard to such, the laws say that they are to be excommunicated.

But others there are who do not often or many times receive such wizards or heretics, but only once or twice; and these are not properly called *receptatores*, but *receptores*, since they are not frequent receivers. (Yet the Archdeacon disagrees with this view; but it is no great matter, for we are considering not words but deeds.)

But there is this difference between *receptatores* and *receptores*: those temporal Princes are always *receptatores* who simply will not or cannot drive away such heretics. But *receptores* may be quite innocent.

Finally, it is asked who are they who are said to be obstructors of the duty of Inquisitors and Bishops against such heretics; and whether they are to be reckoned as heretics. We answer that such obstructors are of two kinds. For there are some who cause a direct obstruction, by rashly on their own responsibility releasing from gaol those who have been detained on a charge of heresy, or by interfering with the process of the Inquisition by wreaking some injury to witnesses on behalf of the Faith because of the evidence they have given; or it may be that the temporal Lord issues an order that none but himself may try such a case, and that anyone charged with this crime should be brought before no one but himself, and that the evidence should be given only in his presence, or some similar order. And such, according to Giovanni d'Andrea, are direct obstructors. They who directly obstruct the process, judgement or sentence on behalf of the Faith, or help, advise or favour others in doing so, although they are guilty of great sin, are not on that account to be judged heretics, unless it appears in other ways that they are obstinately and wilfully involved in such heresies of witches. But they are to be smitten with the sword of excommunication; and if they stubbornly endure that excommunication for a year, then are they to be condemned as heretics.

But others are indirect obstructors. These, as Giovanni d'Andrea explains, are those who give such orders as that no one shall bear arms for the capture of heretics except the servants of the said temporal Lord. Such are less guilty than the former, and are not heretics; but they, and also any who advise, help or patronize them in such actions, are to be excommunicated; and if they obstinately remain in that excommunication for a year, they are then to be condemned as if they were heretics. And here it is to be understood that they are in such a way to be condemned as heretics that, if they are willing to return, they are received back to mercy, having first abjured their error; but if not, they are to be handed over to the secular Court as impenitents.

To sum up. Witch-midwives, like other witches, are to be condemned and sentenced according to the nature of their crimes; and this is true also of those who, as we have said, remove spells of witchcraft superstitiously and by the help of devils; for it can hardly be doubted that, just as they are able to remove them, so can they inflict them. And it is a fact that some definite agreement is formed between witches and devils whereby some shall be able to hurt and others to heal, that so they may more easily ensnare the minds of the simple and recruit the ranks of their abandoned and hateful society. Archer-wizards and enchanters of weapons, who are only protected by being patronized, defended and received by temporal Lords, are subject to the same penalties; and they who patronize them, etc., or obstruct the officers of justice in their proceedings against them, are subject to all the penalties to which the patrons of heretics are liable, and are to be excommunicated. And if after they have obstinately endured that excommunication for a year they wish to repent, let them abjure that obstruction and patronage, and they can be admitted to mercy; but if not, they must be handed over as impenitents to the secular Court. And even if they have not endured their excommunication for a year, such obstructors can still be proceeded against as patrons of heretics.

And all that has been said with regard to patrons, defenders, receivers, and obstructors in the case of archer-wizards, etc., applies equally in respect of all other witches who work various injuries to men, animals, and the fruits of the earth. But even the witches themselves, when in the court of conscience with humble and contrite spirit they weep for their sins and make clean confession asking forgiveness, are taken back to mercy. But when they are known, those whose duty it is must proceed against them, summoning, examining, and detaining them, and in all things proceeding in accordance with the nature of their crimes to a definitive and conclusive sentence, as has been shown, if they wish to avoid the snare of eternal damnation by reason of the excommunication pronounced upon them by the Church when they deliberately fail in their duty.

☆

QUESTION XXXV

Finally, of the Method of passing Sentence upon Witches who Enter or Cause to be Entered an Appeal, whether such be Frivolous or Legitimate and Just.

BUT if the Judge perceives that the accused is determined to have recourse to an appeal, he must first take note that such appeals are sometimes valid and legitimate, and sometimes entirely frivolous. Now it has already been explained that cases concerning the Faith are to be conducted in a simple and summary fashion, and therefore that no appeal is admitted in such cases. Nevertheless it sometimes happens that Judges, on account of the difficulty of the case, gladly prorogue and delay it; therefore they may consider that it would be just to allow an appeal when the accused feels that the Judge has really and actually acted towards him in a manner contrary to the law and justice; as that he has refused to allow him to defend himself, or that he has proceeded to a sentence against the accused on his own responsibility and without the counsel of others, or even without the consent of the Bishop or his Vicar, when he might have taken into consideration much further evidence both for and against. For such reasons an appeal may be allowed, but not otherwise.

Secondly, it is to be noted that, when notice of appeal has been given, the Judge should, without any perturbation or disturbance, ask for a copy of the appeal, giving his promise that the matter shall not be delayed. And when the accused has given him the copy of the appeal, the Judge shall notify him that he has yet two days before he need answer it, and after those two days thirty more before he need prepare the apostils of the case. And although he may give his answer at once, and at once proceed to issue his apostils if he is very expert and experienced, yet it is better to act with caution, and fix a term of ten or twenty or twenty-five days, reserving to himself the right to prorogue the hearing of the appeal up to the legal limit of time.

Thirdly, let the Judge take care that during the legal and appointed interval he must diligently examine and discuss the causes of the appeal and the alleged grounds of objection. And if after having taken good counsel he sees that he has unduly and unjustly proceeded against the accused, by refusing him permission to defend himself, or by exposing him to questions at an unsuitable time, or for any such reason; when the appointed time comes let him correct his mistake, carrying the process back to the point and stage where it was when the accused asked to be defended, or when he put a term to his examination, etc., and so remove the objection; and then let him proceed as we have said. For by the removal of the grounds for objection the appeal, which was legitimate, loses its weight.

But here the circumspect and provident Judge will carefully take note that some grounds of objection are reparable; and they are such as we have just spoken of, and are to be dealt with in the above manner. But others are irreparable: as when the accused has actually and in fact been questioned, but has afterwards escaped and lodged an appeal; or that some box or vessel or such instruments as witches use has been seized and burned; or some other such irreparable and irrevocable action has been committed. In such a case the above procedure would not hold good, namely, taking the process back to the point where the objection arose.

Fourthly, the Judge must note that, although thirty days may elapse between his receiving the appeal and his completing the apostils of the case, and he can assign to the petitioner the last day, that is, the thirtieth, for the hearing of his appeal; yet, that it may not seem that he wishes to molest the accused or come under suspicion of unduly harsh treatment of him, and that his behaviour may not seem to lend support to the objection which has caused the appeal, it is better that he should assign some day within the legal limit, such as the tenth or twentieth day, and he can afterwards, if he does not wish to be in a hurry, postpone it until the last legal day, saying that he is busy with other affairs.

Fifthly, the Judge must take care that, when he affixes a term for the accused who is appealing and petitioning for apostils, he must provide not only for the giving, but both for the giving and receiving of apostils. For if he provided only for the giving of them, then the Judge against whom

the appeal is lodged would have to discharge the appellant. Therefore let him assign to him a term, that is, such a day of such a year, for the giving and receiving from the Judge such apostils as he shall have decided to submit.

Sixthly, he must take care that, in assigning this term, he shall not in his answer say that he will give either negative or affirmative apostils; but that he may have opportunity for fuller reflection, let him say that he will give such as he shall at the appointed time have decided upon.

Let him also take care that in assigning this term to the appellant he give the appellant no opportunity to exercise any malicious precautions or cunning, and that he specify the place, day, and hour. For example, let him assign the twentieth day of August, in the present year, at the hour of vespers, and the chamber of the Judge himself in such a house, in such a city, for the giving and receiving of apostils such as shall have been decided upon for such appellant.

Seventhly, let him note that, if he has decided in his mind that the charge against the accused justly requires that he should be detained, in assigning the term he must set it down that he assigns that term for the giving or receiving of apostils by the appellant in person, and that he assigns to the said appellant such a place for giving to him and receiving from him apostils; and then it will be fully in the power of the Judge to detain the appellant, granted that he has first given negative apostils; but otherwise it will not be so.

Eighthly, let the Judge take care not to take any further action in respect of the appellant, such as arresting him, or questioning him, or liberating him from prison, from the time when the appeal is presented to him up to the time when he has returned negative apostils.

To sum up. Note that it often happens that, when the accused is in doubt as to what sort of sentence he will receive, since he is conscious of his guilt, he frequently takes refuge in an appeal, that so he may escape the Judge's sentence. Therefore he appeals from that Judge, advancing some frivolous reason, as that the Judge held him in custody without allowing him the customary surety; or in some such way he may colour his frivolous appeal. In this case the Judge shall ask for a copy of the appeal; and having received it he shall either at once or after two days give his answer and assign to the appellant for the giving and receiving of such apostils as shall have been decided upon a certain day, hour, and place, within the legal limit, as, for instance, the 25th, 26th or 30th day of such a month. And during the assigned interval the Judge shall diligently examine the copy of the appeal, and the reasons or objections upon which it is based, and shall consult with learned lawyers whether he shall submit negative apostils, that is, negative answers, and thereby disallow the appeal, or whether he shall allow the appeal and submit affirmative and fitting apostils to the Judge to whom the appeal is made.

But if he sees that the reasons for the appeal are frivolous and worthless, and that the appellant only wishes to escape or to postpone his sentence, let his apostils be negative and refutatory. If, however, he sees that the objections are true and just, and not irreparable; or if he is in doubt whether the accused is maliciously causing him trouble, and wishes to clear himself of all suspicion, let him grant the appellant affirmative and fitting apostils. And when the appointed time for the appellant has arrived, if the Judge has not prepared his apostils or answers, or in some other way is not ready, the appellant can at once demand that his appeal be heard, and may continue to do so on each successive day up to the thirtieth, which is the last day legally allowed for the submission of the apostils.

But if he has prepared them and is ready, he can at once give his apostils to the appellant. If, then, he has decided to give negative or refutatory apostils, he shall, at the expiration of the appointed time, submit them in the following manner:

AND the said Judge, answering to the said appeal, if it may be called an appeal, says that he, the Judge, has proceeded and did intend to proceed in accordance with the Canonical decrees and the Imperial statutes and laws, and has not departed from the path of either law nor intended so to depart, and has in no way acted or intended to act unjustly towards the appellant, as is manifest from an examination of the alleged grounds for this appeal. For he has not acted unjustly towards him by detaining him and keeping him in custody; for he was accused of such heresy, and there was such evidence against him that he was worthily convicted of heresy, or was strongly suspected, and as such it was and is just that he should be kept in custody: neither has he acted unjustly by refusing him sureties; for the crime of heresy is one of the more serious crimes, and the appellant had been convicted but persisted in denying the charge, and therefore not even the very best sureties were admissible, but he is and was to be detained in prison. And so he shall proceed with the other objections.

Having done this, let him say as follows: Wherefore it is apparent that the Judge has duly and justly proceeded, and has not deviated from the path of justice, and has in no way unduly molested the appellant; but the appellant, advancing pretended and false objections, has by an undue and unjust appeal attempted to escape his sentence. Wherefore his appeal is frivolous and worthless, having no foundation, and erring in matter and form. And since the laws do not recognize frivolous appeals, nor are they to be recognized by the Judge, therefore the Judge has himself said that he does not admit and does not intend to admit the said appeal, nor does he recognize nor yet propose to recognize it. And he gives this answer to the said accused who makes this undue appeal in the form of negative apostils, and commands that they be given to him immediately after the said appeal. And so he shall give it to the Notary who has presented the appeal to him.

And when these negative apostils have been given to the appellant, the Judge shall at once proceed with his duty, ordering the accused to be seized and detained, or assigning to him a day to appear before him, as shall seem best to him. For he does not cease to be the Judge, but shall continue his process against the appellant until the Judge to whom the appeal was made shall order him to cease.

But let the Judge take care not to commence any new proceedings against the appellant, by arresting him or, if he is in custody, liberating him from prison, from the time of the presentation of the appeal up to the time of the return of negative apostils to him. But after that time, as we have said, he can do so if justice requires it, until he is prevented by the Judge to whom the appeal has been made. Then, with the process sealed under cover, and with a sure and safe escort and if necessary a suitable surety, let him send him to the said Judge.

But if the Judge has decided to return affirmative and fitting apostils, let him submit them in writing in the following manner on the arrival of the day appointed for the giving and receiving of apostils:

And the said Judge, answering to the said appeal, if it may be called an appeal, says that he has proceeded in the present cause justly and as he ought and not otherwise, nor has he molested or intended to molest the appellant, as is apparent from a perusal of the alleged objections. For he has not molested him by, etc. (Here he shall answer to each of the objections in the appeal, in the best and most truthful manner that he can.)

Wherefore it is apparent that the said Judge has in no way dealt unjustly by the appellant nor given him cause to appeal, but that the appellant is afraid lest justice should proceed against him according to his crimes. And therefore the appeal is frivolous and worthless, having no foundation, and not being admissible by the laws or the Judge. But in reverence for the Apostolic See, to which the appeal is made, the said Judge says that he admits the appeal and intends to recognize it, deferring the whole matter to our Most Holy Lord the Pope, and leaving it to the Holy Apostolic See: assigning to the said appellant a certain time, namely, so many months now following, within which, with the process sealed under cover given to him by the said Judge, or having given suitable sureties to present himself at the Court of Rome, or under a sure and safe escort appointed to him by the said Judge, he must present himself in the Court of Rome before our Lord the Pope. And this answer the said Judge gives to the said appellant as affirmative apostils, and orders that it be given to him immediately after the appeal presented to him. And so he shall hand it to the Notary who has presented the appeal to him.

The prudent Judge must here take note that, as soon as he has given these fitting apostils to the appellant, he at once ceases to be the Judge in that cause from which the appeal was made, and can proceed no further in it, unless it be referred back to him by our Most Holy Lord the Pope. Therefore let him have no more to do with that case, except to send the said appellant in the above manner to our Lord the Pope, assigning to him a convenient time, say one, two or three months, within which he must prepare and make himself ready to appear and present himself at the Court of Rome, giving a suitable surety; or, if he cannot do this, let him be sent under a sure and safe escort. For he must either bind himself by the best means in his power to present himself within the assigned time before our Lord the Pope in the Court of Rome, or his appeal must necessarily fall to the ground.

But if the Judge has another case, and proceeds against the accused in another case in which he has not lodged any appeal; in that other case he remains, as before, Judge. And even if, after the appeal has been admitted, and the affirmative apostils have been given, the appellant is accused and denounced to the Judge in respect of other heresies which were not in question in the case from which he appealed, he does not cease to be the Judge, and can proceed with the inquiry and the examination of witnesses as before. And when the first case has been finished in the Court of Rome, or after reference back to the Judge, he is free to proceed with the second.

Let Judges also take care that they send the process to the Court of Rome, sealed and under cover, to the Judges appointed to execute justice, together with a digest of the merits of the process. And Inquisitors should not concern themselves to appear at Rome against the appellants; but should leave them to their own Judges, who, if the Inquisitors are unwilling to appear against the appellants, shall provide their own advocates for the appellant, if they wish to expedite the case.

Let Judges also take note that, if they are personally summoned by the appellant, and appear, they must beware at all costs against engaging in litigation, but must leave the whole process and cause to those Judges, and so manage that they may be able to return as soon as possible; so that they may not be sorely troubled with fatigues, misery, labour, and expense in Rome. For by this means much damage is caused to the Church, and heretics are greatly encouraged; and thereafter Judges will not receive so much respect and reverence, nor will they be so much feared as before. Also other heretics, seeing the Judges fatigued and detained in the Court of Rome, will exalt their horns, and despise and malign them,

and more boldly proclaim their heresies; and when they are accused, they will appeal in the same way. Other Judges, also, will have their authority weakened when they proceed on behalf of the Faith and are zealous in extirpating heretics, since they will fear lest they may be troubled with miseries and fatigues arising from similar appeals. All this is most prejudicial to the Faith of the Holy Church of God; wherefore may the Spouse of that Church in mercy preserve her from all such injuries.

OFFICIAL LETTER OF APPROBATION OF THE *MALLEUS MALEFICARUM* FROM THE FACULTY OF THEOLOGY OF THE HONOURABLE UNIVERSITY OF COLOGNE

THE official Document of Approbation of the treatise Malleus Maleficarum, *and the subscription of the Doctors of the most honourable University of Cologne, duly set forth and recorded as a public document and deposition.*

IN the name of our Lord Jesus Christ, Amen. Know all men by these presents, whosoever shall read, see or hear the tenor of this official and public document, that in the year of our Lord, 1487, upon a Saturday, being the nineteenth day of the month of May, at the fifth hour after noon, or thereabouts, in the third year of the Pontificate of our most Holy Father and Lord, the lord Innocent, by divine providence Pope, the eighth of that name, in the very and actual presence of me Arnold Kolich, public notary, and in the presence of the witnesses whose names are hereunder written and who were convened and especially summoned for this purpose, the Venerable and Very Reverend Father Henry Kramer, Professor of Sacred Theology, of the Order of Preachers, Inquisitor of heretical depravity, directly delegated thereto by the Holy See together with the Venerable and Very Reverend Father James Sprenger, Professor of Sacred Theology and Prior of the Dominican Convent at Cologne, being especially appointed as colleague of the said Father Henry Kramer, hath on behalf both of himself and his said colleague made known unto us and declared that the Supreme Pontiff now happily reigning, lord Innocent, Pope, as hath been set out above, hath committed and granted by a bull duly signed and sealed unto the aforesaid Inquisitors Henry and James, members of the Order of Preachers and Professors of Sacred Theology, by His Supreme Apostolic Authority, the power of making search and inquiry into all heresies, and most especially into the heresy of witches, an abomination that thrives and waxes strong in these our unhappy days, and he has bidden them diligently to perform this duty throughout the five Archdioceses of the five Metropolitan Churches, that is to say, Mainz, Cologne, Trèves, Salzburg and Bremen, granting them every faculty of judging and proceeding against such even with the power of putting malefactors to death, according to the tenor of the Apostolic bull, which they hold and possess and have exhibited unto us, a document which is whole, entire, untouched, and in no way lacerated or impaired, in fine whose integrity is above any suspicion. And the tenor of the said bull commences thus: "Innocent, Bishop, Servant of the servants of God, for an eternal remembrance. Desiring with the most heartfelt anxiety, even as Our Apostleship requires, that the Catholic Faith should especially in this Our day increase and flourish everywhere, . . ." and it concludes thus: "Given at Rome, at S. Peter's, on the 9 December of the Year of the Incarnation of Our Lord one thousand, four hundred and eighty-four, in the first Year of Our Pontificate."

Whereas some who have the charge of souls and are preachers of the word of God, have been so bold as to assert and declare publicly in discourses from the pulpit, yea, in sermons to the people, that there are no witches, or that these wretches cannot in any way whatsoever molest or harm either mankind or beasts, and it has happened that as a result of such sermons, which are much to be reprobated and condemned, the power of the secular arm has been let and hindered in the punishment of such offenders, and this has proved to be a great source of encouragement to those who follow the horrid heresy of witchcraft and has very notably increased and augmented their ranks, therefore the aforesaid Inquisitors, wishing with their whole hearts and strength to put a check unto such abominations and to counteract such dangers, have with much study, much research, and much labour, indited and composed a certain Treatise in which they have used their best endeavours on behalf of the integrity of the Catholic Faith to rebuke and rebut the ignorance of those who dare to preach so gross errors, and they have also been at great pains to set forth the lawful and proper way whereby these pestilent witches may be brought to trial, may be sentenced and condemned, according to the tenor of the aforesaid bull and the regulations of Canon Law. But since it is very right and altogether reasonable that this good work which they have wrought for the common benefit of us all should be sanctioned and confirmed by the unanimous approval of the reverend Doctors of the University, lest by some evil chance ignorant and ill-intentioned men should suppose that the aforesaid Rectors of the faculty and the Professors of the Order of Preachers are not wholly at one in their view of these matters, the authors of the aforesaid Treatise, exactly written out as it is to be printed in fair characters, in order that when it is so printed it may be recommended and honourably approved by the recorded good opinions and mature judgement of many learned Doctors, handed to, and laid before, the most honourable University of Cologne, that is to say, before certain Professors of Sacred Theology, who are commissioned and required to act as representatives of the most honourable University, the aforesaid Treatise in order that by them it might be perused, examined, and discussed, so that should there be found any points which may seem in any way doubtful or hardly in agreement with the teachings of the Catholic Faith, such points might be corrected and emended by the judgement of the said learned Doctors, who shall, moreover, officially approve and commend whatsoever the Treatise contains which is agreeable to the teachings of the Catholic Faith. This accordingly was done as hath been set forth above.

In the first place, the honoured lord Lambertus de Monte with his own hand subscribed his judgement and opinion as here followeth: "I, Lambertus de Monte, Professor (albeit unworthy) of Sacred Theology, and at this time Dean of the faculty of Sacred Theology in the University of Cologne, do here solemnly declare, and I confirm this my declaration with my own hand, that I have read and diligently perused and considered this Treatise, which is divided into three parts, and that, in my humble judgement at any rate, the first two parts contain nothing at all which is in any way contrary to the doctrines of sound philosophy or contrary to the truth of the Holy Catholic and Apostolic Faith, or contrary to the opinions of those doctors whose writings are approved and allowed by Holy Church. Moreover, in my opinion, the third part is to be entirely approved, and is to be put into actual practice, so far as in the trials and punishment of these heretics, of which matters it treats, nothing is done that may infringe the Canon Law. And again on account of the most weighty and salutary matters which are contained in this Treatise, which, even if it were only because of the honourable estate, learning, and good report of these most worthy and honoured Inquisitors, might well be held to be useful and necessary, all diligent care should be taken that this Treatise be widely distributed to learned men and men full of zeal, who thence may very profitably have the advantage of so many and so well-considered directions for the extermination of witches, and it should also be put into the hands of all rectors of churches, particularly those who are honest, active, and God-fearing men, who may by reading therein be encouraged to arouse hatred in every heart against the pestilent heresy of witches and their foul craft, so that all good men may be warned and safeguarded and evil-doers may be discovered and punished, so that in the full light of day mercy and blessing shall fall upon the righteous and justice shall be meted out to those who do evil, and thus in all things God shall be glorified, to Whom be all honour, praise, and glory."

Next the Venerable Master Jacobus de Stralen with his own hand subscribed his judgement and considered opinion thus: "I, Jacobus de Stralen, Professor of Sacred Theology, after having diligently read the aforesaid Treatise, declare that my opinion entirely and altogether is in agreement with the judgement which hath been set forth by our Venerable Master Lambertus de Monte, Dean of Sacred Theology, as he hath written above, and this I attest and witness by my own signature to the glory of God."

In like manner the honourable Master Andreas de Ochsenfurt wrote with his own hand as follows: "In the same way I, Andreas de Ochsenfurt, Junior Professor of Sacred Theology, record that my considered opinion of the matters contained in the said Treatise entirely and wholly agrees with the judgement written above, and to the truth of this I bear witness by the subscription of my signature."

And next, in like manner, the honoured Master Thomas de Scotia subscribed with his own hand as followeth: "I, Thomas de Scotia, Doctor of Sacred Theology (unworthy though I be), am fully in agreement with all that our Venerable Masters have written above with regard to the matters contained in the said Treatise, which I also have carefully examined and perused, and to the truth of this I bear witness by subscribing my signature with my own hand."

Here followeth the second subscription with regard to those discourses which have been pronounced from the pulpit by ignorant and blameworthy preachers. And in the first place it seems good to set forth the following articles:

First Article: The Masters of Sacred Theology, who have subscribed their names below, do much commend the Inquisitors of heretical pravity, who, according to the Canons, have been sent as deputies by the supreme authority of the Apostolic See, and they would humbly exhort them to fulfil their exalted office with all zeal and industry.

Second Article: The doctrine that witchcraft may be wrought by the Divine Permission owing to the co-operation of the devil with wizards or witches is not contrary to the Catholic Faith, but is in *every way agreeable to the teaching of Holy Scripture; nay more, according to the opinions of the Doctors of the Church it is a belief which must surely be held and steadfastly maintained.*

Third Article: Therefore it is a grave error to preach that witchcraft cannot be, and those who publicly preach this vile error notably hinder the holy work of the Inquisitors to the sore prejudice of the safety of many souls. It is not convenient that the secrets of magic which are often revealed to the Inquisitors should indiscriminately be made known to everybody.

Last Article: All princes and all pious Catholics are to be exhorted that they should use their best endeavours always to assist the Inquisitors in their good work of the defence of the Catholic Faith.

Wherefore, these Doctors of the aforesaid faculty of Theology who have already signed above and who have also signed below, have affixed their signatures to these articles, as I, Arnold Kolich, public notary, who have signed my name below, have learnt from the sworn information of John Vörde of Mechlin, good man and true, sworn Bedel of the most honourable University of Cologne, who declared this upon oath unto me, and as (for their hands as signed above and below are well known unto me) I myself have seen set forth as here followeth: "I, Lambertus de Monte, Professor of Sacred Theology, Dean of the faculty, stoutly maintain and entirely approve of the articles here rehearsed, and to the truth of this I bear witness by my signature subscribed with my own hand. I, Jacobus de Stralen, Professor of Sacred Theology, similarly maintain and entirely approve of the articles as rehearsed above, and to the truth of this I bear witness by affixing my signature with my own hand. I, Udalricus Kridwiss von Esslingen, Junior Professor of Sacred Theology, likewise maintain and entirely approve of the articles as set forth above, and to the truth of this I bear witness by affixing my signature with my own hand. I, Conradus von Campen, Professor in ordinary of Sacred Theology, declare that I assent to and am in entire agreement with the judgement of the Senior Professors. I, Cornelius de Breda, Junior Professor, maintain and entirely approve of the articles as set forth above, and to the truth of this I bear witness by affixing my signature with my own hand. I, Thomas de Scotia, Professor of Sacred Theology (albeit unworthy), entirely agree to, maintain, and approve of the opinion of the Venerable Professors who have signed above, and to the truth of this I set my name with my own hand. I, Theoderich de Bummel, Junior Professor of Sacred Theology, entirely agree with what has been written above by the honoured Masters who have signed their names above, and to the truth of this I bear witness by my signature written with my own hand. In confirmation of the above articles I declare that I am wholly and entirely of the same opinion as the above most honoured Masters and Professors, I, Andreas de Ochsenfurt, Professor of the faculty of Sacred Theology, a junior member of the Board of Theologians of the most honourable University of Cologne."

Finally and last of all, the aforesaid Venerable and Very Reverend Father Henry Kramer, Inquisitor, was in possession of and showed us another letter, written out fair on virgin parchment, bestowed upon and granted unto him by the most Serene and Noble monarch the King of the Romans, which parchment bore his own royal red official seal, impressed upon a ground of blue wax, which seal was suspended from and hanging at the bottom of the said parchment, and this was whole and entire, untouched, not cancelled or suspect, in no wise lacerated or impaired, and by tenor of these presents the most Exalted Lord, the aforesaid Noble King of the Romans, in order that for the benefit of our Holy Faith these businesses might be dispatched with the greater ease and expedition, in his royal office as the Most Christian King, wished and wishes that the same Apostolic bull, whereof we have spoken above, should be in every way respected, honoured, and defended, and the provisions thereof enforced, and he takes the Inquisitors wholly under his own august protection, commanding and requiring all and everyone who are subjects of the Roman Empire that they shall show the said Inquisitors all favour and grant them every assistance of which they may stand in need in the discharge of their office, and they shall afford the Inquisitors every help according to the provisions which are more fully contained and rehearsed in this said letter. And this said letter issued by the King commences thus, and concludes thus, as is set forth in order here below: "Maximilian, by the Divine Favour and the Grace of God, most August King of the Romans, Archduke of Austria, Duke of Burgundy, of Lorraine, of Brabant, of Limburg, of Luxemburg and Guelderland, Count of Flanders . . . "; and it concludeth thus: "Given in our good city of Brussels, under our own hand and seal, on the sixth day of November, in the year of our Lord one thousand, fourteen hundred and eighty-six, in the first year of our reign." Wherefore, with regard to all that hath been rehearsed and set forth above, each and every, the aforesaid Venerable and Very Reverend Father Henry, Inquisitor, on behalf of himself and his aforesaid colleague, sought from me, the public notary, whose name is written above and is subscribed below, that each document and all these documents should be officially drawn up and relegated in the form of a public instrument or public instruments, and this was done at Cologne in the house and the dwelling of the aforesaid Venerable Master Lambertus de Monte, which house is situate within the immunities of the Church of S. Andrew at Cologne, in the room where this same Master Lambertus pursueth his studies and dispatcheth his businesses, in the year of our Lord, in the month, on the day, at the hour, and during the Pontificate, all which have been set forth above, there being present there at that very time the aforesaid Master Lambertus, and the Bedel John, as also Nicolas Cuper von Venroid, sworn notary of the Venerable

Curia of Cologne, and Christian Wintzen von Eusskirchen, a cleric of the diocese of Cologne, both good men and true, who bear witness that this request was formally made and formally granted.

And I, Arnold Kolich von Eusskirchen, a cleric of the diocese of Cologne, sworn notary, was also present whilst the above businesses each and all were being performed and were carried out, and to this I give my evidence with the aforenamed witnesses; and in accordance with what I saw and with what, as I have stated above, I heard upon the sworn testimony of the said Bedel, good man and true, I have written out fair with my own hand and engrossed the present public instrument, which I have subscribed, and have caused to be published since I have drawn it up in this official form for publication, and being requested and required so to do I have signed it and sealed it according to the wonted manner with my own name and my own seal, that it may be officially approved and may be a sufficient and legal testimony and probation of all and single that are herein set forth, rehearsed, and contained.